PANIPAT

Vishwas Patil is one of the most acclaimed Marathi writers today. He has written iconic novels like *Mahanayak, Chandramukhi, Pangira, Zadazadati, Panipat, Sambhaji, Nagkeshar* and *Lust for Lalbaug*. He has received the Priyadarshini National Award, the Vikhe Patil Award and the Sahitya Akademi Award for *Zadazadati* and the Gadkari Award for *Mahanayak*. *Panipat* has received thirty-eight awards since its publication in 1988.

Nadeem Khan has been a teacher of English since 1973. He retired as Head, Department of Languages, Shivaji Science College, Amravati in 2010. In 2011, he became the founding director of the Western Regional Centre of the Indian Institute of Mass Communication run by the Ministry of Information and Broadcasting, at which post he remained till 2018. He is currently adviser on English language learning to the Shiksha Mandal, Wardha, an education society founded by Jamnalal Bajaj.

Nadeem Khan has used his wide and eclectic reading to bring body and texture to the translations he has been doing for the past ten years. Other than translating three other novels of Vishwas Patil, he has also brought into English the novels of the young Marathi writer Avadhoot Dongare, as also the works of celebrated writers like Bhau Padhye.

TRANSLATED FROM THE MARATHI BY
NADEEM KHAN

VISHWAS PATIL

PANIPAT

eka

eka

First published in Marathi as *Panipat* in 1988 by Rajhans Prakashan

First published in English as *Panipat* in 2019 by Eka, an imprint of Westland Publications Private Limited, by arrangement with Mehta Publishing House

Published in English in 2022 by Eka, an imprint of Westland Books, a division of Nasadiya Technologies Private Limited

No. 269/2B, First Floor, 'Irai Arul', Vimalraj Street, Nethaji Nagar, Allappakkam Main Road, Maduravoyal, Chennai 600095

Westland, the Westland logo, Eka and the Eka logo are the trademarks of Nasadiya Technologies Private Limited, or its affiliates.

Copyright © Vishwas Patil, 1988
Translation Copyright © Nadeem Khan, 2019

Vishwas Patil asserts the moral right to be identified as the author of this work.

ISBN: 9789395767323

10 9 8 7 6 5 4 3 2

This is a work of fiction. Names, characters, organisations, places, events and incidents are either products of the author's imagination or used fictitiously.

All rights reserved

Typeset by Jojy Philip, New Delhi 110015

Printed at Saurabh Printers Pvt. Ltd.

No part of this book may be reproduced, or stored in a retrieval system, or transmitted in any form or by any means, electronic, mechanical, photocopying, recording, or otherwise, without express written permission of the publisher.

contents

Cast of Characters   vii
The Third Battle of Panipat: An Overview   xv

1. The Pride of the Palanquin   1
2. The Assault on Delhi   87
3. Throne or Faith?   234
4. Dance of Death   353
5. White Cloud   516

Notes   566

cast of characters

Peshwa Nanasaheb	Son of Peshwa Bajirao, prime minister of the Marathas
Vishwasrao	Nanasaheb's eldest son
Sadashivrao Bhau	Nanasaheb's cousin; son of Bajirao's younger brother Chimaji Appa
Raghunathrao Dada	Nanasaheb's younger brother
Shamsher Bahadur	Bajirao and Mastani's son
Gopikabai	Nanasaheb's wife
Parvatibai	Sadashivrao's wife
Subhedar Malharrao Holkar	Important Maratha captain
Ranoji Shinde	Important Maratha captain
Dattaji Shinde	Ranoji Shinde's son
Bhagirathi	Dattaji Shinde's wife
Jankoji Shinde	Dattaji Shinde's nephew
Balwantrao Mehendale	Maratha captain; relative of the Peshwas
Govindpant Bundele	Governor of the Peshwas in Northern provinces
Sakharam Bapu Bokil	Peshwa's secretary (administrator)
Bapuji Hingane	Peshwa agent in Delhi
Naro Shankar	Peshwa official in the North
Nana Phadnis	Young accountant of the Peshwas

CAST OF CHARACTERS

Antaji Mankeshwar Gandhe	Maratha captain
Parashar Dadaji Wagh	Holkar captain
Vitthal Shivdev Vinchurkar	Peshwa captain
Jaanu Bhintaada	Peshwa's officer on household duties
Gangoba Tatya Chandrachud	Holkars' secretary
Ramji Dabholkar	Shindes' secretary
Yashwantrao Pawar	Maratha captain
Surajmal Jaat	Jaat king of Bharatpur
Ibrahim Khan Gardi	Ordnance chief of the Marathas
Shuja-ud-dowlah	Nawab of Ayodhya
Imad-ul-Mulk Ghaziuddin	Dethroned wazeer of Delhi
Ahmad Shah Abdali Durrani	Emperor of Afghanistan
Shah Wali Khan	Ahmad Shah Abdali's wazeer
Shah Pasand Khan	Ahmad Shah Abdali's deputy commander-in-chief
Jahaan Khan	General in the Afghan army
Barkhurdar Khan	Afghan captain
Rehman Khan Barakzai	Chief of the Afghan ordnance
Najeeb Khan	Rohilla captain
Hafeez Rahmat Khan	Rohilla captain
Atai Khan	Shah Wali Khan's nephew
Ala Singh Jaat	King of Patiala
Qutb Khan	Rohilla captain; Najeeb Khan's mentor
Kashiraj Pandit	Shuja-ud-dowlah's ambassador

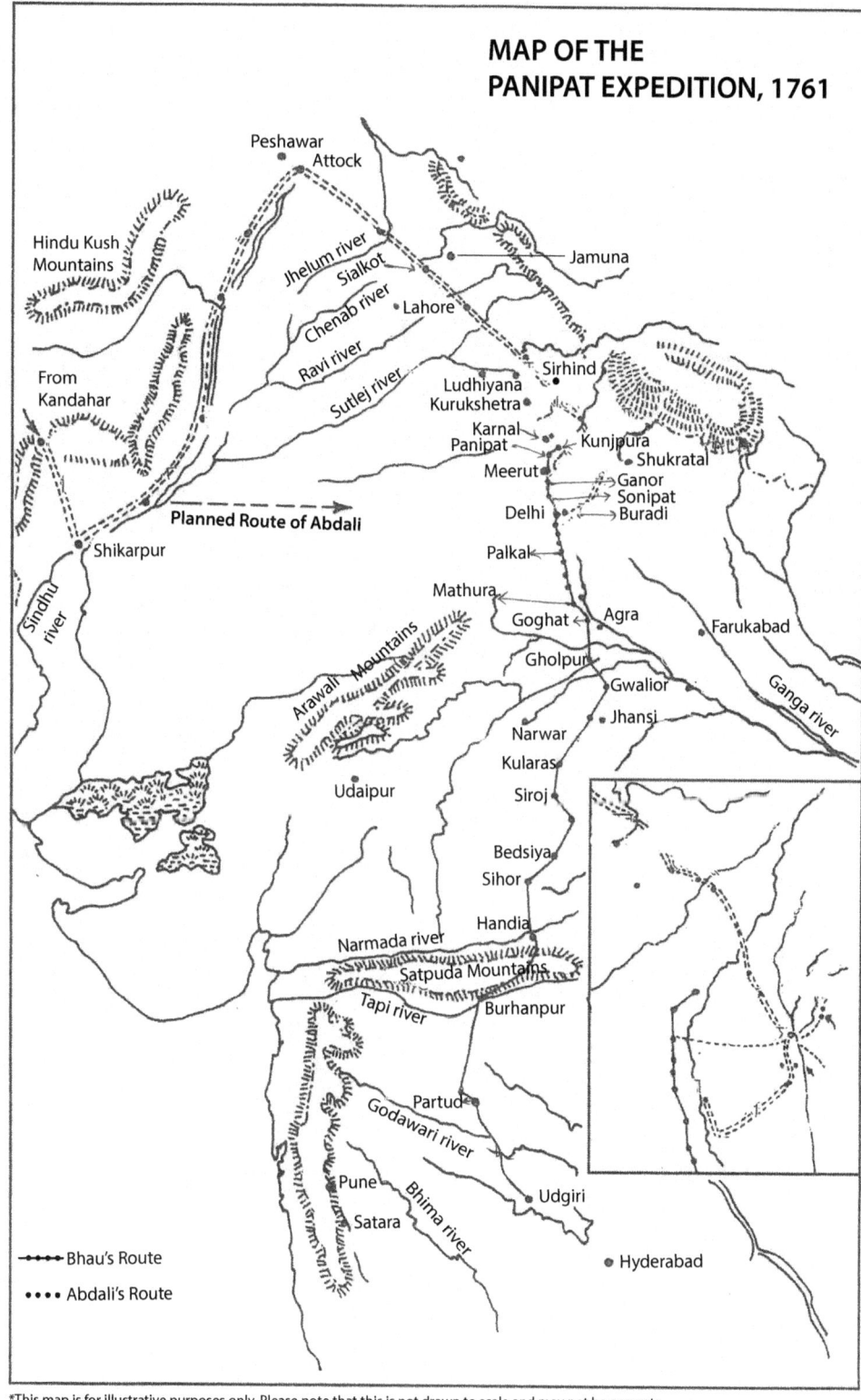

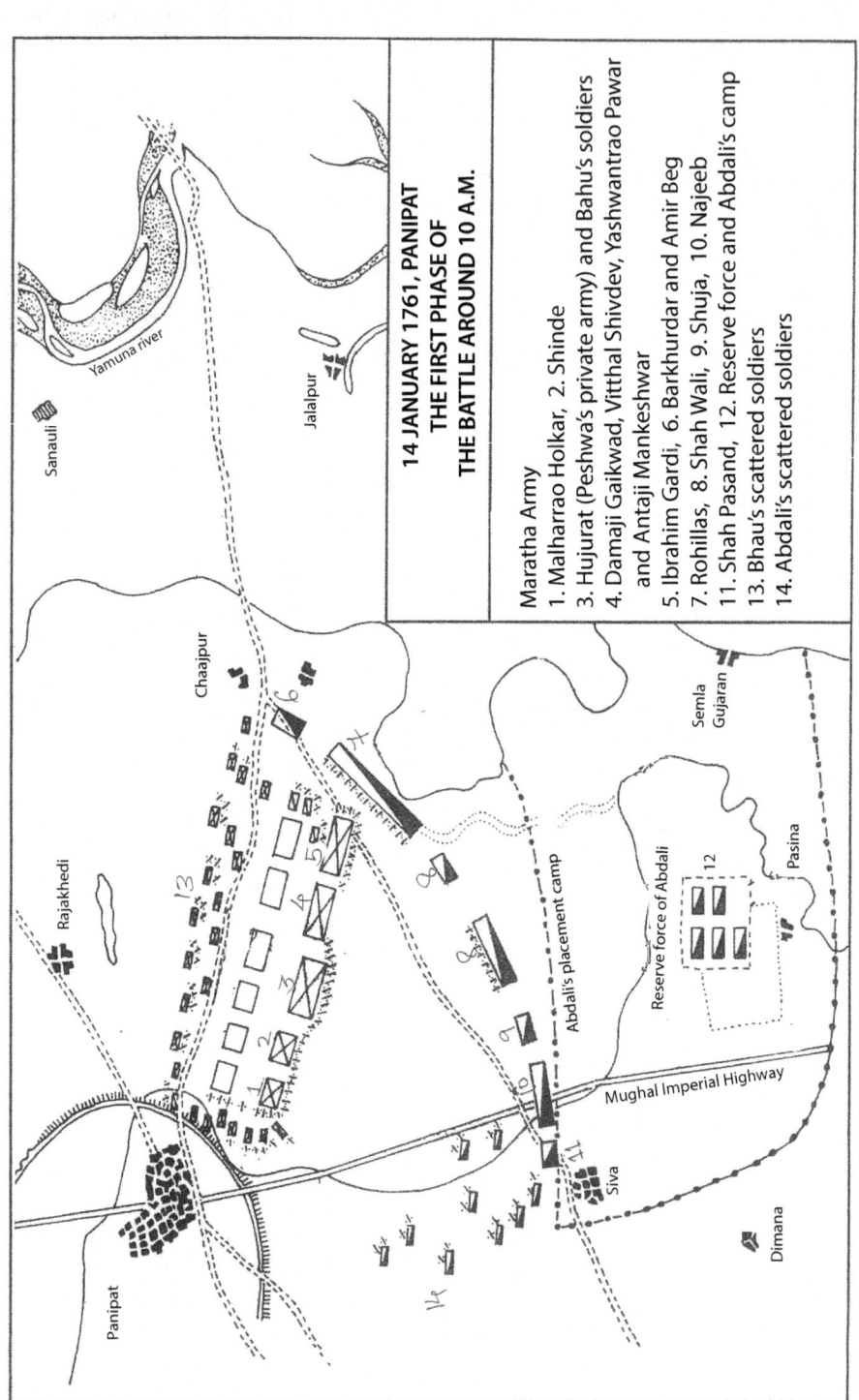

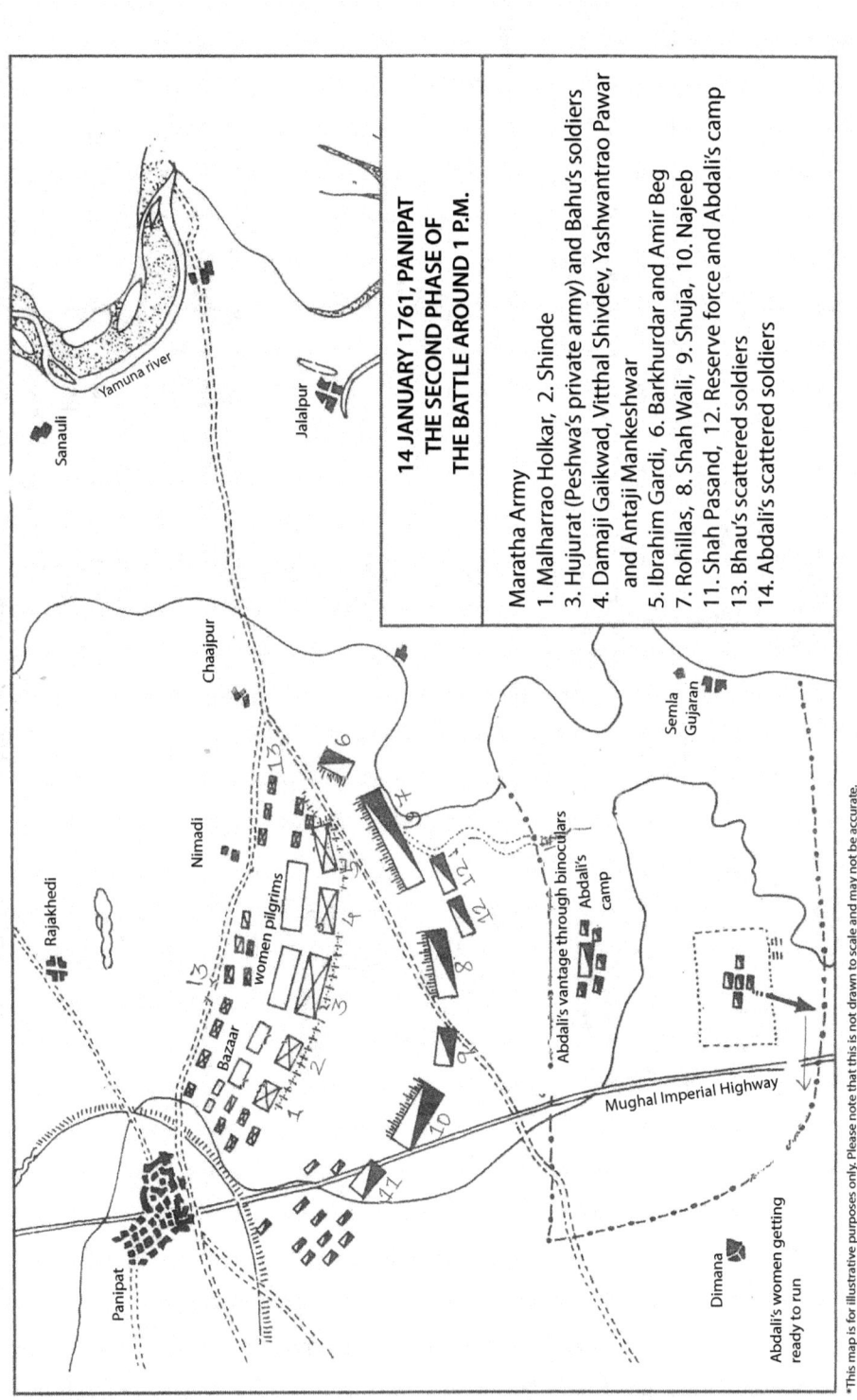

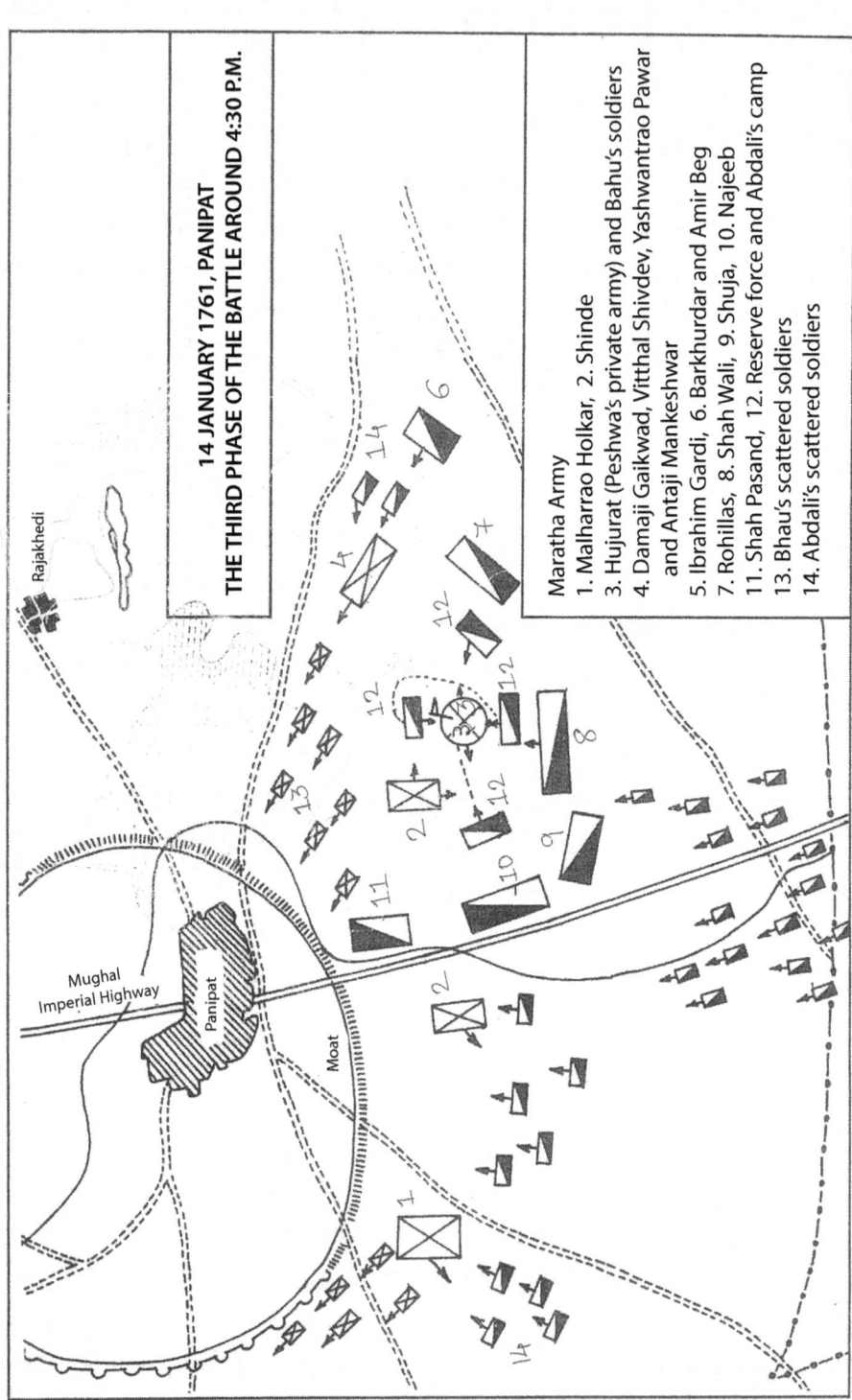

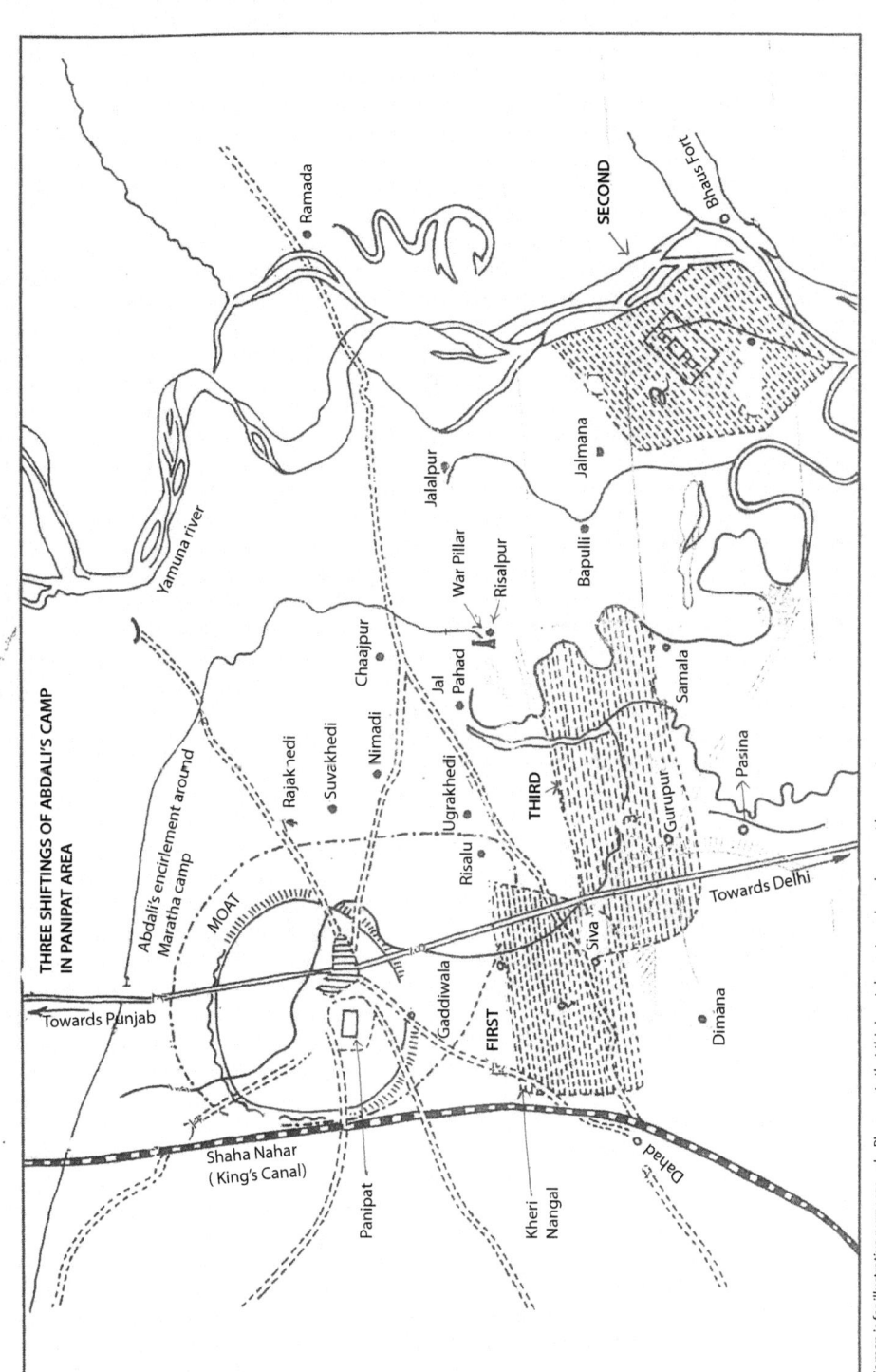

the third battle of panipat
an overview

Panipat … a small township that falls on the Royal Highway that during the Middle Ages began on the frontier towns of Kabul and Kandahar and came all the way down to Delhi via the Punjab. A tiny station in an insignificant little state of those times. But the mere utterance of the word 'Panipat' brings before the mind's eye some of the most significant and turbulent moments of Indian history.

The first and the second battles of Panipat were fought in the years 1526 and 1556 respectively, but the mighty battle that was fought there on 14 January 1761 between the doughty Afghan warriors and the stubborn, indefatigable Maratha soldiers will rank as the fiercest and the bloodiest battle recorded in the history of medieval India.

The battle began at nine o'clock on that fateful day, and the intensity of the combat was such that within eight hours the battlefield was overlaid with the mutilated bodies of 150,000 soldiers and 80,000 animals belonging to both the warring parties. The Mahabharat of Pauranic times was waged on the adjacent battleground of Kurukshetra, but it was a conflict of gods and demi-gods whose story has been handed down to us as India's great epic. The third battle of Panipat, however, is a smouldering piece of palpable, verifiably historical reality. Around 200,000 lives are reported to have been lost when the United States bombed the Japanese cities of Hiroshima and Nagasaki, but it had taken a good four or five days for the toll to reach these figures. Panipat is the only place that gobbled up this number of lives within a matter of hours.

In his mid-thirties, the Afghan king Ahmad Shah Abdali was a battle-hardened soldier. Afghan history eulogizes him as the maker of modern Afghanistan. Through the valour of his sword, he had redrawn the boundaries of six or seven kingdoms of his times. On the India campaign, he had with him his wazeer Shah Wali Khan and his commander-in-chief Jahaan Khan. Even before the fateful battle at Panipat, Abdali had raided India, particularly the province of the Punjab five times, but it was during his campaign in 1761 that he found his return passage blocked by over 100,000 Marathas for a few months. These gritty warriors from the Deccan had given him such a fright that his self-belief had been badly shaken. He had left instructions that in the event of his defeat at Panipat, his wife and concubines should be beheaded.

What were the Marathas doing at Panipat in the first place?

Najeeb Khan, a Rohilla chieftain had sent an appeal to Abdali, requesting him to 'extricate us from the clutches of the wicked Marathas, to decimate this aggressive tribe and drive them back south beyond the rivers Tapti and Narmada'. Najeeb had begun his career as an ordinary foot-soldier assigned to take care of horses. Through intrigue and subterfuge, he had established himself as a Rohilla chieftain of some substance. The town that he named after himself still exists in Uttar Pradesh as Najeebabad.

By this time, the Delhi empire had become so devitalized and shrunken that the washerman would hang the emperor's clothes to dry on the other side of the Yamuna in Jaat territory. In 1751–52, the emperor had struck a deal called the Ahmadiya Pact with the Marathas, giving them charge of defending Delhi and his northern principalities. The task of securing Delhi against foreign invasions provided the Marathas with the opportunity to enter the capital city of Hindustan and to immediately post the Maratha chieftain Antaji Mankeshwar there with an army of 10,000 soldiers. Thus when Ahmad Shah mounted his next raid, it became incumbent upon the Marathas to rush to the north for the defence of the imperial territory.

Thirty-two year old Sadashivrao Bhau, the nephew of the late Bajirao Peshwa, set off towards the north to confront Abdali with a gargantuan army of over 100,000 soldiers. This was when the population of Pune city was barely 20,000. In the north, Najeeb Khan was advertising this confrontation between the Afghans and the Marathas to his fellow-religionists as a 'jihad' between the Muslims and the Hindus; Sadashivrao Bhau, however, was trying to convince the kings of northern India that it was really a fight between the foreign invader and the native forces, and pleading with them to join forces with him. Along with his wife Parvatibai, about twenty-five odd notable personages marched north with Bhau, including crown prince Vishwasrao, Shamsher Bahadur, the son of the late Bajirao and Mastani, Balwantrao Mehendale and Yashwantrao Pawar.

Sadashivrao also had with him the nine-thousand-strong artillery unit of Ibrahim Gardi. This Muslim gunner from the Deccan had taken his training in cannons from the French army situated in the coastal city of Madras, and had joined Bhau's army with his well-trained artillerymen. Shuja-ud-dowlah, the Nawab of Ayodhya and his deewan Kashiram Pandit were strongly inclined to side with the Marathas in this clash, but Najeeb pre-empted this convergence by raiding Ayodhya and dragging the unwilling Shuja by his nose into the Abdali alliance.

A year earlier, Dattaji Shinde had sacrificed his life at the battle at Buradi Ghat. His nephews Jankoji and Mahadji participated in the great battle. While Jankoji was killed brutally by the Afghan chieftains, Mahadji managed to escape with a seriously injured leg. Mahadji went on to lay the foundation of the Shinde dynasty at Gwalior, which later came to be recognized in northern India as the Scindia dynasty.

Govindpant Bundele, the Maratha satrap in the Doab, the land between the waters of the Ganga and the Yamuna, did all he could to keep Bhau's army supplied with provisions. He was, however, decapitated, his death bringing supplies to a grinding halt. Bundele's slaughter brought the Maratha army to desperate straits.

It is true that three months before the battle took place, Bajirao's son, the Peshwa, Nanasaheb, had set off with an army of 40,000 to help his beleaguered cousin Sadashivrao. But he was too far gone as a sybarite, and barely seventeen days before the battle took place, he was celebrating his second marriage at Paithan. Up there in the Punjab, Raja Ala Singh of Patiala was trying his best to send food and fodder to the hard-pressed Maratha army, but that supply too was choked off by some of Abdali's aides racing down from the north. The Maratha soldiers were reduced to starvation. The animals snapped at whatever leaves they could locate on the already denuded trees.

Malharrao Holkar was an important sardar of the Peshwas in the north. For devious political reasons, he had adopted Abdali as his foster-son. He was of the firm opinion that the Pune Peshwas should not be allowed to interfere in the northern region affairs of their two big sardars, Holkar and Shinde. He confided to Jankoji that if the Pune Brahmins got to be overly powerful, 'they won't retain us for so much as tying their dhoties for them!'. It was this Malharrao that became the founder patriarch of the Holkar dynasty of Indore.

As the Marathas got into their mortal combat with the Afghans, not a single king or chieftain of the north turned up on their side on the day of the battle. By blocking the passages of the Afghans back to their homeland for months together, they had begun to seriously asphyxiate them. Amazingly, they were doing this job in a state of near starvation. Finally, finding that they were running out of stamina, they decided on a do-or-die venture. They took stock of their resources, tightened their belts and decided to meet the enemy head on by making the first move towards Delhi. It was nine o'clock of a terribly cold winter morning of 14 January 1761. They moved in a circular defensive formation, perfect for an artillery-dependent army, with Ibrahim Khan and his guns in the lead. For the formation to work, it was important that discipline be maintained and no breach be created. As they advanced, Ibrahim Gardi's guns moved on, blowing huge holes in the enemy front, wreaking mayhem in their ranks and causing Abdali to search for desperate options. It was either retreat or getting blown away. Abdali's squads had begun to disintegrate. The goddess of victory stood all ready to place the crown on the Maratha brow. But the months of hunger and deprivation suddenly began to demand its toll on the Maratha warriors, and the alacrity to get into the breach was missing.

Also, because of differences of opinion regarding the kind of warfare that should be waged, the old guards who wanted the guerilla kind—seniors like Malharrao, Damaji Gayakwad and Vinchurkar—suddenly decided that their own skin was soon to be pulled into the fire. Around afternoon time, they found the opportunity and sneaked out of the battlefield with their troops and turned the heads of their horses south.

The breach that Abdali had been praying for had suddenly been created. He suddenly found himself looking at an opportunity that hadn't existed only a little while ago. This opportunity had emerged from the dissension in the enemy ranks and their state of near complete exhaustion. He got after his own dispirited soldiers, flogged them, turned the fleers round to face the enemy and goaded them into one final effort. The tide of the battle changed. The fatigued Maratha soldiers began to fall like autumn leaves in the face of this strong gust of wind. Even when tens of thousands of his soldiers were being decimated, Bhausaheb fought on in the company of the fifty odd loyals who were around him, till an enemy spear found its mark and brought the bravest of all the Marathas down. History records that after the battle was over, heaps of corpses had sprung up all across the battlefield, and from one of these heaps, Bhau's mutilated cadaver was retrieved later.

It's undeniably true that the Marathas were vanquished in the battle, but at a deeper level of truth, they became stars in the firmament reserved for martyrs. In spite of having won a stupendous victory, Abdali did not carry on his face any sense of achievement. Being the perceptive statesman that he was, he knew how frighteningly close the call had been. The next day after the war, he publicly declared, 'The Marathas went on mounting one murderous raid upon another on our forces. Their raw courage, their harrying of our forces was so unrelenting that if the legendary heroes Rustam and Isfandar of Afghan epics had been around, they would have bitten their fingers in awe and disbelief. It's impossible that this degree of valour, this passion for matching their mettle with the best can be replicated ever, anywhere.'

CHAPTER ONE

the pride of the palanquin

It was twilight time. The cold gusts of wind along the banks of the Yamuna pierced the camp of the Marathas, and set the gilded pennant fluttering. The Holkars had set camp next to Raghunath Rao's, and their flag danced too. The main army had already advanced towards Delhi under the command of Vitthal Shivdev, leaving behind the lame and useless horses that loitered around the camp now. The servants sat warming themselves, huddled round little fires. The wounded soldiers were resting in their makeshift tents. The market facing the commander-in-chief's tent lay quiet, with the merchants checking their accounts and matching their ledgers.

There was certainty everywhere that the Maratha flag would be hoisted very soon atop the Red Fort. The battle games were already being played out in the streets of Delhi between the Maratha soldiers and Najeeb's army. The topic of conversation in the camp was how the valiant Vitthal Shivdev would slaughter Najeeb. Once Delhi fell, Raghunath Dada's next move would be the invasion of the Punjab, and preparations were already afoot. The merchants had to replenish their stocks, the soldiers had to get their weapons battle-ready, the highwaymen and nomads accompanying the army would have to collect grains and other wherewithal on the way, by force if necessary, to keep the army well-fed and well-supplied.

Knowing that Kurukshetra fell on the way to the Punjab, a number of mendicants and ascetics from Pune had latched on to the army: some for the holy sighting of the Ramganga, others for a dip in the Bheem-kund. There had been a near-stampede in the household of Raghunath

Dada for this trip to Kurukshetra. An entire cavalcade of ladies from Pune and the neighbourhood hamlets had tagged along with Baisaheb in the hope of a pilgrimage. Three times before this, the womenfolk of the Holkar household had visited Kurukshetra. So how could the Peshwa ladies be left behind?

Ahmad Shah Abdali had plundered northern India bare and carried the booty to his country, leaving behind minor chieftains and grandees in charge. Raghunath Dada was sure he could send them packing. There was a forty-mile stretch of fertile land lying between the Yamuna and the Ganga, called the Antarved, which was under the control of the Marathas. But Abdali's foray had stripped it bare along with Delhi, Agra and Mathura. Not one had had the courage to stand up to his onslaught. He had looted Delhi in broad daylight, slaughtered its denizens and broken the back of the empire of Hindustan. He hadn't so much as spared the pigtails of the Brahmins. For them it was a choice between losing a tuft of hair or losing the head altogether. The heads of slaughtered Brahmins and cows were strung together and hung on trees. Surajmal Jaat of Vilaspur had found it prudent to abandon the town and flee.

The booty that Abdali carried back was so large that camels' backs creaked under the load. Horses were converted into pack animals, and the horsemen walked alongside. Stray, long-retired horses were put back to work. Even the donkeys of potters and washermen were requisitioned to struggle against their unaccustomed load. On leaving, Abdali had appointed Najeeb as his viceroy. The keys of a treasury had landed in the hands of a thief. By nature a blood-sucking leech, he got sucking whatever came his way—land, jewellery, all kinds of valuables—and sent them over to swell his coffers at Sultanpur.

A mere nobody when he had arrived fifteen years ago from Afghanistan in search of livelihood, Najeeb had appeared to Raghunath Dada an easy pushover. But the rotten-seeming weed had sent down deep roots. Najeeb had erected strong defences around Delhi. The seven gates around the city—Lahori, Dilli, Kabuli, Kashmiri, Turkman, Sindhi and Ajmeri—were guarded by the army day and night. It became evident to Raghunath Dada that the enemy would not be easy to draw out. As a counter-move, he sent a twenty-thousand-strong cavalry to sack the land of the Antarved. Antaji Mankeshwar, Sakharam Bapu and Vitthal Shivdev ran through the banks of the Ganga and the Yamuna, saffron flags fluttering. If today it was Fanand and Kota that were plundered, it was Sikandarabad the next day. The defences of Shikohabad were breached here and Itawa was harried to distraction there. Najeeb's Afghan soldiers at Meerut put up a resistance, but were instantly put to the sword, turning the Antarved earth red.

With the destruction of the Antarved, Najeeb raised his hood. He reinforced the defences of Delhi and increased the surveillance. His Rohilla guards, roaming around Delhi with their torches, looked like phantoms on the prowl. Raghunath Dada was sure that the snatching of the Antarved tantamounted to lopping off Najeeb's limbs. But Najeeb wasn't surrendering yet. Accepting defeat at the hands of the Marathas, the kaafirs, would be shameful. The Marathas rode on and, with a hard push, entered into Delhi. Chandni Chowk reverberated with hoof-beats. Battle cries of 'Har Har Mahadev!' 'Attack!' 'Kill!' 'Plunder!' rent the skies as the Marathas pressed through to the Old Fort. The commander of the fort, Bakhtaar Khan, was an intimate friend of Najeeb's, and he retaliated with great fervour. But he was overpowered and beheaded by Aaba Jagtap of Kenjal. Delhi trembled under Vitthal Shivdev's unrelenting onslaughts. Meanwhile, Wazeer Ghaziuddin had shifted his allegiance to the Marathas, sensing this to be a good opportunity to pull out the fickle Najeeb's thorn from his side. The happy turn of events had lifted the spirits of the Marathas.

Najeeb had taken shelter in the Red Fort. Red as a carrot, Najeeb was a good-looking person. He dyed his short beard with henna. His small but razor-sharp eyes pierced deep into whoever he looked at. Ghaziuddin's betrayal had cut him to the quick. He was boiling with rage. Meanwhile, the Marathas steadily broke through the Rohilla barriers and came closer to the Red Fort. Fire-belching cannons, crumbling ramparts and walls—Delhi was enveloped in smoke and dust and deafening clamour.

☙❧

A shawl wrapped round his shoulders, Raghunath Dada sat reclining against a bolster in his tent. Although a touch feverish, he felt quite on top of the world, and his young face glowed with energy. He was assured of victory when the Marathas broke through the defences of Delhi. When the news of the slaying of Bakhtaar Khan reached him, Dada slapped his thigh in glee. The noose round Najeeb's neck was not going to come loose now. The Maratha flag could flutter atop the Red Fort this very day. A smile began dancing on his lips. His kaarbhaari Sakharam Bapu, a chief administrator of sorts, sat, watching closely the changing patterns of his face. As it turned darker, the servants lit the lamps, making Dada's face look sharper against the dim light. He slapped his thigh and exclaimed, 'Bapu, Vitthalrao is dark as pitch anyway, and today he is likely to descend on Najeeb like fate itself.'

'Quite true, Dadasaheb. Vinchurkar, Holkar, Antaji Mankeshwar, Gandhe, they are all knowledgeable old generals. They have all crossed their sixties in the service of His Lordship, but haven't lost their vigour yet,' said Bapu.

'They are all sons of the Maratha soil, Bapu—resilient, proud, spirited. This Vinchurkar Sardar, now, what was he, to begin with? The son of the Daanis of Saaswad. Was driven out of the house for being a wastrel, and landed in somebody's stable in Satara for grooming horses. Once Shahu Maharaj was out on a hunt. When a boar slipped out of Maharaj's hold, Vitthalrao leapt upon the boar and held it between his thighs like a pup. Maharaj instantly gifted him a fine horse and employed him as a trooper. He has been in service since then. The Siddhi campaign at Janjira, the slaying of Daya Bahadur, the siege of Vasai in the company of Appa, his valiant sword has flashed here, there and everywhere. And today he is going to put Najeeb in chains and present him before me. And I shall dispatch this Najeeb to the mouth of a cannon, I shall.'

'That may not be possible, Dadasaheb,' smiled Bapu.

'Why not?' retorted Raghunath Dada, eyebrows tensing, one eye twitching. 'Why, Bapu? Why may it not be possible? If I flay this rogue alive, you expect Abdali to come thundering down from the mountains to interrogate me, do you?'

'Abdali won't be needed, Dadasaheb. There are some people right around us here, who will not let you touch a hair on Najeeb's head.'

'Who? Who can stop me, Bapu?' Dada's face had turned red. 'The venerable Peshwa himself has ordered—the snake is not to be fed with milk. It has to be squashed!'

Bapu burst into laughter, which irritated Dada further. Bapu managed to get his laughter under control and said, 'Shrimant, if someone were to tell you that last evening the great Najeeb-ud-dowlah Rohilla had visited the Maratha camp in person, and stayed here for an entire hour, would you believe it?'

'What are you saying, Bapu?' Raghunath Dada's face darkened. Eyes flaming, he roared, 'Bapu, who was it that invited that wretch? Why wasn't he instantly beheaded? Who was his host? Give me his name, Bapu, and I'll chop him to bits!'

'Please cool down, Dadasaheb. What would you really do if someone told you that Najeeb was received by no less than Subhedar Malharji Baba Holkar himself, in his own tent, and was seen off past midnight with due courtesy?'

Dada's face fell. The disbelief ... Words deserted him. When Bapu laughed, he didn't know where to look. Collecting himself, he said, 'I have known for some time that Najeeb's agent Meghraj has been making occasional calls to the Subhedar for negotiating a truce. But now Najeeb himself? And that too in Malhar Baba's tent?'

'That's exactly what I've been saying, and this is not where matters end. You will collapse under the Subhedar's pressure and come to terms with Najeeb. This is as clear as daylight, Dadasaheb!'

'Impossible! That is never going to happen! Pat a snake lovingly on the head, and expect it not to bite? Doesn't happen this way, Bapusaheb—bite it certainly will!'

'Even after knowing all this, you will make your peace with him. You will even be generous to him.'

'Never! If ever peace is to be made, I shall not accept a penny less than five million rupees.'

'This exact issue has been discussed earlier, Dadasaheb, and you know what Najeeb's response was: Forget five million! We will not give the Marathas so much as fifty pebbles from the banks of the Yamuna!'

'But think, Bapu, how can we leave holy places in the Antarved like Haridwar and Jwaalapur under Najeeb's control? Shrimant's orders ...'

' ... have become very old, Dadasaheb. Najeeb and Shuja-ud-dowlah are not the milk-suckling babes we take them to be. The Marathas will begin by carrying the saffron flag on pilgrimage to Haridwar, Kaashi, chanting the name of Lord Rama. Tomorrow, they will add a spear to the flagpole and conquer all of the north! They certainly aren't so stupid as to not understand this. So, it would be good, Dadasaheb, to abandon the idea of pilgrimages and their upkeep. Najeeb would rather chop his head and offer it on a platter than let go of the pilgrimages.'

As they were talking, they heard the herald announce in a loud voice: 'Tread soft! Look sharp! The Wazeer of Hindustan!'

Neither Bapu nor Raghunath Dada could withhold their snigger at the empty grandiosity of the heraldry. Ghaziuddin remained wazeer barely in name. The activities of Najeeb and the ups and downs of the power games in Delhi had reduced him to shreds. His distracted face, his unwashed turban and his soiled loose trousers would make one wonder whether this was a wazeer or a runaway clown. The grandeur of the elephants-and-horses days had long fled. With just a horseman or two as entourage, he could as well be an ordinary trooper. Similar misfortune had descended upon Delhi too. Both Nadir Shah and Abdali had looted Delhi to the bone. The famed beauties of the harem had to go hungry. The royal horses now lived the lives of runty stray dogs. The nobles had abandoned the crown in favour of their own well-being, and the Jaats had extended their influence right up to the walls of Delhi. The Rohillas had already penetrated the city from the north, and the land east of the Yamuna had been gobbled up by Shuja of Ayodhya. The washerwomen on the eastern bank proudly proclaimed themselves as of Ayodhya. The Delhi that once ruled all of Hindustan had shrunk its frame in shame.

'Welcome, Khan Saheb,' said Raghunath Dada, pointing at a pillow and signalling for him to sit. 'So, what says your capital city?'

'It lies under your protection, sir.'

'Meaning?'

'Meaning this, sir, that six years ago your commanders Ranoji Shinde and Malharji Holkar had come to an agreement with the emperor of Delhi. Under the agreement, we had turned over one-fourth of the revenue of six of our provinces to the Marathas, in exchange for protection from our enemies. The security of Delhi is the responsibility of the saffron flag, Rao Saheb!'

'It is to fulfill this commitment that we are posted here in person.'

'But even the wazeer finds himself unprotected today, respected sir. My wife has had to walk through the streets of Delhi. If the very clothes on our back cannot be secured, then it's a shame.'

'What are you saying, Wazeer Bahadur?' asked Raghunath Dada, turning grave. 'Who has dared to humiliate the ladies of the royal household?'

'Who else but the adopted son of your Kakasaheb, the Subhedar, the wretched Najeeb? When he got to know that I had joined the Marathas, he raided my mansion in the dark of the night with a few soldiers. He chopped my servants' noses, dragged the ladies into the street, snatched the brocaded clothing on their backs, tore away their ornaments. Even enemies don't stoop to such vulgarities. This one-time gatherer of horse-dung has become the viceroy of India today, Dadasaheb, but his hands still remain covered with filth.

'Rao Saheb, when this nobody had become the landlord of a nothing village, I was the one who had called him over to Delhi. He would rustle people's cattle and horses then, and sell them in the market. I was the person who had let him into Delhi. With the Jama Masjid as witness, he had sworn on the Koran that he would stay true to me to his last breath. And now he should desire to lay hands on my wife's honour? A back-stabber like him would be hard to find anywhere in the world. I beg of you, Saheb, do what you may, but never trust this devil from hell. Don't get into any treaty with him. Show him no sympathy and consideration. One day, mark my words, he will be the downfall of the Maratha empire and bring calamity upon you.'

'Khan Saheb, this Raghunath Dada is no pushover. This is my second expedition to Hindustan. I can count the feathers of a flying bird, and separate the red ones from the blue.' Raghunath was boiling with rage. 'And you too, Bapu, you hear this too. There will be no truce with this Najeeb. No sympathy, no mercy. I swear by Omkareshwara that I shall tear Najeeb limb to limb—throw one part of him to the left of the Yamuna and the other part to the right—and only then will I cross the Tapti and the Narmada to return home.'

☙

The sun had just begun opening its eyes on the horizon, daubing the eastern landscape with a golden hue. Its rays brought the ramparts and the tops of temples and mosques into sharp relief. In their golden slant, the rays stood as a distinct entity on the surface of the calm, awe-inspiring Yamuna. Raghunath Dada stood bare-chested in the water, with just a dhoti wrapped round him. Next to him stood the chieftains Renko Annaji and Janardan Ram, paying their obeisance to the sun god. Some from Wai, some others from Shingnapur and yet others from Nashik—a good bunch of Brahmins, priests and mendicants were absorbed in the ritual of a holy bath. Dada brought his palms together in reverence to the river, lifted some water and let it pour out of his hands while mumbling his prayers.

He finished his ablutions and turned round to move towards the bank. Just then he heard the mendicants cry out: 'Aaarrrghh! What sinful things are these?' They shrank back. Something came floating towards them on the river, and went drifting past Dada. The carcass of a cow. His peaceful face from just moments ago contorted with rage. He cast a searing look at Sardar Paigude. The Brahmin contingent began in an aggrieved tone, 'How long will this abomination go on? This kind of barbarity at such a holy place?'

Raghunath Dada offered no response, just turned round and took another dip. The rest of the entourage followed.

With strong, firm steps, he returned to the camp. In a tent next to his private one was his personal shrine. This shrine accompanied him everywhere. It housed the entire pantheon of gods and goddesses, including Omkareshwar, Parvati, Ganpati, Jyotirlinga and Khanderaya. Dada wouldn't take a gulp of water without first offering his prayers here. Whether he was setting off on a campaign or even on the day of battle, he never stirred out without first visiting the shrine. He wound up the rituals in a hurry today, sipped the holy water offered by the priest, strode out of the tent and barked at the nearest servant: 'Go ask my Kakasaheb, the Subhedar, to meet me at once.' He marched into the conference tent and sat down against a bolster, bare-chested still, and fuming. His generals Sakharam Bapu, Renko Anaji and Paigude stole in soft-footed and sat next to him. It didn't take the camp long to sense that something momentous was afoot. The Maratha soldiers, their wives and children, servants and peasants, weapon-smiths, all began assembling near the private tent. Opinions soon began getting exchanged.

'This really has gone too far!'

'He should have been ripped apart the last time he had been captured!'

'Enemy first becomes my friend, and then my adopted son?'

There was quiet in the tent. Renko Anaji took stock of the situation. 'We've been saying this since the first day, Dadasaheb, that this Najeeb is not a straight person. He is a blight on the fortunes of the Maratha empire. Last year Abdali had raided Mathura. In the land of Krishna, this man had allowed his outrage to peak. This Najeeb had not only whisked away gold statues of gods and goddesses, but also taken away respectable women to sell as prostitutes. That was why, when Vinchurkar had captured him and his associates, we had advised that he be slaughtered and dispatched to hell.'

'It wasn't you alone, Pant!' Paigude exclaimed. 'When the truce talks were in progress, even unlettered women and children had gathered round the tent, chanting that the fiend should not be spared!'

'Truce? What kind of truce was that?' laughed Sakharam Bapu. 'They began with fifty lakhs as punitive imposition, but finally wound up with five. And what has arrived is even short of that, they say. The only gain for the Marathas was the governorship of Delhi for Antaji Mankeshwar.'

'And he was to set off for Saharanpur, we are told, but as of now he has parked himself on the bank of the Yamuna. He will go when he goes; meanwhile, his acts of defilement continue without restraint. Slaughters cows, flings their bones and carcasses into the river. Just the other day, I counted a good twenty to twenty-five cow-heads floating by. If he had been brought before the Peshwa, he would have been pushed over the cliff four times over. Just yesterday, I had an unnerving experience. I was chanting the Gayatri Mantra on the bank. As I finished, I closed my eyes and scooped up a handful of water, and what did I see, horror of horrors, but the entrails of a cow in my palms!' Renko Anaji's face contorted in disgust as he related this.

Everybody laughed. Sakharam Bapu signalled to a servant. The servant brought over a vessel of cow-urine. It was sprinkled on all present, which made the assembled grandees feel cleaner. Renko Anaji was in the mood to carry on with some more episodes, but it occurred to him that it would not be proper for him to lay out the entire list of grievances at one go in the presence of Shrimant. Just about a week or so would have passed since Raghunath Dada had taken that terrible oath of tearing Najeeb apart from limb to limb. It had been proved all over again that Dada was a simple person at heart. When the Marathas had conquered Delhi, and when one great leader after another, one nobleman after another, had come to salute him in his tent, the joy that had suffused his face had been impossible to contain, and spilled all over. Add to that the governorship of Delhi to Antaji Mankeshwar and the provinces of Malva, Gujarat, Ajmer and Agra turned over in writing to the Maratha empire, and Dada was barely an inch away from heaven. Even so, he had never relaxed on Najeeb. The Peshwa instructions were clear: 'Finish off Najeeb,', and he had never forgotten those orders. But then, Malharji Holkar, a person twice his age, had stepped in with the plea, 'Why kill a dead man?' He had gone on to elaborate that Najeeb would distance himself from Delhi.

Malharji was far too exalted a person, and his advice could not be dismissed off-hand. Many a horse had he sent into retirement in his campaign of subduing northern India. His whiskers and side-locks had turned grey during the enterprise. Even now, when the Subhedar led a campaign, enemy soldiers broke into a cold shiver and fled with the cry, 'Malhar aaya re! Malhar has come!' There were other old generals like Vinchurkar in the Maratha army along with the Subhedar. They, therefore, had to be given due respect. But Najeeb had to be punished too. In the early flush of victory, Raghunath Dada had kept the Najeeb issue in abeyance. What, after all, could Najeeb do? But Najeeb had started displaying his 'Najeeb-ness' in a matter of days.

A servant entered announcing the arrival of the Subhedar. Ordinarily, whenever the Subhedar arrived at the conference tent, Raghunath Dada would display extreme respect. But now when he came and eased himself against a bolster, Dada didn't stir at all. Resentment and anger continued to flash in his eyes, if anything, more intensely than before. The Subhedar ran his hands through his stiff moustache and eyed Dada with sternness. The many seasons he had seen, the countless battles he had fought, the myriad places and people he had experienced, they were all starkly visible on his face. In a deep and resonant voice, he said, 'Yes, Dadasaheb, what are your orders so early in the morning?'

'Orders? No! On the contrary, it's we who seek your permission.'
'Permission? From me?'
'Of course!' Dada laughed sarcastically. 'You are a veteran general of the Empire, wise and knowledgeable. Hence we need your permission. As we stand in the waters of the Yamuna every morning to worship the sun god, what oblation should we make? A palmful of water or the entrails of our gau-maata?'

The Subhedar could think of no response. Dada had turned beetroot red.

'Kakasaheb, you have heard of your heroic adopted son's latest achievement? The entire camp has now begun to spit at us. When that snake had landed in our hands, every single Maratha had raised the cry that he should be defanged, if not crushed. But you took him in as your adopted son and hid him in a basket. He has now raised his hood, and he hisses. He has brought our religion into crisis. Tell us what you propose to do about it.'

'I'll talk to him, make him see sense.'

'Don't indulge him like your own progeny, Subhedar kaka!' Dada sprang up and pointed an agitated finger at Malharji. 'It's only out of respect for your age and your service to the Maratha state that I reneged on my oath to Lord Omkareshwar, for your sake alone! Let me tell you this now, if ever this Najeeb of yours desecrates the places of our holy ablutions with cow slaughter, I shall crush him on the spot, and feed his filthy flesh to the vultures. Go and get your adopted son under control!'

Saying this, Dada stomped out towards his private apartment. The Subhedar got up too, and quietly headed towards his tent.

ॐ

Night had fallen. A biting wind blew through the darkness of the Yamuna banks. Fires had sprung up outside every tent. Bouquets of flames could be spotted across the entire camp. Dinners were done with early. The Marathas fed dung-cakes into the fire, stretched out around its warmth, and were soon snoring. The Deccan horses, not used to this kind of cold, rubbed themselves against each other. The bullocks that pulled the cannon tucked their necks into each other's bodies. The camels added a few more bends to their curvaceous necks. The dogs found shelter under the carts. Nod by drowsy nod, the entire camp gave in to the irresistible siren song of sleep.

Taking advantage of the dark, six or seven horsemen slipped out of the Holkar camp and trotted up the bank of the Yamuna. In an effort to protect themselves against the slicing cold wind, they had wrapped heavy Khandeshi blankets round themselves. Leading this little bunch was Subhedar Holkar himself. A couple of miles up, and the enemy camp became dimly visible in the diffused light of the torches planted at intervals. Hearing the indistinct, unfamiliar sounds from a distance, the dogs began to bark and lunge forward. The sentry guards ran with them and relaxed when they saw who it was. Najeeb's soldiers knew Malharji.

The Subhedar's horse halted in front of a big, red tent and the rider dismounted and entered. Najeeb was still awake. Seeing the Subhedar, he extended both his hands and cried, 'Welcome, benefactor! Welcome, abbajaan, welcome, my father. How come you thought of your calf so late in the night?'

The Subhedar looked at Najeeb. His face looked red in the dim light. His feline eyes shone sharper than during the daytime. Some formal exchange of pleasantries, and then the Subhedar turned grave, 'Najeeb, stop your madness. Why do you butcher cows every day and throw their entrails where the Brahmins take their baths? Why do you want to ruin our friendship?'

'Ours is not a friendship, Babajaan, it's a father-son relationship. But the relationship is defined by politics, not religion. Whether I butcher a cow or kill a tiger, what business is it of your Raghunath? It is our private religious matter.'

'But, Najeeb, I am the one who brokered the truce between you two, and the blame lies at my door. Raghunathrao is enraged. He has many generals like me to do his bidding. They talk now of tying you to the mouth of a cannon. Watch your steps, son!'

'Oh, everybody knows how valiant your Raghunathrao is,' laughed Najeeb. 'The Peshwa had sent your Dada to settle scores with Abdali, hadn't he? So, what was he doing dragging his feet in Rajputana while Abdali was around here? As soon as the badshah left for Afghanistan, in comes your Dadasaheb flaunting his fake valour! If he was all that valiant, why didn't he get into a direct confrontation?'

'What has been served on your plate, Najeeb, pay attention to that. I warn you as a friend. Raghunath can be as poisonous as he is good. If the cow-slaughter does not stop, he is going to kill you.'

Najeeb's face turned red. Beads of sweat broke on his face. He gave a tug to his beard and said, 'Go and tell your Peshwa, Najeeb is never going to stop the butchering of cows. Najeeb is ready to lay down his life for his faith. People who die for jihad, our religion knows them as ghaazees. Our fighting force is small, and that is why your Peshwa struts around so. Go tell him, every single one of Najeeb's soldiers is eager to become a ghaazee.'

'You are such a religious person, Najeeb, and you had sworn on the Koran to support Ghaziuddin. Yet, his wife you ...'

'Let go of this pointless needling, Babajaan, and go tell your Peshwa—we are willing to die.'

On the third day, when Raghunath Dada and his coterie assembled before dawn for their ritual bath, a macabre sight greeted them. The riverbank was spattered red with blood. Carcasses of cows were thrown deliberately around their bathing spots. A good fifteen to twenty heads lay around the water's edge. Again and again Dada looked towards the bank, and each time the horns sticking out of their heads pierced him in the heart. He turned round without taking a dip.

The royal kettle-drums began to beat, trumpets rent the air. The entire camp was in a turmoil. 'Up, up, gird up for battle!' went the battle cry. The soldiers actually broke into a dance. Horses that had stood corralled for so long were freed. They shivered with excitement when they felt the saddle strapped on to their backs. Camels heaved themselves up joint by joint. Cavalrymen belted their flowing gowns. War cries of 'Har Har Mahadev!' reverberated from the clouds. The saffron flag was all ready to head into the fierce wind. Every soldier's face was lit up. Not one of them had wanted a truce. On the contrary, they had wanted the wretched Najeeb to be ripped apart and tossed over the cliff. Now that the opportunity had suddenly opened up, they were thrilled.

Amidst this hustle, Raghunath Dada stepped out of his tent. 'Har Har Mahadev!' thundered the assemblage. There was steely determination on Dada's majestic visage. He had a heavily embroidered turban on his head. The emerald necklace twinkled round his neck in the soft early light. The jewel-studded waistband sat unusually snug on him today. Balancing his feet, he leapt into his saddle. The soldiers were astounded when they noticed the absence of any scabbard on his waist. His jewel-encrusted sword glittered in his hand. Its blade gave the illusion of sparks dancing along its length. Dada spurred his horse and shouted, 'Chalaa!'

'Har Har Mahadev!' came the battle-cry. The Maratha soldiers lunged forward to the beat of kettle-drums and the blowing of trumpets. The horses neighed. The soldiers had barely begun advancing when a Holkar horse came galloping towards them. It came straight upon Dada's horse and halted muzzle-to-muzzle. Subhedar Holkar dismounted. The entire army froze. What would happen next? They all held their breath. Dada cast a searing look at Holkar. Holkar stepped forward and held the rein of Dada's horse. 'Where are you off to?' he asked.

'To meet your adopted son, my adopted cousin.'

'I won't let you go.'

'Why not?'

'He is alone, under my protection. It's a sin to kill one who has taken refuge. His force is depleted. A refugee …'

'What does one do when the refugee wants to set the shelterer's house on fire?'

'Whatever it be, I'm not going to let you attack him.'

'We don't care for your opinion, or anybody else's, for that matter.'

Dada nudged his horse a step forward. The Subhedar fell back a bit, held the reins with both hands, and yelled, 'You green-horns will teach us politics? Arrey, your father Bajirao Peshwa himself never ever crossed our word. Such trust and faith he reposed in us—even when the Nizam's begum called him over to her private chamber to have a look at him, he took us along with him …'

'We know all these stories, Kakasaheb. You alone in the entire kingdom could get away with throwing a clod of earth at Bajirao and putting your sword to his chest.'

'That's why I tell you, you will have to do as I say.'

'Even if my own father were to materialize here, I wouldn't stop.'

The Subhedar tightened his grip on the reins and screamed, 'Raghunath, before you flash your sword at Najeeb, you will have to hack me first.'

Dada jumped off his horse and glared at the Subhedar. The old man roared, 'What are you looking at? Lift your sword and sever my head. I've served you all my life. My hair has turned white. Repay the debt now, and chop me to pieces.'

With that, the Subhedar began flagellating himself while the army watched dumbstruck. Commander Vinchurkar came and intervened with folded hands before Raghunathrao. He too was rendered bereft of words. The Subhedar refused to relent. Then, suddenly, Dada's dam burst. 'What are you doing, Kakasaheb?' he begged, tears flowing freely. 'How do I explain? What do I say?' One hand on the hilt of the sword and the other on the blade, he began walking backwards towards his tent. The blade sliced through the skin of his palm and it turned red. The entire camp was left gaping at the scene, shaken to the core.

༺༻

Shinde's soldiers had crossed Ujjain and were well on their way towards the north. The horses were kicking up clouds of dust into the air. The bells round the elephants' necks were creating a rhythm of their own, quite out of sync with the bells round the oxen's necks as they pulled the cannon carts. Jankoji Shinde sat in his brocades on a decked-up howdah atop a dazzlingly caparisoned elephant. Two slaves sat precariously behind him, fanning him as vigorously as they could without losing balance.

Jankoji was about sixteen or seventeen years of age. A look at his young, innocent face would suggest that he had just finished his glass of milk and come. It was on these young shoulders that the Peshwa had placed the responsibility of the north, particularly Lahore and Multan. It had been eight years now since the Ahmadiya pact had been signed, by which the Delhi monarch had turned over the responsibility of his security to the shoulders of the Marathas. Jankoji's father Jayappa Shinde had been personally present with Malharji Holkar when he had signed the royal pact. Jankoji's grandfather Ranoji Shinde had roamed on horseback the entire region starting from Ajmer to Prayag and beyond, right up to Bengal. Jankoji was now the third generation of Shindes devoted to the service of the Maratha empire. Both Jankoji's uncle Dattaji Shinde and Nanasaheb Peshwa himself had placed their trust in Jankoji. The Shindes and the Holkars were the two wheels on which the Maratha wagon rolled in the north. Since the passing away of Bajirao, the wheels had slowed down, they had begun to develop a creak. Yet it was on these two wheels alone that it would move.

Not much time had passed since Raghunathrao had hoisted the Maratha flag on the Attock Fort. He had been called home by the Peshwa on some domestic work, and the understanding was that the Shindes would take over the management of the Punjab. Jankoji would keep getting intelligence from his scouts of both Raghunath Dada and Malharji moving southwards after having vanquished the Punjab. His Kakasaheb Dattaji had gone over to Chambhargonda for his own marriage. Jankoji had been looking forward to participate in the celebrations, but along had come the firmaan from the Peshwa himself for proceeding north. So his wife Kashibai had gone to Chambhargonda, while he was headed northwards.

When Jankoji had set off from Pune, bidding goodbye to the Peshwa's son Vishwasrao had been painful. The friendship between the two had become the subject of much discussion and admiration. They were roughly the same age, and both were extremely tenacious young men. Both had given a great account of themselves in the battle that the Marathas had recently fought at Sindkhed. Bidding each other goodbye had been distressful.

The Peshwa himself had taken a fancy to young Jankoji. His sense of discretion and gravity at such a young age had left a deep impression on the Peshwa. 'Pora,' he had lately told this youngster with barely a trace of hair on the upper lip, 'you and your Kakasaheb are so differently made. That Dattoba is such a tempestuous fighter, god's own soldier. Gives no quarter. I have always told him he should fight like a lord, not like a soldier. But he is so hot-headed that all he wants to do is to pick up his sword and get into the thick of it. You, by contrast, are sober and calm, just like your grandfather.'

☙

The Peshwa's faith in the Shindes was well deserved. It was Ranoji whose valour had won for the Shindes the thirty-six palaces spread across Ujjain, Dhar, Baroda and Bikaner. The Shindes had shed their blood for the Peshwas in return for these treasures. Ranoji wasn't cut out to be carried to the cremation bank on the shoulders of four; he took his last breath in an army camp at Mirpur. Ten years later, Jayappa was killed by the treachery of the Rajputs. Today, the brothers Dattaji, Tukoji and Jotiba had staked their lives for the glory of the Maratha empire. This was Jankoji's first major assignment in what he hoped would be a long innings in the service of the same empire. It was his turn now to range across the north, blowing the trumpet of Maratha victory. It was not his intention to bring up the rear. He would always be in the vanguard, and die fighting on the front when the need arose.

After about thirty miles under the sizzling sun, his men were running out of steam. Once they had arrived within sight of a rather large settlement, they called a halt near a stream with plenty of water. Jankoji dismounted and stretched himself out under a tree in a mango orchard nearby. In a short while, a servant came and stood before him.

'Shrimant,' he said, 'a scout has arrived with news. Raghunathrao's army is barely six miles from here. Dadasaheb is on his way to Pune.'

Jankoji stood up straight at this, grinning from ear to ear. He would soon be face to face with the valiant Dada, who had so recently conquered Attock. For a few months now, he had been receiving an endless stream of stories of Dada's glorious achievements: how he had compelled Abdus Samad Khan to scramble away from Sirhind; how the Maratha chieftains Manaji Paigude, Gangadhar Baji Bhimrao, Gopal Ganesh and Renko Anaji had run their steeds across the Punjab and Multan; how Abdali's son Taimur Shah and his general Jahaan Khan had abandoned everything and fled when Dadasaheb and Subhedar Holkar had blown up the bastions of the Lahore Fort; how a grand reception had been organized for Dadasaheb at the Shalimar Gardens after he had conquered Lahore; how Tukoji Holkar and Sabaji Shinde had hoisted the Maratha flag on the Attock Fort. Jankoji immediately readied his soldiers to welcome his hero.

A puff of dust soon became visible on the distant horizon. The puff soon became a cloud; and as the cloud began swelling east, west and north, the excitement of the Shinde soldiers mounted in equal measure. As soon as Jankoji could discern the outline of the caparisoned elephant in the haze of dust, he made a sign to his gunners, who set flame to powder, and seven guns boomed together in one powerful explosion. Dada dismounted from his elephant and immediately gathered young Jankoji in his arms. The soldiers of both groups began embracing each other.

Jankoji escorted Dada to the cushions that had been laid out under the shadiest tree in the orchard.

'So, Jankojibaba, where's your next halt?'

'I wait for your orders, Dadasaheb.'

Dada suddenly turned very grave. He articulated each word in measured tones as he said, 'Babasaheb, if all our other plans have to be jettisoned, it's all right. If we have to spend another ten million on fresh soldiers, that's all right too, but that motherfucking Najeeb has to be taught a lesson. Do what you have to, but you have to help me here. I myself would have torn that bastard apart, but it was our Subhedar's laments that came in the way. Antarved, Kurukshetra, Kunjpura, a good four-hundred-thousand worth of property has slipped into that wretch's hands. He's our Kakasaheb Subhedar's godson, isn't he? Bijesingh, Madhavsingh, he has any number of godsons, the Subhedar has—each one of them a rascal and a thief. I would have flogged the bastard to death, but that would have offended the ancestor, and that's a great sin.'

Jankoji was uncomfortable and made an effort to change the subject. 'Dadasaheb,' he said, 'after winning Lahore, Sirhind, all of the Punjab, and now having stormed Kabul and Kandahar, what battlefields do you leave for us to foray into?'

'Sending an arrow through this Najeeb's head, this is the important battlefield, Babasaheb. This Raghoba of yours has hoisted the flag at Attock, but hasn't been able to touch a hair on Najeeb's head. This is where I want your help, Babasaheb.'

'What other orders?'

'Once this important job is done, keep a firm hold on the Punjab. Kabul and Kandahar are very much a part of our India. It's been our land since the time of Akbar. We have to reclaim them.'

The heat had subsided. Both the groups had exchanged friendly banter, and they had long distances to go. The two heads exchanged assurances of meeting again, embraced each other and set off in opposite directions.

※

Six days rolled by as Jankobaji's army travelled miles upon miles. They had halted on the bank of a river when a scout brought news that Holkar was about a mile away, on his way to Pune. Jankoji decided to ignore it. In the afternoon, a palanquin was seen approaching their place of rest. Going by its ornamentation, it appeared to belong to somebody important. The palanquin was lowered and, pushing aside the tassels, Gangoba Tatya Chandrachud emerged from it. Seeing the forty-plus, pleasant-faced Gangoba, the Shinde soldiers wondered what the manager to Subhedar Malharji Holkar was doing here. Tatya went up to Jankoji and, bowing and saluting, informed him that the Subhedar desired to come over to meet him.

Jankoji stiffened and responded in a stern voice, 'Tell him we meet next only in heaven.'

Looking at Jankoji's mood, Gangoba decided to use the emotional tack. Adopting a placatory tone, he tried to impress upon him the importance to the Subhedar of this meet. 'Shrimant, the Subhedar is now an old man. Your lordship is a wise person, it's your old Kakasaheb who wants to travel this far to seek your company. Please do not disappoint him.'

With Tatya getting too insistent, Jankoji tried to use the argument of helplessness. 'Look, Tatya, I don't have Kakasaheb Dattaji with me right now. Without consulting him, I cannot speak to anyone behind his back. I shall not. You may go now.'

The palanquin returned the way it had come. Within a little while, the scout came running again, with the news that the Subhedar had set off for the meet that Jankoji had denied to him. He felt a little irritated. But courtesy demanded that white hair be given due respect. He dispatched two horsemen with the message that the Subhedar should stop where he was, and he himself would go over and meet him there.

Malharji Holkar stood on a hillock under a mango tree, from where he saw a bunch of horsemen getting into the climb. On seeing the zestful young man leading the group, he asked Tatya, 'Gangoba, the boy leading the team, is he Ranoba's grandson?'

'Yes, that's him, Jankojibaba.'

'How he's grown!'

His thoughts took him into the past of four years ago, and the Kumbheri Fort belonging to the Jaats floated in front of his mind's eye. This was Raghunath Dada's first sally into the north. Dada had demanded a tribute of ten million rupees from Surajmal Jaat, while Surajmal was willing to part with no more than four million. Neither party was ready to budge from their position. Surajmal was quite decently fortified. He dispatched a messenger with the note that if Raghunath Dada was not willing to accept four million, Surajmal was quite ready to fight. The note had upset Dada so much that he had immediately laid siege to the fort and begun subjecting it to artillery fire. One month had gone by without the fort showing any sign of capitulating. The sandy land had ruled out the possibility of laying mines. Cannonading the bastion was causing injuries to the Maratha soldiers on the other side of the fort. It happened that Subhedar Malharji Holkar's only son Khanderao was on the other side when a cannonball came floating over the fort and hit him like the thunderbolt of fate. No calamity could have been bigger for the Subhedar. On the day the son's body was consigned to the flames, the father swore that if he was his father's son, he would destroy Surajmal, and turn his fort to rubble and throw its dust into the Yamuna.

He went back to battle and tightened the siege of the fort. His assaults got so vicious that the Jaat broke into a sweat. That was when Surajmal's favourite wife advised him to use the offices of Jayappa Shinde for loosening the noose. Jayappa and Surajmal were 'brothers' for having exchanged turbans, and Jayappa exerted himself and brought about a truce between Raghunath Dada and Surajmal. This truce sent the Subhedar into a paroxysm of rage. Truce with a person who had extinguished his lineage, killed his only son? And that brought about by the Shindes? Whatever trust and respect had remained for the Shindes had evaporated in no time.

When the Subhedar saw Jankoji approaching, he was reminded of his dead son Khanderao. He mumbled to Tatya, 'A devil may be trusted once, but the descendant of a Shinde—never!'

'And yet, you are willing to play up to one of them?' Gangoba responded teasingly.

'I have become old now, Gangoba. A dry leaf is bound to fall sooner than later. A score of Ranoba's children and relatives occupy positions of power. I want my solitary adopted son to survive in this crowd. What other desire can I have now?'

On reaching up to Malharji Holkar, Jankoji dismounted and prostrated himself to pay his respect. The Subhedar had him rise and took him into his embrace. 'How you have grown, boy!' he said in a voice heavy with emotion. 'And by God, what striking resemblance to our Ranoba! They're not wrong when they say that the grandfather dies and reappears as the grandson.'

They all sat together, the Shindes and the Holkars. Jankoji and Malharji finished their dinner together and sat exchanging pleasantries. Malharji began reminiscing of old times: during Bajirao's times Ranoji and he would go together on expeditions. Bajirao himself would sit with the soldiers to eat a simple peasant's meal and explain to them the details of the expedition at hand.

The Shinde and the Holkar troops camped together for four days next to the lake. The post-dinner gathering on the eve of their departure got into stride. The Subhedar had decided to depute an attachment of two-thousand soldiers under the command of his adopted son Tukoji to go along with Jankoji. Much discussion was held on this move. Finally, tucking some tobacco in his cheek, Malharji asked, 'So, Babasaheb, what's the next mission on your agenda?'

'Kakasaheb, you have cleaned out everything right from Attock to Multan, Lahore, Sirhind, Delhi, right up to Agra. There's really nothing that you've left behind for us to do!'

'Oh, there is, there is,' responded Malharji in a low voice, 'there is a place from where you can collect plenty of loot on a regular basis. Build pontoon bridges across the Ganga-Bhagirathi and take your armies across into Ayodhya territory. Enough fodder for the animals and victuals for you too. You can then move on to Prayag, and from Allahabad you can think of Bengal too.'

'Building pontoon bridges across the Ganga? Kakasaheb, the rivers here are not like the ones in the south, where you let out a whistle or two and get to the other side! The Bhagirathi swells up to more than two miles across after the monsoons, they say. How can you build pontoons across such width?'

'I know a person who has knowledge of these things.'

'Who?'

'Najeeb Khan.'

'Najeeb Khan?' Jankoji sat bolt upright. 'Kakasaheb, this man has the reputation of a hell-hound. He is a treacherous person, from what I have heard people say. The Peshwa has ordered that this thorn should be removed.'

'Oh, he's a thorn to be removed?' spat out Malharji. 'Yes, once that thorn is removed, the Peshwas get the freedom to run free and do what they like right from Attock in Afghanistan to Rameshwaram deep in the south. It's because Najeeb is firm that the Peshwa conceit is somewhat in check. Once he goes, why would the Peshwas need the Holkars and the Shindes? Get this clear, Babasaheb, once this Najeeb goes, this Brahmin gang from Pune won't want you and me even for tying their dhotis.'

That night, sleep evaded Jankoji for a long time. Was the Subhedar's advice right or wrong?

❦

The Shinde army had been camping on the holy battlefield of the Kauravas and the Pandavas for a week. Dattaji Shinde, Jankoji Shinde and Naro Shankar were delighted at the success of their Kurukshetra journey. Wearied of their battles, invasions and hunting expeditions, the Maratha braves were to set off the next morning for Kunjpura in the Antarved. It had been about eight months since Dattaji had arrived from the south and, in the company of his nephew Jankoji, stamped his presence with great force. The tribute evaders of Delhi had been brought to heels and a Maratha squad had been dispatched to Saharanpur to arrest Najeeb, who had gone into hiding in the mountains of Kumaon. The Shindes travelled to Lahore and Multan in the Sindh province and handed over the reigns of these provinces to Tukoji Holkar and Sabaji Shinde. Dattaji got hold of some local officials and landlords and brought order in the Lahore region with their help. The desire of the soldiers posted here, though, was that both Raghunath Dada and the Holkars should tarry here for a few years.

The locals of Hindustan, from experience, believed the Marathas came in like a storm, raided the place and vanished. It would be so much better if they stayed behind, established order and collected taxes. They preferred the Marathas any day to a foreign plunderer like Abdali. And so they were getting tired of the here-today-and-gone-tomorrow policy of the Marathas.

Peshwadom was trapped in a vortex of debts. The chieftains had created their own individual baronies and fortified them. Each chieftain had his own army. The revenue that reached Shaniwarwada from the districts was mere pittance. The collectors appointed for collecting revenue in the north were busy swelling their own treasuries; they had raised their own mansions and turned into landlords. The Peshwa, meanwhile, was groaning under the weight of debts, and had dispatched Dattaji to Ayodhya-Bengal with instructions to raise a minimum of six million rupees. The worry of a debt-ridden Peshwai was the reason Dattaji was going towards Antarved.

But he had received some thrilling news too. They had barely set foot in Kurukshetra when Bhagirathi had begun feeling nauseous. When he first heard the news, the only thing he didn't do was to break into a dance, and that out of concern for his public image. He hosted a lavish dinner for all his chieftains, distributed alms to the bhikshus by the fistful, dispatched basketfuls of sweets by special horseback couriers to Chambhargonda and Kanherkhed. Since his father was a native of Kanherkhed near Satara, Dattaji had spent his childhood on the banks of the Krishna, playing the usual games of making sand castles and staging mock battles. Ranoji had received the village of Chambhargonda from Shahu Maharaj, built a huge quadrangular manor for himself, and raised fortifications around the village. He got greater joy at being addressed as the Patil, the headman of Shrigonda, than as a chieftain.

Dattaji had been to Shrigonda and Kanherkhed the previous year to get married. The newly married couple had then gone to seek the blessings of Goddess Kanheri, the bridegroom sneaking covert glances at the beautiful girl by his side, barely being able to contain his excitement at the sight of his bride dressed in a green saree, her forearms covered up to the elbow in green bangles. As the two lowered their heads at the feet of the goddess, Dattaji muttered under his breath, 'Mother, a boy first, please!' The temple priest would have read his mind. 'All will be well,' he pronounced. 'The cradle will rock within a year for your little prince!' The shy Bhagirathi had taken the end of her pallu in her mouth and scampered out of the sanctum sanctorum. Here, now, was the first intimation of the prophecy on way to fulfilment, and Dattaji went mad. That evening, when they met, he teased his wife with 'What does my lady prefer, tamarind or aaonla?' Bhagirathi had responded with a look of mock anger.

Once they had settled down in their camps, urgent discussions began among the commanders. Dattaji, Jankoji, Naro Shankar, and their manager Ramjipant Dabholkar would assemble in the conference tent in the evening and sit preparing plans till late in the night. Dattaji was absorbed in the issue of the Peshwa's debts. He was of the opinion that if six to seven millions had to be raised, there was no alternative to crossing the Ganga. It was already the month of June and the occasional monsoon showers had begun. The Ganga could get flooded any day. How would a crossing be possible, then? Hence, seeking Najeeb's help was imperative. During one such discussion, Jankoji said, 'Kakasaheb, these are all matters of experience. Starting from the Peshwa government to everybody else, all say that Najeeb should be beheaded. There has to be some truth in this viewpoint.'

'What you say is quite right, Baba. But who, other than Najeeb, has enough knowledge of the layout of the beds of these massive rivers? We will need hundreds of boats too to make a pontoon bridge across the river. Who is going to supply them to us in this strange land? My opinion is that till such time as we safely reach the other bank, we will need to keep tickling the mane of this tomcat. Once across, it won't take us much time to finish him off. Looks like Malharji's advice is the one that we need to implement for now.'

This was how matters rested for now …

Two days later, Govindpant Bundele came visiting. Pant was a tax collector in the south of Antarved, often acknowledged as the biggest and the most prompt depositor of taxes in the Pune Durbar treasury. Having spent many monsoons of his life in the north, he was familiar with the lay of the land. Many of the recent political upheavals and realignments in Delhi had happened in front of his eyes. He was on easy terms with the power-wielders of many a kingdom around, and thus enjoyed a good equation with Najeeb too. Najeeb was quite sure that a day would come when Dattaji would chop his head off his shoulder. It was necessary for him, then, to find shelter in the space between a powerful pair of legs. How the legs could be hacked when the time was ripe, Najeeb didn't need to learn from anybody. He was desperate, therefore, to get into a more amicable relationship with the Marathas, and had met Pant a few times towards this end. He had taken Pant's wife for his adopted sister, and she would often address him as Govind Daaji, revered brother-in-law.

It was not as if Pant was unaware of Najeeb's true nature, but he was also aware that if ever the need arose for someone who could help him negotiate the terrain, Najeeb would be the man—crossing the Ganga, for instance. He was also aware of the Shindes' desperate need for a pontoon bridge, and accordingly, he sat in the Shinde confabulations as someone with important inputs to give. Dattaji finally decided that the tomcat's mane needed to be tickled.

The Shinde army quickly pulled up its camp at Kunjpura and headed eastward. It crossed the Yamuna at Raamra and rested at Shaamla. When Najeeb got news of the Maratha tents coming up at Shaamla, he was greatly perturbed. The Marathas had now penetrated into the Antarved, and they had the capacity to wreak havoc across many miles of the territory he controlled. Not as if Najeeb was the anti war kind, but he liked them all outside his turf. As of now, he was not strong enough to flash his own sword. If push came to shove, he would have to vanish. And that was why he was frantic to get into some kind of deal with the Marathas.

Govindpant mediated and a meeting was fixed between Najeeb and Dattaji at a mango orchard four miles from the Shinde camp. Why deal with Satan? This was the question to which the entire Maratha camp wanted an answer, but nobody had the courage to pose it straight to Dattaji himself. Bhagirathi too had been quite upset with her husband's work spilling into her private domain. Jankojibaba was not known for speaking with anyone, anyway. Naro Shankar, meanwhile, would sit musing, tying and untying knots in the tuft of hair at the top of his head.

As the day of the meeting neared, tension mounted in the camp. With the Marathas sitting on his chest, no treachery could be expected from Najeeb, to be sure. The slightest foul play on his part, and the Marathas would have burnt down half his territory, and Najeeb knew this well. But the question that even women and children asked among themselves was: when this master of intrigue had as good as walked into their net, why let him get away? Finally, it was Jankoji who broached the subject with Dattaji first. 'When this wild animal walks into our net, wouldn't it be better to put a ring through its nose and tame it?'

'Babasaheb, it doesn't fit into our code of ethics. Even if it is an enemy, when he comes for a dialogue, a dialogue, then, should be the only thing to happen.'

'When has *he* ever bothered about respecting ethical codes? He's gone to the extent of breaking oaths taken on the holy Koran!'

'So, if one person kills a cow, the other goes and kills a calf? It will only be discussions, as arranged. I shall not abandon my ethics.' Dattaji's was the last word. On the eve of the meet, though, the camp couldn't go to sleep. How could such a wonderful opportunity be allowed to slip away?

Taking advantage of the darkness, the most agitated among them gravitated instinctively to a secret spot: Jankojibaba, Naro Shankar, Mankeshwar, and a few others. 'What's the big deal about a bridge on the Bhagirathi? We can do it a thousand times. But this rat Najeeb, who's been gnawing away at the very foundation of the Maratha empire, he must be dealt with tomorrow.'

'I've always been ready for that,' interjected Antaji.

'But I'm afraid of Dattaji's temper,' exclaimed Naroji Shankar.

'There's no cause for fear. That wildcat shouldn't be allowed to go back alive.' All heads turned to see Dattaji's wife Bhagirathi emerge from the darkness, a spear in hand. Jankoji was the first to recover his balance.

'Kakusaheb? You here in this darkness?'

'Yes, I want this Najeeb dead too.'

With Bhagirathi herself joining the conspiracy, spirits rose high. They decided to reconvene at noon. The guards would be instructed to allow nobody else into the tent except Najeeb. As soon as the meet was over, Jankoji would get into the tent with ten others and hack Najeeb to pieces. It would be Bhagirathi's job to pacify Dattaji.

☙❧

The time for the meet had arrived. Dattaji sat resting against a bolster, building in his imagination that bridge across the Ganga. Six horsemen were making rapid progress up the incline on which the tent was erected, with Najeeb in the lead. His sturdy horse was accoutered in a brocade-covered saddle. A string of multi-coloured glass beads danced on its forehead, and it wore silver anklets. The harness was ornamented with silk tassels. Najeeb himself wore a steel helmet draped in red brocade, a brocaded top, gathered at the waist with a gem-studded belt. He was shod in expensive footwear from Lakhnau. As he trotted in, he kept looking around or anything that could arouse suspicion. Right behind Najeeb rode his closest confidantes, Ahmed Khan Afreedi, Saadullah Khan, brother Sultan Khan and a few others.

Najeeb dismounted in front of the tent and carefully examined the cloth wall of the tent. He suddenly turned and looked deep into the guard's eyes and stiffened. There was something odd there. The guards at the entrance looked a little tense too. As he entered the tent, he heard the guards at the entrance blocking the entry of others. Najeeb took a couple of steps deeper inside and looked cautiously around. There sat Dattaji, dressed in white, a welcoming smile on his face. 'Come in, come in, Khan Saheb,' he said, but Najeeb very likely didn't hear it. His ears had heard a low whistle from outside. He quickly looked towards the door and once again met the eagle-eyes of the guard. That was when he noticed Ahmad Khan make a sign. He quickly darted out of the tent, put his foot into the stirrup of his horse and jumped on to the saddle. Six horses galloped away in the direction from where they had come. It was only after they had put a distance of a couple of miles behind them that they slowed down. 'There was something in the eyes of the Marghattyas that I thought looked poisonous,' he said to Ahmad Khan.

֍

Jankoji could see the dots receding in the distance, as he stood chewing his lower lip. The delay couldn't have been more than a minute or so, but that had allowed the prey to escape unhurt.

The Shinde camp had been erected to the north-east of Meerut. Their royal pavilions and tents were pitched just outside the ancient town of Gadmukteshwar. It was around this place that the Hastinapur of the Mahabharat had stood. The Ganga flowed close by. There were tall temples of ancient times, with their stone walls and pillars etched with dancing gods and demigods and demons. The massive banyans had sent their matted locks deep into the earth, and stood witness to the hoary past. This was where Shri Krishna had delivered his lessons to Arjuna. At least two to three thousand out of the three hundred and thirty billion gods had marked their attendance here. No wonder, then, that for the religiously inclined Marathas, this was the ultimate place of pilgrimage.

The camp carried a strange glow about it today. A pavilion for discussion had been erected a couple of miles from the camp. A meeting was in progress between Najeeb Khan, his adviser Chetram, and Dattaji and his manager Ramchandrababa. So many months had drifted by idly, and Dattaji was in a hurry to cross the Ganga.

Jankoji had refused to join the discussions. He had wanted no truck with Najeeb at all. What accord among such discordant notes? He would have settled accounts with him at Shaamli if he hadn't been beaten to it by barely a couple of minutes. It had been a huge waste of effort, because without having touched a hair on Najeeb's head, he had had to suffer the wrath of Dattaji. Dattaji had been livid, and flayed the skin off everyone's back. Nothing could entice Najeeb now out of his lair. He had taken too much of a fright to even think of sticking his neck out of his territory.

Dattaji was required to change tack. On a single day, he dispatched his chieftains in different directions with instructions to raze everything to the ground. The Marathas stormed into every village they crossed in the Antarved and set everything on fire. One-thousand-and-three-hundred villages were torched in one day. In the face of this kind of a murderous assault, Najeeb was left with no choice but to buckle in, and the result was the meeting in progress.

'All we desire for the Khan Saheb to do is to build us this pontoon bridge across the Bhagirathi. We Marathas are land animals, basically, and love to race our horses across jungles and deserts. Your rivers are intractable monsters, and we don't have the legs to span them.'

'Abandon all your anxieties, Prince,' responded Najeeb with a laugh. 'You are our guest, so let us care for your legs. It's our responsibility to take you where you want to go. Your Highness should leave his worries to us. You shall see the bridges you want on the Ganga before the month is out.'

'Whatever we get out of the Ayodhya-Prayag campaign, twenty-five percent shall belong to the Khan Saheb.'

'Who's talking of share, huzoor? In fact, spend your month here at Hastinapur, is what I recommend. It's an important place for your faith. Get into charities, organize prayer sessions, visit holy places, you won't even know when the month has sped past.'

'That reminds me of another thing, Khan Saheb. You just agreed that these pilgrimage places are very dear to us Marathas. You have two very important ones in your territory—Haridwar and Jwalapur. Couldn't you give them over to us? This act will earn you a lot of merit.'

'We'll see about the merit,' Najeeb laughed. 'Get across the Ganga first. I'll hand over your two pilgrimages in the blink of an eye. Meanwhile, as you progress in your present campaign, you will be able to pocket Kashi Vishweshwar. Kashi is the ultimate destination of the religion-obsessed Hindus, isn't it?'

The meeting ended on a cordial note. They exchanged token gifts of bonhomie and exchanged turbans—that made them turban-brothers. Najeeb took Dattaji into his hug.

That evening, as the Shindes sat down to dinner, Jankoji appeared quiet. Dattaji looked towards Bhagirathi and said, 'What's the matter with Baba today? Why so low?'

'What do I say, Kakasaheb?' said Jankoji, his voice weary. 'I fear what you have done today hasn't been good. That double-dealer should never have been allowed to go scott-free. He's going to destroy us.'

The words hit Dattaji where it hurt. He dropped the food back into his plate. 'Baba, *you* alone understand the weal of the Maratha state, and *I* have come this far only to have fun, have I? To me, at least, Najeeb appears clean, and even if he turns out different, I shall smash him and have him for breakfast with stale bread.'

Seeing her husband agitated, Bhagirathi signalled to Jankoji to hold his peace. The sensible thing to do, Jankoji realized, was to exercise patience and withdraw.

Bhagirathi was barely sixteen at this time, but her maturity stretched well beyond this number. After Dattaji had left, Jankoji, Kashibai and Bhagirathi sat for a while with grave faces, when Jankoji finally spoke, 'Kakusaheb, this Najeeb says he will hand over the pilgrimages to us, but

I know that he has settled Muslim colonies near Jwalapur. He has made elaborate arrangements at every pilgrim spot under his control. If this man's machinations are not brought under check now, we go tumbling down the cliff-edge!'

'You know well enough how your uncle is always on a short fuse. Takes offence at trivial things and turns dark as a cloud. It's we who have to play cool.'

'Kakusaheb,' Jankoji let out a deep sigh, 'it's better to be a squint-eyed moron than be the younger person, they say, and they are right.'

ᴏᴊᴏ

It began to rain in earnest. The Ganga went on swallowing farm upon farm. The river that had looked like a lean horse during the summer days had now spread out like an elephant, and it moved in elephantine style too. The Maratha camps began to suffer in multiple ways. Being confined to tents and pavilions had become suffocating. The soldiers went looking for relief in the nearby temples and inns. Dattaji hosted a grand dinner for the Brahmins at the Gadmukteshwar temple as a prayer offering for victory in his latest campaign. It was followed by the usual distribution of alms. The glow on Bhagirathi's face, meanwhile, had started waning, and Dattaji's impatience for his child was hitting new water-marks every day.

Although he had expressed complete trust in Najeeb, there was some doubt that gnawed at his heart. He dispatched five horsemen to Shukratal. The party returned after four days to report that work on the pontoon bridge was in full swing. Najeeb had requisitioned the help of Jaita Gujar and the landlord of Muzaffarnagar. A scroll arrived from Najeeb in the next fifteen days that read, 'The Ganga is in floods because of the rains, and work on the pontoon bridge cannot be finished in good time. Will have to wait for the rains to subside.' Dattaji laughed at reading the missive. Happy with the way things were going, Dattaji and Bhagirathi took advantage of a break in the rains and made a trip to Meerut, rocking all the way atop Javhergunj. They visited the jeweller and Bhagirathi came back richer by the famous Bareili gold armbands and pearl trinkets.

One day, just as it was turning light, a small squad of Maratha horsemen galloped into the camp, sleepless and bedraggled, men and beasts coated thick with slime and mud. They had ridden all through the night from Karnal. The first thing they did was to raise a loud cry in front of Jankoji's tent. They handed him a scroll which Jankoji got an Urdu-reading person to read out to him. The earth appeared to have been pulled out from under his feet. He snatched back the scroll and went running to Dattaji's tent. He pushed the guards aside and shouted in a loud voice, 'Kakasaheb! Get up, Kakasaheb! A calamity has occurred!' His shout was loud enough to wake half the camp up. Some of the nearby soldiers pushed the staked horses and bullocks out of the way and went racing towards Dattaji's tent.

Dattaji stepped out of the tent rubbing his eyes, and asked, 'What's it, Babasaheb, what's the matter?'

'Kakasaheb, the mother fucker has stabbed us in the back! The animal whose back you had been caressing as so soft has now dealt a lethal blow with its tail. It's a calamity, Kakasaheb, it's a calamity.'

'Will you cut out the talk and come to the point? What has happened?' roared Dattaji.

'Look at this scroll, Kakasaheb. It's from Najeeb to Abdullah Durrani that his scouts were carrying to Damascus and Syria. Our horsemen at Karnal got suspicious and stopped them. This is what they found in their possession.'

'Tell us what the missive says,' broke in Naro Shankar, twiddling with his sacred thread.

'This is what Najeeb has to say to Durrani:

'O lord and master of Afghanistan, as you are an Afghan of the highest lineage, my seed is hardcore Afghan too. There are twenty-thousand hardcore Hindustanis here who are ready to jump into the Afghan fire at a sign from me. There are forty-thousand Rohilla Afghans on the other side of the Ganga who swear allegiance to you. I've told you countless times that there are these monkeys from Deccan here who have come and polluted our land. I've kept this big monkey by name Dattaji dallying here on one excuse or another for your arrival. Shuja of Ayodhya will also be willing to join us. So often have I informed the Afghan nobility that valiant Rohilla chieftains like Sardar Dundey Khan, Hafiz Rahmat Khan, Ahmad Khan Bangash and Saadullah Khan are willing to stake their lives for me if you can be persuaded to come. If you have any regard for your religion and for your brothers here, then, O you warrior who can put Rustam in the shade, come racing like the wind and get these Deccan monkeys to....'

'Enough!' yelled Dattaji. He had turned as red as a blade pulled fresh out of the blacksmith's furnace for tempering. His eyes flashed with anger and repentance. He began to sweat profusely. The Marathas were taken aback at seeing their leader in this state. All eyes turned towards him, silently asking the question, 'What have you gone and done, our leader?' Dattaji turned and walked away with long strides.

It was after a mile that he finally halted in front of a small temple on the bank of the Ganga, and went and sat inside in a state of stupor. It was after much cajoling that he was persuaded late in the evening to return to his tent; nothing could persuade him, however, not even Bhagirathi's fervent pleas, to have a mouthful of water or food. He just lay there, stunned, on his mat, uncaring of the bustle outside.

As Jankoji, Bhagirathi and Kashibai sat around him next morning, Bhagirathi suddenly turned pale and nearly fainted. The maid Paaru said, 'Baisaheb hasn't had a bite too since yesterday.'

'What have you been doing, Bhagirathi?' Dattaji snapped. 'Our child inside you would be starving too!'

'It's our tradition not to take a drop of water if the husband hasn't eaten.'

That settled it for Dattaji. With his eating, the entire camp heaved a sigh of relief. After he had forced a few mouthfuls into his stomach, Dattaji's eyes suddenly turned wet, his chest heaved and he let out a long sob. 'What kind of foolish delusion I allowed myself to slip into, Bhagirathi?' he cried. 'Why couldn't I see what was visible to the tiniest tot in the camp? How could I have lost my head so? And now, I've gone and dug a pit for myself!'

'Kakasaheb,' Jankobaji pleaded. 'The spark still hasn't died among the embers. You just have to blow your breath, and every man and horse will burst into flame. We are not fighting for the Deccan land alone, we are fighting for the throne of Delhi, for all of Hindustan. Just one blast from your trumpet, and corpses will jump out of their graves and set after those Afghan Rohillas!'

The camp turned electric at Jankoji's call. Dattaji placed a jaunty turban on his head and stuck a plume in it. He whipped his sword out of its sheath and yelled, 'Har Har Mahadev!' Back came the response from thousands of throats, 'Jai Bhawani!' 'Jai Mhalsakant!' The kettledrums beat louder than usual as the stakes were pulled out for the camp to move. The ropes were untied, the cloth walls and curtains were rolled up and stacked in the bullock carts. Nobody cared for covering the ladies' carts with draperies. Kashibai hopped on to a horse and Bhagirathi got into a palanquin. The twitchings in her womb were strong, but the sight of the Maratha warriors setting off to settle accounts with Najeeb had made all hunger and thirst vanish. She pressed a hand on her stomach and joined the departing hordes. Buffeted by wind and rains, the camp began moving forward along the bank of the Ganga.

The Shinde scouts were keeping them supplied with news from all around. The pontoon bridge across the Ganga was coming along, true, but Najeeb had kept it tightly under his control. His loyal Rohilla guards were keeping it under their surveillance round the clock. Najeeb had found shelter in a convenient bend in the Ganga right there at Shukratal.

With the help of the nearby Saeeds, the Shindes struck camp at Mirapur, two miles to the west of Shukratal. While the Marathas kept a sharp eye on the movements of Najeeb, Najeeb himself kept peeping out at the Shindes like a parrot that had taken shelter in the bole of a tree.

Jankoji took four of his trusted men and went out on a two-day reconnoitering trip. He went around the periphery of Shukratal and ferreted out as much information as he could from his own scouts and the locals. A decent enough picture of the huge Shukratal now stood in his mind's eye. The two rivers Shalini and Malini joined the Ganga a couple of miles up in the north. The riverbank was sandy, unsteady and slimy. To the west of the Ganga, was the holy site of Shukratal. The river here bent like the beam of a palanquin as it flowed through this part. On the inner half-mile square heights, there were huge pits and strange ravines. The tall, windy trees there could easily see the bank of the Ganga for a good ten or fifteen miles. The undergrowth between the trees was dense, interspersed here and there with thick jungle vines. On the tallest point inside sat an ancient Mahadev temple. From the point of security, it was a fortress created by nature. On the east ran the Ganga, on the north and south of Shukratal was horribly soft and boggy land. The west, that was relatively unprotected, Najeeb had cordoned off with huge trees cut and laid across. A battery of cannons was laid out on all three sides. In the inner ring was a trench two-persons deep and ten-arms long. All the land to the east of the bridge belonged to Najeeb, through which camel carts and bullock carts kept him supplied with grains, spices, and whatever else he desired. With a strength of just twenty or twenty-five thousand at Shukratal, he could battle on for months together. Cunning but brave, Najeeb had the Marathas nicely in a bind.

Despite the help from the Mirapur Saeeds, the Maratha army was suffering. With the rains in full fury, it was impossible to stir out too far. While the cost of grain rose up to three kilos for a rupee, Najeeb was getting it all cheap.

Although Dattaji was simmering for revenge, it was difficult to set heavy guns on the sand or to lay mines. One good development was that he received reinforcement from Delhi in the shape of two-thousand fresh horsemen under the command of Jiwaji Shinde and his son Hanmantrao.

For a breath of fresh air if not for war, the Marathas set off one morning for a ride along the Ganga with about two-to-three-thousand horsemen; senior officers like Janrao Wabale, Naro Shankar, Jiwaji Shinde and Dattaji Shinde were among them. In the afternoon, they gathered around Shukratal. When Najeeb's scouts saw such an assembly of Marathas, Najeeb immediately instructed the gunners to stay on the ready. One of the Maratha cavalrymen noticed a Rohilla among the shrubs and fired a bullet in his direction. That started the conflagration. The Rohilla cannons concealed behind the shrubs began spouting fire and roasting the Marathas. This sudden gunfire rattled the Marathas for a minute, but the next minute they jumped off their horses, and using the animals as shields, began returning gunfire with gunfire. The Rohilla ammunition, however, was vastly superior; their cannons began sending the horses up in the air like rubber balls, and their arrows came whizzing out of the bushes.

The sudden conflagration sent Dattaji into a frenzy. He leapt into the fire and slaughtered the gunners before him. A horseman went running back to Jankoji and informed him about the skirmish that had unexpectedly broken out, and that Dattaji had thrust himself deep into the fray. Jankoji immediately tied a sword to his belt, leapt on the horse and dug his spurs into the horse's flanks. When he saw Dattaji surrounded by a large bunch of Rohilla soldiers, snapping at him from all sides like wild dogs around a tiger, he swung his sword in the air, ensuring that each swing brought at least one enemy down. In his rage, he didn't notice a Rohilla creeping up from behind. The soldier got hold of the reins of Jankoji's horse with one hand and swung his weapon with the other. Jankoji swayed aside to evade the swing, but couldn't prevent the sword from grazing the chain armour and shredding it. Jankoji retrieved his balance and sent his sword slashing through the midriff of the assailant.

The Marathas had succeeded in breaking in through a flank and putting the Rohilla guns out of commission. But as they raced in, past the shrubbery, they did not notice the trenches that had been dug on the inner side of the shrubs. They had been advancing with such pace that a good sixty or seventy of the horsemen fell into the trenches along with their horses before the ones behind could apply the brakes on their animals. Those who had not died at the first impact lay groaning, both man and animal, bodies broken and life fast oozing out of them.

On another front, the mounted soldiers of the two armies rammed into each other. It began raining musket balls, bullets, hand-grenades and arrows. One bullet hit the horse under Dattaji's thigh and that brought it down. But just as it was collapsing, Dattaji leapt off it and landed on his feet. A Maratha horseman quickly dismounted and handed over his steed to his master.

It soon turned dark and the skirmish had to end. Dattaji and Jankoji returned tired and wounded to their camp. While Najeeb got away with about fifty Rohillas dead, the loss to the Marathas was heavier. When the count was taken, something like five hundred soldiers and twelve hundred horses had been sacrificed at the altar of Mahadev of Shukratal. Sardar Jivaji Shinde and his son Hanmantrao, who had brought such hope and cheer to the Maratha camp barely two days ago, had lost their lives too. The entire camp was submerged in gloom.

☙

Najeeb Khan's tent, camouflaged under a tree at Shukratal, appeared listless today, its usual conceit diminished. The two posts on which it was erected seemed to have turned limp, the ropes that held the cloth walls taut had developed a sag. The green pennants and the banners of Mohammad, Ali, Zehra and Fatima that otherwise fluttered proudly with every gust of wind had put their heads down. Najeeb sat inside, leaning against a soft bolster, shifting his weight this way and that, as if his buttocks had turned numb. He looked crestfallen, as if he hadn't slept well for the past four or five days. His face had turned into a kaleidoscope of negative emotions: desperation, anger, anxiety. To his left sat his younger brother Sultan Khan; to his right was his bosom friend Ahmad Khan Afreedi, and in front sat his young son Zabeyta Khan. His wife's sister's husband, Saadullah Khan, who wasn't ordinarily invited for such conclaves, was present too. Najeeb addressed them in grave tones:

'You are not just my relatives and friends, you are also people of the same blood. The history of the world since its very beginning shows that it's people of the blood who run to one's aid. That's why I have called you over here, to bare my heart to you. We are caught in the deathly embrace of infidel forces, and our very faith is in danger. Never mind if rivers of blood are made to flow, never mind if we are decapitated, we will make our headless bodies break into a macabre dance, but we shall not surrender before these Marghattyas. What news have you got for today, Zabeyta?'

'Father, despite the havoc we wreaked among their forces, these Marathas refuse to withdraw. Their commander-in-chief, Datta Shinde, is hell bent on revenge. He wants to blow up this pontoon bridge we have built, to disrupt our supplies from Najeebabad. He has been saying he will sever your head and stuff your body with straw before he returns to Deccan.'

'Does he even faintly believe that he can bring to pass such absurd brags? The very opposite is far more likely to happen, when I sever his head and send it as a tribute to King Durrani. I shall then take the king's help and vanquish all of Hindustan, and gather all its riches. I am no molly-coddled bastard child of some Ameer or feudal lord. I have sprung from the soil.'

Talking of the soil took him back to the days of his early struggles. A scene from fifteen years ago floated before his eyes. A full-grown, thirty-five-year-old man belonging to the Yusufzai clan of Kandahar in Afghanistan set off with his wife and child to carve a future for himself in Hindustan. A number of bands of Afghan Rohillas had been trickling into

Hindustan much before Nadir Shah's time. Tall, well-built, aggressive, these Rohillas had immediately started creating space for themselves by flashing their swords. Some joined the services of local chieftains and landlords, some themselves became chieftains by flexing their muscles. Their settlements mushroomed in the land between the upper reaches of the Ganga and the Yamuna. The empire at Delhi had begun crumbling much before this time, and that had given the Afghans the opening to spread their limbs with comfort. Najeeb had begun his innings in Hindustan as an ordinary soldier with Mohammad Khan at the princely salary of two rupees a month. It had taken him no time to display the stuff he was made of. Soon he was promoted to the rank of a sergeant, and his salary was raised to five rupees.

Armies marching off in style, grand durbars, the feudal magnificence, the roaring call of the ushers at the arrival of the grandee, the glitter of rubies and diamonds flashing off every part of his body, the elephant stables, the merry, titillating laughter emanating from the wildly pulsating harems, all of these Najeeb wanted for himself, and wanted them in a hurry. The desire for the good things of life became so overpowering that he hardly knew any peace. His eyes were so blinded by the dazzle of princely splendor that they lost all distinction between good and bad, true and false. It became his driving passion to sit there at the top, and he recognized no obstacle as insurmountable for making his ascent. His first wife, Zabeyta's mother, suffered from asthma, and the malady had reduced her to a coughing, wheezing skeleton. The rumour that did the rounds was that Najeeb had merely set his thumb to her windpipe when she had asphyxiated and collapsed. His soldiers held that he had been eyeing the Afghan prince Dundey Khan's comely daughter for some time, and had believed that wife number one would be a serious disincentive. The calculations, if true, were well made, and once the passage was cleared, the girl walked into his mansion with the key to untold treasures. Along with his daughter, Dundey Khan handed over control of fourteen parganas to his son-in-law, including Nageena, Sherkot, Bijnor and Chandkur.

Landlord Najeeb Khan's steed had now grown a sturdy pair of wings. Dundey Khan had gone ahead and made him an officer of four hundred horses. There was some royal land in Saharanpur contiguous with Najeeb's, and he began nibbling at it unobtrusively but assiduously.

He also began raiding the caravans that carried goods and grains to the Jawalpur and Saharanpur market.

In 1753, a conflict arose between the Sunni and Shia sects at the Delhi court. Safdarjung, the wazeer of Delhi and the Nawab of Ayodhya, was a Shia, and the king had decided to do away with him. When the call came for Ghaziuddin to report to Delhi, Najeeb had been ready and waiting, and he instantly set off for Delhi. It did not matter to him that Safdarjung was a close friend of Dundey Khan, his father-in-law, under whose patronage Najeeb had flourished. Ignoring Dundey Khan's plea for restraint, Najeeb gathered fifteen thousand horsemen by fair means and foul, and raced towards Delhi. Before setting off, he had already procured from the king the promise of the overlordship of Saharanpur. Turning a deaf ear to Hafiz Rahmat Khan, Dundey Khan and his brother-in-law Saadullah Khan, he rode into Delhi with his forces and stood by the Blue Bastion of the Delhi Fort next to the king himself. Spread out before them were the forces of Safdarjung, and standing alongside them were the forces of his own father-in-law. Najeeb brought victory for the king's forces and had Safdarjung flee towards Ayodhya. He stepped out of Delhi only after having secured a baronetcy and the principality of Saharanpur.

Within days of returning, he made Saharanpur his seat and established a big village by the name of Najeebabad. He brought up a new army at the northern end of the Ganga, and improved receipt of revenue. He then fortified Patthargadh, Gaurugadh and Shukratal and reinforced his position there. He went on campaigns and stretched the boundaries of his holdings right up to the foothills of Dehradun. When in the company of his Afghan peers, he was not beyond scratching his nose and causing their bile to rise.

There was no way, therefore, that he was going to let go of his hard-earned prosperity, or abandon Shukratal at any cost. He knew that if he stepped out of his den, he would be slaughtered in no time. He had laid landmines in all directions in the hope of blowing up the Marathas, but it was his misfortune that they wouldn't blow up at the right time. In his imagination, he could see himself standing proudly in front of his vast army like the king of Kandahar; he could see all the Afghan chieftains and landlords of the Ganga-Yamuna belt coming together and rushing to his support; he could see the Nawab of Ayodhya Shuja-ud-dowla extending a hand of friendship. But all these happy visions had still to come to pass. As of now, he had the Marathas sitting heavily on his chest. He turned a sharp eye towards his brother-in-law Saadullah Khan and said, 'Nawab Saheb, I could have dispatched Dattaji long ago, but for that I need all of us Afghans of Rohilkhand to come together. But what do they care for their religion and their clan? On the contrary, for them, I am mad to be bothering so much about these things!'

'You really think they are at fault?' retorted Saadullah bitterly. 'It's you and your devious ways that the Afghans are wary of. When you are in the hot waters of politics, you bring in the angle of religion and talk of 'jihad'. One call from Ghaziuddin, and you went running to Delhi against our joint advice. You swore on the holy Koran and, when the time arrived, you forgot about your sacred oaths when razing his tribe to the ground. The king of Delhi, who made these happy days possible for you, you didn't blink an eye before destroying him and bringing his womenfolk to starvation. There is a whole abyss that separates your behaviour from the call for jihad, Khan Saheb!'

'I am your guest, Nawab Saheb,' Najeeb changed tack, 'and an occasional minor intransigence of one's own people can be forgiven. People go spreading canards about me and you …'

'People spreading canards, eh? And what about my own experiences?' Saadullah was in no mood to let the man slip away. 'I am your wife's sister's husband, your own brother-in-law. After this closeness, have you spared my own lands? Haven't you flogged every excuse, big and small, to buttress your own wealth?'

Najeeb was defeated. He turned his eyes down, and then looked up piteously at his inquisitor, suggesting that he should be spared the humiliation in the presence of company. Khan Afreedi stepped in and changed the subject. 'Any message,' he asked, 'from Shuja-ud-dowla in Ayodhya?'

'Not yet,' responded Najeeb, 'but he has no choice but to send his forces to help me. I have made it crystal clear to him that if the Marathas ever cross the Ganga, the next thing they will do is to mount a campaign against Ayodhya for tributes, that is certain. Once this infidel community finds a toehold anywhere, it is bound to stretch its limbs out. This pilgrimage town today, that territory tomorrow, there will be no end to their demands. For all you know, tomorrow the Marathas may well prop up Ghaziuddin as the Nawab of Ayodhya! Shuja will remember this Najeeb's warnings then!'

'Khan Saheb, it was just a few years ago that you had risen up against Shuja's father Safdarjung. You had fought against him for being a Shia. You had been instrumental in driving him out of the seat of the wazeer at Delhi. You expect Shuja to forget all the humiliation?'

'Khan Bahadur,' laughed Najeeb, 'you should have been a poet instead of being a ruler. Only poets think the way you do. This is politics, brother, where bonds are made and unmade according to the circumstance. If he can truly understand the gravity of the danger that looms over him, he will send his forces post-haste. Or else, he will be destroying his own self.'

It was while these deliberations were in progress that Kaarbhaari Chetram rushed into the tent, turban in hand. His face was glowing. One look at his face, and Najeeb asked, 'What's the news?'

'I have great news.'

'Spill it out, then!'

'A scroll has arrived from the commander-in-chief of the Afghan army. It says the King of Afghanistan, Badshah Durrani is due to reach the borders of Hindustan in a fortnight.'

'Subhaan Allah! Praise be to Allah!' the cries rang out in the tent.

Najeeb was so tickled with the news that he was immediately transported into another world. He saw Dattaji Shinde lying spread-eagled on the blood-soaked ground, like a bullock whose throat had just been slit. And all those Afghan overlords and chieftains, who had been sneering at his desperate calls for help and had stayed pointedly away, he saw them filing in one behind the other, heads down, as if their spines had snapped from the neck. He saw Shuja of Ayodhya lowing like a lost calf, desperately trying to catch Najeeb's eye. Najeeb, of course, had no time to waste on such insects as these. He sat on the royal swing, exchanging pleasantries with Badshah Durrani himself.

He immediately sprang up and ordered that a feast be prepared for all the guests. His over-vaulting thoughts had already flown past the clouds and were in intimate conversation with the stars.

While Najeeb's camp was feasting that evening, the Marathas were making plans on how to cross the Ganga from the upper reaches of Haridwar. Four days earlier, they had come together to celebrate Dussehra, the festival of crossing of borders. They had all assembled—commanders, chieftains, petty lords, soldiers, workers and camp-followers—to reaffirm their loyalty to their overlord Dattaji. Addressing them, Dattaji said:

'My esteemed Maratha brethren, this enterprise has turned out to be really heavy. In earlier times, Dussehra would be the time when your ancestors and mine would set off for collecting their revenues from their holdings. But this Dussehra has been quite an ordeal for us. It's four months now since our campaign began, and victory is nowhere in sight. While we and our animals starve here for food and fodder that wretched Najeeb has been bloating on all the victuals he gets across from the Antarved over his pontoon bridge. What do we do?'

'Shrimant,' Jivaji Bhoite responded, 'one way to bring Najeeb to his knees is to attack the bridge and loot his supplies.'

'The bastards have been keeping a watch over the bridge like ghouls,' piped in Jankobaji. 'Attacking them directly would require creating barricades on the river, but the barricades are not likely to stay on this monster of a river. Najeeb's cannons will roast us, and we would lose lives pointlessly.'

'What does one do, Shrimant? My fingers are itching to get round Najeeb's throat. But all the slime and mud here doesn't allow us to make a hit. We can't get a good vantage point for blowing up their bridge. The Maratha horses and elephants go up to the banks and turn back disappointed because they can't cross the violent waters.'

'That's true, of course, but if we want to survive, some vantage point will *have* to be found,' growled Dattaji.

'You are quite right,' said old Govindpant.

'I don't want a word out of you, Pant,' Dattaji snapped at Govindpant. 'It's Marathas like you who have been an obstacle to our progress. You Marathi people who have settled in North India have not cared for the well-being of your native soil. Here we have launched our expedition against the King of Delhi, and you people go befriending rogues like Najeeb. He's your brother-in-law now, isn't he? Addresses you as Daaji, I have seen!'

'You have to take your words back, Shrimant,' he said, mopping his eyes. 'Just because he addresses me as Daaji, you shouldn't think that he is any intimate of mine. Shrimant, my hair has turned grey in the service of the Maratha confederacy. I know you carry doubts in your head, so I swear by Lord Maha-Ganpati of Wai, within four days I shall find a suitable point for crossing the river, and take the Maratha army across right up to Najeebabad. We shall blow their pontoon bridges, I swear, and it won't matter to me if I fall victim to a cannonball. No better way to die than gaining martyrdom on the banks of the holy Ganga.'

※

The oath taken by Govindpant on that Dussehra day was now in the process of being fulfilled. Pant had been the revenue collector in these parts for decades, and had gained considerable familiarity with the land and its people. He had returned at the crack of dawn after a quick visit to Muzaffarpur, and had brought with him Jaitya Gujar. Gujar was the person who had helped build the pontoon bridge for Najeeb at Shukrataal. He knew every bend and curve, every rise and dip, every stone and rock in the area intimately, and he was an unrepentant mercenary. He would be willing to help anyone who gave him sufficient money.

The Marathas set off with Jaitya that very same night, and reached close to Haridwar after two days of journey. It was towards the upper end of Haridwar that Jaitya showed them a place where crossing the river was possible. Jivaji Bhoite was the first to get his elephant into the water. The elephant waded through the very wide expanse towards the other bank, followed by some Maratha braves. The water was just about navel-high; once the depth was ascertained, the army went delirious with joy. A thrilled Dattaji turned towards Jaitya and gifted him with an elephant, a horse and a jewel-studded walking stick on the spot.

It was already midnight, and they had decided to cross the Ganga before the day broke. The land on the other side was Najeeb's land, and his sentinels would be keeping an eye out. The raiding party had to at all costs sneak into Najeebabad under the cover of darkness. Eight thousand horsemen crossed the river under the leadership of Jivaji Bhoite and Tatya, the son of Antaji Mankeshwar. On the bank, Govindpant tied a length of woollen cloth round his head and shook hands with Dattaji before setting off.

'Pant, let at least Jankojibaba join you,' said Dattaji in a heavy voice.

'No, no, Shrimant, let this expedition be mine alone.'

The Deccan men and horses began racing though the bitter cold of Najeeb's land. When daylight arrived, the secret of the Maratha raid was laid bare. Najeeb's posts around that area mounted a resistance against the invading Maratha forces. Flashing swords and flaming torches began with their game. Najeeb's land was being razed. In village after village, walls and houses were being levelled by gunfire. Massive holes were being punched into the battlement walls, and the houses were crackling as they went up in flames.

Govindpant soon laid siege to the Najeebabad Fort. Its ramparts were strong. The Marathas began digging trenches and laying mines. The guardian of the fort staked his life to protect it. In the first two days, the Marathas managed to capture an enemy elephant, five carts full of arrows, and also a few camels and horses. Najeeb's caravan was trapped inside the fort. His wife stood shivering. It would have been quite easy for the Marathas to take her hostage, but that was not how they worked. They ensured she did not come to any harm during the four days of their assault on the fort.

When he saw smoke and dust rising up in his territory, Najeeb was at first stunned. He crossed the pontoon bridge with a select band of soldiers and got into his patch. The temerity of the Marathas had set him on fire. But Abdali was hundreds of miles away, and the only person who could be accessed was Shuja-ud-dowlah of Ayodhya. He had sent desperate letters to the Afghan king long ago with the message, 'Oh king, it will be your shame if we have to die a dog's death at the hands of these sinners while the King of Afghanistan breathes. Till as long as I have life left in me, I propose to keep fighting against these demons, even if left alone.' But the Afghan king was caught in his own problems: Nasir Khan on one side and Herati on the other, both had risen up in revolt. Caught in these domestic hassles, Abdali would take a long time coming to India.

As soon as he got news of Govindpant crossing the river, he dispatched an urgent appeal to Ayodhya: 'O king of Ayodhya, jewel among men, the sinful ghouls have caused mayhem in the Antarved. Once they're finished with this obstacle in their path called Najeeb, they are going to attack you. If you really want to die at the hands of these sinners, suit yourself, but remember that you still have it within your powers to save Islam. All this business of Shia and Sunni, they are limbs of the same body, aren't they?'

When the Afghan grandee Dundey Khan learnt of the siege laid by ten thousand Maratha horsemen of the Najeebabad Fort, with his daughter trapped inside, he decided to overlook Najeeb's intransigence, and for the sake of Afghan pride, got into the battlefield with fellow grandee Hafiz Rahmat Khan. They put up a stiff resistance against the rampaging Marathas, but the momentum of the enemy soldiers was too much for them to withstand for long; they were steadily getting pushed back. The Marathas began advancing towards the pontoon bridge in the east. Najeeb had lost all hope, but there was all that arsenal stocked on the other side of the river that would fall into enemy hands, and so, he fought on desperately. But with Dundey Khan also slackening, he was overtaken by fear for his life, and he fled with his two-thousand-strong army to seek shelter in the eastern mountains.

With the resistance falling limp, the Maratha forces pressed on harder. When they came within sight of the bridge, they let out a loud yell and ran towards it. Once upon it, some began digging up the earth coating, some others began undoing the ropes that held the boats together. Some others took the bridge to be Najeeb himself and began hammering at it furiously.

Najeeb was racing frantically towards the safety of the mountains. He had to live to fight another day. He would have progressed a couple of miles when he saw a cloud of dust approaching him from the front. What new calamity could this be? Believing that this was the end, he was about to dive into the bushes on the side, when he noticed the green pennants fluttering in the vanguard. He slapped his thigh in glee and laughed. When they came closer, he recognized them as the army of the Gosavi brothers Umraogiri and Anupgiri. This Hindu Gosavi army under the vassalage of Shuja was reputed for its toughness and resilience. Big built and courageous, they were fierce warriors. Najeeb's anxiety vanished at the sight of them. Addressing Umraogiri, he said, 'Sardar Saheb, you have arrived like a breath of life in the nick of time. Any later, and it could all have been over for this nobody.'

'It's not us alone, Shuja-ud-dowlah himself is coming right behind.'

'That's great news,' burst out Najeeb, mopping his moist eyes. 'See, Sardar Saheb? The Hindus and Musalmans of Hindustan are like Ganga and Yamuna. But these monkeys from the Deccan won't let us people live in peace. Let's find a permanent solution for these Deccanis for the well-being of Hindustan. Come along, my ghaazees, let's beat the hell out of these sinful Deccanis once and for all!'

Gosavis, Nubians, Muslims, they all began racing towards the battlefield with renewed vigour, with Najeeb leading from the front. As they rode together, Najeeb let the word go round among his neighbouring riders that Abdali was coming too. The cry was taken over by the soldiers and they started shouting as they rode, 'Abdali's come! Durrani's come!'

The Marathas had barely scraped the first layer of earth and would have loosened the ropes of a boat or two, when they heard the clamour of the approaching horde from a distance. Along with the drumming of the horse-hooves, they also heard the yell of 'Abdali's come! Durrani's come!' That was enough to send shivers through them. They dropped their weapons. Somebody shouted in panic, 'We're done for! Run! Run!' When the first ten or fifteen of them ran, the rest lost heart too, and began running pell-mell. Nobody wanted to hold on and think. Those of them that could jump on to their horses bolted. Those that were caught with their feet in the stirrup began falling to the arrows that came flying. Soon the entire army of the enemy was upon them, and they began falling to the swords that had begun flashing all around them. Riderless horses were running out into the open not knowing which direction to take.

It was evening when the Marathas who had set off first reached Najeebabad. Seeing their panic-stricken mates running for their life, the five-thousand odd soldiers at Najeebabad also decided to flee while there was time. Umraogiri and Najeeb were not very much behind the soldiers they were chasing. In the darkening twilight, the Marathas were running for their lives, with the Gosavis bearing down upon them like avenging furies. The terrorized Marathas somehow made it to the northern reaches of Haridwar, and rode their horses into the part of the river from where they had crossed earlier. Because of the darkening loam, however, and sheer panic, many of them got the spot altogether wrong and were quickly swallowed up by the water, horse and all. Many of those who had got their spot right couldn't do it quick enough, and became easy pickings for the Gosavi bowmen on the bank. The sheer disorder of their race to the other bank meant that some would die of the push and pull of the melee.

Najeeb was egging the Gosavi archers to dispatch their missiles faster and faster. 'We've got these Marathas to scamper like ants,' he said laughingly to Umraogiri Gosavi. 'Who can stop us now?'

⁂

Dattaji had withdrawn his Mirpur camp some seven or eight miles behind. Fate had marked the Maratha army for its favourite punching bag. A new calamity would stand up to be measured every day. Govindpant's valiance had ended in disaster. Well upwards of two-thousand soldiers made it from Haridwar to the main camp in rags that barely hid their shame. Covered in dust and caked blood, they could easily have been mistaken for the wretched beggars of Gudmukteshvar. But when the battered and beaten regiment of Tryambak Bapuji began filtering in from the Punjab, it made even these bedraggled soldiers drop their jaws in astonishment.

Ahmad Shah Abdali's son Taimur had raided the Punjab and devastated all the posts that the Marathas had established. General Jahaan Khan had piled pyramids of bodies in every village he had passed through. The news now was that Ahmad Shah had himself set off for an expedition to Hindustan. Taimur's name had been proclaimed in Lahore, and prayers had been offered to him as the new badshah of the Punjab. The villagers had got wind of the dire straits of the Marathas; consequently, even petty highwaymen had become bold enough to denude them of whatever they carried on themselves: ornaments, their swords, even the clothes on their back. They would often smash their heads for fun. Fighting against these impossible odds, Tryambak's beaten soldiers would often smear themselves with ash and try to pass off as mendicants. When they finally managed to reach Dattaji's camp, they bawled out in relief and had the first decent meal in weeks. They were given two sets of clothes each.

Maratha thanedaar Sabaji Shinde too had arrived, managing to escape from Multan. Even before that, the local landlords that Dattaji, Raghunathrao and Malharji had appointed as caretakers had begun creating their own rumpus. As a result, Lakshminarayan, the caretaker of Adina Beg and the children of Saadiqa Beg, had also run in to take shelter with the Marathas. With hardly enough to feed their own, the Marathas were now having to provide for these peripherals.

While Abdali, Taimur Shah and Jahaan Khan were descending into Hindustan from the Punjab with a fresh army of fifty thousand, Najeeb, on the other side of the river, driven by the obsession of burying the Marathas, had begun gathering his Afghan friends and relatives. The Marathas were getting trapped from both sides, as if in a nutcracker, and the entire camp was in a state of distraction. Soldiers had cocked their ears for the consultations that were on in the private tents. The traders had gathered up their merchandise and were ready to wind up their camp enterprises. The gypsies and the suppliers of fodder sat in small huddles, discussing in their strange language which region to go to now, how to gather grains.

With the enemy adding a new twist each day into an already complex situation, Dattaji was tied up in knots. Bhagirathi didn't want to add to her husband's worries. She would conceal her teary eyes with heavy lines of kohl applied with a flatter finger.

ॐ

It was a star-studded assembly of grandees that had gathered in the conference pavillion. It included big-wigs like Janrao Wabale, Jankoji, Govindpant, Phaltankar, Somajibaba Bhosale, Tryambak Bapuji, Jivaji Bhoite, Saabaj Shinde and Naro Shankar. Somajibaba said, 'That Najeeb is a hound straight out of hell. With Abdali closing in from Sirhind, Madho Singh from the Punjab, he himself from across the Ganga along with Dundey Khan, Hafiz Rahmat Khan, Kutub Shah Guru and Shuja-ud-dowlah, and Ahmad Khan Pathan from Farookhabad, they have got us properly in their clutches, like a python round its prey. Why, then, should his agent Chetram have come yesterday to talk the sweet language of truce?'

'It's pure charade,' opined Tryambak Bapuji. 'Once Abdali arrives, why would he care a bad penny for this truce?'

'And who's started this talk about Abdali Durrani, anyway?' chipped in Janrao Wabale. 'The mere mention of his name makes people go pale.

The emperor of Hindustan, whose duty it is to lay down his life for the defence of his realm, he is looking for a safe hole to hide himself in. He and his wazeers have all sent their clansmen packing towards distant Agra for security. Marwaris, tradesmen, petty entrepreneurs, not one of them wants to hang back in Delhi. They have all tied up their bundles and vanished. Delhi has turned into an abandoned wasteland, they say.'

Reports from scouts and spies had been pouring in even while the conference was in progress. Most of the scrolls sent in dealt with Abdali's campaigns. As the discussion dragged on, Jankojibaba suggested, 'There's not much point in staying here too long. We should wind up our effects and leave. Najeeb's persuasions are not worth a straw.'

'We've had a taste of his wile once, so why let him sidle near again?' asked Dattaji. 'Every movement we make from here on has to be precise and cautious. With so many of our soldiers having come over here from all over the Punjab, our army is well over forty-thousand-strong. It makes no sense to sacrifice such a huge army for no worthwhile gain.'

The servant Rajaram entered to give the message that the wazeer of Delhi, Ghaziuddin had arrived. 'What's that man doing here at such an early hour?' wondered Dattaji. He stood up to receive him. 'Come, Khan Saheb. How come so early here, and that too alone?'

'I'm not alone. I have with me Nagarmal, Surajmal Rupram Katare's agent and his infantry of five-thousand men.'

'Which way is the wind blowing in Delhi?'

'You would have heard, I'm sure, that we have assassinated the emperor of Delhi and tossed his corpse over the fort into the Yamuna below.'

This was shocking news. 'When did it happen?' enquired a worried Dattaji. 'Why?'

'Just three days ago. We have placed the Mughal Prince Saani on the throne and had prayers read in his name.'

'Why did you have to worsen the situation with such a precipitate move?'

Everybody's attention was focussed on the dark-complexioned wazeer. He already carried public rage against himself for having done away with an emperor before. The unexpressed question on every face was: what further mischief would be triggering off by killing yet another emperor? Ghaziuddin, however, looked quite sure that what he had done was the most appropriate thing to do. 'Shrimant,' he began, 'you are probably not aware; I wasn't aware either, till such time as the emperor's and Najeeb's secret letters travelling towards Kandahar landed in my hands.'

'The emperor's letters going to Kandahar?' stammered an unbelieving Jankojibaba.

'Yes, gentlemen, the emperor as well as Madho Singh of Jayanagar had dispatched their scrolls to Kandahar. Now, the emperor, whose job it is to protect Delhi, if he turns the wheel the other way and invites an enemy to invade his own capital, what should I have done?'

The wazeer threw a pouch at them and asked them to examine its contents. The contents of the scrolls from Najeeb, Madho Singh and the emperor stunned them. Dattaji was rattled. 'What misfortune is this?' he exclaimed. 'Here we are, three hundred miles from our native land, wearing our bones in this heat and storm, and the emperor, whose duty it is to protect Hindustan, he himself is opening the doors for the enemy and readying to welcome him! However, whatever happens, we are not going to let it affect our faith. We will not let Najeeb carry on with his diabolical games. We will not return before drowning him in the Ganga.'

Ghaziuddin left for his tent to stretch out for the night. The conference was nearing its end. A scout ran in with another piece of intelligence: Abdali had raided the Punjab and his Haroli army had reached Ambala. As soon as the scroll was read, Dattaji declared, 'It won't do for us to tarry at a single place. If we don't move briskly, Abdali may cross the Yamuna at Kunjpura, and before we know it, he and Najeeb will join forces. We need to stop Abdali's advance before this happens. Let's take an account of Abdali on the fields of Kunjpura and Kurukshetra. If we can tackle him, Najeeb is a mere pushover.'

'But Abdali is no raw recruit,' Naro Shankar reminded the assembly. 'He tamed Iran and Afghanistan with the strength of his arms.'

'He may not be raw,' growled Dattaji, 'but I shall tear him apart like a wolf and eat him raw. Raw meat tastes better than cooked meat, they say!'

'All right, then, let's lock horns with him. Let's see what Abdali is capable of,' said Somajibaba Bhosale, and that brought the meeting to an end.

Kettle-drums were beaten and trumpets sounded. Orders were issued to pull up tents. Within a matter of three hours, the entire camp was ready to move. Dattaji and Jankoji sat on the howdah mounted on Javhergunj. With an eight-month-heavy womb, Bhagirathi was loath to move. Riding on an elephant or on a she-camel was simply out of the question; even a palanquin ride had become difficult for her. Hence a special palanquin was rigged up for her, which was put in charge of the most nimble-footed bearers. Jankoji's wife Kashibai's palanquin travelled alongside her. From time to time, she would push aside the tassels, peep out towards her friend, and check on her. There were seven she-camels and around forty slaves and servants of Adina Beg's man Lakshminarayan that travelled with the caravan. Also in the entourage were the wives and kids of Saadiqa Beg, the entire crowd that had fled from the Punjab and sought shelter with the Maratha army. The five-hundred strong foot-soldiers that Surajmal Jaat's wazeer had brought also walked with the army with tense faces and timid, uncertain steps. There was no sign of the weaponry, the zest, or the determination that the Maratha soldiery had carried before. They were a load that Dattaji's caravan would happily have done without. They were grievously short of food and resources to begin with. The Shindes would have convulsions at the thought of having to feed forty-thousand persons and looking after their horses, elephants and camels. Over and above them were the eight thousand freeloaders belonging to the wazeer who had lately dispatched his emperor to the other world—all of them consuming more than they paid back to the earth.

They crossed the dark bank to the south of Kunjpura and reached somewhere in the vicinity of Kurukshetra. The Maratha scout Bhimaji Naik met them on the way and delivered the intelligence that Abdali's son Taimur had been camping on this side of Ambala in Chhat, Banora and Laldu two days back. He had now split his forces into right and left flanks. He was travelling in the middle of those flanks. Every twenty to forty miles, he was getting his squads on both sides to beat the shit out of the Hindustanis that fell in their way.'

The army stopped midway to get some rest. The elephants sat where they stood. As soon as the load of the riders got off their back, the horses gave a big shiver and shook their legs. The palanquin bearers had developed knots in their calves and welts on their shoulders with days and nights of continuous walking. They flexed their waist and midriff and sat down to massage their calves and shoulders. For two days the marchers hadn't had a proper meal. As soon as a halt was announced, the soldiers brought over rocks to make temporary hearths. They fished out their griddles from their baggage. While some sat to knead the dough, some others spread out to gather dry twigs for fire. Soon the hearth was blazing and thick bhaakari, unleavened jowar bread, began being distributed all around. People began wolfing it down with whatever was available—green pepper, powdered red chillies, or just water.

The nobility had no time for setting up their hearth. Accordingly, the soldiers passed on whatever they had cooked to their officers. Dattaji, Jankoji, Govindpant, all ate where they stood. Just then, two Maratha spies appeared with confirmation of the message they had brought earlier. Dattaji turned and said, 'Jankojibaba, Govindpant, this crowd of women, old people and children we are carrying is just so much of load on a donkey's back. If we have to stop Durrani and finish him off, we will need to separate our army out of all this. The enemy is descending upon us in three bunches, and we need to prepare ourselves to give them adequate response. I suggest you take charge of this overload, take away all the women and kids, take away the wazeer's wives and brood with you; as for the heavier guns behind, turn them round and take them back with you and park with them at Kunjpura. I just want the brave, the hardy ones—soldiers who will happily leap into the fire with me. Please take the rest away.'

'Kakasaheb, I cannot let you face this alone. I don't care if I lose my life in the battle, but wherever you are, that's where my place is,' Jankoji said forcefully.

'Jankojibaba, I can get after the enemy with abandon if I can ensure the security of all of these people here. You have the blood of my brother Jayappa flowing through your veins. I know that you cannot sit easy at home when there is a battle in progress. But it is absolutely necessary that one of our family stays behind to take care of the women and children. There's only you I can trust with this job. So, please go.'

As per Dattaji's instructions, the entire camp was split into two. Young, spirited, aggressive fighters were made to gather on one side, while the elders, the wounded, the women and children gathered on the other. On the other side were also the freeloaders: the Delhi wazeer's retinue and Rupram Katarya's soldiery. Dattaji put the elephants, the older camels, the rundown horses, as well as the heavy, lumbering guns under Jankoji's charge. He didn't even take his favourite Javhergunj with him. Instead, he got astride Lalmani, a dark auburn, big-boned young horse that could hardly stand still with the energy racing through it. It trembled when it stood still, and danced with its tail up when excited. As Dattaji was doing his round of the soldiers selected for battle, he spotted among the young soldiers the seventy-year-old Somajibaba Bhosale astride a young steed, his hand placed arrogantly on his thigh. Some of the youngsters were ribbing him for his white hair. Dattaji pulled his horse in front of the old man and asked, 'Baba, what are you doing here?'

'Datta, my boy, my life is nearly over. Another couple of years at the most. Instead of getting burnt on the pyre back at home, it is so much better to die fighting on the battlefield. I can hope to be released from this cycle of birth and death and rebirth!'

Dattaji had no answer to that. He went ahead and finished the inspection. The separation had been done, and it was time for the two divisions to move their separate ways. Dattaji thought of his wife and turned his horse in the direction where the ladies had assembled. When he reached Bhagirathi's palanquin, he pulled aside the brocaded curtain and peeped in. Bhagirathi had knowledge of where her husband was headed, and why. She tried to hide her anxiety behind a fake smile, but she wasn't altogether successful. Dattaji's eyes turned moist at his wife's disquiet. He looked at her pale visage and thought, 'What strange times, these! She should have been stretching out at the manor of the Bhapkars at this time, rocking softly in the swing under those trees. She would have been surrounded by friends and caring relatives. The Bhapkars would have converted their manor into the ultimate place of comfort and ease for her. And who does she have for company here? Harbingers of death like Durrani, fiends like Najeeb, traitors like Shuja—the most depraved among human beings are due to assemble here soon. The life growing inside her womb is my seed, and it should have been resting now on a bejewelled bed on soft, silken cushions. That little thing inside you, through what hostile lands and through what trying times is it being made to roam, Bhagirathi?'

Jankoji made the sign for the palanquin to be raised. Bhagirathi spoke in a low, anxious whisper, 'Please take care of yourself, and keep praying to goddess Jagdamba!'

Dattaji fought hard to press down the storm of emotions that was threatening to explode, nodded a goodbye to Bhagirathi, and tapped the spur into Lalmani's flank. His gallop towards Ambala had begun.

⚛

Before setting off, Dattaji had given careful instructions to his deevaan Ramjipant. It was his duty to stay alongside Jankoji and keep the Kunjpura camp under tight security. The slope along the Yamuna was to be kept under strict vigilance and protected at all time. If Abdali happened to slip past Dattaji, it would be Jankobaji's responsibility to block his further progress. In this eventuality, it would also be his responsibility to dispatch a couple of she-camels to Malharji with the message that he should set off with whatever forces he had.

Dattaji got information that Abdali's forces had reached close to Thaneshwar. That would mean that the collision with his forces would happen in the jungles of Kurukshetra, which suited Dattaji well. It was his plan to search him out among the trees, and tear his forces to shreds.

Valiants like Jivaji Bhoite, Somajibaba Bhosale, Tata Mankeshwar and Naikji Bhoite launched their assault on Durrani's forces. Intense battle ensued. The head of this first company of the Durrani forces was the general Shah Pasand Khan. He spotted the Maratha army, got his small-cannon camels to sit, and let loose a volley of arrows and fireballs on the enemy forces. The Marathas' cannons were not in order, so they took cover behind trees and began shooting their own arrows in the direction of the Afghans. Very soon a hand-to-hand combat began. The two armies swung their swords and hacked into each other's flesh. The air became thick with yells and shrieks and groans. Limbs were chopped and heads severed. Great destruction of life was wrought. The mayhem stopped only when it became too dark to see.

The next morning, as the Maratha force was getting ready for another day of bloodshed, a spy ran in with the news that Abdali had crossed the Yamuna at the Budhiya Ghat into the Antarved, and set off towards

Najeeb. He had given them the go by. As Dattaji strolled around the battleground, he saw the slaughter of the previous day. Headless, limbless bodies lay scattered everywhere. There was an old body among them, with a necklace of tulsi beads lying close. Dattaji couldn't prevent tears from springing up. 'It was a good choice you made, Somajibaba,' he muttered hoarsely. 'Much better to have left your body here in Kurukshetra than on a funeral pyre. Your release from the birth-cycle is assured.'

The other soldiers also identified the bodies of the father-son duo of Jivaji and Naikji Bhoite. Abdali had to be confronted, and there was no time to waste. The soldiers gathered all the corpses and heaped on them whatever dry wood they could collect. Dattaji set fire to the mound and watched the flames gather strength. Leaving the fire to take care of the six or seven hundred martyrs, Dattaji set off from there.

'Dattaji,' commented Tatya Mankeshwar, 'Abdali seems to have taken fright of you and crossed the river in the dead of the night.'

'No, Tatya,' laughed Dattaji. 'These Pathans are a shrewd tribe. Their combat with us yesterday was merely to test our strength. He has now gone towards Najeeb. They will all combine forces there and then mount their assault on Delhi. Whoever holds Delhi holds the key to Hindustan. Without a king, Delhi, as of now, is a widow; we need to rush to its protection immediately. Those bastards shouldn't be allowed to get into Delhi even if I have to shed my blood; else, the entire political structure raised by our forefathers after years of hard work will come crumbling down.'

Dattaji moved fast and hit their base at Kunjpura in a day's time. From there, while keeping track of Durrani's movements, Jankoji, Govindpant and Dattaji began moving along the eastern bank towards Delhi.

❦

When the Shindes had set off from Panipat, Dattaji had decided to carry the formidable cannon called 'Attock' with him. Before leaving for the Punjab expedition, this heavy cannon had been left in the temporary care of a landlord at Panipat. When he had first seen this massive weapon with the emperor at Delhi, Dattaji had fallen in love with it. Ten arms long and two-and-a-half arms wide, made of an alloy of five metals, it was a weapon to make the eyes pop out. It could not be mounted on any but the strongest battlement. The weaker ones would crumble under its sheer weight and impact.

It was out of love for this gun that Dattaji had decided to carry it along with him now. Accordingly, one-hundred-and-fifty pairs of bullocks were put under the yoke and were made to pull the monster with heavy chains. Whips began raining on their backs. The animals strained till the whites of their eyes showed. Some even shitted and urinated with the effort, but the cannon refused to budge. When they were prodded and poked to apply still more effort, the chain snapped and the animals went hurtling forward. Many of them got injured. Attock had been dragged there from Delhi by a good seven or eight elephants. Dattaji now didn't have the time or facility to repeat the exercise backwards. There was no saying when the enemy would invade Delhi. Finally, the cannon was handed back to the landlord's care and the army moved forward without the cannon.

☙

Dattaji and Jankoji knew no peace of mind. Delhi had to be secured before the enemy could lay its trap. Barely four days back, Shinde had settled his people in Delhi. The ladies of the royal household, their minions, expensive and heavy articles—all these had been shifted in small units to the custody of the Jaats at Revadi. The spies had brought intelligence that Abdali, Najeeb, Shuja and all the Afghan cheftains would be assembling in Luni on the other side of the Yamuna in a day or two. It would be difficult to counter them if they managed to cross the Yamuna into Delhi. Dattaji, therefore, proposed to block them and incapacitate them before they could do so.

For the last few days, a small team of Maratha scouts had been keeping a close watch on the Yamuna banks snaking around Delhi. Where could the enemy sneak in from? A secret pathway from some ghat? A sharp slope somewhere? How deep was the water at this spot or that? The slopes in the riverbed could have sunk deeper in many places too.

It was January, and the flow of the river had slackened substantially, creating the prospects of potential crossings. At the crack of dawn,

Dattaji sent elephants into the water at Rajghat opposite Daryaganj to test its depth and the strength of the current. A short distance downstream was located a very thin strip that could be forded at neck-deep. One false step, and that would be one more offering to the Yamuna. The spot, however, looked vulnerable, and Maloji Shinde was posted at Rajghat at the head of 2000 soldiers. Govindpant was stationed at the Majnu hillock that lay between Delhi and Jagatpur. Upstream of Jagatpur was the Buradi Ghat, and Janoji Wable was posted there. Dattaji, thus, went about posting pickets along the riverbank to ensure the security of Delhi.

Dattaji had set up camp about twelve miles behind the Buradi Ghat. Tents, big and small, stood shivering in the January cold. Depositing their light baggage as well as their heavy guns in the camp, the squads had set off with their swords and spears, and stood guarding the areas assigned to their care. The main army, fifteen-to-twenty-thousand-strong, remained stationed in the camp. Accustomed to moving bare-chested in their native land, the Maratha men didn't know how to cope with the marrow-freezing cold. Waistbands went round the ears and the dhotis were wound round the torso; pieces of blanket were put into service too. When all this swathing didn't help, some scooped out holes in the Yamuna sand and buried their feet in them, as dogs scoop out the earth to bury their bellies in. Teeth chattered violently. The cold felt like lumps of ice sliding in through the ears, setting off paroxysms of shiver through the entire length of the body. They, however, stood on, battling against the elements, waiting to test their strength against the enemy.

Wrapped in warm woollen blankets, Dattaji had set off for Delhi in the dead of the night astride his horse Lalmani. With him rode four hundred of his bravest men. Shinde's contingent was due to have left the previous day for Revadi, but Dattaji hadn't a moment to spare for personal issues. Bhagirathi had given up on waiting for him. Within a month from now, she would be peering into the lovely little eyes of her own child. Her entire body felt heavy. Her heart felt heavy too. In her present state, she had so fervently wanted Dattaji by her side. She craved for the comforting caress of her lord and master; but such joy was not for her. Instead, in these war-ravaged times, she scampered from one place to another, carrying the precious cargo in her womb.

To insulate their seeds from the conflagration that raged in the air, Jankoji and Dattaji had decided to send Kashibai, Bhagirathi and their domestic entourage to Jaat territory. Bhagirathi was housed in the large mansion of the landlord, Bhagatram. When the clatter of horses' hooves reached her ears through the darkness of the night, a wave of energy surged through her tired limbs. She heaved herself out of bed and made for the mansion gate. In the dim light of the torches lighting the portico, she set eyes on her husband's face after a gap of seven days. The dusky Dattaji looked darker. Despite the fatigue written all over, his eyes were as bright as the torches around them. As he entered, Bhagirathi said, 'Finish with your bath.'

'At this hour?'

'Lordship seems to have forgotten that it's Sankrant eve today.'

'Oh, yes, true.'

'It's so long since I've poured water over you, and one doesn't know when I'll have the next chance.'

'You talk of giving me a ceremonial bath, Bhagirathi,' said Dattaji, laughing softly, 'and that Abdalya and Najibya there are looking to set the Peshwa empire on fire. The main Peshwa army has gone to serve the Nizam in Ahmadnagar. No sign of Malharjibaba. The Peshwa has sent him repeated orders to come and help us. Will come in four days, he's replied, but as of now, we have no one. Things look difficult, but the Peshwas expect us to pull through. The crocodile's embrace, however, is heavy this time. Let's see what the gods have in store for us.'

A maid brought a tray full of dishes. Bhagirathi took the tray over from her and examined the dishes. She had got the khichadi, kheer and ghee prepared with special attention, and fixed the twelve-vegetable course required as ritual food for the occasion. But Dattaji's mind was not on the food. He called over his manager Ramji Dabholkar and asked, 'All ready to shift to Revadi this evening?'

'Yes. Just waiting for the chieftains to finish, and we'll be off.'

Dattaji hadn't a moment to spare. He washed his hands, and was ready to go.

Bhagirathi lowered her head to his feet and said, 'Lord, please don't rush in on Abdali or Najeeb. They are snakes. Let Malharji arrive, then do as you please.'

'But, Abdali's advance has to be blocked, my dear. Delhi has to be protected, even at the cost of our lives. Else, the long years of our efforts at winning and retaining will have come to naught.'

Then, with a signal, he asked the maid to leave the chamber, reassured himself that no one was around, and glided his palm over Bhagirathi's bulging stomach. A shiver of joy ran through her body. Dattaji placed his right ear over her stomach and said in mock surprise, 'Hey, does this slave of yours ever go to sleep? I can hear some rumpus inside. Could he be playing around?'

Warm teardrops landed on Dattaji's cheek. He wiped the tears from Bhagirathi's eyes and said, 'Take care of this fellow.'

Bhagirathi nodded.

'In case ... something ... untoward happens, don't throw yourself at my funeral pyre. It's a terrible sin for a widow to burn herself if she's carrying,' Dattaji shot it out in a single breath.

Bhagirathi grasped Dattaji tight and broke into a wail. Dattaji's dam burst too, and he wept without restraint. He passed his hands over her and brought his sobs under control.

'Forgive me, love, for speaking so candidly, but if my lineage is secured, I'll be happy in heaven. Will peer down proudly at my son as he dams the currents of the Ganga and the Yamuna. Take care of my little one. Raise him well. Whether I survive or not.'

Kashibai and the other women came in to bid goodbye. Dattaji looked into Kashibai's eyes that were silently asking, 'Why hasn't he come?' 'I'll tell Jankoji,' responded Dattaji's eyes. With a heart heavy as lead, Dattaji bid farewell.

When Dattaji reached the camp, Jankoji and the other nobles were waiting for him. In a little while, a message arrived. The enemy soldiers had begun to gather since dusk in Luni. Najeeb, Qutb Shah, Shah Wali, Jahaan Khan, and Abdullah Durrani himself—they had all reached. Right behind them were the armies of Shuja-ud-dowlah, Dundey Khan and Hafiz Rahmat Khan. Jankoji instantly ordered the army to get into full alert. No blowing of trumpets or beating of drums; the enemy was about eighteen miles away, Dattaji let everybody know. Night patrolling was increased. Up early tomorrow morning, and any time from there, they could head towards the battlefield, and that would keep them on their feet all day. The soldiers began retiring to bed early.

⊙⊤⊙

A conference was in progress in the large Durrani tent. Ahmad Shah Durrani sat leaning against a bolster stuffed with soft downs. His calm but sharp face would readily convince any observer that despite being just thirty-seven, this man had encountered a wide variety of men, manners and lands. But a look at his clean, white Afghan robe, trousers and simple turban didn't quite proclaim him as the emperor of Afghanistan. On either side in front of him sat Afghan and Indian nobles leaning on their bolsters, looking towards him unblinkingly. As they sat in their resplendent brocades and jewellery, the king, by comparison, seemed no more than a butcher's boy. To his left sat Najeeb, and to his right was his chancellor, Shah Wali Khan Bamezai. In front, to the right, was Commander-in-chief Jahaan Khan, his deputy Shah Pasand Khan, as also other chieftains like Barkhurdar Khan, Noor-ud-din and Abdullah Khan. To the left in front sat the Indian nobles: Shuja-ud-dowlah, the Nawab of Avadh, Najeeb's father-in-law Dundey Khan, brother-in-law Saadullah Khan, son Zabeyta Khan and Hafiz Rahmat Khan. With the exception of Jahaan Khan, the Afghan nobles were not one whit interested in Najeeb's litany of grievances.

Najeeb was entreating Abdali with all the passion he could muster: 'These Marathas get into our land and throw grit into our grain. But there has to be a limit even to harassment and persecution. Zille-Subhani, Shadow of God, we were willing to enter into a truce with that Datta Patil but he abandoned the siege of Shukratal halfway and came up here to confront you. What does it mean? It means that once he has seen you cross the borders of Hindustan over to the other side, we here are sunk. These Marghattas are sure to feed our bones to the wolves …

'Your Majesty, you came to Hindustan as the savior of Islam, and the subjects here will never forget this favour. They'll carve their heart out to support the army. That's why, huzoor, we must immediately launch an offensive, and cleanse Delhi of these sinful Marghattas. There are so many differences among them, huzoor, so many factions and collusions, that they will slaughter each other for a patch of farmland. Once they infiltrate somewhere, they don't readily come out. If they capture Delhi, they'll certainly send all of Hindustan into turmoil. Tie them to a tree, and they run away with it; such is the viciousness of their race. They are best kept out of Delhi.'

'Let's mount an offensive on Delhi in a couple of days,' suggested Shah Wali Khan.

'Tauba, tauba!' cried out Najeeb, 'but this delay won't do. My spies have brought news that Datta Shinde Patil is alone now, and he should be decimated before Malhar can join him. Whoever holds Delhi holds the key to Hindustan.'

'He's quite right, Your Majesty,' chipped in Commander-in-chief Jahaan Khan. 'This is our moment to attack the Marghattas and dispatch them to hell.'

Not many days had passed since Dattaji Shinde's army had killed Jahaan Khan's son in the Punjab. The wound was still fresh, and Jahaan Khan was raring to get his teeth into the Marghatta throat. The conference had now reached a high pitch, and Badshah Durrani intervened, 'The people of Hindustan are bitter fighters. Our surveillance has to be put on high alert. During my previous two invasions, they made me eat dirt—that Meer Manu and then Safdarjung from Ayodhya.'

The badshah laughed as he looked at Shuja as he pronounced Safdarjung's name. Shuja felt mortified at the thought of his valiant father. How his father had stood against the foreign invader and what he was doing now embarrassed him for a moment. Najeeb cast a sharp glance at him, which read that the past was past, and the Nawab should put it all behind him. The conference got over, and as the badshah moved towards his private apartment, he ordered, 'The first contingent shall cross the Yamuna at daybreak under Najeeb and Qutb Shah.'

❦

10 January 1760. In spite of the freezing cold, the Yamuna waters were warm. A blanket of fog covered the river and lay thick across at least half a mile on either side of the banks. Little clouds of fog came rolling out of the wide expanse like so many giant chicks hatching out of their

eggs. Janrao Wable had stationed his four-thousand-strong army on the western bank, and was guarding the Buradi Ghat. The troopers were trying to get the shivers out of their system; they had lit little fires out of the refuse they could collect, and were gathered round them in groups of five or six. The smoke curling out of these fires slowly dissolved into the mist. The early streaks of dawn could not persuade the fog to budge, and the soft-flowing Yamuna gurgled along, only heard, but not seen.

The water having receded considerably, the Buradi Ghat wore a transformed look. The main flow had split into two, with an island in the middle now, a good twenty-four-feet high, covered with dense shrubs. There were depressions so deep on either bank that a horseman could ride through them without being easily spotted. A number of large streams had joined up with the river on both banks. The flow of the water had bulldozed the loam, creating ravines on the riverbed massive enough to conceal a cavalry five-to-six-hundred strong. There were dense jungles along either bank, with the space between the trees overgrown with brambles. The river having shrunk, footpaths had emerged that connected one bank to the other, making it possible for two or three horsemen to ride across shoulder to shoulder.

It was now nine. The sun had risen, and the fog had begun to lift, but the joints of the horsemen were still stiff; the thawing hadn't quite begun. As they sat in bunches on the nearer bank, one bunch couldn't see the other four steps away. The place was covered with reeds as tall as men. The cold eased a little bit, and the fires began to die down. Just then, a sharp-eared soldier heard a plonking sound in the water. Must be one of the guys, he thought, getting into the water for the morning ritual, and relaxed. But in no time, the plonking and the squelching began to multiply. The soldiers sprang to their feet. This was the tell-tale sound of horses and camels wading through the water. If they are not ours, they are the enemy's. They picked up their spears and swords and ran towards the bank. What they saw beyond the island in the middle made their jaw drop in awe. The enemy forces entering into the water appeared as if an anthill had burst open: caravans of camels and horses butting each other forward; mahouts trying to work out ways of getting a few elephants into the water, the small cannons on their backs rocking with their movement; the camels swinging their long, curvaceous necks as they moved with their load of artillery; muskets on shoulders, the Rohilla infantry creeping forward with heavy steps.

'Enemy!' shouted the Maratha guards, 'enemy!' Janrao Wable rushed towards the bank. The fog had lifted by now, and it began lifting from Maratha eyes too. The Rohillas on the far bank looked like so many wraiths as they flitted in and out of the thick vegetation. When the Maratha cry reached them, it sent them into a frenzy. The muskets on their shoulders came down and began spitting fire. The camels squatted where they stood, and the artillery pieces on their backs started belching flame, roasting the Marathas like bread. The Rohillas just kept coming like water squirting out of multiple holes punched in a water-skin. The cannonade turned the Marathas into bamboos falling off a burning roof. The sudden charge completely rattled Janrao Wable, and he instantly dispatched a horseman to Dattaji for help.

Dattaji and Jankoji stiffened when the news of the assault reached them. The Maratha regiments were ready and waiting. Sabaji Shinde and Bayaji Shinde got their orders, and seven thousand set off on a gallop to the field of battle. The plan was to confront and destroy the enemy while he was still on the riverbed. There wasn't enough time to mobilize the heavy guns. They couldn't have lowered the heavy gun carriages on the riverbed anyway. Dattaji quickly decided to split his forces into two. He put Jankoji in charge of five thousand troops, and asked him to move to the east bank with the State flag. As Jankoji spurred his horse, he said, 'Kakasaheb, please be cautious; don't leap into the fray.'

'Baba,' responded Dattaji, 'till such time as Malharji arrives, we have to defend the ghats, not die fighting.'

The fifteen-thousand-strong Maratha army raced towards the battleground, the Peshwa banner fluttering in the lead. Dattaji, in full gallop astride Lalmani, was like a man possessed by a raging fury. The reins and spurs had whipped the horse too into a state of high excitement. Froth and sweat bubbling at the nostrils, it carried its rider inexorably forward. Trumpets blowing, kettle-drums beating, the Maratha army surged forward like a tidal wave.

When the Rohillas on the other bank heard the clamour on the Maratha side, for a moment they were bewildered. Najeeb shot his spine straight in the manner of a cobra raising its hood. The very word 'Maratha' was enough to send the fire of vengeance coursing through his veins. His mentor Qutb Shah was with him. He sprang from behind one tree to another, screaming at the top of his voice, 'Kill the infidels! Destroy them!' Just then, Sabaji's son Bayaji entered the riverbed with his seven thousand men. They wielded their spears and aimed for the chest with telling effect. Pain-racked screams of 'Ya Allah!' and 'Ya Khuda!' rose from the fallen Rohillas. But the Marathas had barely a musket among them; all their artillery was resting in the camp. Thus, when the enemy took recourse to its small artillery, muskets and mortars, they began to drop like flies. Blood streamed into the sand and the water, and the trampling whisked the riverbed into a strange hue. The pits and furrows stretched across the floor made it maddening for the Maratha horses to get any purchase. The horsemen too became easy targets for the Rohilla marksmen, and began jumping off their steeds to escape getting hit. Getting behind tall reeds for concealment, they used spears and arrows to bring the enemy down.

The father-son duo of Sabaji and Bayaji had run away from the Punjab to escape the wrath of Abdali's assault. Bayaji was often ribbed by his colleagues for being a deserter. The same Bayaji was now in the midst of the enemy, swinging his sword with great skill and guts. Streaming with sweat and blood, as he pushed his horse deeper into the melee, a bunch of ten or twelve Rohillas surrounded him and began slicing him from all sides. Horse and rider collapsed together in a heap, half on the sand, half in the water.

When Dattaji reached the bank, he was greeted by disheartening news: an Afghan squad had ripped Maloji Shinde's regiment posted at Rajghat to shreds, with Maloji himself having disappeared into the boom of the cannons and the constellation of the dead. The remnants of Maloji's regiment had run to Buradi Ghat to save their lives. No good news arrived from Govindpant either. The enemy had mounted attacks at three different spots simultaneously and besieged the Marathas. When Dattaji realized this, his battle-instincts completely hijacked his senses. With an impassioned cry of 'Har Har Mahadev!' he made Lalmani buck and leapt into the reeds on way to the enemy. Helmeted and chain-mailed, Dattaji crashed into the enemy like Nemesis.

Jankoji was putting up a spirited fight around his banner. Jahaan Khan, on the far bank, spotted him and lined up a few cannons. The guns soon began belching fire and began blowing up the Marathas like fluff. For how long could they really have carried on matching their swords against enemy guns and muskets? The Maratha bank of the Yamuna was soon littered with mutilated bodies. An arm smashed here, a leg blown off there. Smoke soon took over the space that the fog had only just vacated on the Yamuna waters. The boom and roar of the cannonade was deafening. It sounded like massive fort walls being blown up with mines. As the Marathas were getting rapidly decimated, Tanaji Kharade came running to Dattaji and screamed, 'Patilbaba, we are being turned to rubble. No sign of Govindpant, Maloji's missing too! Our banner lies exposed. Let's roll it up and withdraw with whatever honour we can!'

'That's impossible!' roared Dattaji. 'If the banner is rolled up, the entire army will turn tail. Then what will I do? Scamper away too? Never!'

'But, Shrimant, the gods themselves have sometimes had to abandon the battlefield!'

'Then their divinity can't have lasted long. Tanaji, your name holds a place of honour in our history. Don't bring it to shame. If we die, well, then, we die. We'll take that, but no way are we going to let those filthy sinners climb up to this bank. We'd rather be buried here!'

As the dance of death reached a crescendo, men and animals started going mad. The clangour, the thunder, the maimings, the killings, the thrust and parry—for two frenzied hours, brutal mayhem reigned. As Jankoji strained, defending the standard, a bang was heard, and he went tumbling off his horse. A bullet had torn through his upper arm, shattering the bone. The four Rohillas in front noticed Jankoji falling and rushed in to drag him away. In the nick of time, Yesaji Bhoite and Janrao Wable pounced in and pulled the unconscious man out. They put him on a litter and rushed him towards the rear. A few menials had seen Jankoji falling, and had no idea what had happened next. They ran towards Dattaji, screaming out their lungs, 'Baba! Jankojibaba has been killed!'

When these words fell on Dattaji's ears, he was beside himself. Rage, frustration and vengeance set aflame every pore of his body. The images of Ranoji, Jayappa and Jankoji stood before him. 'Jai Kaneshwari!' he roared, as he shot forward and rammed into the Rohillas in front, swinging his sword with maniacal fury. Just then, he spotted Najeeb's face ahead, and fired by the desire for revenge, he began cutting his way through to him, hacking with a savage sword all who stood in the way. Soaked in blood and sweat, he saw before him Yashwantrao Jagdale turned to pulp by a cannon shot. He saw Piraji trying to retrieve his brother's body. He saw the ghoul-like Rohillas pulling the body in the other direction. 'Pull the body!' he screamed. Suddenly there was a loud bang of mortar-fire from the front, and a streak of lightning flashed out of the clouds and went right through Dattaji's ribcage, smashing Lalmani's back. In the blink of an eye, Dattaji and his horse lay twisting and turning on the ground, blood gushing out of gaping holes.

'Dattaji has fallen!' rose a loud cry. When Qutb Shah and Najeeb Khan heard this, they jumped off their howdahs and rushed to the spot. Faces contorted with hate and bloodlust, they circled around the fallen hero. Dagger in hand, Qutb Shah closed in on Dattaji. Noticing a tremor in the fallen man, he shouted out, 'Datta!' Dattaji stirred, opened his smouldering eyes and fixed them on Qutb Shah. 'So, Patil,' snorted Qutb Shah, 'some more fight?'

Dattaji gathered whatever strength remained in him, rallied his failing voice and grated, 'Why not? If I live through this, I certainly shall!'

This response incensed Qutb Shah so much that he sat astride Dattaji's prostrate body and riddled his chest with his dagger. Najeeb took a scimitar and brought it swinging down on the neck, decapitating his body. He then ran a pointed spear into the cavity and raised the horrifying head for all to see. The macabre sight paralyzed the birds on the trees. The flow of the Yamuna froze for a moment. The Rohillas stood gaping at the macabre head on the spear, as if hypnotized. Najeeb broke the spell with a yell, 'Wretched bastards, what are you ogling at? The Marathas on the bank are fleeing for life. Go slaughter them!'

⁂

Abdali had a decisive victory. Drums were beaten, horns and trumpets blown. Najeeb, on the way to meeting him, did the circuit of the streets, dancing as he went along, his gruesome trophy nodding diabolically on his spear.

The Marathas were being hunted down relentlessly right through that fateful day. Hideous groans and gut-churning screams of the dying permeated the air. A massacre was of such humungous proportions that it could as well have been goats and chickens getting slaughtered. Pools of blood stood everywhere along the Yamuna bank.

Night finally fell, and darkness descended. Rajaram Chopdar and his four associates emerged cautiously from the shrubbery where they had concealed their contraband charge—the cold, stiff, battered, headless body of Dattaji. Stealthily, they went around collecting whatever dry wood they could gather—a twig here, a dead branch there. On the far bank were the shattered gun-carriages whose wood could be put to use. It was brought over. A pyre was erected on the sand. One of the group undid his dhoti to serve as a shroud for the martyred leader. Whatever betel leaves and nuts they could dig out of their pouches were placed on the pyre. The food-pipe sticking out of the severed neck was taken for the mouth of the dead man, and a little water was poured in. The bone-chilling night wind howled and the Yamuna gurgled on as, under the open sky, the body was surrendered to the flames.

It was the festival of Sankranti in Maharashtra that day. Every household was in the mood for celebration. Confections of sesame, jaggery and sugar were being made in every home and distributed among relatives, friends and neighbours. People feasted till their stomachs were ready to burst. And here, the headless body of one of their own, Dattaji Shinde, of village Kanherkhed, a boy who had grown up playing on the banks of the Krishna river, was being consumed by a roaring fire on the banks of the holy Yamuna.

❦

The Shinde army was being shredded thread by thread as it moved farther and farther away from Delhi—the Delhi that Raghunath Dada had won on horseback, the Delhi for which Dattaji had laid down his life. The news of Dattaji's death had shattered the morale of the entire force. As soon as they realized that they were defeated, the horsemen had made a beeline for the base camp. They gathered all that they could lay their hands on and began bolting away. With the shadow of death dancing on their heads, all they wanted was to create distance. The leaders were not far behind when it came to picking up their soldiers' effects. There was no distinction left between senior and junior, elder and younger, as men and animals scampered to save their own lives.

The hurry and disorientation was such that they kept tripping and knocking and bumping into each other. The issue was of taking care of the body measuring three-and-a-half hands in length, and no length was too much to traverse to ensure its safety.

The deep wounds that Jankoji Shinde had suffered didn't allow him a moment of relief. As he thrashed and groaned in intolerable pain, Janrao Wable brought him over to base. There was nobody to carry him any further as the palanquin bearers had all vanished. Yesaji Bhoite decided to take things in hand. He collected a couple of blankets, folded them fourfold, and placed them in front of the saddle on one side of the mane. He then loaded the injured Jankoji across the blanket, face down. Next he undid the length of cloth round his waist and used it to secure Jankoji to the horse. He carefully got into the saddle, kept one hand on Jankoji's back, and with the other hand guided his horse forward. Every time the horse took a false step, Jankoji writhed. As the horse gathered a little pace, the wounded man simply passed out in pain. The cloth wound round him was soon drenched in blood which, in a little while, began dripping down to Yesaji's feet locked into the stirrup. Yesaji, however, was too engrossed in managing the horse to notice. The enemy was after Jankoji with a vengeance, and his duty was to take him out of harm's way.

The Rohillas had begun their race towards the Shinde base camp. Lakshminarayan, the deewan of the Adina Beg contingent was getting his flock together when the Rohillas descended. The Afghans pounced on them and started swinging their swords wildly. His beaten-down four-thousand foot soldiers were like sitting ducks for the marauding hordes. They were cut down like sugarcane ready for harvesting. Everything that fell within the raiders' sight was looted: tarpaulins, tents, grains, beddings and utensils. While some Rohillas broke into the treasury, some others began rounding up the horses and mares that were roaming aimlessly. They also gathered some ten or twelve elephants and a large number of camels. They had thrown a ring round the camp, into which they herded the frightened animals before corralling them.

Javhergunj was the Shindes' favourite elephant. Since the time Jankoji's father Jayappa had brought it from Malva, the Shindes' good days had begun. The entire army knew how much both Dattaji and Jankoji had doted over it. Javhergunj's caretakers Badey Khan and Rajaram would look after it like their own child. Now, when the camp was descending into pandemonium, Badey Khan took four men with him and first got the heavy, bejewelled howdah off its back. With gentle nudges on its formidable neck and a twisting of the ears, he got the massive animal moving, with four horsemen as security. The bells round its neck rang loudly, as if tolling the death-knell of the Shinde army.

By twilight, some of the fleeing Marathas had gone a distance of over twenty miles while some had done barely ten. Soon it was pitch dark. The road was unfamiliar, the turns unknown. The horses limped along, stumbling against unseen stones and pits. Every time the Gilchas caught up with them, there was violent slaughter, followed by dismemberment of heads, fingers and toes to extract the gold or silver necklaces and rings out.

Javhergunj would have travelled about ten or twelve miles, widening its button eyes as large as it could. Its mouth had turned frothy and it would raise its trunk from time to time. Badey Khan's throat had turned hoarse with all the coaxing and shouting he had had to do to keep it moving. That was when a posse of about forty enemy horsemen caught up with them. The four security horsemen surrounding Javhergunj lammed it into the desert before the Gilchas closed in. Badey Khan's frantic cry of 'Stay! Let's give them a fight!' made no sense to them at all. Badey Khan, however, had a debt of gratitude to repay to his masters and their favourite ride. Death was certain, anyway, so, might as well die fighting. He patted the animal's neck and turned it towards the advancing horsemen. With skillful manoeuvering, he spurred the beast on towards the advancing enemy horseman. One blow from the powerful trunk, and the first man went flying into the air and descended with a crash, never to rise again. It caught the other one in the bend of its trunk and lifted him off the horse as if he were a log of wood. It then struck the man so hard against its own massive leg that the man simply crumpled. Seeing the destruction that the elephant was causing, one horseman balanced his spear on his shoulder and sent it flying on the mahaut. 'Ya Allah!' screamed Badey Khan and fell off Javhergunj's neck to instant death. The enemy soldiers then formed a ring round

Javhergunj and, using their lances, began moving it in the direction they wanted it to move.

Yesaji Bhoite's steed was struggling on with the burden of two men on his back. The land was rough, stony and cluttered with undergrowth, none of which made the animal's journey easy. Its hooves took bad hits and its shins were lacerated with thorns. Despite the swoon in which Jankoji moved, the jolts would bring an involuntary groan out of him. There was also the thirst, and he would occasionally mumble for water. Yesaji heard all that, but there was no way he could respond to his pleas. He had no time to take a pause. With about twenty-five or thirty miles covered, the horse was getting exhausted too. Yesaji turned round to see that there was no sign of the Gilchas. As soon as he hit the next hamlet, he pulled his horse to a halt. The forty or fifty horsemen riding with him halted too.

With the sound of so many horsemen stopping, the village got tense. Yesaji banged on a door, but the inmates didn't want to risk opening it in the darkness of the night. Four soldiers pushed their shoulders against the door, and the latch inside gave way. Yesaji stepped in and told the terrified inmates, 'Please don't be afraid, we won't harm you. All we want is a cot and some water to drink.' The frozen inmates refused to budge. Yesaji eased out the ring he was wearing round his finger and tossed it at them, picked up a cot and brought it out. He laid Jankoji on it. Feeling a little reassured, the people of the house stepped out and gave them earthen pots full of water. Yesaji poured water through Jankoji's parched lips, and little by little, he gained consciousness.

'Yesaji, where is my Kakasaheb?' he mumbled.

'Oh, he's right behind,' Yesaji said, avoiding Jankoji's eyes.

Janrao Wable borrowed some turmeric from the house, ground it and applied it on Jankoji's wounded arm. The horse ride had so drained the poor man out that he had no strength even to sit up. Yesaji and Janrao secured the injured man to the cot and began their march. The rest and the water had brought back some energy to the men as well as the horses.

By dawn, the contingent stopped at the outskirts of a village. They noticed a few covered palanquins and carts, a few horses and about fifty or sixty people stretched out in the open. On noticing their arrival, some of the sleeping men sprang to their feet, lifted their weapons and shouted, 'Arrey, fellows, up! The Gilchas have arrived.' The cry set the little encampment aflutter. Yesaji shouted out to his own men, yet loud enough for everybody to hear, 'Stop, stop! Don't panic! It looks like our own people.' Identities were established. It was a part of the Dattaji-Jankoji contingent that had left the previous evening. The horsemen and soldiers met and embraced each other. The women had stretched out a little beyond, with a sheet stretched over them. Kashibai and Bhagirathi got up. They recognized Yesaji Bhoite and Janrao Wable in the distance and quickened their steps. Seeing the state to which the soldiers had been reduced, they tensed up. Then they noticed the cot that had been lowered in front of the men. Kashibai ran forward and removed the blanket from over Jankoji's face. It was covered with bruises and blobs of congealed blood. He had begun groaning for water again. The sight was too much for Kashibai to withstand. 'Maazhya daulitechey raja, king of my life,' she cried, 'how can you be reduced to this state of begging for a mouthful of water?'

As soon as some water was poured into his mouth, Jankoji became alert again. 'Where is my kaka?'

The people around him stood mute, with their head hung low. Bhagirathi looked in terror from one person to another, and when not one pair of eyes was willing to meet Jankoji's or hers, she knew that her worst fears had come true. She let out a loud, heart-rending wail. Jankoji was devastated too. 'I'm left rudderless, Kakasaheb!' he bawled like an infant. 'Why could I not have died in your stead? What use am I now without you?'

He looked around with such helplessness and despair, and cried so inconsolably that Bhagirathi had to put her own sorrow aside to help him retrieve his balance. 'How can you lose heart like this, Baba?' she reasoned softly. 'With your Kakasaheb gone, your responsibility has now more than doubled. The entire Shinde army looks up to you for survival. If you break, the enemy will simply sweep us out with a broom!'

'No, Kakusaheb, no! Without him to guide me, everything has lost all purpose. My world has lost its mooring. I'm like a dead leaf now, a plaything for every wind that passes by.'

'Stop this self-piteous wailing, Baba!' Bhagirathi said in a stern voice. 'Look at me! I am a woman, your Kakasaheb's widow. If I can find the fortitude to live for his child that I carry, you carry a far bigger responsibility. Get a hold on yourself and stand up for your illustrious family, for your army of which you are now the head, for all of us who have now become your responsibility, as your Kakasaheb always did; the enemy is knocking at the door, Baba, looking for any chink through which it can sneak in. You cannot be that weak spot. We have no time to lose. Let's get moving from here and save whatever is left of the Shinde clan.'

It was a stirring display of courage from a young woman who had just lost her most precious possession in the world. She lifted the spirit not only of Jankoji, but of all the others present there. The bedraggled, broken army gathered up the bits and pieces of its tattered glory, and resumed its grinding advance towards a safe haven.

❦

Word had spread about the beaten Shinde army moving through its lands, and the villages on the way swarmed over it like vultures over a wounded stallion. Janrao Wabale shooed them away as well as he could and trekked on. Filling in for a grievously injured Jankoji, Bhagirathi, despite being in her ninth month of pregnancy, had plumbed her deepest recesses and found the toughness to assume charge. She turned over her palanquin for the needier Jankoji and got astride a horse herself. Every bump or jerk sent terrible pain radiating in all parts of her body, but she clenched her teeth and soldiered on.

It was next day in the evening that the battered caravan reached Kotputli. They were bone tired from the relentless marching on an empty stomach. Their rations had run out a couple of days ago, and they had been surviving on whatever they could gather on the way, including grasses and leaves. As they sat shivering in the bitter cold, a miracle occurred. It was as if Goddess Kaneshwari had suddenly decided to intervene. A unit of Subhedar Malharji Holkar's army entered Kotputli. When Malharji got information of the Shindes being four miles away, he took a bunch of horsemen with him, his wife Gautamabai and his son's widow Ahilyabai accompanying, he rushed to meet them.

When the Shinde horsemen came face to face with the Holkar contingent, it was as if they were meeting long lost relatives. A victorious army is felicitated with songs and dances and fireworks; a beaten army is not noticed by so much as a dog. The Shinde forces had actually been ravaged by good-for-nothing village louts. The sudden appearance of the Holkars, therefore, was nothing short of angels descending from heaven.

When Malharji saw the broken Jankoji stretched out on the cot, with not enough clothing on him to keep the shivers away, he was moved to tears. He held the young man's chin in his fingers and cried, 'Jankobaba, what calamity has come crashing down on us because I couldn't set off from Jayanagar fast enough! You are my Ranoba's grandson, and that Dattaba was the toast of the entire Maratha tribe! And now destiny has snatched him away from us. This was the land where with Bajirao himself, Ranoba and I had ground the enemy to dust, and what has this same land done to you boys now? God Khanderaya, what account have you been settling with these boys?'

'Kakasaheb, let's forget about the past,' Jankoji said, 'and see what we can do from here on.'

'Baba, I may be in my sixties, but I am nowhere near tired. I won't let that Abdali get away with this, I swear. If I am my father's own son, I'll skin him, fill him with sawdust and hang him at the city gate.'

While Malharji tried to comfort Jankoji, his wife Gautamabai went up to Bhagirathi. The sight of a Maratha princess shivering in the cold during the last month of her pregnancy made her stomach churn. Her eyes flooded. She took the shawl off her shoulder, wound it round the distraught-looking girl and locked her in embrace. For three days now, Bhagirathi had sealed her mind against the infiltration of any emotion by a sturdy wall that she had built around herself. In the warmth and comfort of this old woman's embrace, the wall suddenly collapsed, and the pent-up agony broke all dams and came bursting out. She howled into Gautamabhai's shrunken old shoulders, and the old woman held her and rocked her softly, moving her gnarled fingers through Bhagirathi's tousled hair.

'Yes, pori, yes,' she whispered into the young woman's ears, as if telling her to feel no shame in grieving publicly. 'You are a brave girl, you are one of a kind.'

Gautamabai had instructed a servant to get a good fire going, and now they sat by it, letting the warmth get through their skin and into the bones. Ahilyabai walked in with a set of her own white widow's clothes, and quietly handed them to Bhagirathi. That was when Bhagirathi realized that she hadn't even smashed the bangles on her wrists, as widows were required to do. She accepted the clothes with a hint of hesitation, kept them on the cot and walked over to the post in the centre of the tent with leaden steps. As she banged her wrists against the post, the tears and sobs again took over. When the last bangle was broken, she held the post in her two hands, leaned her forehead against it, and stood keening inconsolably. Ahilyabai placed her hands softly on her shoulder. Bhagirathi turned round and surrendered to Ahilya's hug, her keening building up into a louder wail. 'No point crying, Bhagirathi,' Ahilyabai murmured. 'We get married not to our sardars, but to their swords. Once the sword falls, we are undone.'

'Baisaheb,' Bhagirathi managed to speak between her sobs, 'when Khanderao Saheb left, you at least had the good fortune of bidding goodbye to his mortal remains. I had no such luck. The enemy took away his head dancing on the tip of a spear, I hear. And the rest of his body? Only god knows whether it was consigned to the flames or whether it ended up inside the stomachs of wild dogs.'

'Shhhh, shhhh! Don't think such thoughts! Destiny has its own master plan, and we are helpless against it. I had wanted to burn myself on my husband's pyre and become a sati, but my parents-in-law were so old, and they had nobody to live around. I had no choice but to give in to the Subhedar Malharji's plea and live on. '

'Whose pyre would I have burnt myself on? This soil here? My lord is now one with the soil, and it is to the service of *this* soil that I shall devote myself. I have to live for Jankojibaba and this little life that will soon spring out of me.'

Ahilya, Gautamabai and the Subhedar left to make arrangements for their lately arrived horde of guests. Tents were erected, clothes were distributed. While the royals ate together, the Shinde soldiers were provided with plentiful meals and bedrolls. The little fires in the camp warming their tired limbs seemed like a luxury to them.

After he had ensured the comfort of the Shinde soldiers, Malharji entered his private tent. His wife Gautamabai lay stretched out on the bed. When she heard his footsteps, she sat up. He had hung his turban on a peg and turned round when Gautamabai said, 'So many times your camels and your couriers arrived carrying messages, while you hung around playing your games with Madho Singh at Jayanagar! It was our delay that cost Dattaji his life!'

This sudden attack from an unexpected quarter caused Malharji to freeze midway. Bristling with resentment, he snapped, 'You too have started shooting your mouth like an enemy agent? I can swell my chest with pride and say that no other person has served the Maratha empire with as much dedication as this Malharji has. This Sadashivrao who now wants to gobble more than his mouth can hold, his father Chimaji Appa had laid siege to the Ajinkya Fort in Wasai. When the fort could not be breached, he had thundered, 'Tie me to the mouth of a cannon and blow me up in that direction! At least my head will travel to the other side of those walls!' The mines that were laid for blowing up the battlements of that fort, it was this Malharji who had lit the fuses of those difficult mines! Whether it was settling scores with the Nizam along with Bajirao, or it was the hoisting of the Maratha flag with Raghunathrao at Attock, for the last few decades, this Malharji has been at the forefront of every expedition, every campaign. From the coast right across to the Attock river, the very earth stands witness to the exploits of this man, if nobody else does. If these new-fangled foxes howl their doubts about Malharji's loyalty to the Maratha flag, I don't care. But you too?'

'I had no intentions of casting aspersions on your lordship's integrity,' Gautamabai responded in a soft voice, 'but what surprises everybody is how you could have let that Najeeb Khan go free. It's that demon that slit Dattaji's throat and drank his blood. With Dattaji gone, an important pillar of the Maratha empire has collapsed.'

'Gautama, it is a sacred tradition among us to grant life to a person who has taken shelter. I had no idea then that he would turn out to be such a rogue. But why do these Peshwa and Shinde people spread canards against me? It was I who had brought Dattaji's father Ranoji Shinde into the service of the Maratha empire, hadn't I? How then, can these Shindes accuse me of having got Ranoji's son Jayappa assassinated? I was, of course, furious when Jayappa had gone and made a truce with the Jaats, who had caused our son Khandu's death. But can you imagine that I would stoop so low as to set hired killers after Jayappa? Wasn't Ranoba's son like my own? And yet, these …'

'But who's making these baseless accusations?' Gautamabai asked. 'Have you ever heard Dattaji and Jankoji speak in this vein?'

'The servants say what their masters say, what else? Why should they keep under their wings their wretched deewan Ramji, who is known have to caused this rift between the Shindes and the Holkars? Isn't there any regard for me? At every step, I have served the Maratha empire with honesty and loyalty—and these young cockatoos have the gumption to point finger at me! Nanasaheb Peshwa is at least a little senior in years, but what about Raghunath Dada and that Sadashiv, who are less than half my age? How dare they come and talk morality to me?'

'Whatever anger you have, you should sort it out directly with Raghunath and Sadashiv Bhau, but that Najeeb Khan, you can't let that snake come too close. He is as poisonous as he is attractive.'

'Najeeb? What, after all, is this Najeeb? Will it take me longer than a minute to set him right? But what I ask is, why do these people keep raising the bogey of Najeeb? Can't see an entire pestle in their own eye, but readily see a tiny bristle in somebody else's! The real royalty among them all was our Peshwa Bajirao, a real companion, a real friend. We've roasted bread at the tip of our spears and eaten together, he and I. We've munched on raw corn and drunk off the stream together to create the Maratha empire. That was a truly great man, and he knew how to respect. It just needed an utterance and the great man entrusted the entire Indore province into my lap. And look at what's going on now—mere childish pomp! We stake our lives carrying the load of all of north India, and there, in Pune, they sit at their desks and go through our accounts. In these seventeen years, has the Peshwa ever crossed the Tapti and the Narmada and come to the north? If there is a military expedition, send Raghunath, if it is accounts hand it to Sadashiv! And what does the Peshwa himself do? He sits indulging himself with dance and drama. That son of our Appa, that Sadashiv Bhau, one blackguard he's turned out to be. Always checking ledgers, always asking for accounts, for revenue deposits; no other work he seems to have, for ever glued to his quills! Try a sword some day, someone should tell him!'

'Look, I am a woman, after all; what do I understand of state matters?' Gautamabai sighed. 'But what I do understand is that these differences will disappear in time, but this Ahmad Shah Abdali has descended like doom upon the entire Maratha empire. Your lordship began life minding sheep on the banks of a stream. When you came of age, you dropped the shepherd's hook and picked up a sword and got so many kings and kingdoms to run bleating like sheep. It was you who helped the Maratha empire expand its boundaries, who will be so ungrateful as to forget that? But when the dark clouds of these Rohillas hover so threateningly over Hindustan, it won't do for your lordship to sit on your hands, growling at the Maratha royalty. It can well bring disgrace to your deeds and make you the subject of vicious gossip. Subhedar, you have no choice except to sharpen your sword again.'

'Gautama,' laughed Subhedar Malharji, 'you speak like the true wife of a valiant man. What is the worth of these miserable Gilchas in my eyes? I'll pluck all these Pathans out like millet stalks and feed them to the cattle. I'll destroy them root and stem!'

The exchange between husband and wife went on. It was well past midnight when suddenly a commotion erupted. 'Run, run!' screamed panic-stricken voices. 'Run, the Gilchas have arrived!' The soldiers were jolted out of their sleep, women and children began screeching, the furore increased. Malharji strode out of his tent and leapt on his horse. Ahilyabai mounted the horse next to his. 'Halt!' cried Malharji. 'Stop! Don't panic!' But the Shinde soldiers were in no mood to pay heed. It didn't take Malharji any time to understand that this talk of the Gilchas arriving was purely rumour-driven. It took a full half hour for Malharji and his men to bring the terror-stricken Shinde soldiers under control. As Malharji was heading back towards his tent after bringing a semblance of order among the troops, Yesaji Bhoite came alongside him on his horse. 'Kakasaheb,' he moaned, 'the entire Shinde army has become thoroughly demoralized, and I don't know whether they have begun infecting your army too with their own dread. The ordinary horseman now believes that if such a valiant soldier like Dattaji couldn't hold his own, what will they count for in Abdali's presence? I suspect that what we need now is fresh soldiers and powerful guns from the south.'

'Pora,' Malharji assured him, 'there is still a lot of relevance left in Shivaji's variety of guerilla warfare. We will mount guerilla raids across the country on these Gilchas and drive them out from here.'

Yesaji was not convinced. 'We'll do what we can with guerilla tactics, but what we need now is fresh soldiers and English armoury to confront the enemy guns. If we continue battling with our arrows and spears, we will only be repeating the Buradi Ghat catastrophe and get wiped out.'

※

Badshah Ahmad Shah Abdali's camp was erected right outside Anoopshahar. Green flags fluttered atop red tents. Since the camp was to stay for a fair duration, the workers had gone for double-ply tent walls. The poles and stakes were also of the heavier kind, and thick ropes were stretched tight to hold the tents firm and taut. Soldiers from Abdali's slave regiment were erecting their tents too according to pecking order. Summer was round the corner, and once it arrived, the Kandahari soldiers would find the Hindustani heat difficult to withstand; hence the soldiers were busy erecting thatched huts. Those who had got their huts up were giving it a coat of cowdung slurry. A few of them had even paved the floor with a mixture of cowdung and clay.

A special meeting had been called by Badshah Abdali today. Friday was his favourite day. For the past twelve years since his coronation, he would arrange an assembly every Friday of the select intellectuals of his kingdom: judges, priests, historians, astrologers, researchers, and the like. But there had been a break in this exercise for the past four months or so. He had been busy uprooting the posts the Marathas had established in the Punjab—right from Sirhind to Attock—after driving away his son Taimur. Then there was that intractable Maratha warrior Dattaji, who had launched a murderous assault on his interests, and brought him hurrying back to Hindustan. Dattaji had hardly been taken care of when the sixty-seven year old Malharji had put him into a spin. Here today, somewhere else tomorrow, the badshah's enemies had kept him perpetually on the run, to the point of exhaustion. Only recently had the Durrani army cut the armies of Malharji and Gangoba Tatya to size near Sikandra. They had then brought the Jaats to their knees. It was after a long time, therefore, that he had found some time for himself, and he was determined that there would be no running for him this Friday.

The personages invited to the pavilion were great warriors like the senior Wazeer Shah Wali Khan, Jahaan Khan, Barkhurdar Khan and Prince Taimur, and great historians like Mirza Bahadur. The young emperor sat leaning against a brocaded bolster, a dark red conical cap on his head wrapped around with a white, bejewelled Afghan turban. He wore a soft, very loose-fitting muslin shirt that reached up to his ankles; his loose Afghan trousers were strikingly visible through the muslin of the shirt. Round his waist was a band with floral patterns done in typical Kandahari thread-work. His five-hand long Pathan sword lay by his side in its sheath. The jewels and precious stones embedded on the sheath in intricate patterns of inlay work demanded the attention of all present. The emperor seemed to be in a happy and relaxed mood.

The meeting began with an address by the historian, Mirza Bahadur. He stroked his long beard that flowed right down to his chest and said, 'Zille-Ilaahi, you smashed through the invincible Ramgadh Fort of the Jaats, and imposed upon them a punitive tribute of four-and-a-half-million rupees. We, your Afghan brethren, are immensely proud of this achievement of yours. On behalf of the assembly here, I offer our good wishes to you. During your coronation, you assumed the title of 'Durrani', which means, as this assembly well knows, the emperor of emperors. With your latest victory, you have again given evidence of how apt this title is for Your Highness. We wish your fame to spread in all directions. We pray that your mighty exploits reverberate not just in Afghanistan, Persia and Hindustan, but through the entire world.'

'I have tremendous respect for religious scholars, teachers and intellectuals, and pray to Almighty Allah for their well-being,' the badshah began in grave tones. The assembly listened to him in rapt attention. 'There have been any number of crusaders in the world that have come and gone; but being valiant is not enough—valour needs to be accompanied by luck and the grace of Allah too. If it hadn't been for these two accompaniments, I would not have been able to travel from where I was to where I stand today. Mirza Bahadur, I remember the times I have travelled through very well. My father was an ordinary landlord. Before I took the lead, Afghanistan didn't know what a king or a kingdom was. Our warring clans were a scattered lot. There was internecine warfare all the time, but Persia had no intention of letting a native king emerge. My father struggled for an indigenous Afghan kingdom, for independence. After my father, it was my elder brother Zulfiqar who raised the banner of revolt for independence. Persia detested our Kandahar and Herat. When that great Persian, Nadir Shah, devastated Herat in 1732, I was barely ten years of age. Nadir Shah reduced us to dust and rubble. When Zulfiqar and I were fleeing towards Kandahar, the landlord Meer Hussain caught us and threw us into a dungeon. For four long years, we did not see sunlight. When there wasn't enough food, we ate insects and cockroaches. So many years without sunlight on our skin, we had turned white like lizards. We were not sure whether we would see sunlight again. But the Nadir Shah we were fighting against—he was the one who freed us. We managed to survive in the shade of a great tree. We managed to secure for the Afghans their own country, their capital city, their banner and their self-respect. If it hadn't been for the grace of Allah, we would still have sat rotting in that lightless dungeon.'

'How can you stop here, your lordship?' nudged his wazeer, Shah Wali Khan. 'You were just sixteen years of age when you first came to Hindustan as a mere soldier in Nadir Shah's army. When Nadir Shah stormed into the Red Fort, what had the Nizam of Hyderabad told you when he had seen you near the filigreed door?'

The emperor look pleased at this, and smiled as he continued, 'The Nizam Bahadur was as good an astrologer as he was a valiant soldier. Nadir Saheb had great faith in his prophecies. He started when he set eyes on me. He checked out my eyes and my nose and proudly proclaimed, 'This boy is going to become an emperor one day.' Nadir Saheb then called me over and said, 'When you do become an emperor, don't forget me.' And saying that, he marked me out with this token.' Abdali showed the company the scar he had on the lobe of his right ear.

Prince Taimur had often heard tales of his father's coronation. Noticing the flow into which the emperor had got, he said, 'Babajaan, I've heard so many stories of your coronation ceremony from others' mouths. I so much want to hear it all straight from you.'

Abdali laughed. His dark eyes turned darker. Slowly pushing open the doors of his past, he said, 'This story is twelve years old. Nadir Shah was a great king. That was the reason why we chieftains of the Sidozai, Abdali and Ghazni clan served him faithfully. But though he was mettlesome, as he grew old, he started having fits of insanity. Not only would he order the destruction of a passing subject, but he would often send his soldiers to an undeserved death too. Sometimes he got as many as four hundred soldiers executed. He would drown people in hundreds just for fun. Once he brought out a firmaan that all the soldiers guarding his harem should be killed as they slept. That was the night when the plan to assassinate him was hatched, and was also put into effect. The Persian nobles who had executed this plan had decided to first rob his Afghan contingent at dawn before they announced the death of the king. This was where my fate stepped in. One of Nadir Shah's wives, named Bibi Saheba, belonged to an Afghan clan, and she fed this intelligence to me. That very night, I slipped into the palace and stood before the emperor's dead body. I pulled the signet ring with the royal seal out of his finger and also took into my charge the unparalleled Kohinoor diamond that he wore round his neck. We were in the land of the Persians, and I suspected that we wouldn't be able to go far without being caught, hence we Afghans decided to clear out immediately. We got on to our horses past midnight and bolted.

'Day and night we rode on, till we reached this village called Nadirabad, about sixty miles from Kandahar, and halted there to catch our breaths. It was just flat, bald plains for miles around. No structure except for the shrine of Shaikh Sarook Saheb standing all alone, with not a soul in sight. It was at this place that the Afghans called a conference. As you need a shepherd to drive sheep, you need a king to run a kingdom. Without a king, people behave no different from shepherdless sheep. There had to be someone to control them. The Afghans were certain that they needed a king to bring their society into a semblance of order. The preceptor Mohammad Saabir Khan suggested my name for kingship. I was completely nonplussed. I was elected the king, all right, but what kind of a king was I? I had no treasure, no throne to sit on, no seal of authority! I was wondering in my heart what I could do to bring all these things together, when Saabir Saheb picked up a fistful of earth where he stood, and placed it on my palm and said, 'This is your seal of authority.' This was how I was anointed king. There was no sprinkling of perfume nor the showering of flowers. My companions looked around for some tufts of grass, and that is what they showered me with. I still haven't forgotten the aroma of that earth. Even if I didn't have currency, I had with me broad-chested Pathans and sturdy Kabul horses that would jump over any fire. To slake the hunger of my poor country, I began raiding other countries. Hundreds of banners have I snatched away, thousands of canopied kings have I toppled off their elephants. This is my fifth expedition to Hindustan.'

'Aalam-panaah, refuge of the world,' bleated Mirza Bahadur, 'this assembly is grateful for the narration of your inspiring story.'

The conference that had begun immediately after the morning namaaz got over after the afternoon namaaz. The assembled men of religion, scholars and nobles left for their tents. The badshah too was getting ready to go towards his harem. The only person left with him was his wazeer, Shah Wali Khan. A slave entered and informed that Najeeb-ud-dowlah was outside, requesting an audience with the king. With a sign of hand, Abdali told the servant to allow him in. Najeeb entered and bowed low in the emperor's presence. Abdali asked with a laugh, 'Khan Saheb, can you tell me who my two main enemies are, here in Hindustan?'

'Huzoor,' Najeeb responded with a smile, 'one is the harsh Indian summer, and the other is these Marghattas of Deccan.'

The answer delighted the king. He asked again with a chuckle, 'So, what arrangements have you made for beating the first enemy?'

'Jahaan-panaah, special posts and cloth walls have been ordered from Delhi, with the sturdiest ropes to hold them erect with. Whatever grass that the villagers had, all of it has been confiscated for preparing thatch roofs. Your shelter has been so constructed that summer will turn into a cloud and float away. The pulse of all of Antarved rests in the hands of this Najeeb of yours. Thousands of mules, asses and ponies have been requisitioned to carry on their backs the best that is available in the markets of Delhi, Agra, Mathura and Bareili for your pleasure.'

'And what news of my other enemy?'

'Malharji has been given a thrashing near Sikandra. He and Gangoba Tatya had hatched an ingenious plot of looting ten lakhs worth of our treasure, but against the counter-plot of the Pathans, it failed miserably. Malharba's state is now of a rusted sword. He keeps cooking up schemes, but he is now touching seventy and can't ride a horse for too long. Yesterday was shimagi poornima, the full moon night when the Holi fire is lit. The harems of the Holkar-Shindes are at Sambalgad beyond Chameli. The spies say that Dattaji's widow delivered a baby boy at Sambalgad. The event was celebrated with much fanfare and bursting of sparklers and crackers, and even the firing of guns. But much to the misfortune of the Marathas, the infant died within a few days. People say that the woman was crying like the monsoon clouds. There's nothing left for her now, no husband, no child. The Marathas in Hindustan have become totally dispirited. A war can happen only when they get fresh reinforcements from Deccan.'

'Anything else?'

'Aalam-panaah, Delhi is now under your thumb. Yaqoob Khan has nicely garrisoned both the Red Fort and the Old Fort. Guns have been lined up all along the Yamuna bank. Your Highness, if it pleases you to stay in Delhi for some …'

'That will be folly,' Abdali cut him short. 'Delhi is just Delhi, what else? If there isn't a grain of food to eat, what is Delhi or Kabul or Kandahar? Or even Istanbul? A graveyard would be far better. What is left in Delhi now? Nadir Saheb, we ourselves, the Marathas, the Jaats—we have plundered Delhi over and over again. For the last ten years, Delhi has been in the state of a woman who has lost her husband. The attitude of the peasants there is to work their fields for bare survival and no more. Where's the point in slogging all the year round and have someone snatch it all away? This Anoopshahar is so much better by comparison. It is well-supplied with all that grows in the Antarved.

'You can be sure that the Marathas are going to dispatch a big force soon. We killed Dattaji, all right, but he was no ordinary horseman. He was their sun, moon and stars. The Peshwa is not going to take this loss lying down. That Raghunathrao, who drove my son away from Attock, he may arrive, or that fellow Sadashiv Bhau may arrive. People talk a lot about this Sadashiv Bhau. Both of them may come together, perhaps. By the time the war begins, the rains would likely have begun. These huge rivers may be a bigger obstacle to their progress than our armies. It may well be the Yamuna that becomes our defence line.'

Najeeb was bowled over as he listened to the emperor's closely reasoned calculations; he felt ashamed too. The notion he had fancied of being the smartest operator around took a battering. The emperor had sketched out for him in details the contours of the next confrontation with the Marathas. He said in complete admiration, 'Lord of the World, we have in your leadership an enterprise that is no less than Rustam's; with you at the helm, we cannot lose any war.'

'Things are not as simple as that, Najeeb,' the badshah retorted. 'I suggest you join us in our Friday meets; we have historians there who carry the history of Hindustan on the tip of their tongues. Don't forget that Hindustan has given birth to great warriors like Shivaji, Rana Pratap and Sher Shah Suri. As I was anointed king with a fistful of wild grass, Rana Pratap's anointment was no different from mine. There have been great men, great warriors and great leaders in every part of India, but the misfortune is that this land does not have enough discernment to appreciate their greatness today.

'Why go very far back? I'll tell you of my first three expeditions of Hindustan in these last ten years. There was one Qamruddin, with whose valour I had been so impressed that I had conferred upon him the title of 'Farzand Khan Bahadur, Rustam-e-Hind'. It is his young son Meer Mannu that I remember even today. He wasn't the emperor of Hindustan, he was just the Subhedar of Punjab. I had come with the arrogance that I would plunder Hindustan blindfolded. With this conceit I first attacked the Punjab, and that was where I ran into the forces of this Meer Mannu. He gave me such a thrashing that I just about managed to escape to Kandahar with my life. I spent an entire year preparing to launch my second assault, but even that fetched me no results, and I had to return beaten and disappointed. I got into another two years of preparation, gathering around me some of the toughest fighters from the vales and mountains of Afghanistan.

'I mounted a third raid, and besieged the Lahore Fort. I burnt down all the land within a hundred-and-fifty miles of Lahore, and razed it to the ground. There wasn't a grain of corn left in any Lahore basket. People began to die of starvation, horses collapsed in their stables, but this Meer Mannu refused to surrender. He hung in there, in the insane belief that help would reach him soon from Delhi. But you Delhi people have never understood the worth of Punjab; nor will you ever understand. The people of Lahore began to die on the streets, begging for a mouthful of food. The city fell into a state of unprecedented turmoil. It was then, out of concern for the lives of the citizens of Lahore, that this braveheart stepped out of the fort with a white flag in his hand. Even as he surrendered, his spine was straight as a palm tree. In the darkness of the night, he walked boldly into our tent. I asked him why he had not surrendered earlier.

'I was working for another master then,' he replied.

'Why didn't your master send you aid?'

'My master believed that I was competent enough to handle the situation.'

'What would you have done if I had fallen into your hands?' I asked him.

'I would have decapitated you and sent your head as a gift to my master at Delhi,' he replied, without batting an eyelid.

'Well, now you are in my hands. What should I do with you?' I asked.

'And this was his reply: 'If you are a trader, you will sell me as a slave. If you are a butcher, you will chop my head. But if you are a king, you will forgive and forget.'

'There are still plenty of high-spirited Meer Mannus here in this land of Hindustan even now, Najeeb, don't forget. It was among these Marghattas that an invincible warrior like Shivaji was born. Why go so far back in time? If these two barons Holkar and Shinde had come together with all their heart, they would have stopped my horse from crossing the Punjab and beaten the hell out of me. Allah himself would be proud of the virtues that these Marathas possess—valour, courage, determination, resilience. When I shall fight the final battle with them, they will eat the dust, but they will not withdraw. They also have plenty of cracks in their bastions—internal discord, nepotism, envy, conceit, and so on. It is by exploiting these cracks that we shall beat them.'

Suddenly the emperor fell silent. Najeeb decided to stay silent too. He had no idea what new thoughts would have flitted across the great man's mind. It was the emperor himself who broke the spell. 'My barons and chieftains keep pleading with me that from here on, I should not stay on in Hindustan during the summer. We are Kabul grapes. Once the temperature begins to rise, we fall off the branches. Our men and horses cannot withstand this heat. I have begun to think they are right. If needed, we should come back after the monsoons.'

It felt like somebody had pierced a thorn into Najeeb's heart. He was in a state of panic. 'What are you saying, Lord of the World?' he blathered. 'How can you think such calamitous thoughts, my badshah? You should know that the moment you cross the frontier of Hindustan, these Marghattas will rip me apart. They will rip apart the fabric of Islam too. You won't see a beard left on anyone's chin. Each one of us will carry a tuft on our heads like the tail of a snake. Masjids will begin housing idols, and the crescent moon and star of Islam will settle permanently behind a cloud in all of Hindustan. The names of Hasan and Husain will have vanished. People will forget their namaaz and get into yogic Surya Namaskaar contortions. The blame for the decimation of Islam will lie at your door, Zill-e-Subhaani. Do whatever you have to, but you cannot abandon us to the mercy of these Marghattas. How could Jahaan-panaah have forgotten the instructions of Shah Waliullah Saheb?'

The only thing that was left for Najeeb to do was to put some dust in his mouth and roll on the ground. The very thought of Abdali leaving them in the lurch was a nightmare for him. The emperor felt a pang of pity for the desperate man. He softened on hearing the name of Shah Waliullah pronounced. He let Najeeb finish with his pleadings, and then said, 'Khan Saheb, it is my duty to defend Islam, and I shall not be wanting in doing my duty. But I am not a complete mullah in this matter either. An army marches on its stomach. It needs food, fodder, money. All the scrolls you sent me before I left for Hindustan, I have them all in my bag. How do you expect treasure worth ten lakhs of rupees to be adequate for an army that measures fifty to sixty thousand soldiers? I didn't bring along such a huge, lumbering army for buying sweetmeats in the Bareili market. Talk of wherewithal.'

'Forgive me, Your Highness, I shall never let you fall short of anything from here on.'

'Najeeb, you are a cheat and a hoax. You can trick all of Hindustan, but you cannot deceive me. I care a great deal more for Islam than you do. You first have to see about food and fodder. There were so many missives that you had sent to me with reference to Madho Singh; how many days have we spent trying to reach him? That Nawab of Ayodhya, I didn't even realize when he had disappeared. Whatever cash you have to arrange, you do it yourself. Don't point other people's houses to me.'

'Forgive me, Your Majesty. From here on, nothing shall ever be wanting in the service of the badshah. Finish these Marghattas off for me, and I shall be your servant for life. When you head home after demolishing this community, I shall load so much of plunder on your men and animals that they will break their backs carrying it. I shall hand over such wealth to you that not one part of Afghanistan will want for anything after that.'

CHAPTER TWO
the assault on delhi

The Marathas had spread their base camp out all around Daulatabad. Tents and pavillions had been erected at the foot of the Devgiri hills on all three sides. Torches were belching out thick smoke into the night. Dinner was long over, but the chieftains and their horsemen still hadn't retired.

It seemed that time had seated himself in the conference room atop the Devgiri Fort and was looking down at the Maratha camp with admiration. The flames of the thousands of torches blazing around seemed to proclaim their pride in the Maratha Empire. The Marathas had joined the select band of a handful of conquerors who had earlier succeeded in hoisting their banner atop this invincible fort. The fort had had to wait for centuries together before it saw an assaulting force gain victory over it. Even the founder of the Maratha Empire, Chhatrapati Shivaji had not reached anywhere close to Devgiri. If he could have had the good fortune of hoisting the saffron flag on Devgiri, he would have become the lord and master of all of Hindustan with the greatest ease, this even Devgiri knew. It was through cunning machinations that Muhammad Tughlak had managed to insinuate himself into Devgiri. He was obsessed with the idea of establishing the throne of Hindustan in this impregnable, redoubtable fort. It was from here that he had overseen the administration of Hindustan for a few years. It was in remembrance of all this history that the brocaded banner that fluttered atop Devgiri's brow throbbed with joy. The conquest by Sadashivrao Bhau and Raghunath Dada had put the triple-tiered bastions of the fort to shame. Even if the enemy managed to penetrate these bastions, there were the secret passageways that would mislead the infiltrator into perilous pits or send them flailing down cliffs; there were magical doors that could slit an intruder's throat before he could step back. All these passages, pits, cliffs and doors had been outwitted by the Marathas now. All they could do now was to watch sheepishly as the Maratha soldiers spread themselves all over the place.

The entire camp was bubbling with excitement. Two days later, they were to celebrate Holi. This festival of colours was one of the favourites of the Maratha soldiers. They loved its merrymaking, but the joy they would derive this time would be of an altogether different order. The armies that had set off from Pune had torn the Nizam's lands to shreds. Storming through one territory after another, they had left them to rot and die. This fusillade had caused the Nizam thorn to come loose, and compelled the cranky ruler to come scurrying to the table for negotiation. The result was that along with the resplendent fort at Udgir, other areas like Burhanpur, Asirgadh, Daulatabad, Ahmednagar and Mulher—territories that together yielded over four-and-a-half million in revenue—had been turned over to Maratha control. Another one-million-and-a-half was on its way as one-fourth share of the collections. The great Nanasaheb Peshwa himself had had to stir out of Pune after a long time and take to the field for this campaign. There were other notables, too, who had got into the campaign: Nanasaheb's younger brother Raghunath Dada, who went rampaging right up to Attock in the north; his cousin and chief administrator of the Peshwa empire, Samba Sadashivrao 'Bhau', who had brought Karnataka to its knees; his elder son, Vishwasrao, on whom the responsibility would devolve to carry the Peshwa lineage forward; and countless other barons. The Peshwa's base was at Ahmednagar. On the forefront of the conflict were Sadashivrao Bhau, Raghunath Dada and Vishwasrao. Sadashivrao Bhau held the reins of this campaign and punched a hole in Devgiri's indestructible legend. The Marathas were ecstatic with this decisive victory, and the festival of Holi this time would be special.

However, both Sadashivrao Bhau and Raghunath Dada were feeling a distinct sense of unease. An inexplicable constriction in the chest, despite the joy of winning Devgiri. The news from the north was that both Najeeb-ud-dowlah and Ahmad Shah Abdali had been trying to cramp their lion, Dattaji. Dattaji had thrown himself fully into the task of protecting Delhi, and had set off full speed towards it. The Peshwa had dispatched countless messages to Malharji Rao in Jainagar to rush to his aid. For a message, even a quick one, to travel from the Antarved took a good twenty-four days. There hadn't been any news for the entire fortnight that had gone by, and that had put the royal household, including the Peshwa, on the edge.

In the royal pavillion, Sadashivrao Bhau and Raghunath Dada were in discussion, as seventeen year old Vishwasrao sat soaking up every bit of the conversation between his uncles, his kakasahebs. Out in the camp, people were noisily preparing for the coming festival. The horsemen were going through their gymnastics that they would present before Peshwa Nanasaheb, who was slated to celebrate with them. The entertainment artists—singers, dancers, instrumentalists, drummers—were determined to put up their best performance and were busy rehearsing. With forty or fifty cavaliers gathered around him, a balladeer was getting into the upper octaves, the beats of the tambourine rising up to meet the notes.

Four or five tamasha troupes were putting their skills on display, vigorously shaking their buttocks while two thousand soldiers crowded around them, whistling and clapping and cat-calling without restraint. Aba Kalal had brought over barrels of liquor from Khultabad by the cartloads just the previous day; hence the soldiers were nicely primed for the fun that had just begun. They rocked to the beat of the dholaks and did their best to get in among the danseuses. With the Peshwa himself stepping up to patronize them, good days had arrived for the tamasha companies. No better place for them now than Maratha cantonments for making good earnings. In three days' time, the Peshwa would be present in person to appreciate them and to give them handsome gifts; no wonder, there was much zeal in the manner they threw their peacock pallus in the air and gyrated like pigeons, throwing killer glances all round.

Carts full of sacks of colour-powder—green, yellow, red—had begun to arrive from Aurangabad. No efforts were being spared to make the festival memorable this time round.

The conversation between Sadashivrao Bhau and Raghunath Dada was still in progress when a camel rider hurried up to the pavillion and demanded to be shown into the presence of the princes. 'A rider has come from Hindustan, Shrimant,' announced the herald. 'He says he has arrived with a scroll from Ramji Dabholkar, the deewan of the Shindes, and requests immediate audience.'

'Send him in immediately,' ordered Sadashivrao Bhau.

The man stumbled in and handed over the scroll with head bowed, and hands trembling. Bhau would have read barely four lines when he turned pale and his eyes tense and moist. Looking at that, Raghunathrao began to fear the worst and shouted, 'What's it, Bhausaheb? What does the letter say?'

Sadashivrao tried to shape some words with his lips, but they began trembling uncontrollably. He put his head down, broke into sobs, and handed the scroll over to Raghunath Dada. 'How could this have happened?' he screamed, after reading the first few lines.

Sadashivrao took the scroll back from his hands and reread it, face contorting with grief and rage. 'At the Buradi Ghat, it reads,' he said. 'The Shinde army has taken a terrible hit. Yashwantrao Jagdale, Bhoite, Phaltankar, Bhosale, some of the doughtiest warriors have been brought down. Delhi has been taken over by the Pathans. The Afghans of the Antarved have all come together, and have joined hands with Madho Singh, Shuja-ud-dowlah and Najeeb. The Holkar army has been badly mauled too. All the Maratha posts in Hindustan have been uprooted.'

Young Vishwasrao, who had been listening to the conversation of his Kakasahebs with rising anxiety, had a knot in his stomach as he asked, 'What's the information on Jankojibaba, Kakasaheb?'

'Wounded all over. Lies broken on the yonder side of Chameli. The Shindes have lost their greatest wealth. The guerilla tactics started by Malharji haven't met with much success either. The blood of two generations of warriors has gone to waste.'

Hearing of the disturbances emerging out of the royal pavillion, the other barons—Shamsher Bahadur, Sakharam Bapu, Balwantrao Mehendale and a few others, came running. It seemed as if a ship had been wrecked. That was when another scout arrived from Ahmednagar and handed over a letter from the Peshwa. He too had been brought abreast of the devastation in the north through a letter from Jankoji. So, the news was true, after all. He had left for Partud, and the army was to follow early the next morning. The disintegrating ship of the Peshwas had to be rebuilt, plank by plank.

Sadashivrao Bhau gave the signal, and the kettle-drums began to beat and trumpets began to blow. The hills surrounding the camp echoed and amplified the sound till it rattled the eardrums of those who were sleeping or drowsing, causing them to jump out of their beds and go scampering towards the royal pavillion. It appeared that the army would have to set off for somewhere, and the colours kept aside for another day. It didn't take long for thousands of soldiers to gather in front of the pavillion. When they heard of the massacre of Dattaji, they exploded like an ammunition dump hit by a spark. They broke into tears.

As Sadashivrao collected himself to speak out, the gathering went pin-drop silent. 'Dattaji has sacrificed himself for Hindustan,' he roared. 'The Ahmadiya pact with the badshah had committed us to protect the Delhi throne, and our Kohinoor has now been turned to ash in the furnace of that commitment. We now have to avenge ourselves on the Gilchas and chase the foreign enemy out of Hindustan. Fate has been very unjust to the Marathas in snatching away our priceless Kohinoor diamond. What's happened cannot be undone, but there's only one thing to do from here: fight! The direction we take is a little unclear now, but we should have it right in the next couple of days. Such has to be our hurry that when the sun rises tomorrow, it shouldn't have so much as a piece of thread to look at in this camp.' Sadashivrao and Raghunathrao were awake till late in the night, putting things in order at Devgiri. The army was up at dawn and moving. By the time the sun was properly up, it wasn't the Maratha army, but a fifty-thousand-strong township, elephants, horses and all, that had left Devgiri about fifteen miles behind. Sitting on their elephant, Sadashivrao and Raghunathrao would frequently look behind. The Maratha flag fluttering atop the Devgiri Fort looked red to them. It seemed to be soaked in Dattaji's blood, and it hurt them deep inside. Vishwasrao, sharing space atop the elephant with them, could see the anguish that had settled on their faces.

The colours had turned murky for the Marathas. A month earlier, Dattaji had played Holi with his own blood on the banks of the Yamuna. Peshwa Nanasaheb, who should really have headed to Devgiri to flag off the grand festival of colours, had, instead, now reached Ambey Partud.

It was here that the strategies for their responsibilities in the north would be worked out. The Maratha army had to chart the what and the how of their next moves. Light tents and pavillions had been erected on the bank of the Purna river. The heavy equipment hadn't been rolled out yet. A select band of Maratha grandees had assembled in the royal pavillion that included Peshwa Nanasaheb, Sadashivrao Bhau, Raghunathrao, Vishwasrao, Mahadji Purandare, Balwantrao Mehendale, Sakharam Bapu Bokil, Shamsher Bahadur, Manaji Paigude and Sonaji Bhapkar. The glow of victory had faded from Nanasaheb's face, to be replaced with anxiety. The nobles sat leaning against their bolsters with grief-ridden faces, waiting for Peshwa Nanasaheb to speak.

The Peshwa let out a deep sigh and began, 'Dattaba was God's own soldier, and there won't be another one like him. He died in the service of Ranojirao Shinde's lineage and glory. If the Shindes and the Holkars had got together as a unified force, they would have vanquished the Pathans long ago. The boy has been pointlessly wasted.'

Much to the satisfaction of everyone present, Peshwa Nanasaheb then passed instructions to Sadashivrao that the feudal rights of twenty-four villages should be transferred to the name of Dattaji's widow Bhagirathibai. He then continued, 'Raghunath Dada had been sent north earlier to demolish Abdali, but for one reason or another that didn't happen, and now the entire game is in tatters. Going by all the intelligence from there, one of the royal princes will now have to go with the best guns we possess, otherwise it will be curtains for the defeated Maratha forces stranded over there.'

'Wouldn't it be better if one of the chieftains is sent at the helm of a fresh force, instead of the royal princes?' asked Sakharam Bapu.

'It *has* to be a royal prince!' Sadashivrao napped. 'There's no way our flag will fly again without a prince jumping into the fray. It'll be best if Raghunath Dada sets off immediately.'

'Let's not repeat our errors,' said Nanasaheb. 'The Delhi badshahi that we are sworn to protect will survive only if we strain every nerve.'

'The demand of the Maratha people there is that the Peshwa himself should visit the north in the company of Sadashivrao Bhausaheb,' Raghunath Dada interjected.

'Why we now? We've done enough running around in the north fifteen-twenty years ago. Our years of hopes are behind us. It's now you people who should be doing the fighting. Raghunath Dada, you should prepare for departure. Just remember, the mistakes we commited earlier must not be repeated.'

Raghunath Dada stiffened. 'I'm not sure I got the Peshwa's drift.'

Sadashivrao stepped in. 'Nanasaheb is saying we need to find a permanent remedy for this ailment. That sinner, that creep Najeeb still lives. Raghunath Dada, while that thorn was still sticking in the side, instead of pulling it out first, you decided to go ahead and plant our flag at Attock in faraway Punjab. Now that thorn has dug deeper and begun to tear the inside of the Maratha empire. How much more damage it will do from here on, one can't say.'

'Bhausaheb, planting the flag at Attock was no child's play,' replied Sakharam Bapu, smarting at the jibe. 'That was Raghunath Dada leaping up to the sun. A region that was not even a part of Akbar's empire, Raghunath Dada brought it under the Maratha heels. But who seems to care? There would be more plaudits for someone if he were barely to win a ghat at Katraj close by Pune!'

'Please don't say that, Bapu, that is not true,' replied Sadashivrao with some annoyance. 'When Raghunath Dada vanquished Attock, all of Maratha land had turned ecstatic. The balladeers had taken to the streets. The common people too had sung paeans to him. This single achievement is enough to put Raghunath Dada's name right on top in the annals of the Marathas. But in the process of hoisting that flag, a few mistakes occurred, and they are costing us dear.'

'Bhausaheb need not be so indirect in his criticism. He should specify openly the errors he thinks were committed,' Raghunath Dada said, acid in his voice.

'Well, you have undertaken two missions to the north in a matter of four years. The entire administration expected that you would attempt to resolve the tensions that exist between the Shindes and the Holkars. It may be your courteousness, your non-confrontational nature, or the simplicity of your heart; you could do nothing on that front. The Shinde-Holkar conflict continues to fester. Meanwhile, chieftains and agents of the north like Govindpant Bundele, Antaji Mankeshwar and the Hingane brothers have gone on swelling their own coffers. The revenues collected there have never ever reached in full to the desks at Pune. There are huge inconsistencies in their books. They have mainly been busy erecting their own manors and palaces, and carving out huge properties for themselves. It's these shirkers and traitors that are the real enemies of the state. Forget cutting them to size, you went on to add the renegade Gopal Barve to that list of thankless chieftains. Being the Peshwa's brother, if not for any other reason, how could you decide to ignore these developments instead of putting them under check?'

Sadashivrao Bhau's words stabbed the hearts of both Raghunath Dada and Sakharam Bapu. Each statement hit Raghunath Dada like a whiplash and raised welts on his face. But Sadashivrao Bhau was a full four years senior to him in age, and back-answering him in the presence of the Peshwa required the kind of foolhardiness that he didn't possess. While Nanasaheb occupied the throne, it was really Sadashivrao who actually ran the affairs of the state. As Chimaji Appa had devoted his entire life to the service of his elder brother, Bajirao Peshwa, so had Chimaji's son Sadashivrao, alias Bhausaheb, dedicated himself to run the empire on behalf of Bajirao's son Nanasaheb. Everybody believed that whatever Bhau wanted done was what got done in the Peshwa administration. Raghunath Dada had no choice except to suffer the bitter words that Bhau was spewing.

As the discussion about the north progressed, Bhausaheb said, 'Whoever finally goes to the north, his most important task will be to drive the foreign enemy out of the land. Ten years ago, the Marathas had sworn to protect the Delhi Empire, and we have to live by that promise. Shuja-ud-dowlah and Madho Singh are Hindustanis; we will iron out whatever differences we have with them in due course, but an outsider like Abdali has to be chased out.'

'If the enemy could so easily wipe out the celebrated army of the Shindes, we will need to carry the best quality of armory to settle accounts with him,' Nanasaheb said. 'But the debts that the Maratha empire is groaning under have only been increasing. Hence this mission has to be undertaken with a sharp eye on the expenses, not by bringing a debt of eighty-thousand rupees on our heads.'

Sakharam Bapu and Raghunath Dada exchanged looks of surprise. It was under Sadashivrao's financial supervision that Raghunath Dada had undertaken his two campaigns. It was he who had measured out every penny for the purpose. Thus, these words coming out of the Peshwa's mouth appeared strange to Sakharam Bapu. Before he could say anything, Sadashivrao Bhau spoke up, 'The Peshwa's words are worth their weight in gold. The empire is getting crushed under millions of rupees worth of debts. With money not arriving in the central treasury on time from the provinces, it has become impossible for me to manage the accounts. From here on, whoever sets off on missions will have to raise their own resources as they go along. These campaigns should bring money into the treasury, not a sackful of debts. This profligacy has to come to a stop.'

These words were more than Raghunath Dada could stomach. When he saw Sakharam Bapu turn a bitter face towards him and blink uncomprehendingly, he couldn't hold himself back any further. 'I have no personal desire to make a third visit to the north, but if his lordship continues to insist on sending me, then he will have to arrange for eighty thousand as running expenses and hold another ten million on standby. If this can be done, we will go and measure Ahmad Shah Abdali's worth; otherwise it will be impossible for us to take responsibility of this mission.'

Sadashivrao said, 'Accounts have to be balanced if a state has to be run. Festivals can't be celebrated on borrowed money. Living on half a slice of bread under such circumstances is our duty as Marathas.'

Sadashivrao's friend Balwantrao Mehendale had been observing Sakharam Bapu's steadily contorting face for some time. He took the opportunity to take a snipe at the man by saying, 'Those who raised such a mountain of debts on the pretext of Attock—did they ever make an effort to confront Abdali, despite so many opportunities?'

An already agitated Raghunath Dada flared up at these words. Turning beetroot-red, he turned towards the offender and spat out, 'Mehendale! Move out from behind your accounting desk and step into the battlefield some day. Scratching figures on a slate and fighting on the battlefield are two very different things. Let the entire empire know who is a valiant soldier and who is a pen-scratcher!'

Although Raghunath Dada had addressed these words to Mehendale, the real target was Sadashivrao, and the entire gathering knew it. His face turned hard as he turned to look towards Nanasaheb. Nanasaheb didn't like the slight either. In an effort at reconciliation, he cut in loudly, 'Take your words back, Dada. Just because you were dispatched on the northern campaign, does it mean that Bhau doesn't know of the battlefield? His mission to Karnataka along with Mahadjibaba, his invasion of the fort at Bahadur Bhendi, his shredding of the Nawab of Sawanoor, the victories he brought in Tungabhadra and Koregaon, and his latest exploit of taming the Devgiri Fort, can anybody ever forget them? If defaulters fear the ink of his pen, so do brave warriors who have tasted the poison of his sword.'

The conversation had suddenly veered towards personal criticism. Although there was much left to be discussed, the Peshwa decided that this would best be done another day, and, bringing the meeting to a close, he left for his personal quarters.

❖

Sadashivrao sat in his private pavillion. The tiny lamps burning here and there shed a dim, diffused light as his childhood friend Nana Purandare and he sat leaning against bolsters for a post-dinner chat. Nineteen-year-old Parvatibai sat on a mattress in a corner. The border of her deep yellow Paithani saree twinkled wherever the gold strings caught a ray of the dim lamps. The diamonds in her nose-ring refracted the rays and caused much brighter twinkles. The Kashmir shawl wrapped round her shoulders brought out her fair complexion. Her eyes would return again and again to the mien of her husband, who was looking graver than usual. The news of Raghunathrao having back-answered him in the conference had spread all around the camp. Nana Purandare, sitting next to him, also looked on guard. It was he who finally broke the icy silence and said, 'Bhausaheb, it won't do for you to be so tense. You are, after all, the chancellor of the exchequer and the principal administrator of the Peshwas. You have to show breadth of heart and mind and ignore the intransigence of others. You have to be forgiving. How can you allow ash to settle in your head? It's a small matter. Just dust it away'

Tall, big-boned and well built, Sadashivrao remained silent for a while. His breathing became a little heavy and the muscles of his taut body swelled and contracted slowly in the subdued light. He mopped the beads of sweat that had broken on his brow and said, 'Nana, there's sense in explaining when somebody is willing to listen, but whatever has been happening is well beyond my wits to resolve. It's as if I have been pulling this Peshwa cart for my own personal ends. I have been a loner since childhood, Nana, and I continue to remain a loner. I don't have even hazy memories of my parents. I was barely four weeks old, they say, when my mother passed away. My father would always be out on missions with his elder brother, Bajirao Peshwa. Once he left after Dussehra, he would return to Shaniwarwada only with the arrival of the monsoons. It was only like migratory birds that we met for a brief while. Even during the monsoon months when he was home, he would be engrossed in bookkeeping. Add to that the frequent trips to the king of Satara. I had barely begun to understand things. I had just begun to make sense of the victory bugles of my Kakasaheb Bajirao Peshwa, and his younger brother Chimaji Appa, my father, around which time Bajirao passed away. They were as intimate with each other as milk and water. With one passing away, the other began to unravel. My father's grief at the loss was so intense that he simply fell apart, and was ready to pass away eight months down the line. I continued being a loner. Those were exciting times for Shaniwarwada. Victorious armies were returning home from all four directions, battle-drums were beating and the saffron pennant fluttering. But I was experiencing what it meant to be a lonesome boy without a father or mother. If it hadn't been for grandmother Radhabai Saheb, there would likely have been no Sadashivrao today.'

'Who can say, though, that the late Peshwa didn't shower enough love on you?' Parvatibai's voice came from her corner.

'I am surely not such an ingrate as to forget my cousin Nanasaheb's kindness to me. Whatever little stature I have, it is entirely his gift to me. But again, I didn't have the opportunity to spend any part of my childhood in his company. Whatever Raghunathrao may say today, grandmother had made arrangements for all of us youngsters' education in Satara. Shahu Maharaj, of course, considered us Peshwa children as a part of his household, and gave us lessons in statecraft. It was on the soil of Satara, on the banks of the Krishna river that we grew up—Raghunathrao, Janoba and I. We would be at the banks of Mahuli one day, splashing in the water, playing hide-and-seek in the Ajinkya Tara Fort another day, or go galloping to the neighbouring province of Jawali when the fancy took us. As we raced past dense, thick vegetation, we would be transported back to the times of Shivaji Maharaj. Athletics, horse-riding, wrestling, yoga—we learnt all these skills in Satara. I still remember the wrestling sessions we lads used to have on the sands of the bank of Krishna. The king would seat us boys around his throne and give us lessons in how to run a country. He would occasionally send us to neighbourhood hamlets like Mahuli, Koregaon, Warney and Ninam-Padali to resolve local issues. Raghunathrao was eight and I was twelve when Nanasaheb became the Peshwa. While Nanasaheb was on his way to Delhi, he had sent a scroll for Raghunathrao from Udaipur, and Raghunathrao had come running to me, waving the scroll excitedly. Those were the days when Nanasaheb showered his benevolence on me. He would forever be admonishing Raghunathrao to learn his lessons under my tutelage. After my father's death, it was Nanasaheb Peshwa whom I considered my guardian, my parent. These are all childhood stories, though. Maturity arrives, times change. Thrones and emperors change, too, but people remain the same, although hearts do change. When differences between yours and mine begin to emerge, then everything changes.'

'Bhausaheb, we have heard that Nanasaheb would take time out from his busy schedule and discuss with you aspects of statesmanship, Raghuvansh, the teachings of Chanakya and also the Mahabharat. I remember you telling me that if there was something that you didn't understand, he would sit and explain it to you at length. But now, it seems, some kind of distance has crept up between the two of you, however small. My question to you is, what could be the real reason behind this?'

'Look, with her ladyship Gopikabai entering his life as his wife, some change was bound to come, wasn't it? With the passing of time, she has begun to influence the Peshwa so that he is no longer the independent decision-maker that he was before. What the wife doesn't approve of doesn't happen now.'

It was for the first time that Parvatibai was hearing the ups and downs of her husband's life from his own mouth. Sadashivrao continued, 'Some people are born with all the luck they can want. They just stretch out under a tree, and a luscious fruit detaches itself from the branch and falls straight into their mouth. Even when they are not hungry, the most delicious fruit gets stuffed into their mouth. But for unfortunate ones like us, we don't even get to see the fruits. Even after the victories I have achieved in life, they seem like defeats. Every one of my victories is framed in defeat. There's been conflict at every step. Never has any reward arrived by itself. When the great Bajirao Peshwa died, Appa took Nanasaheb with him to Satara. Shahu Maharaj handed over the stamp and seal of the Peshwa to Nanasaheb. During Rao Saheb's time, Appa was the second-in-command. When Nanasaheb was appointed the Peshwa, I was appointed as his second-in-command. Although I grew older, I was still biding my time in Satara. No message came from Pune. Finally, it was the king who sent a stern reminder, wanting to know whether I was going to be called over to Pune at all. That was when my summons for Pune arrived.'

'So that was when the trouble began, then?'

'Of course! Gopikabai Saheb was carrying Vishwasrao at the time. Then, after he was born, and was still in his cradle, she was worried about who the next Peshwa would be. I was considered as the smartest of the boys growing up in Shaniwarwada, and that was being held against me. When I arrived in Pune, I was not given any work. Just joined the family at mealtimes and sat writing unimportant things in the office. I would see people leaving on missions every day. There would be despatches to war, clarions would be called, drums beaten. When I saw the howdahs go rocking on elephant backs for this campaign or that, I would be livid with rage, my blood would boil. After all, it was Appa's blood that was running through my veins; how could it let me sit quiet? I would stand in the columns and watch the elephants set off on missions and listen to the neighing of the horses like a commoner. The sight would kill me, but I just stood waiting, hoping that my turn would come one day or another.'

'Bhausaheb, Karvirkar had offered to make you a Peshwa; so, what was your reaction to it?'

'I was thrilled, of course! It was an opportunity for me to do something worthwhile on the banks of the Panchganga, and earn a name for myself, instead of just sitting in Pune, twiddling my thumbs. I had made all preparations to set off for Kolhapur. That was when the reverend Peshwa saw my hunger for work, and got a little flustered. Although his interest in me had faded a little bit with time, his inner bonding with me had remained. He came down strongly against my plan to shift, and prevented my departure to Kolhapur. In the interest of keeping the peace between us cousins, Mahadjipant vacated the principal administrator's post and handed over the reins to me.'

Nana Purandare was all sincerity and concern as he said, 'Bhausaheb, the name of Bajirao and Chimaji Appa as a pair earned fame and repute across the world; people say that Nanasaheb and you make a similar team. There could be occasional differences, but it is important for you to exercise some forbearance.'

'I agree that there is enough respect for me and appreciation of my work here, but deep inside I am seen as an outsider. Although I am ready to sacrifice my life for the empire, there is hardly any trust reciprocated. This distance, this superficiality has hurt me a number of times.'

'But, Bhausaheb, I haven't ever heard of Nanasaheb having treated you with any coolness.'

'You heard what Raghunathrao said in the presence of so many today, didn't you? The finances of the Peshwa have to be strengthened, his revenues are drying up, his wealth is drying up; this is the one reason why I began looking after his accounts and spent hours upon hours scratching figures sitting at the desk. Let someone stand up and in the name of Lord Gajanan tell me in which conflict I have fallen short! When the invasion of Karnataka took place, I was barely sixteen! The enemy still remembers me for the havoc I had wreaked among its ranks. Who can forget the Koregaon-Tungabhadra battles? After I have only recently planted our flag on the invincible Devgiri Fort, how can Dada insult me by calling me a mere pen-scratcher! I don't think I know the Dada of today. These thoughts couldn't have sprung from his head. I have no doubt that there is somebody from the inner circle who is planting these thoughts into his head. I have now decided that I shall go straight to the Peshwa and tell him to handle his pen-register and office himself. I am setting off on the Hindustan campaign—'

'Please don't take decisions in such a hurry, I beg of you!' Parvatibai said with a lump in the throat.

'Nothing shall ever make me change my mind!'

'But, Bhausaheb—'

'Yes, Purandare! I am no mendicant or beggar waiting in line to be served food and sweetmeats. Along with knowing the accountant's desk,

I also know well enough the battlefield. Once there, you don't care two hoots for who stands before you; you don't give a damn for death either! Death and I have been not just acquaintances, but close friends. My mother, my father, his second wife who became my next mother—all of them left me while I was still a child. When I grew to adulthood, I met this dream in human form when my first wife, Uma crossed the threshold to enter my house. She spread the fragrance of the bakul flowers in every corner of my house and turned it into a veritable heaven. The twin sons that were born to us departed from the world before they could relish a whiff of that fragrance. It was like a sand-castle collapsing for us, and we spent the entire night in mourning. And then, as the soft light of dawn rises and vanishes within moments, so did my Uma after a brief illness. With Uma breezing out of the life of this Samba Sadashivrao, Parvati breezed in. Fate took away two lives that issued from her womb too. That's why I say, I have had many encounters with death. I have met death as one meets acquaintances on the riverbank. If I meet death on the battlefield, I shall take him in my arms and swallow him as the earth swallows up a bolt of lightning. I will at least have earned the merit of driving a foreign enemy out of Hindustan.'

The pain that this picture raked up was more than Parvatibai could bear. She stuffed the end of her saree in her mouth to stifle her sobs. One look at her, and Nana Purandare turned towards Bhausaheb and said, 'You have to think of baisaheb too! There is no reason for you to get into the battlefield yourself.'

'Not even the gods can make me change my decision now,' declared Bhausaheb. 'From here on, nobody in the inner sanctum will be able to say that Bhau has his eye on the Peshwa's throne. For the valourous man, the battlefield is the ultimate heaven, and his permanent throne rests in this heaven. This is the throne that I desire to make my own. I have to once again demonstrate to the world that Appa's boy is not just any pen-scratcher, but a warrior of the first order. Chimaji Appa disdained death, cocked a snook at it, and it is his blood that races through my veins and screams to be expressed. It will never let me sit in peace, never!'

Nanasaheb had removed his turban, tossed aside the sheet that covered his chest, and stretched out on bed. Two girls stood fanning him on either side. The fatigue was showing on the forty-year-old Peshwa. He had been fighting a number of ailments for the last two years. It was now twenty years since he had been the Peshwa, the wazeer of the Maratha kingdom, and for the first ten or twelve years of his Peshwadom, he had led some zealous campaigns in Hindustan.

When he had been handed over the stamp, seal and robe of the Peshwa by Shahu Maharaj in his court at Satara, powerful personages like Babuji Naik of Baramati, Raghuji Bhosale of Nagpur, Dabhade and the regional chieftains had mounted a strong opposition to the move. The throne of the Peshwa was not hereditary, and the important question before the Maratha empire had been: who should be Bajirao's successor? It was Chimaji Appa's diplomacy that had compelled the king at Satara to bestow the robe of honour to Nanasaheb in the face of bitter opposition. Appa had persuaded Shahuji that this twenty-year-old son of Bajirao would earn a name for himself. Besides, Nanasaheb had spent his early years learning his lessons in Satara. It was in the same conference that both Chimaji Appa and Mahadji Purandare had been bestowed with their robes of authority. When Nanasaheb had bowed before the king while accepting his position, Shahu Maharaj had placed his hand upon the young man's shoulder and said, 'Become as great as your father. Rule over the entire world.'

Nanasaheb had been fired up by the idea of a Hindu empire, and had embarked on his campaign to North India. For the next two or three years, he had gone on a rampage in the valleys of the Ganga and the Yamuna. Between 1751 and 1752, his chieftains Shinde and Holkar had signed the Ahmadiya pact, under which the Marathas had taken over the responsibility of providing security to the Delhi Durbar. Antaji Mankeshwar had been posted permanently in the capital city of Delhi with his army of five-thousand soldiers.

'Nanasaheb, the Peshwa robe you wear is made of fire,' Chimaji Appa had cautioned him as they were returning to Pune from Satara. Keeping that lesson in mind, Nanasaheb had crushed the Nizam twice in Sindkhed; brought Devgiri to its knees; crushed Damaji Gayakwad's revolt and brought him to heel; he had got half of Gujarat under his control and defeated Tulaji Angre with the help of the British. It was a life of adventure, during which Nanasaheb faced a variety of events and personalities. It was a moment of pride for him when Raghunathrao had hoisted the flag at Attock. Thus straining under the complexity, the turbulence and the rough-and-tumble of running an empire, when he had found both Raghunathrao and Sadashivrao coming into their own, he had felt greatly relieved. Little by little, he had transferred the responsibility of the empire to their young shoulders and slipped into a life of ease. Indulgence, luxury and romance soon soft-footed their way into the vacuum and began spreading out insidiously. Alongside, his health had begun to slip in the last few years, sending him into despondency.

He wasn't feeling very well that day either. A touch of fever, perhaps. The royal physician had prescribed some medicines. On top of his ill-health had come the devastating news of the fiasco in the north, throwing him completely out of sorts. He couldn't go to sleep, nor did he feel like getting out of bed. That was when Gopikabai walked in energetically and the two fan girls slipped out. She felt his body for any sign of fever and sat down beside him. Adjusting the shawl she wore on her shoulder, she began, 'Is it true that your lordship and Bhausaheb are heading towards Hindustan?'

'The situation there is so bad that the people there believe they need a prince from the Peshwa house to bring things back into order. It's been a long-standing demand of the valleys of the Ganga, the Yamuna and the Antarved that Nana and Bhau together get into Hindustan with a powerful army. I had made up my mind to do so too, but my health won't allow me to. That's why I informed the army this morning to get ready for the campaign.'

'In other words, Bhausaheb is being given the campaign because Raghunathraoji has been considered incompetent. Anybody can see the impropriety of this move.'

'What is proper and what is improper, only time can tell,' replied Nanasaheb, gravely. 'Besides, we have already given two opportunities to Raghunathrao to prove his gallantry.'

'So he didn't prove to be gallant enough, did he? Who was it, then, who hoisted the flag at Attock?'

'I am just as proud of Raghunath Dada's achievements as anybody, but the circumstances now are different. The Pathans there, that Durrani from Kandahar, the landlords beyond the Ganga, the smaller landholders—they have all ganged up together and wreaked havoc. It is important to bring round the chieftains settled there and to bring them together. Antaji Mankeshwar, the Hingane brothers, Gopalrao Barve, Govindpant Bundele and some other of our men, who had been sent north to look after our possessions, have begun to line their own pockets. Somebody needs to place a hand on their shoulders and persuade them to mend their ways and get back into the struggle. It's a delicate situation that requires mature handling. It needs a disciplined general and a skilled diplomat. Our Dada is too innocent and simple-minded to handle the intricacies of the situation. Under the circumstances, we need a shrewd and strong-headed person like Bhau. There are some who believe that Bhau carries greater traction than me with the army as well as the diplomats, and I think they are right. The last two expeditions of Dada's have raised a mountain of debts. The soldiers too are a little unhappy with him for not having received their allowances on time. In contrast, they are very happy with Bhau for his recent capture of the invincible Devgiri Fort. With the excitement and enthusiasm over this latest exploit still hot, the Maratha army will easily vanquish the Rohilla-Durrani assembled in the Ganga-Yamuna belt. Besides, Bhausaheb has already decided on this campaign and Raghunath has backed off on account of allowance issues. The only sane course here is to give our blessings to Bhausaheb.'

Nanasaheb, the diplomat, was busy displaying what an effective political strategy he had put into place, but the furrows on Gopikabai's brow refused to soften. They only deepened as his lordship sang paeans to Bhausaheb. Now that he had finished, he sat watching his wife's face. For a good while, neither of them spoke. Finally, Gopikabai broke the silence and said, 'I suggest that your lordship give the entire plan a rethink. It's because Bhausaheb looks after the administration here that your lordship can stay away from the tensions of running the state. It's Bhausaheb who sits poring over the revenues and the accounts. You are busy with your own shenanigans ...'

Gopikabai noticed the angry glare that Nanasaheb threw at her for the frivolous term she had used, and she pretended to lower her head.

'Your dislike of Bhau is not right. However much you try to cover it, it's not just all of Shaniwarwada that knows of it, but half of Pune does too. It was only when Shahuji Maharaj applied the pressure that Bhau finally made it to Pune. The expression on your face when that young boy walked in was worth seeing. I still remember it clearly. When Bhau had set off to crush the revolt in Karnataka, you had a thousand doubts as to what he would achieve. It was on account of your unrelenting nagging that I sent a message to him, asking him to turn back. When he did not return, you compelled me to go chasing him forty miles. Why this level of distrust? After all, he is Appa's flesh and blood. You think he doesn't register this shameful treatment?'

'But our—'

'Our own children will be left roofless, right? How many more times do I have to hear this from you? Not everybody has brothers such as these. If your sons have capabilities in them, they will rise in life on their own strength, under their own steam, to occupy seats of power. But this business of getting so overly obsessed with your own sons' future and casting aspersions at Bhau at the drop of a hat, how does it make any sense? It's you who have poisoned Raghunathrao's mind with regard to Bhau, so much so that he humiliated Bhau by calling him a pen-scratcher in the presence of the entire gathering today. Has Bhau so much as whispered his desire for Peshwadom in anybody's ear? As Appa stood firm as my father Bajirao's shadow behind him, so has Bhau—'

'What shows is different from what actually is. When the offer of a Peshwa's post arrived from Karvirkar, all of Pune knows how he went flaunting it around town.'

Nanasaheb cast a scorching look at Gopikabai and said, 'You were so stunningly young and beautiful at the time, weren't you? All of my subjects know that their Peshwa has a weakness for youth and beauty. I gathered your beauty in my embrace and your poison travelled along with it. The distinction between right and wrong vanished. The brother who was dearer to me than life before my marriage became a stranger, an unwanted person in my eyes. Life for the poor, orphaned boy became a mess. He hadn't come to Shaniwarwada as a mendicant who would be happy to find a place in the row of diners and nothing more, day after day. The chivalrous blood that ran through him, how could it allow him to sit quiet? In my book, it was no sin for him to accept Karvirkar's offer, or anybody else's for that matter.'

'I had expected no other answer from you.'

'Your tongue has begun to wag quite freely these days, hasn't it? You just threw that 'shenanigan' barb. Yes, I indulge in drama and the arts, and spend time on the good things of life, and you never seem to stop rubbing it into me. You see me in a vulnerable state, and you go about poisoning ears about my near and dear ones, just so that you can increase their misery. Well, I guess, Bhau will have to accept whatever destiny throws his way.'

'Is Bhausaheb setting off alone?' she asked after a little while.

'His wife Parvatibai may go with him.'

'Oh, really?'

'Why? What's wrong with that? Haven't you been with me to North India during my campaigns? My grandmother had learnt this lesson when my father had taken a mistress for himself. Maratha warriors are out of their homes for eight months in a year, leaving their wife and kids behind; no wonder they get hooked to some unwanted habits and "shenanigans". So it's better they can take their wives along. It was on this argument that you began accompanying me on campaigns, and the palanquins of other chieftains too began moving with them. In the last ten or fifteen years, it has become a tradition. Besides, poor Parvatibai has no children to keep her busy here either. Also, Bhau is an inveterate workaholic, who forgets meals and rest when he is in the middle of an enterprise. Parvatibai's presence is going to keep his health in order, at least.' Gopikabai waited till the fraternal emotions that had welled up inside Nanasaheb for Sadashivrao subsided. Then she slowly said, 'I have decided that Vishwasrao will also go on this campaign.'

Nanasaheb was startled. 'Rao? For this campaign? Why?'

'Should he sit in Shanivarwada playing girlish games, then? Shouldn't he too learn the skills of military campaigns, diplomacy, administration and the like?'

'Who says Rao doesn't have experience of battles? He was on the forefront in the battle of Sindkhed, and proved his valour beyond doubt. But this campaign is complex. Why do you want to send my strapping young son, barely seventeen years of age, into the heat and dust of the north? He's handsome enough to put the moon to shame. Why do you want him to be struck by the evil eye of the enemy? He has a long life ahead to go to as many battles as he wants.'

'I am more concerned about his skills as a statesman, about his abilities as the future Peshwa, than about his good looks,' retorted Gopikabai.

'See? See, Gopike? How suspicious you are of Bhau? If he wins this time, he will go and crown himself as the emperor of Hindustan, you fear, don't you? I see no other reason behind this move of yours.'

Gopikabai turned stiff and decided to give it back to Nanasaheb without mincing words. 'Let your lordship think whatever he wants to, but this I have to say straight out: I cannot let my children grow into fat and flabby hedonists. I don't want them to be bullocks spending their time chewing the cud in the Peshwa's barns. They should take swords in hand and match their skills with the enemy. I wouldn't like it if people were to call them tin-soldiers and paper-tigers. They should earn fame across the world as their grandfather did.'

Nanasaheb could think of no suitable response to her argument. After a few minutes' silence, he said, 'Well, all right, I don't want to stand as an obstacle to your plans. Only, I don't want it happening out of any distrust of Bhau. I don't mind if Vishwasrao is being sent to learn military skills. He is Bhausaheb's ward and disciple, anyway. If Bhau gets hurt, he winces; if a single hair on Vishwasrao's head comes to harm, Bhau will destroy the world to protect him. I am quite sure taking our son along will not pose any problem to Bhau.'

'The campaign should be under the command of Vishwasrao, the funds should be released in his name, all deals and pacts should be signed in his name. Let me tell your lordship in the clearest terms, when I think of the humiliation we went through sixteen years ago, it makes me break into shivers. That horrible night, the sarcastic laughter of the wicked wada inmates, the Peshwadom slipping out of our hands, the entire world slipping out from beneath our feet— what can be worse than that? Let me repeat this for your lordship, I want to live as the Peshwa's wife, or the Peshwa's mother. I don't want to be sent out on the street.'

Gopikabai's words shook Nanasaheb to the core. Despite sixteen years having rolled by, that event of 1744 had the power to reopen the wound and bring back the pain as if it had happened yesterday. Naik of Baramati,

Raghuji Bhosale, Dabhade, the Brahmin coterie had ganged up with the other chieftains to bring Nanasaheb down. They had gone and poisoned Shahu Maharaj's ears; as a result, the king had taken the post away from Nanasaheb for a full month. Nanasaheb had understood well, then, what a flag-post means without a flag, what a body feels without its head, or a king feels without his throne. The memory of that conspiracy still had the ability to make his skin break into blisters. It wasn't like Gopikabai was entirely wrong, he realized. He placed his hand on her shoulder as a mark of sympathy.

⁂

The decision to send Bhausaheb on the Hindustan campaign was confirmed. This would be a difficult campaign. He had to put plenty of things in order. He stayed in his office submerged in work. The campaign bug had bitten him hard all over. He had been taken over by a wild frenzy of preparations. He did not sleep and did not rest. He had no time for home or wife either. It was quite late when the message reached Parvatibai that he would not be returning, and would spend the night working. Midnight came and went while Bhau sat scratching his pen on charts and tables. At the crack of dawn, he woke up and went to the bank of the Purna for a dip. While his servants stood shivering on the bank, Bhau seemed immune to the icy coldness of the water as he took a quick splash and stepped out. He quickly finished his early morning prayers and got back to work as the first trace of light began spreading across the east. A missive had to be sent to Govindpant Bundele in the north, and he sat preparing the first draft.

When it became light, it occurred to Sadashivrao that it was the morning of Holi, and prayers had to be performed. The celebration, this time, however, was muted right across the camp. It had been decided long ago that all the fanfare would be given the go by. Dattaji's death had taken the fun out of all festivals. What Holi and what puran-polees and other sweetmeats? Earlier, when the Marathas were on campaign, the sweet Holi puran-polees made in the camp tasted better than they did at home. Now, however, nobody had any joy left in either making those sweets or consuming them. They would stick in the gullet. The priests had decided that five pancakes would be made for the gods as a ritual, and that would be it.

Twigs, logs and cowdung cakes were assembled in front of the royal pavillion, and the work of stacking them up began. A few minions held a castor-oil plant in the middle, while the others arranged the dung cakes and the twigs round it. The priests handed over the consecration plate to Nanasaheb, who performed the prayer. The privilege of lighting the Holi pyre always belonged to the Patil, the village headman. For years, the tradition had been for the head of the Shinde Patil household to do the honours. Dattaji's younger brother Mahadji stepped forward, with all eyes turned towards him. One look, and it was clear that the memory of his beloved brother was overwhelming him. He set the heap on fire, threw the torch into the burning heap, and turned round with his fist in his mouth, not being able to suppress the sobs that were consuming him. Two steps down, and he broke into a loud wail and lamented, 'Why, Dattaji? Why? Why did you leave us to become one with an unknown battlefield among unknown people? How could you have deserted us so, Dada?'

The Maratha chieftains, horsemen and cavalrymen lifted the end of their turbans and stoles and wept into it. With the royal Holi thus set alight, people dispersed to burn their own smaller stacks. Shells were blown up, and a pall of smoke spread across the camp.

※

Sadashivrao got into the office pavillion. A lot of work had still to be done. A number of experienced and responsible administrative officers like Balwantrao Mehendale, Nana Purandare, Hari Shivram Khajgiwale and Mahipatrao Chitnis had been assigned to accompany him on the campaign. Not one of them had arrived. Each one of them was busy finishing off with his individual Holi, and that was holding work back. Sadashivrao began turning restless. The Holi of the Maratha people has already been set alight, he thought. What's left now to celebrate? As he sat fretting, the doorman announced the arrival of Vishwasrao.

As Vishwasrao entered, Sadashivrao could not take his eyes away from the young man. Tall, slim and fair, Vishwasrao was a particularly attractive person to look at. His shapely, jet black eyes had a distinct glitter in them. Rose-petal lips, tapering chin and a sharp nose. A trace of soft downs had just begun to sprout on his upper lip. It was rightly said in the Maratha kingdom: the most beautiful woman—Mastani; the handsomest man—Vishwasrao. He could easily stand among the best sculptures and be mistaken for a statue. He carried his clothes with great style too. It was, of course, the clothes that gained grandeur from being worn by him. Sadashivrao was worried about how he would carry such a treasure of a boy with him on his campaign.

'Why do you look at me so, Kakasaheb?'

Sadashivrao snapped out of his thoughts and said, 'Come, come, Rao, sit. The question I was trying to resolve was whether the enemy will swoon at the sight of our Vishwasrao. So, what plans have you worked out for our campaign?'

'Kakasaheb, with you as my teacher, why should I sit making plans? My only plan is to implement your orders, that's it.'

'Son, Najeeb and Abdali have made such massive preparations that this is not going to be any ordinary skirmish. This is going to be a major war. It may take on a good colour or a bad one, but you have to participate in it not as the Peshwa's son, but as a gallant warrior. You have to bring glory to the name of your lineage, and to the empire.'

'Kakasaheb, under your guidance, we shall undoubtedly be successful. I want to melt like iron in the conflagration of war as an ordinary cavalryman rather than as the Peshwa's son.'

'If we prepare well, we should be able to clash with Abdali's forces by June. There are three more months to go for that. Besides, we got into an argument with Raghunath Dada on the issue of expenditure. Therefore, now that we have given our word, we will have to raise money for this campaign from outside.'

'Whatever you say, Kakasaheb.'

In a little while, officers like Purandare, Mahipatrao Chitnis, Hariram Khajgiwale arrived at the office pavillion. Knowing that Bhausaheb would be upset at their late arrival, not one of them looked him in the eye and buried their noses in the maps and charts.

Sadashivrao looked towards Purandare and said, 'You know, Nana, with all the penmanship I have been indulging in, it may well create serious blemishes in my career as commander-in-chief of the army now.'

'Didn't get you, Bhausaheb.'

'Oh, the meaning is quite clear. All this time, I have been taking our Hindustan chieftains and revenue collectors to task for proper accounts. All of the empire knows how I scoured the Hingane brothers who had erected such a palatial mansion in Delhi. I reduced Antaji Mankeshwar, Naro Shankar and Pant Bundele to dire straits. For a person who has to keep accounts, keeping a finger on every pulse becomes unavoidable. A commander-in-chief may manage for a little while on borrowings, but if an accountant turns lax, the entire empire will crumble. In the process of being a conscientious accountant, I have really had to get after some people. Not even Malharji has been exempt from it. Now, as commander-in-chief, getting all of them together is going to be a tough task.'

'Why did this subject crop into your head now?'

'Well, the first urgent letter we have to dispatch is to Pant Bundele.'

Mahipatrao Chitnis sat to write the draft. Sadashivrao ran through the rough draft and began dictating the text:

> You are among the eminent chieftains to have hoisted the Maratha flag in Bundelkhand. The empire points towards you as the promptest depositor of revenue in the state exchequer. You will be required to carry a major burden for this campaign too. There is no Marathi person more worthy of trust north of the Vindhyas than you. Please keep a sharp eye on Shuja-ud-dowlah of Ayodhya, and extend whatever help you can to the Shinde and Holkar sardars. It will be nice if Shuja can be reminded of past favours and persuaded to join our side. After all, it is for the sake of the Delhi emperor that we are mounting this struggle. Nothing can be worse than this foreigner Abdali managing to find a base in Hindustan.

Bhausaheb paused to organize his thoughts and continued, 'Yes, write this:

> Please arrange for two million by the time we reach Malwa. Also, keep your account books for the past two or three years ready.'

Sadashivrao could see the hesitation with which Mahipatrao was writing the latest dictation. 'I realize too, that this is not the best time for me to bring up the issue of money. But what choice have I got? If one goes on a campaign, food and fodder have to be arranged. That needs money, and getting the money needs discipline. I know it's tough, but I don't see any alternative to it.'

While finishing his letter, Sadashivrao did not forget to remind Pant that news from Hindustan should keep reaching him all the time, it should reach him fast, and it should be detailed. After that, he shot off another eight or ten letters. When he had finally finished, Vishwasrao asked him, 'Kakasaheb, the Shindes and the Holkars tried so hard that Ayodhya should stay with Shuja's father Safdarjang, didn't they? So Shuja should remember the debt and join up with us, shouldn't he?'

'What you say is perfectly right, Rao Saheb. Shuja-ud-dowlah and his province of Ayodhya are tremendous assets. Its strength lies in the vast and fertile lands on the banks of the Ganga, its plentiful stock of equipment and its valiant chieftains like Anupgiri and Umraogiri Gosavi. Whenever we clash with Abdali, Shuja's presence or absence, whose side he is on will make a critical difference to the outcome.'

'We have to strain every nerve, then, to get him to join us.'

'Yes, we are doing all that we can to get him round.'

The pavillion had become a bee-hive of activity. While Sadashivrao was busy running through documents, he heard a bustle outside the pavillion. The guard entered to say that some five or six hundred cavalrymen were kicking up a rumpus outside. They wanted an audience with him at all cost, and immediately. Letting out a sigh, he stepped out and boomed at the gathering, 'Yes, gentlemen, what do you want to meet me for?'

'Bhausaheb, so many of us have not received our allowance for an entire year. How are we going to fight, then? Mere talk of conquests doesn't help fill stomachs, saheb!'

'Bhausaheb, how many months have gone by since the Sindkhed conflict? Our horses were taken away from under us. How long can cavalrymen survive without their horses? And if such is our state, how do you expect us to join this campaign?'

'Give us allowance for horses!'

'Give us our saddle allowance!'

'We are not coming for the campaign!'

'Not at all!'

'Silence!' roared Sadashivrao. 'None of this clamour! You think I don't know all that you have been shouting about? This rebelliousness is going to take you nowhere. Everybody has to come for the campaign, you hear me? I know what you are going through, but you are not going to get a penny now. You will have to find a way out of these bad times. I promise you here, within fifteen days of setting off, I shall settle your accounts. You will get your horses and your allowances, but for that, you have to show some patience. The empire is groaning under a debt of twenty million; if you act sensibly, it will survive, else it will disintegrate.'

These words from Sadashivrao brought solace to the soldiers and they dispersed.

◈

The task of separating the two accounts was in full swing. Also being discussed among Sadashivrao, Vishwasrao, Shamsher Bahadur, Nana Purandare and Balwantrao Ganpatrao was the formation in which the army would move: which regiment would be on the front, which would be at the back; whose kettle-drums, and who would be the royal guards; who would carry the army flag in front, and so on. An order was instantly dispatched to the superintendant of Ahmadnagar Fort to make immediate arrangement for flintstones, gunpowder, lead and fuses for cannons. Five hundred bullock carts were dispatched to Nagar for more gunpowder. Barons, chieftains, individual soldiers and cavalrymen were instructed to take stock of their horses and load-carrying animals like mules and asses. Only the best saddles should be carried, the rest left behind. Sadashivrao called over some of the headmen and discussed with them how the Pendharis—the food and fodder gatherers—would keep the army supplied in their respective regions once they crossed Burhanpur. Dusk was approaching and the end of the work was nowhere in sight. Sadashivrao could barely lift his head from the table.

He suddenly got up, looked at Purandare and said, 'Nana, send a man to Damaji Gayakwad with the message that I am setting off right now to meet him.'

'You yourself? To meet Damaji? He can be called over here just as well!'

'No, it's I who should go to his pavilion.'

There was a flutter among the servants. Two of them ran with the message to Gayakwad. Sadashivrao and Vishwasrao mounted two of the most elegant horses that were lined up in front of the pavilion. The news of them riding out spread like wildfire among the thousands of soldiers camping along the Purna river. As they passed by the tents, their faces glowed with a strange radiance. The soldiers stood in front and bowed to mark their respect to the royal pair. They looked in admiration at the Kakasaheb-nephew duo that was soon to lead them into a major campaign.

Though they knew of the bitterness that existed between the Peshwas and the Gayakwads, neither Nana Purandare nor anybody else could fathom why Sadashivrao should want to meet Damaji at this point.

The Peshwas had raised a demand for the Gujarat region that was under the control of the Dabhades and the Gayakwads. The Dabhades were from Talegaon and the Gayakwads hailed from Dawadi, and there was considerable cordiality between the two. Ten years earlier, Umabai Dabhade had strongly opposed the handing over of half of Gujarat to the Peshwas. During this period, the anti-Peshwa Tarabai of Karveer had started bringing together a number of old chieftains, and Damaji Gayakwad had joined Tarabai's faction. The old chieftains carried strong feelings against the Peshwas running the empire. Umabai Dabhade would openly wonder why the Maratha sardars allowed the Brahmins to purloin the empire from under their noses. The Peshwas, during this period, were out on their Karnataka campaign. Damaji's army began advancing in the direction of Pune and triggered off turmoil in the city. Tryambak Mama Pethe quickly brought Radhabai, Kashibai and the treasury under his charge and took shelter in Sinhgadh. But the Gayakwad forces, instead of moving into Pune, headed towards Satara via Jejuri. At Wadutha on the banks of the Krishna, Damaji's forces ran into the forces of other chieftains of Shahu Maharaj. A serious conflict ensued, and Vitthal Shivdev took the father-son duo into custody and held them in detention at Lohgadh. The Peshwas returned from Karnataka and set afoot frantic efforts at healing the rift. Peshwa Nanasaheb signed off half of Gujarat to Damaji. Loading him with important-sounding titles and robes of honour, he dispatched him with honour to Gujarat. The pay-off was that Damaji would send to the Peshwas a regiment of ten-thousand soldiers whenever the need arose. Damaji was as irascible and obstinate as he was brave. The Peshwas did their best to bring about a meeting of hearts, but all they finally managed was the agreement. The bad taste in Damaji's mouth remained. He could not rid himself of the ache he felt in the heart each time he thought of the humiliating incarceration, despite the assurance of safe-passage. As a marker of his continued resentment, Damaji would always salute Nanasaheb and Bhausaheb Sadashivrao with his left hand.

Thus, it was mystifying that Bhausaheb should want to make a personal visit to such a temperamental chieftain.

There was commotion in the Gayakwad camp when the news arrived that Bhausaheb was on his way to meet Damaji. Damaji stepped out and welcomed him with a loud, 'Welcome, Bhausaheb, welcome. What a rare honour that you should take the trouble to visit us!'

'Not just you and I, sir, but the entire world knows that there is still some distance that exists between the Peshwas and the Gayakwads. If this distance can be reduced by my taking a few steps towards you, well, why not?' smiled Sadashivrao.

'Well said, Bhausaheb, very well said,' acknowledged Damaji.

The two sat down for a one-on-one. Sadashivrao was so caught up in the campaign that he held forth on that subject for a long while. Finally, he said, 'Such being the circumstances, it is wrong that there should be any distance between us. If there are pending issues that need resolution, let's resolve them right now and set off on our mission with a single mind and heart.'

'Bhausaheb, the Gayakwads have never been remiss in their service to the empire, but those bitter memories are impossible to put behind. You were on your Pune campaign then, all of you. The rumour that we were marching on Pune created such a stir that no less a pair than Bajirao's wife and mother ran to seek shelter in Sinhgadh. If the Gayakwads had really been harbouring evil intentions, a lot of mischief could have been wrought. It would have been easy for us to tie Pune's honour to the stake for five or six days at least. But we did nothing of the sort. We completely ignored Pune and marched straight ahead. There was a skirmish, yes, but because we were granted safe-passage, we stayed at the banks of the Vena. Although it had been agreed to sort things out with civility, some two-bit chieftains of your camp suddenly materialized and began looting our tents while we were busy with our baths. We stayed true to our word, but the treachery and knavery of your people that day was such that even today my blood boils when I think of it. That was not the way chivalrous people should have behaved, Bhausaheb.'

Bhausaheb let Damaji spill all the bile out. After sufficient pause, he began, 'Damaji, we were not complicit in any way in that shameful incident. But if you think we were, all we can do now is to offer our sincerest apologies. Let's give all the past bitterness a final burial. The occasion that confronts us now is colossal. The conflict that we are getting into is not between Hindus and Muslims, but between the common Hindustani and the foreign intruder. This war is not of the Brahmin or the Maratha or the Muslim or any other caste or creed. This war is of the entire nation of Maharashtra. All of Maharashtra is racing forward to protect the badshah of Delhi. All of Maharashtra is determined to stand in the battlefield and repel the advance of the foreign foe. It's for this mission alone, Damaji, that we have to come together, heart and mind, to fight to the last drop of our blood. There are some demands of yours regarding the palace at Gujarat that are still pending, but we promise to resolve that issue after we return from this campaign, rest assured. As for now, let us resolve to leap into the fire together with a singularity of purpose.'

The confabulation went on for a long time. As the two finally stepped out of the pavilion, they embraced each other. Damaji walked a few steps with Bhausaheb Sadashivrao to bid him goodbye. The glow that showed on Damaji's face suggested that the meeting had brought peace and pride back to his wounded heart. This time when he saluted Bhausaheb, it was with his right hand.

☙

Not many days were left for Sadashivrao to set off on the campaign. The two armies had to be separated, and the work pressure had quite obliterated the difference between night and day for him. In fact, he had virtually shifted residence to the office pavilion; that was where he washed and ate and collected his forty winks. The administration of Peshwadom had to be handed over to Sakharam Bapu, and that required that he should bring the books and registers into order. It wasn't in Bhau's nature to brush aside any mismatch in the accounts, however tiny. It had to tally to the last penny, and that had kept him awake till well past midnight. He hadn't found time to visit his private quarters.

He got up with the crow of the first cock. On an ordinary day, he would first have put in a thousand to fifteen hundred Surya Namaskaar, the yogic exercise with which he began his day, but today his mind was extraordinarily distracted; he couldn't have done more than a couple of hundred. He was far too preoccupied, dreaming of moves and counter-moves for the impending campaign. In the company of a few servants, he walked to the banks of the Poorna for a dip. A quick prayer to the river goddess for success in his mission, and he was back to his tent where he plunged straight into work.

The day dawned. Balwantrao Ganpat arrived early, but seeing Bhausaheb deeply engrossed, he waited outside the pavilion. Shamsher Bahadur, Mahipatrao Chitnis, Tryambak Sadashiv alias Nana Purandare and Khajgiwale arrived within minutes of each other. Every one of them belonged to Bhausaheb's innermost circle; a number of them had grown up with him. The hubbub outside brought Bhausaheb to the surface, and he signalled to his servant to invite the assembled group in. As Balwantrao Ganpat sat down on the mattress, he remarked, 'Sleep seems to have become a rare commodity for you, Bhausaheb.'

'Watch it become rarer as we move on,' laughed Sadashivrao.

A fair, slim seventeen year old walked in. Ostrich neck, thin, razor-sharp nose, he was delicate to the point of being an apparition. Balaji, alias Nana, was the son of Balwantrao Ganpat's sister Rakhmabai and Janardan Bhanu, the former Phadnis, the accountant of the Peshwas. During the northern campaign of Dadasaheb, Janardanpant had died of a mysterious stomach ailment. Balwantrao Ganpat was a childhood friend of Bhausaheb, and his prestige in the durbar had increased since the Savnoor victory. Sadashivrao took a liking for Balwantrao's nephew and conferred upon the young boy the robe and seat of his late father. Though young in age and delicate in constitution, Nana possessed a sharp mind. He had a good understanding of bookkeeping too, with the result that Sadashivrao had confidence enough in him to hand over important documents for assessment. Even now, as Nana sat poring over the sheets, he would lift his dolorous eyes and sneak a furtive look at the assembled guests.

Mahipatrao Chitnis asked, 'Bhausaheb, what time should we set off?'

'That's what's been bothering me,' replied Bhausaheb. 'This is the most ambitious campaign of my life, and they have still not identified an auspicious enough moment for getting it started.'

'We have such competent scholars and astrologers like Jereshastri, Punalkar Joshibuva and Bhargava Pandit with us in the army. Why, then, should this task be so difficult?' asked Khajgiwale.

'Instead of getting after this scholar and that,' chipped in Mehendale, one of Bhausaheb's advisers, 'why don't you consult Govind Deekshit of Paatan? If you remember, he was the person who had given us the propitious time for the Udgir campaign. In fact, because of the success in that campaign, the Peshwa had gifted him a village with a revenue of five thousand. With such an exceptional astrologer available on call, why should we get after anybody else?'

'That's quite true, Balwantrao,' agreed Sadashivrao. 'I too have faith in that man. Just yesterday I was talking to him and he has even carried my horoscope. It looks like we may have to set off by the Shiv-likhit moment, otherwise there are no favourable dates this month. We may have to wait for a couple of months if we miss this, he says.'

'So, what difference will a month or two of waiting make?' said Mahipatrao Chitnis. 'It's always good to set your foot forward after ensuring that the moment is well chosen.'

'The moment has to be chosen carefully, of course,' said Sadashivrao gravely, 'but other important facts have to be factored in too. We cannot afford a delay of one month. That blight named Abdali and that demon of Najeebabad would have razed all of Hindustan by then. Let's take the Shiv-likhit as propitious enough, as Deekshit says.'

'The Shiv-likhit is not all that bad a choice,' piped up Nana Phadnis. 'Deekshit is no ordinary astrologer; I have studied plenty of his almanacs.'

'Balwantrao, your nephew seems to be quite an accomplished astrologer,' said Sadashivrao with a smile, setting off a good-natured chuckle all round.

He then came to the subject of preparations for the army. How big should the army be? What about food and fodder? How many chieftains?

What about gunpowder and cannonballs? Would there be a shortage of paper for the wicks for the cannons? What could be done about it? What arrangements could be made for additional gunpowder and lead? As the talks progressed on various aspects of getting the army battle-ready, the absence of Ibrahim Khan Gardi was sharply felt. The man had a deep understanding of the paraphernalia required for equipping an army, and no discussion would be adequate without him.

'Why is the Nawab Saheb so late in coming?' Sadashivrao Bhausaheb wondered aloud, and immediately dispatched a servant to fetch him.

'Oh, he would be busy with his exercises,' laughed Balwantrao. 'Whatever you may say, Gardi is as disciplined as those whites. He has to go for his exercises every day in the morning. Gives himself a proper sweating. His exercises are as important for him as our ritual bath is for us. Look at us Marathas, putting our legs up in the four monsoon months, gorging on festival delicacies, and setting out only with the first signs of autumn in Dussehra. Meanwhile, the discipline of the battlefield is placed under total suspension. Gardi, however, never relaxes his fitness regimen.'

'Oh, yes, we too must learn to change with the new world order,' said Bhausaheb. 'We've been familiar for ten years now with the striking power and the regimen of Gardi and the French. It was ten years ago that I was accompanying the Peshwa to settle accounts with the Nizam at Ahmadnagar. Moving along Kalas, Khed and Wadgaon, we crossed the river Kukdi. We had been hearing for some time about this artillery unit of the Frenchman Bussey working for the Nizam. We had heard of Ibrahim Khan, too, who was working as Bussey's assistant. It was a full-moon night when we crossed the Kukdi; there was to be a lunar eclipse, and that gave us the rare opportunity of earning merit with some special prayers. Accordingly, the revered Nanasaheb and I got into the river along with our men and a few other notables. We had our gold and silver utensils with us along with the prayer material. It so happened that Bussey's unit was on its way back from Pune and they found us thus exposed. They attacked us instantly and their European weapons began belching fire. We were battered mercilessly, and the casualty ran high. A couple of dozen lost their lives. We ran out of the river, with our wet dhotis sticking to our legs. The Peshwa and I jumped on to the bare backs of our horses, somehow managed to give the dodge to Ibrahim Khan and and his mentor Muzaffar Khan in the neighbouring fields, and reached our shelter with our lives. The next morning, when we visited the site of our discomfiture, we saw hundreds of our men and animals lying scattered everywhere, their skins roasted off their bones. That was when the efficacy of the French weaponry hit us hard. We knew then that the days of swords and spears and bows and arrows were over. Tomorrow would belong to muskets and cannons, and we decided to procure those French weapons as early as we could.'

'We have heard that the Peshwa had sent a petition to the English governor at Mumbai, requesting the services of four European experts to train our men in modern weaponry,' said Shamsher Bahadur. 'What was their response, Bhausaheb?'

'Yes, the Peshwa had made considerable efforts in that direction, but those whites were in no mood to indulge us. This was the magic weaponry with which they intended to break our backs, so why would they want to share its knowledge with us? In fact, we went beyond and tried to get the services of this French gunner Bussey, but we didn't succeed, and had to finally settle for Muzaffar Khan.'

'But I remember your allergy for this man. You were insisting that we kept this Muzaffar at a distance!' said Nana Purandare.

'That's true. From the very first sight of him, I knew that he couldn't be trusted. Like a prostitute changes her clothes four times a day, Muzaffar was the kind who would change his patrons with the same frequency. He had even plotted to murder the very same Bussey from whom he had learnt the art of gunnery. I had strongly advised the Peshwa to have no truck with such a treacherous person, but we Marathas are poor judges of character. It was the same old theme of being kind to a person who seeks shelter. The Peshwa appointed him despite my resistance. But when the time arrived for Muzaffar to stand up and fight, he promptly made a deal with our enemies and hopped over to the Savnoor camp. He stayed with them a few months, and was back again at our doors, begging for mercy. The Peshwa again gave him shelter, and that was how he landed in our service.'

'But Ibrahim Khan was this Muzaffar's protégé, wasn't he? So why was Muzaffar so envious of his own man?' asked Shamsher Bahadur.

'Muzaffar was forever riled up at you since the time Ibrahim came into your service.'

'There are some fruits that are by nature bitter. Whatever you mix them with—sugar, butter or whatever—their bitterness doesn't go away. We were on an outing once when his son-in-law Hyder Khan mounted a murderous attack on me. I was lucky that Nagoji Gujar was by my side, else I would have been done for. That's the kind of fiend Muzaffar was.'

'The Peshwa didn't take time to settle accounts,' laughed Mahipatrao Chitnis. 'Without bothering to set up any inquiry, he got the father-in-law and son-in-law duo beheaded in a single day.'

'It couldn't have been any other way,' opined Balwantrao Chitnis. 'There are some forces that, for their own selfish ends, are always trying to drive a wedge between Nana and Bhau. As young children, we have seen with our own eyes the affection between them. One got hurt, and the other's eyes would turn moist.'

'Bhausaheb, you may not agree, but since the time that this one Gardi mounted his attack on you, my trust in all the Gardis has disappeared. It is a treacherous, faithless community of people. Some senior chieftains often express their surprise over how Bhausaheb continues to trust one of their tribe even after the heinous attack. How can you place so much faith in Ibrahim Gardi?' asked Nana Purandare.

'It's never a tribe or a community that is treacherous,' reasoned Bhausaheb. 'It's a matter of an individual's own character. During Chhatrapati Shivaji's times, did the people from his own soil show any less treachery? But I don't know why, from the first time that I saw him, this Ibrahim Khan has struck me as a loyal and straight-forward person. He has risen up from extreme poverty. He began as a young boy, running with a flag in hand as a pilot of Bussey's band, and see where he is today. Only recently did he bomb the hell out of Devgiri and brought the Nizam to his knees. It was his unit that broke the back of the Nizam's forces. His amazing knowledge of European muskets and cannons, his readiness to jump into the fray at a single order, his ability to convert the toughest bulwarks into dust in no time—these are the magical qualities that he possesses and we have all seen them in action. If he were to go looking for an opportunity in Hindustan, every single king would welcome him into his fold. This is the treasure we possess, and we have to use his abilities to the hilt in the coming campaign.'

As they were talking, a servant ran in to announce the arrival of Ibrahim Khan Gardi. All eyes turned towards the door as the man walked in: very short, strongly built and pitch dark; as he walked at a slow, measured pace, he gave the impression of a black rock rolling in. His sable visage was further marred by deep craters that smallpox had left behind. His red, bulbous eyes completed the resemblance to the frightful buffalo-god Mhaisoba. His walk, his carriage and his apparel were altogether European. His head was covered with a red hat popular with French soldiers, his orange-coloured coat reached down to his knees, and his fancy leather boots swallowed his legs right down to the hem of his coat. The white feather stuck on the hat fluttered as this eye-catching figure walked with deliberate steps into the gathering and bowed ostentatiously low before Bhausaheb and said, 'Assalaam alaikum.'

'Walaikum assalaam,' responded Bhausaheb with a light bow.

'I seek forgiveness for my impudence, huzoor, but when your message arrived, I was still on my gunnery exercises, hence it took me time to come. Please accept my apologies.'

'Don't worry, Nawab Saheb, please take a seat.'

Permission granted, Ibrahim Khan tried to sit down on the mattress like the others; but his clothes were too tight for that, so he had to sit without folding his legs inwards. He had been with the Marathas for a little over six months, but whenever he had time on hand, he would occupy himself with his military exercises.

Bhausaheb and Ibrahim began their conversation, while the others sat and listened. Bhausaheb set the ball rolling with expressing his admiration for the gunner. 'Nawab Saheb, as you very well know, our entire campaign depends upon your platoon. Our earlier artillery is just so many old pots and pans. It's your responsibility now to roast the enemy with your latest guns.'

'Huzoor, you shall not find your servant remiss in his duties. Once a commitment is made, this Ibrahim is forever a slave to that commitment. No matter if this head is severed from the shoulder, even as I die, I shall carry a hundred odd enemies with me.'

'Military tactics have changed dramatically now, and it's a new world into which we have entered. What's the use of our old artillery unit now? We are very satisfied with the way your gunnery squad has achieved its victories, my trust in you is complete. We do have great warriors among us like Vitthalrao Vinchurkar, Malharrao Holkar, Damaji Gayakwad, Manaji Paigude, old veterans who have seen the Maratha empire through its spring and autumn, through its victories and defeats, through its good and bad times, through its summers and rains; well, so be it. But these great and valiant soldiers have turned old; they still continue to keep faith in their old-world guerilla strategies, and refuse to acknowledge the efficacy of the newer ones. In my opinion, the enemy we are going to confront is not going to be the Kabuli or Kandahari simpleton of old who can be blown away like so much fluff. When we clash with each other for the final and decisive round on the battlefield of the Antarved, it's your European cannons that will make the difference. Otherwise, for sheer, raw courage, was Ranoji's son Dattaji any short? We don't want his fate to be visited upon any of us, and that's why I am alerting you well in advance: ask what support you want, and it shall be provided to you; but this time round, Nawab Saheb, we have to show the Kandaharis the stuff that we Deccan people are made of.'

'Gentlemen, the trust and generosity that you have showered on me and my squad shall not go in vain. I am beholden to you for your steadfast belief in us. We have already shown you in Devgiri what we are capable of. All these Durrani-Turranis will become no more than fodder for our guns. So violent will our attack be that along with the two rivers of the Antarved, the Ganga and the Yamuna, there shall be a third river flowing: that of Afghan blood.'

'As you know, the misdemeanor of your Muzaffar Khan has brought the name of the Gardis under a cloud. This blemish on your community ...'

'We shall wash it away, huzoor, of this you may be sure,' responded Ibrahim Khan. 'If one fruit happens to be cankerous, do we black-ball the entire tree? How can the perfidy of one Muzzaffar Khan be used as an excuse to tar the entire community of Gardis? Bhausaheb, you are offering us this opportunity to get into battle for you, and for that you have my boundless gratitude.'

'I believe that our guerilla strategies are not going to be of much use at the Antarved. Looking at the fate that the armies of the Shindes and the Holkars have suffered, we have arrived at the conclusion that strategies need to change according to the terrain and the circumstances of war. We hear that Abdali's cannons are invincible, impenetrable ...'

'Shrimant, punching holes in the impenetrable is our speciality,' Ibrahim broke in. 'But, Bhausaheb, with heavy cannons to carry, our movement is going to be slow, while your Maratha horsemen will be riding on the wind. We don't have legs on which to run; we are legless, actually. If the enemy comes thundering in and your horsemen do the vanishing trick ...'

Sadashivrao laughed and patted Ibrahim's back reassuringly. 'Nawab Saheb,' he said, 'you may abandon your doubts. If ever the moment of reckoning arrives, we shall forfeit our lives but not the battlefield. We never break our faith. Wherever you stand, there I shall plant myself. My word to you shall never fail.'

Promises were exchanged. Both parties gave each other gifts as tokens of affection for each other. They gathered each other into their arms and gave a tight squeeze.

❦

Sadashivrao quickly finished his prayers and got ready to set off towards his office pavilion. Parvatibai stepped forward and handed him his stole. As he threw the stole over his shoulder, Parvatibai said, 'Nana Phadnis's mother Akkasaheb Rakhmabai had come to meet you yesterday.

'Oh, really? What does Akkasaheb have to say?'

'That she and her household are accompanying you.'

'To the campaign?'

'Not *to* the campaign, *with* the campaign—a visit to the three holy pilgrimages of Kashi, Prayag and Mathura. It's been her desire for years, to see Kashi Vishweshwar and the feet of Vishnu, and this desire is now going to be fulfilled in your lordship's company.'

This information stunned Bhausaheb. For a moment, he did not know what to say. Finally, in a worried tone, he asked, 'Who told Akkasaheb that we are going to Kashi-Prayag? Our battle is going to be fought around Delhi, don't you know? Why would we go to the triad of Kashi-Prayag-Mathura?'

'Well, Akkasaheb said that Mathura is on the way to Delhi, so a visit to Shri Krishna's land is guaranteed. Go a little north, and you have Kurukshetra and Haridwar. Besides, as Akkasaheb says, once the battle is over, it's finished, isn't it? Once Abdali has been vanquished, she would persuade your lordship to move down the Ganga towards Kashi. The entire army will earn the merit of visiting these holy places.'

'Amazing! One doesn't understand how to explain things to you women! Sitting here in the south, you cannot imagine what the north is like. Besides, the places you talked about, they are not a *little* above or below Delhi. They are all hundreds of miles apart. Basically, we are completely ignorant about the north. Our estimates are built almost exclusively on hearsay, on the information provided to us by scouts and other people's experiences. How, then, can all this business of pilgrimages be made possible?'

'It's not Akkasaheb alone, the wives of all the chieftains and grandees, a few hundred of their relatives, and another few hundred of their village friends are setting off with you for the pilgrimage.'

'Oh, we are a truly blessed people!'

As Sadashivrao Bhausaheb left for office, he encountered on his way a few of these prospective pilgrim groups. Each of these groups was five- or six-hundred strong, comprising women, children, and plenty of doddering old people. There were mendicants and renunciates with their begging bowls in hand. Every group had its mules, donkeys and other load-bearing animals laden to breaking point with all kinds of paraphernalia. There were pots and pans of various sizes, household appliances and even musical instruments sticking out of their backs. Long before the military campaign could organize itself, the pilgrims were ready and raring to go.

By the time Bhausaheb arrived in office, his group of intimates like Balwantrao Ganpat, Nana Purandare and a few others had already taken their seats. The first question that Bhausaheb shot at Balwantrao was, 'How many groups of pilgrims are riding with us?'

Balwantrao gave Bhausaheb a startled look. Before he could respond, Bhausaheb continued, 'Look, I have nothing to say about Akkasaheb. She is your sister, your closest relative. I also know that there are the wives of a few other sardars who plan to join the pilgrimage. But I notice now that people with no connections at all, a motley crowd of all and sundry, are all gathered and ready to get on to the bandwagon.'

'Bhausaheb, people who have no patrons, for them the Peshwa himself is their lord and protector, and you are in his shoes now. The patronage that the sadhus and sanyasis received during Nanasaheb's reign, they couldn't have got even during the times of the Puranas. The Peshwa's glory has spread across all the three worlds, stretching across Kashi, and Prayag right up to Bhuvaneshwar. Who else do the people of our land go to for shelter? Kashi, Haridwar, Gadmukteshwar, Prayag, Kurukshetra, these are truly far-off lands. If these pilgrims were to make their journey alone across thousands of miles, they would be easy prey to all kinds of thugs and thieves and robbers and confidence-tricksters. Then there are the priests at the other end, waiting to fleece every innocent pilgrim they can lay their hands on! But if they go under your protection, it will be that much easier for them, and the merit you gain out of making their pilgrimage possible will release the punyaayi, the merit-force of another Ganga, and your army will sail through on its waves.'

'Balwantrao, keep aside all these fanciful tales of merit-earning and use your head for a minute. With so much non-combatant, useless lumber to take care of, how will the army be able to retain its agility? Besides, how are we going to feed so many mouths? You should know that jobless people eat a great deal more than usefully occupied ones. To keep them well fed, we will have to starve our army, and that will be a great way of bringing deliverance for our soldiers.'

Jereshastri was listening with great interest to Bhausaheb's ignorant prattle, the furrows on his forehead getting deeper with every statement. When it got too much for him, he gave a scornful laugh and intervened, his rudraksha beads rattling furiously, 'Bhausaheb, you have no conception of God's ways. A man may be as brave and valiant and invincible as he wants, but he can't hope to match the powers of divinity. The gods alone can perform the miracle of converting men into monkeys and monkeys into men. Let calamities mount one on another, but if you have the gods backing you, they are all bound to melt away. There's the famous story of Shivaji going to listen to Tukaram's religious discourse. The enemy got wind and thought it a good opportunity to apprehend Shivaji. The gods then got into the game and so mesmerized the enemy that every single assembled devotee looked an exact image of Shivaji. All right, rascals, whom will you arrest now? Exactly in the same manner, if you carry these thousands of devotees to their pilgrimage, whatever catastrophe falls your way, be it famine or epidemics, or your two-penny worth Abdali, Lord Shri Krishna Himself will incarnate by your side and behead Abdali with his Sudarshan-chakra. But for that, Bhausaheb, you need the blessings of holy men.'

'What Shastribuva says is absolutely true,' Mahipatrai Chitnis chipped in. 'Bhausaheb, the Peshwa has earned so much of merit that this Abdali is going to get inundated in its flood. In any case, when your army measures in hundreds of thousands, how can a bare fifteen-thousand pilgrims be of any count? You won't even notice them.'

After belting out a few more homilies, Jereshastri left. Balwantrao Ganpat said, 'Bhausaheb, you are thinking only in military terms, but gods and religion have such a hold on us people that if you hum and haw, it will create many unexpected problems. I suggest that you bear this with patience.

'Besides, you and Dadasaheb are often at odds on this issue or that. You know how devout he is. Wherever he goes, he carries his entire pantheon of divinities with him in a separate pavilion. When he was in the north, he gifted away so many villages in the service of this god or that. So many village revenues he has assigned for feeding the brahmins. Your military language is not going to go down well with Dadasaheb's faction,' advised Mahipatrao Chitnis.

'Look, Mahipatrao, I am not an atheist either, but I have to meet the expenditure of this campaign from the outside, without having to touch the Pune treasury. All occasions are not the same, and my fear is that my army may have to starve on account of the non-functioning load we are carrying. It will be a disaster if my fears come true.'

A mere two days were left for departure. Bhausaheb set off with Mahipatrao Chitnis and Balwantrao for last minute consultations with Peshwa Nanasaheb. Nanasaheb was ensconced on his cushions, with Raghunath Dada on one side. They were surrounded by a coterie of brahmins and scholars of all hues. Nanasaheb was driven by the desire to get the Hindustan campaign done with successfully and expeditiously. He responded to Bhausaheb's salute with a nod and continued with whatever he was dictating to Sakharam Bapu. Bapu was diligently taking notes.

'Yes, Sakharam Pant, write to Gopal Govindrao to continue with the drums at Ma Bhavani's temple at Tulzapur night and day. Attach a village for the purpose. Make arrangements for the drums to continue at Pandharpur too. Inform Hari Damodar to get the Markand Tirth of Vaijnath at Parli in good repair. Arrange for a couple of priests to attend to the temple there. Make arrangements for the devotional lamps to be perpetually fed with oil in the sanctum-sanctorum of all the four gods at Nimgaon. Assign half the revenue of the villages Ubad and Kushaatarpan for the welfare of the brahmins. Send orders to Sadashiv Paagey that he should attach the revenue of a thousand-rupee village to the service of the goddess at Ambejogai. He should immediately arrange for a prayer service there, and start a mess for twenty-five Brahmins. Lamps should be lit for other gods too at state expense. Also, tell him to invest the revenue of the Lonar region and the Tonke pilgrimage for setting up an annual pension for the brahmins. Ask him to plant trees on either side of the road that connects the Mukund Tirth to the Narsinh Tirth.'

It didn't take Bhausaheb a minute to understand that Nanasaheb was distributing all these goodies among gods and brahmins for the success of the campaign, and he was deeply touched. This was Nanasaheb's way of showing the deep affection in which he held Bhausaheb. Nanasaheb went on scratching his head, trying to remember which god or goddess might have been missed. 'Oh, yes,' he continued, 'tell this to Hari Damodar too, that he should take the help of Kesopant Patil at Bhima-Shankara and construct an inn for travellers for one-and-a-half-thousand rupees. He should arrange for a couple of brahmins to keep the prayers and the lamp going at all times at Bhima-Shankara. Ask Tryambakrao Mama too to arrange for prayers at the Tryambakeshvar. Send a note to Naro Appaji here in Pune that he should get peepal trees planted along the road, starting from Pune through Paashaan, Vitthal Wadi, Katraj and Alandi right up to Thewoor. The trees should be at a distance of fifty arm-measures from each other. Naro Appaji and Shivajipant have to personally supervise this work.'

The number of gods and goddesses that the Peshwa could remember! One moment he instructed for mango orchards to be planted at Junnar and Pune and at far off Baleghat for the acquisition of merit. The next moment he thought of the Shooleshwar Temple at Bhingaar that had got submerged in water, and ordered for it to be rescued out and rebuilt. He ordered for hundreds of dilapidated temples to be repaired, and for food to be served to the poor and the brahmins in this village and that. Then suddenly his brow creased and his eyes turned moist. 'Jai Vyankatesh!' he said with folded hands. He looked at the chieftains and grandees, brahmins and scholars, who sat around him and said in a loud voice, 'The Shri Vyankatesh Temple at Deulgaon near Sindkhed is a particularly vibrant temple. In the name of that temple, I make this pronouncement: when Bhausaheb or Malharrao or any other Maratha sardar brings victory to our army by decapitating Abdali, we shall gift ten-thousand gold coins to the Vyankatesh at Deulgaon. Sakharam, send an immediate order to the administrator at Jalnapur that he should expend two-thousand rupees every year in the service of Shri Vyankatesh.'

The assembly was impressed by Nanasaheb's largesse. Dattopant Agnihotri looked up at the sky and brought together his palms as a mark of thanksgiving. He wiped his moist eyes, turned towards Bhausaheb Sadashivrao and said, 'Bhaurao, set off on your campaign without any ifs and buts in your mind. To please the God of Victory, the Peshwa has rained such a vast amount of gifts, and with such obvious devotion that your Abdali is sure to be swept away in the flood of merit that will ensue. If he ever dares to stand up to that flood, he shall surely be incinerated on the spot. Forget all worries. The job of worrying now belongs to the gods, not to you. Whether you fight now or you don't, victory is assuredly yours!'

Bhausaheb had arrived to have a heart-to-heart discussion with the Peshwa. He had wanted to tell him openly and forcefully that in all this business of pleasing the gods and arranging pilgrimages, the real issue of war should not be forgotten. But the mood of the assembly was such that there was no way he could turn the subject round to the mundane, practical issues of moving an army and conducting a war.

'It's been a long-standing desire of mine,' said Nanasaheb, 'that the holy places of Kashi and Prayag come under our control. There are demons there, obstructing the path of gods. When will the day dawn, oh Lord Ganesha, when the Marathas will be able to set out on these pilgrimages without a fear in their hearts?'

'Our Dadasaheb's thoughts echo your thoughts exactly, my lord,' said Sakharam Bapu. 'When Dadasaheb had stepped into the Kurukshetra area six years ago, the entire Hindustan had begun to resound with the trumpet of his devotion. It had been a part of Dada's plan to win control of these other pilgrimages too.'

'It's quite true,' the Peshwa replied, 'that many of our generals have bent their backs towards this goal. The Shinde-Holkars had once made a pact with Shuja's father for the holy Kashi to be handed over to us, but, unfortunately, the words never materialized into action.'

'I hear that this time many more than a thousand pilgrims have gathered to accompany the army northwards,' said Dada.

'What choice do they have, the poor wretches?' said Nanasaheb. 'Going on a pilgrimage is an ordeal like none other. The roads are treacherous, there are huge mountains and massive rivers on the way, and then there are the highwaymen.'

༺༶༻

The month by the Hindu calendar was Phalgun, March by the English calendar, the eleventh day of the waning moon. The day was Thursday. The auspicious moment for the departure was in the evening. Patankar Deekshit had located this nearest available favourable time for departure. With Thursday fixed as the day for departure, the camp had gone into a frenzy on the previous day with last minute preparations. Petty traders had folded up their tents and loaded their goods. The troops of the royal regiment had collected their weaponry, and the tents and pavilions of the nobility had been rolled up before noon.

By afternoon, the regiments had begun to assemble at their assigned places. The royal troops stood in the centre. The vanguard regiment was at the periphery. They were to set off the previous evening, identify a good spot for the next halt, and get the royal pavilions and tents erected before the arrival of the force. But this being the first day of the march, it was also required of them to be present at the formal rituals of their departure. Once the movement began, they would have to rush to the point of next halt, which would be Sindkhed. They would have to scout for the right spot for the army to camp, and also erect Bhausaheb's pavilion in good time for the commander-in-chief's arrival. As of now, they stood waiting restlessly for the auspicious moment to arrive.

As soon as the sun went behind the hill, a signal was given and the gunners set light to the wicks of the massive guns. Five cannons boomed in unison with a massive, eardrum-shattering boom. Horses neighed and stood on their hind legs, elephants lifted their trunks and trumpeted. The kettle-drums and pipes joined in to complete the cacophony. The giant army began to move ahead. The elephant with the royal pennant began trundling forward at a regal pace.

Gopikabai, Nanasaheb, Raghunath Dada, Visaji Krishna, Sakharam Bapu and other nobles had gathered to bid goodbye to Bhausaheb and Vishwasrao. Gopikabai began the send-off ritual by circling the earthen lamp round Vishwasrao's handsome face, and applied vermillion to his forehead. She then handed over to him the jewel-studded sword off a golden tray. Vishwasrao, who had been holding himself rather well, lost control of his emotions and took his mother in his embrace with a loud wail of 'Aai Saheb!' The mother's sturdy heart melted too at her son's cry. She patted him on the back and wiped the tears off his face and her own. Vishwasrao then went down on his knees and lowered his brow at his father's feet. The Peshwa lifted him up and held him tight in his arms. Gopikabai then performed the same ritual with Bhausaheb and handed him another jewel-studded sword of European make. Bhausaheb bent low before his sister-in-law and exclaimed in a hoarse voice, 'Vyanisaheb, I promise to give this sword the dignity that it demands. I shall rip the enemy apart with its blade, or in the process, lay my own life ...'

Before he could complete his statement, Gopikabai placed her hand on his mouth and said, 'No inauspicious statements, please, Bhau! I have no doubt that you will come back victorious.'

Sadashivrao then went on his knees before Nanasaheb, who raised him to his feet and gave him a warm embrace. At office, in diplomatic meets, on the battlefield, in household matters, it was this man who had stayed with him like a shadow at all hours of day and night; the Peshwa was overwrought while bidding him goodbye. In a voice choked with emotion, he said, 'Bhausaheb, I have never seen you as a brother. You have held the same place in my heart as Vishwasrao has. My state now is quite like Dashrath's. I doubt if he would have felt the same pain while bidding goodbye to Lord Rama as I do now!'

'My state, Shrimant,' responded Bhausaheb, 'is like that of Bharat. I carry with me your footwear to foreign parts. I now have to see how I can help it inspire me to hoist the flag of victory in all directions.'

'Keep sending messages. Ask for whatever you need. Never hesitate for a moment. You are well and truly the son of Appasaheb, the kind who can set alight a ball of fire even inside a conflagration. But please exercise caution while playing with fire. If you go, the world will go to bits.'

'The lord Peshwa may set his mind at rest. I shall exercise all caution,' Bhausaheb assured him.

As Sadashivrao turned his back, the simple-hearted Raghunath Dada could not hold himself back. 'Bhausaheb,' he cried and stepped forward. Hearing his name called, Bhausaheb turned round and saw Raghunath reach up to him with extended arms. As the two took each other in their embrace, Sakharam Bapu turned his face away with distaste. 'Bhausaheb,' continued Raghunath Dada in a hoarse voice, 'anything untoward, and you just have to send a message. This Raghunath of yours will come riding the wind and bring the earth and the sky down on their knees for you.'

Bhausaheb was too overcome to trust his own voice. 'Yes, thank you,' he somehow managed to utter, and took leave of everybody.

Beside Bhausaheb stood his favourite steed Chandrasen. Snow-white, strong, tall and muscular, Chandrasen was of the Panchali breed. The mane on its graceful neck blew in the wind like the tresses of a nubile damsel let loose after a bath. On its forehead danced tassels of silk and gold. The saddle on its back was made from heavy brocade, and its harness and reins were woven in silk. The anklets on each of its four legs were made of gold. It was the kind of animal that would stand out in a herd of thousand. Next to Chandrasen stood Gajendra, Bhausaheb's favourite elephant. Imagine a huge black boulder rounded smooth after eons of steady grinding under a waterfall, and that would be Gajendra. Vishwasrao had already taken his seat on the grand canopy placed upon Gajendra's back. Bhausaheb nudged Chandrasen close to the elephant, and with one leap on its back, he climbed over to the seat next to Vishwasrao. Once again the air shook with the boom of five cannons fired in unison. The ladies of the royal household—Akkasaheb, Parvatibai, Lakshmibai and others—got into the howdahs of the elephants lined up behind. Nanasaheb looked around and remarked, 'Why don't I see Nana Phadnis anywhere in this crowd?'

'He's indisposed, Shrimant,' somebody responded. 'He is not in a state to travel on horseback or even on a howdah. He is being carried in a palanquin behind us.'

The word 'indisposed' brought a snigger on Sakharam Bapu's lips. The rolling out began, with the royal elephants leading. Behind them were the big and small palanquins, followed by the units of the other chieftains. Behind them was the army, the traders with their wares packed on animals, the water-carriers, the servants, footmen, the players of the kettle-drums and trumpets, the palanquins of the tamasha women, after them the sanitation workers, the clerks, dancing troupes, novitiate brahmins, beggars, monks, mendicants, holy men of various hues and persuasions, scholars, soothsayers, astrologers, brahmin cooks, non-brahmin cooks, odd-job men, instrument players, drummers, bards, minstrels, balladeers, travellers, horse-trainers, grooms; this was as eclectic an assembly of human beings as had ever moved together as a single, massive body.

Nanasaheb stood watching this tidal wave pass by. This parting from his son Vishwasrao, and particularly his cousin Bhausaheb, had affected him deeply. As he stood wistfully looking at the wake, he turned to his wife and murmured, 'Gopikay, I remember so vividly the time when I was returning to Pune after leaving Bhausaheb behind for his studies in Satara. He had come right up to the palace gates to bid me goodbye. In fact, he had trailed me right up to my horse and stood holding its harness. The eyes of that little boy had filled up with tears; I had had to dismount from my horse to pacify him. And now that same boy has grown into such a composed individual. In fact, it is now I who have become a little boy who can't hold back his tears. For a person barely into his thirties, how much maturity this boy has acquired!'

The sun had set behind the mountains, and its rays had scattered themselves into a hundred thousand threads all across the western horizon. The silhouettes of the distant pennants, spears, howdahs and the bobbing heads of the horsemen had begun to dissolve in the haze of the dimming light. As Nanasaheb stood looking at the massive ocean of humanity melting into the distant horizon, he had the strange sensation of walking in step with his brother, his son, and with his comrades of many a former battle.

❦

On the fourth day of the month of Chaitra, 1681 of the Hindu calendar, 4 April 1760 A.D., the Maratha army had reached Burhanpur. Bhausaheb had planned for one thing, and what had actually been happening was quite another. At Partud, he had talked of finishing off the enemy in three months. The assumption had been that, as always, the Afghan raiders would want to return to Kandahar before the monsoons arrived. One of the frequent barbs thrown at Dadasaheb had been that he had never ever sought a face-to-face confrontation with Abdali; Bhausaheb was keen that no such barb was shot in his direction, and had determined that he would catch him before he returned and exterminate him. That was the reason why he had been planning for the encounter to happen in three months. As per the schedule, they should have reached Burhanpur in eight days, but when they actually took twenty, Bhausaheb was quite perturbed. The circumstances, however, were such that there was little that anybody could have done about it. The news of Dattaji's downfall arrived, and the decision to leave for Hindustan had to be rushed through. The earlier campaigns would always start off from Pune and there would be enough time to organize all aspects at ease. But this time round, they were barely back from the Udgir campaign when they had to set off for the Hindustan campaign with quite the same cavalry, horsemen, animals and soldiers. A number of days had thus to be spent in pruning out lame and wounded animals, identifying fresher men and animals to fill the space, and having them sent over from their villages to join the force.

The next stop after Partud was Sindkhed. As Bhau had promised, the soldiers who had been moving around without horses for the past two years were provided with money. A few more units from Ahmadnagar and Aurangabad joined in. Meanwhile, the pilgrims from various villages kicked up a rumpus, which led to the creation of two bases at Sindkhed. Moving forward thus, bit by bit, via Parli and Kanaar, Bhausaheb had to use up twenty full days to cover those one-hundred-and-twenty miles to Burhanpur.

It was fairly early in the morning, but Bhausaheb was up and sitting in his pavilion, immersed in work. The pressure of all the travel and the account-keeping was substantial. Three weeks of sleepless nights had turned his eyes flaming red. His unceasing prodding had drained out Balwantrao Ganpat and Mahipatrao Chitnis too. Shamsher Bahadur sat in a corner of the pavilion, patting his thick whiskers as he took stock of the ordnance. Bhausaheb wrote a letter to Madho Singh urging him not to support an alien foe and to keep Hindustan free of foreign intruders. He also wrote to a few Rajput kings and landlords of Agra, pleading with them in persuasive words to fight alongside his Maratha army. After a good eight or ten of these letters were written, he put his reed down, wiped his brow with the end of his stole and said, 'All right, Mahipatrao, I'm done writing to Madho Singh. Let's see now what stance he and the rest of the Rajput group take.'

'Good you have written to all these people, but how come Madho Singh? He was the one—'

'—who actually invited Abdali to India and positioned himself against the Marathas, right?'

'Yes!'

'Well, let's see, we have to make all the efforts we can, haven't we? He will take his own call, of course, but there have been occasions when people have transformed dramatically.'

Shamsher Bahadur asked, 'Any news from Govindpant?'

'Not yet, but then, it takes time. It takes three weeks for the post to reach. But we are running short of funds. It'll be a blessing if some money reaches us soon.'

Balwantrao said, 'Bhausaheb, you had fixed some taxes for all the chieftains and landlords who were earlier a part of the Maratha empire. The Shindes and the Holkars had also agreed to pay those taxes. Have you received any funds from them?'

'I had planned to put all that into force this time round, but then this campaign intervened. They have all come up with a hundred excuses for defaulting. Peshwadom is groaning under a mountain of debts. Gangoba Tatya of the Holkars informs that they are in a deep hole on account of expenses. What does Gangoba know who really is in the bigger hole?'

'But, Bhausaheb, you were the person who established accounting practices for the payment of tithe. You prodded them into coughing up their dues!'

'Oh, yes, I did a lot of this revenue fixing work at Shaniwarwada. I had Ramchandrababa to guide me. Fixing accounts, land revenue, bookkeeping, appointing clerks and accountants for the exercise, it was a lot of hard work that we went through for putting a system in place. Took to task Antaji and those cheats, the Hingane brothers. That is exactly why this Bhausaheb is such a demon to all these shysters and their relatives and friends. But if you want the empire to be self-supporting, all these bitter doses of medicine must be administered.

A servant entered and announced, 'Some carts have arrived from the fort-keeper of Ahmadnagar, Shrimant: their men are waiting outside.'

'From Narobabaji Nagarkar?'

'That's right, Shrimant. Shall I let them in?'

'No, I'm coming out myself. Come, Shamsher, let's see how much of the arsenal has arrived.'

Bhausaheb, Shamsher Bahadur, Mahipatrao and Balwantrao stepped out of the pavilion. They took the waiting men along with them and walked out of the camp through the army bazaar. Three-hundred-and-fifty bullock carts had lined up in the open space outside the camp. The bullocks looked spent after a full night's journey. The plod through mountains, valleys and jungle tracks had brought froth spewing through their mouths and nostrils. Not wanting to extend the agony of the animals, Bhausaheb instructed Mahipatrao and Nana Phadnis to take an immediate count of the munitions. Narobabaji had exercised sufficient care while dispatching the arsenal. Every cart had been covered with tarpaulin, canvas and leather to protect the ammunition from getting wet or sweating with rain or dew. Chitnis began the count: there were eight-score measures of lead and forty-score measures of gunpowder and ninety-nine-thousand cartridges. Bhausaheb looked at the list and burst out, 'Mahipatrao, just eight-thousand big cannonballs? We need a minimum of nineteen thousand!'

'Narobaba has drained out whatever he had at the Ahmadnagar Fort. A letter has been dispatched to Pune to send over whatever they have. We should be receiving some cannonballs from Burhanpur too.'

'We will need something like two-thousand reams of European paper to make the wicks for the cannons, and all we have got is sixty-five!'

'Quite right, Bhausaheb, we should begin looking out for them.'

'All right, Mahipatrao, even if we haven't got as much gunpowder as we want, this is good enough to begin with.'

While the talk was on, an official from the fort stepped forward and said, 'Shrimant, two-hundred-and-fifty out of these three-hundred-and-fifty pairs of bullocks have been brought on hire from Ahmadnagar. These bullocks belong to the grocers there. They parted with their animals on our word that they would be brought back immediately from here. My apologies, but your lordship will have to make arrangement for new animals.'

'Heard that, Chitnis? Send people immediately to the neighbouring villages. Buy at least four or five hundred pairs. We will need a lot of animals to pull the cannons. We have the Vindhya and Satpuda ranges to cross. Where ordinarily you need a hundred-and-twenty-five bullocks for one cannon, there you will need two hundred. Buy as many animals as you can in the next four days. We will lose a number of animals as we move along, factor that in too. At Bundelkhand, too, we want a good two or three thousand young studs, send a letter to Govindpant.'

Having been required to leave in a hurry from Partud, Bhausaheb had decided to use two or three places in Burhanpur to make good the deficiencies they had left with. He set off on horseback to make the round of the camp. At one end of the camp, Manaji Paigude was supervising the repairs of saddles, harnesses and stirrups. Some five-to-seven-thousand cobblers had assembled on the ground, and they were busy stitching tears, patching holes, refixing strings, and applying oil to leather gone dry and brittle. Some cobblers were cutting out fresh leather to make brand new seats. When Bhausaheb arrived, they stopped their work and tried to get up to pay their respects, but Bhausaheb waved them down with a sign of hand. 'No, no, don't get up, continue with your work.'

On another side sat the weapon-smiths with their furnaces blazing. They fed coal into the red hot braziers, shoved swords and spears into the coal and bellowed the braziers till the weapons turned white with heat. The weapon-smiths and their gypsy assistants then pulled out the white hot weapon and hammered the edges sharp. A goodly crowd of soldiers had assembled around each of the braziers, all intent on tempering their swords before they set out to temper Abdali.

At a third spot were the tents of the gunners, where Ibrahim Gardi was getting the gun-carriages repaired under his direct supervision. Lakshmanrao Panse was right adjacent, getting his own gun-carriages fixed. Some of Ibrahim's Telangas were busy oiling and greasing the cannons. Blacksmiths were heating and hammering rings into shape to fix on the wooden wheels. The carpenters sat with them, repairing damaged beams, spokes and yokes. When Ibrahim noticed Bhausaheb trotting astride Chandrasen, he saluted him warmly.

'How goes the preparation for war, Nawab Saheb?' asked Bhausaheb, solicitously.

'My cannons and missiles are absolutely ready, huzoor, just point out the enemy, and I shall blow him to pieces.'

'Shamsher,' said Bhausaheb, 'stay with Khan Saheb and see what all he needs, and make sure that he gets them without delay.'

While Bhausaheb's retinue moved on, Shamsher Bahadur walked in with Ibrahim into his tent. Ibrahim served him lemonade and sat looking at him unblinkingly: his rugged face adorned by big, thick whiskers, his physique strong and big-built, his eyes sharp. Shamsher noticed the gaze and asked laughingly, 'Why are you looking at me as if at a woman, Khan Saheb?'

'Not at a woman, Rao Saheb, but at the young, handsome cub of the lionhearted Bajirao. As a child, I would go into a daze at the very mention of Bajirao's name. Let me look at his son's face, at least, to my heart's content.'

'What's there to see in me? I am neither here nor there; neither a Hindu nor a Muslim—' said Shamsher with a tinge of bitterness.

'You are a human being, aren't you? Shamsher, you are like the musk deer that has no idea of the perfume it carries inside its navel. The beautiful Mastani from Hindustan and the valiant Bajirao Peshwa of the Deccan—you are the product of the union of beauty and valour, and you should be proud of it.'

'Khan Saheb, if a person wants to live in peace here in Hindustan, he should carry the stamp of his caste. A man without a caste is a dog without a chain.'

'Shamsher, huzoor, such bitter words don't sound nice coming from your mouth. You are treated with all the respect you deserve at Shaniwarwada, we hear.'

'This respect and dignity has arrived only lately, Khan Saheb. I was earlier a thorn in the path of some. With the passage of time, I am no longer a thorn now, but a sentry posted at the bastion. Since I have understood the facts, I find all this respect and dignity meaningless. You talked about the union of beauty and valour, and you are quite right, of course. Valour was charmed by beauty, and Mastani came over to meet Bajirao. She did become his, but the rest of the wada saw her as a seductress of an alien race, a sorceress—and she was treated accordingly. We were made to live in a separate palace. I was barely two when guards were posted at our gates. My mother would pine for the sight of my father like a fish thrown out of water. She had to suffer the blasts of hot desert winds. My father did lavish his caresses on me; he would take me to see the river flowing in full spate past Shaniwarwada; he would show me the poetry of the star-studded sky, explain its magic to me. It was his desire to perform the sacred thread ceremony for his son Shamsher.'

'If it was the desire of the great man himself, who could have dared to stand up against it?'

'Khan Saheb, caste and religion are such powerful meshes that even the bravest of men can get trapped in them like chicken in a coop. Great scholars and savants got into the ring and flaunted the authority of the holy books to declare that a son born of an alien womb can never be a Hindu, even if he is Bajirao's seed. There was fear in the inner chambers too, that if today Bajirao was pushing for the sacred thread, who could say, tomorrow he might well push for a coronation. The tribulations that my mother and I have suffered, they were unheard of. She was a votary of valour, and she took bravery for her husband. Despite being a Muslim by faith, she observed all the rites of a devoted Hindu wife. But for all her soul-searing efforts, she remained an alien for all of Pune. The religious big-wigs decided to stay away from all ceremonies at the Peshwa house, to boycott us in all matters of church. Their demand was that Mastani should be banished from Pune. And towards that end, they started building up pressure. They refused to officiate in Sadashivrao Bhau's first marriage, and stayed away from Dadasaheb's thread ceremony. Strong personalities like my grandmother Radhabai and Bhausaheb, however, came to stand behind my mother. My grandmother openly declared that if the Pune brahmins refused to perform their religious duties by the Peshwa, they would call brahmins from Kashi. If it hadn't been for my intrepid grandmother, god alone knows which jungle or desert my mother would have been made to wander. I was barely six years old when my father, who made the sky bow to his wishes, passed away, and soon my mother, who had hovered like a protective shadow over my head, vanished too. My travails, however, were far from over.'

'But, Rao Saheb, there were all these efforts made to take you into the Hindu fold just before your marriage!'

'That's quite true. Both Bhausaheb and Dadasaheb were very keen on it, and Nanasaheb had also given his consent. It was more out of respect for my late father than any love for me. But even that didn't materialize.'

'Is it? With the Peshwa himself giving the clearance, who could have stood against it? Netaji Palkar had converted to Islam, and yet Shivaji had happily taken him back into the Hindu fold, hadn't he? How, then, could the great Bajirao's son run into obstacles?'

'That era is long past, Khan Saheb. When the revered mother of our Vishwasrao and the chief consort of the Peshwa—Gopikabai Saheb—makes a pronouncement, there's nobody who can stand against her wishes. Unfortunately, for her I am nothing more than the brat of that sorceress, that alien seductress.'

'Ah, yes, I see. So she wants no partner in power, and therefore, she wants no intimacy with potential competitors—isn't that the case?'

'Who can stand up to the pressure she can exert? This son of Bajirao had to settle for marriage to Lalkunwar, daughter of Lakshavilpatrai, formerly a Hindu and now a Muslim. I have been displaying the prowess of my sword since I was barely thirteen years of age. Whether it's been the northern campaign of Raghunath Dada, or Tulaji Angre's conflict at the seaboard, or the Bundelkhand episode, this Shamsher has been true to his name—a flashing sword—in the field of battle.'

'How unfortunate, really, that you should not have been embraced, in spite of being Bajirao's seed!'

'With people like Bhausaheb to shower their care and affection on me, I have no reason to feel neglected. We two are similar in that we sit quite close to each other at the table that misfortune has laid out for us. I don't feel upset at all for not being allowed to convert to Hinduism. I have no regrets for being the product of a Muslim womb either, because our ultimate caste and lineage is that of the naked sword. We are children of the battlefield; it's the theatre of war that gives us our roots, our identity, our caste and lineage; it gives purpose to our very existence. You shall be there this time to give us company, Khan Saheb, and we shall convince you of our pedigree in the coming conflict.'

'Shamsher Rao Saheb, people like you and Bhausaheb are the offspring of fire. Destiny has granted glory to your swords, although it has also lodged a few thorns into your soles.'

'Khan Saheb, this ineffable, imponderable, untamable power—some know this power as Allah, some others as Ishwar. It's a crafty power, this; never grants anything at one go. It often gives with one hand and takes away with the other. That's what keeps its divinity alive, doesn't it?'

After inspecting the artillery, Ibrahim Khan and Shamsher Bahadur set off towards the pavilion. While they were on the rounds, many of Ibrahim Khan's team—Telangas, Nubians and Europeans—would point Shamsher out to each other as Bajirao's son. The sound of their whispers reached Shamsher's ears and made him swell with pride. It was such whispers that had given him the courage to fight with his circumstances.

⁕

The tent appeared like a mobile war-office. Dozens of clerks sat scratching their reeds on paper. Books and registers of revenue and expenditure lay scattered all around them. Dusk had fallen, and Bhausaheb had not moved from the seat he had occupied since morning. As had been happening often, he had again let lunch go by, and made do with a few fruits and a jug of water.

The masterplan had been to meet the enemy in three months' time; three weeks had already drifted past and they were barely a hundred-

and-twenty miles into the journey. The rest of the journey would be done through highways and jungle tracks to reach the land between the Ganga and the Yamuna—the Antarved—where the clash was expected to happen, and that was still a good eight hundred miles away. These were the thoughts that were somersaulting in Bhausaheb's mind, leaving him restless. A scout handed him fresh intelligence, which he now sat sharing with his advisers. 'The latest news is that Abdali is still in Aligarh. If we want to confront him where he is before the monsoons arrive, we have to cross the Yamuna, and for that, we have to put pontoon bridges in place for the army to cross over.'

'Kakasaheb, haven't you sent a note to Govindpant asking him to suggest names?' asked Vishwasrao.

'Orders have to be implemented in time, haven't they? Where's the point in playing the flute later if you let the cobra in hand slip away? I guess I should send another note to him today.'

'But Bhausaheb,' intervened Shamsher, 'how appropriate is it to place the entire weight on Govindpant's shoulder?'

'What you say is quite right, but what choice have we got? For one, all our satraps in the north are a treacherous lot. Govindpant is the only one among them who remains loyal and deposits his revenues on time. Old and experienced, he has been running Bundelkhand as our most prosperous province for many years now. This entire campaign has sprung up so suddenly, we are left with nobody except Govindpant to look to for help.'

Bhausaheb immediately began dictating the matter for Mahipatrao to write:

> *'It's necessary for us to construct a pontoon bridge over the Yamuna before the monsoons arrive. Expenditure on the army has increased substantially, hence we will need about twelve-hundred thousand when we reach Malwa. Meanwhile, please see if you can send about six-hundred thousand immediately. We haven't been receiving news from the north with any regularity; our delivery system has to improve. It's essential that Shuja-ud-dowlah join forces with us, hence you must keep sending him missives every second day.'*

The letter was handed over to a rider who got on camel-back instantly and left. Bhausaheb then sat and had detailed discussions on the issue of ordnance with Ibrahim Khan and Shamsher Bahadur. That done, he set about sending instructions to chieftains, grandees and landlords in various places along the way to dispatch wherewithal for the army.

'Yes, Mahipatrao, write:

> *At least a thousand quivers of arrows should arrive in eight days from Nashik. Twelve-score measures of gunpowder should reach us from Bagalkot, and about ten-score measures of lead from Kalyan. A thousand muskets should arrive for Khan Saheb from Goa.*'

Bhausaheb was conscious of nothing else—not of the passage of time, not of the hunger pangs of his army of clerks, not of his advisers shifting weight from one buttock to another ... And then suddenly, he seemed to notice the discomfort of the people around him and asked, 'Shamsher, what is the time?'

'It's getting to be midnight, Bhausaheb.'

'So late?' He looked at the assembly, laughed and said, 'Look, from tomorrow onwards, as soon as it is twilight, you people should begin leaving without seeking my permission. My thirst and hunger have long disappeared; my life, my death, my hunger, my thirst, my darkness, my light have all rolled up into one single phenomenon—war!'

॥

The Maratha army was camping in the hills of Sihor. On the thirteenth day of Vaishakh, 28 April, the army had left the village Sihor behind and moved beyond.

When it had started turning dark, the general expectation was that Bhausaheb would call a halt for the night, but the order that arrived from him was that torches should be lit and the forced march should continue. The people whose business it was to provide torches—Maang, Mahaar, Chaambhaar, Kunbi, Musalman—lit their torches and began helping the army find its way along the treacherous track peppered with brambles, pits and stones. When the cold night wind began, the flames buzzed and fluttered and began blowing out. So they went back to striking the flint and setting the torches alight again. But through all this confusion, Bhausaheb refused to relent. After setting off from Handia Ghat, it had taken a full twelve days to cross the twenty-five miles of wilderness, the reason being that the Ahirs of Ahirwada, the cowherd community of that region, had erected barricades at a number of places for mounting raids upon the passing army. All kinds of calculations were racing through Bhausaheb's mind. What was the point of making a halt? Crawling at that speed would throw all calculations out of gear. The enemy had to be confronted before it moved out. A thousand-strong force had been sent four days earlier under Sardar Vitthalrao Shivdev Vinchurkar to settle the Ahir issue, but there was no news at all from them. Men and animals hadn't had enough to eat for the past two days, and it was only compulsion that was making them drag on. The state of the pilgrims travelling with the army was bad. They could barely lift their feet; and the older women had begun to sit down on the road to ease their aching limbs. The women of the nobility who were being carried in palanquins had become stiff-jointed too, and the palanquin-bearers had started feeling weak and dizzy. The children of the pilgrims began to bawl with stomach cramps. As the clamour gathered volume, it became obvious that the march could not go on any further. When they came to a rivulet, Bhausaheb finally ordered a halt at its banks.

As soon as the orders arrived, the travellers sat where they had stood. Once they had got back their breaths, they began to unload their animals. They gathered whatever twigs they could collect in the dark and began lighting up their hearths. Those who had flour quickly made bhaakaris and wolfed them hungrily with those around. The Maratha soldiers dipped into their saddlebags and pulled out griddles. The cooks of all the sardars pooled their stock of flour and got bhaakaris ready for their men, which they consumed in the blink of an eye. Then they threw some fodder before their horses and spread themselves out flat. The valets erected shelters for Bhausaheb, Vishwasrao, Shamsher Bahadur and the other nobles. It was merely an overnight halt; like nomadic settlements, everything would be pulled out the next day at the crack of dawn and set in motion. Hence, neither the nobles nor the soldiers cared for where they were parked. The mahouts found an open area where they stabled the elephants; the royal ones and the labourers forgot the difference between them, and sat silently next to each other, flapping their massive ears and ruminating philosophically.

As the night advanced, the bonfires lost their vigour, with barely a spark left to flash. The soldiers slept in a circle round these dead or dying embers, with stones doing duty for pillows. It was around a month-and-a-half ago that they had set off, and the continuous bouncing up and down on horsebacks had rattled every bone and joint in their body and knotted their intestines into a tangle. Every pore of their body ached and screamed, and it didn't take them a minute to pass out when they had stretched themselves around the bonfires. The pilgrims too had locked themselves into each other's embrace, and made do with the warmth that their partner's bodies exuded.

Bhausaheb had fared worse, if anything, than his men. The travails of the journey, added to the anxieties and the sleepless nights of the commander-in-chief, had taken a heavy toll on him. His eyes had turned blood-red, and had now started oozing fluids. Every inch of his body screamed for rest, but that was one thing he simply couldn't afford, at least not immediately. He got a special shelter erected next to the rivulet where he set up his office. His men had erected canvas screens to secure the torches from getting blown out by the strong wind. There he sat with his legs folded under him, poring over the papers under the flickering lights of the torches.

Meals over, Bhausaheb called an emergency meeting of his deputies. Balwantrao Ganpat, Manaji Paigude, Shamsher Bahadur, Vishwasrao and Nana Purandare were among those who assembled in the office pavilion. Crossing the flat lands from the Handia Ghat to this point had consumed as many days as crossing the Satpuda range. The distance hadn't been much, but the highwaymen and brigands belonging to the tribes of traditional bandits like the Ahirs, the Umats, the Khechis and the Saudiyas had unexpectedly pestered the army with their pounce-grab-and-run tactics, causing it to bleed from a hundred random cuts.

'Shamsher Rao, who is arranging for the guards today?'

'Ibrahim Khan himself is mounting guard today with his Gardi pawns.'

'That's good. If Khan Saheb has taken the responsibility, we have nothing to worry about. Otherwise, the slightest rumour of an Ahir raid triggers off hysteria among our men.'

'Bhausaheb,' said Nana Purandare, 'these Ahirs, Umats and other such tribes are congenital thieves and robbers. Stealing, mugging, stick-ups, conning travellers, these are skills they learn at their mother's lap. Look at how they come raiding, all coated in mud, with twigs and branches sticking out of them. You wouldn't know them from a tree if they come and stand next to you. Just the other night, they divested Rakhavlal Manchharam of four of his best horses and four- or five-thousand worth of valuables. They let the army settle down for the night, ooze out of the darkness, mount their assault and disappear into the trees where our horsemen can't reach them; and we don't have enough foot soldiers to go chasing them into the bushes.'

'We are writing now to Pant to arrange for foot soldiers, but our Vitthal Shivdev had set off four days ago with a thousand-strong force, and he still hasn't returned,' said Bhausaheb. 'He may as well return after settling the Ahir issue for good.'

'It'll be wonderful if that happens,' Shamsher said, 'but Ahir and Umat gangs don't let a leaf crackle under their feet as they move. Besides, they know these jungle tracks like the back of their hands. They create shelters on the tops of these hills, and it's nearly impossible to flush them out of there.'

'The food-stock for the army is critically low, and there is no sign of any replenishment,' warned Mahipatrao Chitnis.

'In fact, whatever ration was left has already been distributed. There's nothing left,' informed Manaji Paigude. 'The soldiers have retired on half-filled stomachs, and the horses have been going hungry too. How can they undertake such exhausting marches on empty stomachs? They may start raiding the wayside villages too!'

'I have a fair idea of the dismal state of affairs, but when there is no help forthcoming, what does one do? I've been sending a missive or two to Govindpant every day, and yet not a coin arrives. Got a letter from him a couple of days back. The farms in the Antarved have been hit by hailstorms, he writes, and standing crops have been levelled. The farmers have no grains, and the collection has plummeted to nothing, hence he has nothing he can send. We have so many vassals all over the Antarved and the Bundelkhand regions, but does even one of them part with a single pie? And all our men like Barve and Khandekar, they are just sitting warming their butts!'

'Forgive me, Bhausaheb, but allow me to speak openly on this. The timing of this venture is wrong. It's along this same route that Dadasaheb carried his forces to Delhi; the forces of the Holkars and the Shindes have roamed through these areas, and they continue to do so. The peasants have had to suffer the Muslim invaders at one time and the Jaats the next. All these invaders have stripped the poor peasants of the shirt on their backs. Despite paying annual tributes as protection money, they find that nobody takes on the responsibility of really providing them protection of any kind. Pant Mankeshwar sits there in Delhi, providing security to the badshah and soaking up lavish parties, but what about the peasants? How much do you think we can gain by looting a community that has already been reduced to rags?'

Bhausaheb silently heard Shamsher Bahadur out. Shamsher had visited Hindustan twice before this, and had even administered the Bundelkhand province for a fair period, hence his opinion was supported by the weight of experience.

Mahipatrao Chitnis took over and said, 'Bhausaheb, there isn't a splint of wood available from any village for lighting up hearths. We get no fodder for animals even after flashing money. The villages have built battlements around themselves. So, even before you confront the villagers, you first have to get past these barriers and the forces mounting these barriers.'

'Which should mean, I guess,' said Vishwasrao, 'that we cannot depend upon raising money on our way for this campaign. We will have to ask Pune to finance the enterprise.'

One could almost hear the clicking of eyeballs as they turned towards Vishwasrao in surprise. Bhausaheb's criticism of Dadasaheb's Hindustan campaigns had been over the expenditure of eight million rupees paid from the Peshwa treasury; how would Bhausaheb now ask Pune for money? Circumstances had now turned on their head. How, now, to go pleading for help, and how to manage the circus without doing so? What about the money that should come from the revenue collectors? The expenditure of running the army was running beyond six-hundred thousand rupees a month—Ibrahim Khan's regiment alone ate up two-hundred thousand of it. 'When is the full moon night?' would be the most frequent question one soldier asked to another. That was the time when he was given his monthly allowance. But two full moon nights had come and gone, and allowance disbursement there had been none. If the rations required for bare survival were discounted, the miserable men had got pretty much nothing from the army for all the toil.

Bhausaheb picked up the quill and began drafting a letter to Govindpant:

> 'Arrange to send at least a million rupees in the next eight or ten days under any circumstance. The Ahir menace hasn't abated. Please send three-thousand young foot-soldiers to take care of the problem. And, yes, pay them a month's advance salary before you dispatch them.'

As he was finishing the letter, he was reminded of the Gardi regiment. The guns still hadn't arrived from the south. What's a soldier worth without his weapons?

> 'Govindpant, purchase three-hundred guns and a hundred muskets and dispatch them with the greatest speed.'

༺༻

It was past midnight when Bhausaheb headed towards his private quarters. The wicks in the lamp were flickering on a low flame as Parvatibai sat waiting for the arrival of her lord and master. It had been ages since she had had a few peaceful moments with him; maybe she would find some this evening. Bhausaheb staggered into the room with tired, unsteady steps, as a drunk wobbles in. The over-exertion had drained all the strength out of his legs. Parvatibai rushed forward to collect his footwear. As she removed his turban, the touch of his skin felt distinctly warm. By the time she returned after depositing them in their places, her husband had stretched himself out on the bed. She sat down by his side and reached out for his brow. As she slowly ruffled his hair, she noticed he had passed out instantly. A source of satisfaction, that.

The Gardis of Ibrahim Khan were on their beat, guns and swords in hand, their dark visage making them look like a pack of ghouls in knee-length firangi jackets. Their blood-red eyes flashed like rubies every time they crossed the torches stuck at regular intervals. Ibrahim Khan himself was on horseback doing the round of the entire camp, eyes peeled and peering into the surrounding darkness like a nocturnal bird of prey. In the process, he also ensured that the guards scattered around on the periphery were on full alert.

The darkest part of the night was over, and indications of dawn were about. The air had turned nippier. Suddenly the dogs accompanying the pilgrims began barking loudly, sending the Gardi guards scurrying towards the noise. A number of the light-sleeping pilgrims got up with a start and kicked up a clamour, panicking their more drugged travellers out of their slumber. The word went round that the enemy had struck.

'Lord! You are our protector!' the cry went up.

'Up, up, run!'

'Oh God, God! Where's my baby? Where's my little one?'

'Mother, gather your things, quick!'

The women began wailing and clinging to each other, the children caught the infection and began to bawl. The uproar began building up. Ibrahim came riding in and yelled, 'Shut up, you idiots! What's all this hullaballoo about? Guards, start caning these morons into sense!'

With that he galloped in the direction of the barking dogs, with a couple of hundred of his mounted guards at his tail. As they neared the river, they could hear the approaching hoof-beats. One of the guards came up to Ibrahim and said, 'Nawab Saheb, shall I set fire to the matchlocks?'

'Wait! These are no highwaymen's horses, these sound like better-bred animals. Let them come a little closer.'

As the soldiers began gathering and taking position, the approaching horsemen halted. As Ibrahim sat on his steed quickly assessing the situation, they heard a loud cry from the other side, 'Har Har Mahadev!' It was immediately followed by 'Long live, Bhausaheb!' 'Glory to Vishwasrao!'

Everybody heaved a collective sigh of relief. It was the long-awaited Vitthal Shivdev Vinchurkar's regiment finally come back. Within minutes, the two groups were mingling into each other with hugs, backslapping and booming laughter. Word reached the commander's tent of the return of the Shivdev contingent, and soon enough a page came running and said, 'Bhausaheb desires immediate audience with the Sardar.'

'The boys are still awake?' asked a surprised Shivdev.

'Yes.'

Bhausaheb stepped out of his tent with a shawl wrapped round himself. In the flickering light of the torches, he saw Sardar Vinchurkar riding in with great dignity. He looked the quintessential warrior of Shivaji's times: the same energy, the same zest, the same excitement, his beard and whiskers glistening white, big-boned, sporting a turban of rough, coarse wool. Four years ago, Vinchurkar had turned sixty, but he was fit enough to challenge anyone who mistook his white hair as a sign of debility. His booming voice jolted Bhausaheb out of his thoughts. 'Bhausaheb, still awake?'

'Ah! Yes, wasn't really asleep. Then I got to know of your arrival. Dismount and relax a little. Any special news?'

'Not the right time for dismounting and discussions. You can happily surrender yourself to sleep. We have settled the Ahir issue.'

'Really? What exactly happened?'

'The posts on the route that the Ahirs had grabbed, we have wrenched them back from them. We chopped off the heads of as many as we could, but a majority of them escaped into their mountains and their ravines. We gave chase and brought down a number of them. We have ensured they will not bother you again. We have left behind about seven hundred men with Radhe Govind and established checkposts and regular security beats on the way. Abandon all worries. We have broken the backs of the Ahirs well and proper.'

As he lay stretched out on his bed, the images of Bajirao and Shahuji flashed across his mind. These two had combed the nooks and corners of Maharashtra to form a hardy band of warriors—Ranoji Shinde, Malhar Holkar, Baba Vinchurkar and others—each worthier than the other. This was the mark of a great ruler—the ability to spot talent, and win over their loyalty. They form the foundation of ... Before Bhausaheb knew it, he had slipped into a peaceful slumber.

☙❧

Bhausaheb got up late by his standards the next day—the sun had already begun to rise. Feeling guilty at this indulgence, he had a quick bath and finished off with his prayers.

The regiments of the nobility were moving quite close to each other. Some of the sardars had preceded them, and were more or less at the head. The petty traders and the pilgrims had more or less merged with the army in the middle part. From their canopy atop the royal elephant Gajendra, Bhausaheb and Vishwasrao were taking in the landscape they were crossing. Bhausaheb's frisky horse Chandrasen was trotting in front of the elephant as if it were a herald of the imperial dominance of its master. The clouds of fog trapped in the vegetation had begun to vaporize. From his height on the hill, Bhausaheb suddenly noticed smoke billowing down below, and he was startled. Just then, three or four horsemen galloped in and stood panting at Gajendra's feet. 'Yes, what's the matter?'

'Shrimant, there's been a skirmish between our soldiers and the villagers down there. Our soldiers have set fire to some stacks of hay there.'

'Chandrasen!' yelled Bhausaheb, at which the horse turned round and came and stood by the royal elephant. Bhausaheb leaped off the canopy onto the horse's back and heeled it forward. As the soldiers joined in from behind, Bhausaheb asked, 'Why did our soldiers have to go to the haystacks and set them alight?'

'They were desperate, Shrimant! Some of the contingents got barely a handful of grass yesterday to feed their animals. A bunch of frantic horsemen wanted to enter the first village they came to this morning, but the villagers got on top of the bastion walls and shot missiles on our men. Our men then broke into the village by breaking down the gate, and a ruckus ensued.'

Bhausaheb left for the village. When the villagers noticed a grandly dressed man approaching, they knew it was royalty riding in. They noticed the soldiers freeze; they looked flustered and embarrased. Some of the elder men lowered their arms and advanced towards the approaching horseman, telling the others, 'This is the king of the Marathas. Let's talk to him!' When Bhausaheb had come close enough, the oldest among them touched his feet and said, 'Saheb, if every passing soldier indulges in this kind of vandalism, how will our wayside villages survive? We live hand to mouth, anyway. Even if that little were to be snatched away, what are we going to live on?'

Bhausaheb turned his gaze to his errant soldiers. Not one of them had the courage to meet his eye. Bhausaheb knew the desperation that had driven them to such low deeds. He turned towards the villagers and said, 'My army is marching towards Delhi to free it from the clutches of foreign intruders. If my men and animals do not get food and fodder on the way, how are we going to move towards our mission? On behalf of my men, I offer my apologies to you all, and request that you forget their misdemeanour. I shall compensate you for all the losses they have caused you, but I also request that you help procure sustenance for us, so that we may move ahead.'

The villagers were floored. The headman nodded vigorously and the village was transformed from being obstructive to becoming a facilitator. Bhausaheb called over his treasurer and immediately made payments for whatever the villagers offered.

❦

The Maratha army had found a suitable spot beyond Gwalior to camp for a little while. The assembly of nobles that sat discussing the state of affairs included Shamsher Bahadur, Vishwasrao, Manaji Paigude, Mahipatrao, Vitthal Shivdev, Balwantrao and a few others. Vishwasrao was telling the audience, 'The news is that Abdali and Najeeb are bickering. They seem to be punching at each other. Abdali is baying for Najeeb's blood because Shuja has not joined their forces. His army has begun to grumble too. Abdali has dispatched Taimur Shah's mother-in-law Malika-Zamaan to Lakhnau. He is doing all he can to persuade Shuja to join.'

'Bhausaheb,' said Shamsher, 'we should bring Shuja on our side at all costs. Whichever side he joins will gain a big advantage.'

'That's exactly why we dispatched Shaamji Ranganaath to Lakhnau a fortnight ago. He is going to present our case with great force. Besides, the letter he carries from me is quite expressive too. I've told him that both of us are equally concerned about the prestige, the well-being and the honour of Hindustan, as we are sensitive to the esteem of the Delhi empire. The Afghans have always been uncaring of the glory of Hindustan. We both know how Abdali and Nadir Shah razed our country to the ground and looted it of its last dime. They look down upon the

Muslims of Hindustan, and are hell-bent on not letting any native ruler live in peace and prosperity. He is the ablest among the rulers of Hindustan. I have begged him to believe that the Afghans will talk sweet till as long as they need him, and when their needs are met, they will toss him away like a fly in their milk. I have promised him that if we emerge victorious, God willing, we will instate Shah Alam on the Delhi throne, make him the commander-in-chief of Hindustan, and return to the Deccan. I am not even insisting that he should have his army fight on our side; even if he stays out of the conflict, it would be good enough. Shrimant Bajirao and Shuja-ud-Dowlah's grandfather Saadat Khan were great friends and had entered into a pact. I stressed on that and suggested that we should keep the friendship going, and it wouldn't help either party if he were to hold us in disdain and join forces with a foreigner. With all that I have written to him, I feel quite confident that he will side with us.'

'We cannot, perhaps, rule out the possibility of Najeeb himself going to Ayodhya,' suggested Shamsher.

'Oh, that charlatan is capable of any chameleon act,' laughed Bhausaheb. 'He can cross over to heaven as an advocate of the devil. He can also make a deal with the gods and represent them in hell. Only if we had understood him well enough earlier, the Marathas wouldn't have had to see these bad days. But I can tell you, the Nawab will gain nothing but misery by tying up with him. The best thing for him, clearly, is to fall into step with us; else he will suffer badly.'

'But Kakasaheb,' asked Vishwasrao, 'what if he still casts his lot with them?'

'How can he?' snapped Bhausaheb. 'How can he possibly do that? Look, in the next ten or fifteen days, we will have crossed the Chambal. We will take our army across the Yamuna. A strong redoubt like Itaawa is under the Marathas' heels, with Govindpant sitting astride it. To the north of Itaawa is Najeeb's territory, and to its south is the Nawab's land. Our forces are going to be entrenched there; so there's no way Shuja's forces can leap past us to join Abdali.'

'But, your lordship,' interjected Ibrahim Khan, 'the rains would have arrived by then, so crossing the Yamuna will be—'

'Khan Saheb, we have taken that into account and planned for it. I don't think we should start worrying about it so early in the day. Yes, there will be an odd shower now and then, but the real rains will be about a month away. That's when the Yamuna will get flooded. And even if we do have some rains, Govindpant will arrange for boats. We will have Malharbaba summon the Jaats in, if the need arises, but we should be able to cross the Yamuna comfortably, and snuff Abdali out before Shuja can join him.'

As the nobles sat listening to Bhausaheb's battle plans, hanging on to every word, an agitated servant burst in and blurted out, 'Shrimant, a couple of dozen horsemen have just ridden in from Ahirwada, and seek audience with your lordship.'

'Tell them to meet me tomorrow!' said Bhausaheb. 'Don't you see an important meeting is in progress? How dare you come and talk about horsemen?'

'But, Shrimant,' stuttered the servant, 'they are in bad shape! Wounded! Their armour is all blood-spattered. Some important—'

'Huh?' Bhausaheb paused. 'Shamsher, go see what the matter is.'

Shamsher hurried out and came back in a little while, looking tense. 'The news is bad,' he said. 'We had a hundred men under an officer at the Kadwai Fort in Ahirwada. The Ahirs have once again risen and killed the officer and a good sixty or seventy of our men. This may well set off a chain reaction, and our other posts in Ahirwada are in danger of slipping out of our control. Some landlords of Malwa seem to be in cahoots with them too.'

'What's this, Vinchurkar?' growled Bhausaheb, looking daggers at the man.

He had already started turning pale and tense when Shamsher was reeling out the news. 'But … but, Bhausaheb,' he stammered 'I had settled everything there, I'm sure! I'd left Ragho Govind fully in command, and put our squads and sentinels in place everywhere! I was sure we had smashed the Ahirs!'

'Who has smashed whom, Vinchurkar?' snapped Bhausaheb. 'A leader who has such a presence in Hindustan, how can he fail in such a simple exercise? This is most disappointing, and smacks of incompetence and negligence. It doesn't suit your age and experience at all!'

Vinchurkar's grey beard dipped into his neck. Did he have to be insulted in front of so many? Wouldn't it have been better done in private?

Aah! Bajirao's times are now history, and it's these brats who now rule the roost. This pup Sadoba, this Ganpat of the Mehendales, this rank outsider Ibrahim, that quill-pusher Mahipatrao, spoiled brats, all! How would they know of our glorious past? If Malharba had been here, he would have shown them their place!

Shamsher was still standing, watching the scene unfold. Trying to ease the tension, he said, 'Bhausaheb, the horsemen are waiting outside to meet you.'

'To hell with them!' yelled an incensed Bhausaheb. 'What has happened to our officers here? The land in which Bajirao ripped apart Daya Bahadur, how can bandits and crooks like the Ahirs dare to cock a snook at the Marathas? And what do our officers and chieftains do? Turn tail and run! Where do these rebellious ruffians get their gumption from, after all? It's ... it's ... because our men here are worthless. They don't have the spine to keep our posts intact. No brains for collecting revenue either. There's scope for collecting revenue worth anything from fifty to a hundred thousand here in Ahirwada, but they just can't do it! Even in the Antarved region, my spies tell me, Pant's own officers are abandoning their posts and fleeing. If they can run at the mere whisper of 'The enemy has come!' they are not true to their salt. Who will respect them? Who will fear them? Station officers are feared when they are willing to die fighting. It's their corpses that should leave the post, not their trembling legs!'

The conference tent had gone completely silent. They were all subdued by Bhausaheb's red-hot rage. He paused a little for breath, turned his gaze towards Sardar Manaji Paigude and said, 'We've been struggling so hard and sweating blood here. Our armies are often marching on empty stomachs. Just a fortnight back, we received funds of a hundred-and-eighty thousand rupees from Pune, and we cleared the debts of the moneylenders of Ujjain and Indore. Such a huge sum disappeared in a day's time. We don't have the resources to pay even ten rupees as wages to our horsemen. The royal entourage's expense alone is a good two-hundred thousand! Our army, our men and animals are fast disintegrating, and yet there is no money coming from our vassals from Antarved and Bundelkhand! All right, even if they don't send the money, why can't they at least protect the posts that their ancestors won across

Hindustan at the cost of their blood? How can they not meet at least this basic responsibility, Paigude? All of Hindustan is falling apart! Even the Rajput Ranas seem to have withdrawn help!'

'Can I speak frankly, Bhausaheb?'

'Frank speech is what I want, Paigude!'

'Well then, Bhausaheb, there is a reason why money has stopped coming from these areas. The peasants, the nobles, the station officers, they are all in a quandary. The forces of Shinde-Holkar have bitten dust, Dattaji was slaughtered on the banks of the Yamuna, Malharba has taken refuge in the hills of Rajputana ...What are the chances that Sadashivrao will be able to turn the tide for the Marathas? They are all afraid, and the enemy's morale has been waxing. It's the fear of backing the wrong side that has sent these people into a freeze. Who will then want to collect taxes and who will do the dispatching?'

Paigude had spelt out the changing equation in Hindustan. The facts on the ground had become evident to everybody, including Bhausaheb. The mood of the conference turned yet more sombre. As they sat sulking under the weight of a dark, brooding silence, a page entered the tent and handed over a scroll to Bhausaheb. Bhausaheb's face turned darker with every word he read. As he paused to wipe the moisture from his eyes, the rest just stared at him, mute and expectant. After a tense pause, Bhausaheb let out a deep, painful sigh and said, 'Man can only propose, they say, but it is God who disposes. Where has this Pant disappeared? Why do I feel that our bastion is getting dismantled, stone by stone? The great Maratha bravehearts that have spent their entire lifetimes in Hindustan, why have they turned silent in our moment of greatest need is beyond comprehension. Itaawa has been under our heels for six years now; we had been badgering Pant and Hingane to collect enough boats and barges for crossing the Yamuna. It was from Itaawa that we had planned to launch into the enemy forces and scatter them to the winds. Well, that ... Itaawa ... has ... fallen.'

'Whaaat! Itaawa has fallen?' everyone looked at Bhausaheb with eyes popping out of their sockets, as if a bolt of lightning had struck them.

As the import of the intelligence began sinking in, they looked at each other and back at Bhausaheb with fear-filled eyes. Bhausaheb again took a deep breath and said, 'All right, friends, this is how the wheel of life turns.

Good and bad days come, good and bad days go. They have come and gone before, and they will do so in the future too. But nothing can excuse the losing of courage. Paigude, you said a while ago that the enemy is so powerful that our people here are terror-stricken. But what I say is that however strong the enemy may be, our chests are no less wide, we are not short on valour. However powerful the enemy, nobody can snatch away our right to die fighting on the battlefield. I must confess that when we had set off from Udgir, I hadn't imagined this campaign would be so testing, but it's turning more and more challenging with each passing day. After all this, the choice for me is clear: I may or may not succeed in driving the enemy out, but I shall certainly stake myself for the honour and glory of Hindustan.'

His resolve rang out, leaving everybody stunned. Mahipatrao Chitnis was the first to find his voice. 'Whatever you may say,' he said, 'the Shinde-Holkars have far greater experience of these regions than we have. You will be meeting Malharrao in a few days from now, but meanwhile, there have been some letters from him, which should be read and discussed.'

'Sure, Mahipatrao, read them out.'

Mahipatrao began reading loudly:

'Bhausaheb, station yourself at Gwalior. You shouldn't think of crossing Gwalior and then crossing the Chambal. Just give us the armies, and see what we do with the enemy.'

Having read this piece, Mahipatrao looked round at the others.

Bhausaheb laughed and asked them all, 'So, what do you say? I'll stay put here in comfort, and you people will move ahead, yes?'

'What rubbishy talk is this?' growled Ibrahim Khan. 'Bhausaheb, there's no room left for you to turn round now. Strike a tree at the root, and it will dry up—there'll be no more sprouting.'

'This is impossible!' thundered Shamsher and Balwantrao.

'Kakasaheb,' Vishwasrao sprang up from his seat, 'we will die fighting next to you, but—'

'Shhhh! Don't say such inauspicious words, Rao Saheb. You are the future Peshwa!' said Bhausaheb.

'Kakasaheb, let me put this straight: as long I have you next to me, the cremation ground would be a holier place for me than any royal court.'

With the first issue settled, Mahipatrao read on further:

'Please leave your women, your pilgrims and your free-loaders behind. The Jaat king Surajmal is quite willing to take over the responsibility of feeding them.'

Bhausaheb sat up at this, but before he could respond, Ibrahim Khan beat him to it and said, 'This is quite true. The battlefield is not a harem for women, but the mad-house of men.'

Bhausaheb laughed at the analogy and said, 'All of us should consider this point carefully. The expenses on the army are mounting with unseemly speed, with relief coming from nowhere. My advice to you gentlemen is to give this matter deep thought. We will meet again tomorrow evening and arrive at a consensus. Then, we will have to set off at the crack of dawn the day after.'

༺༻

The news spread with the wind that Bhausaheb had proposed to leave the pilgrims, the ladies and the free-loaders behind. The pilgrims were livid. There was an uproar among all the parties affected. 'We don't care a fig for your political moves and countermoves,' was the refrain, 'but how can you want to deprive us of our religion and our gods?'

'This was our opportunity to see the three holy places, so we came along. Now, what's this new thing you are telling us?'

'It's three years since my husband passed away. I have been preserving his ashes like it's gold, in the hope of submerging it in the Ganga. Should I scatter it to the winds here and turn around? The poor man gave his life in battle, and there's no way Bhau's army will escape from his curse!'

'Hundreds of us pilgrims have come along with the army with such hopes! Ditching us thus midway won't do any good, that's for sure. The gods haven't turned blind yet!'

'His Peshwa brother there has been distributing largesse with both hands to the brahmins from his Shaniwarwada's doorstep, and here it's the whims of the Gardis and Pardhis that seem to count!'

'If he disregards the brahmins and scuttles the pilgrimage, it will bring complete ruination!'

'It's that brat of that Muslim woman and that darkie Ibrahim who've been poisoning Bhausaheb's head.'

'If the pilgrimage doesn't happen after having travelled so far, I propose to fast here till I die.'

The agitated pilgrims and soldiers had gathered in big and small huddles around astrologers, soothsayers, palmists and men of magic, desperate to know what the consequences of Bhausaheb's proposed sacrilege would be. There was this matted-haired, ash-smeared, red-eyed wraith with his parrot. The bird was pottering around in its cage with a peepal leaf in its beak. The voodoo-man managed to collect a crowd around him and shouted, 'Aalya mantar, kalya mantar, chhoooo! Oh you servant of the mightiest gods!' he pronounced with a frightening boom, 'oh feathered creature from across the seven seas! Hooooo! You carry that holy leaf in your beak! Hrrrr! If Bhausaheb does not carry forward with him these holy, devout servants of your master, tell us, bird, I put you on oath! Tell us whether his mission will succeed or fail. Hear me, bird?' he screeched at the nervous-looking bird. 'If Bhausaheb will return victorious after leaving the pilgrims behind, dance on your tail, hear me? But if his army is going to be routed for this sin, drop that leaf from your beak before I finish counting five. Hear me, divine bird? One ... two ...' He shouted louder, as the crowds milling around him ogled tensely at the cage, 'thr ...' And before he could complete the number, the bird dropped the leaf and began circling along the wires of its cage. A groan broke from the audience as the bird confirmed what they had already known. 'The army is going to be wiped out!' the bird-man announced with ringing finality. 'Every single one of them will be slaughtered!' The crowd showered coins on him to ensure that no evil stuck to them.

The holy men with their beards and ash-smeared faces sat at whichever convenient spot they could find, looking suitably grave. Women tossed coins on the outspread horoscope charts of the astrologers, and begged for a peek into the future. The wise men waited till they had sufficient incentive to get started, and finally asserted, 'Bhausaheb's stars are not well-aligned. The most deleterious of planets have crowded in. Devastation, the heavenly bodies say.'

There were specially trained divining bulls, but they hadn't been trained to be consistent. When asked whether the army would swim through or sink, they would shake their bovine heads and jingle the bells round their necks, sometimes to indicate yes, some other times to mean no. The milling crowds around them took both answers in their stride with sufficient credulity.

Among astrologers, there was no one anywhere close to the stature of Jereshastri. Sardars of the eminence of Paigude and Vitthal Shivdev had ensconced themselves in his tent, and were eagerly awaiting his diagnosis as he sat poring over the charts. 'Things don't look nice for Bhausaheb's army from here on,' he finally pronounced. The other astrologers and pundits too had checked their charts out from all directions—up to down, down to up, sideways, diagonally—done furious number crunching on the digits of their fingers and come up with similar forecasts.

Soothsayers and fortune-tellers of all shapes and hues had got into the act: cloth artists, monkey-men, bead-tossers, stick-throwers, and the self-sufficient trance specialists. All frantically racked their brains and peered into the dark to find their answer. Nana Phadnis hadn't been keeping well, and hadn't stepped out of his tent. His mother, however, had strong faith in his forecasts. Nana was telling her, 'Bhausaheb has pointlessly offended the gods. Oh Shiv, Shiv! The future looks forbidding, go make him see sense.'

Mayhem reigned supreme right through the day. Around dusk, Rakhmabai Akkasaheb collected a few women and descended on the office pavilion. Bhausaheb, as always, was engrossed in work, but when he noticed the ladies, he gave them a welcoming smile and said, 'Welcome, Akkasaheb, what are your orders?'

'Bhausaheb, however elevated a person be, he cannot rise above the gods and the brahmins.'

'Akkasaheb, this entire empire survives on the blessings of the gods and goddesses.'

'Ah, forget it! If Raghunath Dada had been around, he wouldn't have required so much explaining,' said Rakhmabai. 'One shouldn't let advice from infidels stand in the way of service to religion. I have visited a few astrologers and your stars are on the ascendant. You will not only win this war, but also accompany us to Kashi and Prayag. Kashi-Vishweshwar hasn't gone to sleep, he knows very well the mischief that the Muslims are up to.'

'But politics and religion shouldn't be allowed to mix, Akkasaheb!'

'Really? You think all the merit earned by these thousands of pilgrims will go waste? Bhausaheb, the Peshwa himself has promised to offer a thousand gold coins to the god at Shri Vyankatesh. You should try and understand the impact of that prayer.'

༺༻

The grandees sat down to confer after dinner. Bhausaheb had been given a clear enough picture of the turmoil in their camp. Vitthal Shivdev began the discussion. There was a sharp edge to his voice as he said, 'It was on account of your assurance that people have brought their women and kids with them. In the wars we have raged for the past twenty years, haven't the sardars carried their harem with them? And yet they came back victorious, didn't they?'

'That's quite true,' chipped in Paigude. 'All of the Maratha empire knows that Nanasaheb himself went on the northern campaign in the company of Gopikabai.'

'And, Mastani travelling with Bajirao Saheb was never an impediment to his wars and campaigns,' said Vinchurkar, looking at Shamsher to shoot a tangential barb.

Bhausaheb sensed where the argument was heading. The issue of shedding some human load had been brought up before, of course, but not one of the senior grandees wanted any reduction in their entourage of their women, servants and guests. Chieftainhood required a retinue, slaves, servants; Nana Purandare alone had twenty-four minions travelling with him, while the others had many more than that. Bhausaheb began to wonder whether he had done the right thing by needlessly riling up all these chieftains and their gods and goddesses. The issue of leaving behind the pilgrims, women, and their brood at Gwalior had arrived by itself, and got resolved by itself: they had come together so far; now they would roam together or die together the rest of the way.

Parvatibai accosted him at night. 'Your lordship proposes to leave people behind, I hear!'

'That thought has been abandoned long ago.'

'That's good,' she commented. 'Such a large number of people are using this opportunity to finish their pilgrimages. They would have felt terrible had they been left behind. A lot of them are either our own acquaintances or the relatives and friends of the other chieftains.'

Bhausaheb let out a deep sigh. 'What can I say here? That's the kind of people we are. Find a person who is doing well, and relatives and guests swarm around him and stick like leeches, and suck as much out of the poor man as they can. These relatives, guests and acquaintances blind the poor working man with fanciful emotions. The harm they have done to our Maratha culture, not even all our enemies put together can equal it.'

⁂

Shamji Ranganath, the special envoy of Bhausaheb, was surveying Faizabad in the royal horse-carriage. Kashiraj Pandit, the chief manager of Shuja-ud-dowlah, was taking him around different parts of the city. Kashiraj was a Maharashtrian Brahmin by birth, but he had migrated to Ayodhya at a very young age. He had started off at the court, and excelled at accounting. He rose through the ranks, and on the strength of his integrity and hard work, he had established a name for himself in the Faizabad court. The entire province of Ayodhya was aware of the closeness Kashiraj enjoyed with Nawab Shuja-ud-dowlah; no surprise then, that when they saw his jewel-encrusted horse-carriage approaching, the subjects bowed low to accord him respect.

Shamji Ranganath was bowled over by the vast, rolling lawns of the Lalbagh and Motibagh gardens. The Nawab had collected flowering plants of varied hues and fragrances from different parts of the world and made them bloom in these beautifully manicured spaces. The sight of Asifbagh and Bulandbagh had completely enamoured Shamji. As they rolled along, Kashiraj was saying, 'It's barely fifteen years since the battle of Buxar was fought. When our Nawab Bahadur lost in the battle, he shifted his capital from Lakhnau to Faizabad. Our Nawab Saheb is a connoisseur of beauty by instinct. Five years ago, this town had a crumbling wall round it. Nawab Saheb not only got that wall repaired, he got two more walls constructed alongside the old one. So, it's behind this three-tier screen that our beautiful township flourishes.'

For the entire week gone by, Shamji Ranganath had been soaking in the eye-popping opulence of the capital city of Faizabad. His eyes raced like a deer for miles along the long, wide, straight-as-arrow streets. The magnificence of the city had him spellbound: majestic mosques and temples; dense green trees blooming with colour and fragrance on either side of the roads; the battlements of the forts peeking out from above and behind the trees; the city wall standing tall and proud; the red-and-black uniformed soldiers marching up and down its battlements round the clock; the wide streets abuzz with fast-racing bullock-carts, horse-carriages, palanquins, caparisoned elephants and the occasional gun-carriage. The splendor was enhanced by the music that filled the air: the call to prayer from the mosques, the chiming of the temple bells, the occasional sound of kettle-drums—the sights and sounds together created the illusion of the city of Indra, the King of Gods.

Kashiraj was waxing eloquent. 'As you had Shah Jahan in Delhi, so we have Shuja, the Nawab of Ayodhya.'

Shamji sat peeping out of his carriage. There were endless food-stalls laid out under the trees: stacks of sweetmeats, vessels full of gulab-jamun, hot, spicy meals, kebabs being grilled on skewers, fried parathas; next to them were shops selling faaloodas and biscuits. When the gourmand had indulged himself to his heart's content, he would let out a loud belch and walk over to the big earthen jars for washing it all down with delicious cool water. As Shamji sat watching it all with joy tinged with envy, the thought uppermost in his mind was: nowhere else can one find a happier people and a more magnificent king.'

The horse carriage turned round at Lakhnau Gate and headed for the Nawab's palace. Feeling a little fagged out, Shamji Ranganath said, 'Pandit Saheb, I think I have seen enough of this Lakhnavi splendour for the day.'

'Is Your Excellency feeling a little under the weather?' Kashiraj now had the Lakhnau culture running in his blood. In the most persuasive voice, he went on, 'Huzoor, you are our royal guest. If our hospitality is falling short on any count—'

'No, no, no, don't say that, Pandit Saheb. If I had come here as a pleasure-seeking tourist without any workload, I would never have turned round,' remonstrated Shamji. 'The dazzling resplendence of your city, the swinging chandeliers that bring a glow to the nights of your palaces, the ankle-bells of your gracious dancers, and the wail of the saarangi piercing the heart of the dark night— these are things that have no parallel anywhere. But the burden of the mission that my patron has placed upon me does not allow me peace of mind.'

'Who's your patron? And what's your mission?'

'Panditji, have you forgotten that this nobody is the slave and servant of Sadashivrao Bhau? Your Lakhnavi tradition of submerging a political envoy in sugar syrup as if it were a fly is quite interesting.'

Kashiraj ordered the driver to pull the carriage to a halt at the gate of a garden. They walked in and sat down at a comfortable and secluded spot under a tree. Once nicely settled, Kashiraj said, 'All right, now, we can talk in peace. It's not the walls alone that have ears here, every leaf and flower has ears too. You have no idea, Shamjipant, what a network of spies we have everywhere. They say they patrol all of Hindustan, but they send fortnightly reports from as far away as Afghanistan—and your Pune, too.'

'What are you saying?'

'Nawab Saheb has upwards of ten thousand spies reporting to him. You may think, Shamjipant, that this Brahmin is of the same stock as you, so he will keep you well-informed. I'll be frank with you. I do have great affection for the land of my birth, but I am a devoted servant of Nawab Saheb, and I shall never do anything that hurts his interests, not even by mistake or oversight. There is some pull that my native land exerts over my heart, so I shall help you to some extent; but please understand this clearly: do not delude yourself by thinking that I am a hundred percent your man.'

Shamji looked steadily at the fair-skinned, forty-five-year-old Brahmin sitting by him. Thirty years of service to the Nawab had certainly cost him all the hair on his head. 'Panditji, see if you can answer me this,' he said. 'Bhausaheb and Abdali will soon be locked in combat. Which of these two warring sides do you find better?'

'Justice and good intentions lie on the side of Bhausaheb alone. He is clearly fighting to support the Empire at Delhi and for the well-being of all of Hindustan.'

Shamji digested this information in silence, thought for a while, took the measure of the situation and said, 'Panditji, it's difficult to ascertain where the Nawab's heart lies.'

Kashiraj laughed.

'So, yes, Panditji,' Shamji went on. 'For how long do we live in expectation? With no message reaching him from me, Bhausaheb would have lost all his peace of mind. The great person that he is, he has been labouring day and night for the success of his mission. Every day, he dispatches at least four or five letters, one of which is always addressed to Govind Pant. His deepest desire is that the Nawab Bahadur of Ayodhya join sides with us. He has sent many messages to Nawab Saheb to this effect.'

'Assume for a moment that Nawab Saheb does not join your forces. What difference is it going to make to your war?'

'Oh, you want to hear the praises of your patron from our mouth, do you? Well, so be it. Try pointing out another ruler, with two parganas of fertile land on the banks of the Ganga, so resourceful, affluent and powerful, and you'll know. You have an eight-thousand-strong regiment under Khizarbaksh who had trained under Nadir Shah himself, which you have further reinforced. Under your wing stand the tenacious ten-thousand fighters of the Naga Gosavi sect of the Ganga banks. Under their leaders Anupgiri and Umraogiri Gosavi, they descend like avenging fate upon their enemies, and there isn't a single kingdom of Hindustan that has not taken a merciless thrashing at their hands. Not only are these Gosavis valiant, but they are also skilled in the black arts. These bearded leviathans get into their abracadabra act and swallow up the enemy's cannonballs as if they were luscious fruits, says all of Hindustan. Your artillery is of the highest quality. With so much of power and pelf behind him, the Nawab Bahadur can tilt the scales towards whichever of the two sides he chooses to join.'

'Wonderful, Shamjipant, wonderful!' responded Kashiraj and broke into a loud laughter.

'What does this laughter mean, Panditji?'

'Oh, the meaning is clear. We had thought that our spies were the best in the country, but it is obvious, Shamjipant, that your network is of the highest quality too. You have information on every twig, every leaf and every stone that rests in Ayodhya. But, Pant, you are toiling under pointless apprehension. Why harbour baseless anxieties? Your commander-in-chief is a lion among men. We had been hearing about him for a long time, but now we are convinced that after Bajirao, there has been nobody in the Peshwa clan who can compare with Bhausaheb in the matter of valour or wisdom. I feel a sense of pity, Shamjipant, that your Peshwas didn't think it worthwhile to send a person of Bhausaheb's calibre on the Hindustan campaign earlier. How could they keep such a man nailed to the accountant's desk at home? If he had crossed the Narmada and travelled through this country even once, perhaps Abdali would have never reached Anupshahar. You just talked about the letters that Bhausaheb has sent to the Nawab Saheb; you haven't mentioned anyone else's name.'

'What does that mean?'

'Ah,' laughed Kashiraj, 'perhaps you have no inkling. Our Nawab Saheb's mother Sadr-un-nisa Begum exercises such influence upon her son that she can summon him to court or berate him in the public square anytime. Bhausaheb skillfully extracted this priceless information and wrote an appeal to her, requesting her to join forces with the Marathas. What a quill he possesses! What persuasive writing! He delicately reminded the Queen Mother of how the Shinde-Holkars had extended support to the Nawab's father during his time of need.'

Shamji Ranganath was stunned. 'I really had no idea about this leap that Bhausaheb had taken. But the important question is: what impact did it have on the Queen Mother?'

'Ah, that I don't think I can tell you,' Kashiraj responded cautiously. 'All I can say is that as of now, the stars are favourable.'

'We know that too! But Panditji, why this silence of the graveyard? The horse refuses to budge, neither forward nor backward, neither to the left nor to the right!'

'It's an Ayodhya horse, sir,' laughed Kashiraj.

Winding up their conversation, the two headed towards the main palace. The resplendence of the palace walls made of translucent white marble struck the observer dumb with awe. Was that hard stone or the purest rose petals brought delicately together by magic? The heady aroma of the grape garden inside came wafting right up to the gate.

The fountains inside the garden could have been peacock-eyed beauties frolicking among themselves. That was when the bugles sounded and the kettle-drums began their tattoo. Ushers and mace-bearers carrying sticks of gold and silver cried out in unison, 'Alert, alert! Stand alert with all respect and all consideration! Mirza Jalaluddin Haidar, Shuja-ud-dowlah, the Nawab of Ayodhya, is due to manifest His Gracious Presence in a moment! All eyes to turn suitably down!'

Shamji Rangnath instantly turned his head towards the royal avenue and noticed fifteen or more horses of the highest breed come trotting down towards the palace. Shuja's Arab roan led the pack with proud, mincing steps. Anybody could see that the grand animal had a good four or five saloons where it was decked up. On its back was first laid a length of cloth heavily embroidered in threads of gold and silver; on top of the cloth was a richly brocaded saddle. Round its neck glittered multiple loops of precious stones strung on gold threads. The stirrups were gem-encrusted too. On either side of the cloth hung heavy, multi-coloured tassels of silk inter-woven with gold and silver. The steed exuded such extreme opulence that the observer would know that it could belong either to some god in heaven or to the Nawab of Ayodhya.

On either side of the roan trotted a couple of horses of the Panchali breed, carrying two spectacularly beautiful maidens. An outsider would never guess that these were merely maids, and not the Nawab's begums. The other officials riding behind the Nawab had a host of labourers running behind their horses, equipped with trowels and pickaxes. By now Shamjipant had got quite used to this custom of the Nawab to roam around the city morning and evening, with artisans in tow.

Fair and handsome, twenty-eight-year-old Shuja-ud-dowlah had an arresting personality. Eyes dark as rain-bearing clouds, red lips, spirited face, the dignity of his posture on the rocking horse, a flowing muslin frock covering his chest, velvety footwear studded with gems, scarlet-red, tasseled turban, strings of necklaces studded with diamonds and pearls worn with as much abandon as a cow-herd wears his shells—if a person were to suddenly wake up from sleep and see this grand phenomenon, he would know that it was the Nawab of Ayodhya.

As he dismounted from his horse, Shuja cast a fleeting glance at Shamjipant, whispered a few words to Kashiraj standing next to him, and entered the palace, curtly acknowledging the elaborate obeisance of the ushers, the grandees, the poets and scholars, and his personal servants who had gathered around.

Shuja was known to be a hedonist, a lover of the finer things in life, but he had seen plenty of ups and downs too, even at this young age. His father Safdarjung was a valiant Muslim of the Shia sect. His grandfather Saadat Khan had also earned great renown for himself. When Ahmad Shah was on the throne of Delhi, Shuja's father Safdarjung was the wazeer of all Hindustan. During the five years of his wazeeri, Safdarjung had earned for himself great fame, and of course plenty of wealth. By that time, Shuja himself had done great work as the head of the artillery. When the Durrani king, Abdali had first attacked Hindustan, Shuja's father had brought the invader's rampaging horse tumbling down to earth. Every time the battle of Manpur was remembered and Safdarjung's exploits talked about, the chests of the denizens of Ayodhya would swell with pride.

Safdarjung knew well that the Rohilla Pathans had no right to settle in the Antarved. They were foreigners. The Hindus and the Muslims native to the soil could and did live in complete harmony. There would be occasional tiffs, but soon they would be back to roaming arm in arm. But if the foreign Durrani clan ever settled down there, it would slit their throats, for sure, Safdarjung knew. The settlements of the Rohillas had begun to grow in number and size in the regions of Najeebabad, Muzaffarnagar, Shaamli, and nearby areas. If they began stretching limbs further, they would soon reach Ayodhya, which was to the south of that territory. A heap of sand could never make a comfortable pillow, Safdarjung thought, and he decided to nip the Rohillas before they became too adventurous. He mounted an offensive on them with the help of Shindes, Holkars and the Jaats. During the battle of Farookhabad, the Rohillas came together and joined forces; but Dattaji's father Ranoji and Malharjibaba staked their lives and decimated the Rohilla forces. Safdarjung was saved.

The battle of Farookhabad was fought in 1751, but in the next three or four years, the winds began to change directions. Imaad began to poison the Delhi emperor's ears so as to win the wazeer's post for himself, as a result of which relations between the emperor and his then wazeer, Safdarjung soured. This was the time when Imaad insinuated Najeeb into Delhi politics for the first time. The lure of filthy lucre made the Shinde-Holkars turn their backs upon Safdarjung, and the person for whom they had staked their lives three years ago suddenly became persona non grata for them. When the lion lies ailing, little mice start nibbling at its buttock. In the same manner, Najeeb began hounding Safdarjung. Shuja-ud-dowlah too became wary of the Marathas' blow-hot-blow-cold politics. He saw his valiant father Safdarjung come scampering back to save his life in the shelter of his home territory of Ayodhya. The wound of his father's humiliation was still raw and festering inside Shuja. He wanted to ride up the Delhi road astride an elephant, with all the pomp and ceremony of the wazeer of the country, down which his wazeer father had been compelled to flee like a thief. He was forever looking for an opportunity that would help him realize his dream. The experiences of the past had turned Shuja cautious about each step he took. He could see that both the Marathas and Abdali had arrived at the threshing floor. It would be best if he took his time before deciding on the course of action.

Shamji Ranganath's patience was being severely tested. The last he had met Shuja was seven days ago. Since then Kashiraj had gone on giving him assurance of another conference the very next day, and that next day would go on getting pushed to the next. He was very well aware of the kind of taskmaster Bhausaheb was. He would be roundly reprimanded for this kind of delay. Bhausaheb had dispatched him to Ayodhya when they were in Gwalior. The Maratha army would have arrived in Agra by now. For how long could this procrastination carry on? As he stood looking in despair at the retreating back of Shuja, Kashiraj's hand rested on his shoulder and broke his chain of thoughts. 'Please stop worrying, Shamji, Nawab Saheb proposes to meet you in the durbar today—alone!'

Shamji Ranganath could not believe his ears.

The meeting began in the resplendent durbar hall of the palace. Kashiraj stood by their side. Shamji Ranganath presented to the Nawab the expensive gifts that Bhausaheb had sent for him. Shuja-ud-dowlah's face remained blank and expressionless. Only his eyes appeared to speak, 'You talk. I shall simply listen.'

'Bhausaheb has prayed for the health and prosperity of Nawab Bahadur at the temple of Shri Gajanan and sent the prasad, the sacramental sweets, for Your Highness.'

'It's Allah's Grace that the kind wishes of the great Bhausaheb are with us.'

'Nawab Saheb, we Marathas have begun to feel that we have somehow incurred your displeasure.'

'All of Hindustan knows of the old bonds that exist between us and the Marathas.'

'That's exactly why the Marathas seek your affection, huzoor. Bhausaheb requests to be given some token of that affection.'

'The stamp that each of us carries in our heart, let it not lose value by being put on paper.'

Shuja-ud-dowlah was glib of tongue. He began to talk in circles: 'We have for years been each other's well-wishers, haven't we? Where's the need for any urgency? We are all in Hindustan, aren't we?' Such was the line Shuja had decided to adopt. Shamji Ranganath tried all kinds of tacks to get Shuja to reveal himself one way or the other, but the Nawab was too swift-witted to give the harried man the slightest peek.

Shamji sensed that the time for dismissal had arrived. He had begun breaking into a sweat when suddenly a servant appeared with a scroll in hand. Kashiraj handed it to his patron. As Shuja began reading it, his face registered confusion and tension. He turned towards Kashiraj and said with feigned concern, 'Panditji, what's this I see? Such an important envoy of the Marathas has been sitting with us for so long, and no refreshments have been served? No sherbet, no fruits, nothing? Is this how we Lakhnavis treat our guests?' Kashiraj immediately disappeared through a door and returned with a retinue of servants carrying trays of drinks and delicacies.

In the morning, Shuja had whispered into Kashiraj's ears that the meeting should not extend beyond ten minutes. The conversation should not stretch to a point where a word should slip out inadvertently. But neither of them had anticipated the news that arrived with the scroll. Sadashivrao Bhau had already arrived at the bank of the Yamuna. There was no saying when he would arrange for the boats and cross over into Ayodhya. Shuja began addressing Shamjipant as if he were a long-lost friend. 'We want friendship with the Marathas. We are both from Hindustan, and would prefer an intimate neighbour to an unknown foreigner any day. There's no wisdom in siding with people from a far-away land. Sadashivrao has always been a close friend.'

Shamji was nonplussed by Shuja's sudden volte-face. But this was not the time to sit scratching one's head. The balance had tilted in his direction, and that was all that mattered. Thrilled beyond measure, he joined heartily in the pleasant conversation that followed. 'My apologies, Pant. It's been our tradition to regale our honoured guests with musical soirees. It's been so many days since you arrived, but on account of being indisposed, we couldn't attend to you well enough. We shall set matters right by organizing a grand performance of the most beautiful girls of Lakhnau this evening.'

Shamjipant was enamoured by the warmth that Shuja exuded. The invitation for the evening revelry was offered and gleefully accepted. Just then a servant entered and whispered something urgently in the Nawab's ear. He immediately stood up, offered Shamji a paan as a symbol of taking leave, and hurried inside. Shamji bowed, turned round, and walked out of the durbar wondering what could have happened to cause the Nawab to leave in such a hurry.

Shamjipant waited till late in the evening for the invitation for the evening soiree to arrive. What he finally received was a regret message. The Nawab Saheb was feeling a little under the weather, hence the evening revelries had been called off. Shamji sat wondering what health problems the Nawab could have developed between afternoon and evening. Before he got into bed, his spy brought him the intelligence that Malika Zamani, the begum of King Mahmood Shah, had arrived from Delhi. An elaborate dinner had been arranged for the royal consort at the palace. The news ensured that sleep wouldn't return to Shamji for a long while.

Where could this thunderbolt have descended from? What if it brought their carefully laid out plans crumbling down? Abdali had played a powerful card by dispatching Malika Zamani, who was known for her pronounced tilt towards the Turani faction at the Delhi Durbar. The potential fall-outs of this meet were frightening. Oh Omkareshwara! You alone can know what heartstrings of the Nawab this silken-tongued siren from the netherworld would play on.

The royal repast was over. The minions had cleared the tables, offered the royals their post-meal indulgences and withdrawn. Shuja-ud-dowlah invited Malika Zamani into the adjacent chamber to sit for consultations. Malika shrewdly requested Shuja's mother Sadr-un-nisa Begum to join them. The conversation warmed up, but Malika Zamani could not divine which way Shuja and his mother were going to swing in the imminent war. She forcefully presented reasons why Ayodhya should team up with Najeeb and Abdali. After this had gone on for a while, Sadr-un-nisa broke in to say, 'Badi Saheba, why should we think of the Marathas as our enemies? On the contrary, it was the Shinde-Holkars who had rushed to our help when the chips were down for us.'

'Begum Saheba, you surprise me with your short memory! Weren't the Shinde-Holkars in the forefront of hounding Nawab Safdarjung Saheb out of Delhi?'

'Those were different times, Badi Saheba. In any case, the Najeeb-ud-dowlah, whose case you are advocating, was the villain-in-chief who was hell-bent on crushing Nawab Saheb.'

Malika Zamani could see that Shuja and his mother were in no mood to relent. She let some time go by and said, 'Look, we have great affection for your house. Forgive me if I offend you, but I should talk straight. Najeeb and Abdali will be here in a couple of days after razing the Maratha posts on the way, and when that happens, they will make war on you. Have the good sense to see which way the wind is blowing, and make your peace with them before calamity strikes.'

'Thanks for the concern, and for the information,' said the Queen Mother, 'but why do you think Bhausaheb is going to give Najeeb and Abdali time for all that?'

'What do you mean?'

'I just got a message today that they have touched the Yamuna.'

'Yes, but crossing Mother Yamuna is not something within their abilities,' responded Malika Zamani. 'Where will the Marathas get boats from? The Peshwas have given that old crow Govindpant orders to collect boats, but that's not a task he can see through. My belief is that instead of cozying up to the infidels, you should side with the brotherhood. The final call is, of course, yours.'

Shuja had lost his sleep. He knew how desperately both sides were wooing him. If Bhausheb did manage to procure the boats, he would cross the Yamuna in no time and soon be upon Ayodhya. He would then bring to bear the pressure of his army to pull him to his side and strengthen his forces. On the other hand, if he was not able to cross, the Marathas would stay stuck on the yonder side. Meanwhile, Abdali wouldn't merely be sitting and waiting. He would let loose his men to burn the countryside, and may even lay siege. Both sides were hell-bent on doing all they could to get him to join. What was he to do?

The following day, Shamjipant organized a rendezvous with Kashiraj in the office palace. He asked, 'Panditji, there is unusual silence in the palace premises since morning—no kettle-drums, no bugles, nothing! Is everything well with Nawab Saheb's health?'

'Nawab Saheb left at the crack of dawn with his retinue towards Patna to meet Shah Alam. There is no saying whether he would return for the next four months. He is in fine fettle. I suggest that both you and the Afghans begin caring for your own health,' he added laughing.

❦

Shuja-ud-dowlah had decided to stretch himself out at his Mahdiganj palace for a few days. He wanted neither Bhau's company nor Abdali's embrace. All that he had wanted fifteen days ago was to take care of his Ayodhya, but the Marathas as well as the Afghans were so eager for his help that they would not let him sit in peace. He had never been subjected to such discomfort in his own palace: sit down for lunch with Bhausaheb's envoy and then entertain Abdali's representative over dinner. Dodging the advances of the former and then of the latter had got his head into a serious muddle. It was in the hope of dislodging both from Faizabad that he had set off for Patna. The intention was to stretch his limbs out for the next few days with Shah Alam. By then, either the Marathas or Abdali would surely be decimated, and that would bring him out of the squeeze. The Marathas, at least, would have been satisfied with bare good wishes, but Najeeb certainly would not have let him get away so cheap.

The Malika Zamani strategy did not work. Abdali also knew that the Maratha envoy still sat stuck like a limpet to Shuja's door. Finally,

Commander-in-chief Jahaan Khan and Najeeb-ud-dowlah set off from the Antarved with their armies in the direction of Ayodhya. Bhausaheb would barely have reached Chambal from the south when Najeeb and Jahaan mounted their attack on Itaawa. Govindpant's Itaawa posts in Bundelkhand were considered strong redoubts. But despite the presence of five- to seven-thousand Maratha soldiers, everybody, including the petty officials, had disappeared even before the enemy soldiers had arrived. Another twenty or twenty-five posts fell, including Shikohabad, immediately after Itaawa. Jahaan Khan and Najeeb now marched up to Bidur. They blew up the obstacles Shuja had erected around Kanpur, and now stood on the border of Ayodhya. A few of their horsemen entered the bordering villages and towns of Ayodhya and began running amok. A bit of arson and a few killings resulted. When Shuja, who was on his way to Patna, got news of this, he instantly turned round and headed straight for Delhi, without even stopping at Faizabad on the way. He made a stop at Mahdiganj about thirty miles away from the border. He and his mother Sadr-un-nisa Begum were receiving reports from their spies and reinforcing their surveillance by setting up additional pickets.

Sleep had abandoned Shuja. The Ganga flowed hardly a mile away. His palace at Mahdiganj stood on its banks in the middle of a dense mango orchard. It was in this beautiful, serene, cool palace that Shuja had spent many a hot summer day, soaking up all the pleasures that youth had to offer. But he was haunted by a sense of insecurity this evening. Both parties had been so set aflame by the desire to recruit him to their side that anything could happen any time. The cool wind had barely lulled him to sleep when he was jolted awake by sounds coming from the riverbank. He stood up and yelled loudly for the guards. 'What's this ruckus?' he growled at them. Are the soldiers manning the posts awake, or have they been buried? What's this noise I hear drifting in from the river?'

'Your Highness, the soldiers are wide awake at their posts. It could be that our soldiers or some fishermen have gone to catch fish. Or it could be some woman in labour, who has set off towards the town for help, and so a boat has been lowered. No reason for worry, huzoor.'

'Hmm, all right. But keep a strict vigil, do you hear? The times are bad.'

'Your wish is our command, Your Highness.' Shuja went back to bed, but he couldn't get the noise he had heard out of his mind.

Who could be out there under the pitch-black sky so late in the night? Restless spirits? Demons? Najeeb Khan? Shuja sank into slumber, albeit a little disturbed.

His fears, however, were not misplaced. The notorious stealer of people's peace of mind stood on the other bank of the Ganga with a posse of sixty horsemen. He had introduced himself to the sentinels as the envoy of Abdali. Many of Shuja's soldiers knew him. Fishing boats were requisitioned to load the horsemen, and they were sent floating down the current. After sailing down a couple of miles, the boats hit the opposite bank, and Najeeb disembarked at Mahdiganj with his squad of battle-hardened storm-troopers.

As the word of his landing spread, Beni Bahadur, the deewan of the Nawab presented himself to pay his respects to Najeeb and said, 'Huzoor, I would have informed Nawab Saheb of your arrival immediately, but he hasn't slept well for the past few nights, and the Queen Mother's instructions are that he should not be disturbed till ten tomorrow morning.'

'Don't you worry, Deewan Saheb, we will take care of that and wake your Nawab when the time for it arrives.'

Satisfied, the deewan made requisite arrangements for Najeeb's stay in quarters that suited his stature. As soon as they were settled, Najeeb turned to his brother-in-law and said, 'See, Jahaan Khan Saheb? My sources can never go wrong. That old fogey Govindpant Bundele will meet the Nawab at lunch tomorrow to persuade him to strike a deal.'

'But it appears that he still hasn't reached here.'

'Oh, he's a cunning old fox, believe me. He would be camping somewhere close by in the woods. When the time for the meeting arrives, he will materialize like a ghost. He's spent his entire life studying the contours of this region. He is the last trustworthy source of information left for Bhau.'

'How did he manage to arrange an audience with the Nawab in such quick time?'

'It's that old crone, Begum Sadr-un-nisa, the Nawab's mother. She's in love with the Marathas. She's the one who has set up all this drama. She's issued instructions to the guards that nobody should be allowed to get close to the Nawab till his conference with Govindpant gets over.'

'Which obviously means, Khan Saheb, that we should break in before any deal with the Marathas is struck.'

'Abandon all worries, Khan Saheb, You have Ghazi Najeeb with you here!'

⚜

The rays of the morning sun had lit the sky, but the soldiers and their sergeants still lay stretched out groggily. Their chieftains hadn't left their beds either; they lay shaking the sleep out of their limbs. The sentinels posted outside Shuja-ud-dowlah's palace carried the weight of sleep on their eyelids, while two Telanga minions were rubbing tobacco in their palms to keep their battle with slumber going.

The sun slowly lifted itself out of the horizon and Najeeb called the Telangas over. The men shook their bleariness away and ran to attend. As they saluted, Najeeb laughed and said, 'This is truly impressive! The night has fled, but the watchmen are still alert! Never seen this devotion to duty even in Kabul and Kandahar, let alone Hindustan!'

'It's a matter of survival, huzoor. Besides, the Queen Mother's instructions are quite clear: not to let anyone see Nawab Saheb before lunch,' said one of them.

'Of course, of course!' Najeeb cast an appreciative look at them. He fished out a couple of gold coins from his pocket and said. 'I have this gold from Saharanpur. What do you think of it? Looks pure?' He placed one coin each on the two outstretched palms.

Two pairs of eyes sparkled. 'This looks absolutely genuine, huzoor!' blurted one of the Telangas.

'It does, doesn't it?' said Najeeb, 'Then tuck them in your turban. Collect all the good things you can, says the Koran.'

The two guards looked hesitantly at Najeeb-ud-dowlah, pocketed the coins and said, 'How can we be of service to you, huzoor?'

'I want a meeting with the Nawab Saheb in the next ten minutes.'

The guards' faces fell in unison. 'Huzoor, the Queen Mother's instructions —'

'Yes, yes, you have told me that,' Najeeb said with great sympathy, as he pulled out two more gold coins from his pocket and placed them in eager hands. 'But, then,' he said with a laugh, 'on the banks of the Ganga here, don't you have snakes and scorpions crawling all over the place?' As he looked at them meaningfully, the face of one of the two guards suddenly lit up. The man flashed a crooked, conspiratorial smile, stretched out his palm again and said, 'Yes, huzoor, there are plenty of snakes and scorpions here.'

Najeeb laughed out aloud, gave the two one more gold coin each, and patted one of them on the back. 'That's my man. All right, then, get busy.' With that, he turned round and walked back towards his door.

He instantly heard the two screaming at the top of their voices, 'Hey, get up! Get up! Cobras! Three of them, big, scaled cobras!'

The other guards snapped out of their drowsiness and came running. The two terrified-looking guards pointed towards the palace and screamed, 'Three huge cobras have just gone slithering from under the palace door! Alert the chamber guards!' In no time, it became a shouting contest, with everybody running helter-skelter searching for a stout stick. The noise reached such high decibels that Shuja-ud-dowlah himself stepped out in a dishevelled state.

'What's going on? What snakes are you yelling about?' he shouted.

'Huzoor,' croaked one of the guards, 'Another guard and I saw three big cobras slide into the palace from under the door!'

Pandemonium took over, with guards and servants fanning out in all directions inside the palace in search of the reptiles. As Shuja stood confused and flustered, Najeeb-ud-dowlah took the opportunity to walk into the Nawab's presence. Shuja was startled. Was this one of the snakes that his minions got frantic about? He was left with no alternative but to force a smile and welcome the biggest of all reptiles into his chamber.

As the servants appeared with sherbet, Shuja asked after Najeeb's health and that of the badshah. An uncomfortable silence followed this exchange of courtesies. Najeeb took the opportunity and offered to Shuja the scroll of the proclamation that the badshah had issued. Shuja unrolled the scroll and first noticed the stamp and seal of Durrani's authority. Then he began to read: Issued by the King of Kings, the Scion of the Royal Lineage of the Durranis, Emperor Ahmad Shah Abdali. The proclamation was written in Arabic, appointing Shuja-ud-dowlah as the Wazeer of Hindustan.

Looking at Shuja's bewildered face, Najeeb laughed and said, 'Nawab Saheb, I offer my gratitude to Allah for having made me and the badshah the instruments for fulfilling your greatest desire. Congratulations.'

'I stand beholden to you, Najeeb Saheb,' Shuja stuttered, 'but, really, where was the hurry for all this?'

'This was just to reassure you that the badshah lives by his word, and would rather embrace death than let his promise go unfulfilled.'

'Anything else?'

'We now await your arrival, huzoor. The honour of the Durrani Emperor lies rolling in the dust of Ayodhya. You, with your fists of steel, can reinstate his dignity.'

'Please do not embarrass me, Najeeb Saheb,' Shuja managed to say. As Najeeb looked at Shuja with widening eyes, a couple of servants came panting in. 'Huzoor, the Queen Mother is most indisposed, and requests your immediate attention.'

Shuja shot up with an anxious look. Najeeb stood up too and asked, 'What could the Queen Mother have suddenly taken ill with?'

'She has been suffering from stomach cramps.'

'Nawab Saheb, I have a couple of doctors in my company. Should I send them over to the palace?'

'Doctors? Oh, no, no! We have our own Lakhnau physicians who've been looking after her, and they understand her illness. I apologize for having to leave you in such a hurry. If you can be so kind as to wait, I shall hurry back as soon as I can.'

As Shuja hurried away, Najeeb broke into a sweat. He turned to Saadullah Khan and said, 'See the old crone's machinations? How could the stomach ache have sprung up right at this moment? What a wile move the old hag has played. She is determined to make the Marathas win the war.'

Shuja rushed frantically to his mother's palace only to find Sadr-un-nisa locked in conversation with old Govindpant Bundele. As soon as he joined them, Sadr-un-nisa warned him, 'Son, don't ever put your trust in Najeeb. He is as complete a hell-hound as I have ever seen. I cannot forget the manner in which he set about destroying your father to secure the wazeer's seat for Ghaziuddin. There is a variety of snakes on the banks of the Ganga that change the colour of their skin to match the environment:

they turn green in grass and look brown in the dust. Najeeb is one of that kind, changes shape and form according to his needs. He can cry, he can roll at your feet, he can even lick the dust off your boots. Once his needs are met, he will bare his fangs and destroy his benefactor without blinking an eye. Your father had told me on his death-bed that I should teach you to trust the devil before you trusted this evil man.'

Shuja's spine tingled. His mother's advice had touched the right chords in him. Times were bad. What should he do now? He turned towards Govindpant. 'Well, Pant, what's the latest from your end?'

'Nothing new, Nawab Saheb, it's the same old story. But I have brought a fresh letter for you from Bhausaheb.'

'I have already received two or three missives from Bhausaheb before this.'

'I still request that you read this one carefully.'

Shuja-ud-dowlah was as erudite as he was handsome. He knew the Arabic and Marathi languages along with Urdu and Hindi. He began reading Bhausaheb's letter:

'I have sent letters and scouts at the Nawab Saheb's doorstep before this one too. Let me clarify once again: we are getting into this war not for a share of revenue from your territories, but for safeguarding the Empire of Hindustan. Our humble request to the Nawab Saheb is that he ride along with us in the conflict. If, for some reason, that is impossible, it is requested that Your Highness stay away from the war altogether. We are not insisting on contribution of funds, arsenal or armaments; we just want your word that you will sit out. You should not allow that sinner, that charlatan Najeeb anywhere close to your door. You should not offer space to that Afghan infiltrator who has pillaged Delhi and turned it to ashes twice or thrice before this. The Nawab Saheb is requested to remember the blood that our forefathers shed for Ayodhya in the past. The differences that exist between us can be resolved any time we sit down together, but under the present circumstances, the foreign enemy must be annihilated.'

Shuja gave it another careful reading. Sadr-un-nisa put her weight behind the letter and said, 'Son, the Maratha stance appears just and fair to me. If you can't support them, you can at least stay neutral.'

'That's our humble appeal to you, Nawab Saheb. Just stay away if you cannot join us,' reiterated Govindpant.

'Bhausaheb has already declared that the wazeer's post of Delhi is yours,' chipped in Naro Shankar, who was the sardar posted to Delhi.

Shuja sat silent for a while. Then, he got up and gathered his mother, Govindpant and Naro Shankar in a single sweep of his glance and said, 'Well, all right, Pant. Meet me again after four days. After all, you and I are made from the same clay—we are Hindustanis. If I enter the war, it will be from your side; else, I shall stay out altogether. I have to leave now. I left my meeting with Najeeb half-way; I must get back to him.'

As he stepped out into the lawns, he paused when he noticed a bustle in the garden. A few snake-charmers had come over with their flutes in the hope of luring the cobras that were reported to be lurking in the premises. They were being tailed by about a dozen soldiers.

The suspended talk with Najeeb resumed. When Najeeb realized that Shuja was refusing to offer him any quarters, he flared up and said, 'Nawab Saheb, don't you see that Allah has offered us an unprecedented opportunity to chase these Deccan monkeys out for good? While these infidels are hell-bent on enslaving all of Hindustan, you sit here unmoved! What should we make of your indifference?'

'What you actually mean is that we help you drive the Marathas away, so that Delhi, then, comfortably falls into your lap, right?'

Najeeb hadn't expected such open resistance. He quickly got a hold of himself and said, 'Huzoor, is this your opinion of us? Please, I don't hanker after Delhi. I have just given to you the message carrying the seal of the Durrani king appointing you wazeer. If your lordship is ready, this Najeeb can easily persuade Durrani to place the crown of Delhi on your noble head.'

'Khan Saheb, I have never coveted the throne of Delhi, I do not do so now, and will never in the future either,' Shuja responded hotly. 'But what crime, do you think, have the Marathas committed, anyway? In fact, it is your Nadir Shah and your Abdali who have looted Hindustan time and again, looted it with a ruthlessness that has no precedent in world history. The Marathas, by comparison, are a whole lot better, besides being of the same land too.'

'Nawab Bahadur, you talk in this tone because Bhausaheb has landed on the yonder side of the Yamuna. But please know, he will never be able to cross the river.'

Shuja's face turned red with anger. He fished out Bhausaheb's scroll and pushed it under Najeeb's nose. 'Read this, it is in Bhausaheb's hand. He gives reassurance here of staying friends even after the war, and he gives a clear impression of being a trustworthy person.'

Irritation written all over him, Najeeb read the missive and returned it with disdain, adding, 'Don't go by these honey-traps, Nawab Saheb, these are the moves of a cunning spider. Before you know it, you get trapped in the web that he is weaving around you.'

The sound of the snake-charmers outside was gathering volume. Najeeb pressed on aggressively with his case, 'Why are you showing us this missive of Bhausaheb's, huzoor? Why don't you pull out the letters from the Peshwa to his satraps that your spies have intercepted? The Peshwa wants all the pilgrimages for himself, doesn't he? Prayag, Kashi, Mathura, Haridwar, Kurukshetra! How can it escape the notice of a keen statesman like you, that today the Peshwa wants them as pilgrimage, tomorrow he may want to place his throne there?'

The pilgrimage issue pushed Shuja a little on the backfoot. Just then an emissary entered with hot news. As the Nawab read the scroll, he turned pale. Najeeb knew exactly what it was about. He had orchestrated it all. It had been arranged that as soon as Najeeb left for this assignment, Jahaan Khan should raid the villages on the border of Ayodhya and burn them to the ground. Since the Nawab was quartered close by, he would get the news even as his talks with Najeeb were on.

After reading the missive, Shuja handed over the scroll to his deewan. Thirty villages being burnt down was no small matter. The imminence of Jahaan Khan setting off for Lakhnau in a couple of days was no pleasant thought either. It was also true that crossing the Yamuna would not be an easy task for Bhausaheb, whatever the determination. Added to that, Shah Wali Khan of Delhi and his disciples had gone on a campaign in the mosques and madrassas of the border villages, proclaiming that Islam was in danger, and the coming war was nothing short of jihad; it was a religious war between the believers and the infidels of the south. Shuja was left with very little space for manoeuvering.

The snake-charmers outside were still blowing upon their pipes. Najeeb raised his voice a few decibels. In the manner of the conjurers toiling outside, Najeeb knew that the reptile in his presence was more than ordinarily intractable. He straightened his spine, gathered his best arguments, summoned his most persuasive voice and continued, 'If there have been some misunderstandings during our conversation, I offer my sincere apologies, but as a true Muslim, I have to tell you this. The war soon to descend upon us is not between friends and enemies. Nawab Saheb, it is not even between the Afghans and the non-Afghans, nor between Hindustan and Iran. It is not between those of the Deccan and those from Hindustan either. Nawab Bahadur, it is out and out a war between the believers and the infidels. You as a good Musalman know as well as I do, that when a jihad is being fought, coming out in support of the infidel is a sin. For a person of your exalted lineage, it will be the supreme sin. In the name of the Protector of us all, can you think of a bigger transgression than standing up for the disbeliever in a battle of the holy versus unholy?'

With Najeeb hitting below the belt, Shuja lost his balance for a moment; however, he quickly recovered and retorted, 'Khan Saheb, why do you talk to me of jihad? You need me now and you talk religious bonding. Once the war is over, Abdali and his chieftains here will shake me by the nape of my neck, demanding tribute, because I am not one of them.'

'Ya Allah! Oh dear lord!' Najeeb looked dramatically at the roof and lifted his hands. 'When will You bring home to this Nawab that we are all from the brotherhood of Islam?'

'Najeeb, you people sing this tune in times of need. But tomorrow you will all jump at my throat because I am a Shia and you are Sunnis. Besides, my father had roundly vanquished Abdali twelve years ago in the battle of Manpur. How can he forget that? The fire of vengeance would still be burning inside him.'

Najeeb let out a laugh and said, 'Huzoor, does the right hand ever tell the left hand that it is the left one? Does the left hand say this to the right one? Even if the hands are two, the entity, the body, the soul are one and the same. It's the same with the Shias and the Sunnis. But Nawab Bahadur, if you do not join the jihad, and if we are defeated, every mosque in Hindustan will be razed to the ground. The one Koran will be replaced by eighteen Puranas, the one and true Allah will be substituted by thirty-three lakh gods and goddesses. Even the thought of such an eventuality makes my bile rise. Among the Hindus, it is the Brahmins that have the strongest taste for religion and rituals. That Sadashiv Bhau is a Brahmin from Pune. They call the Brahmins and sadhus from Kashi and Prayag and distribute alms. The issue of pilgrimages brings them together like soulmates. If we don't settle accounts with them today, it's the Hindus that will celebrate Bakri Eid and lead the Muslims to the slaughter house as so many sacrificial goats. Nawab Saheb, once the infidels have been defeated, I promise to visit Ayodhya every day, and wash your feet and drink that water four times in a day. But today you must stand up and defend the dignity of Islam.' Najeeb's eyes began to stream as he belted out the passion-laden peroration.'

'Look,' responded Shuja a little tentatively, 'I have no faith in the good conduct of Abdali's sardars once he wins the battle.'

'Who's Abdali, and who are his sardars?' snorted Najeeb. 'It was I who got after that ass to ensure that Islam survives in Hindustan. His sardars like Jahaan Khan and Bahadur Khan are mere nobodies. I swear to you in the name of Allah, if Abdali so much as casts an angry eye on you, I shall pluck those eyes out of their sockets with my own fingers. If Najeeb falters in this promise by so much as a blink, then he is not the son of his father. After becoming the wazeer of Hindustan, why do you let petty worries bother you? The one-hundred-and-fifty-thousand Indian Afghans of the Antarved are your subjects. You simply have to issue orders!'

None of Najeeb's honey, however, could make Shuja fly to the bait. His eyes seemed to suggest that he was measuring up the man, and not liking what he saw. When Saadullah Khan also tried his persuasive tactics and failed, Najeeb began to lose patience. 'Nawab Saheb,' he proceeded in a desperate voice, 'here I have been turning blood to water in the hope of persuading you to do the right thing, but I see no positive response from you. Well, so be it. It is possible that you have already given your word to the enemy envoy. If that is so, I request that you rise now and accompany me to Abdali, merely for a meeting. If that too is unacceptable to you—'

Najeeb suddenly stood up dramatically and pulled out the dagger that hung from his waist-band. Shuja's bodyguards instantly swished out their swords, but he signalled them to stay away. The dagger shone like silver-colour fish swimming in clear waters. One hand holding the dagger, Najeeb wiped the tears off his eyes with the other one and said,

'Here, Nawab Saheb, if you find a visit to Abdali unacceptable, take this and chop my head off. I'd rather die at the hands of a Muslim than be desecrated in the battlefield at the hands of infidels. My fame, perhaps, will reach Makka and Madina that a Muslim called Najeeb went back to his Maker out of love for Islam, while another Nawab of the finest lineage—'

'Stop, Khan Saheb!' shouted Shuja, finally succumbing to Najeeb's wiles, 'please don't say another word.' His eyes turned moist. Najeeb threw the dagger clattering to the floor and reached out to wipe the tears from Shuja's eyes. He looked up at the roof and incanted, 'Ya Allah, grant success to us fighters in the cause of your Faith!'

The agreement was reached. Shuja committed himself to fight on Abdali's side. Pounded, bruised and battered by Najeeb's harangue, all that Shuja could say to Najeeb as he turned towards his private quarters was, 'Please don't leak this to anybody for the next four days. The envoys of the Marathas are still in the vicinity.'

※

It was during the season of the Orion constellation that the pavilions of the Maratha nobility started coming up on the northern bank of the Chambal river. The office and the private tents of Bhausaheb were being erected even as about half of the army was in the process of crossing over. It was for the first time that the Maratha soldiers were looking at a span as wide as this, in comparison to the Mula-Mutha and the Indrayani rivers back home in Pune. Four firm strokes, and one could cross the Mula with ease, but this furlong-wide span of the Chambal was an unnerving stretch. After leaving Gwalior, they had first crossed the small tributary of Kumari before they got a glimpse of the banks of the Chambal. They could see huge pits all the way to the water. As they moved on, they had to negotiate patches of land that had been gouged out as if by a mountain-sized plough. Herding elephants and horses past these craters to the river was a challenge. To heap one misery over another, the sky suddenly clouded up and started pouring over the hapless travellers when barely five to six noblemen had crossed with their retinue. This unexpected onslaught from the skies took them by surprise, and brought everyone's spirits plummetting down, Bhausaheb and the other sardars included. As the night descended, it found the army sundered into two clumsy parts, one on each side of the river, while the rains battered on relentlessly. There were a few old temples on the yonder side where some kind of makeshift shelter was rigged up for the women of the royal household.

Bhausaheb had posted four sardars on the riverbank to help the late crossers wade out of the water. The sudden downpour had unsettled him. What had been pits and gouges had now become treacherous puddles, the sludge and slime making foothold extremely precarious. Having stayed out all night in the rains, men and animals had turned stiff in the joints, Now, with the earth inches deep in the slurry of mud, the slightest misstep would send them sprawling. The load-carrying mules had to watch their steps too as they negotiated the wet sand. The worst to fare were the poor bullocks that had been detailed to pull the heavy cannon carts. It was only the goads and the whips falling on their backs that kept them straining to pull the carts out of the water, snorting, frothing and sweating despite the wet, cold winds.

For one reason or the other, the campaign had got terribly behind schedule. Bhausaheb had begun with talking of finishing off Abdali within three months; he was still floundering in and around the Chambal even though three months had slipped past. According to the original calculations, the Maratha forces should have wiped out Abdali and stood at the gates of Delhi by now. The army, however, was nowhere near ready for such an eventuality. Even the tarpaulins or other equipment for erecting shelters hadn't been bought. Bhausaheb was consoling himself with the thought that Malharji would arrive in a day or two, and after due consultation, they would cross the Yamuna three or four days later. He had asked Malharbaba's advice on where the Chambal should be entered from, and it was on his instructions that the army had begun crossing the river. He continued to hope that his forces would be joined soon by fresh Shinde-Holkar troops, and that would fit them out to launch a devastating attack on Abdali.

By the time the evening winds began blowing, almost the entire army had crossed the river. Bhausaheb decided to set camp near Dholpur-Karoli, which was about four or five miles ahead, and the army moved with urgency. A scout ran up to Bhausaheb's elephant and handed over a scroll to his master seated under the canopy. Bhausaheb smiled wryly as he read the missive, causing Vishwasrao to cock a quizzical glance. 'Oh, nothing urgent. Hafeez Rahmat Khan is arriving tomorrow to meet us.'

'To meet us?'

'To look for some deal.'

'This means that the Kandahari king has finally relented and wants to negotiate. His conceit has deflated a little bit, has it?'

Bhausaheb laughed and cast a look at his nephew that suggested that he still had some growing up to do. 'This Abdali is good at playing games,' he said. 'The ruse is to lure the chicken with some grain and then lunge at it and twist its neck. They pretend they are ready for talks, keep us deluded, and attack when we are distracted: this is their game. They would have got the news of us having crossed Malwa long ago, hence this move.'

They struck camp at night. Rakhmabai Akkasaheb heard that Muchkund was nearby. She instantly spoke to her brother Balwantrao Mehendale's wife Lakshmibai Saheb. Akkasaheb, who had set off for a pilgrimage to the three main holy places of Kashi, Prayag and Mathura found the sudden possibility of a pilgrimage to Muchkund a rare piece of luck. When she used to listen to or recite the *Hari Vijaya*, Akkasaheb would love the tale of Muchkund. Bhausaheb's wife Parvatibai was thrilled too.

The whiff of Muchkund's proximity reached the other pilgrims too: the Brahmins including Jereshastri, Agnihotri, and the motley crowd of mendicants, monks and recluses. Jereshastri instantly made his way to Akkasaheb's tent and said, 'Akkasaheb, this is no ordinary piece of fortune, the opportunity of our feet touching the dust of the consecrated land of Muchkund. Muchkund is one of the holiest saints to have battled demons before he settled down in these parts. Passing him by without worshipping at his shrine would be a grievous sin!'

Jereshastri was shrewd enough to know how to break through Bhausaheb's resistance. Working through the good office of Akkasaheb and Parvatibai, Bhausaheb's wife, he weaved in the keenness of the soldiers too for the Muchkund pilgrimage. In practical terms, Bhausaheb knew he was trapped, and he gave his nod, however much against his wishes, with the injunction that the entire exercise should not exceed a couple of days.

Batches of pilgrims began to set off for Muchkund Tirth the same afternoon. Nana Phadnis too found that he was feeling strong enough to travel in a palanquin along with his mother. Sardar Paigude's father had passed away the previous year, and being the dutiful son he was, he had brought his father's ashes in a gold urn to release them into the waters of the mighty rivers. The minimum he had hoped was to consign the ashes to the Yamuna waters. He was thrilled when his priest informed him that submersion of the ashes at the Muchkund pilgrimage would earn him the same merit too. Accordingly, a grand ritual was organized at the banks of the river, where all the relatives and friends in his army were in attendance since early morning. Paigude took care that all the religious rites were observed to the minutest detail.

The army got so engrossed in the pilgrimage that they didn't register how three days had leaked away. As it was finally gearing up to leave Muchkund, Jereshastri set off an uproar, screaming, 'The day after tomorrow is the thirtieth day of the month of Jyeshth! There will be a solar eclipse! How can you even think of resuming the journey on a day as holy as that?' The devotees were thrilled. They thanked Jereshastri for the reminder and decided that they would not move till the benefits of the auspicious day were gathered.

Bhausaheb himself experienced the immediate advantage of placating the gods when a scroll arrived from Shuja-ud-dowlah with the message, 'I shall be joining your side within a few days.' Bhausaheb was over the moon. The very news of Shuja joining the Marathas would puncture the hopes of Abdali, and his army that had been compelled to suffer the harsh Indian summer was bound to wend its way back home. That was when the Holkar's manager, Gangoba Chandrachud, came with the news that his patron would arrive in a couple of days. He also updated Bhausaheb on all the developments in their camp, including the visit of Abdali's envoy Hafeez Khan looking for a deal.

Holkar's imminent arrival meant hanging on. Meanwhile, the occasion of the solar eclipse was also given due reverence. The entire army took holy baths. Another two days passed, and soon the Holkar pennants were fluttering alongside the Peshwa flags. Both the armies were overjoyed. The heralds announced the arrival of the great patriarch Malharjibaba with loud calls to the hoi polloi to stand in reverence and attention, eyes suitably turned down.

As he saw the old but steely form of Malharjibaba Holkar, Bhausaheb instantly got up to pay his respects. Malharjibaba strode forward and warmly gathered Bhausaheb in his arms. 'When did you arrive, Bhau?' They sat down and made polite enquiries about each other's health. 'Bhausaheb,' said Malharbaba, 'just because I've turned old, you shouldn't think my senses have taken leave of me.'

'Don't understand you, Kakasaheb!'

'You spring lambs, you continue to address me as Kakasaheb; well, all right, doesn't matter. When you crossed Gwalior, you would have received my earlier letters. Why should the Peshwa dispatch an important prince like you on such a trivial campaign? The blood running through these veins is still hot, there is strength in the sinews still, and courage in our hearts.'

'Why do you say this, Kakasaheb?' laughed Bhausaheb. 'You are going to lead the campaign. We shall stay by your side and fight under your guidance.'

'Bhausaheb, yes, there have been differences between the Shindes and the Holkars. But can anyone contest the fact that it is the two of us who have traversed every patch of the battlefields here and demolished the enemy?'

'There are no two opinions on this count, Kakasaheb, but your vassals here in Hindustan, from Bundele onwards to everybody else, have been so awfully remiss in depositing their due revenues, despite so many reminders. What have they been doing?'

'Well, yes, the revenue collectors have turned lax. On top of that is the fear of Abdali.'

'Kakasaheb, the expenses on the army have crossed the sixty-thousand barrier. There isn't a dime coming from Pune. How does one raise funds?'

'Bhausaheb, I hear that you carry in your army a regiment of eight-thousand Gardis?'

'That's quite true.'

'Why do you carry those black-faced Telangas and those foreigner sons of the devil? The Gardis should never be trusted, and you are carrying such a huge contingent of them!'

'Kakasaheb, these Gardis have the latest in artillery. From here on, wars will be won only on the strength of this latest arsenal.'

'I can't trust them for a minute. Our guerilla strategies are any day superior.'

'We shall sit together and jointly decide what strategy to use. But meanwhile, how do we block the advance of the enemy before they descend like rain upon us?'

'We shall first cross the Yamuna, where the Jaats will come to our help. I've had detailed discussions with them. We should also receive some food consignment from them in a couple of days. A few cartloads had set off from Bharatpur four days ago.'

'This is great news, Kakasaheb. This will at least settle the issue of feeding the army.'

'The Jaats can be put to other uses too.'

'If the Delhi Empire has to survive, whoever steps up to help us at this juncture is welcome. Any news from Shuja?'

'That boat seems to be rocking a bit, from what I can guess. You have any news from him?'

'I had received a message from him a couple of days back, expressing his decision to join forces with us.'

'Well, my information is different. Both Najeeb and Jahaan Khan have touched Ayodhya for consultations, I hear.'

'What are you saying, Kakasaheb? Najeeb?'

This jolted Bhausaheb and caused a knot to form in his stomach. Bhausaheb and Malharjibaba Holkar sat talking for a long time. It was decided that they would wait for the supplies from the Jaats to arrive, and then cross the Yamuna to try to scuttle the possibility of a deal between Shuja and Najeeb. If possible, they would place Govindpant's territory at their back and beat the hell out of the Najeeb-Abdali duo.

Malharbaba left for his tent, but the latest intelligence about Najeeb kept Bhausaheb rooted to his seat for a long time.

The Shinde contingent arrived after two days. When Jankoji Shinde entered the private pavilion, nearly all the important noblemen were present there to welcome him. When, after crossing so many hurdles, this seventeen-year-old son of Jayappa Rao Shinde and the nephew of Dattaji Rao Shinde came and stood before him, Bhausaheb leapt forward and gathered the young man in a tight embrace. Jankoji returned the affection with equal intensity, in the manner of a son hugging his father on returning from a long exile in the wilderness. He began to sniffle like a child. Bhausaheb patted his back and sat the boy down beside himself. Wiping his own moist eyes, Bhausaheb began, 'When that Muzaffar Khan had mounted his vile attack on me, Dattaji had sent me a letter of consolation from the north. It must now be about a year since that episode. Who should console whom now, Jankojiba? When I look at you, dear boy, the image of that valiant man springs before my eyes; I think of the proud and intrepid warrior Dattaji, who was forever rearing to jump into the cauldron of war in search of conquests.'

'The sacrifices made by the Shinde family in the service of the Maratha Empire are without parallel,' said Balwantrao Ganpat. 'Ranojibaba became a martyr on the battlefield; Jayappa Shinde, and after him, Dattaji, gave up their lives fighting for the glory of the Marathas.'

'The person singly-handedly responsible for these grievous losses is that misbegotten hell-hound Najeeb-ud-dowlah,' said Jankoji. 'After offering a hand of friendship to my uncle, he stabbed him in the back. He looks for chinks, whether of caste or religion or other divisive factors. Once the crack is located, how much time does it take to fill the crack with dynamite and blow up the best defences?'

While the entire court was offering condolences, Malharbaba was looking at Jankoji unblinkingly. Jankoji and Vishwasrao sat on either side of Bhausaheb and threw covert glances at each other. The two boys were meeting after a very long time, and were sending unspoken messages to each other. Sitting in the rear, Gangoba Chandrachud was telling his neighbour, 'See this? We toil hard too, but the people that the Peshwas care for are only the Shindes!'

The arrival of the Shindes' and Holkars' forces breathed new life into the Maratha army. Here were people who knew these parts well, who were familiar with this soil. With them by the side, their days of crises would soon be over. The Shinde-Holkar armies were also feeling rejuvenated. The last five or six months had been bad for them, with relentless misfortunes and defeats breaking their spirits to the point where they had stopped believing in themselves. They simply couldn't shake off their bad memories: the unceasing flight of the Shindes since their defeat at the Buradi Ghat, the ordeals of the Holkars in the mountains of Rajasthan, the shameful chase given to Gangoba Tatya and his men through the jungles and heaths of Agra and Mathura when they had gone to waylay Abdali's treasures. The wounds were still raw. They were like cattle who had found shelter after being chased by a tiger. They were now among their own people, and suddenly began feeling capable of taking in their stride whatever good or bad came their way.

Hundreds of grain-laden carts dispatched by the Jaats began rolling in. Like the sharecroppers back in their native villages, the soldiers began swarming around the carts. The millers of the army, along with the Kunbi women, began grinding the grains in the hand-mills till their spines creaked and their fingers broke into blisters. The hearths were set alight with a new joy. The soldiers gorged themselves on crisply baked bhaakri eaten with chutney prepared from the red-pepper of Bundelkhand. Nobody could say when the next meal would come, and so they ate and ate till they could eat no more, and then they stretched themselves out with a contentment they had not experienced in a long, long time. The monks and mendicants looked around stealthily, quietly folded a few bhaakaris and slipped them into their bags. Who knew where tomorrow's sun would take them?

After a good afternoon siesta, evening was time for merrymaking. The dancing boys and the eunuchs kept the soldiers regaled. For the serious ones, the balladeers sang songs of valour, and the hymn singers gave them compositions of Tukaram. Slowly, the merriment came to an end and they finally hit the sack. The animals too had not had it so good before, and they settled down flicking their tails with the satisfaction of a full stomach.

As dawn broke, the drums began to beat, shaking the camp rudely out of its slumber. The soldiers sprang up and began rolling up their belongings. The workers pulled out the stakes and brought the tents down. Bhausaheb had alerted them the previous evening, and they too were ready to depart. The bullocks were yoked to the cannon-carts and the horses and mules were loaded with household effects. The travellers, however, remained disoriented for a while. They had been yanked out of such deep, early morning sleep. Why had these soldiers begun such a rumpus so early in the morning? The last few days had been spent in such wonderful prayers and meditation, and now it was back to the hurry and scurry of an army on the move. Up now, and back to the never-ending hassles of travel! The biggest howls and moans came from the women and children. Collecting their belongings and getting them travel-ready was enough to test the patience of a saint.

For the Shinde and the Holkar armies, this was familiar territory, and they set off to form the vanguard. The Marathas had no idea in which direction they were heading. Bhausaheb had sorted the issues out with the Shindes and the Holkars the previous evening.

Vishwasrao had abandoned his seat on the royal elephant, and was now riding his favourite horse alongside Jankoji. The friends had met after a very long separation. Two years back, both of them had put their courage and swordsmanship on display in the battle of Sindkhed. Vishwasrao carried no conceit of being the crown-prince. Jankoji too did not feel the need to maintain any distance with the eldest son of the Peshwa. On the contrary, the bonds of friendship were getting woven tighter and tighter between the two. Both of them were exemplary warriors at such a young age, and reminded onlookers of Lav and Kush, the twin sons of Lord Rama.

It was Vishwasrao who set the ball rolling. 'Baba,' he said, 'your Kakasaheb has earned undying fame for himself. It needs seven lives to earn the merit of dying fighting on the battlefield.'

'The gods played a cruel game with me by sending me into a swoon,' Jankoji said gravely. 'If I had been in my senses, I would either have brought that Najeeb down or got blown up by a cannonball and accompanied my Kakasaheb to heaven.'

'Hush! Why should death be playing on your mind?'

'Rao Saheb, does this life have any purpose? We have just been hopping up and down like puppets. Mother Goddess Kaneshwari has blessed us with such robust bodies. Yet, if we cannot wreak vengeance upon our enemies, we are surely fit material for hell.'

'Rid your mind of all worries, Jankojibaba. This Vishwasrao will happily stake his life on the battlefield and join the martyrs.'

The sky should really have brightened a good four miles earlier, but today it was heavily overcast. Dark clouds had gathered across the sky like dense billows of smoke. The humidity was such that men as well as animals began to perspire profusely. By afternoon, rations for the next four or five days had been distributed to the soldiers. When they hit upon a mango grove, they called a halt and pulled out their stale bhaakris. A number of the Marathas stood leaning against their horses as they chewed down their food, and after they had finished, went over to the nearby well to wash it down. There was a bit of a melee as the men searched for shade. They would have stretched their limbs for barely an hour or so when the drums began to beat, and the army was ready to move again.

Bhausaheb couldn't shake off his restlessness. The news of Najeeb setting off towards Ayodhya kept niggling him. He looked unseeingly at the dark, heavy atmosphere around him, and suddenly arrived at a firm decision. They had wasted enough time on the way. There would be just one more stop in front, and half a day beyond that would be the Yamuna. There wouldn't be much water in the river now. If Govindpant had made even some stop-gap arrangement for boats, then he would get some of the soldiers to cross over. He would then send criers to the nearby villages and gather a few boatmen. He would pay them double rates and get a pontoon bridge built across the river in four days' time, and get the entire army to cross over ... Bhausaheb could see in his mind's eye that mile-long bridge rocking gently in the water. He could see elephants, camels and horses walking carefully across with their escutcheons. The regimental flags were fluttering in the river breeze.... His dream was rudely shattered by a loud crashing sound: Booom! Booom! Rumble! Crash! The sound rent the sky and a bright electric crackle went racing across the gloom overhead, wiping out the darkness for a split second. The pontoon of his dream instantly turned to vapour and an icy hand clutched at his heart. Please, please God! Not this assault!

The darkness intensified. They ran into a big inn on the way, and found shelter for the women. There were a dozen or so temples and a few mosques a little ahead, towards which the sardars crashed their way. Blinding flashes of lightning would dispel the gloom and flash upon the soldiers spread out half a mile beyond the inn. Bhausaheb, Malharbaba, Jankoji, Vishwasrao, Balwantrao, Yashwantrao Pawar and some other grandees had found shelter under the outer verandah of the inn. As they sat on their haunches watching the dance of light in the sky, suddenly there was a louder crash than before that caused the bullocks to pull at their yokes. As the camels snaked their necks this way and that and the horses shivered, the sky opened up and the rain began falling in sheets. The wall of water was so thick that everything beyond it disappeared from sight. The entire army was blanketed out by an impenetrable screen of water. The travellers began crowding in the temples and mosques. A vast majority of horsemen sought shelter under whatever trees they could spot and stood dodging the stream that fell upon them from above.

Bhausaheb groaned, 'Time is playing such games with us! Who knew the rains would begin so early?'

'I've lived through so many monsoons in these parts, but never have I seen such torrential rains descend so early,' commented Malharbaba.

'What now, Kakasaheb?' asked Vishwasrao and Jankoji in unison.

'No getting disheartened. What we have decided, we have decided. There's no turning back now. This downpour will not last for more than a day or two. In any case, it is not going to hold us back. Govindpant would surely have made some arrangement, however inadequate. I had sent scouts to him four days back. We will certainly get news from him this evening. Whatever equipment we can gather, we shall use it and cross the Yamuna, and cut Najeeb and Abdali to pieces in the Antarved.'

Two camels came to a stop in front of them and a peon came scurrying up to them with a scroll secured in a cylindrical sheath. Bhausaheb pulled the scroll out of the soaking wet sheath, shook it open and began to read. Curious, Vishwasrao asked, 'Boats arranged?'

'No boats yet, but the news here is far worse,' Bhausaheb spoke in a hoarse voice. 'Rao Saheb, a stable, trustworthy, righteous boat has just sunk.'

'Meaning?'

'Shuja has joined up with Abdali. Najeeb's machinations have borne fruit,' he said in a low voice.

For the half-starved Maratha nobility that sat on their haunches in the gloom, the information came as a huge blow. Jankoji and Vishwasrao looked at each other in panic. Malharbaba, for all his bluster and tough exterior, looked shaken. Nobody spoke a word. The blast of the wet wind had begun turning their limbs numb. Despite the loud clatter of the rains, despite the water surging and swirling at their feet, despite the company of their brethren, each one of them felt despairingly lonely. Bhausaheb broke their musings with a painful sigh and said to Malharji, 'See, Subhedar kaka? The lesson here is that we should never do others any favour. All our agreements, all our affection, all that we did for the throne of Ayodhya, all of that didn't count for anything with him in the final tally, and he went and bonded with that foreign intruder Abdali. With this act, Shuja has done incalculable damage not only to all of Hindustan, but to himself too.'

The painful silence returned and lingered for a long while. Finally, Bhausaheb spoke out again. 'All right, my esteemed friends, get up and find some place to stretch out, however cramped. If we sit frozen like this, we will certainly die. Whatever confronts us tomorrow—deluge, storm or earthquake—we will cut our way through all obstacles. We shall cross the Yamuna and devastate Shuja's land. We shall cut Abdali down too. We shall die but not talk the language of withdrawal.'

One by one all the nobles disappeared to hunt for a place to lie down. Mahipatrao Chitnis alone remained sitting by Bhausaheb's side. Bhausaheb was finding Shuja's treachery impossible to digest. In a burst of fury he barked, 'Pant, before you go to sleep, draft letters to all our vassals in the Antarved. Instruct them that they should not let Shuja know a moment of peace. All these provincial chieftains should raid Shuja's land and burn it down. The landlords of his own province should be subjugated by whatever means, at whatever cost. Give them cash and get them to go rioting everywhere. Issue this decree to all: complete anarchy should descend upon the land beyond the Ganga; it should go up in flames.'

At dawn, Bhausaheb set off towards the Yamuna with a band of five thousand men. Ibrahim, Shamsher, Jankoji, Malharbaba, Vinchurkar and Yashwantrao were among those riding with him. The horse-borne contingent squelched its way through the sludge to reach the bank as the sun was coming out. The four to six furlong span of the river was too wide for the eyes to take in. It was a veritable sea that had broken its embankment and run amuck. Heavy rains would have lashed the Antarved side of the river too. All hopes of leaping across to the other side had been dammed by the swollen Yamuna. Dotted right across the wide stretch could be seen innumerable whirlpools the size of giant cartwheels. Tossing and swirling inside those eddies were trees twisting and turning as if they were twigs. What kind of a pontoon bridge could ever be strung over this vast, mad, untamed water? How was it to be negotiated? There was no sign of any boat and no trace of Govindpant either.

Four floats were readied, each with two boats strung together. With a fervent prayer to god, they were pushed into the water with carrier-spies with the best swimming skills aboard, bags of scrolls tied round their waists. Despite the swirl trying to hurl them off their floats, the spies bowed to Bhausaheb with a loud 'Har Har Mahadev!' Their full-throated screams were no match for the roar of the waters, but that did not dissuade them from continuing to shout the mantra anyway. They did not know how many miles downstream they were likely to dock at the other bank, if they docked at all.

As Bhausaheb turned his horse round, he looked back one more time at the violently bobbing floats, and let his tears mingle with the rain water that was lashing his face. All his grand plans of chewing up Antarved had been washed away by the storm and the flooded river. His body had turned as stiff and heavy as his mind had. His horse Chandrasen was carefully picking its way across the slush with its mane bowed. Malharrao came up from behind and patted Bhausaheb's wet back. 'Don't worry, Bhausaheb, we will take the help of the Jaat king and find a way out.'

On reaching his tent, he threw himself listlessly on the bed with his wet clothes still on him. An anxious Parvatibai coaxed him into changing into dry ones and called the astrologer Deekshit Patankar over for help. 'What do I do, Patankarbuva?' Bhausaheb spoke in a choked voice. 'Every card I throw is getting trumped.'

'Stop worrying, Bhausaheb,' Patankar tried to assure him, 'a remedy will surely emerge from this mess. We are fairly close to the plains of the Ganga. Send instructions to your servants in those regions to send a regular supply of the water of the Ganga. Bathe in the holy water every day. Mother Ganga-Bhagirathi will not send you back south in shame.'

⚜

Bhausaheb's army was stuck twenty miles on the west side of Agra. All his plans of racing to Agra in the next two days had come to naught. The huge river that stood in the way had blocked the advance of the Maratha army. The monsoons had arrived much earlier than anticipated. The rains had beaten the stuffing out of the land, the ravines and the riverbanks, uprooting trees everywhere and converting the trails to sludge. They had also reduced Bhausaheb's strategies to slurry. He had started off from Partud expecting to clash with the enemy near the Yamuna, and before the month of Jyeshtha arrived. But nature had made a mockery of his plans. The rains had converted the sandy terrain that lay between the Chambal and the Gambhir into a knee-deep mire, and the army had got stuck in it.

Whenever there was a small respite, Bhausaheb would make a tour of the banks of the Gambhir river in the company of Ibrahim Khan, Shamsher and Malharji, and turn back each time with a heavy heart. The Gambhir was nowhere as grand as the Ganga or the Yamuna, but in its present state, it still spanned a furlong and a half. The momentum of the water was such that those who foolishly entered their horse into the stream would find the horse sucked into its whirlpool. Hence the locals had given the river the name of ghoda-pachhad, the horse-wrestler. The Maratha horses had occasionally been nudged by their riders to close in on the banks, but one look at its murderous intent, and they had backed away chastened.

Bhausaheb sat in his tent, completely focused on the work at hand, while the rain played its unrelenting drums on the roof above. The supply from the Jaats had resolved the food-and-fodder issue temporarily, but they still had a long distance to go, and there were many issues that required his unflagging attention. As he had set off for the campaign, he had dispatched his envoys and representatives to dozens of kings and royal houses, inviting them to join the Maratha forces in protecting Hindustan from foreign intruders, and the responses had been trickling in—just this morning, a pair of spies had returned from Jaipur and Bundikota. Till date, the feedback had not been heartening at all; hence, what the spies had brought back this morning hadn't surprised him, it had just turned him graver. Some of his close companions like Vishwasrao, Balwantrao, Shamsher, Mahipatrao and Tryambak Sadashiv sat with him. He finished off his fourth letter and kept the quill aside. He looked up to find that Vishwasrao looked very grim.

'Rao Saheb,' he addressed him with half a smile playing upon his lips, 'you look very anxious.'

'Kakasaheb, how many people have you written to till now? Whom all have you invited to join you?'

'To everyone whose name came to my mind, to friends and to enemies—to Hindupat of Bundelkhand, Madho Singh and Bijesingh of Rajputana, to the Rathods of Jaipur, the Rana of Bundikota, Khechikar of Bhopal, in fact, even to Kamaal-ud-din Babi of faraway Gujarat.'

'And your envoys even now sit twiddling their thumbs in these many courts! Why haven't any of them shown the courtesy to respond? Hasn't my grandfather, the great Bajirao Peshwa done a few good turns to Bundelkhand? How is it that Hindupat should stand up against us today? After all, the Marathas do consider themselves as long-ago descendants of the Rajputs and Rajput lineages, don't they?'

'That's true. The great Chhatrapati Shivaji himself belonged to the Sisodia lineage.'

'Then, why don't these Rajput Ranas come to our help during our time of need? Why don't they at least respond to your missives?'

'Oh, the responses come, they have come. But Vishwasrao, during these difficult times, each one of them is doing some close calculations—who is likely to win, who is likely to lose. Without a major win in a major confrontation, they are not likely to run to us with help.'

'But, Bhausaheb, despite Abdali being a foreigner, the Rohillas and the Pathans of the trans-Ganga region have gathered under his banner. Why, then, can't the Rajput kings gather under ours?'

'You and I are paying for the sins that we have committed earlier.'

'What sins would the Marathas have committed for which they are paying the price today, Kakasaheb?'

'Rao Saheb, what has gone wrong before is our entire policy relating to northern Hindustan. Our forces would sit on the chests of these Rajput kings to collect tributes. The story of the king of Bundikota is particularly heart-rending. The sister of Savai Jaising of Jaipur was the queen of Bundikota. Her step-son occupied the throne, and she had immense influence on the king. She helped him run the kingdom with the help of her brother Savai Jaising. For some reason, sister and brother had a falling out, and the sister ran for help to the Shinde-Holkars. Our sardars got her to shell out six-hundred thousand rupees before setting off to help her.

'We Marathas consider the kingdom of Udaipur as the epitome of religious and national pride. This is one house that has never offered its daughters to the Delhi kings as appeasement. Our Peshwa Bajirao paid a visit to this kingdom and was felicitated in court in the presence of thousands of courtiers. Rao Saheb displayed his reverence to the throne of Mewad and sat next to it. He bowed his head to the holy throne that had once been graced by Rana Pratap.'

'He was a great man, my grandfather,' said Vishwasrao.

'However proud these stories make us feel, Vishwasrao, we Marathas showed no generosity in the matter of extracting money out of our friends. Seventy thousand in cash were immediately gathered as tribute, and a revenue share of a hundred-and-sixty thousand per year was imposed upon them.

'In the Jaipur war of succession too, our policy was deeply flawed. Ishwarsingh, the eldest son of Jaisingh, laid claim to the throne, while the younger son Madho Singh demanded half the inheritance. Ranojibaba was lured by a vast sum of money into siding with Ishwarsingh, while the younger bought Malharbaba over with a bait of two-hundred thousand. The two brothers fought, and Madho Singh was defeated. He reached out to Pune for help. Attracted by the a hundred-and-fifty thousand he had to offer, the Peshwa changed sides, and put up a charade of bringing about rapprochement between the two brothers and imposed heavy tributes on both. Accordingly, Malharbaba reached Jaipur to collect the tribute from Ishwarsingh. The already enervated Ishwarsingh lost heart.

He was so terrified and so disgusted with life that one night he managed to procure a poisonous cobra from a snake-charmer. He closed the doors of his chamber, got into bed with the snake and provoked it to bite him. His four queens also preferred the bite of a cobra to the bites of the Marathas. This happened ten years ago. You may say that their blue corpses are symbols of the faulty Maratha policies.'

The story sent cold shivers down Vishwasrao's spine. 'Kakasaheb,' he asked, 'is it because of this incident that Madho Singh became our enemy? Is this why he preferred to go with Abdali?'

'Malharbaba turned over the throne vacated by Ishwarsingh to Madho Singh. The new king was ready to pay a million rupees as tribute for this favour, but our hunger was insatiable. We got after him to give us as annual tribute at least one-fourth of the revenue collections, if not one-third. From then on Madho Singh turned more and more bitter. He tried a couple of times to assassinate the Marathi sardars, but failed. It then happened that about four-thousand Marathas arrived in Jaipur for sight-seeing, and Madho Singh saw his opportunity. He hosted a lavish lunch for them and had all the gates closed at noon. The Rajput soldiers and the citizens of Jaipur then launched a murderous assault on the Maratha soldiers, and a blood-bath ensued. Barely seventy-eight of the four thousand managed to escape somehow, many with bleeding and broken limbs. Our earlier sins had converted Madho Singh into a sworn enemy. It was our behaviour that sent him into the lap of the Rohillas and the arms of Abdali.'

'This means that we cannot expect any support from the Rajput kings,' said Balwantrao.

'That's what the messages to us till date suggest. We have been steadily forgetting Shivaji's principle that collecting revenue from a region comes with the responsibility of the welfare of the subjects of that region. Look at the image that the people of Hindustan have of the Marathas today. For a fistful of grain, they are willing to place a knife on somebody's throat, kill for material gains and make life miserable for the ordinary people. For the people here, there is no difference, really, between the Pathans and the Marathas.'

'But Bhausaheb,' interjected Shamsher, 'the message circulating here is that we have set off to protect Delhi from the foreigners.'

'Even if that is true, will the ghosts of our past abandon us? They stick to us like our shadows. Our path now lies through the thorns that we laid out earlier, and the pain will be substantial. Circumstances have turned so convoluted now that withdrawal too is out of the question. Shuja has gone, the Rajput Ranas refuse to come, the feudal lords are turning their backs. It's a lonely furrow we have to cut. These are bad times for gathering companions.'

'The Jaats continue to be with us, though,' said Shamsher. 'They are the ones who have kept us supplied with food and fodder.'

'It's our good fortune that Surajmal Jaat continues to be on our side, despite the departure of Shuja,' laughed Bhausaheb.

There was one king backing Bhausaheb's enterprise. When his son Khanderao had fallen during the siege of Kumbheri, Malharbaba had sworn that he would uproot Kumbheri and toss it in the Yamuna. This animosity for the Jaats had certainly subsided in the past two or three years. In fact, it was to Jaat shelter the Holkars and Shindes had run after their latest confrontation with Abdali. Although Malharbaba was not the forgiving and forgetting kind, he had found the strength to change his attitude and close the distance with the Jaats. It was he who had created the link between the empire and the Jaats, and this was a matter of great satisfaction to Bhausaheb.

'Mahipatrao, issue this proclamation and circulate it in the army: once we cross the Gambhir river, we will be in Jaat territory. When this happens, there should be no disturbance, no harassment, no arson and pillage in any of the villages or hamlets. Anybody indulging in mischief will be severely punished.'

When the Holkar deewaan Gangoba Tatya Chandrachud and the Shinde administrator Ramji Anant Dabholkar noticed that there were no Holkars or Shindes present in Bhausaheb's office, they went to the tent and sought his audience. 'Of course let them in,' said Bhausaheb. 'They are not merely administrators of our sardars, they are as much officials of the empire.'

The strikingly fair Gangoba Tatya took his seat opposite Bhausaheb, while Ramjipant sat next to him after looking around with flustered eyes. 'We got the news that as administrators, you tried very hard to arrange for a meeting between us and Abdali in the Jaat territory,' Bhausaheb began. 'You also met Hafeez Khan a month ago, we have heard.'

'That's true, but our efforts didn't bear fruit,' Gangoba responded.

'How could they? After all, the pawn Najeeb, who was chosen to speak on behalf of Abdali, and for whose safety and security the entire conference was intended, how could he ever be acceptable to us? Anyway, speak, what urgent matter brings you here?'

Gangoba laughed and said, 'We have come with a request.'

'Yes, what is it?'

'Bhausaheb, you should not cross the Gambhir and pointlessly put your life at risk. We will take care of vanquishing Abdali. If you wish, we will chop his legs and offer them to you as our homage.'

'Hmm. What have you got to say, Ramjipant?'

'I agree with Tatya. Your life is much too valuable to be exposed to pointless risk. Give us the responsibility and we will it see through.'

'You mean, you two will confront Abdali with the forces of the Shindes and the Holkars?'

'No, it's not quite that,' they said in unison. 'You and Vishwasrao should stay behind, and hand your army over to us.'

'Aha! You don't want us two, but you want the army?' Bhausaheb laughed. 'Well, where is the point in discussing things that will not happen? Talk about something else.'

Gangoba and Ramji fell silent as if they had suddenly got blisters in their mouths, and after a while, they took their leave.

Bhausaheb's face suddenly turned grave. He signalled to Shamsher to stay behind while the others trooped out. 'Shamsher,' Bhausaheb began, 'there's this riddle I have not been able to solve. Since the time we left Gwalior, this Gangoba has been chanting that we should stay behind and not get into Hindustan. He came for the second time today with the same request. We had talked and come to a consensus on this with our sardars Shinde and Holkar, and they never brought it up again. Why, then, should their managers continue to play the same stupid game?'

'What do you mean?'

'There is a drip somewhere. Keep these two under observation. Set spies on them to find out who they are talking to, the places they visit, the way they conduct themselves, and so on. Man is a strange creature, Shamsher, you simply don't know who will behave how and when.'

❂

Exploiting the opportunity of a clear sky, Bhausaheb, Surajmal Jaat, Shamsher Bahadur, Yashwantrao Pawar, Malharbaba and others set off with their retinue. There were servants around them, holding parasols over their masters' heads. Suddenly the sky darkened again and it started raining, rendering the parasols useless. The grandees were soaked to the bone in no time. Their brocaded attires stuck to their skin. The land along the riverbank had big pockets of trapped water, and the horses were wading through it, tongues hanging out a foot, and with their bellies touching the water. After reaching a raised patch of land, Bhausaheb brought Chandrasen to a halt. The horses of the other nobles clustered around to find whatever space they could squeeze into. Bhausaheb's eyes surveyed the distance between the retinue and the other bank of the Yamuna. He said to Surajmal Jaat, 'Raja Saheb, do you think a small boat or a dingy can cross over to the other side?'

'Bhausaheb, not a single boat has crossed these waters in the past seven days. If somebody tries, he is certainly inviting a watery grave.'

'What news from the other side?'

'We are locking horns, to the extent we can, with Abdali. When the enemy left Ramgadh to move to Anupshahar, our troops conquered Ramgadh. It's only a week back that Abdali's pressure slackened. We sent a good two-thousand barrel-chested men across by boat, and despite a heavy downpour, our braves captured all the posts in the surrounding areas.'

'Raja Saheb, how different this northern scenario is from the one in the south! Your rivers are not so much rivers as the sea broken loose. Such invincible armies we possess, but a river blocks our way, and we become legless!'

Bhausaheb was happy that at least the Jaat king Surajmal had reached out on his own to help him. The Jaat territory was spread all over Mathura. To the north was the boundary of Delhi; to the south was the bank of the Chambal; to the west was the frontier land of Jaipur; and to the east lay the Yamuna bank. In the middle was the Jaat territory. If one travelled from the south towards Delhi, the road from the Chambal river to Delhi would pass through the land of the Jaats. The Jaat kings considered themselves to be of the Yadav lineage. The holy places of Mathura, Goghat and Dwarka were the pride of Jaatland. Gopal Jaat, an ancestor of Raja Surajmal, had resisted Aurangzeb for many years. It was with great difficulty that Aurangzeb had finally managed to capture and kill him. The rebellion ended with the death of a successor, King Bhajja Singh Jaat. Badansingh was another valiant king born among the Jaats, who captured Mathura and Agra and gave himself the title of Vajra-raj. Badansingh's son Surajmal was particularly heroic. He conquered Bharatpur and made it his capital city. Surajmal's father Badansingh had three hundred wives and twenty-seven other sons from them. The place of honour among all the princes, however, belonged clearly to Surajmal, and he had established it firmly through the strategic use of power.

While setting off from the south, Bhausaheb had had doubts about how enthusiastic the Jaats would be to join forces with the Marathas, but the changing political landscape had left the Jaats no alternative but to shake hands with them. In his previous raid, Abdali had gone on an unrestrained pillage of Mathura and Vrindawan, reducing an affluent, flourishing kingdom to utter destitution. This time round too, Abdali had not spared them. His forces had brought the Aligarh and Ramgadh forts down at the very first shot and razed all their trans-Yamuna posts to the ground. If the primary intention of these foreign intruders was to collect a booty of diamonds and rubies, there was no way they would return without marauding the kingdom of the Jaats. Delhi had already been done and dusted, and there wouldn't be much to gain from the smaller fries in the neighbourhood. Shuja-ud-dowlah's land was too far away, while the Jaats were next door to Delhi. The horses that the Delhiites brought to the Yamuna for a wash would often cross over to the other bank and chew up the standing crop from Jaat fields, while the Delhi washermen would hang their clothes out to dry on Jaat fences.

Abdali had been getting information that Bhausaheb was going all-out to entice the kingdoms of Hindustan, and so he had made his own moves to woo Surajmal. But Surajmal was wary, and didn't see much benefit in joining with Abdali. He would have the privilege of rubbing shoulders with royalty, but in the end, he would be left picking up the tab for their food and fodder. Having been used before, Surajmal had no desire for any friendship with Abdali. Besides, there was Najeeb Khan, who would not think twice before breaking every Jaat bone to fill up Abdali's coffers and his own.

His relationship with the Marathas had been steadily improving for the past four months. Neither party was likely to forget the bitter memories of the Kumbheri conflict, but it was to the Jaats that Jankoji Shinde and Malharbaba Holkar had run for shelter when Abdali was giving them the chase. Surajmal and his favourite queen Hansiya had given them personal attention. The queen, true to her name Hansiya, the ever-smiling one, had been particularly kind and considerate towards Dattaji's widow Bhagirathi. She had political shrewdness, but she was philanthropic too. When the Marathas were refusing to lift the siege of Kumbheri, she had advised that an envoy be sent to win over Ranoji by acknowledging him as an elder brother. She had the astuteness required to bring about a rift between the Shindes and the Holkars. Later, when Malharbaba had seen the hospitality provided to them as refugees in the Bharatpur Palace, he had remarked, 'It's not enough to say that she is just a hospitable Jaat housewife. To my eyes, she is the quintessential Maratha housewife dressed in a nine-yard saree, serving her guests with affection and diligence.'

It had been a matter of routine for the Maratha forces moving from south to north to pillage the villages and destroy the standing crops on their way. Surajmal had sent a letter to Bhausaheb, requesting that his armies be restrained, and in return he would willingly provide them with food and fodder. He had also dispatched carts of grains and other essentials along with the missive as a token of his intent. In response, Bhausaheb had honoured the generosity of the Jaats and issued strict instructions that his forces should in no way cause harm to Jaat people and property. He knew this spirit of cordiality would stand him in good stead in the war that was to come. He had taken two steps to Surajmal's one to welcome the Jaats as friends. And now he was pleased to have the heavy-built, thick-whiskered, bulbous-eyed Jaat king Surajmal riding with him in these heavy rains. The former wazeer of Delhi, Ghaziuddin, after being driven away, had found shelter in the Agra Fort, where he was recovering from cold and fever. 'What news of the great wazeer,' Bhausaheb asked. 'How is he doing?'

'He's a little under the weather, but quite happy and content. The very man he had nurtured, that Najeeb, looted his caravan and drove him away from his seat. With Bhausaheb having arrived now in person, he is delighted, He now believes better days are round the corner.'

'Being delighted is fine, but the seriousness with which he should have run the empire, that gravity your friend does not possess. On the contrary, he is being reviled as the wazeer who plotted the murder of two kings through treachery, and abandoned Delhi at the news of Abdali's arrival.'

'What you say is quite true too. He is that kind of person, but Bhausaheb, I believe that he will improve under the influence of a generous and principled person like you.'

'Well said,' said Gangoba Tatya.

'Gangoba, don't talk, and concentrate on your horse. It is getting pasted with slush. You get stuck, and you will hold us all back.'

When all the horses had arrived at the high patch of land, Bhausaheb called out, 'Shamsher!'

'Yes, Bhausaheb!'

'Check how many boats there are at the bank. It will be tough rowing to Delhi against the current. It isn't easy to pull them to the bank either, but get as many pulled out as you can and start moving towards Delhi. As many boats as you can spot from Mathura onwards, have them all head towards Delhi slowly and steadily. I am assigning Yashwantrao Pawar and Damaji Gayakwad to help you with this. Gather as many boats and boatmen as you can and enter the neighbourhood of Delhi. Put posts on every track that leads to and from the banks.'

The sardars bowed before Bhausaheb Sadashivrao and instantly set off to implement the orders. Surajmal Jaat was nonplussed at the instructions; Malharbaba was bemused too. Surajmal couldn't suppress his curiosity and asked, 'What is your lordship's strategy? I'm quite confused.'

'What strategy now? We just have to stick our chests out and launch an attack straight at Delhi.'

'Attack Delhi?' Surajmal asked, surprised.

'Absolutely!' responded Bhausaheb. 'Look, the waters of the Yamuna are not likely to subside for another three months, which means that neither Abdali can cross over to this bank, nor can we cross over to that. Hence, it makes more sense to move the forces towards Delhi than to let them stay rotting here. If we can win Delhi, the morale of our soldiers will rise, to say the least. It is my desire to see the Maratha flag flutter atop the Delhi Fort in a fortnight's time.'

While the assembled nobility felt their chests swelling at Bhausaheb's forceful rhetoric, Surajmal was perplexed. 'Bhausaheb,' he said humbly, 'it doesn't look right for a small person to talk big; after all you are the lord of all Hindustan, while I am merely a small landlord, but I consider it my duty to alert you to facts as I see them. All over Hindustan you are regarded as a conqueror, but your opponent's reputation is greater. Go ahead if you have to, but do so with the minimum baggage. Leave your heavier guns behind, either inside the Gwalior Fort or in any of the burrows in Kumbheri or Bharatpur.'

'What you say makes sense,' Bhausaheb replied, 'but I don't know why I have immense faith in my artillery. If the balustrades of Delhi have to be brought down, how will mere muskets help? We must carry with us cannons that can blast the eardrums with their power. I have great faith in Ibrahim Khan's guns.'

'In other words, Bhausaheb,' queried Malharbaba, 'you want to fight your battle the Mughal way?'

'Well, no, I don't want to fight altogether the Mughal way, but I do want to use my French cannons.'

'But, Bhausaheb,' pleaded Surajmal, 'what are you going to do with the huge number of freebooters accompanying your forces? I apologize for speaking frankly, but these crowds will rise against you earlier than your enemies can. You must leave them behind.'

The moment the fellow-travellers were brought into the picture, Bhausaheb's shoulders sagged, his passion leaked away. Turning a morose face towards Surajmal, he responded, 'Raja Saheb, you have hit the nail on the head. Twice before this, I tried to din sense into these pilgrims, but failed miserably. Their obsession with religion is so maniacal among our people that sense and reason don't stand a chance. You are absolutely right when you say that this obsession with religion hurts practical matters. In our country, when a thorn penetrates the heel and settles there, we call it kuroop, a corn. It gets so embedded that you can neither walk nor pull it out. All these pilgrims are corns that have got into our heels, and we have to step very carefully. However, in all other circumstances, we will have to hand these travellers to you another day.'

'But why, again, do you want to stake your own life?' piped in Gangoba Tatya. 'You stay behind here with these pilgrims and hand your forces over to us. We will do the conquering.'

'Gangoba,' Bhausaheb responded with asperity, 'you can't handle even your own administrative affairs and talk of wielding the sword and go around distributing unsolicited wisdom! I am no petty trader to sit here and send my army to do the fighting. A shopkeeper may sit in one place and manage a shop in some other place, the general of an army cannot.'

Looking at Bhausaheb's fury, Gangoba broke into cold sweat. The other nobles too were taken aback. Bhausaheb continued in a rasping tone, 'Gangoba, I don't know why but some people don't want that I head towards Delhi. I cannot break away from this army and live. I shall fight with them and I shall die with them.'

※

Shamsher and Yashwantrao instantly got busy with their assignment. A count began for the number of boats on their side of the Yamuna. Efforts began to work out strategies to pull the small boats out of the water. With constant submersion in the water, the wood of the boats had swollen. They had become so heavy that the ropes used to pull them out would keep snapping. The slush on the bank would cause the boats to skid and slip. Some of Shamsher's ablest and strongest men were bending their backs in the effort. With mud everywhere, getting a firm foothold in the earth was near impossible.

It turned dark. The reflections of the battlements and minarets of the Agra Fort began to disappear from the water. After three batches pitching in their all without a break since the afternoon, merely three small boats had been dragged out of the water. In the darkness, the water-soaked boats looked like fearsome creatures of the deep that had been stranded out of their natural habitat. What was one to do with them now? Was it at all possible to row them against the current all the way to Delhi? With the banks more than knee deep in sludge and potted with puddles all the way, they could not be dragged along the bank either. Shamsher and Yashwantrao felt their heads spinning, quite like the logs of wood that swirled round and round, trapped in the many whirlpools they had seen in the river.

ॐ

23 June 1760. Abdali had pitched his tents in an elevated spot on the northern bank of the Ganga. The security guards of the camp, toting flaming torches in their hands, looked like dread creatures from hell as they patrolled round the emperor's pavilion in the dark. Ten or twelve loaded cannons always stood in readiness round his pavilion. No tired gunner had the temerity to let his head droop the tiniest bit, despite the invitation offered by the cool breeze from the river. Naked swords glittered in the light of the torches. The bank afforded them only a narrow strip, causing the army to spread out along the length of the river. The lights of the torches on the banks twinkled on the Ganga water. The reflection of the army tents too could be seen dimly dancing on the waves. The commander of the army, Shah Pasand Khan had laid a tight security ring around the camp. When he set out with about fifty Ghaznavi and Kohati bodyguards to check on the alertness of the guards, the men would shiver in fear.

Three months ago, they had parked in Aligarh-Ramgadh. The posts at Ramgadh were rather strong, and Abdali's army had had to work hard at winning them from the Jaat fort-keeper Durjansal. The battlements of the Ramgadh Fort were strong too, but with fifty or sixty thousand men and around forty thousand horses and mules to look after, a good waterbody nearby was imperative. Also, with such a vast number of men and animals defecating and urinating, health issues were bound to crop up. Those three months of stay at Aligarh had created an unbearable stink in the air. In direct contrast was this new spot where they now had to see the monsoons through. The huge Ganga was flowing close by. The spot where the army laid its camp was comfortably elevated, and it was serviced by strong winds and allowed the rain water to drain out instantly, leaving neither stink nor puddles.

Strategically too this was a well-placed location. On the west flowed the Yamuna; it would be impossible for the Marathas to cross the rain-swollen river. Besides, the land of Shuja and the Rohillas was close by; food and fodder could be procured from there without any problem.

King Ahmad Shah Abdali sat reading some documents in the dim light of a lamp with nobody for company except his Wazeer Shah Wali Khan. When he finished reading, the wazeer said, 'Jahaan-panaah, you would certainly have finished reading the missive from Madho Singh.'

'Yes, of course, wazeer,' laughed the king. 'I can stop worrying about Rajputana now. What bothers me is the Sikhs and the Punjab. There are some hot-blooded youngsters there.'

'Huzoor, you should stop worrying about the Punjab. It is true that it has a few hot-heads like Allajat. I too had this fear of the Sikhs and the Marathas coming together. There is some affection between the Hindus and the Marathas, true. But earlier, too, the Marathas had established a few posts in the Punjab. They ruled and exploited their subjects there. The Sikhs don't want anything to do with the Marathas now. Besides, at this moment, I cannot see any Maratha leader who has the capability to crossover to the Punjab and win over the Sikhs.'

'That's a great comfort, Shah Wali. Read Madho Singh's latest letter out to me now.'

Shah Wali undid the knot of the silk pouch, pulled out the scroll and began reading:

'Refuge of the World, benefactor of Hindustan, scion of the Sadozai clan, Ahmad Shah Durrani Saheb, Madho Singh bows before you. In obedience to your lordship's instructions, I have sent letters in every direction. The Rajput Ranas from Mewar, Marwad, Jodhpur and Jaipur, all of them have sworn their commitment to you. We are taking care that not one of them will extend even a finger to the Marghattas. Dattaji's nephew Jankoji and the deposed wazeer of Delhi, Imad-ul-Mulk, had visited a month ago, with Jankoji pressing hard to persuade us to join up with the Marathas. He sought forgiveness for earlier mistakes and reminded us of being Hindustanis, and so on, but we did not pay any attention to his talks. The Marghatta Sambashiva's envoys are still parked in the town, hopes still flickering. We too have left them hanging with their hopes so that the simple-minded Sadashivrao will continue to wait. We are beholden to the

affection of the Supreme King of the World, which is surely the reward for the good deeds of our ancestors.'

Emperor Abdali felt a pleasurable sensation spread through him. Shah Wali paused and said, 'May I be permitted to ask a question, huzoor?'

'By all means.'

'This brother of the Peshwa, Sadashiv, has been moving upwards with a huge army. The news is that they have already crossed Malwa, and will be touching Agra in a few days' time. With him steadily moving northwards, why has your lordship allowed the Rajputs to stay on in their palaces instead of ordering them to join you here along with their forces?'

'That would be a foolish thing to do, Shah Wali. You don't know this Sadashiv well enough. I have been collecting information about this man for a long time. He is brave, resilient and courageous, and in spite of being a Maratha, he has a sharp mind. If the rajas of Rajputana were to be called over here with their armies, he would instantly move into Rajputana and get the entire region under his control. As a result, our battle will have to be fought around Jaipur. The Marathas would then have their supplies coming from Gujarat and Malwa. That wouldn't suit us at all because we would be sucked far away from our own supply sources in the flourishing land of the Rohilla-Pathans. It's so much better that we meet Bhau in the vicinity of Delhi. He would then be surrounded on three sides by the land of the Rohillas, Najeeb and Shuja, and that would make the battle very difficult for him. Why dissuade the animal away from entering into the cave?'

Shah Wali Khan was impressed by the emperor's war strategy.

'Shah Wali,' said the emperor, 'write this letter for Madho Singh.'

'As you wish, huzoor.'

'We are delighted at the love you bear for Hindustan. We are grateful for the manner in which you have organized things at Rajputana. Your service and your esteem for us will be duly rewarded. Once the war is over, we shall re-set the clock of Hindustan. Exercise great caution in one matter: that Malharba Holkar is a very dangerous man. Rajputana is a land he knows well; you won't even know when he mounts a raid on you. Be very careful of that man's movements. We have received news that the demon named Sadashivrao is moving towards Agra. To the extent possible, plant secret posts of soldiers in

his way. Harass him by creating obstacles all along. He should be exhausted before he finally clashes with us. We have stayed on in Hindustan despite the murderous summer. Our feet will remain planted through the monsoons too. When winter comes after the rains, we shall all go to the southern land. We shall enter the houses of our enemies and drive them out. We shall give you permanent liberation from the menace of these Marathas.'

Once the dictation was over, Abdali crinkled his eye-brows and asked, 'Shah Wali, what's the news from Najeeb and Jahaan Khan?'

'I have already brought your lordship abreast of the information we received two days ago. Although the tug-of-war between the Marathas and our envoys continues in the Lakhnau court, victory shall certainly be ours.'

'Don't speak in ifs-and-buts. What is the actual situation?'

'Shuja shall join us.'

'But when? That infidel Sadashiv has been getting stronger by leaps and bounds. We have received intelligence that the Jaats have been providing supplies to his men and animals.'

'This is bad news, huzoor!'

'The really bad news is still to come. If the Yamuna hadn't been kind, that Satan would have entered Ayodhya and Shuja would then have joined the Maratha forces. Shuja is not dependable. This entire Hindustan belongs to the infidels. This slow pace is not going to help us at all. You have to stay alert all the time, Shah Wali!'

As the king and his wazeer were locked in discussion, a servant entered to announce the arrival of Najeeb. The king signalled for the man to be allowed in immediately, and a tired Najeeb made his entry. Abdali pointed at the mattress for Najeeb to sit on and threw a piercing look at him. Najeeb laughed and said, 'Lord of the World, please abandon all your worries.'

'Give us the details.'

'Huzoor, Shuja-ud-dowlah will join us.'

'Wonderful! But where is he right now?'

'He is coming behind us.'

'Meaning?'

'He couldn't be more than ten or fifteen miles behind us.'

'But how did you come ahead like a wedding guest? The guest has arrived and the bridegroom on his horse is still trailing?'

'Lord of the World, Shuja is still wary of your lordship. He wants a copy of the Koran and a written guarantee that there will be no treachery.'

'Give it to him, then! Allah alone knows how many more assurances we shall have to give to get this anti-Maratha alliance in place. Send another letter of promise to him.'

'With pleasure, huzoor.'

'Najeeb, I killed that Dattaji and drove Malhar away; so, what remains now? However valiant my soldiers may be, they are people with wives and families! They have been stuck here for six months now, let them go back to their clansmen.'

'Lord of the World, the death of one or two chieftains is not enough to drive the Marathas away. With you gone, we will be reduced to the state of an elephant with a broken spine. Please do not worry about wealth and food and fodder. Whatever you desire shall be procured. Once the campaign is over, we the Afghans of Hindustan will be true to our salt. We'll fill sacks upon sacks with gold coins, we willl distribute diamonds and rubies in charity.'

'Najeeb, I still have some faith left in you. Don't betray us after this battle is over.'

☙❦❧

18 July 1760. Abdali's army was in the midst of unprecedented merrymaking. The emperor who had placed an embargo on the playing of musical instruments had removed all restrictions for the evening. Trumpets and oboes and bassett-horns were blown, drums and other percussion instruments made the air thrum, Qawwals had assembled in large numbers to sing Sufi poetry. The court was due to assemble in the afternoon, where the Nawab of Ayodhya Shuja-ud-dowlah would be given a royal welcome. Najeeb had stationed himself five miles from the venue, while Abdali's son Taimur stood three miles away.

For Shuja, the relief of having finally decided which way to go meant something. A great weight had been lifted from over his heart when he had received the letter of guarantee from Abdali, complete with his peacock seal, that he would be treated with fairness and dignity. He had thought things ten times over as he left Faizabad with four thousand horsemen and twenty small guns to meet Abdali. Once the decision to join him was taken, what would be the obstacles he would have to face in the future? Was it all that easy to break connection with the Marathas? They were well known for their courage and daredevilry. What if they got it into their heads to challenge the might of the flooded Ganga-Yamuna and succeeded? While he would be celebrating in Abdali's court, they would have lined up their cannons against the battlements of his palace. The thought made Shuja's stomach churn. Today Abdali was in Hindustan, and circumstances favoured all this fun and frolic. But tomorrow when he returned to his own land, would the Marathas let him breathe in peace? Keeping a possible Maratha raid in mind, he had erected defensive pickets along the western border of his kingdom, and had left the main army of Ayodhya in charge of his son Mirza Amani Asaf-ud-dowlah and his friend Raja Beni Bahadur, with instruction that there should be round-the-clock patrolling of the city walls. His mother Begum Sadr-un-nisa was to keep an eye on the affairs of the state like a hawk.

The noblemen closest to Abdali had taken their seats on mattresses covered with soft velvet. Among them were Wazeer Shah Wali Khan, commander-in-chief of the Army Shah Pasand Khan, General Jahaan Khan, Sardar Noor-ud-din, Barkhurdar Khan, Abdullah Khan, Saadullah Khan, Dundey Khan and Ahmad Khan Bangash. It was a rich mix of native and foreign grandees. They all looked resplendent in their brocades. The triumphant expression on their faces suggested that with the arrival of Shuja-ud-dowlah, the battle had already been won; all that was left was to carry the Maratha corpses to the cremation ground. When Shuja came near, Abdali got up from his seat with delight, and with a loud cry of 'Welcome, son!' he gathered Shuja in a tight embrace. Shuja responded with equal fervor. Two cannons were fired on cue and musical instruments began to be played. The festivities in the court had begun. Abdali gifted him with rolls of the highest quality of richly brocaded silk, velvet and broadcloth. A garland strung with a thousand-and-one gold coins was placed round his neck. A dagger and a sword, their hilts embedded with precious stones, were presented to him, as also a richly caparisoned elephant. The whisper that was doing the rounds among the Iranian and Kandahari troopers was that no other king had received such a grand welcome at the hands of their emperor. Ahmad Shah Abdali declared in a loud voice, 'Till now I believed that I had only one son in Taimur. But I realized later that I have another son, in Hindustan, and his name is Shuja-ud-dowlah.' The extraordinary welcome accorded to Shuja was received with awe by the assembled noblemen. There was a large gold plate in front of the emperor, with something kept tantalizingly covered in a piece of velvet. It had become a subject of curiosity among all who saw it. Abdali walked towards the plate, and again addressed the audience. 'Crusaders of Iran and Hindustan,' he said, 'the throne of Hindustan, which has had such a glorious history, appears to be lying vacant. Shah Alam, whom we had declared as the emperor of Hindustan, that unfortunate man is wandering homeless in some jungle of Bengal on the other side of Patna. But we have with us here his partner in governance.'

He paused dramatically, pulled the velvet cover off the plate, and revealed an aigrette studded with rubies and emeralds winking in the light of the chandeliers hanging from the room. Lifting the aigrette from the gold tray, he lifted the ornament so that all could see. Walking towards Shuja, he said, 'My valiant friends, I am no lying Sadashiv Bhau to write letters of false promises to Shuja-ud-dowlah. This aigrette is not of paper, but of the costliest gems that money could procure. We present this ornament to the gallant Nawab in this durbar and declare him the wazeer of Hindustan.' Trumpets and drums broke out in celebration and the court resounded with claps and shouts of congratulations. But the hero of the celebration shook his head and, lifting his hands in refusal, cried, 'No, Lord of the World, please do not give me this aigrette of the Wazeer of Hindustan.'

Abdali was stunned. 'Why? Have I done something wrong?'

'No, your lordship. I am trully grateful for the honour you have bestowed upon me today, but please don't give me this aigrette. Whose wazeer will I be, after all? If you were to occupy the throne of Delhi, I would happily serve as your wazeer. Hindustan today has a throne, but no emperor, and where the emperor is, there is no throne. Such being the circumstances, please do not confer upon me the robes of the wazeer and save me from an endless sea of troubles.'

When Abdali saw the state to which Shuja had been reduced, he immediately withdrew. Shrewd as he was, he deftly distracted the attention of the flustered nobles towards other things with his pleasant talk. Soon the company got involved in light-hearted conversation. Just as the mood had warmed up, a courier came with a scroll and respectfully handed it to the emperor. As Abdali read it, those present couldn't help noticing his face turn grave.

Abdali looked up and said, 'My nobles and sardars are assembled in this court, and therefore I shall not keep this important piece of intelligence concealed from them. The news is not particularly heartening, yet I believe I should share it with you all. Sadashiv Bhau reached Agra four days back where that wretched Raja Surajmal Jaat welcomed him. As they could not find any way of crossing the Yamuna, they both have left Agra and begun advancing towards Delhi.'

The gathering turned cold. A blight descended upon the merrymaking. Najeeb's face was pitch-dark as he said, 'Lord of the World, I had been alerting you all along about how treacherous the Marathas can be, and how hell-bent they are on destroying Islam, but you weren't entirely convinced. This move only confirms my beliefs.'

'All right, Najeeb, this is no time for getting into arguments,' replied Abdali. 'We'll have to ensure that our army reaches Delhi before them. We'll set off towards Delhi at the first opportunity that the Yamuna allows us. I consider today as a day of happy coincidence. It was the Nawabs of Ayodhya who, with their conquest, consecrated the land of Hindustan. By the grace of Allah, a scion of that very family, Nawab Shuja-ud-dowlah, is present here at this hour of our need. He knows the lanes and by-lanes of this land better than anyone else. I instruct him to set off for Delhi this very evening. He should examine every inch of the Yamuna bank for places from where a crossing can be made. If no point is spotted for us to cross, he should identify a spot opposite Delhi where our army can be assembled on this side of the Yamuna. I too propose to set off at the crack of dawn. The prestige of Hindustan resides in Delhi, and we shall not let it fall to the Marathas at any cost.'

'Lord of the World,' Shuja responded, 'I happily accept the aigrette for this responsibility, and I shall fulfill it with dispatch.'

The durbar had suddenly turned anxious. Shah Wali Khan spoke in a tone of conciliation, 'Refuge of the World, if Hafeez Rahmat Khan can bring about truce with the Maratha forces, my humble opinion is that we should accept it. Our men have been away from their homes for upwards of seven months, and they keep asking me when they will return to Kandahar. The greatest of warriors have taken recourse to compromise, and I am sure there is no reason to feel small on account of it.'

Abdali turned his wazeer's suggestion over and over in his mind. He then looked at the desperate faces of his foreign soldiers and said, 'Look, I have no objection to a deal. I shall be happy to accept an honourable compromise if it can be arrived at. It is not proper to entangle the army in a race for dominance and abandon one's responsibilities towards one's home country for months and months on end. If an honourable agreement can be reached, why not?'

'I am in agreement with Your Highness,' said Shuja-ud-dowlah.

While these opinions were being exchanged, Najeeb's face had been turning darker and darker. 'What are all these deals and agreements?' he finally shrieked. 'Merely a few lines scratched out on a piece of paper. Lord of the World, I fall at your feet a thousand times. The misfortune of this Najeeb is that nobody else has been able to understand the Marghattas as well as I have. When the emperor's horse turns its face towards Kandahar after signing a deal, even before the ink on the paper has dried, these very same Marathas will turn upon the Rohilla-Pathans of Hindustan and shred them to bits. Rivers of blood will flow, copies of the Koran will be set aflame, Islam shall be wiped out for ever from these parts. There is only one Pathan emperor in the world—that's you, huzoor. If you care for the honour of Islam and us believers, oh emperor, you will have to abandon this defeatist talk of agreements. Let there be one last and final battle. Let the wicked, sinning, greedy monkeys from the south be taught one final lesson.'

ॐ

Surajmal had made wonderful arrangements for Bhausaheb in Mathura. Mathura was the equivalent of Kashi for the Jaats, one of the leading pilgrim spots of Hindustan. The Jaats had constructed four big palaces there. They considered themselves as belonging to the clan of the Yadavas, they drew a direct line of descent from Shri Krishna himself, hence Mathura held a special place in their hearts. One of the palaces was reserved for Bhausaheb and Vishwasrao, while the other three accommodated all the other nobles.

While setting off from Agra, the thought that their next stop would be Mathura itself had overjoyed the pilgrims in Bhausaheb's entourage. Even the soldiers and troopers were thrilled. Even as the spires and domes of the temples began rising on the distant horizon, the devout travellers, the soldiery included, could hear the sweet notes of Krishna's flute come towards them, floating in the air. Even before they had reached the town, many had taken dips in the water on whose banks the divine cowherd used to graze His animals.

Jereshastri, Agnihotri and Punalkar Joshibuva had reached the holy spot a day before Bhausaheb. Rakhmabai Akkasaheb hadn't allowed her palanquin-bearers a moment of rest, thus ensuring that she was the first to reach the holy town. Her son Nana Phadnis had fallen ill again, and so he was constrained to move at a slower pace, reaching Mathura only the next afternoon. The soldiers and horsemen began wandering around the lanes and alleys of Mathura. The local priests, the pandas, came the very same evening along with Jereshastri, Agnihotri and the others to meet Bhausaheb. Within only a day of knowing each other, Jereshastri and Agnihotri had developed ten years worth of intimacy with the pandas and the administrators of the temples and other pilgrimage spots. They talked and behaved as if they had been childhood friends. Bhausaheb welcomed them all and said humbly, 'How can we be of service to the citizens of Mathura?'

'Please don't say that, Shrimant,' replied Brahmadev Pandit. 'You come from the land of Maharashtra, the land where the Hindu religion and its rituals have flourished, where the nectar of the holy books has come alive, where Gods have been given back their godhood after aeons. You are the brother of the great Balaji Rao Peshwa, who has practised the holy way of life in these evil times. It is we, the people of Mathura, who have now been blessed with the opportunity of serving you.'

'You may say that it is we who have been blessed with your arrival,' said another scholar.

'What do you learned men have to say?'

'Bhausaheb, you are setting off from this holy place to annihilate the enemies of our religion. It is clearly stated in the holy books of ancient times that the performance of a yagya and certain other rituals increases wealth and brings about the destruction of enemies. Our appeal is that you should not skip past this holy place without performing the rituals that our religion prescribes. We hear that you are halting here for four days for. Add another three days to it, so that you may be able to perform a small seven-day yagya.'

'Seven days? That's impossible!' replied Bhausaheb in horror.

'An entire kingdom sinking should be preferred to religion sinking, great saints have said,' said Jereshastri. 'We, of course, don't want either to sink, we want them to swim across, hence this yagya.'

'Besides,' Brahmadev Pandit continued, 'you're passing through Mathura during the days of shraavan. The days of shraavan—the period of the barren month—are a big opportunity for a devout Hindu to earn blessings, and that too in the holy land of the great Lord Krishna!'

'I am bound by the oath of the Kshatriya, the warrior caste,' Bhausaheb said firmly. 'It will not do for me to forget the enemy that lies ahead and get sucked into these rites.'

Punalkar Joshibuva chipped in, 'Bhausaheb, we are not talking of homa, the holy fire for making burnt offerings, because we are also eager that our lineage should flourish. As we burn ghee here in the homa, your Najeeb and Abdali will begin to burn there. They will get destroyed. Perhaps you could send a few of your chieftains ahead to fight your war while you stay behind for a few days. They will win with ease, and that's certain.'

'Look, if your high priests insist, I don't mind our ladies going and sitting by the sacrificial fire. But I have absolutely no time for all this.'

'Well, all right, you could just come and bow before it and join the holy meals afterwards. Parvatibai, Lakshmibai and others will sit by the sacrificial fire. It should be enough if the royal ladies tie a coconut to the end of their sarees as a substitute.'

At the insistence of the Mathura priests, a huge pavilion was erected the next day where around five thousand people could sit. The army supplied the wood and the roofing cloth for the pavilion. The masons got together in a hurry and by afternoon they had six rings ready where the homa fire would be burnt. Cowdung was coated over the masonry. The army also arranged for lumber, the sacred leaves and grass, the sacrificial sticks, turmeric, kumkum, saffron and ashtagandh, a perfume with eight fragrances. Holy books were recited, mantras were incanted, rites were performed. Parvatibai, Lakshmibai Balwant and the members of the Paigude family sat round the homa. Some six to seven hundred Brahmins, including those who had accompanied the pilgrims, joined the incantation. A good three or four thousand people marked their attendance during the ritual. No less than seven or eight thousand devotees and mendicants sat in rows for the food that was served.

With around a hundred-and-fifty thousand Marathas having descended, Mathura wore the appearance of a religious carnival. Locals there had long known of the Maratha penchant for charity. The pilgrims, soldiers and troopers would get up at the crack of dawn and set off on foot, on horseback or in their palanquins, doing the rounds of Gokul, Vrindawan, Mathura, and all the temples in the vicinity. Rakhmabai's pious heart was in a state of high excitement. She had brought her late husband's ashes with her in an urn, and a part of this burden she tossed into the Yamuna waters. Nana Phadnis had joined in to pray for his father. Commensurate with the reputation of the Phadnis family, six thousand people were served meals. As required by the holy books, horses and gold rings were given away as alms, heads were shaved and even penance for past sins was done.

After Mathura, Nana Phadnis went with his mother Rakhmabai Akka towards Vrindawan. Nana was overwrought at the sight of the town that was so steeped in holiness and so tightly woven with the legends of Radha and Krishna. Rakhmabai bowed her head at the pool where Krishna had slaughtered Kalia Nag, the wicked cobra of the netherworld. Nana set off to hunt for the kadamb tree where Krishna would sit after having whisked away the clothes of the bathing cow-girls. When he could not find the tree, he asked one of the travellers about it. The man laughed and replied, 'This is kaliyug, son, the age of evil. Where would you find Krishna and his kadamb tree in this age?' A local priest's son overheard the conversation. Sensing an opportunity, he took Nana and Rakhmabai to a point on the Yamuna bank where he unearthed some roots. 'These are the roots of the tree you were searching for,' he said. Mother and son were ecstatic. They immediately went down on their knees, rubbed their brows against the earth, and applied turmeric to the roots. The boy, of course, was suitably rewarded.

Was it even conceivable to go without taking a dip at the Kalia spot? Nana took twelve of them. He had been suffering from a strange ailment. He would be haunted with visions of alluring faces of nubile girls, and that would send excitement soaring. He would yearn to indulge his carnal desires. There was no way he could rid himself of sinful thoughts. In an effort to cure himself, he had even performed the Maha-Rudra, but that hadn't brought down the temperature of his racing blood. That was when he had got news of Bhausaheb's northern campaign. A visit to the three holy pilgrimages would surely cleanse his mind of filthy thoughts, his sins would be washed away too. This was why he had joined the expedition with his wife. Thus, after his twelfth dunking, his face suggested that all prurient thoughts had been rinsed out. That was when he saw a few young girls bathing, in a state of semi-nudity, some distance away, and his heart again lurched. What should he do now? Well, there was nothing much left to do except take five more dips.

ᘐ

Bhausaheb did not sit twiddling his thumbs in Mathura. He summoned all the landlords from around the Jaat territory, and convinced them to organize help for the expedition. Shamsher Bahadur, Yashwantrao Pawar and Damaji Gayakwad had set off for Delhi along the Yamuna bank, taking the wharves on their way under their control and confiscating whatever boats they could find. Bhausaheb had resolved that there would be no rest for him till Delhi was won. On the fifth day of arriving at Mathura, he dispatched the armies of Malharbaba Holkar, Jankoji Shinde, who knew well the lanes and bylanes of Delhi, and Balwantrao Mehendale. It would not be difficult to capture Delhi after subduing the small contingents of Pathans posted there.

When Balwantrao Mehendale was preparing to leave for Delhi under the orders of Bhausaheb, his wife Lakshmibai couldn't stop her tears. 'Don't cry,' Balwantrao tried to pacify her. 'In barely four days you will also be setting off for Indraprastha.'

'Even four seconds of separation from my lord and master is difficult for me to bear!'

'You are all insane, you Maratha women! You are travelling with the army for the precise reason of minimizing separation. Do you want us to carry you piggy-back to the battlefield now?'

This would be the very first confrontation with the enemy. To ensure Balwantrao's victory, Lakshmibai got eleven Brahmins to sit and propitiate the gods. Nervous as a cat, she began sitting at the homa along with Parvatibai.

Just when the seventh and last day of homa got over, a courier came astride a camel bearing news. Vishwasrao ran with the glad tidings to Bhausaheb and shouted, 'Bhausaheb, we are blessed. Praise be to Lord Gajanan. Delhi is—'

'Speak, boy, speak!'

'Our forces have been victorious. Here, read this letter from Balwantrao! The day they reached Delhi, they set up barricades along the fort and climbed over the walls with ladders. Kakasaheb, we have won Delhi!'

Bhausaheb's face lit up. Winning Delhi was no mean feat. Delhi, the city that had brought so many great men to heel and ground so many vaulting ambitions to dust! So many valiant soldiers had died in the effort to rein it in! How many of its insane lovers had it adorned with a halo! How many more was it going to drive insane? How many more was it going to deprive of sleep and rest? How many sacrifices did it want, how many soldiers— entire armies—did it want slaughtered at its altar before it knew contentment? Broadly speaking, Delhi was under the protection of the Marathas since the Ahmadiya pact; but today, when the Maratha flag had been flown atop the fort in the real sense, Shivaji and Bajirao in heaven would have turned moist-eyed with joy. Many times before, Delhi had come under Maratha control, come and slipped away like a child playing hide and seek. Bhausaheb's eyes were streaming with tears of unrestrained joy. A cloud of sorrow suddenly spread over his face, which Vishwasrao noticed. 'Why the sudden grief, Kakasaheb?' he asked with anxiety.

'Rao Saheb, the joy of planting the Maratha flag over Delhi has suddenly reminded me of Dattaji Shinde. The hero leapt into the fire of Buradi Ghat only so that he could protect this Empress of Hindustan from the blast of foreign winds. If only he could have been present among us to hear these glad tidings!'

The news had sent the entire army into a tizzy. Cannons were fired, trumpets blared and kettle-drums were beaten. The soldiers came out singing and dancing and throwing colours on the streets. Raja Surajmal was grinning from ear to ear as he went and congratulated Bhausaheb. Looking at him, one would think that the robes of a wazeer had already been awarded to him. Jereshastri arrived and began, 'Seen the glory of god's power? In the next two days, Najeeb and Abdali will go up in flames too. Bhausaheb, you have Delhi under your thumb. Very soon you will be ruling the world.'

Lakshmibai was over the moon at hearing of her husband's success. She gave the Brahmins praying on her behalf double the promised honorarium.

Bhausaheb declared his intention to set off for Delhi that very afternoon, but Vishwasrao said, 'Kakasaheb, please stay back tonight. We can leave tomorrow morning.'

'I've had enough of these religious rituals. What more do they want?'

'It's not about the rituals, Kakasaheb, but our Janardanpant Bhanu Phadnis's son Nana—'

'What happened to Nana?'

'His fever has suddenly shot up. His condition's become worse. Hence Rakhmabai Akkasaheb has requested for another day's halt.'

'Oh no! This boy is barely eighteen.'

The departure was delayed by a day.

To celebrate the conquest of Delhi, the Jaats threw a lavish dinner party for the noblemen.

Breaking his routine of many days, Bhausaheb retired early to his private quarters. Parvatibai said, 'The gifts that the Peshwa bestowed upon Lord Vyankatesh were bound to show results. And the results of the homa are also right before us.' Bhausaheb surrendered himself to a relaxed sleep.

༺༻

The drum-beats of departure jolted Bhausaheb out of his sleep. Was he late in getting up, or had the drums begun to beat a little early? He peeped out of the palace window with heavy lids, and noticed that it was still dark. Dawn was still some distance away. Why this drum-beat, then? He heard a cry from outside, 'Kakasaheb, get up! Get up, Kakasaheb!' It was Vishwasrao.

Bhausaheb rushed out. 'What's the matter, Vishwasrao?'

'Kakasaheb, it's a huge mess!'

'What happened? What mess?'

'Kakasaheb, we have not conquered Delhi.'

'What?' Bhausaheb felt a cold hand grip his heart. He felt the entire palace swirling over his head. He steadied himself and continued, 'What are you saying, Vishwasrao? Didn't the messenger say our soldiers had climbed over the outer wall?'

'It's true that our soldiers had scaled the walls, but Balwantrao got carried away and sent the news that Delhi had been conquered.'

'So, then, what happened next?'

'Our men got down on the other side and, instead of first finishing off the enemy, they got busy looting the town.'

'Looting before eliminating the enemy?' Bhausaheb roared with rage. 'So, our Marathas can't keep themselves from showing their true colours even at this critical juncture!'

'Kakasaheb, the fort-keepers got into action and cut down our soldiers who were busy pillaging. They also fortified their balustrades. Our sardars are still attacking the fort from the outside, but it refuses to fall.'

'What might be the strength of the enemy inside the fort?'

'Certainly more than a thousand.'

'What a shame! Three sardars with their armies, and they cannot get past a mere thousand defenders? Vishwasrao, we are setting off right now! Any delay now will reduce the Maratha empire to ruins.'

By afternoon, Bhausaheb's force had covered a good twelve miles on way to Delhi. Bhausaheb and Vishwasrao were both riding their horses while the rest of the family was travelling on elephant-back well behind. Something caught Vishwasrao's attention on the other bank of the Yamuna, and he shouted, 'Look, Kakasaheb, see what's going on at the other side.'

Bhausaheb's heart sank at what he saw. A mile beyond the other bank of the river, he could see elephants, horses, camels, mules and foot soldiers moving in the direction of Delhi, dragging with them heavy cannon carts. He shouted out to Nana Purandare, 'Come on, Nana, rush the Gardi regiment to the front. The enemy is advancing fast. Come on, move faster. If Delhi does not bow, we shall make it bow. If it doesn't bend, we shall make it bend!'

By morning, the Maratha army had crossed Ballabhgarh and Palwal, and was speeding on course towards Delhi. Bhausaheb's eyes roved all over the landscape. The soil was fertile, the rains were aplenty, the Yamuna was flowing full, yet the farms were bare. The farmers had not bothered to grow crops beyond what was required to meet their needs. Why take any harvest? Delhi was one of the renowned capitals of the world, yet its subjects knew no security. So many times during the last ten years, armies had plundered away their grains. They knew that Abdali had arrived in Delhi with a force of seventy-five thousand soldiers. They also knew that the Marathas had set off towards Delhi with an army of a hundred thousand to a hundred-and-fifty-thousand men. If they had grown some crop, one of the two forces would certainly have snatched it away from them. Much better, then, to let the land stay fallow. The empty fields had got Bhausaheb worried. Even if they did manage to capture Delhi, what would they do for food and fodder?

The outlines of the domes and minarets of the Red Fort, Jama Masjid, the Old Fort, and the spires of temples began coming into sight. The fortifications of the city also became visible. The soldiers quickened their steps. Bhausaheb had insisted that the Gardi regiment reach there first; accordingly, Ibrahim Khan had skipped the night halt and marched on without a break. Alongside ran Lakshmanrao Panse's ordnance.

Soon the Maratha army was upon the Delhi fortification. A hundred thousand soldiers gathered in the neighbourhood of the walls. Numerous chieftains, thousands of horsemen and troopers, banners and pennants, howdahs, camels, bullocks, mules, caravans of pilgrims; all taken together, they were no less than the sea in high tide. As this wave began moving forward through the streets and settlements of Delhi, young boys and girls watched them from the balconies of their houses, jaws dropping and eyes popping out of their sockets. Not since the times of the Mahabharat would Delhi have seen an army as huge as that. Bhausaheb felt a pang of pity for Delhi. Such a massive city, built upon the valour of great men, had been reduced to destitution because of the incompetence and treachery of their descendants. The ease with which it fell into Maratha hands, if only Shivaji had been able to get it with equal ease! Bhausaheb instantly reined in his thoughts. There was no cause for him to be so infatuated with Delhi. What if the city had fallen on hard times? The enemy was still in control of the fort. He quickened his pace towards the Red Fort.

⚜

Bhausaheb finally arrived at the Red Fort. The forces of Vitthal Shivdev, Malharbaba Holkar, Jankoji Shinde and the royal guards that had reached before him had already laid a siege. Some Maratha soldiers were busy digging trenches at many places. The work of putting together earth and stones for mounting the cannons was also proceeding apace. Horses that had been standing before the bastions for the past four days looked cramped and stiff. A few of them would let out a loud neigh and look towards the fort. When the soldiers posted at the fort noticed the arrival of Bhausaheb, they turned suddenly alert and let out loud battle-cries of 'Har Har Mahadev! Jai Bhawaani! Jai Mhalsakaant!' The freshly arrived soldiers immediately responded with loud cries of 'Har Har Mahadev!' and immediately ran up to the fort. The Maratha army looked like frothing waves crashing from all sides upon a small island in the sea. The enemy soldiers watching from the balustrades saw this vast sea of soldiers and took better cover behind the walls.

Vitthal Shivdev, Malharbaba, Jankoji and Balwantrao went up to Bhausaheb, who surveyed the walls of the Red Fort with a sharp eye and dismounted. The chieftains then moved to the temporary tent that the Holkars had erected closeby, and an emergency meeting was immediately under way. The first thing that Bhausaheb did was to throw a searing look at Balwantrao and bark, 'What was the meaning of behaving so childishly, Balwantrao? Why did you have to report a conquest even before the fort had fallen? What kind of impetuosity was that? As a result, we sat there at Mathura celebrating a victory that never was! If we hadn't received that premature letter, we would have come racing to the fort a good two days earlier. It's these kinds of things that create misconceptions among the people, our armies collapse out of fear of the enemy and disaster results.'

Balwantrao couldn't lift his head up out of shame, while the other chieftains remained silent. After a little while, Bhausaheb's temper cooled somewhat and his face turned a little softer. He turned towards Malharbaba and said, 'All right, Subhedar kaka, please give me the details of what exactly transpired.'

'Bhausaheb, on the first day our forces came and rammed into the city walls. In an hour or two, we breached the wall and entered the city through the side of Javed Khan's mansion. We laid siege to the fort. Our contingent that was gathered in front of the Asad bastion tried very hard to break open the gate. The Shinde and Holkar forces set themselves against the Delhi Gate, Jankojibaba and I myself bent our backs against the wicket gate, but to no avail. It seems to be made of zinc and copper. It seems to be reinforced with a mesh of steel rods from the inside. No amount of effort can make it budge. A few of our and Vitthalrao's brave soldiers climbed down into the fort, but instead of opening the fort gates for us, they got into looting. The fort-keeper Yakub Khan took advantage of their folly and cut them down. Some of them jumped off the bastion into the Yamuna and broke their limbs. The fort-keeper is now on full alert.'

'How many of the irregular soldiery, do you think, are inside the fort?'

'No more than a thousand or two.'

'What does the fort-keeper propose to do?'

'Bhausaheb, he is obviously waiting for help to arrive from Abdali, and therefore he is fighting on with whatever little force he currently has.' Jankojibaba said.

'How many cannons and how much ammunition do they have inside?'

'What cannons and what ammunition?' said Antaji Mankeshwar. 'While Abdali was in Kolkojaleshwar, he packed off the good artillery of Delhi two or three months back. At best, the fort may be left with twenty or twenty-five muskets and matchlocks.'

'See?' Bhausaheb exclaimed with disappointment. 'The enemy has not only destroyed Delhi, but stolen its cannons too.'

'If only the troopers who had entered had shown some patience and opened the doors, the fort would have fallen long ago!' groaned Malharbaba.

'There was no controlling them as they entered Delhi. Started despoiling as soon as they stepped in. If this level of indiscipline continues, they won't think twice before fleeing away from a conquered Delhi at mere rumour. No need for any discussions here. Let's just keep beating the Red Fort and turn it black and blue!'

Bhausaheb took the nobles along with him to do a round of the fort. They also had for company Raja Surajmal Jaat, who knew the city inside out. Ibrahim Khan was immersed in the job of creating platforms for his cannons on the bank of the Yamuna. As Bhausaheb passed by, he patted him on the back and said, 'Khan Saheb, the day has dawned today only to witness the miracle of your masculinity.'

'Don't you worry, huzoor! The sun will set today only after having seen our heroism in action.'

The fort was surrounded from all four sides. Not a single enemy soldier could be seen on the walls and balustrades. They did their patrolling behind whatever protection the walls had to offer. A cold evening wind had begun to blow. Everything had now been put in readiness. Ibrahim Khan had installed three big guns on the bank of the Yamuna. One of the cannons looked straight at the dome atop the Asad bastion, mulling, as if, whether it wanted to chew it or swallow it. The second cannon looked as if it had settled the issue: it would simply swallow the eastern fortification. The third one sat aiming at the harem, eavesdropping on the flutter it had created among the women inside. Right since the afternoon, the gunners had stuffed the monsters with sulphur, lead, pellets and gunpowder; they now stood looking at it with a mixture of pride and awe.

Bhausaheb gave the signal, at which Ibrahim shouted, 'All right, let it go!'

The gunners who had stood with burning torches in their hands set the wick alight, ran into the Yamuna water and clamped their ears as tight as they could. The others around followed suit. The crackle couldn't have lasted for more than a few seconds when it was followed by a boom that no Maratha there had heard before. Despite the tight press they had given to their ears, they couldn't help feeling that their eardrums had surely blown a massive hole. The gunners on the water dunked themselves into it to escape the blast of heat that the guns had released. When they looked towards the fort, they found that the dome of the Asad bastion had disappeared. What could be seen was mangled masonry that was letting off smoke and dust as if it were on fire. Large chunks of masonry stones were still traveling in the air, forming their trajectory downwards either on the land below or into the Yamuna water. The cannonballs had penetrated right into the Deewaan-e-Khaas, the private audience hall of the emperor, and instantly reduced its wall and a few pillars to rubble. The shock wave of the blast had travelled to the Rang Mahal and the Moti Mahal and etched deep spidery cracks all over. Some of the buildings inside had caught fire. The inmates broke out into loud, terrified screams. The shrieks of women and children added a poignant touch to the pandemonium that reigned inside. The fort-keeper Yakoob Khan was himself badly rattled, but he did all he could to bring back order. Bhausaheb was thrilled at Ibrahim Khan's marksmanship. Even Subhedar Malharbaba Holkar was impressed enough to go and pat Ibrahim Khan on the back.

The sun was setting. Everybody was agreed that the fort-keeper would not be able to hold his charge together through the night. He would be compelled to hand the fort over to the Marathas sooner rather than later. The soldiers who were not on duty got busy with their pots and pans. Darkness had still to descend when some soldiers turned to look at the other side of the vast expanse of the Yamuna. They saw Abdali's army assembled a mile beyond the bank, and in front could be seen a horseman astride a very restless horse. That was Abdali himself, for sure, Bhausaheb surmised, frustrated at seeing the Red Fort pass into Maratha hands. There was no way he could cross the turbulent river, and could do nothing but dance in rage. Looking at the flares of torches on the other side, Bhausaheb ordered, 'I don't care whether people live or die, but I want the fort under our control before break of day, do you hear?'

The fort-keeper was pacing frantically like a fish out of water. The rumble of the Yamuna that reached him through the dark night sounded like the rumble of doom to him. The food supply had reduced to nothing, and with the river in flood, there was no way it could be replenished for the next two months, despite Abdali being right across.

The thunder of Ibrahim's cannons was still resonating in his head. Under the circumstances, the sanest thing would be to respectfully surrender the fort to the Marathas and save the lives of the inmates. Accordingly, he sent a messenger carrying a white flag and invited a team for talks. A group of seven or eight persons including Surajmal, Shinde's manager Ramji Dabholkar, Holkar's manager Gangoba Chandrachud and Antaji Mankeshwar went into the fort.

The entire army stayed awake to hear the results of the deal. Ibrahim Khan still stood by his primed cannons, prepared for all eventualities. The constant roar of the flooded river added a macabre tone to the night. Around midnight, the contingents of Shamsher Bahadur, Yashwantrao Pawar and Damaji Gayakwad went towards Bhausaheb. As soon as his eyes fell on Shamsher, Bhausaheb asked, 'Shamsher Rao, what security arrangements have you made?'

'Please don't worry, Bhausaheb. We have confiscated all the boats we could locate in the ten or fifteen villages along the left bank of the Yamuna, and anchored them under the fort. We have posted pickets everywhere, and every quay and wharf has been put under strict surveillance.'

'Excellent.'

'Bhausaheb, I beg your forgiveness, but I have come with information that knocks the bottom out of any faith that man should place on any other human being. I consider it my duty to pass this information to you.'

'Really? Out with it then, Shamsher!'

Shamsher bent his head and mumbled a few tense words in Bhausaheb's ear. Bhausaheb's face turned red, and he snapped, 'Are you sure of your facts, Shamsher?'

'Absolutely, Bhausaheb, as Bajirao's son, I wouldn't pass on half-baked stories.'

'One-hundred-and-fifty thousand? At Kumbheri?'

'Yes, Bhausaheb.'

The outrage on Bhausaheb's face was contrasted by the moisture that filled his eyes. With super-human effort, he swallowed his fury and his grief and turned his eyes towards the fort. He saw a couple of torches materialize at the gate and move in his direction. In a little while, Gangoba Tatya reached Bhausaheb, and when he noticed his flaming face, his heart missed a beat. Bhausaheb shot a rasping question at him, 'Yes, Gangoba, what deal have you struck?'

'Shrimant, Yakub Khan is ready for a deal. He seeks assurance of safe passage for himself, his clan and the soldiers trapped in the fort. He has no other demand besides this. He is willing to hand over the fort if he is given a firm commitment.'

'All right. Mahipatrao, draft a letter of assurance on paper carrying the seal of our government. Write—'

'Just a minute, Shrimant,' interrupted a nervous Gangoba. 'Yakub does not want an assurance on your seal.'

'Whose seal should it be, then?' asked Bhausaheb in a raised voice.

'He wants the assurance from Shinde-Holkars, Wazeer Ghaziuddin and the Jaats. He also says that after being evacuated, the fort will be handed over to the wazeer, and not to you.'

'Shut your filthy mouth!' roared Bhausaheb in uncontrolled anger. 'Another word from you, and I shall have your tongue pulled out! My men stake their lives and shed their blood to bring the fort down, and the fort be handed over to that battle-fleeing coward Ghaziuddin? Gangoba, take your dirty face back to that fort-keeper and to that Jaat and give my message. If he wants to vacate the fort out of our desire, he will have to take the assurance on our seal. If he thinks that he still has some heat left in him that needs cooling, he should say so. I shall set my cannons roaring and my guns rattling again. I shall turn the Red Fort to dust, do you hear? Now get lost!'

It was after two hundred years that a flag of the native soil had begun to flutter atop the Red Fort. Yakub Khan had surrendered the fort to the Marathas and crossed over to the other side of the Yamuna. Bhausaheb's health had suddenly taken a hit. As he lay stretched out on his bed, the clouds that had gathered on his face were refusing to melt and disperse. For the last two days, Vishwasrao had been observing the unusual sight of grief playing on his Kakasaheb's visage, and when he found the opportune moment, he quietly asked him, 'Kakasaheb, in the name of my father, your esteemed brother, I beseech you, please let me in on what has been eating away at your heart. Clearly you are not at peace with yourself. Surely, you consider me close enough to take me into confidence.'

Bhausaheb thought for a moment and heaved a sigh. 'You are right, Vishwasrao; after all, you are going to be the next Peshwa. You have to learn and understand the various shades in which the soil of our country comes. Why were Shinde's manager Dabholkar and Holkar's manager Gangoba not keen on our crossing the Chambal and coming here? Why were they falling at our feet, requesting us to halt at Gwalior?'

'Why?'

'They had already struck a deal here before we came. Not many snakes this venomous are likely to take birth anywhere in the world, people who can go to such lengths to betray the Maratha soil that has nurtured them.'

'What exactly has happened, Kakasaheb?' asked Vishwasrao, turning tenser by the moment.

'What do I say, Rao Saheb? These two, Dabholkar and Gangoba, the trusted managers of the two clans of the Shindes and the Holkars—the two wheels on which our empire moves—these two have taken a hundred-and-fifty thousand rupees as bribe from the Jaats and Wazeer Ghaziuddin. They had worked out a conspiracy to confine us to the other side of the Chambal, take our army with them and shed their blood to win Delhi, and then deposit the prize in the lap of the wazeer of Delhi. They would then hand over the administration of Delhi as well as the Agra Fort to the Jaats, swell their coffers enough to last for the next seven generations, and spend the rest of their lives in the north in unimaginable ease and comfort.'

Vishwasrao turned livid with rage. 'Kakasaheb,' he roared, 'let's have them crushed under the feet of elephants, or throw them over the walls of the Red Fort instantly.'

Bhausaheb, however, remained a picture of patience. 'Rao Saheb,' he said in a calm voice, 'we will certainly visit upon them the punishment they deserve, but now is not the time for it. These two are no streetside ruffians, they are the managers of the Shindes and the Holkars. Their bosses, of course, have no idea of the treachery of their servants. Taking action now will lead to a lot of talk. This talk may well make the cracks within our ranks visible to our enemies and give them a handle to beat us with. Disaster may well result. Once we have finished with the final battle, we shall bring the black deeds of these monsters out into the open. We shall strip them naked, place them on donkeys, whip them with lashes as they are carried up and down the streets of Pune, and finally we shall hang them on a gibbet right in front of Shaniwarwada. But as of now, let's please hold our horses.'

Bhausaheb sat quietly on his bed for some time, with Vishwasrao sitting beside him. Suddenly his eyes filled with tears. A disconcerted Vishwasrao asked, 'Kakasaheb, with our Maratha flag flying atop the Red Fort, why should you be crying?'

'Rao Saheb,' replied Bhausaheb, after somehow getting himself under control, 'such a great achievement, and yet I am left unmoved.' He stayed silent for a while, let out a painful sigh and continued, 'Vishwasrao, what I feel miserable about is this: the Marathi soil has always had the power in its arms to hold Delhi by its shoulders and shake it till its bones rattle, not once but a thousand times, but a few things have prevented us from realizing our potential. Our internal squabbles, our nepotism, treachery, sycophancy, our desire to have our egos tickled on the pretext of self-esteem, or our desire to propitiate all and sundry—these are the shortcomings because of which Delhi has always been far in spite of being so near, and it shall always be so.'

CHAPTER THREE

throne or faith?

Abdali's forces had set up camp on the other bank of the Yamuna right across Delhi, with Patparganj in their rear. Hearing of the Maratha army moving towards Delhi, he had set off with as much speed as he could muster. He hadn't let his men rest during the day or sleep at night. If ever Najeeb noticed either man or animal catching a breath, he would rush to Abdali and begin dancing like an ape. 'Aalam-panaah, Refuge of the World, let's keep moving. Those infidels have chewed the capital to bare bones. We can't wait!' It was a matter of Abdali's honour too. The slipping away of Delhi was the losing of the spine; without it, the trunk and limbs were of no use. They ran into heavy rains and squalls. The streams refused to recede. When they crossed through bogs and puddles, the horses often had to wade across water chest high. The cannon-carts would skid and groan and jam. In any case, they had to be carried along elevated land, as far away from the water-logged, low-lying land as possible. It was a half-starved army that finally reached the vicinity of Delhi. When Abdali saw the Red Fort on the other side of the swollen river, what with the thousands of torches of the Maratha men running this way and that, it looked as if an entire mountain was dotted with jungle fires. He looked at the raging water, and it was the same lights dispersed and thrown across the waves. The fort itself looked as if it had been cut into ribbons and tossed into the river. Right in front of his eyes, he could see the enemy holding the fort in its pincers. His men were stuck there, and he could do nothing to rescue them. With a fifty-thousand-strong standing army of his own, supported by a dozen or two Hindustani sardars and their men, thus after having a hundred thousand men at his command, all that he could do was to see the fort slip into infidel hands. What shame could be bigger? Abdali, who had prided himself on his composure even during times of difficulty, could not prevent the bile from rising this time. He looked up at the dark clouds and groaned, 'Oh mighty Allah, why this?' All that he heard in reply was the battle-cries of the Maratha soldiers from across the raging waters, 'Har Har Mahadev!'

It had been raining continually for two days now. It was on the previous day that the Maratha flags had begun to flutter on the Red Fort walls. The fort-keeper Yakoob Khan had somehow managed to procure four boats and managed to transport about a thousand of his people across the water. The Yamuna went on swelling. It continued in its irrepressible course, sucking into its insatiable mouth whatever lay within the reach of its monstrous tongue—man or beast or material.

The rain finally showed signs of letting up that day. Shelters were erected under Najeeb's supervision. Some grass was spread and covered with thick rugs in front of the royal tent and a few bolsters were laid out. On it sat the sprightly, thirty-eight-year-old Ahmed Shah Abali, looking unblinkingly at the Red Fort. The sight of the Maratha flag fluttering there made his innards spit and fume as water does when sprinkled on a hot griddle. He went on his knees and raised his hands towards the sky as if to pray.

Shah Wali Khan laughed. 'Why do you let it bother you, huzoor? After all, what's left there inside Delhi for them to crow over? We have picked it clean of the tiniest vestige of flesh. What are those infidels going to gain by conquering it now? If they need wood, they will need to pluck them out of fallen buildings; if they need shingles, they will have to pick them off roofs that have fallen to the ground. We had reduced Delhi to a land of destitutes long ago, now these Maratha beggars have only gone and swelled the crowd.'

'Destitution and penury does not reduce the importance of Delhi, Shah Wali,' responded Abdali. 'The name contains within itself the essence of all the epics that have ever been written on Hindustan. Uncountable are the ambitious warriors who have turned to stone waiting to win the city over. In direct contrast stand those vagabonds who have had Delhi fall into their undeserving lap. All they have done is to strut around and build memorials of their misbegotten rule. In the eyes of the world, he who has held Delhi in his power has held all of Hindustan, he who has lost Delhi has lost Hindustan too.'

'Oh Lord of the Day of Judgement,' cried Najeeb, throwing a sidelong glance at Abdali, 'why didn't You drown me in the flooded Yamuna instead of having me see Delhi slip into infidel hands?'

'Cut out your farce, Najeeb. I can feel the grief of losing Delhi a thousand times more intensely than you ever can. I had first stepped into this fort more than fifteen years ago as a camp-follower of Nadir Shah. It was in this fort that the Nawab of Hyderabad had prophesied that the boy who stood before him would one day be king. The Delhi that I have vanquished and plundered now lies under infidel control. Have you anything worse left to show to your slave, oh Allah?'

'But these Margatthas—'

'Your worry is not ill-founded, Najeeb. I remember a Friday evening when I sat in a conference of historians and scholars. I don't remember the context or the name of that scholar, but he told us the legend of the king of the Marathas, Shivaji, attending the court of Aurangzeb. Do you know why the Mughal Emperor had kept Shivaji standing at a distance of fifteen steps? He had wanted him to realize the glory and grandeur of the empire, and to realize how inconceivably outside the grasp of the Margatthas Delhi was. Allah did not bless that man with a long enough life, otherwise the valiant man would surely have shaken the throne of Delhi long ago. All told, like the Holy Grail, Delhi has stayed out of the grasp of these Deccan Marathas.' Najeeb moaned as he mopped the tears from his eyes. 'Lord, bad times have arrived. That son of Nana Peshwa, that brat Vishwasrao will now become the emperor of Delhi.'

'Shut your filthy mouth!' shouted Abdali, turning red with rage. Managing to regain control, he added, 'Najeeb, if anyone else had uttered these sinful words, I swear I would have pulled his wicked tongue out from the root. We will chase those Margatthas out of Delhi.'

'Shah Waliullah's mansion is in Delhi. How heartbroken he must be at seeing this infidel army milling around the town!'

'Quite right,' said Abdali and shook his head.

That was when there was a series of deafening booms, and balls of fire described a parabola across the Yamuna waters and crashed into their army camp. Right in front of Abdali's tent were stabled about twenty-five horses. One cannonball fell in their midst, at which the animals lifted themselves on their hind legs with loud neighs. They were so terrified that they broke their tethers and ran helter-skelter in confusion. The cannonball had descended straight upon one of the horses, causing its shredded and burnt pieces to fly in all directions. Some of them suffered terrible burns, and were rolling in the wet earth and ploughing their hooves into the ground in a vain effort to mitigate the agony. A second ball fell at the other end of the camp, setting a number of tents on fire. Mayhem broke loose in the camp, and Barkhurdar Khan had to instantly rush in and bring back some semblance of order. He yelled at them and ordered them to fetch water from the Yamuna in pots and buckets to throw upon the raging fire. The third ball fell on the left wing and burnt itself out without causing much damage.

Abdali had climbed atop his horse. He patted its rump, looked around in anger and screamed, 'Jahaan Khan, are the Marathas the only ones with long-range cannons?'

'Huzoor, ours too have been mounted on their bases and primed up with powder. They merely await your orders. As your lordship knows, when you are in camp, it is you alone that can issue orders.'

'So set the wicks alight and blast those infidels out!'

Jahaan Khan rode up to the gunners and screamed, 'Fire!' Five cannons were torched and they boomed out within seconds of each other. The flaming red missiles went whistling and screeching across the Yamuna and crashed into the Maratha encampment, making it burst like an anthill. The first one that landed threw a small bunch of bullocks into the air, tearing every limb apart. The second set fire to a few tents of the pilgrims. This was their first experience of cannon-fire, and they began running in panic like headless chickens, screaming and shouting, 'Hey Bhagwanta!' 'Hey Panduranga!' A score or so of the soldiers also perished in the attack.

After this volley, Abdali waited for a long time for the response to arrive. His chieftains had, meanwhile, gathered around him. Collecting all in his gaze, he growled, 'The Marathas have turned very bold and ambitious these days, haven't they?'

'After having swallowed up half of Hindustan, they think no end of themselves!' exclaimed Najeeb.

'When we launch our raid now, it should be so terrifying that the very mention of Rohilla Pathan should make them quake!' said Abdali.

By late afternoon the next day, a number of Abdali's squads began moving westwards. He turned to Shuja and Najeeb and asked, 'Have the boats been arranged?'

'Huzoor, all the boats have been assembled at the Buradi crossing.'

'Will it be possible to make a crossing given the current state of the river?'

'Huzoor, the men will surely be able to cross,' responded Hafeez Khan, 'but, how can we ferry heavy cannons on these small dinghies?'

'Well, taking a few hundred horsemen across and creating a clamour among the enemy ranks, nothing wrong with that, is there?'

'Nothing at all, huzoor!' Hafeez Khan smiled.

It was getting to be dusk, and darkness had begun to settle on the Yamuna. Forty Rohilla Pathans armed with muskets got into a boat, and the boatman's long bamboo began poking the river floor to lever the boat into the current. The boat would have travelled barely a few feet into the water when a huge monster of a wave rose up from one side and rained an avalanche into the vessel, filling it with water and causing it to list dangerously to one side. 'Allah, save us!' screamed the soldiers; but the roar of the water apparently crowded out their frantic pleas from reaching Allah. Another wave hit it at the hull and the boat turned turtle, catapulting its passengers out and send them tossing with the current like logs of wood.

It was after a long wait that the men on the bank gave up the count: barely twelve of the original forty had managed to make it to the land. Abdali was shaken, but Najeeb was not willing to give up. 'What does the loss of one boatful of men matter, Aalam-panaah? Let's put another boat into the water.'

'No, Najeeb, no! We shall not make the same mistake again. We need enough men for the final battle. We will stake our soldiers out when the time for it arrives, but now it will be wrong. The infidel is in readiness on the other bank. Before our forces can set foot on that bank, he will roast them alive.'

As they rode through the darkness, Abdali asked, 'Hafeez, where does such a big city like Delhi get its supplies from?'

'From here, from the Antarved, and from Ayodhya.'

'But how are the loads of grains carried across the river? From where?'

'Your lordship, the village right behind us, Patparganj, that is the granary of Delhi. The grain from the entire region gets collected here. The wharf we just came from, that is where the grain transporters sit watching the rise and fall of the water, and take their small boats across when they see the opportunity. In fact, they often manage to cross during floods too.'

'Shah Pasand!'

'Huzoor!'

'Set up posts tonight on this bank here, twenty miles on each side. Not a grain, not a blade of grass should cross over to the other side, you hear me?'

'Your wish is our command, huzoor!'

'Lordship, this is a master stroke!' Najeeb burst out in glee. 'With no grains and fodder crossing over from this side, what will the Marathas survive on? Sands from Rajputana?'

The bonfire in front of the royal tent stayed alive till late in the night. Hafeez Rahmat Khan and the emperor sat pulling on the hookah side by side. Around midnight, Abdali threw a glance at the Yamuna and said, 'Khan Saheb, fighting a war on the waters of the Yamuna is impossible. When does this river begin to subside, ordinarily?'

'Huzoor, my hair has turned from black to white roaming up and down the banks of the Yamuna in all three seasons. But once the Yamuna rises with the monsoon floods, it doesn't come down for the next three months at the very least.'

'Three months?'

'More, perhaps, but never less.'

Early the next morning, a firmaan reached the Hindustani Pathans like Saadullah Khan, Faizullah Khan and Dundey Khan to report immediately to the royal tent. When they had all assembled, Abdali addressed them, 'From here onwards, only Shuja-ud-dowlah, Najeeb and Hafeez Rahmat Khan will stay here with me. The rest of you are to return to your provinces.'

'Lord, have we sinners been remiss about something?' asked a couple of chieftains in anxiety. Abdali laughed. 'Dundey Khan, Saadullah,

Ahmad Khan, war won't be possible over the Yamuna waters for the next three months. Till then, it makes so much more sense for you to return to your lands. Eat well, rest well, and regain your strength and energy, you and your animals. Whenever the need arises, or when the waters of the Yamuna recede, our firmaan will be dispatched to you, and that's when you must return refreshed. That's when we will settle accounts with the infidels. That's when we will push them across the Narmada with renewed vim and vigour. After the rains, we will burn the entire Deccan down to ashes.'

❦

Surajmal Jaat had established his base camp at Tughlakabad. It was during the morning hours that Ghaziuddin had arrived at the camp for consultations with him. Suraj had not finished with his morning bath yet. From a window of his tent the Red Fort could be seen, as also the pennants of the Marathas flying on their long poles atop the Delhi gates. There were saffron banners on other balustrades too, and they were not a pleasant sight for Ghaziuddin by a long shot. The struggle he had faced for the past four years to retrieve the wazeeri of Hindustan! When the letters of the Mughal Emperor inviting Abdali to Hindustan had fallen into his hands, he had got the emperor killed and tossed his body over the Red Fort into the sands of the Yamuna. He was willing to go to any extent to get the wazeer's seat back under his thighs. It was only last evening that he had stepped into the mansion from where Najeeb had so unceremoniously driven him out. Three or four hours of rest in his own house revived him somewhat, but the cinders inside him were still alive. When he had first heard of Bhausaheb's Hindustan campaign, he had been delighted, but once he had arrived, Ghaziuddin couldn't remember a single occasion when the great Maratha would have sent for him. On the contrary, whenever Bhausaheb turned his gaze towards him, he couldn't help noticing more than a trace of contempt in those eyes. Despite the fact that Shuja had joined up with the foreigner, Bhausaheb still held him in respect, Ghaziuddin could see, but there was no such respect visible for him. He was getting more and more convinced that the wazeeri would not come his way via the Marathas, and that was a disheartening thought.

A servant entered with the message that Surajmal had arrived, and soon enough he entered the tent with strong, confident steps. Ghaziuddin rose and welcomed him with a bow which suggested that Surajmal was his one final hope. When both of them were seated, he started, 'Raja Saheb, you were the one to subdue the Delhi Fort, but the flags that fly atop it belong to the Marathas? It was very wrong of Yakoob Khan to hand the keys over to Bhau. We had such expectations from Bhau, but they seem to have turned to dust.'

'That's quite true, Ghaziuddin,' sighed Surajmal. 'It should really have been your forces or mine that should have entered the fort. Not one of our cards seems to be falling right. That Gangoba and that Dabholkar had sworn by the holy Ganga that, through whatever means, they would ensure that the administration of Delhi would come to us and the fort would be handed over to your charge.'

'So, why isn't it happening? Why the delay?' asked Ghaziuddin.

'We have all fallen victim to a serious delusion. Gangoba and Dabholkar's assessment of Bhausaheb Sadashivrao has been altogether wrong. They believed that Bhau was a backstage person who knew nothing beyond his office and his account books, a mere pen-smith who would be out of his depth on the battlefield and on the political diplomacy front. Based on this conception, they had hoped that once Delhi was won, they would be able to sweet-talk him into accepting their advice.'

'Yes, but what have we finally got?'

'Well, we came here with the belief that something would fall to our lot. Look, these people of Delhi and we on the other side of the river are tied together by ancient bonds, even by ancient abuses. As a matter of fact, ours are the true rights over Delhi. It's you people who call it Delhi today, but the ancient name of this city is Indraprastha. We Jaats are of the ancient lineage of the Yadavas, who ruled over Delhi for centuries. Look at the distance from where these Margatthas have arrived. Can you imagine even the tiniest thread connecting them to Delhi? They are people who care only for tithes and tributes, and hence roam across heaths and forests with leaves tied to their soles. Why would they want to possess Delhi?'

'The final outcome, Raja Saheb, is that neither you nor I will meet our goals here. I will have to abandon my dream, permanently, of ever becoming the wazeer.'

'Why?'

'It appears that Raja Saheb is still not aware of yesterday's developments.'

'No, I don't think I am. Anything special?'

'The Marathas were climbing down the steps of the bastions yesterday after planting their flags. Devidutt happened to be there.'

'Who's Devidutt?'

'Shuja's envoy. He had gone to hold talks with Bhausaheb. Shuja's offer was that Shah Alam be instated as the emperor of Hindustan, with he himself as his wazeer. Alongside, if Bhau was ready to move his forces out of Delhi and head back south, Shuja would persuade Abdali to return to Kandahar. We've of course known a long time the inside plan of having Shuja placed on the wazeer's seat.'

'What a load of rubbish!' replied an irritated Surajmal. 'No matter what happens, Bhau cannot afford to abandon us. Can he point at one person north of Narmada and call him a friend? And look at the other side of the Yamuna now: Abdali and Najeeb have gathered all of Hindustan under one flag.'

'Raja Saheb, without the wazeer's post, what is my life worth? I have been criss-crossing the wilderness for the last four years with just one single purpose. No grandeur, no palanquins, no canopy atop an elephant! This one-time wazeer of Hindustan has had to go from pillar to post, and stand at people's door like a mendicant's boy begging for the seat. Do what you have to, Raja Saheb, but my head has to be graced once again by the wazeer's crown.'

Surajmal laughed and said, 'If you are so desperate, why don't you do one thing?'

'What?'

'Cross the Yamuna and beg for it there.'

Ghaziuddin didn't know whether to laugh or cry at this suggestion. 'Forget getting any wazeeri there, it will be a problem crossing back with my life. That wicked Najeeb will keep dunking me again and again in the Yamuna till I die. He will keep pushing me back into the river as the sati is pushed back on her husband's pyre.'

Surajmal turned a little grave and said, 'Wazeer Saheb, while every door seems closed for you on the yonder bank of the Yamuna, there is a tiny crack that may still be open for us.'

'What crack?'

'Oh, there is one.' Then Surajmal Jaat fell into a brooding silence. He then resumed, as if talking to himself, 'But, no! That headache is best kept at a distance. Confabulating with the mischievous can leave only mischief behind. All of Hindustan knows how Abdali reduced Delhi to tatters on his previous visit. And the mayhem he had let loose in our Mathura! Rivers of blood had flowed, women and gods and goddesses were dragged into the street and shamed. Look at Bhau, on the other hand. Even if the settlement is not to your taste, he won't harm a hair on your head. But that foreigner and his dog Najeeb will certainly burn us alive. So, why jump from the frying pan into the fire?'

'But Raja Saheb, you still have one string you can pull to make Bhau dance: why can't you cut off his food supply?'

'What have we given to the Marathas in the last fortnight, after all? But Bhau is not the kind who will soften with the cutting off of food supply. He is a particularly obstinate and resilient person.'

'Then it's best for us to wait and watch. Let's get to know what Bhau has in mind. Why don't we go and meet him right away? We can't suffer this uncertainty for very long.'

❈

The Maratha camp was pitched in the southern part of Delhi. A large part of the army was still divided into pickets around the Red Fort. Abdali's encampment was clearly visible on the other side of the Yamuna from the fort, their animals grazing here and there as also the movements of their men. Abdali, of course, didn't have the guts to cross the river to launch an attack; however, Bhausaheb had taken the caution of placing strong pickets two miles in either direction along the waterfront. There were soldiers' tents standing everywhere. Right in the middle was Bhausaheb's own pavilion, marked by a gold spire. A few heavily-caparisoned elephants stood in front of the tent. A contingent of about a thousand armed soldiers stood on the alert outside. Huge bronze vessels containing drinking water were placed outside. Animals, women and children were loitering everywhere, creating their own buzz. Valets and doormen bowed to every chieftain that passed by.

Jankoji Shinde and Malharbaba Holkar were sitting in conference with Bhausaheb. Jankoji was saying, 'Bhausaheb, there is shortage of food and fodder in the army. The enemy has blocked all supplies coming from Patparganj across the Yamuna. We are now having to ration out the fodder to the elephants and horses. Under the circumstances, we need to take the Jaats into confidence.'

'So, how do we take the Jaats into confidence?'

'I mean ... I mean we should make him feel hopeful.'

'Have we ever shown lack of confidence in the Jaat king?'

'Bhausaheb, when Dattaji had fallen at the Buradi Ghat, we were in a terrible shape. No one across Hindustan was willing to take in Shinde-Holkars. It was the Jaats alone who had given shelter to our armies at Kumbheri and looked after them. How can we forget that?' said Malharbaba.

'Kakasaheb, we never ever forget anybody, and will never do so either,' responded Bhausaheb in a tired voice. 'Look, Kakasaheb, thinking about the Jaat means deciding who to place in charge of Delhi, isn't it? All these matters are bound to be settled today or tomorrow, aren't they? But there's the monster of an enemy that's planted himself right across the river at the moment. Just walk up to the door of the tent we are sitting in, and you'll see the enemy forces flexing their muscles. If we hustle and settle right now who gets Delhi and who gets to be the wazeer, we may well spoil the political pitch.'

Jankoji and Malharbaba fell quiet, although the expression on the latter's face read, 'Here I am, the elder statesman, offering valuable suggestions, and this chit of a boy just tosses them away; how right is this?' That was when the usher entered to announce that Dabholkar, Gangoba, Surajmal and Ghaziuddin had arrived outside. Bhausaheb started a bit, then ordered the usher, 'Allow Raja Saheb and Ghaziuddin in. Tell that Dabholkar and Gangoba to disappear. Tell them they should not be anywhere within sight while the nobles are discussing matters here.'

Bhausaheb welcomed Surajmal and Ghaziuddin and invited them to a seat. Once they had settled, he enquired politely, 'Yes, Raja Saheb, any special instructions for us?'

'It's not our worth to issue instructions to you, Shrimant. You are the Peshwa, the lord of the Deccan, while I am merely a landlord. All we seek is not to fall from your grace, Shrimant.'

'I don't quite understand what you're implying, Raja Saheb.'

'During the surrender of the fort, the fort-keeper Yakoob Khan merely sent a message that a Jaat contingent be sent over, and that seems to have upset your lordship, we have heard. Yakoob was talking on the basis of prior acquaintance with us, there was no subterfuge in that message, Shrimant.'

'Subterfuge there may be or may not be, Raja Saheb, but it is not proper for you either to misunderstand the direction of our anger.'

'We also hear that Shuja's envoy has established camp in the Maratha forces.'

'Raja Saheb, this is war time. During times such as these, it is a custom of statesmanship for envoys to keep coming and going, irrespective of whether the terms that are tossed around for an agreement are acceptable or not. What do you find objectionable in that?'

'Your lordship seems to place inordinate trust in Shuja, but it seems to a dim-wit like me that Shuja will never fall into your hands. The only thing he is concerned about is how he can protect his province in this battle between you and Abdali.'

Bhausaheb laughed and said, 'But this seems to be the attitude of everyone around these parts, doesn't it?'

'But, Shrimant, while on the one hand, he talks of arriving at an agreement with you, on the other hand, he has been persuading the others to join up with Abdali. I myself received a letter to this effect before I left my province. Your lordship may want to read it.' With that, he fished out a scroll bag from his tunic and handed it to Bhausaheb.

Bhausaheb undid the knot, pulled out the scroll and began reading it attentively:

Greetings to brother Kunwar Saheb.

My heart has been yearning for a get-together with you. I haven't received any letter from you either. I hope the affection between us hasn't diminished.

All the chieftains of Hindustan have applied the dust of Abdali's foot to their forehead and sworn their fealty to him. They have committed themselves to stand united and fight against Bhausaheb. Bhausaheb's crossing the Chambal has thrown all of Hindustan into a turmoil. Anyone who stays outside the alliance of all the chieftains of Hindustan that Abdali has brought together may consider himself unfortunate. What is your opinion on it? If you are thinking of shaking hands with Bhausaheb, you will have to stay away from us. Bhau has been swelling these days on the strength of his power and authority....

God willing, I shall be happy to plead your integrity with Ahmad Shah. I should also be able to procure for you a letter of agreement and indulgence from Aalam-panaah. If you decide to leave your province behind and rush to the service of Ahmad Shah, you will earn the goodwill of the emperor, your power and pelf will expand. At the very least, you should relax at ease in your province and watch the future unfold itself, but you should not commit the folly of offering so much as a blade of grass to the Maratha forces. You are wise, experienced and foresighted. Not much more needs to be written to you.

Bhausaheb finished reading the letter and said laughingly, 'This Abdali has nicely put all these chieftains of Hindustan on leash.' With that, he handed the scroll over to Malharbaba and Jankoji. Ghaziuddin was watching Bhausaheb's face with expectation. Bhausaheb organized his thoughts and began, 'The chieftains of Hindustan have all decided to become this foreigner's doormats; they are competing with each other to wash his feet and drink the water as nectar. With this scenario as background, I am satisfied to note, Raja Saheb, that there is this Jaat King who has decided to stand up to him and move over to our side. But I don't know why, but this little flutter that has been in your heart for the last two days doesn't seem quite right.'

Surajmal shot a startled look at Bhausaheb.

'Yes, Raja Saheb, you may call it the efficiency of our spy network, or consider me as a great reader of faces, but there is a flutter in your heart, and that's certain.'

'Our only desire is to stay within your lordship's grace,' Surajmal swallowed hard and mumbled.

'Raja Saheb, in what manner have we offended you? Just give us one single example,' Bhausaheb pleaded. 'When we were on the other side of the Chambal, we received your note: we should not cause any disruption as we passed your territory. Such a huge army passed through your land, but did they step over a single twig? Out of the tribute that was fixed during the battle of Kumbheri, you still owe us seven hundred thousand. Despite our army marching half-starved, have we demanded anything of that?'

'Bhausaheb,' intervened Malharbaba, 'we have taken the Jaats as our friends. Seven or eight months back, the Jaats took in hungry Maratha soldiers and families. In acknowledgement of this favour, I request that half their debts be written off.'

'Granted.'

'Let's also write off four years of tribute from here on,' chipped in Jankojiba.

'Granted.'

'It's been a drought year; the blight of the invader has also visited us. Therefore, could you stretch the exemption by another year, and make it five?' pleaded Surajmal.

'Granted this too.'

'Please also make a land grant of fifty or sixty thousand to our envoy Roopram Katare, Shrimant!'

'Agreed. This too is agreed,' responded Bhausaheb with a laugh.

'Shrimant, the fort at Agra falls in our territory. This too should stay with us.'

'It's as good as in your control as of now, but it shall not be possible to give it over to you in writing at this moment,' Bhausaheb stated upfront. 'Such demands can be considered after the war is over. The urgent need is for us to stay together and protect the Hindustan empire. The rest can be sorted out later.'

The short shrift set Surajmal a little aback. Ghaziuddin, meanwhile, had been steadily looking at Surajmal, his eyes saying, 'Sort out all that you can right now. Who cares for anyone once the war is over?' Surajmal looked a little bothered, but he steeled himself one more time and said, 'Fine, Shrimant, we will discuss the Delhi-Agra issues after the war. But meanwhile, is there any obstacle to declaring Ghaziuddin as the wazeer of Hindustan now?'

'Raja Saheb, till such time as the enemy doesn't go past Attock, Hindustan cannot be said to be under our control. Crowning a person without a throne in sight will be too pretentious.

'Shrimant, you regard us as your sole allies in this war,' Surajmal persisted. 'So, what difficulties do you see in seeing this little thing through?'

Bhau turned towards Ghaziuddin and saw desperation on his face; every atom of that visage was begging for the favour. But Bhau could find no sympathy in his heart for those frantic looks. Here was a man who had done two emperors to death to serve his wicked ends. He was the person who had fled Delhi at the very rumour of Abdali's arrival. He had turned his back on Dattaji and let him die unsupported on Buradi Ghat. A corrupt, wicked, spineless person like him to become the wazeer of Hindustan? Unthinkable! Bhausaheb intoned in a low but firm voice, 'Raja Saheb, whatever you may say, but I am not in a position to take a stand on this issue as of now.'

Ghaziuddin's face fell. Surajmal bowed his head too. They quietly got up and left. Bhausaheb too set off for his private tent. Surajmal's incongruent behaviour mystified Bhau, of course; but what also bothered him was the guilty looks on the faces of Holkar and Shinde.

The next day, Mahipatrao Chitnis came running to Bhausaheb and cried, 'Bhausaheb! I come bearing some bad news. The Jaat left straight for Ballabhgadh last night with his forces. Ghaziuddin left with him.'

Bhausaheb was furious. 'Why wasn't I informed immediately last night?'

'Nobody got to know when they left, Bhausaheb. They quietly pulled out their tents and simply disappeared. They took care even to remove the bells that hung round their elephants' necks.'

Bhausaheb was thunderstruck. The complaints of severe food shortage in his army had intensified since the previous night. On top of that, the only friend of the Marathas slipping away in this manner was terrible. Bhausaheb had never wanted to set eyes on the faces of Dabholkar and Gangoba, but he was left with no choice. He called the two over, added Mahipatrao to their company, and said to the three of them, 'Go after the Jaat. Accept whatever big or small desires he expresses. Do what you can to get him round, but have him come back to us.'

The three returned the next morning. Mahipatrao couldn't lift his head as he said, 'The Jaat has reached Ballabhgadh. He is in a sulk. Refuses to talk or listen. Won't come back either.'

'Well, if he refuses to come, so be it, then,' said Bhausaheb in despair. 'You can't block the way of a person who is bent on going away. You can't contain a passing breeze in your arms. All that is left for us to do now is to face the imminent hurricane.'

Bhausaheb lay stretched out on his bed under a quilt. Parvatibai lay beside him observing his face. She knew that although her husband's eyes were shut, he had been awake for a long while. Suddenly Bhausaheb opened his eyes. 'When did you wake up?' he asked.

'It's months, I have seen neither the day dawn or the night fall in your company. Even before the first streak of light, your lordship leaves for office. Fifty times I send the servant enquiring about your meals—'

'Fifty times? I don't remember even one!'

'What can the poor men do? They make the rounds of your office, find you submerged in work, so they don't have the courage to break through your trance and deliver my message.'

Bhausaheb laughed loudly and said, 'Parvati, you will have to see these bad times through for another few months. Once we are done with the enemy, we will go not to Pune, but to Peyn, your parent's home. We'll go spend time at Janjira, and chat through the evenings, just you and I, in the cool breeze of the beach, I promise.'

In her mind's eye, Parvatibai could already see the deep blue sea, and the romance of the sea-breeze rose in her. The expression on Bhausaheb's face, however, was serious as he said in a heavy voice, 'How the present crisis is going to be resolved, though, the Lord alone knows.'

As the darkness outside began to melt, Bhausaheb got out of bed and hurried through his morning bath and prayers. Then he left for his office immediately. Ibrahim Khan Gardi was standing astride his horse in front of the office. On seeing Bhausaheb, he immediately dismounted and bowed low before him. Even in the faint early morning light, Bhausaheb could notice tension writ large on his face; his eyes looked red. 'What's this, Khan Saheb?' Bhausaheb asked solicitously. 'Do I see tears in your eyes?'

'Calamity has struck, my lord. At least forty of our cannon bullocks have died in a single night.'

'What are you saying?' Bhau was shocked.'

'There's no saying how many more may die soon. Strong healthy bullocks, all turning into carcasses, all! It's a horrible sight, lord!'

'Let's go and see!'

The Gardis had tied the legs of the carcasses of the dead bullocks, strung them on stout poles and carried them out of the camp grounds.

When Bhausaheb saw the stiff bodies of the animals laid out in rows, his heart sank. 'You brought them all out in a single night, Khan Saheb?' he asked in awe.

'What other option did we have, Shrimant? If we hadn't removed these dead animals immediately, another hundred could have caught the disease.'

'What's this new blight that has struck our campaign?'

'Shrimant, this cold, wet air of the Yamuna banks does not suit our animals from the Deccan that are attuned to higher temperatures. Our animals also die of dehydration if they contract dysentery. Our horses, too, seem to be losing weight in this weather, look!'

'What measures are you taking to keep the rest of the animals safe?'

'Have collected all the vets and physicians of our army. The animals have been put on a course of herbs and extracts of green vegetables. The voodoo men have also been put to work, making threads and talismans for the animals to wear. We are doing all we can, but—'

'But what?'

'But if our animals keep falling like this, how will we manage?' Ibrahim Khan's face was contorted with anxiety. 'Shrimant, our enemy is armed with the best cannons. Whenever the war breaks out, the entire burden of the war will be carried by the artillery on both sides. Each of our guns has the power of elephants. Every single shot is guaranteed to mow down a hundred of the enemy men. But for that, we need enough bullocks to pull the cannons to the battlefield.'

All that Bhausaheb could do was to nod his head in assent. 'Don't worry, Ibrahim,' he finally said, 'don't take these deaths to heart. We shall certainly find a way out of this.'

But Bhausaheb couldn't get the animals out of his head. If they didn't have enough healthy animals when the moment of reckoning arrived, how would they be able to confront the enemy? The riddle of the ailing bullocks needed to be solved quickly.

When Bhausaheb dismounted in front of the office, a large number of cavalrymen crowded round him. 'What's the matter?' he asked in a loud voice.

Some six or seven of them started speaking together: 'Shrimant, it's now been two or three months since our horses died under us, and we have been moving on foot, which is tough for people like us. A horseman without a horse is like a body without a head. How long can we carry on like this? Please provide horses to us, as also our allowances.'

Bhausaheb saw their gaunt, tired faces, their frayed footwear and their cracked feet, and felt deeply saddened. 'My brave warriors,' he addressed them, 'in whom have you put your trust for these many days?'

'In you, Shrimant, who else?' they roared.

'Thank you. I beg you with folded hands: endure for a few more days. Don't imagine I would ever throw you before the enemy in this state. We are here to win the war, not lose it. Return to your tents without any worry. God is watching over you. We shall put the reins of high-quality horses into your hands before the bugle of war is sounded, rest assured.'

Mahipatrao Chitnis, Nana Purandare, Nana Phadnis and a few others were waiting for him inside the office. When the usher announced Bhausaheb's arrival, they rose from their seats to welcome him. 'How much of our funds still left, Mahipatrao?' Bhausaheb asked.

'Not enough for even a week's allowances, Shrimant!'

'With what fanfare we had made our entry into Delhi barely a week ago! We had drunk in the sight of the Red Fort to our heart's content, organized a special court and got the chieftains to offer their tributes to Vishwasrao; it had felt for a while that by conquering Delhi we had conquered the world. But now, the scales seem to have fallen. What kind of Lords of Delhi are we? 'Lords of the Wasteland' describes us better ... Lord Gajanan will find a way out for us, let's hope ... Mahipatrao, send a letter to that Govindpant.'

'Yes, my lord.'

'Mahipatrao, how many letters would we have written to Pant till date?'

'Can't give the exact figure, but certainly one letter every day, and often two.'

'And what good have they done? Well, let that go. Here, write. He can only behave according to the sense the Good Lord gives him. Yes ... write:

> There is provision in the government for bullocks for the artillery unit. They are an absolutely essential need. A number of bullocks have died of diseases. Many more are in a terribly emaciated state, and they are dying even as I write. Round up about five hundred strong, healthy bullocks in and around

Itawa and have them dispatched immediately. There is no scope for any delay, as their shortage has left the army seriously compromised.

Despite having written so many letters to you, and made so many requests, all that we have received from you till date is a bare two hundred thousand rupees. How can this be considered adequate by any measure? The dues from you have been steadily mounting. There are sufficient resources available in your province. Please arrange to send them at the earliest. Men and animals here are close to forgetting the taste of food and fodder. When the nobles themselves are finding it hard to procure food, what can be said about the common people? You will have to make arrangements for a minimum of two-and-a-half million rupees and send them immediately on receipt of this letter.'

Just as the letter to Govindpant came to an end, Vishwasrao and Jankoji arrived, followed by Balwantrao Ganesh. Bhausaheb addressed Balwantrao in an anxious voice, 'Balwantrao, all ways here have led to a dead end. Should we send a demand to Pune, then?'

'Absolutely, Bhausaheb. What's wrong with that?'

'Kakasaheb, we should certainly ask for assistance from Pune. We should call for reinforcements. We are caught in a terrible bind here. If we don't access Pune for help, where do we go? Kandahar?' said Vishwasrao all charged up.

'Rao Saheb, six weeks back we had sent a letter to Pune, requesting them to instruct the revenue collectors of the Antarved to deliver half their collections here at the warfront and send the remaining half to Pune. We haven't received any response yet.'

'Bhausaheb, the post gets delayed during monsoon,' said Balwantrao.

'I don't feel good asking Pune,' said Bhausaheb with visible embarrassment. 'Vishwasrao, Mehendale, Nana, I am sure you would remember the time when we were discussing the Hindustan campaign at Partud. What a stink I had raised regarding the debt of eight million rupees Raghunath Dada had run up during his Punjab campaign! It is such a shame that I too am doing the same thing: asking Pune for funds, instead of raising them on the field!'

'There is no reason for shame at all!' Vishwasrao's fair face had turned red with passion. 'Kakasaheb, a campaign of this kind has never been undertaken in the history of the Marathas. The events we are having to confront, they may not come to pass in the next seven lives of most armies. Please, I beg you, write to Pune without shame or hesitation.'

Bhausaheb felt a deep sense of satisfaction at this display of maturity by the crown prince. He signalled to Mahipatrao Chitnis and began dictating the text of the letter:

> '... In Hindustan, here, the matter of raising resources and collecting revenue has become quite complex. I reported this to Shrimant in my previous letter. The crops were hit by blight this year, resulting in poor harvest for the farmers of the Antarved. Besides, Abdali and Najeeb's raids have weakened our hold on the local landlords. The debts on Govind Ballal keep mounting, but there is nothing forthcoming from his side. Also, given our uncertain relationship with the Jaats at present, we cannot demand our dues with any great insistence. The land looks devastated. Animals are dying of disease. Sustenance has become difficult to procure—'

His voice turned hoarse and began to break. He steadied himself, tried to stealthily mop up the moisture around his eyes, and continued:

> 'For the rest, even if we defeat the Pathan, there is little possibility of raising any revenue here till Dussehra. It is requested that Shrimant immediately dispatch strong letters to the local landlords here. They should be compelled to deposit their entire collection of revenue right here in Hindustan. Circumstances here are grave. I feel bad for having to ask for money from home, but no options remain. I have always believed in raising money wherever one goes, and whining for help is not a good thing to do. But, Shrimant, circumstances have been steadily worsening since Dattaji's passing. We have reached a point where we have to dip our hands into our own treasury, and that makes me feel miserable. It stings and bites. But in these difficult times, I don't see any other way out.'

Both Jankoji and Vishwasrao were grieved to see their hero suffer this way. Suddenly there was a loud clamour outside the tent. Shamsher Bahadur entered, looking harassed. 'What's going on, Shamsher?' asked Bhausaheb. 'What's all this noise outside?'

'What do I tell you, Bhau? Many of our regiments have been going hungry for the past two days. The pilgrims have also been creating a rumpus. Camels and horses cannot survive on a diet of water. They can't stay on their feet, and once down, they can't lift themselves up again. If this continues, the spine of the entire army will smash, everything will be ruined. Bhau, a way out of this has to be found, that too, quickly.'

When he saw a tough person like Shamsher floundering, Bhausaheb knew they were in dire straits. He sprang up from his seat. 'Call our fort-keeper over and let's go visit Delhi right now. Let's see whether we can raise some money there.'

As Bhausaheb rode out with his retinue, heads started popping out of the tents they crossed. It seemed that even the animals pricked up their ears and threw doleful glances at him. Women and children too turned their beaten eyes towards him, with just a tiny flicker of hope. It was only after he had ridden out of the defeated, emaciated crowd that Bhau could again begin to breathe.

The newly appointed fort-keeper Naro Shankar and his assistants Meer Khan Thokey and Baloji Palande soon joined the retinue. Bhausaheb's heart wept at seeing the barren, plundered Delhi that lay before him. The blank faces of the populace spoke of the misery of many years. The brocades on their backs had begun to shred. Delhi looked devastated, as if hit by famine. The horses rode past Chandni Chowk and headed towards the goldsmiths' lane. Most of the doors on the way were locked from the outside. When his horse Chandrasen entered the moneylenders' row, Bhausaheb wondered for a moment whether the deserted platforms were for the moneylenders to do their business or for laying out corpses for cremation. The doors through which once one could look at jewellery on display were all sealed shut, their shutters coated with thick layers of dust. The lanes that once used to be crowded with excited shoppers were bare, with an occasional mangy dog lying scratching itself under a bench. So many of the locks on the kiosks had turned rusty, so many of the doors had been nailed shut. When a few dead-beat traders stepped out of the few open doors to pay their respects to Bhausaheb, he asked a grocer, 'Where have all the traders gone? Why are all these doors closed?'

'Huzoor,' replied the man, 'which trader would want to stay on in this forlorn city? Delhi is now a widow with no one to protect her. Just about anyone can come and molest her. The traders who lent money have lost it all. Those who had wealth to bother about disappeared for keeping their possessions safe. Your two armies are circling over Delhi like birds of prey. The traders will return when one of you emerges a clear victor.

Till then, this city will remain dead as a corpse. Life will return only after the war is over.'

It was as if the barbed wires strung round the big shops and the mansions pierced Bhausaheb's heart. Without resources, without food and fodder, how could he turn his army round even if he had wanted to? No land to ransack, no grain to feed the hungry stomachs, it appeared that he had run out of all alternatives. Jankoji read Bhausaheb's mind and said, 'Kakasaheb, there is one way out of all this.'

'What? Where?'

'Inside the Red Fort. Come with me, I'll show it to you.'

Within a short while, they rode into the Red Fort. Right beyond the gate was the Deewaan-e-Aam, the Hall of Public Audience, of the king of Delhi, Shah Jahaan Saani. The entire cavalcade of the emperor had not received food supplies for two days. Bhausaheb held the puppet emperor installed by Ghaziuddin in contempt; but the Marathas had found no replacement yet, therefore, whether he liked it or not, the upkeep of the dummy king remained his responsibility, thought Bhausaheb. And it wouldn't be the emperor alone—there was his harem, his army of cooks, his hangers-on and the rest of them. The expenditure would run to over a hundred thousand, Bhausaheb calculated. His army required fifty or sixty thousand per month. The men hadn't been paid their allowances for months now. This emperor now adding to the burden like the bridegroom's horse was not a pleasant thought. Bhausaheb ignored the Deewaan-e-Aam as he rode on.

Jankoji brought Bhausaheb near the Deewaan-e-Khaas, the Hall of Private Audience, and made him stop. This was the palace where the grandees of Delhi would be called for conference, where the great Mughals would hold discussions with their peers. Though this hall rested on a number of pillars, not one of them obstructed the view of the throne from any corner. The architects had ensured that the emperor's eyes reached everywhere and saw everyone. As soon as the troupe entered the hall, their sounds began reverberating. Every word they spoke was accompanied by a resonance.

Jankoji drew Bhausaheb's attention to the palace roof. It was plated right across with silver, with fanciful fleur-de-lys patterns carved all over. Half of this silver-plating, however, had been torn away by rude hands.

Pointing towards those ravaged areas, Bhausaheb asked, 'Who could have torn off the roof?'

'Ghaziuddin cleaned it out,' said one of the Delhi residents.

Bhausaheb stared unblinkingly at the remains of the plating that continued to hang, sending sharp spears of light wherever sunlight struck. In that shaft he saw descending cascades of silver coins, and suddenly in those coins he saw the sorrowful eyes of his starving men and animals. He tightened his fists in determination and ordered Naro Shankar, 'Fort-keeper, call over all the carpenters and masons from the fort and tear the rest of the plating down!'

The people around him were stunned at hearing the order, and many began exchanging alarmed glances. Some of the bolder Delhi denizens mustered up courage and stammered, 'M'lord, please don't visit this catastrophe on the Deewaan-e-Khaas. It's the pride of Delhi. So many invaders have come and gone, but they have not desecrated the holy etchings of this magnificent hall! It can only bring bad luck!'

'Really?' roared Bhausaheb in rage and scorn. 'Can't you choose better things to lie about? How do you explain half the ceiling missing? When Nadir Shah had carted away the Peacock throne and the Kohinoor diamond fifteen years ago, in broad daylight and from right under your noses, which mouse-hole had you scurried into? This Abdali camping across the river was a soldier on the forefront of Nadir Shah's forces, looting and razing all of Delhi. Who among you had the spunk to throw questions at him? How can you stand there and talk of pride and honour?'

At a sign from him, the assembled carpenters and masons arrived and set up their ladders against the filigreed pillars. As they began the wrenching and tearing, the die-hards among the Delhi men gave it another shot and pushed the ill-luck theory harder. When they continued grovelling for the ripping to stop, Bhausaheb thundered, 'I don't want this wealth for squandering,' he shouted. 'I want to keep alive the men and animals who have travelled all the way here to protect Delhi, and are now dying of hunger on this soil. Anybody who raises obstructions against my sacred duty shall be cut down.'

The entire plating was ripped off, and now lay in a heap on the floor. Bhausaheb estimated that the silver should fetch him at least seven to eight hundred thousand rupees. Shamsher Bahadur's squad was already waiting at the palace gates. The men gathered the silver in sacks, loaded them on horses and were ready to depart under the protection of five thousand well-armed soldiers. When Shamsher bowed to take leave, Bhausaheb said to him in a heavy voice, 'Shamsher, you haven't a moment to waste. Set your horses racing and take this silver to Bharatpur, Bareli, anywhere, but try your best to return tonight. Remember that our starving men and animals will be waiting for you here with eager expectation.'

※

Life had returned to the Itaawa of the Bundeles. Najeeb Khan and Jahaan Khan had launched their attack on Itaawa two-and-a-half months back and stretched Pant Bundele's forces to the limit and beyond. Those two-and-a-half months had been bad for the entire region of the Antarved stretching from the banks of the Yamuna right up to the Ganga. Najeeb had blown up the posts of the Jaats on the eastern bank of the Yamuna and marched into Govind Pant's province, razing to the ground Maratha territories like Shikoha, Bithoor and Itaawa. Pant's manor at Itaawa had not escaped Najeeb's wrath either, and had been subjected to ruthless arson and pillage. The furniture and fitments of the inner rooms had been torched too, reducing the beautiful, luxurious Mughal-style structure to a black, charred shell. When Abdali got news of Bhausaheb's army rapidly advancing towards Delhi, he immediately set off with his army, thus reducing the pressure on the eastern part of the Antarved. Pant took immediate advantage of this slack and mounted ferocious raids with his eight-thousand-strong army. One after the other, the forts fell to his force, and he soon cleared the province of the Pathans-Rohillas.

Govind Pant was the seniormost, the most experienced feudal lord of the Peshwas in the north. The province he held under his sway was no tiny patch either. His control spread right from Sagar at the bank of the Yamuna to Gadhakota, Patharia, Balhai, Hatey, Kota and Jaitpur to Damoh. When Bajirao Peshwa had received the territory of Bundelkhand, he had arranged for its security by appointing a young Pant as the revenue collector. Pant had then gone on to capture the surrounding country and seriously increased his heft. The other chieftains recognized him as the boss of a good half of the province of Bundelkhand and began addressing him as Bundele. As time passed, Pant virtually forgot that his real family name was Kher, and happily took for himself the surname of Bundele. During his twenty-seven years of overlordship of Bundelkhand, he had seen plenty of summers and rains, and watched his hair go from black to white. His two important offices were located at Raipur to the south of the Yamuna and Itaawa on the other side of the river. He had brought over good clerks from the Maratha countries Konkan and Desh and established them in his two offices, thus creating a good and tight administration in his feudal lands. When the time for revenue collection arrived, he would visit his fiefs in person and camp there till all the collection was done. During the wet monsoon months, he would sit in his office and get his account books into order. His firm, well-organized administration had earned for him the fear and respect of his village headmen and petty officials, and getting them to deposit their dues on time had become easy.

Pant had established his headquarters in a town called Saagar by a beautiful lake; there he had constructed a strong fort and posted intrepid soldiers to guard it. There were a number of chieftains who had received land grants from the Peshwas in the regions of Malwa, the Antarved and beyond, but nobody ran his province as efficiently as Pant did.

A brocade-laced kerchief thrown over his shoulder, short and portly Pant was immersed in the papers in his office. He had entered his sixties a few years ago, but the energy and enthusiasm he exuded would be a rare sight in a person forty years younger. Most of his earlier records had been burnt to ashes in Najeeb's invasion, and now Pant was busy creating a new set virtually from scratch. Next to him sat his old friend Neelkanth Shastribuva, watching with admiration the commitment that Pant brought to the work at hand. As he saw the new rolls of paper covered with matter freshly drafted in a beautiful hand, Shastribuva remarked, 'Pant, with such invasions taking place every once in a while, it would be seriously disrupting your administrative clock!'

'What else?' groaned Pant. 'I have been looking after the administration of this province for the past twenty-seven years. How many times I would have yelled into the Peshwa's ears for the setting up of a standing force of thirty thousand men here in the Antarved, but what does he care? If only he could have made a permanent arrangement here, so much of unnecessary headache would have been avoided!'

'They say, Pant, that looking at your sense of responsibility, Bajirao handed over Bundelkhand to you at a very young age. Was it just this, or are you also in any way related to the Peshwas?'

'You think this kind of thing comes to pass on account of relationships?' laughed Pant. 'My family comes from a village named Newara near Ratnagiri. Although I was an adopted child, both my adopted father and my natural father were poor people. I would have been barely fifteen years of age when our entire family crossed the mountains and landed at Wai in search of livelihood, and settled down in a village called Bawdhan. Not finding enough work there, I came over to Pune around the time that Balajirao was creating waves in Hindustan. The trumpets of his victory blared everywhere in the north. Look at the coincidence here: Bajirao's mother Radhabai hailed from the house of the Barves from our own village of Newara. I used this connection to catch the attention of the Queen Mother and managed to find shelter at Shrimant's doorstep. Sheer chance!'

'But again, as people say, you began life as a commoner at the court, so how did you suddenly rise to becoming an important chieftain?'

'It's quite true that I began as a nobody under Bajirao's tutelage, and I have no sense of shame in confessing this; in fact I am proud of it. But I am surprised that you should not know how his lordship turned his benevolence on me.'

'Well, I really don't know!'

'The entire court knows about it. Anyway, as it happened, his lordship was on his way to Hindustan to settle accounts with Bangash Pathan. The armies of those days were lean and swift; it was only much later that this business of carrying wife and kids crept in. There was nimbleness in Bajirao's campaigns. We would rest for barely two or three hours in the night and get moving again. After three continuous days of advance, our army rested by the side of a river. Everybody, including Shrimant, was famished, and the responsibility of arranging food for his lordship fell on me. In that wilderness, we had enough grocery with us, but what we couldn't find was fire and logs for burning. Shrimant, meanwhile, was stamping his feet for some quick food. As I walked up the bank, I noticed a pyre burning by the water. Even as the body was burning, I dragged out some burning logs from the pyre, kneaded the dough and quickly roasted the bhaakari over it. After his lordship's dinner was over, someone who had noticed me in the act went up to him and disclosed my impertinence, in the hope of getting me severely chastised. Shrimant sent for me, and I went and stood before him with trembling legs, expecting severe punishment. His lordship asked my name and the name of my village and said, 'The boy is enterprising; he should be put to use.' My life changed. In due course, I was given the responsibility of looking after Bundelkhand. That was how a nobody called Govind Kher transformed into Bundele.'

They sat laughing and chatting about old times when a page entered with a scroll sleeve. 'From which part?' asked Pant. 'Desh? Delhi? It's from Bhausaheb, right?'

As the page nodded, Shastribuva asked, 'How many scrolls do you get from Bhausaheb in a day?'

'One is guaranteed; sometimes two.'

'Quite a bother, this!'

'Why a bother? Bhau is caught in a difficult situation, what else can he do?'

Mumbling the name of god, Pant pulled out the scroll and began reading.

> *Greetings from Sadashiv Chimaji to Govind Ballal, the deeply respected knight of the realm.*
>
> *Received your letters that pleaded that I should not bother you with trivial matters; you do not have money; there's trouble in the provinces; once arrangements are in place, you propose to visit with the accounts; you will act according to the orders given to you. Pant, I have put such trust in you, and yet you talk of accounts?*
>
> *Expenses here have been very heavy; how far can the two hundred thousand go that you have sent? Please deposit about two years' worth of revenue in advance with the government. Finances in your region are in good shape; raise loans. I have written to you a number of times how desperately money is needed here. Please send over two-and-a-half million as soon as you receive the letter. Raise it whichever way you have to, but the money has to be dispatched immediately; no excuses.'*

Pant broke into a sweat. As he was wiping his face with his kerchief, his son Balaji Pant arrived. 'What's Shrimant's command?'

'Two and a half million, and that too urgently. Shastribuva, I have no idea where to get this money from. Revenue has not been coming in from the small peasants. It was just during sowing time that Najeeb and Jahaan had mounted their raids, preventing the farmers from getting on with their activities. The crops of so many who sowed were hit by disease. Those with healthy crops will get nothing in hand till Dussehra, so no payment of dues till then. Bhausaheb says, raise loans; but the traders and moneylenders have all vanished. They don't want to pour their capital into the pit of war, as there is no guarantee of the money coming back. Whatever moneylenders there were have scattered in all directions. In spite of such straitened circumstances, I managed to gather two hundred thousand to send to him. When I ask Bhausaheb whether I should show him the account books, he flares up. How does one raise loans during times of such dire emergency?'

'Pant, I speak to you as a friend; please don't take offence,' said Shastribuva. 'Ever since Malwa, Bhausaheb had been writing again and again for boats to be arranged. But when Bhausaheb reached the Yamuna, he saw neither you nor the boats. People say that if you had arranged for the boats, Bhausaheb would certainly have crossed the river and finished off the enemy. After having served the Peshwa with such sincerity all these years, all that you get now is a black mark.'

'Shastribuva, there is one thing you are missing out. However big a landlord I may be, I'm not a voodoo man. I do not possess magical powers. How many things can a single person do at one and the same time? I have no desire to lay blame on Shrimant Bhausaheb, but there are limits to which a person can stretch himself. Itaawa is hundreds of miles from Shukrataal. 'Go help Dattaji', and I went. It was sheer luck that I returned alive from there. I had barely returned when the Durrani-Rohilla armies came tailing me. Our western border abuts Rohilkhand, so that makes it a bit like our in-laws' land. They then brought along a friend, Abdali, and the forts and the province we had raised brick by brick over twenty-seven years were levelled to the ground as we watched. Since we didn't have a big army of our own, we were just brought down like sitting ducks: Bithoor today, Itaawa tomorrow, the villages just fell one after another. A game that took twenty-seven years to assemble fell apart in a fortnight. On top of that comes Bhau's instruction: meet Shuja by whatever means, turn him round towards the Marathas. My own province was in flames when I sprinted towards Ayodhya. Lakhnau-Faizabad are not round the next corner, are they? And that champion schemer Najeeb had reached there. Wasted days dodging that hell-hound and trying to bring Shuja round. Meanwhile, Bhau had crossed the Chambal. It was only on returning from there that I started retrieving my stations one after another. Till such time that I bring order back in these places, how am I going to collect money? How much can a person run at this age, and where all? Yet I managed to scrape up two hundred thousand. But all said and done, we are the Peshwa's troopers, and propose to be of service to our last breath. It's my misfortune, though, that I could not arrange the boats for Bhau at the time of need.'

'You have to say this about Bhau: despite all difficulties, despite all the obstacles that keep springing up, Bhausaheb has been hacking his way through and moving on. I have never seen a person as spirited and competent as this man for a long, long time.'

'Never was a truer word said,' responded Pant. 'Through his resilience, his passion, this Bhau has earned the credit to be called Chimaji Appa's son. The fervour with which he has been driving his men, the astuteness with which he has laid out his political strategies, he hasn't allowed a seasoned enemy like Abdali's to have his way. When I see this zeal, Shastribuva, I feel that I should have been young enough and strong enough to ride shoulder to shoulder with a valiant general like Bhau.' Balaji told his father, 'We've got news that Sardar Gopalrao Barve is coming to pay you a visit this afternoon.'

'Sardar Gopalrao Barve? What is it that we owe him yet?'

'Besides, there is a person by the name of Rasadullah Khan who has been desiring an audience with you.'

'Rasadullah Khan? When did he come? Balarao, send this man over and you move on. I have some important matter to discuss with him.'

Balaji left as instructed, leaving Shastribuva bemused. 'Pant,' he asked, 'who is this Khan fellow? I hear your neighbour Najeeb Khan addresses you respectfully as Daaji, so is this other Khan some relative of his?'

'Don't be absurd!' growled Pant, but it was obvious that the unexpected arrival of this Khan had pushed Pant into a rather discomforting corner. His awkwardness increased when this rather dandily dressed person presented himself and greeted him, 'Salaam, Saheb.'

'Salaam to you Khan Saheb,' Pant responded with a pasty smile. 'How are you? You would have received the stuff I sent you!'

'Yes, I received the stuff you sent,' replied the Khan, catching on the conspiratorial mood, 'and forwarded the purchase to where you had wanted it sent. Such delicately beautiful figures, such loveliness of complexion, such melodious voices those birds have—'

'Khan Saheb!' Pant had turned red as he screeched. 'Our work is done, why get into all these details? Thank you for your help. Goodbye.'

'My apologies, Saheb!' Khan looked a little hurt. He thought he had been playing the game well. 'Any time you need help in this department, please remember this servant of yours.'

When Rasadullah was safely out of earshot, Shastribuva burst out laughing and said, 'What's this, Pant? Developing new tastes at this age?'

'What rubbish, Shastribuva! You know I have always had a fondness for animals and birds. So, when I got to know about these singing birds—'

'Birds with melodious voices is fine, but since when have these birds sprouted beautiful figures and delicate complexions?' Shastribuva asked teasingly.

Pant knew that any effort at concealment was futile. He lowered his eyes and looked straight at Shastribuva and said, 'Look, I have no connection with this dismal affair.'

'But you were the one who counted out the money, didn't you? The man even talked about having dispatched the goods to the desired location. Where is this palace where you have housed these mellifluous birds?' Shastribuva couldn't keep himself from taking a dig at his friend.

Pant knew that the only way out of this embarrassment was laying it all bare. He went up to a trunk, pulled out a letter from the bottom, and gave it to Shastribuva. 'Shastri, read this, and then forget that you have ever seen it.'

Shastribuva took the letter and began reading with great interest. It was written by Nanasaheb Peshwa himself about a month ago. '... The government has arranged for a theatre academy this time. Hence, look out for beautiful young girls of the purest caste and send them over. Make sure they are of the best quality.' The letter was dated 17 July 1760.

As Shastribuva read the letter over and over again, Pant remarked, 'What are you getting so excited about? There are any number of festivals and gatherings in the royal court. They would need dancers there, wouldn't they?'

'But why do they need to be of the best quality, beautiful, young, and of the purest caste?'

'Shastribuva, that's enough nit-picking for the day. In from one ear, and out from the other. Why should we get after whatever Shrimant does?'

'Who's getting after anyone? But what shocks me is that there is Bhausaheb on the one side, who has been sending frantic letters asking for guns, ammunition, food and fodder for the army, and on the other is the Peshwa himself, asking for pure-caste, beautiful, young—'

Pant clamped his hand upon Shastribuva's mouth to shut him up, and placed the letter back in the trunk. He then insisted that his friend join him for lunch. Without bothering to enquire whether Gopalrao Barve was coming at all, the two sat down for their meals. Their chat continued, with Shastribuva asking, 'Pant, Gopalrao enjoys considerable intimacy with the Peshwa. Now you sent whatever you could to Bhausaheb; how much of his treasury did Barve empty out?'

'Would have sent tens of millions,' laughed Pant. 'Let's not get into reviling our seniors. But yes, I wonder what glory the Barves would have brought to the Peshwa crown. Here I am, who have for the last twenty-five years turned my blood to sweat and sent half my earnings to Pune, and there he is, with his one qualification being that he is Janakibai's brother and Raghunath Dada's brother-in-law.'

Pant was otherwise a careful talker, but when the topic of Gopalrao cropped up, he found his tongue running away a bit with him. 'In our land of Maharashtra,' he said even while vigorously chewing his food, 'there are very few who have risen up by sheer dint of ability and work. Never mind whether they are Brahmins or Marathas or any other caste, if people have had the right connections, they have moved up at the durbar. We have this saying in our village: wife's brother, softer than butter. I didn't climb up the ladder by having to hold somebody's fingers. It was as a boy that I crossed the mountains and landed at Wai. The Rana from

Bundelkhand had given this property to Bajirao; but later his descendants began plotting to get it back. Now I have not been a big-time soldier, but I managed to assemble an army and settled the issue. Twenty-seven years I sowed into this land, and what I reap today is the result of my hard work.'

'So, can it be said that Dadasaheb brought pressure to bear for half the province to be handed over to Gopalrao?'

'When you are up against power, it's good not to be too smart. When it's a matter of the Peshwa's in-law, who do you go to and say a province should not be split?'

'But then, in such times of trouble, the in-law should be sending good funds to Bhausaheb, then!'

'Who is he obliging by sending and not sending?' Pant growled in anger. 'Even when the province was split, the palace in the difficult northern area facing the Rohillas was tied round my neck, while Gopalrao eased himself into the Prayag side, with lovely, fertile lands to rule over. The revenue collections there are substantially more than mine.'

The news of Gopalrao's arrival was announced soon after lunch was over. Pant entered the reception area and advanced with a smile to welcome the man. After the exchange of pleasantries, Pant got straight to the issue and asked, 'You would have received letters from Shrimant Bhausaheb!'

'Yes, they keep coming, off and on.'

'How much funds have you dispatched?'

'Oh yes, I have to send that. Ganesh Khandekar hasn't sent anything either. I thought I should check with you before I sent the money. I have made all the arrangements, though. How much have you sent, by the way?'

'I have sent two hundred thousand, but he has been pressing for two hundred thousand.'

'What? Two-and-a-half million? Well, yes, I have been getting urgent messages too.'

Govindpant's voice turned anxious as he said, 'The Marathi people who have been employed in various jobs in the Antarved have taken a fright and have begun winding up their households and leaving for their native villages. Bhausaheb has heard of it too, and has sent desperate letters to me.'

'What else would these people do other than packing their bags and leaving? With war clouds turning denser, they would want to return to the security of their native lands, wouldn't they?'

'But as feudal lords here, we should be preventing them from leaving, shouldn't we?'

'Well, yes, that's true, too.'

After a little while, Barve remembered something and asked, 'Have you received letters from Sakharam Bapu, Pant?'

'The ones that ask for half the funds to be sent to Pune and the other half to Bhausaheb?'

'Yes, those ones.'

'Yes, I've got them.'

No great intimacy existed between Pant and Barve, it was evident. After a little more discussion over fruits, Barve got up to leave, and Pant escorted him up to the portico. Barve then rode off with his manager Dasopant Nervekar by his side. 'Did you see, Dasopant?' Barve said, 'He too hasn't sent the kind of money he was expected to. None of the others have done it either.'

'But the demands have been unrelenting from both sides!'

'Take advantage of Bapu's letter and start writing to both sides.'

'How?'

'Write to Pune that the money has been sent to Bhausaheb, and tell Bhausaheb that the money has gone to Pune.'

'But what if this ruse gets exposed?'

'How can you be so innocent, Dasopant? With such a huge war looming in front, who has the time to sit cross-checking accounts?'

As Pant saw Barve recede into the distance, he remarked to Shastribuva, 'These were the kinds of people who had gone and poisoned the Peshwa's ears about me. I had to run to Pune with my account books, there were inquiries, and what was the result? It's we, the companions of the Peshwa, who have risen from the soil, that will stake their lives for the empire when the need arises; but I can assure you, Shastribuva, that during times of crises, people like Gopalrao are going to be of no use at all. What relationships and what affections? When the going gets tough, one's own children are known to turn their backs. When there is power and pelf, there will be plenty of friends and relatives crowding around you; any number of brightly feathered birds will fly in to dip their beaks in the plate. But when the season turns to autumn, when the leaves begin forsaking the tree, they will all disappear. Fair-weather friends, all!'

⁂

It was pitch dark, and the rain was falling in sheets. Abdali's army had stretched itself out in relative comfort, battling the rain and wind as well as it could. Abdali, actually, had managed to camp his army decently well. The Marathas had abandoned the Yamuna bank in the south of Delhi and moved to the west, erecting their tents and pavilions all around Shalimar Bagh. When the rival camps were on either side of the river, the horsemen and soldiers of either side would sit watching each other's movements hour upon hour. There would be the occasional exchange of gunfire—men and animals would fall victim, tents would go up in flames. Two or three weeks had passed in this manner when the Marathas suddenly decided to change their base camp. Abdali's men were so thrilled at the disappearance of the Marathas from the other side that they began celebrating. Some of the Afghan Rohillas brought out processions, as if the enemy had already been defeated. Abdali and Najeeb had to come down upon them with harsh words: 'Stop this tomfoolery, you idiots! The battlefield is still some distance away.'

That very night, the emperor called a conference in his pavilion that went on till late. The same night, Abdali, Najeeb, Jahaan Khan, Shuja and Shah Wali rushed towards Shahadara, located a site on a rise and began shifting their tenting equipment. There were no Marathas to be seen now on the Yamuna banks. Their base now was at Shalimar Bagh. Abdali had posted his sentinels up and down the bank on his side to secure it from a sudden Maratha raid.

With Abdali sending back some Rohilla sardars to their lands for the next two or three months to regain health and energy, the pressure had reduced on fifteen to twenty thousand of Abdali's soldiers. The army had split into two divisions: the Sunni Rohilla Pathans to the north, and the Shia soldiers to the south. Thus, it was in the northern wing that the Emperor Abdali, his Wazeer Shah Wali Khan, Commander-in-chief Jahaan Khan, Barkhurdar Khan, Najeeb Khan and the other grandees had their pavilions. In the south, it was primarily the Shia Shuja-ud-dowlah and his officers and soldiers. Earlier, Shuja's men had carried their tent material to the north and had begun stringing up their structures. The Pathan soldiers kicked up a ruckus at this and shouted, 'Look which way the wind blows, and then see where these Hindustani Shias are pitching their tents. We are having to suffer their stench that comes blowing downwind; it is not acceptable to us. Dump them in the south, we want the northern part.' The chieftains found the men's complaint reasonable, and Shuja's men were told to carry their stuff south.

Shuja's tents now stood on the plains, shivering in the cold, wet wind. Shuja-ud-dowlah sat in the conference chamber of his Nawab's pavilion. Fine, delicate partition screens made of reed hung from all sides, with tastefully placed tassels adding to the impression of grandeur. Finely carved boxes of perfumes, both Indian and foreign, rested on tall tables. Trays of fresh rose and jasmine flowers interspersed with the aromatic kewada grass made the air thick with exotic redolence. Never mind that it was a battlefield 'palace', but one look would convince the observer that it could belong only to the nawab of Lakhnau.

A sandalwood bed stood in the middle, covered with a thick mattress. The deep red, crinkled fringe along the four sides of the bedcover reached down to the floor. The mattress was secured to the four legs of the bed with silk threads, so that however much Shuja tossed and turned, the mattress and its cover would remain in place. The bolsters placed on the smaller seating mattresses around the bed were covered with soft muslin. While Shuja reclined on the bed, his most trusted advisers Sardar Anupgiri, Kashiraj and Maulvi Sultan Baba sat below with a few others. His robe was made of the finest white muslin; the delicate floral patterns round its collar and sleeves had taken the best artists months of embroidering.

Maulvi Sultan Baba said, 'Nawab Saheb, it was the hypnotizing tongue of Najeeb that duped you into coming here. You actually invited calamity upon yourself for no rhyme or reason. We now have to suffer insults at every step. There was all that talk about saving Islam before we came here, but clearly it was all politics, the garb of the religion cloak.'

'You are quite right, Maulvi Saheb, I invited this calamity upon myself, and now I am trapped in a dark cave, as it were. Can't see any way out of it, at least not till the war gets over.'

'Nawab Saheb,' spoke up Sardar Ismail, 'our Lakhnavi style of life, our spirit, our manners and courtesies should stay unobstructed wherever we go, we justly preen ourselves on it.'

'Where can one find any equal to our Lakhnavi way of life? The kebabs of Bareili and the nawabs of Lakhnau are famous the world over for their distinctiveness. So, where's the controversy?'

'Nawab Saheb, I feel ashamed to have to repeat it before you,' said Ismail, 'Our army of four thousand valiant fighters is accompanied by a harem and our servitors that measure up to another thousand. You know what Najeeb calls these non-combatants? Litters of a sow.'

'Things haven't stopped there either, Nawab Saheb,' joined in Sultan Baba. 'That uncouth Najeeb Khan says that this litter of piglets does not have any place in the Afghan army. If the Nawab is so fond of this cavalcade, he should cross over and join the forces of the Marathas on the other side of the river.'

'If he disdained us so much, what was he doing wearing out the doorsill of my palace?' growled Shuja. 'Sultan Baba, the mistake is altogether mine. I fell for his sweet talk and wore this snake like a bracelet on my wrist. Now that, true to its kind, it has bitten, who can I go and complain to?'

'Nawab Saheb, there is a prohibition in the emperor's army for anybody other than the emperor himself to sit in a canopy,' informed Kashiraj Pandit. 'However big a chieftain, and however many elephants he has, he cannot be seen astride his animal. When these chieftains see our canopies rocking in front of your pavilion, their filthy hearts turn black with envy. I've even heard the Pathan soldiers gripe that the nawab cannot consider himself greater than the emperor of Kandahar, and so on.'

'This is nothing,' Sultan Baba piped in. 'Nobody can blow the trumpet in the army without the emperor's orders, but we are not the vassals of the Durrani king, are we? Nawab Saheb, I have to bring this to your knowledge that a few of our trumpeters were rounded up this afternoon by some Afghan ruffians for playing their instrument, and were given physical chastisement.'

Shuja-ud-dowlah was deeply mortified at hearing these tales of petty insults. 'How is it that they have suddenly remembered all these sanctions?' he snarled. 'When the Marathas were rolling at my doorsteps begging for friendship, I rejected them and came over to Abdali. Who was it that clanged cymbals, beat kettle-drums and blew on trumpets? His army had taken out a procession, with the emperor himself ordering the blowing of trumpets; and now it is a punishable offence?'

'Nawab Saheb,' Sultan Baba said, 'you remember the speech Abdali had delivered when we had decided to join him? He had gushed about having such a variety of people in his army. He had even given an assurance that the Hindustanis among them would follow the traditions of their land. Why, then, this sudden recourse to beatings?'

'There is only one answer to all these questions,' Shuja responded gravely. 'However much we support them, provide them with wherewithal, even lay down our lives for them, in the end these Rohilla Pathans will never forgive us for being Shias, even if we are Muslims. It is their conceit of being Sunnis that makes them behave so ill with us.'

'Nawab Saheb, this is the month of Muharram. In the next couple of days, we will be coming out with our processions. There is a strong possibility that the fanatical among these Afghans will cause disruptions. We need to exercise great caution,' said Sultan Baba.

'We will take as many precautions as we have to, but I had never thought that matters would descend to such lows,' Shuja groaned.

Sultan Baba threw a sharp glance at Shuja, ran his fingers through his white beard, and said, 'Nawab Saheb, the tenth day of Muharram is the day on which the battle of Karbala was fought; it is also the day for commemorating the sacrifice of the martyrs. Nowhere else in Hindustan are condolence meetings held and processions taken out with as much gravity and fervour as in the province of Ayodhya. It's not just Lakhnau and Faizabad, the entire province of Ayodhya gets immersed in profound grief. Nawab Saheb, please narrate to us the sacred story of the battle that took place at Karbala. It's been a long time since I heard it from your lips. No teller of stories, no raconteur can narrate the martyrdom of Imam Hasan and Imam Hussain with as much pathos as you can.'

The others took up the refrain and turned towards Shuja with great excitement and expectation. Kashiraj Pandit too added passionately, 'Please Nawab Saheb, please do narrate that story to us. Our ears are most eager to hear it in your words.'

Shuja-ud-dowlah composed himself and began, 'The prophet of Islam was our Paighambar Saheb. When he moved on to heaven, who would be his successor? This question our Paighambar had answered even before he was called back to Allah: his successor would be appointed by common consent. Three caliphs came and went after our Paighambar Saheb passed away. Imam Ali, the Prophet's son-in-law, was a valiant fighter for the cause of religion. Every time each of the three caliphs was selected, his claim was overlooked. Our sect of the Shias believes in the Imamate of Ali.

'Imam Ali became the fourth caliph. Upon his death, his son and the Prophet's grandson Imam Hasan became the next caliph. Mu'aviyah, the governor of Syria, challenged the caliphate of Imam Hasan, and to avoid bloodshed, Imam Hasan handed over the caliphate to Mu'aviyah, on condition that he treated his subjects well, and did not make the post hereditary. But Mu'aviyah later broke the pact and appointed his son Yazid to succeed him as caliph. Imam Hussain, the second son of Imam Ali Saheb and the grandson of the Prophet, refused to accept Yazid as caliph. Yazid then began to put pressure on Imam Hussain to get him to yield, but Imam Hussain was adamant.

'Tiring of the persecution of his people at the hands of Yazid, he set off towards Kufah, Iraq, with his band of followers, as also the women and children of the clan, some on horseback, some atop camels, and some on foot. The journey through the baking desert was very difficult. Children began to cry with hunger and thirst.

'On the way, they came upon the bed of the river Dajla, and at some distance, in the desert land of Karbala, they could see the glitter of small ponds and puddles. As they raced towards the water, they were blocked by the enemy soldiers, who were under instructions to not allow the travellers access to water. As men, women and little children cried for water, Yazid's men towered over them and laughed. Meanwhile, the sand under their feet had begun to scorch the soles of their bare feet. Imam Hussain, however, was determined not to give in to these diabolic pressures and accept the caliphate of Yazid. Instead of dying of thirst and hunger, Imam Husain and his loyal followers preferred to stand up to the tyrant and die fighting. They pulled out their swords, a band of seventy-two against a besieging army of four thousand armed men, and they died fighting, every one of them. This happened on the tenth day of the month of Muharram, known as the 'Ashura'. After they were massacred, their bodies were decapitated, and their heads, including that of Imam Hussain's, were carried on spear-points amidst raucous, demoniacal celebration. This was how Imam Hussain was martyred. This is the story of the battle of Karbala.'

The story had reduced the raconteur and his audience to tears. Wiping his eyes, Shuja carried on, 'So, this was how Imam Hussain stood up against a power-drunk tyrant and preferred martyrdom to surrender to the forces of evil. Many such calamities like the Karbala keep raising their heads in the path of Islam, but our faith finds the strength to stand up against them. Hussain's martyrdom was, in fact, the death knell for Yazid. As the poet has said:

> The passing away of Hussain was but Yazid's demise
> After each Karbala, Islam again does rise.'

The audience recorded their appreciation of Shuja's talent for storytelling, and decided that, in spite of being so far away from Lakhnau and Faizabad, they would hold condolence sessions on the day of Ashura, bring out banners and pennants in remembrance of the battle of Karbala and the beheading of their Imam, and carry the taaboot—a replica of Imam Hussain's shrine made of bamboo, cloth and paper—in procession as they did at home.

The day of Ashura, the tenth day of Muharram dawned. Shuja's army had begun preparing the taaboots quite a few days in advance. Servants had been dispatched to Bulandshahr to collect the material for preparing the structure. Bamboo sticks were slit thin and intertwined to the shape of the dome of a masjid. The dome-shaped frame was then pasted over with paper in various colours and further daubed with paint. Each one of these taaboots rose to the height of a full-grown tree. Early in the morning, Shuja and his chieftains had dressed themselves in the dark green, ankle-length tunics of fakirs, taken begging-bowls in hand, and begun doing the rounds of the entire camp crying for alms. 'Give in the name of Allah,' they sang, 'give in the name of Ali, give alms to this beggar.'

Shuja went and stood in front of Abdali's pavilion and cried out, 'Give alms in the name of the martyrs of Karbala!'

Emperor Durrani stepped out in person and deposited fruits in Shuja's begging-bowl with suitable reverence. The Sunni Pathans held in disdain this ritual of the Shias to turn fakirs and go begging on the streets. A number of the Afghan soldiers sniggered at the sight of the Shia nobles and commoners with their begging-bowls; some even made fun of them.

Shuja's army stayed busy all day arranging for the taaboots to be carried in procession in the evening. In the afternoon, Shah Wali Khan went to Abdali and said, 'Aalam-panaah, the Shias will take their taaboots out in procession this evening for immersion in the Yamuna. I have secret information that some of our fanatical Afghans plan to disrupt these processions.'

'This should not be allowed to happen,' snarled Abdali. 'It will be the ruination of all our plans. It's important for all of us to fight as a single army. Release an imperial ordinance; tell them that anybody found indulging in these disruptive activities will be severely punished. Plant soldiers at every important point in the camp, and along the route of the procession.'

It was now four o'clock. Shuja's thirty-five-hand tall taaboot stood right at the head of the procession. Its beautifully built dome and the arches in all four of its walls were covered with delicate filigree work. Not just coloured paper and sheets of silk, but the jewellery of the begums had also been skillfully incorporated into the structure. In the hollow inside, the taaboot was the replica of Imam Hussain's grave, draped in a sparkling white shroud. On top of the grave were scattered basketsful of flowers, and a turban was balanced upon it.

Five cutouts of the human palm with the five fingers spread out, called the *Pan Jaatan Paak*—the Sacred Palm—were carried on poles. They symbolized the five males of the Prophet's family. The red flags carried by the processionists symbolized the blood of Imam Hussain spilt in Karbala, while the green flags symbolized the blue-black blood of his elder brother Imam Hasan, who had been poisoned to death. Imam Ali's invincible sword 'Zulfiqaar' was carried swinging and flashing in front of the procession. The entire procession was to wind its way through Abdali's camp and finish off at the Yamuna bank, where the tall taaboots would be immersed into the water.

As the taaboots began to move, they were led by maulvis, raconteurs and professional singers singing elegies recounting the martyrdom of the brothers Imam Hasan and Imam Hussain. The words in which the elegies were written were straight and simple, but the story they narrated was so charged with passion that both the singers and their audience were soon reduced to bawling in grief. Thus the procession moved forward, resonant poetry invoking images of the battlefield of Karbala, its hot, unforgiving sand, its parched, dry landscape, and Imam Hussain's caravan of valiant soldiers, and hungry, thirsty women and children marching into the mouth of certain death. The processionists were dressed in mourning black, heads uncovered and feet bare. As the proceeded, they kept shouting in rhythmic refrain: 'Hasan! Hussain! Hasan! Hussain!' A number of them had removed their tunics and were slapping themselves hard on the chest, shoulder and back as they chanted the mesmeric slogan, 'Ya Hasan! Ya Hussain!'

As the procession crept forward, more and more of the processionists began removing their tunics and began beating themselves violently, so violently that the skin on their chest and back soon broke, turning them into a mass of flesh and blood. The flagellation, though, continued without respite, to the beat of their agonized shouts of 'Ya Hasan! Ya Hussain! Ya Hasan! Ya Hussain!'

Soon the procession was crossing Abdali's pavilion. The crowd turned denser and the cries of 'Hasan! Hussain!' turned louder. A number of Sunnis had also joined them in mourning of their Shia co-religionists. There were a few pageants that moved along with the procession. A couple of camels covered in black cloth walked as emblems of the unfortunate caravan that had accompanied Hussain that fateful day. Round and round them hopped and swirled boys with naked swords in their hands, in imitation of the soldiers of Yazid, letting out an occasional snarl and a demoniacal laugh. The procession would have wound past half the camp of the Afghan army when a couple of hundred fanatical Afghan horsemen broke into the procession, waving their naked swords over their heads. 'Deen! Deen!' they shouted, as they launched into the taaboots. For a little while, the crowd thought that it was a part of the pretence of playing Yazid's soldiers, but soon it became apparent that these latest intruders meant serious business.

Once their riotous intent became evident, panic overtook the onlookers as well as the processionists. The noise of the bedlam soon became loud enough to reach Abdali's pavilion. He sprang up instantly, pulled out his sword, jumped upon his horse and waded into the crowd with a loud cry. 'Kill these renegade soldiers,' he screamed in rage. The emperor's guards soon isolated the disruptors and rounded them up. It was only after Abdali had personally supervised the reorganization of the procession and the clearing up of the remaining distance to the Yamuna that he returned to his pavilion.

The conference in the royal pavilion went on till late into the night. Shah Wali, Shuja, Jahaan Khan, Najeeb, Barkhurdar Khan, and all the assembled nobles sat throwing terrified looks at Abdali's face. Abdali's mien was a kaleidoscope of the most negative emotions, anger, disgust, disappointment and frustration, chasing each other as he walked up and down the pavilion, slapping his biceps in annoyance. 'The next time this kind of bedlam breaks loose in my army,' he spat, looking daggers at his nobles, 'the next time this display of intolerance for others happens, I shall hang everyone on the gibbet, and I shall personally hammer the nails in. Idiots, all, don't you have any brains whatsoever? I have now been here for ten months, seen the entire summer through, and now the monsoons are about to end, and we are still stuck in Hindustan. The infidel on the other side of the river is growing stronger by the day. Despite shortage of food and fodder, Vishwasrao Bhau's self-belief today is no less than of a rampaging lion. The thrones of so many kings have I kicked out my sight, I have twisted and turned the boundaries of so many states like one bends a supple bamboo, and yet I can't get a good estimate of which way this campaign, this war is heading. The complexion this time is altogether different—impossible to say with certainty who will win and who will lose. The reason, clearly, is that Bhau—that infidel with such unflagging self-confidence. Any chance of a deal has altogether disappeared. The final battle is still to be fought. Learn to live with discipline. Those Shinde-Holkars have their palaces nearby; if they lose the battle, they still have their own country to run to, even if half broken and half dead. But, you nincompoops, how far do you think your Kabul and your Kandahar are? If we are defeated, forget our bodies, not even the hair on our head has any chance of reaching our native land. That is why, brainless oafs, learn to live with discipline, not with arrogance.'

❦

It was well past noon. With the wind having dropped, the saffron flag atop the band-room of Shaniwarwada was also fluttering half-heartedly. The guards posted on the Delhi Gate also stood listless, while work at the office moved at a snail's pace.

The entire atmosphere was so different from when Bhausaheb ran the office of the Peshwa. He was known for keeping a close watch on the servants and the interns right up to the sardars who came visiting. Everybody behaved with decorum and due courtesy. Whenever he took the round of Shaniwarwada, his hawk-eyes would absorb all, missing nothing. Whenever he crossed, the greatest of them would stiffen their backs; even the caparisoned elephants before the wada would freeze the flapping of their ears. He would arrive immediately after finishing his morning bath and a quick obeisance to the gods. Once he had occupied his seat, he would immerse himself in work and continue till his back began to creak.

It was now seven months since he had left for his campaign to northern Hindustan. The Peshwa administration was now being run by Raghunath Dada Saheb, and the important office of civil issues was handled by Sakharam Bapu Bokil. Nanasaheb Peshwa hadn't been keeping good health, and would mostly stay confined to his palace. Raghunathrao would get up after sunrise, and then spend a few hours in his bath and rather extended prayers. It was only towards the afternoon that he would drift into office for about an hour. 'So, Bapu,' he would drawl on arrival, 'how is it going? Anything unusual? Any special news?'

Sakharam Bapu would then rise from his seat with a cheerful smile, point towards Bhausaheb's seat, and say, 'Welcome, Shrimant, welcome your lordship! Our empire seems to be peaceful. No complaints, no petitions, nothing. When your lordship is at the helm, there can only be calm and contentment. Dadasaheb would then occupy his seat, tuck in a paan or two, potter around with the stationery a bit, and within an hour he would be ready to return to his palace. Very often he would be too lazy even to make this perfunctory visit to the office. Instead, he would call Sakharam Bapu over to his palace if there was some specific work or some desire he wanted fulfilled. If there was no message for some time, Bapu would paste a pleasant smile on his face and himself make a visit to Dadasaheb's palace to pay his respects. After a long exchange of pleasantries there, he would stop next to pay his courtesies to Nanasaheb. A little more while there, and then, on his way back, he would drop in at Gopikabai's palace to keep her abreast of the latest happenings in the empire. Thus, after having collected the dust of the three palaces, when Sakharam Bapu returned to office, there would be some of the Peshwa's strut in his walk as he made for his seat.

The complaints and petitions from the populace had reduced substantially. If any appellant did come along, Bapu had made arrangements for the person to be stopped at the Delhi Gate. An ordinary clerk would interact with such visitors, and that would free up Bapu to do his own thing. Who was there to question him once he had done the round of the three palaces? He would now have the time to sit gossiping about life with a bunch of admiring friends and relatives who now gathered regularly in his office.

'It was twenty-five years ago that the work of constructing the Shaniwarwada had begun,' he would lean back on the bolster and recite, 'and this Sakhoba was just an ordinary clerk appointed to keep the accounts. I can tell you how the foundation was laid, how brick was placed upon brick, where the bricks are well roasted, where they are not, where the lime is more, where it is less, everything. Although I was merely a clerk, as soon as the masons and workers were paid in the morning and the account balanced, I would roam around the wada all through the day and keep a sharp eye on every brick that was put into place. The soles of my feet would break into blisters and turn red. My mother would apply oil to them and ask why I was wearing myself out, and I would tell her that it was no less than the Peshwa's wada that was coming up, and although just a clerk, I considered it my duty to stay on the beat. I had to make sure that everything was in order. My mother would then remind me that I was nothing more than a clerk, and was not expected to take such a load upon myself. I would then tell her that the Peshwa's empire was a subject of reverence for me, and it was my dearest wish to see the empire expand

and spread across in all directions; hence I couldn't sit in peace and felt compelled to do the rounds. My mother would then bless me and say that my wish would certainly be fulfilled—the Peshwa's empire would spread across the length and breadth of Hindustan, I would not remain a clerk and rise to be a great chieftain, visit every state and province of the country. Well, my mother's words have come true. One way or the other, the Maratha empire covers the entire stretch of the Mughal holdings right from Attock to the deep south. So, gentlemen, what is the central message of my narration? Let's see if you have the answer.'

'Bapu, your riddles are beyond comprehension,' someone piped up softly.

'This is no riddle,' Bapu laughed. 'The meaning is crystal clear. The structure that is the Peshwas' empire is now spread across all of Hindustan. Whatever the state or province, this Bapu alone has the knowledge of how many bricks and how much mortar went where, where the lime is less and where more. The final conclusion? Nobody can take us for a ride.'

It was thanks to Mahadji Pant Purandare that Bapu had gained entry into the Peshwa administration. Mahadji was a manager with the Peshwas and Bapu had done his internship under him. The post of an accountant at village Hivara on the Karha plateau in the Divey Ghat had been with Bapu's family for many generations. An ancestor by name Mahadji Yamaji had earned great fame while in the service of Shivaji Maharaj, and Bapu was immensely proud of the fact. However, bad times had fallen on the family in the intervening years, and Bapu had been reduced to doing menial jobs at a very young age. But Bapu was sharp, hardworking and had the faculty of attracting the attention of important people, and he put these talents to use to improve his own lot and that of his entire family.

He had done the tour of Kashi, Prayag, Mathura and other places in northern Hindustan in the company of Nanasaheb Peshwa twenty years ago; he had been in the Karnataka campaign with Bhausaheb; but his real affection and loyalties lay with Raghunath Dada. It began with his participating in Dadasaheb's campaign in Gujarat. During his next two campaigns to northern Hindustan, Bapu was the chief administrator. He had actually danced in the Festival of the Lamps that was held in the Shalimar Gardens at Lahore to celebrate the hoisting of the Maratha flag at Attock. He considered himself blessed to be able to trail Dadasaheb like a shadow. Now, of course, the entire administration of the Peshwa empire had fallen into his charge—Nanasaheb was either unwell, or too deeply engrossed in his drama academy to bother, while Raghunath Dada was lazy, and had unshakeable trust in Bapu's word. As a result, Bapu was now convinced that he was the supreme authority in the office, and suspected that the royal flag atop Shaniwarwada fluttered at the behest of the signals his eyes sent.

As of this moment, he sat in easy comfort in his office seat, with a few of his well-wishers gathered around him. 'Bapu,' queried one of them, 'you must be carrying a load of responsibilities now?'

'Well, what choice do I have except to see it through?' Bapu responded with more than a touch of smugness. 'Right from the times of Shivaji Chhatrapati up to Nanasaheb Peshwa, our family has had the good fortune of being of service to the empire. It is our supreme duty to keep this tradition going.'

A servant came running in to announce that Dadasaheb was on his way to the office. Bapu shot up from his seat and placed his turban on his head as the Raghunathrao arrived. Bapu flashed an ingratiating smile and bent low as he intoned, 'Let your blessings be on us, Dadasaheb!'

Dadasaheb returned his smile, took his seat, and said, 'So, what's special today, Bapu?'

'Nothing truly special, Shrimant, but maybe you may find it interesting.'

'Yes, what's it?'

'A letter has arrived from northern Hindustan,' Bapu said in a low voice.

'Whose letter? Bhausaheb's or Govind Pant Bundele's?'

'It's from the honourable Bhausaheb.'

'So, how's Bhausaheb's campaign going?'

'The news of Bhausaheb capturing Delhi reached Shaniwarwada four days ago, and has now gone stale.'

'Anything beyond that?'

'Bhausaheb writes now that there's famine in the army. There's no money left, and men and animals are dying of hunger.'

'Really?' Dadasaheb looked surprised.

'This is what Bhausaheb writes,' he said with a trace of amusement. He paused for a moment and then continued, 'Dadasaheb, I know it is wrong for small people like me to overstep boundaries and meddle in the matter of their superiors, but there is something that I cannot rest without saying, if I may have your permission.'

'Go ahead.'

'Dadasaheb, writing about winning Delhi in one sentence and about famine in the army in the very next one … now you tell me, Shrimant, can the words Delhi and famine go together? It's the untold wealth of Delhi that has attracted invaders from all over the world, hasn't it?'

'Please read Bhausaheb's letter first, will you? What exactly does he say?'

'Yes, Shrimant, I was just going to do that,' responded a slightly flustered Bapu. 'He says that even if the Pathan is defeated, there is no way that money can be raised before Dussehra. He wants the Peshwa to dispatch strong letters to the feudal lords, instructing them to deposit funds directly in Hindustan. The situation is grave, he says. 'It's true that one should raise money where one works, but the circumstances have turned such that I am constrained to seek money from the home treasury. I feel terribly ashamed for doing so, but I do not see any other way out.''

Dadasaheb had turned grave. 'Do you think things have turned so grim there, Bapu?'

'Well, Shrimant,' Bapu responded in a low voice, 'when you are carrying an army, complexities are bound to arrive. We ourselves have gone on two campaigns to Hindustan, haven't we? You remember the discussions we had had at Partud, and all the heated arguments about who should lead the Hindustan campaign? It was Bhausaheb himself who had said then that winning provinces on money drawn from home couldn't work. He was so upset at the eight million debt you had run during your Hindustan campaign, and had yelled for you to submit accounts!'

'Yes, that's true,' Dadasaheb said with a smile. 'I guess now Bhausaheb would have realized how difficult it is to run an army, what responsibilities it entails!'

'And, Dadasaheb, your army hadn't sat on its heels in Delhi, it had marched right on to Attock beyond the Punjab! How beautifully we had managed everything, Shrimant!' Adding a little more sugar to his voice, Bapu went on, 'Dadasaheb, your statements take on the gravity of an epic.'

'Meaning?'

'Shrimant, hadn't you said then that there is a world of a difference between an office and a battlefield? Penmanship is easy, but swordsmanship is another kettle of fish altogether.'

Dadasaheb burst out laughing. Getting his breath back, he enquired, 'Our feudal lords and revenue collectors would have sent the money to Bhausaheb, wouldn't they?'

'Dadasaheb, did Bhausaheb forge cordial relations with at least one of our Marathi people up there in the north? While he sat in office here, he had taken every one of them to task. The Hingane brothers, Naro Shankar, Govind Pant Bundele himself—there were inquiries, investigations, and punitive actions against every one of them. I don't say that they would not have accumulated personal wealth, we are dealing with human nature, after all. But shouldn't there have been some consideration?'

'You are quite right, Bapu.'

'Look at the case of your brother-in-law Gopalrao Barve.'

'What about him?'

'Tell me, Shrimant, what's wrong if close relatives bask under the shelter of royalty? Should they just admire from a distance and spend their lives under a leaking roof? Bhausaheb hadn't liked it one bit when a part of Bundele's province had been handed over to the Barves.'

'I am aware of that, Bapu.'

'Why just this? Your relation by marriage, Antaji Mankeshwar! For ten years, he stayed in Delhi with his army, protecting it with all the alertness he could muster, and how did Bhausaheb reward him? He instituted inquiries against him, didn't he? And why? Simply because he was related to Dadasaheb by marriage?'

The conversation shifted to other subjects. Dadasaheb then suddenly remembered something, looked around to ensure that they were alone, and then asked, 'Bapu, what does your spy ring report?'

'What about, Shrimant?'

'What's news from our Vyanisaheb, sister-in-law's house?'

'It's been a long time since his lordship and his wife have met, Shrimant. Many internal squabbles. Things are not as pleasant as they used to be.'

'Aha?'

'Exactly. The affection between the two of them seems to be fading fast. A number of girls have arrived from the north at his lordship's drama academy. His lordship settles scores with his ladyship by being immersed in them. Meanwhile, there are flares that keep shooting out from her palace too.'

As they were exchanging these secrets, a page arrived from Gopikasaheb, with the message that the two of them had been summoned. The two repaired to her palace immediately. Dressed in a heavily brocaded Paithani saree, her neck loaded with gold jewellery, thirty-seven-year-old Gopikabai stood haughtily in her palace, waiting for the two to arrive. Her fair mien carried more than a suggestion of annoyance, and her eyes flamed. She welcomed Dadasaheb and had him take his seat. Bapu, conscious of his status as a servant, stood deferentially, a gratuitous smile pasted on his face. The first question that Gopikabai shot was, 'Any news from Hindustan?'

'Bhausaheb has sent a letter informing that the army needs money from the treasury.'

'That we have already read.'

Dadasaheb threw a startled look at Bapu, who suddenly got interested in his toes. Gopikabai continued, 'Dadasaheb, we do not need to indulge overmuch this force that has gone to Hindustan. As it is, it is in Bhausaheb's hands; besides, we have that Muslim woman's brat Shamsher Bahadur too.'

A look of displeasure settled on Dadasaheb's face. Gopikabai noticed it instantly and said, 'Sorry, Dadasaheb, you do not like my words, perhaps. But whatever you say, I do not trust these Muslims one bit.'

'Vyanisaheb, please don't say such things. Shamsher Bahadur is a valiant soldier. There's no denying he is our step-brother. Everybody knows him as Bajirao Peshwa's son.'

'So what? He was born of a Muslim woman's womb, wasn't he?'

Dadasaheb turned his gaze away, suggesting that he did not want to dwell on this subject. Gopikabai continued, 'Dadasaheb, you seem to have forgotten the hell Bhausaheb raised on the issue of your debt of eight million. If the army has to be run on treasury money, why do we need Bhausaheb there, then? Any brat can do these hunting raids efficiently enough. Bapu, from here on, you will deliver letters arriving from Hindustan to me first, understand?'

'Yes Vyanisaheb. Your servant has implemented your orders even before they were delivered.'

'Bhausaheb writes particularly sweet letters, as if they have been dipped in a jar of honey. Our lordship here falls for the honey trap every time he reads them. He's always had a soft corner for him, anyway; doesn't understand the simple difference between one's own and others. It was a good thing I walked into his life, otherwise he would have been so grateful for Bhausaheb's services that he would have hung the entire Peshwai round his neck. I know very well what a simpleton our lordship is.'

'You are right, Vyanisaheb,' said Dadasaheb, nodding in agreement.

'What do you mean 'You are right'?' responded Gopikabai angrily. 'You are his lordship's brother, and are as much of a simpleton as he is, so you don't say a word! How you managed to find your voice at Partud only Goddess Bhawani knows. Haven't I seen it a million times? Every time you and he have talked, you have just looked at your toes and nothing else, like a girl.'

'That's very well said, Vyanisaheb,' giggled Bapu.

As they were talking, some disturbance was heard outside. Two pages came panting in and announced, 'His lordship has arrived.' When they heard the news, both Gopikabai and Dadasaheb shot up from their seats. Bapu too tried his best to disappear into the floor. Nanasaheb entered the palace dressed in sparkling white clothes. One look at him showed that his health had plummeted in the last three months. All colour had disappeared from his face, leaving it pale and bloodless. He walked slowly, nearly dragging his feet. As he took his seat, he asked, 'So, what plottings are afoot here?'

He then turned and stared at Bapu who was trying to shrink into himself and asked, 'Yes, Sakharam Pant, how's your work getting along?'

'Very well, Shrimant.'

'What do you mean, 'Very well, Shrimant'? It's barely six months since Bhausaheb has been away from Shaniwarwada, and look at the state to which it has descended. The entire wada, all the palaces have begun to look deserted. The servants have all lost their discipline. All the minions loaf around aimlessly doing nothing at all. The fountains used to trill and sing when Bhausaheb was around, and now they are all starved for water. Looks like you have decided to convert this wada into a wasteland, Sakharam Pant.'

Dadasaheb was struck dumb, Bapu was altogether petrified, but Gopikabai refused to be cowed down. 'How come the Peshwa suddenly remembered his dear brother? Have your lordship's drama school inmates gone for a round of the parks that he's found the time to visit us?'

'Well spoken,' Nanasaheb responded with a deep sigh of helplessness. 'It's only on account of my falling into stupid addictions that absolute nobodies have suddenly grown wings. Sakharam, where is Bhausaheb's letter that arrived two days ago?'

'Yes, yes, Shrimant!' Bapu stuttered.

'When it was addressed to me, how did it not reach me?'

'Shrimant ... Shrimant ... I had come to your palace immediately on receiving it ... but the gates of your palace were shut, Shrimant!'

'You find this excuse meaningful? Or useful? Why was I not woken up? Who knows how many such important letters have disappeared on the way?'

Shaking in terror, Bapu pulled the letter out of his tunic and handed it over to Nanasaheb. As he read it, his face turned dark. 'Who knows what state the army has been reduced to.'

Gopikabai could not hold herself back. 'It was Bhausaheb decision to go on this campaign. He should now handle it the way he thinks fit. Shrimant has no reason to get anxious.'

'If he can't turn to us for help, who else should he go to? To Abdali?'

'Delhi is the capital of Hindustan, and that Bhausaheb has conquered. How can Delhi be in want? It's hard to believe that Delhi is running short of resources.'

'Small people like me shouldn't meddle in the matter of their superiors, but I can't hold myself back either,' butted in Bapu. 'We have Dadasaheb here as witness. When we had last reached Delhi in Dadasaheb's company, Abdali had just left it after pillaging it to the bone. There was so much he had made off with that not a single pack animal was left in any household, not even a lame one. But I am sure that there still is untold wealth lying in the basements of Delhi manors, they just need to be searched out.'

Bapu's sliminess did not go down well with Nanasaheb. 'Don't you dare spew your wise declamations before me, Pant, do you hear?' Nanasaheb snapped. 'Have you dispatched my letter to Hindupat, asking him to extend help to Bhau?'

'Yes, Shrimant.'

'And have you sent instructions to the landlords and revenue collectors that they should dispatch half the collections straight to Hindustan?'

'Long ago, Shrimant!'

Peshwa's concern for Bhausaheb was not at all to Gopikabai's liking. She broke in bitterly, 'People who are expected to fill the pots with water are punching holes in them. Look at the resources that have been dispatched to Bhausaheb already: all the gunpowder from the Nagar Fort has gone, the Shaniwarwada arsenal has been swept clean and sent over too. While Bhausaheb was in Malwa, he was once sent two hundred thousand, and then again one-hundred-and-eighty thousand. Govind Pant Bundele has sent him funds too. Does money grow on trees here?'

'Gopikabai,' replied Nanasaheb, 'all that you can see is Bhausaheb's accounts. I don't see you cast an eye on your own expenditure ever. There is no doubt that I'll have to arrange for money for the forces in Hindustan soon, tomorrow if not today.'

'Your love for Bhausaheb is simply gushing over. But one thing your lordship will do well to keep in mind: trusting one's brother is risky enough, here you are dealing with only a cousin. He will keep sending false reports of Delhi, and one day he will quietly install himself on the Delhi throne. Vishwasrao will go and tend cattle then, when all his inheritance vanishes.'

The barb buried itself deep in Nanasaheb's heart. He groaned like a wounded animal and said, 'Gopikay, God will never forgive you for your contempt for Bhausaheb. When he hoisted the royal flag on the Red Fort, he arranged a special durbar, seated Vishwasrao on an elevated seat and got the chieftains to pay their tributes to him. There's Bhau with a heart as vast as the ocean, and here you are, with a stinking puddle for a heart. Whatever my state of health, whatever my addictions, one of these days I too will have to set off for Hindustan to help our forces there. You stay ready for it too, Dada, do you hear?'

Dadasaheb was startled at this decision of Nanasaheb. Bapu hung his head and Gopikabai turned red in the face. Burning with rage, she spat out, 'It's enough that you've dispatched a hundred thousand men with Bhausaheb and that Muslim brat, Shamsher Bahadur. If you carry the rest of the force with you, there'll be nothing left to guard us here. No further Peshwa force is going to leave from here on!'

'Silent!' Nanasaheb roared in uncontrollable anger. 'This is the Peshwa's wada, not some street corner! It's only the Peshwa's writ that runs here! I have allowed myself to be distracted earlier by your beauty and your cunning, but if I continue to go by your misbegotten urges, I shall certainly bring this empire to ruin. No longer will I be ruled by a woman's mind! I refuse to push my men into the jaws of a foreign monster. I want them back, and I want them back alive!'

Suddenly Nanasaheb was out of breath. He took to bed for many days.

✧

Emperor Abdali sat in his conference pavilion. Giving him company were his trusty Wazeer Shah Wali Khan and one of his most valiant soldiers Sardar Barkhurdar Khan. Attempts had been made earlier to bring about a truce between the Marathas and the Afghans, but they had come to naught. On the one side was Shuja-ud-dowlah, struggling with might and main to bring it about; on the other side was Najeeb, struggling with equal ferocity to ensure it didn't come about. But the forces on both sides of the Yamuna had become sick and tired of starvations and deprivations of different kinds; the talk on both sides was, 'See if you can do something, please. A little this way or a little that, a little give and take, but let's get out of this mess!' A good agreement was what both sides wanted. Abdali told his wazeer, 'It's now been nine months that our forces have been stuck in this land. A way out has to be found. Our soldiers have not seen the thresholds of their houses for nine months now. How much longer can they stick it out in a foreign land, after all?'

'And Aalam-panaah, we have nothing to show for so much time spent!'

'We don't care for the crown of Hindustan, which we could have snatched, if we had wanted to.' Abdali turned towards Barkhurdar Khan and said, 'See if a truce can be hammered out. Take cognizance of Najeeb Khan's main demands. As far as we are concerned, we want to be decently compensated for the losses suffered by our forces. If Hindustan has to be fractured for making a permanent settlement, so much the better.'

'Aalam-panaah, I am certain that some deal can be struck,' said the wazeer.

'Well, yes, I think so too. But Barkhurdar, you have to take care. I don't want to have to listen to Najeeb's gripes every morning, and I don't want these Marathas to be running all over the place either.'

Barkhurdar Khan bowed low and left the pavilion. He had to hurry across the river and get into a talk with the Marathas. Najeeb had been waiting for Barkhurdar to emerge from the pavilion to head for the river. He got into step with the general. He had put his resources to work to ensure that it would be Barkhurdar who went for the talk, without the good man knowing anything about it. The emperor had earlier decided to dispatch his seniormost officer, Shah Wali Khan himself. As soon as Najeeb had got wind of it, he had got after Commander-in-chief Jahaan Khan to orchestrate some tweaking. Najeeb knew the wazeer was desperate for the army to head homewards, and would very likely agree to some of the absurd demands of the Marathas, and all the travails they had been through would have gone waste. 'How can a truce be made with these monkeys who slew your son in the Punjab?' he had told Jahaan Khan. 'It is much better to send a stronger person for the talk who would not settle for a truce on easy terms.'

Jahaan Khan had seen substance in Najeeb's argument, and had decided to take the matter up with the emperor. 'Who doesn't want a truce?' he had told the emperor. 'But why send your wazeer into the Maratha camp? They are treacherous people, these Margatthas. What if they decide to put him under arrest? It would be a serious slap in the face of the entire Afghan empire. It would be wiser to send somebody senior enough but not as senior as the wazeer.' The emperor had readily accepted Jahaan Khan's trusted lieutenant Barkhurdar Khan for the job.

Najeeb was trotting alongside Jahaan Khan and his men as they rode towards the river. He handed over a list of demands that Jahaan Khan should present to Bhausaheb. Barkhurdar Khan laughed and said, 'Why don't *you* go for the peace talks instead of me?'

'I? Najeebullah? To the Maratha army?' laughed Najeeb. 'You have a good sense of humour, Barkhurdar! I cross over to the other side for good, and you have fun here. If I fall into Maratha hands, you can be sure that this war will come to a close. They will either chop me into tiny bits, or if they are the more romantic kind, they will tie me in chains and carry me home. They will then put me on display in a bird-cage in the public square.'

Jahaan Khan and Barkhurdar Khan laughed at this macabre image. Najeeb continued, 'Sardar, good if a truce can be brought about, but remember that it is a wicked thing to shake hands with the infidel.'

Barkhurdar Khan got into the boat with his four companions. The boat sailed away, white flags fluttering atop it.

ॐ

Bhausaheb had decided to lead the talks with Abdali's envoys himself. Shuja-ud-dowlah's man Devidutt had been camping with the Marathas for the past two months, and was keeping a sharp eye on the latest developments.

Bhausaheb sat calmly in the pavilion where the conference was to be held. Everybody was curious to know the names of the two trusted advisers who would sit in on the meeting with him. The first call went to Malharbaba, who instantly grinned from ear to ear, put on his turban and swaggered over to the conference chamber. When Jankoji Shinde heard of the invitation to Malharbaba, he was quite upset; so were the young officers like Vishwasrao, Mahipatrao, Balwantrao, Shamsher Bahadur and Nana Purandare, who had arrived with the army from the south.

Malharbaba lowered himself into his seat and said laughingly, 'Bhausaheb, where's your second adviser?'

'He should be here soon.'

'Who could he be?'

'Our Ibrahim Khan Gardi,' replied Bhausaheb calmly.

The name sent Malharbaba into a shiver of rage. 'What? That black-faced Gardi? What are you saying, Bhausaheb?'

'Yes, Subhedar kaka, that Ibrahim is a person I find completely trustworthy.'

'Oh, that darkie merits your trust, and what are we? Untrustworthy?'

'Subhedar kaka, you are experienced, you have seen the Maratha empire through its ups and downs, and that is the reason why you have been invited here to offer guidance. So, how does that make you untrustworthy?'

'Bhausaheb, place your trust in a block of stone, but never on this Gardi clan. Don't you remember, at Garpir, it was one of their men, Muzaffar Khan, who—'

'—had attacked me? No, I haven't forgotten that. But God knows why, this man Ibrahim has seemed trustworthy and honest to me since the first time I set eyes on him. When bad times descend on me, when I am close to the jaws of death, when poisonous fangs are on the point of penetrating my flesh, I don't know how many of my hundred thousand friends are going to rush to my side; but of the few that do, this brave Ibrahim is certainly going to be in the forefront.'

'Well, if this is the extent of faith you place in him, what can I say?' said Malharbaba in disappointment. 'Yet, I cannot hold myself back from saying this to you. You have just referred to my being experienced. It hasn't been with your father alone, but also with your Kakasaheb, with Bajirao Peshwa himself, that this Malharba has galloped across all of Hindustan. I have spent my entire life battling the elements. Please show some consideration for my seniority and allow me to say a few things.'

Bhausaheb responded with a stony silence. That was when a horse neighed outside and word was brought in that Ibrahim had arrived, and Malharba decided to seal his lips. Ibrahim Khan entered and Malharba turned his face away. Bhausaheb informed them that it would be good to call Shuja-ud-dowlah's man over and suss him out before Abdali's emissary arrived. As soon as Devidutt arrived, Bhausaheb fixed his gaze on him and said, 'Devidutt, Shuja-ud-dowlah, you and I have emerged from the same soil of Hindustan. We can sit with each other a thousand times and resolve our differences. But why do you have to become a camp follower of this foreigner Abdali?'

'Shrimant, to tell you the truth, it's my patron the Nawab Saheb who has been making efforts from the very beginning to bring about a truce. It's for this exact reason that I have been posted here for the past two months and more.'

'Why doesn't the truce happen, then?'

'There's that black-hearted schemer Najeeb sitting there on the other side. It's because of him that every effort fails.'

'What are your main demands, anyway?'

'The Nawab Saheb's desire is that the wazeer's post be given to him.'

'Both sides are in complete agreement on this!' Bhausaheb laughed. 'What else?'

'The Nawab Saheb also believes that the administration of Delhi should be handed over to him.'

'All right. Anything else? Any claims on boundaries?'

'None at all, Shrimant.'

'What do you think are Najeeb Khan's main demands?'

'He wants Delhi for himself. He wants the Marathas to leave the Delhi region for good and return south.'

'Oh, what a man, this Najeeb!' Bhausaheb laughed.

Devidutt handed over a scroll to Bhausaheb and said, 'Shrimant, a letter from the Nawab Saheb. He wanted it delivered to you before any negotiations happened.'

Bhausaheb began reading:

Bhausaheb, it is my misfortune that I have been trapped in the net that this Satan had cast. All routes of escape are blocked now. My forces are suffering humiliation at every step, but what do I do? I am stuck in a morass here. But Bhausaheb, let me take this opportunity to alert you: Najeeb has been running a vilification campaign against you in all directions, to the extent that the critical economic and political issues have become secondary. The war has been given a religious colour. Such being the circumstances, it would be best to arrive at a truce.

Bhausaheb was lost in thought after reading the letter. The neighing of horses outside reached their ears and a pair of pages ran in. 'Shrimant, the delegates from the other side have got into their boat. They should be here soon.'

Bhausaheb made a sign and Devidutt disappeared. There was a quick round of discussions finishing with Bhausaheb declaring, 'Whatever efforts we can make without selling our dignity, let's make them.' To which the other two nodded vigorously.

Barkhurdar Khan arrived in a short while. Although he was barely twenty-five, Bhausaheb was quick to spot the intelligence sparkling in his eyes. Barkhurdar bowed low and handed over an expensive looking ring to Bhausaheb, saying, 'The emperor has sent this diamond-studded ring as an offering for your lordship. If worn on the little finger, it will serve as a memento of friendship and goodwill.'

'The emperor's graciousness delights us. How is his health?'
'Excellent. He has sent good wishes for huzoor's health too.'
'We are obliged. How is Najeeb Saheb's health?'
'In the pink, huzoor.'

'His health is always in the pink; it is other people's health that he causes to change colour,' Ibrahim taunted, triggering a burst of laughter from everyone, including Malharbaba, with Barhkurdar joining in heartily too. After a little more of formal chit-chat, Bhausaheb broached the central issue. 'So, what does Durrani Saheb have to say?'

'He is ready to leave Hindustan at a moment's notice.'

'But on what conditions?'

'The question of boundaries and tributes, of course, exists. But importantly, he wants Najeeb's demands to be looked into.'

'What does Najeeb-ud-dowlah want from us?'

'Why don't you read his letter?'

Barkhurdar handed over Najeeb's letter, which Bhausaheb held as one would hold a dead rat by the tip of its tail. Shaking it open, he began reading:

Pride of the Deccan, dear Bhausaheb, I am well aware of the anger you nurse against me. If I have erred in some way, I appeal to your large heart to grant forgiveness. I can arrange to send your enemy out of Hindustan; however, for that, I request that four little things related to my welfare be granted. My feudal lands, my provinces in the Antarved comprising Najeebabad, Saharanpur and Shamli may kindly be allowed to stay with me. You should kindly abstain from taking upon yourself the bother of looking after the administration of the Delhi empire, nor should you bother Shuja-ud-dowlah with that responsibility, and leave it for your slave here to carry the burden. With your blessings, I shall prove to you that I have the competence to do it efficiently. There are some other requests from the emperor and me that Barkhurdar Khan Saheb will tell you about; they may also be favourably considered.

Bhausaheb rolled up the scroll and shot a look at Barkhurdar and said, 'All right, speak.'

'The first important thing: if the terms and conditions for the truce are acceptable to you, they will need to be guaranteed by statements written under Malharrao Holkar's signature and seal.'

'All right. It's no small thing that there is at least one among us whom your emperor can trust. Well now, get on with your other conditions.'

'The next important question is that of the boundaries: upto where the emperor's boundary should stretch, and upto where the Marathas'.'

'There's no cause for confusion on this issue. We have Subhedar kaka here too. When our Raghunath Dada got his Deccan horse to drink the water of the Attock river, that became the boundary of Hindustan. On the other side of the river is Afghanistan, your own country.'

'Bhausaheb, there's some confusion here. Probably you have not got the drift of my argument. When you talk of the boundaries of Hindustan, why do you push in the boundaries of the Marathas?'

'What do you mean?' Bhausaheb let his irritation show in his voice. 'What exactly are you trying to say? We Marathas are not Hindustanis? This Hindustan is ours. It's mine. The Deccan land is not different from the rest of Hindustan. In fact, it is the iron fist of Hindustan.'

'All right,' said Barkhurdar in a heavy voice, 'I don't have the authority to decide on policies, it's not within my ambit to take decisions. I am a mere representative. I only voice the instructions I was given on the other side. If Abdali's boundary is the Attock river, the boundary of the Marathas is on the other bank of the Narmada.'

'This is not at all acceptable to us.'

'Peshwa Saheb, if we are looking for truce, we may have to show a little flexibility. We need elbow room to shift here or there, a little backward or forward.'

'What exactly do you want to say?'

'Attock as boundary is not at all acceptable to Emperor Abdali. Move a little bit towards Hindustan, please.'

A shadow of worry flitted past Bhausaheb's face. He, Malharbaba and Ibrahim looked at each other. The truce horses seemed to be stumbling on the rocks of the boundary issue. A decision was taken to take a small break and the three of them repaired to a quiet section of the pavilion for a secret conclave. Bhausaheb's heart and mind were labouring under a heavy weight. The hoisting of the flag at Attock was the theme of the ballads that were sung in every nook and corner of Maharashtra. Foregoing claim over Attock, therefore, was an unthinkable proposition. But not relenting on the issue would bring the truce wagon to a grinding halt, which, of course, would mean ... all those men and animals ... so many mouths to feed ... the severe shortages ... famine ...! The consequences were frightening to imagine! What was one to do?

After an hour-long break, the three of them returned to the conference pavilion. With his tongue turning to lead, Bhausaheb intoned with difficulty, 'All right, Barkhurdar, we are willing to shift a little bit; but what are you going to do in return?'

'We will let you mark your boundary a little north of the Narmada.'

'Lahore.'

'The emperor will not agree to that. Allow some distance south, please, give the emperor some space.'

Bhausaheb sat chewing over the demand for a while, and then said, 'All right, we will come down upto Sirhind.'

Barkhurdar broke into a smile. 'We are willing to let you spread out by the same distance too. Peshwa Saheb, if I am not wrong, the distance between Delhi and Sirhind is exactly one hundred and sixty miles, and the distance between Delhi and the river Chambal is one-hundred-sixty miles too. We are willing to leave all the land up to the Chambal for the Marathas. Come to the next point now.

'You talk. Come out with your next demand.'

'The issue that remains is who will become the administrator of Delhi.'

'That is no longer an issue of contention, Khan Saheb,' Bhausaheb came back with some heat. 'It was resolved a good ten years ago.'

'How is that?'

'It appears that you have not heard of the Ahmadiya pact, Khan Saheb,' Bhausaheb said with asperity. 'That pact was signed from the Maratha side by Jayappa Shinde and our Malharbaba sitting here. According to the terms of the pact, the emperor of Delhi had placed the responsibility of the empire in the hands of the Marathas. We propose to continue that way. Anyway, what exactly does Emperor Durrani have to say about the administration of Delhi?'

'In his opinion, both the wazeership and the administrative responsibility of the Delhi empire should be handed over to Najeeb ...'

'Never!' both Malharbaba and Ibrahim burst out together. 'This we shall never accept!'

'But the Marathas will continue to receive one-fourth of the revenue …'

'The devil takes the one-fourth revenue!'

Bhausaheb let out a scornful laugh and said, 'Let's assume for a moment that we accept this condition, what other demands does the emperor have?'

'He wants a large tribute for distribution among his soldiers.'

'Ah, I see, indulge Najeeb, and then indulge the emperor! Take care of me, and take care of my little puppy too, right? Go tell your emperor, this kind of a truce is not even fit to be thrown on a trash heap!'

Barkhurdar put his head down. As he made to leave, he asked, 'Any message for the emperor?'

'Oh yes, please deliver this message to him: such a renowned emperor, for whom I had carried respect in my heart, I had never in my wildest dreams dreamt that he would place such wretched conditions for a deal. The city of Attock that occupies such a pride of place in our history, he thinks we will ever part with it? Abandon the Ahmadiya pact and hand Delhi over to a cattle-thief? If I were ever to accept these conditions, even little brats from my land of the Deccan would throw dung at my face. Yes, my forces do not have enough provisions, yes, my valiant soldiers are dying of hunger, but does that mean we'll say yes to your humiliating conditions? I will never let my land down in this fashion. Go, tell your emperor, my soldiers shall see you in the battlefield.'

***

Some of the loftiest lords, chieftains and religious bigwigs had gathered around Bhausaheb's pavilion, searching desperately for a way out. Vishwasrao and Jankojiba waded past them into the pavilion without being announced in; the ushers were too listless with hunger to spring to their feet quickly enough. Ibrahim Khan and Malharbaba were already inside. Ibrahim was saying, 'Shrimant, this matter of hunger has to be resolved, for men as well as for animals. If there are no bullocks left to carry the artillery, it will be disastrous.'

'Bhausaheb, the men-folk may yet be able to take some beating, but the women and children accompanying the army need something in their bellies fast.'

'Kakasaheb, we have been hearing for the past two days of sacks of grain arriving from the Shinde-Holkar provinces, but there's no sign of them yet.'

'We are just as anxious, Bhausaheb,' said Malharbaba. 'Food and fodder need to arrive fast. Such big animals, our army elephants, but see how they have begun to droop. The moment succor arrives from our provinces, we will distribute them to everybody.'

Bhausaheb's gaze shifted to Sumer Singh, the chief of the nomadic community travelling with them. His longish, tapering Kashmiri cap, his footwear from Delhi, the flowing Lakhnavi tunic and trousers tightening below the knees, all of them proclaimed him as the leader, but his face was crestfallen. Bhausaheb turned towards him and said, 'Sumer Singh, there are as many as ten thousand nomads travelling with our army, which had led us to believe that we would never fall short of food. It was such a joy to watch your bullocks off-load sacks upon sacks of grain in our kitchens. But you too have tucked your legs under, I notice.'

'Rajaji,' pleaded Sumer Singh, 'the fault is not ours at all. It's just that bad times have suddenly descended upon us. The roads on the other side of the Yamuna are blocked. Your forces and Abdali's taken together amount to more than three-hundred thousand mouths to feed, and you have been here for four months. So many animals, so many human beings, where can so much of food come from? The entire region within fifty miles of us on every side has been eaten clean. The markets have closed down, the villages are deserted, there's no food for us to buy or snatch.'

'Sumer Singh, this defeatist tone doesn't become you. You have been our supplier since the times of Dadasaheb's campaign.'

'Please don't misunderstand me, Shrimant,' Sumer Singh responded, 'but money was not in short supply during Dadasaheb's times; nor had the crops been so bad then. Prices today have gone through the roof. We still haven't received money for the supplies of the previous two months. It's no longer possible for us to bring sacks from such long distances. Our community needs to survive too.'

'All right, Sumer Singh, keep doing your work. I'll arrange for the payments in a couple of days.'

Mazbar Khan, the chief of the highwaymen had also been waiting for a long time for an audience with Bhausaheb. He had been the grain supplier for Malharbaba for many years now, as a result of which the highwaymen's army had developed close contacts with the Holkar forces. Bhausaheb addressed him, 'Mazbar, your army of highwaymen is noted for facing all kinds of crises with aplomb. Your community is known for bringing grain even over flooded waters by erecting pontoon bridges. What's happened to you now under these testing circumstances?'

'Rajaji, our horses, our mules and asses have bent their backs before to bring provisions for your Maratha armies. But times are bad now. We have to look far and wide now before we can locate a handful of grains to bring. We will continue to strive, Shrimant, to keep your men from going hungry.'

'All right. What else?'

'Nothing else, Rajaji, just some money is needed.'

Bhausaheb nodded vigorously, suggesting that he would soon fix the problem of money, and Mazbar Khan left within minutes of Sumer Singh. Bhausaheb sat silent, not knowing what to say, with Malharbaba, Vishwasrao and Jankoji looking worriedly at him. Malharbaba finally broke in, 'Bhausaheb, I have seen so many wars, but never have the times been so bad. Even the nobles' wives have begun to have only one meal a day.'

'Kakasaheb' chipped in Vishwasrao, 'Kakisaheb Lakshmibai Mehendale had to sell some of her jewellery to procure some grains.'

Bhausaheb's brow furrowed. Malharbaba continued, 'Bhausaheb, why don't you call Bapu Hingane in? As the agent of the Maratha empire here, he has tucked so much of wealth under his belt! He's made himself a luxurious palace here close to Jantar Mantar; where did he get the money from? He owns a few palaces in the Antarved too! He owes a lot to the Peshwa empire; now is the time to call him over, twist his ears and make him cough out the money!'

'Subhedar kaka, there are some people whose faces one doesn't want to see. But since you insist, we will call him over. Mahipatrao, send an order immediately.'

Mahipatrao departed to issue the order, and Malharbaba continued, 'Bhausaheb, when I see our hungry army, I think of Surajmal Jaat. We should not have let him go away in a huff.'

'We did try very hard to retain him, but Subhedar kaka, whatever deals and pacts one has to make, they have to stay within the limits of dignity. It's not in my nature to abandon my self-respect for immediate gains.'

'There's news that Abdali is trying to reach out to him through Shuja,' Vishwasrao said.

'I am absolutely sure that he is not likely to lean in their direction,' opined Bhausaheb. 'His sympathies will always stay with us, the Jaat is ours.'

'Why, then, does he refuse to send us provisions?'

'It's just that we are going through bad times, Kakasaheb. One of our own men has gone and told him that once we settle with Abdali, we are not going to let the Jaat get away.'

Shamsher Bahadur, Damaji Gayakwad and Manaji Paigude had just returned from Rajputana. When they presented themselves to Bhausaheb, he asked in a calm voice. 'Managed some provisions?'

'Bhausaheb, the land has been hit by famine. Persecuted by both our forces, entire villages have disappeared. The only people left behind are the weak and old, those who didn't have the strength left to move. They move around in the rags on their backs, and live off whatever leaves and roots they can lay hands on. It was only at the border of Rajputana that we found four villages that had some grains. Managed to procure around a thousand sacks.'

'What's a thousand sacks for a hundred thousand mouths?' worried Malharbaba.

'Well,' sighed Bhausaheb, 'it's not altogether insignificant. 'Shamsher, don't hang around here. Distribute the grains among the women and children. Don't give anything to the men as of now.'

Shamsher left to carry out instructions. Bhausaheb suddenly remembered Govindpant, and started drafting a letter to him. All the agony that was running through his veins began oozing out through the reed, as also the anger at Govindpant's dereliction of duty:

> ... *how can you be so unconcerned when it is time for you stand by us? Both you and Gopalrao Barwe should head for the Sorab Ghat and assemble an army. Abdali has sent Faizullah Khan, Saadullah Khan and other Rohilla chieftains back to their provinces to rest and recoup during the monsoon months. The monsoons are on their way out, and these Pathans would be*

readying to return and gather together. Decimate them before they can do so. The Yamuna blocks our way and allows us no scope to tear them apart. You should get busy creating mayhem in the territories of Shuja and the Rohillas. Block the provisions reaching Abdali. Plunder the villages. Enter the Sorab Ghat immediately. Ravage the villages along the Ganga and the Antarghat as you move along. Do not wait any longer, Pant, create terror in every village, on every road, using guerilla tactics.

Nothing has grown here, ensure that something grows there. Sowing time is slipping away, but we have been getting news that your subjects have not done any sowing. We don't know how long this conflict will last. If there's no sowing, there'll be no harvest, and if there is no harvest, what'll be there to eat? Give your subjects all the encouragement they need, but get them to sow.

You are the holder of such a huge fiefdom, and yet not much is happening from your end. After having served the empire for so long, why do you show this indifference now? We desperately need money and provisions here, not excuses. Dispatch a million and a half instantly. You possess valiant men, Pant! Rise up, pillage, burn, and send the proceeds to us immediately. Do not tarry!

The camel post left with the letter as news reached that Bapuji Hingane had arrived outside, but still hadn't presented himself. Instructions went out, and Hingane stole in, eyes downcast. Bhausaheb signalled for him to sit and began, 'Bapujipant, as we were moving out from the south, we had huge expectations from you as the agent of the empire, and from our Delhi resident chieftain Antaji Mankeshwar. We had hoped that velvet carpets would be rolled out for us as soon as we reached the gates of Delhi. But our hopes and expectations have turned out to be empty dreams. Our army has been stranded here for two months now, fighting against rain, cold winds, hunger and deprivation. It was during such times of need that we had expected you—our agent for sixteen years—and Antajipant—our chieftain for ten years—to be our anchors and navigators. But while we have been waiting for you every day, you two have been ducking and hiding from us like petty thieves!'

Bhausaheb's words got Bapuji perspiring profusely. He mopped his face with the end of his shawl and stuttered, 'Shrimant ... Shrimant ... if there has been laxness in our service, I offer my sincere apologies.... My father and I have considered it a privilege to be of service to the Peshwa.'

'Silence!' roared Bhausaheb. 'Ask us, Pant, what your entire life has been spent in. In brazen violation of our express instructions that our agents should not gather property in their places of residence, you have gone on to accrue enormous wealth. You have signed false pacts under our name to get huge tracts of land transferred to your name. You have constructed a grand palace for yourself at Jantar Mantar. You have pocketed bribe in millions from wazeers, kings, the Rajput Ranas and sundry chieftains by promising to buy them the Peshwa's favour for one thing or another. Whose agent have you been, Bapujipant, and towards what end?'

'My apologies, Shrimant, but you have been misinformed,' blabbered Bapuji, nervously. 'We have served your lordship alone, and not indulged in any questionable activity.'

'What a liar this man is!' screamed Malharbaba. 'I swear by Lord Khandoba, Bhausaheb, the emperor's palace at Agra was to come to the Holkar-Shindes, but it was this Bapu that poisoned the emperor's ears. He filled up his own coffers and turned the palace in the direction of Madho Singh.'

Bapuji Hingane couldn't take his eyes off the floor when Bhausaheb shouted, 'Heard this, Pant? Got evidence to counter these accusations? A mere bunch of beggars from Panchvati near Nashik, how did you transform yourselves into being lords? And the empire that brought you all this grandeur has been dying of hunger at your doorstep, and you don't have a fistful of alms to give to it?'

Bapuji began to weep. 'We could have erred, and we have taken sufficient punishment from your lordship earlier. You had taken away our authority from us six years ago and confiscated our houses. We had paid a fine of two million to the empire. Dadasaheb too sent us to prison two years ago. We may be put into chains again if Shrimant desires.'

'My men are dying of hunger. How much food can you supply?'

'Whatever I have ... two or three hundred sacks!'

'Two or three hundred sacks?' Bhausaheb couldn't believe his ears. 'Anybody around there?' he yelled. 'Haul this man out of my presence immediately. I can't bear to see his face any longer!'

Bapuji Hingane quickly scuttled out of the place. Bhausaheb looked helplessly towards Malharbaba and groaned, 'See, Subhedar kaka? One reaps as one sows. Great people like you and Dadasaheb carried the Maratha flag right up to Attock, ransacked sixteen big Mughal provinces, expanded the Maratha empire right up to the border of Afghanistan, making our chests swell with pride. But what good came of conquering all these provinces and palaces and forts? For every inch of land that we won, we left so many of our valiant Marathi men buried in that foreign soil. After shedding such priceless blood for winning these lands, who did we hand them over to? Selfish, reprobate, wretched, treacherous rascals interested only in gathering land and erecting palaces for themselves. My revered father was not a good judge of character. Incompetence ruled over the conquered lands. Our valiant men had to shed their life-blood to win territories and then they installed scoundrels for representatives who fleeced the populace to stack their own treasuries! We could never really establish true Maratha rule in any of our captured lands. Look at Shivaji's reign, what a sharp contrast! It may or may not have been as big as even a Mughal province, but he established uniformity in rules and administration in all the lands he brought under his rule. Fixed the revenues and gathered the blessings of his subjects. He held not only his subjects and his employees under his sway, but also ruled over the winds that blew across his country.'

Bhausaheb fell silent for a while, and then in a voice filled with passion, he said, 'Although the task we have undertaken is as tough as lifting the bow of Lord Shiv, I shall do it if all of you support me as you have supported me so far. I shall not only lift the bow, but twirl it round my finger.'

The passionate declamation sent a bolt of lightning through the veins of those present. Both Shamsher Bahadur and Jankoji sprang to their feet. Trying desperately to prevent his voice from breaking, Shamsher said, 'Bhausaheb, time has placed the steers of this boat in your hands. Now whether tempests break over our heads or the boat capsizes, all of us here have placed our complete trust in you. We won't care if we drown in the effort, but we shall not desert you.'

'Kakasaheb!' sobbed Jankoji, 'the army is hit by famine today, and we are all starving. If it comes to that, we will eat wet mud, but we will never ever leave your company.'

Bhausaheb's eyes turned wet. He said, 'The war is far from over; in fact, it has yet to begin.'

While the conference was in progress, cartloads of grain arrived from the lands of the Shinde-Holkars. Bhausaheb was informed that the supplies were substantial enough to serve them for another two days at least.

Bhausaheb walked out of the tent with Jankoji and Vishwasrao. He got astride his horse Chandrasen, and with an escort of twenty-five trusted horsemen, set off towards the north, riding past the soldiers' tents. Shalimar Bagh had lost all its charm. The trampling it had suffered of over a hundred thousand men and a good forty thousand animals the last few months had robbed it of all its attractions. The trees were leafless now; where once the air was redolent with the fragrance of fragrant flowers, it now stank of dung and urine. Branches had been rudely yanked off trees and the vines had been pulled out by their roots. But the arrival of the carts from the Shinde-Holkar territories had begun to bring life back into the Bagh. Hearths were being fired at various places, smoke had begun curling up into the sky. Queues of excited men had begun forming wherever the carts were parked; the nervous hubbub that ran up and down the lines laid bare the anxiety that the grain could run out on them.

As the band of horsemen rode out of the camp, Vishwasrao asked, 'Where are we going, Kakasaheb?'

'Towards Buradi Ghat.'

'Buradi Ghat?' Jankoji repeated in a startled voice.

'Yes,' was the calm response.

They rode along for about fifteen miles and came to a halt on an elevated piece of land. Horse and rider stood looking mutely at the wide expanse of the swollen Yamuna. It could have been mistaken for a sea gone wild. The sun had begun to set, turning the turbulent water a fiery red. Grey and white clouds could be seen ambling across the horizon in the far distance. The riders nudged their uncertain horses forward. As the Buradi Ghat came closer, Bhausaheb's heart began to beat faster and a strange tension showed upon his face. Jankoji pulled up his horse and whispered hoarsely, 'Kakasaheb, this is the spot. This is where our forces had put up camp. It was from this spot that Dattaji leapt towards the battlefield when Bhoite's men collided with the Afghans.'

'Where is that battlefield?'

'Right here,' said Jankoji, pointing towards the roaring expanse of water.

Bhausaheb turned his gaze across the expanse. He took in the site of the fateful battle. As the horse neared the water's rim, its steps slowed, as if they had turned to lead. Bhausaheb reached up to the edge to see the sun dip below the horizon. Darkness had begun to swallow the entire landscape: the vast, roaring river, the four directions, and now the sky. Bhausaheb dismounted from his horse. Even as the darkness deepened, the rumble of the waters rose in both pitch and volume. The winds gathered a new urgency and whistled to create a wild symphony. Bhausaheb suddenly felt the presence of Dattaji standing beside him, taking an estimate of the violence that resided in those turbulent waters. *The river refuses to indulge, does it? But this intrepid warrior, he wants to fly across the waters on the wings of destiny; wants to slice off the golden spires of the royal pavilion as Santaji Ghorpade had done, and on his way back, wants to bring back Najeeb's head tucked under his armpit as a trophy! Bravo, comrade, what a man! An entire age has passed since we last met! But, why is your body covered in blood? Why, my dear friend, why?*

'Bhau kaka?' Jankoji's voice suddenly jerked Bhausaheb back to consciousness. 'Kakasaheb, let's clear out of here. This place gives me the shivers!'

'Why should you be afraid, Jankobaba?' Bhausaheb said with a trace of a smile. 'When the ordinary die, they turn into ghosts. But the great martyrs are born for eternity. These martyrs stay with the valiant till the end of time. Sites such as these sanctify us; where's the place for fear here?'

As he walked down the soggy bank, his footwear gathered mud and turned heavy, but he kept walking as if in a trance. Suddenly he stumbled over something. He bent down to scoop out a circular object. It turned out to be the wheel of a small cannon. Could well be a relic of Dattaji's forces! He handed it over to one of his servants. As he walked on, he asked, 'Where exactly did Dattaji fall, Jankoji?'

'I had fainted, Bhau kaka, and I was denied the blessing of knowing where exactly my Kakasaheb received his martyrdom.'

'But you people have talked of the mouths of the streams, the twists and turns of the riverbed, those ferocious islands!'

'All of that is submerged in the water. The river runs over it now.'

Dattaji would surely have been cremated somewhere close by here. Where would that spot be? Bhausaheb bent low, lifted a fistful of wet earth and smelt it deep. He then caressed it. What a burden of wounds you carry all over your body, my friend? Bhausaheb dipped his fingers in the mud and applied it across his forehead. He then collected another handful of mud, carefully emptied it into the corner of his shawl and tied it up in a knot. Another thought struck him: maybe a grain or two of his ash was scattered somewhere here? He picked up a fistful first from one place, then from another. Could it be here? Or there, maybe? His mind in a swirl, he lifted his eyes towards the sky and looked around. There? How foolish he was being, trying to confine Dattaji to a tiny space. Dattaji is everywhere—here, there, in that water, in the dark, deep pool inside there, all across the sky, he has permeated the entire cosmos, his Dattaji has!

The horses finally sped through the darkness of the night and began galloping towards Delhi. The wind began singing in Bhau's ears. It brought with it deep, resonant sounds from the ravines far away, sounds that morphed into a heavy reverberating voice, a call that seemed to breathe with each gallop. 'Bhau! Bhau! Bhau Raayaa!'

Bhau felt as if a streak of lightning had passed crackling through his entire being. Through the medium of the wind, he began responding to Dattaji's call. 'Dattaji!' he cried, 'Datta! Datta! You laid down your life for the defence of Delhi. I shall not let the blood that you have shed go in vain, friend! Don't lose heart, my gallant friend! I shall sever a hundred Afghan heads and sprinkle their blood at your feet! I am coming! I am coming to meet you soon!'

⊕

Najeeb had collected qazis, maulvis, imams, ulemas and sundry religious leaders in his pavilion. His face was contorted, as if he had just downed some very bitter medicine. Nailing his glance at the Delhi Fort, which could be seen through his window across the Yamuna, he continued his harangue, 'So, brothers in Islam, this is the last alert we are giving you. These nights are the nights of retribution, stay awake. Awake, my dear brothers, Islam is in danger. The infidels are determined to wipe out the last traces of Islam from Hindustan; it's for this reason that the wicked Sadashivrao from the Deccan has smashed the throne of the emperor, which has for hundreds of years served as a symbol of Delhi's pride and self-respect.'

'Ya Allah, forgive us,' screamed a few of the maulvis, 'has the throne actually been smashed?'

'Not just smashed, but broken into bits,' continued Najeeb, warming up to the theme. 'None of the infidels gathered there had the courage to commit such sacrilege, but this Sadashivrao then had a blacksmith's sledge-hammer called over and stepped up to the throne with it. A few respectable citizens of Delhi ran up and tried to dissuade him from committing such a horrible act, but he shooed them all away and proceeded to assault the throne till its pieces fell apart.'

The information gave the gathering a rude jolt. Najeeb removed his turban, ran his fingers dramatically through his wavy hair, and looking towards Delhi, he exclaimed, 'Friends, the Jama Masjid that you can see from here has been the emblem of Islam for thousands of years. Take your eyes' fill of it now.'

'What do you mean?' a few asked.

'I mean that it won't be there in the next four days; it is going to be razed to the ground.' The assembly went mad with rage. Their faces and eyes turned blood-red as they roared, 'Who are these infidels who want to demolish our sacred mosque? Give us their names!'

'We shall dispatch them to hell in no time!'

'We shall slit their throats and drink their blood!'

Najeeb signalled them to be quiet and continued, 'The name of that infidel is Sadashiv. Do you know which Hindu god bears this name?'

'Shankar, their Lord Shankar!' replied a mullah.

'You are right, it is Shankar, Shankar of the matted locks, the lord of those Hindu sinners. This man has begun to believe that he is the incarnation of their Lord Shankar, the Destroyer. He has taken oath that he will not allow a single mosque to stay standing anywhere in Hindustan. He has sworn to smash them all and replace them with temples to Lord Shiv, and house the pind, the phallic symbol, in each one of them. He has declared that he will demolish Jama Masjid and build in its place a temple bigger and grander than the one at Kashi.'

'We shall not let this happen! We shall fight!'

'We will lay our lives against this satanic act!'

'Allah-o-Akbar! Allah-o-Akbar!'

Najeeb again raised his hands to silence his audience said, 'Friends, that sinner Bhau has stripped the shrines of Nizamuddin and Mohammad Shah of all its gold and silver. What I am going to tell you now is yet more shocking: he has anointed Vishwasrao, Peshwa's brat as the emperor of Hindustan.'

'Allah have mercy!'

'He didn't stop at that. He got coins minted in this Vishwasrao's name and had his ascension read in the khutba as official recognition of his emperorship. So, friends, just think, these sinners who have so quickly desecrated the throne of Hindustan, do you think they are likely to leave our religion alone for long?'

The mullahs broke into loud cries of: 'Jihaad! Jihaad!' 'Allah-o-Akbar!' 'Let's march to Delhi!' 'Death to the infidels!'

After Najeeb had let them spend their passion somewhat, he resumed, 'You are erudite gentlemen and I am a mere ignoramus, who knows only action. But this I know, that if you merely shout slogans and cross the Yamuna on their strength alone, you will all drown. Instead, I advise that you go back to your villages and towns.'

'What do we do there?'

'Let everyone know that doom is due to descend on Jama Masjid and Delhi. Provisions continue to reach the infidel in a stealthy manner; loot them on the way, block all their routes. When the war starts, persuade the young men of Islam to join in this fight to defend their religion. Create dissensions among the enemy.'

It was with these instructions that Najeeb's day-long conference came to an end.

Najeeb was now alone in his pavilion. He looked pleased with himself. Bhau, you ass, you have been flaunting your high and mighty ideals of fighting for the Delhi empire, haven't you? You talk your fancy talk of the war being between natives and foreign infiltrators, don't you? My dear boy, you still haven't understood the power of my poison tongue. Look what I have done now: fired them up in the name of jihad; so who remains a native and who the usurper? The war now is between the Hindus and the Muslims.

His reverie was broken by an usher. 'Khan Saheb,' he said urgently, 'the emperor desires an immediate audience with you.'

Najeeb quickly patted his hair down, donned his turban, and presented himself in quick time at the emperor's tent. He entered with a wide smile on his face, but switched it off on seeing Abdali's grave face. Abdali signalled him to take a seat and said, 'So, Najeeb, any news?'

'You must have heard of the conference I called of the preachers today. I have set them on fire with the call that Islam is in danger. All of Antarved will get into turmoil now. Villages will be torched, the infidels will find their paths blocked in every direction.'

'Najeeb, your love of Islam has held us back in Hindustan for the last ten months, but for religion to survive, the armies have to be saved first.'

'Any inadequacies on our part, huzoor?'

'Our Kandahari horses have begun to die in this climate. Also, the fodder available here is not good. Five thousand of our horses have died. As with the infidels, our forces are having to confront famine too, people are starving. How do you propose to solve this problem?'

'Forgive my impertinence, huzoor, efforts for procuring food and fodder are on, but as in Delhi, not much sowing has been done in the Antarved either. But may I offer a suggestion, huzoor?'

'Speak.'

'Aalam-panaah, Ayodhya is a province that produces twenty million. We have with us Nawab Shuja-ud-dowlah, whom you have promised the wazeership of Hindustan. It took so much persuasion to have him join us. Is there anything wrong in causing him a little discomfort now?'

'A message has been sent to him too. You may leave now; I have to discuss certain things with him in private.'

Najeeb bowed his way out of the pavilion. Shuja-ud-dowlah arrived in a little while. As he sat down, leaning against a bolster, Shuja kept his eyes fixed on the emperor and noticed his grave face. After sweets and drinks were served, the emperor began, 'Shuja-ud-dowlah, the ordinary Hindustani points to you as a person of great resources and affluence. You have a revenue of twenty million rupees under your seat. Our forces are suffering from famine, and the men have reached the limits of their endurance. You will have to give us provisions.'

'But, Jahaan-panaah,' Shuja got back, 'when I departed from Ayodhya, I had been delivered a guarantee bearing your seal, and there was no mention in it of providing sustenance of any kind. The pact was that we would be treated with respect and dignity.'

'Nawab Saheb,' Badshah Abdali responded in a raised voice, 'we had not invited you to entertain your royal entourage. This is no child's play, you should not forget, we are at war. You have to eat with joy what falls in your plate. When the time comes, you will fly your victory flag and consume the sweets, won't you? In the same manner, if a little bit of poison falls in your bowl during the war, that has to be tasted too!'

'Yes, Aalam-panaah,' replied Shuja in a cold voice.

'Nawab Saheb, your province is close by. Arrange for provisions in the next four days, there should be no slackness here. Providing for a bare eighty or ninety thousand soldiers, can it be beyond the resources of the Nawab of Ayodhya? Who will ever believe it?'

Shuja lowered his head and walked out of the royal pavilion. The person closest to him in the entire Afghan contingent was Shah Wali Khan, who held a deep hatred for Najeeb. In his opinion, they should not have tarried for another hour in Hindustan, but he couldn't take any step against the emperor's wishes. Rattled by the emperor's threatening tones, enraged by Najeeb's reneging on promises, Shuja went to Shah Wali Khan in the state of someone with a fishbone stuck in his throat and, in a broken voice, told him what had transpired. 'It was on your assurance that I came,' he groaned, 'and now look at the treatment I am being given.'

'What assurances are you talking about? And who had given you these assurances?' Shah Wali shot back. 'During times of war, assurances and sentiment have no meaning. Pacts, agreements, assurances, all of these empty words look nice only on paper. The crookedest of people put on the robes of honesty and dance on marble floors with filthy feet.'

'But what crime have I committed, huzoor? That Bhausaheb had been breaking his back to persuade me to merely stay confined to my kingdom if I did not want to sign any treaty. I drove him away and brought along my force of four thousand and my powerful artillery to fight for you; was this my fault?'

Shah Wali laughed out loud and said, 'You have committed one grave sin, and that was to fall for the persuasions of that king of liars. I had never given you any assurance of any kind, so what was the need for you to cross rivers to join us? Who, do you think, would have crossed the mighty Ganga to launch an assault on Ayodhya?'

'What, then, do I do now?' Shuja groaned.

'Do what you want to, but don't get on the wrong side of the emperor, else you've had it.'

Shuja returned to his pavilion defeated, and said to Kashiraj, 'Pandit, send our messengers to our western border towns and villages and ask them to open up our granaries there. See what they can do to have the provisions reach here in the next four days.'

༄

18 October 1760, the first day of the Navaratri, the festival of nine nights. A strange silence pervaded the Maratha forces. It had rained heavily for ten days. The men had their eyes peeled on the Yamuna water level. Its obstinate refusal to subside had washed away all their plans and strategies. The rains were withdrawing but had only swelled the flood on their way out. It became obvious to all that the Yamuna that should have begun to subside within the next fortnight or so now threatened to take at least a month. Anxiety began to reach new highs. The ladies of the royal pavilion too began to feel the pangs of hunger. And now Navaratri had arrived. Parvatibai and Lakshmibai Balwant began rigorous fasts in the name of Goddess Amba. Shamsher Bahadur's wife Meherbai also joined in the austerity. Who cared whether it was Allah or Goddess Amba who brought them relief? All they wanted was deliverance from their tribulations. Rakhmabai Akka announced to the women of the chieftain households, 'We shall all observe strict austerities during the Navaratri. Kurukshetra is not too far away from here, they say. We shall do the fulfilment rituals there.'

A hassled Bhausaheb sat in conference with his most intimate colleagues. There was a contingent of horsemen that had been out on another campaign since the Dussehra of two years ago; they had been ordered to join Bhausaheb's forces straight from Udgiri. Away from home for almost two years, these forces had forgotten how the wind blew in their homes; and now another Dussehra was almost upon them. They sat dreaming of the doors and windows of their homes, the children somersaulting in the courtyards, the woman of the house standing behind the door, the pallu of her saree pulled over her face, looking out every once in a while, like a bird peeping out of its nest, for the return of her husband.

It was all right for Abdali's men, they were professional soldiers for whom the army was a full-time occupation. But with the Maratha forces it was different. Except for a few thousand horsemen and troopers of the Peshwa's personal guards, the rest of them were primarily farmers, whose rhythm of life was quite different. Sowing would begin with the arrival of the first showers, and the next few monsoon months would mean almost constant attendance on the field—weeding and redoing the furrows and transplanting, and so on. Around Dussehra time, the air in the farms would turn fragrant. The grain would ripen, it would be harvested, threshed, and then left out to dry in the sun. Around the time that half the crop had been dried and stored, summons would arrive either from the Peshwa in Pune or from the local chieftains. Drums would be beaten. The farmers would let the remaining half of their harvest dry while they pulled out their weapons and hurriedly sharpened them on whetstones. Soon they would jump into their saddles, slap the quivering rump of their fresh steeds who had been gathering their strength for four months and set off on their campaigns.

These farmers had not returned home for two full years now, so how would they know whether harvest operations had been completed on time and what harvest their farms had yielded? Would the buffalos have been taken for insemination? Would their daughters have been brought home in time for their confinement? Grandson or granddaughter? These and a thousand other questions would haunt them. It was four months since they had laid down camp at Delhi. They were stuck there like animals caught in the mire. On top of that, no food for their bellies and no fodder for their animals! No allowances in their hands and no victory feathers in their turbans! How long could one carry on with this life of pain and deprivation?

Bhausaheb was battling on. However, he was never quite certain of the rightness of his acts. Could he be deluding himself? What appeared to be resilience on the surface seemed to lose its firmness on a little scratching. The army was writhing with hunger pangs, and a few dozen animals were dying each day. The cold of the northern region was too bitter for their southern bones; now coupled with unseasonal rains, it had acquired a demoniacal form. Chills, fevers and diseases had found themselves a congenial environment to flourish in, and troops and cavalry had begun to fall like poultry struck with sleeping sickness. Eyes had turned to stone staring at the road running south to Pune for help. The Afghans on the other side were not relenting, nor was the excitement of war showing any signs of flaring up. That required spirit and energy, and that, in turn, required food and fodder. Thus, in the end, whichever side you looked at it from, it all boiled down to priming up the stomach.

☙

Sardar Manaji Paigude, who was sitting next to Bhausaheb, said, 'Bhausaheb, Dussehra will be upon us in the next ten days; it is particularly dear to Maratha soldiers like us. It is on this day that the brave among them set out for hunts and campaigns. It is the day for shaking the dust of the farm off our clothes and walking into the fields of battle. Should we, then, stay stuck in these bogs when Dussehra arrives? This logjam has to be broken somehow.'

'You are absolutely right, Manaji,' responded Bhausaheb. 'It was on this day that Lord Rama had beheaded the conceited, power-obsessed Ravana.'

'We have to step out of here,' said Holkar. 'Four unbroken years of war and slaughter and arson has devastated the land around these parts. If animals cannot find a blade of grass, what can you say about humans?'

'I have been thinking of mounting an assault on Kunjpura,' said Bhausaheb.

'Kunjpura? What's there in Kunjpura?' some chieftains asked.

'We set off northwards from here on the imperial highway towards the Punjab. Kunjpura is a town about eighty miles from here. There is a fortress there overflowing with grain. Since it is on way to Afghanistan, Abdali has got it stacked with provisions worth millions for emergencies. We'll raid this post.'

'Shrimant, we are with you in this,' the chieftains said in unison.

'We've also heard that there is a good route across the Yamuna near this town. We can cross into the Antarved using that way. On the other side is Muzaffarnagar, Najeeb's territory. We can land there and then capture Najeeb's other posts like Najeebabad and Sultanpur.'

'Bhausaheb, how do you think Abdali will respond to this move?'

'The Yamuna allows Abdali no scope hereabouts for getting in. A mile or two up the imperial highway, the Yamuna runs north to south. Sonipat is thirty-six miles from Delhi, Panipat is fifty-six miles and Kunjpura is at the eightieth milestone. The Yamuna expanse along this entire run is deep and wide. Abdali does not have the courage to cut across to our side in this area. This act would require a heart the size of a winnowing basket. Once we set off from here, even if the Afghans move up with us on the other side, they can cross the Yamuna only at Kunjpura to confront us. The plan is to capture Kunjpura and lay waste Najeeb's territory before they can cross over. Let's break their back before that.'

'Let's celebrate Dussehra in Kunjpura this time, then,' said Sardar Vinchurkar excitedly, and everybody seconded the proposal.

'Kunjpura has yet another attraction,' continued Bhausaheb. 'After Dattaji Shinde was killed, the person who beheaded him and carried the head on the tip of his spear is at present in the Kunjpura Fort. His name is Kutb Khan. I want to see his head on a spear too.'

The mention of Dattaji's killing fired up the brothers Tukoji and Mahadji, who had been his childhood friends; and Jankoji spoke, 'Bhausaheb, give us your guidance and your blessings. We shall ravage Kunjpura this Dussehra, and chop the heads off the Afghans' necks.'

Shamsher Bahadur, however, got up and brought the attention of the gathering to a matter of great gravity and concern. 'Bhausaheb,' he began in a measured tone, 'we should most certainly set off for Kunjpura at the first opportunity and blow off its fortress, but before we do so, we should take some important decisions with regard to Delhi here. The news that reaches us from the neighbouring provinces is worrisome. Najeeb has spread a lot of disaffection among the people there. Villages are being set alight. The rumours he has circulated everywhere are that Bhausaheb has anointed Vishwasrao as the emperor of Delhi, literally smashed the throne, and that Islam is in danger of being obliterated.

'That's not all. He has also let the lie spread that Bhausaheb has undertaken the mission of razing all the mosques to the ground, including the Jama Masjid. There is a very strong presence of Muslims in these parts, and Najeeb's machinations have set them all afire. If this continues, not one of our posts in the Antarved will remain safe. Calamity can descend on our soldiers who are minding the fords on the river. If the entire population rises up in revolt, it will spell disaster for us. We have to take immediate action to set matters right.'

Bhausaheb looked anxious now. Information on Najeeb's incendiary activities had been reaching him earlier. Quite certainly, he would have to take some firm decisions before they decided to move out of Delhi. The Wazeer Ghaziuddin had got Alamgir II assassinated and placed Shahjahan Sani on the throne. That hulk of a puppet now lay rusting in the Red Fort like a forgotten item in the cupboard. It was important to remove him and to make some alternative arrangement. Because Alamgir had been killed, the sympathy of the people lay with crown prince Shah Alam for ascending the throne, but the terrified prince had fled to Patna and gone into hiding to escape the gallows. If he were now to be declared as the emperor of Delhi, it would bring considerable comfort to the people in and around Delhi, and corroborate Bhausaheb's claim that the war was for the defence of Delhi and against foreign invaders. Making Shah Alam the emperor would be an astute political move, Bhausaheb decided—it would bring down two birds with a single stone.

Shah Alam's mother Zeenat Mahal was in Delhi at the time. With the Marathas in Delhi, Abdali had not been able to do touch her in spite of having come within range. Zeenat Mahal had been making repeated visits to Bhausaheb's pavilion beseeching him to institute her son on Delhi's throne. She would talk of paying him ten million for the effort. Bhausaheb asked Naro Shankar, 'You think the emperor's mother would be able to shell out two million or so in a hurry?'

Naro Shankar laughed. 'She goes by the name of Queen Mother but owns not a hut. She may just manage five or six hundred thousand at best.'

'Oh, is that so?' Bhausaheb laughed back. 'That doesn't stop her from talking big, though! Anyway, comparing the weakness and strengths of Shah Jahan and Shah Alam, Shah Alam appears to me worthier for the throne. Lives a life of courage, even if it is in faraway Patna. Take whatever little money that comes, and help bring Delhi to life.'

'Bhausaheb,' asked Holkar, 'what's the decision on the wazeeri?'

'Let's declare Shuja as the wazeer.'

'Malharrao didn't like the decision. The faces of Gangoba Tatya and Ramji Anant fell a mile. Shamsher Bahadur, however, welcomed the decision, 'Bhausaheb, this is a wonderful counter-move to punch Najeeb in the nose.'

'Considering that Shah Alam is not here, on whose head would you place the crown?' Malharbaba enquired.

'Let's keep the throne vacant. Meanwhile, his son Jawaan-Bakht is very much in Delhi. Let's declare him as the crown prince, seat him by the side of the throne and get the khutba read in his name.'

Once the decision was taken, Bhausaheb instructed that the investiture should happen the very next day. Nana Purandare, Lakshman Ballal Kher, Ramji Dabholkar and Naro Shankar were put in charge of the programme. After all the decisions were taken, Bhausaheb said, 'Naro Shankar, we are leaving behind three thousand horsemen and an equal number of foot soldiers for Delhi's security. Keep this in mind all the time: Delhi is the key to the politics of Hindustan. You may not find a smashed pearl here today, but Delhi, in the final count, is Delhi. This is the Delhi we leave behind in your care. Protect it with all your might. Whatever happens to the campaign in the north, you must never abandon Delhi. Defend it like Dattaji would have done. Stake your life for it, if you have to.'

'Bhausaheb,' replied an emotionally charged Naro Shankar, 'till as long as there is breath left in the body, this Naro Shankar shall not let go of Delhi.'

Bhausaheb then turned towards Shamsher Bahadur and Damaji Gayakwad and said, 'We shall set off at the crack of dawn. You two follow us a little later, and plant a few soldiers on every wharf along the Yamuna. We don't know what may happen in the battle ahead, but if Abdali tries to jump into the river and make a crossing, our soldiers on the western bank should finish him off mid-stream.'

The conference was drawing to a close. Before turning towards his private quarters, Bhausaheb looked at the assembly and said, 'This Kunjpura mission is no cakewalk. Our animals are weak and the distance to cover is long. If you wish, you may get started right now. Whatever you find on the way, in the fields and in the villages, feed them to your animals.'

The tents were dismantled, the cloth walls and bamboos rolled up and tied. The animals began their slow march, nibbling at whatever little vegetation fell in their way.

Naro Shankar visited Bhausaheb at night and said, 'Shrimant, the khutba for the new emperor will be read out tomorrow. Shrimant should mark his attendance at this important ritual before he proceeds north.' Bhausaheb replied, making a sour face. 'Naro Shankar, I have no desire to hang behind for this meaningless ritual.'

'Well, then, at least Vishwasrao—'

'How can he stay behind? He is the son of the Peshwa!'

As he turned to leave, Naro Shankar stole a look at Bhausaheb's face. It had an expression of distance. It seemed to say, why stay behind for such a lowly programme? We do the fighting, we spill our blood. He fled away despite being the prince. We now announce him as the emperor even while he is absent! Who takes the bullets and who carries away the biscuits? All this is quite clear, but circumstances allow no room for manoeuver. Oh destiny, destiny, you are ultimately the greatest! Although I carry Delhi in my Marathi fist, the earth of my own Maratha land is so far away! What deceptions you practise, destiny, what deceptions!

☙

Kunjpura was a prominent town, eighty miles from Delhi, on the Imperial Highway to the Punjab province. Located on the banks of the Yamuna, it had houses, temples and mosques built under the shelter of large, shady trees. The river bank was lined with short, umbrella-shaped trees laden with flowers, filled with birds of many kinds and other arboreal creatures. It was the unbroken stir and scamper and hum and chatter everywhere that had given this historic town its name. The holy land of Kurukshetra began a few miles from here; thus people on their way there—saints, ascetics, mendicants—tarried in this beautiful, peaceful town before proceeding further.

The impressive battlements of the Kunjpura fort-complex could be seen sticking their heads out proudly from among the dense foliage that surrounded it. The entire town was encircled by a wall. Right in front of the town was a big, strong fort on level ground. The fort was as central to the fame of Kunjpura as the Red Fort was to Delhi. The outer ring of battlement was punctuated by three huge gates: the Karnali Gate on the west, the Nyavali Gate on the north-west and the Mohammadi Gate on south-east. These massive metal gates were strong as sheets of rock. They were further protected by stone-masonry walls a few feet in front, making it impossible for the gates to be blown away by cannon fire or brought down by maddened elephants. These walls thus protected the fort from a frontal attack. A few feet beyond the periphery of the fort walls was a moat ten arms deep, filled with water round the year. With the Yamuna flowing so close by, the moat would be perpetually supplied by underground springs. In earlier times, the moat would be infested with alligators; but even if there were no such monsters now, there were enough poisonous snakes that found the waters of the moat congenial.

Despite being located on a busy route, Kunjpura was a quiet post. It had not been subjected to any major assault. The town hadn't paid any heed to any of the rulers of Hindustan either. The post at that time was under the control of Najeeb, and his trusted cousin Najabat Khan was the fort-keeper. Once you crossed the Yamuna that was visible from the fort, you got into the Kirana sub-division of Muzaffarnagar. Once the Yamuna receded, brisk trade would begin between Kirana and Kunjpura. During the summer months, there would be plenty of boats travelling to and fro between the two banks.

This Kunjpura was suddenly jolted in the afternoon by the sound of the big bell, the huge, unwieldy, frightful bell that hung in the porch of the fort. It took two men to pull the rope that swung the clapper. It was rung only during times of grave emergency, such as invasion by a foreign army, and such a crisis hadn't struck in many years. Rumours had been rife for the past two months of an imminent attack by the Marathas, but when the bell suddenly began to boom that afternoon, panic took hold of the town. The crescent moon on the mosques and the spires of the temples tried to peep over the walls. The townspeople climbed over the bastion walls and peered at the Karnal-ward road. There … there … a couple of miles down, the Maratha forces could be seen, kicking up dust clouds, closing in rapidly with their flags fluttering, a storm of locusts vaster than a glance could encompass. The entire village was whipped into a state of panic. People went into a frenzy, and began gathering their valuables and secreting them in pits and holes under the floors of their houses.

Fort-keeper Najabat Khan was a person who walked to the beat of his own drum. He was not the kind to drink water off another person's palms. Despite being Najeeb's appointee, he liked to keep his distance, and Najeeb was sensible enough to respect the man's sensibilities. Najabat Khan lived in the fort with eight thousand Rohillas. When he saw the war clouds gathering around Kunjpura, he turned nervous.

The threesome of Najeeb's teacher Kutb Shah, the Subhedar of Sirhind Abus Samad Khan and Momin Khan had set off from the Punjab with the intention of crossing the Yamuna at Kunjpura and entering the Antarved. They wanted to go down the eastern bank of the river and meet up with Abdali. But the river was showing no signs of receding, and moving with such great quantities of war equipment was difficult. Najabat Khan had collected two hundred thousand sacks of wheat and stocked them in the fort. The plan was to move ahead with the wheat as well as a huge quantity of gunpowder. Kutb Shah, Samad Khan and Momin Khan were travelling in the company of twelve thousand spirited Kandahari horses ridden by twelve thousand big-built, strong-armed, strapping young horsemen. They had wanted to join up with Abdali as soon as possible with the purpose of vanquishing the Marathas and returning home in the company of Abdali's forces.

With the waters refusing to slacken, the three chieftains had got stuck on this side of the river. They were aware of the stiff and standoffish nature of Najabat Khan. Although a native of Afghanistan, he had been resident in Hindustan for thirty years now. Najeeb's three chieftains were extraordinarily proud of the soil of Kabul and Kandahar. As the chief of the Kunjpur post, Najabat Khan had offered them the palaces within the walls of the fort, but the Iranian Sardars had decided not to get under the obligation of the stubborn Hindustani fort-keeper. Accordingly, Samad Khan and Momin Khan had pitched their camps outside the fort walls, and erected their own tents in the space between the moat and the walls. Miyan Kutb Khan, on the other hand, had not bothered to take much cognizance of Najabat Khan, and had pitched his pavilion facing the Nyavali Gate from the outside.

It was the primary responsibility of Najabat Khan to protect the village and the fort. He had received information that a huge Maratha army was on its way to his fort. He put forth the suggestion before Najeeb's chieftains that they should bring their armies together and confront the enemy, but both Samad Khan and Momin Khan were dismissive of him, while Kutb Shah was still wrapped up in his conceit. Najabat Khan was left with no alternative but to make do with his eight-thousand-strong force as best as he could. He posted the men on the inner side of the gates, close to the balustrades, and near the ordnance. He placed round-the-clock patrols; yet, with all his efforts, he wasn't sure he had done enough. The chieftains could afford not to care, but for Najabat Khan, it was a life-and-death issue.

Najabat Khan espied the fast-approaching Maratha forces from the bastion walls, and his heart sank. He immediately jumped on his horse and galloped out of the Nyavali Gate. Miyan Kutb Khan was relaxing in his pavilion when, to his surprise, he saw the arrogant fort-keeper heading towards him. 'What's the matter, Khan Saheb?' he enquired. 'What's the hurry about?'

'The Maratha forces are travelling up the Karnal road. I saw them.'

'What else?'

'Miyan Saheb, I am a Pathan by race, and owe allegiance to Abdali. I am Najeeb's cousin.'

'I, as it happens, am Najeeb's teacher,' laughed Kutb Shah.

'That's why I say, we are all joined together by bonds. The emperor needs provisions, I keep getting constant reminders from him. I have gathered two hundred thousand sacks of wheat for him, along with a lot of high-quality gunpowder. Shouldn't I be concerned about safeguarding all these provisions?'

'Are you suggesting that these cannot be safeguarded?' sneered Kutb Shah. 'Fort-keeper Saheb, you seem to have accepted defeat even before the fort has been assaulted. Are you so afraid for your life?'

'Not one bit, but what is wrong with being concerned?'

Kutb Shah stood up with a flourish, and swinging his arms in the manner of a wrestler, he said, 'Fort-keeper Saheb, you see these strong, muscular arms of mine? It's these very arms that ripped apart that Datta Shinde at the Buradi Ghat last year. The Margatthas thought of Dattaji as a cheetah, but I tore him apart as one yanks off a chicken leg.

I have estimated well and proper the heft of the Marathas. You have no reason to worry.'

'Shah Saheb, circumstances have changed now. They are bringing with them a hundred-thousand-strong force backed by a strong artillery unit.'

'A hundred thousand, is it? Who cares if they are twice that number? This swarm of ants and insects won't be able to touch a single hair on this Kutb's head. You may go back to your fort without a worry. Take a nap. Abandon all fear. I stand here at your main gate like an immovable rock. If the Margatthas are foolhardy enough to come face me, I shall throw them into the moat and drown them to death.'

'There are no two opinions about your courage, Shah Saheb, but I still believe that your forces and those of Samad Khan should get behind the shelter of the fort walls. With the fort as our shield, we should together be able to eliminate the enemy.'

Kutb Shah broke into laughter. 'I've told you, fort-keeper saheb, get back into your fort without a worry. I am no pansy to use your walls as shields to fight my battle. I had torn that Dattaji into pieces out in the open. This Kutb Shah does not believe in the cowardliness of trapping an animal in a cave for hunting it down. We will show the Margatthas the stuff we are made of in the open battlefield. That not a single Margattha comes within touching distance of your walls is our responsibility. Go, go back without a fear.'

A disappointed Najabat Khan turned round to walk out of the pavilion when a scout hurried in with a post-bag and handed it over to his master. Kutb Shah quickly read through the missive and laughed in delight. 'See, fort-keeper saheb?' he waved the scroll at Najabat and said. 'The Afghans have enough merit going for them. This missive is from Emperor Abdali. He seems to have got intelligence about the Marathas' movement much earlier than we did. A force of nine thousand hardy men is moving up the other bank, and should be here to help us in the next couple of days. It had set off quite early. So, fort-keeper saheb, just stop agonizing. Have trust in Allah, He is the ultimate Giver.'

Najabat climbed on to his horse and sped away. He took a round of his fort to ensure that the defences were in place. 'Stake your life if you have to,' he told the soldiers on guard behind the gates, 'but the doors should not be opened at any cost. Even if the world outside is on fire, do not open the gates without my express instruction.'

⁂

By afternoon the Maratha forces had begun gathering around Kunjpura. Jankoji Shinde had turned ablaze the moment he had set foot on the Kunjpura soil. The monster who had decapitated Dattaji, the devil who had danced on Dattaji's body as he lay taking his last breaths, where could that Kutb Shah be? Jankoji's eyes were scanning all directions with such passion that if they had teeth, they would have chewed the fort walls to a pulp. 'Kutub Khan!' they screamed, 'Either I dispatch you to your Maker now, or die in the process!'

Malharrao Holkar and Vitthal Shivdev had both traversed these lands right up to the Punjab, and grown old in the service of the Maratha empire, yet their excitement today was as sharp as that of the youth. They knew that this could be the decisive encounter. What happened here would determine the course of the main war later, and their old bones did not want to let this opportunity slip unaccounted. Damaji Gayakwad too was letting the blood rush to his head and urging his horse to greater speed. Bhausaheb had taken him in his arms before they had crossed the Vindhyas, and wiped out all misgivings, misunderstandings and distances. He was eager now to display the sharpness of his sword in this new battlefield of Kunjpura.

As light began to soften, the Maratha men began laying siege to the fort. The forces of Damaji and Shamsher Bahadur stood now face to face with the men of Kutb Shah in front of the Nyavali Gate on the north-west. From Delhi, they had moved up along Samalkha, Sonipat, Panipat and Karnal, planting pickets all along the big and small wharves on the way. Before touching Karnal, they had met up with Vishwasrao and Bhausaheb's men and Ibrahim Gardi's contingent. Gardi's ten thousand men accompanying around two-hundred-and-fifty cannons were moving briskly in regular battle order, but there was no way the foot soldiers could keep pace with the cavalry. They had the responsibility of the heavy moving guns too. Bhausaheb's royal guards were in the vanguard, with the pilgrims bringing the rear with their mules and other pack animals. Damaji and Shamsher's troops had left the caravan behind and shot forward that morning.

Shamsher spotted Bhausaheb's elephant Gajendra rocking through this sea of men in a trance of its own. Both Damaji and Shamsher bucked their horses and came abreast of the animal. Damaji raised his right hand to salute Bhausaheb and Vishwasrao who sat in the canopy, and Bhausaheb let out a hearty laugh in return. 'Move on briskly, Damaji,' he shouted, 'we'll destroy Kunjpura tonight.' Damaji nodded enthusiastically. Shamsher positioned himself broadside of the canopy and got his thoroughbred to stand on its hind legs. The horse crossed its forelegs in the manner of a human being joining palms as a salutation. This was Shamsher's usual way of paying his respects to Bhausaheb on the battlefield. Bhausaheb accepted the salutation and asked anxiously, 'Shamsher, the arrangement at the wharves—'

'It's all in perfect order. Not an ant can cross over to this bank.'

'Very well, then. Go on and get into battle formation.'

'Your wish is my command, Shrimant.'

By dusk, the forces of Gayakwad and Shamsher stood facing the Nyavali gate, putting their men in position a short distance away from the moat. Fate had given him a raw deal, thought Shamsher, it had abandoned him, but the battlefield was the one place where he was free to make his own destiny. He licked his lips in anticipation as he saw the rays of the setting sun play on the ramparts of the fort.

Yashwantrao Pawar's troops were getting into formation in front of the Mohammadi Gate in the south-east, along with the squadrons of Manaji Paigude, Antaji Mankeshwar, Darekar and Rethrekar. In front of the Karnal Gate in the west stood Jankoji Shinde, glaring at the fort unblinkingly. Alongside him were Balwantrao Mehendale's men and the royal guards who had hurried on ahead and were taking their positions.

Curiosity seemed to have got the better of caution with many of the denizens of Kunjpura. Every vantage point that offered some kind of cover was spilling over with people: balconies, roofs and even temple spires. The Maratha forces surrounding the fort from all sides made it look like a black island in the middle of a sea. Soldiers and troopers were closing in on the fort, like waves whipped to a froth by strong winds. Najabat Khan stood sighing on the bastion of the fort wall as he watched the crowds gathering around him. Kutb Khan too had stepped out of his pavilion to observe the Maratha movements. He had placed his men at strategic spots along the moat. At the other wing, Samad Khan and Momin Khan had lined up their forces on the land that lay between the fort walls and the moat. Both sides were guaging the rival's preparedness.

The sun was close to dipping below the horizon, but the Gayakwad-Shamsher army knew no cooling off. They started raining arrows on Kutb Shah's men on the other side of the moat. The guns began to crackle too. Kutb Shah's men returned the volley. When Najabat Khan saw the face off begin down below, he gave a sign to his men on the bastion and his Afghani guns began to crackle too. Gayakwad's squad that had moved forward began being hit, and before they knew it, a number of his horsemen in the vanguard had fallen. The survivors immediately turned round to regain the safety that distance offered, dragging as many of their injured brethren as they could. Reorganizing themselves, they resumed their fusillade of arrows on Najabat's men on the fort wall.

Jankoji was so swept away by the excitement of the battle that he began to nudge and spur his horse. 'Kill!' he roared, 'slaughter!' His men were equally excited. They shot arrows at the bastion and brought down a couple of dozen gunmen. 'Ya Allah!' 'Ya Parvardigar!' came the agonized cries as the Afghans fell to their death in the moat below. While it was 'Har Har Mahadev!' on the outside, the roars that rose from inside the walls were 'Allah-o-Akbar!' The cries and counter-cries kept the men on both sides too busy to notice the sun disappear altogether from the sky. The gathering darkness merged with the smoke and dust all around and reduced visibility to naught. The gunfire soon ceased on both sides.

༺༻

As Bhausaheb was crossing Karnal in the afternoon, his army had created a flutter among the natives. Word had got round that a great king of the Marathas was crossing their town with a massive force, and they had gathered in large numbers on rooftops, on tree-tops and on the balconies of the bigger houses to see the tidal wave go past: thirty-five to forty thousand men on horses and no less than fifteen thousand foot soldiers.

It was for the first time in their lives that they were seeing an army of this dimension pass by their town.

Beyond Karnal was the town of Nyaval, from where the road to Kunjpura began. There was about three miles of desert on the way. It was still afternoon, and the hot sand began to scorch the hooves of the animals. The foot soldiers of Ibrahim Khan's brigade too found it difficult to move over the baked land. With great difficulty, they managed to cross half the desert. The bullocks pulling the cannon carts were exhausted. They had been weak from starvation while leaving Delhi; what followed was a taxing journey of seventy miles in five days' time. Fortunately the royal canal ran alongside the imperial highway going from Delhi towards Panipat and Kunjpura. The land on either side of the canal was covered with plenty of vegetation—grass and bushes—for them to feed on. The army also managed to purchase some dry fodder in the villages around Sonipat. Thus, when the bullocks began to tire, the cart-men would unyoke the animals and let them wallow in the canal. The sun-scorched animals would cool themselves for a little while, come out and graze on the fresh juicy grass on the banks, and then get yoked again to pull the cannons with new vigour. Ibrahim pressed upon Bhausaheb to buy a thousand bullocks at the Sonipat market. Where earlier there were fifty bullocks pulling a cannon, now there were ten more, which made the job of pulling much easier.

Bhausaheb knew that carrying the cannons through the desert would take time; hence he instructed Ibrahim to make as much haste as he could and went forward with his royal guards. The drag of the sand and the changing wind on the desert brought both animals and men to a state of desperation. After covering a couple of miles with great difficulty, the animals could take it no more. The tired Gardis unyoked the animals and themselves lay spread-eagled. Lakshmanrao Panse and Ibrahim had realized that the animals couldn't be persuaded to rise without an hour or two of rest. They prodded the herders to empty the water-bags in buckets and place them before the animals. After the bullocks had drunk their full, the rest of the water was poured over their sweaty backs. Much to their relief, a cool evening breeze had also begun to blow.

It had begun to turn dark when Bhausaheb reached Kunjpura. The gunfire he had been hearing from a distance had now gone silent, making him wonder for a minute whether it was real or imagined. As he moved closer, he saw that the armies of Shinde, Holkar, Vinchurkar, Gayakwad and Shamsher had surrounded the fort. Except for the soldiers in the forefront, the rest were busy erecting their tents and setting up hearths. Earthen pots were bubbling with the jhunka gram-paste that would be eaten with hot bhaakaris.

The troopers had erected four pavilions for Bhausaheb and the royal ladies during the afternoon in the mango grove adjacent to their camp. As his elephant Gajendra came to a halt, the servants ran with ladders, but as always, Bhausaheb put his foot out of the canopy and jumped onto the back of his horse Chandrasen that stood alongside. He patted the rump of his horse and drank a jugful of water in one breath. He took Vishwasrao along with him, and with the armed camp sentinels as guards and a host of men carrying torches, set out for an inspection tour.

There were some fifty or sixty injured soldiers stretched out in Damaji's pavilion. As they lay groaning, healers were treating them with herbs and potions. Bhausaheb exchanged a few words of encouragement with the men and congratulated both Damaji and Shamsher for their men's bravery. He congratulated them both and asked Damaji, 'What is your sense of the enemy's strength?'

'The Afghan contingent is lined up out in the open at the foot of the fortress. They are a fierce lot.'

'Shamsher, have you noticed any weak spots?'

'Bhausaheb, it looks like they have enough guns both outside and inside the fort, but only a small cannon or two on the bastions.'

'Are you sure?'

'I am quite sure, Shrimant.'

'Mahipatrao,' he ordered, 'send a few scouts down the way we came. Ibrahim Khan would be four or five miles away. Tell him to move like the wind, and ensure that our cannons are here and mounted before dawn.'

Bhausaheb resumed his round and soon reached the Holkar camp. Malharbaba applied the sacred turmeric powder of Lord Khandoba on his forehead. Vitthalrao Vinchurkar was also present, and they discussed the deployment of their forces. Finally, Bhausaheb said, 'Subhedar kaka, don't you notice a flaw in the siege we have laid today?'

'What could that be, Bhausaheb?'

'The fort is quite nicely encircled, covered from all sides, but the village looks free.'

'Yes, that's quite true.'

'Kakasaheb, I suggest that we let these young boys assault the fort, but as soon as the conflict starts, you and Vinchurkar should get into the village from the other side. Najabat has a big mansion at Kunjpura, I have been told. Who knows some reserve force might have been posted there? Smoke them out and kill them.'

☙

Ibrahim Khan got the bullocks yoked to the cannons again. In the light of the torches, the battalion of the Gardis began moving forward, the creak of the carts and the clank of the chains adding their notes to the night wind. Ibrahim Khan planned to continue this way till they left the desert behind. They would then take a break, finish their dinner and rest till midnight. They would then resume their march and reach the Kunjpura fort by daybreak. But just as they had stepped out of the sands, he received the summons from Bhausaheb and immediately revised his plan.

It was around midnight when the Maratha artillery reached the Mohammadi Gate at the south-eastern face of the fort. The torches of the sentinels on the bastions burned bright enough to reach the moat. Yashwantrao Pawar's men stood on guard behind whatever cover was available. That was where, dodging the eyes of the enemy sentinels on the bastion, the dark-faced Gardis began erecting platforms for mounting the cannons. They looked ferocious enough to give even the darkness cold shivers. Jereshastri and Punalkar Joshibuva arrived at Bhausaheb's pavilion at about eleven. 'Yes, Shastribuva,' Bhausaheb greeted them, 'what is it?'

'What does one say before Shrimant?' sighed Jereshastri. 'Not a leaf moves in our army without Patankar Deekshit's horoscope. It was he who decided the muhoort, the auspicious time for setting out of Partud; it was he again who drew the muhoort on touching Delhi. But look at the results all his muhoorts have given us—the army is starving, the animals have nothing to eat. It's now the eight or nine months since we left home, Shrimant, and what have we to show for it?'

'Well, why don't *you* tell us a good time for tomorrow, then?' Bhausaheb responded with a laugh.

'Tomorrow is maha-ashtami of the month of Ashvin; there cannot be a more auspicious day. Let's set fire to the cannon-fuse three hours past sunrise, and sit back and watch the results. If that does not spell success for us, this Jereshastri swears never to touch a horoscope again.'

'All right, then, let's begin tomorrow at your suggested time.'

'Please alert that Ibrahim Gardi not to be in undue hurry. He has itchy fingers and tends to jump the gun.'

Bhausaheb immediately arranged for the message to be conveyed to Ibrahim Khan. Anticipating an early morning battle, the soldiers retired early to bed, with only the night guards doing their rounds of the camp. A little past midnight, Ibrahim Khan's cannons were securely mounted on their platforms, and with the herders to help them, the gunners began stuffing the cannons with gunpowder. The fort, as it were, stared unblinkingly with its red and black eyes at the Maratha army gathered at its feet.

Jankoji lay on his bed staring at the fort bastions. Where could that hell-hound Kutb Shah be? The night advanced, but the wicks in Jankoji's eyes kept burning.

Dawn broke and Ibrahim Khan's guns placed in front of the Mohammadi Gate began booming, throwing the troops on both sides into a frenzy. The battle had begun. Mahipatrao leapt on to his horse and raced to Ibrahim Khan. 'Khan Saheb, what have you done? Shrimant will be furious!'

'What's the matter, Chitnis?'

'The auspicious moment is a good three hours away!'

Ibrahim Khan laughed and said, 'Why does good work have to wait for an auspicious moment? Give my message to Bhausaheb, and tell him not to worry. I will win the fort for him.'

When they heard the sound of cannon-fire coming from the Mohammadi Gate, Damaji Gayakwad and Shamsher Bahadur too got into the spirit for battle. When they learnt that the forces facing them on the opposite side of the moat were none other than Kutb Shah's, they began shooting arrows across furiously. The effect was immediately visible; the enemy had begun feeling the heat. Some enterprising archers made it literally hot by shooting paraffin-soaked, flaming arrows into the enemy lines. One such arrow found Kutb Shah's pavilion, and it immediately caught fire. In very little time, the neighbouring tents had caught fire too, spreading panic among the six or seven thousand men that Kutb Shah's battalion comprised.

Fire raging behind them, arrows raining in front, they didn't know which way to run, where to find shelter. Noticing the confusion among Kutb Shah's forces, Damaji and Shamsher began letting out loud war cries of 'Har Har Mahadev!' Shamsher suddenly noticed a narrow part of the moat and took measure of the distance. He patted his horse, gave it a sufficient run to take off and flew across the moat to the other side. When Damaji saw this, he knew that he could do it too, and he too leapt over to the other side. In no time at all it became a sport, with all the Maratha horsemen leaping over and across the water. Kutb Shah started making last ditch efforts to boost his men's courage by loud cries of 'Kill! Kill!' Swords clashed against swords, horses rammed into horses and men began cutting each other up, causing squirts of blood to shoot into the air.

The war was now joined on all sides, the cannon fire drowning the clamour of men and animals each time it boomed. Holkar and Vinchurkar's men went and dashed against the walls of the town. They charged up the elephants to bang against the gates and sent them crashing down. The forces of the two generals poured into the town and slaughtered whoever fell in their path. The roads were soon spattered with human blood. Holkar took his men with him and set them up against Najabat Khan's stone-walled mansion. Taking as much shelter of the walls as they could, a good thousand or two soldiers got engaged in mortal combat.

At the Karnal Gate to the west, Jankoji's and Momin Khan's archers were shooting missiles at each other across the moat. Arrows and bullets crossed the water thick and fast in either direction. One of Jankoji's braves picked up a spear, balanced it on his shoulder, took careful aim and flung it across the water. The missile described a neat parabola and found its target with perfection. It pierced the chest of Momin Khan sitting atop his elephant and brought him crashing down in a pool of blood. The fall of their chieftain broke the courage of his men; they began to flee from the battleground. Jankoji's troops saw their opportunity and threw long planks across the moat to make the crossing. Reaching the other side, they brought the fleeing enemy down in heaps.

The boom and roll of Ibrahim Khan's cannons was deafening. In front of him on the other side of the moat stood Abu Samad Khan of Sirhind with his seven or eight thousand strapping Pathans. Their zest was undimmed, but they did not have the cannons to put it to use. Ibrahim Khan's guns, on the other hand, were belching fire incessantly. The fusillade of lead balls they spat out went and hit the fort walls in a continuous stream. The moment a cannon had shot out its charge, the gunners would run and load it with lead and gunpowder, tamp it hard, place a wick and light it up again for the next dispatch. The men around sweated profusely as the ambient temperature shot up. The air had turned thick with smoke and dust. The big monster guns finally began bringing the stones of the fort walls tumbling down. Gaps were opening up, wide enough for a couple of boats to pass through. The bastions started crumbling like stone mansions shaken up by a massive earthquake. As the cannon balls punched massive holes, Najabat Khan's gun-toting Pathans posted on the bastions began falling over along with the collapsing masonry of the walls. Bhausaheb mounted on Chandrasen. 'Kill!' he screamed. 'Slaughter! Smash them all!' Loud cries of 'Har Har Mahadev!' resonated from all sides.

It became evident to the Pathans that they would not last long in the face of this onslaught. The news of Momin Khan's death disheartened them completely. 'Ya Allah! Ya Khuda!' screamed Abu Samad Khan's men at the Nyavali Gate as they abandoned their weapons and began to run. That was when the survivors of Momin Khan's battalion also came running in, tripping and falling over each other, and joined the melee that was making a dash for dear life towards the Nyavali Gate. When Abu Samad Khan realized that there was no holding back his men, he too leapt off his canopy and joined his fleeing troops. They all began banging at the unyielding gate with whatever they could lay hands on, and raised a loud furore with cries of 'Open, please brothers! In the name of Allah, please let us in! We shall be slaughtered out here!' There was no way these desperate cries for help would not have reached Najabat Khan's men inside, but they were under strict instructions not to open the gate under any circumstance. Ibrahim's cannons were rapidly converting the fort walls into rubble. Soon half of the bastion lay in a heap of dust and stones, and wide gaps began opening up exposing the pulverized interiors of the fort. A good bit of the masonry fell into the moat, creating a passage for the Marathas to cross over. At a signal from Sardar Yashwantrao, Ibrahim brought the gunfire to a halt. The cannons turned silent, letting off residual smoke, drooling, as if, at what more they could have brought down. Yashwantrao Pawar then galloped in with his horsemen to chase the Pathan towards the Nyavali Gate, which was finally opened from the inside. Meanwhile, Gayakwad and Shamsher were giving the fleeing Abu Samad Khan a hot chase. The entire fortress was buzzing with excited Marathas putting to death whichever Pathan they could espy and prise out. The seriously wounded fort-keeper Najabat Khan fell into their hands alive along with his entire clan. The Maratha flag was hoisted on the fort to the accompaniment of trumpets and kettle-drums, with the delirious soldiers jumping and dancing to the beat. A few of the men lifted Ibrahim Khan over their shoulders like a victorious wrestler, and they went dancing with him in every direction. They couldn't get over the euphoria of the victory that they had been coveting for so long. Horsemen and troopers gathered each other in their arms, overjoyed. The pilgrims joined in the display of unadulterated joy. Although the fort had fallen, the looting in the village continued for long.

A good eight to ten thousand soldiers had gathered round Bhausaheb's pavilion, raising loud cries of victory in his and Vishwasrao's name. His face beaming with unrestrained pleasure, Bhausaheb raised his hands and acknowledged their greetings. Parvatibai arrived with a tray to welcome the victor with an aarti and applied vermillion on her husband's forehead. When their eyes locked, neither could hold back tears.

In a little while, an elephant with a canopy on its back was seen lumbering towards the flag-post, with hundreds of soldiers walking in its trail. The seat in the canopy was occupied by a bedraggled prince of sorts. On either side of the elephant were Damaji and Shamsher on their horses, nudging the elephant forward. Bhausaheb stood wondering who that could be. Then from somewhere in the crowd a loud cry broke out, 'Kutb Shah! Kutb Shah!' Damaji and Shamsher had managed to capture him alive. At the very name of Kutb Shah, Bhausaheb's placid face turned red with anger. He shouted, 'Who has placed that demon in the canopy? Pull him down instantly!'

Kutb Shah was dragged down from his seat and made to stand at the flag-post. As swords were pulled out of their sheaths, Bhausaheb went up to the man and snarled, 'Who killed my Dattaji?'

Kutb Shah stared at Bhausaheb. He knew that his time was up, never mind whether he spoke up or stayed silent. However, no fear showed on his face. He looked into Bhausaheb's flashing eyes and said, 'It was I who beheaded him.'

'Why?'

'I merely observed the rituals of warfare. It is an old tradition with us to decapitate the fallen enemy and carry the head on a spear in procession.'

The fire of vengeance was racing through every drop of blood in Bhausaheb's body, rising to a crescendo with every beat of the pulse. 'What are you waiting for?' he shouted at the men with the naked swords. 'Hack this monster to bits!'

Before the guards could move forward, a loud shout came from behind. 'Stop!' All heads turned to find Jankoji Shinde sitting astride his horse, his feet firmly planted in the stirrup. The wide-bladed jamdada in his hand glittered in the afternoon sun, matching its glare with the fire that flashed in his eyes. 'Nobody lays a hand on him! He is my prey!' He took aim at Kutb Khan's neck. The sword flew in the air and found its mark to perfection, separating the head from the body like a scythe slicing through a sugarcane stick. As the head and the headless body fell to the ground, a fountain of blood shot out off the severed neck, creating a puddle of bright red where it fell.

Jankojibaba's revenge was not yet over. He jumped off the horse, picked up the head with a spear and mounted his horse again with the macabre trophy. His men had waited for a full year, dreaming of this moment.

Suddenly there was chaos among a section of the crowd. A huge black elephant, almost like a massive, rolling boulder, was cutting its way through the gathering of Jankoji's men, a broken chain trailing behind it. The soldiers were scampering out of the way crying, 'Mad elephant! Run!' As it passed close enough for Jankoji to see, he yelled ecstatically, 'Javhergunj! Javhergunj, here, here!' The elephant juddered to a halt and turned its head round. It lifted its trunk and tested the air, and trundled towards where Jankoji stood. When it was close enough, it gently curved its trunk round its prince and lifted him off the ground. When Jankoji was deposited back and released from its grip, he clung to the elephant, wept and kissed it repeatedly.

With drums and trumpets escorting him, Jankoji moved regally towards his pavilion on his beloved elephant, still pumping vigorously the spear with the gruesome head grinning atop it. His Dussehra celebration had begun.

News arrived that the grievously injured Najabat Khan had given up the ghost. Abu Samad Khan had been slaughtered too. When the body count was taken, four thousand Pathans had lost their lives against seven hundred Maratha soldiers dead. A huge quantity of ordnance fell into Bhausaheb's hands. Holkar and Vinchurkar laid at his feet the loot they had collected in the village, while the fort yielded eight hundred thousand in cash. None among the Marathas could in their wildest dreams have hoped to land this quantity of wealth. Two hundred thousand sacks of wheat lay stacked in the fort warehouse, worth more in value than all the jewels of Hindustan. Dussehra was barely two days away. The Marathas got busy preparing for the festival.

※

While Badshah Abdali's officials Shah Wali Khan, Shah Pasand Khan, Najeeb Khan, Barkhurdar Khan and others sat with their faces red and heads down, he paced to and fro, terrifying even the cloth walls and curtains of the pavilion into hushed silence.

'Can there be a bigger humiliation than this?' he roared. 'Shame, shame on this wretched life. Look at me, the all-conquering King of Kandahar! Commanding a presence that makes the mountains shrink and crumble, the earth quake in fear, the birds hide in their boles and the trees forget to flutter their leaves! With such an emperor alive and breathing, three of his stalwart generals are slaughtered in broad daylight and their corpses desecrated! And all this happens in barely two hours of skirmish! If the emperor's close associates can be subjected to dishonour and slaughtered while his heart still beats, what right does he have to continue living? So much better, isn't it, to surrender to the embrace of death? Such gallant men, supported by the best Hindustan-Afghanistan troops, overflowing ordnance, and yet this disaster? Pluck the fancy feathers and decoration pieces out of your turbans, all of you, go to the markets at Bareili and buy bangles for yourselves!'

Najeeb was the only one with the brazenness to respond. Shedding tears like a child, he bawled, 'All has been washed out, Aalam-panaah. The Day of Judgement has arrived. Two hundred thousand sacks of wheat, treasure worth a million, all the priceless ordnance, all snatched by those Deccan ruffians! We have been destroyed, Aalam-panaah, annihilated!'

'Stop your bawling, Najeeb!' roared Abdali. 'If you and our people had been the slightest bit concerned, how far away was either Saharanpur or Najeebabad from Kunjpura? Why didn't your men show courage? Why didn't they launch an assault on Kunjpura? It's only we, foreign Pathans, who should turn to dust fighting for you, while you happily come over to rule?'

'Forgive my impertinence, huzoor,' snivelled Najeeb, 'but what did *we* gain from the fall of Kunjpura? Those wretched Marathas killed my cousin Najabat Khan, who was also a dear, loyal friend. My post has been destroyed.'

'Our entire battalion of strapping Afghans has been wiped out,' said Wazeer Shah Wali Khan. 'Such a valiant bunch of soldiers has been wasted!'

Badshah Abdali sat brooding for an hour. His mind had turned numb; nothing seemed to interest him, no suggestions held any appeal. In fact, he was finding it difficult to tolerate the very presence of the chieftains standing before him. Finally, he barked out in anger, 'Go, get up and go, all of you, and don't show me your inauspicious faces. Go to the villages nearby, search out some boatman, a fisherman, a float-maker or somebody. Find a spot from where we can make a crossing. Till such time as I carry my army across and trample, roast and totally destroy those wicked demons on the other side, I shall know no peace. Return only when you find a crossing, otherwise jump into the river with your wretched faces and drown in it, you hear? Go!'

The chieftains filed out with their heads lowered. The Yamuna banks had been examined time and again, but there was no ford or wharf within seven miles that was open for even a difficult crossing, they all knew.

However, both Najeeb and Nawab Shuja-ud-dowlah dispatched teams to the nearby villages to look yet another time. A couple of hours had passed by when the badshah sent again for Najeeb and Shuja. The two walked on trembling feet back to the emperor's quarters feeling like a pair of goats heading for slaughter. There was no softening at all in the fury that showed on the emperor's face. He was pacing the room as frenetically as before. 'You two believe that you are the dominant figures of Hindustan. This gentleman here is no less than the Wazeer of Hindustan, the famous Nawab Shuja-ud-dowlah of Ayodhya, yes? And this other great man is the Mir Bakshi of Hindustan, Najeeb-ud-dowlah Rohilla, right? Wants to run the empire of Hindustan all by himself, doesn't he? Officious fool, you, you had the smartness to send your brother as envoy to faraway Kandahar to invite me to this campaign; if you had had enough smartness to look up four good crossings on the Yamuna, I would have thanked Allah for it. All in all, every Hindustani—right from the foot soldier to the biggest chieftain—is a worthless nicompoop.'

'Yes, Najeeb,' Abdali barked, 'where are these Margatthas likely to go after having captured Kunjpura?'

'Huzoor, my guess is that in the excitement of their victory, they will very likely go towards Kurukshetra. It is very close from Kunjpura.'

'Does either of you have any proper information beyond mere guesses?'

They had no response to the emperor's question beyond staring mutely at him. Abdali lashed out. 'Nature works in strange ways. Even if the tree is the same, the fruits can be startlingly different: some just don't ripen; some arrive late and have to be ripened in straw; but there are some fruits that ripen on the tree. That Bhau Peshwa is of the last kind, ripening at the top of the tree. He had never been provided the opportunity before, so no one had known the sweetness of that fruit. It's only now that the world has got to see his worth.'

Praise for his enemy from Abdali's mouth set Najeeb on fire. He couldn't hold himself back and said bitterly, 'Aalam-panaah, such praise for a worthless infidel, that too from you?'

'He is not worthless, you are stupid. Do you have any idea of the plan he has worked out? There is this Sikh landlord by the name of Ala Singh Jaat near Patiala in the Punjab. You may have heard of this blackguard; this hooligan uses rough-arm methods and has declared himself the king of Patiala. He has browbeaten the landlords and small fief-holders of the neighbourhood into submission and spread anarchy in the region.'

'What about him, huzoor?'

'That's what I am coming to. Bhau has established contacts with this Ala Singh Jaat.'

'Ya Allah!' Najeeb exclaimed.

'Fortunately, we have a strong espionage network. Our scouts have got hold of some correspondence between the two. Ala Singh is stationed at a village called Manuk in Kurukshetra right now. The possibility of a meeting between Bhau and Ala cannot be ruled out. Besides, there are some chieftains and some Sikh gangs in Patiala and Sirhind that are inclined to accept this Bhau as their emperor. I don't find these eventualities improbable at all. After all, whenever Afghan raiders set off to launch their attacks on Hindustan, they first burn the Punjab on their way to Delhi. The Sikhs would naturally be sick and tired of us, suffering us since the time Nadir Shah marauded Hindustan ten or fifteen years ago. So it is not surprising that they should find in Bhau an ally. If in the next week or two, the proclamation goes round of Bhau as the emperor of Hindustan, where will I hide my face? If those turbaned Sikhs and the Margatthas of Deccan come together, the tide will turn in all of Hindustan. The way back to my motherland passes through the Punjab. If immediate action is not taken, it will mean disaster for us; not one Afghan will be able to reach Kandahar alive.'

The information made the earth shake under Najeeb's feet. If the Sikhs and the Marathas came together, he knew that his game would be over. Reading Najeeb's face, the badshah continued, 'That is why I say, Najeeb, it is critical for us to cross the Yamuna before the Marathas and the Sikhs come to some agreement. We have to snatch back the wealth that has landed in their hands, we have to annihilate them, else our army is done for.'

Having delivered the punch to Najeeb, Abdali hurried out of the pavilion, mounted his horse and rode into his army. The wazeer, the commander-in-chief and other officials came running in. Bugles were blown and they were all instructed to stand at their appointed places. While the neighbouring villages were busy preparing for Dussehra, an air of gloom hung over the Abdali army. They had all heard of the massacre of Abu Samad Khan, Momin Khan, and Kutb Shah along with ten thousand of the best Pathan soldiers. The clash at Kunjpura was the first face off between the two armies since Bhausaheb had departed from the south and reached the northern areas, and his soldiers' might had shaken Rohilla-Durrani warriors to their core. It was important, therefore, for Abdali to create some semblance of activity so that his men did not lose heart. Word got round that a head-count of the army was being taken. Abdali located an elevated piece of ground and stood on his roan watching his men in movement.

The entire army was camped within a two-mile radius of Abdali's pavilion. Abdali had two thousand personal camels that carried small cannons called jamburkas with them, with two gunners riding each camel. The army also carried forty-eight big cannons and another couple of hundred small cannons called sutarnaala, also carried on camels. Some six thousand horsemen and eight thousand foot soldiers moved under the flag of Najeeb, while Shuja-ud-dowlah had with him two thousand horsemen and an equal number of footmen, along with about fifty Ayodhya cannons. Ahmad Khan Pathan Bangash had brought with him two thousand horsemen, about five hundred foot soldiers and a few cannons.

Badshah Abdali dispatched orders that morning to the Rohillas Dundey Khan, Hafeez Rahmat Khan, Saadullah Khan and Faizullah Khan, who had returned to their principalities two months ago to get somerest and replenish supplies, to rejoin the army within a couple of days. Counting forty-five thousand horsemen and thirty thousand foot soldiers, Abdali thus had a total of seventy-five thousand men under his command. Besides, the army had in its shelter thousands of orphans who had nobody to call their own. Abdali's own guards had a few. The number of these orphans ran up to twenty thousand, and all of them carried a horse each under their seats. These were all healthy young men, and could be of considerable use during battle. Any time that a battalion won a battle, these orphans would descend upon the enemy, and loot and kill. They were the Afghan equivalent of the pendharis, the provisioners, but they could wield a sword when the need arose.

Abdali finished his inspection and set off for his pavilion, ordering his subordinates to get ready for departure. 'We shall leave this place with the bare army within an hour. The orphans' battalion, the tribes and the cannons can start tomorrow. Locating a crossing point is very unlikely for the next five or ten miles, so let's make Baghpat our next destination.'

A skeleton army thus left the spot that every afternoon. The forces moved rapidly, putting behind them twenty miles to reach Baghpat some time after midnight. They went ahead two more miles and set up camp. Abdali's small tent was up and ready two hours before daybreak, while the rest—soldiers as well as chieftains—dumped their bamboos and tarpaulin on the ground and stretched their tired bodies out on the grass under the dark sky. While those put on guard duty moved around like zombies, the rest were snoring in no time. Badshah Abdali felt his eyelids turn heavy.

Ah, I see the way. But who are these wraiths standing on the way that leads to my motherland? Black-faced, teeth long as fate, not one of them with familiar a familiar face? Where is my canopy? I don't see my flag either, nor my minions! Where's my army? What heaps do I see here laid out on this desolate landscape? What's that red stream flowing? Those heaps couldn't be the corpses of my army, could they? Who's that person raising such a loud lament? Wazeer Shah Wali? What state have you been reduced to? And you Jahaan Khan, my commander-in-chief, why are you so soaked in blood after being ...

All right, this was Allah's will, so I'll take it. But Shah Wali, you, at least, shouldn't have been crying. You remember the terrible night on which Nadir Saheb was killed? Saabir Saheb had placed a fistful of dust in my hands at Shaikh Serku's shrine, and had pronounced that that dust would be my throne! You were the one who had anointed me king by throwing a handful of grass on my head as if they were flowers! You remember those events well, don't you? So why cry so inconsolably? Because we have been beaten in Hindustan? Actually, the earth of this place is bad. No reason to lose courage, though. There, there you can see my Kandahar palace. Come, let's raise another army.

What's this? I stand at my own doorstep, and who are these strangers? Who are you? And how dare you put me in chains in my own land? Who am I? I am Durrani, the emperor of emperors, and this is my palace, and I shall have you thrown off my castle walls. Hey, who is this snake that sits coiled on my throne? The face looks familiar. Hello! This is my own nephew Abdul Khaleeq Khan! Treacherous rogue, is this the game you want to play? But, boy, I had been aware of your dark intentions from when you were a child, so why didn't I strangulate you before I left on my campaign to Hindustan?

What dark dungeon is this? Looks darker than the cell of my childhood years! I saw a streak of light there, even if it was after five years. How many years here? A lifetime? 'Ya Parvardigaar! Ya Allah!'

Abdali began to weep in his sleep. His wife came running and shook him by the shoulder. 'Aalam-panaah! Aalam-panaah!' The king woke up with a start and looked around with frightened, disoriented eyes. He wiped his streaming face with a kerchief.

Sleep had now deserted him. Against his wife's advice, he tossed a shawl over his shoulders, mounted his horse and began riding through rows of his sleeping men. The day had broken. In a little while, the wretched dream faded away, but his palace in Kandahar and the face of his nephew refused to leave his head. It was as if a cork had been pulled out, and his heart was being drained of blood. He kept riding this way and that till the sun became quite bright.

Once the army was awake, Abdali left his tent and pitched another one on the bank of the Yamuna. He called for a meeting and dispatched Shuja and Najeeb's men and the royal guards to the nearby villages to fetch over the headmen, the petty revenue officials and the landlords. A detailed search of the bank was instituted, with all the boatmen, fishermen, and a few taut-bodied wrestlers joining in the hunt for a ford. Emperor Abdali refused to budge. Everybody who could swim was pushed into the river. Those whose arms were weak flailed and bubbled and drowned in the water, but those with adequate strength heaved and puffed and panted and finally managed to reach the other bank, dripping water from every pore. This obsessive search sent at least ten to fifteen men to a watery grave, but the emperor didn't turn a hair. He just sat there watching the sun rise and set on the Yamuna plains.

Two days of intense, unrelenting search. On the third night, Abdali's hopes began to sink. He went on his knees to Allah, and prayed fervently. He also went on a fast that tested his capacity for endurance.

The dawn of the fourth morning saw Abdali twisting and turning on his bed. His appetite had disappeared, and the rare occasions on which he slept, he would be woken up by dreadful dreams. He felt feverish all over. It was then that he heard the timid, tentative cry of an usher, as if afraid to wake his master from sleep.

'Who's it?' Abdali shouted.

'Aalam-panaah, commander-in-chief Jahaan Khan is here, and expresses the desire to meet you urgently,' came the voice from outside.

'Why so early in the morning?'

'Huzoor, he has brought a person with him who knows a crossing on the river.'

The word 'crossing' rang in his ear like a beautiful piece of music. He rushed to the conference tent. Jahaan Khan pushed before him a dark, well-built man dressed in rags.

'What's your name?'

'Gulab Singh Gujar.'

'Where do you live?'

'At Gauripur-Panwaadi, huzoor.'

'Where is this crossing? How far from here?'

'About two miles away from here, huzoor, near my village.'

'How do you know about it?'

'Huzoor, I have spent my entire life by mother Yamuna. I also had a boat once, huzoor, hence I know the water here very well.'

'Come, let's go right away.'

'Huzoor, what about my reward?'

'Reward?' Abdali laughed aloud. 'Just show me that crossing, and I shall happily give you my neck if you ask for it!'

Abdali took a few of his trusted men and reached the upper end of Gauripura. Gulab Singh had materialized from nowhere as an answer to their prayers. They gathered at the shrine of a holy man, and Gulab Singh pointed a finger towards the Yamuna. The hillocks of silt on either side had narrowed the course of the river considerably. The narrowing had, of course, increased the current in the water, and the bank on this side had been cut away. The sedimentation on the other side appeared to have converted the far bank into a mire.

Gulab Singh was an expert swimmer. And he had brought such a great king over; the reward he would receive would be great too. So almost all of Gauripur had turned up to see their boy honoured. Gulab Singh tightened his loincloth around his waist and said to Abdali, 'Huzoor, before I dive into the water, you will have to propitiate Mother Yamuna.'

'What do you mean?'

'Huzoor, please offer a paan along with five gold coins to the Mother with your own hands. That will prevent any mishap.'

Abdali bent and scooped water in his cupped palms. A paan and five gold coins were placed in his palms, which he then tossed into the water. Gulab Singh leapt into the water and went swimming some distance. He then began to indicate the depth of the water to the spectators by raising his hand and allowing himself to sink in. In the first dip, the entire hand had disappeared. He then swam a little further and repeated the same exercise. This time, his fingers remained out of the water. Still further on, his head stayed out, and beyond that the water ran up to his neck. The water, it appeared, ran deeper towards the eastern bank. The middle seemed as if it had been lifted by the gathering of silt on the river floor. The sand on the eastern bank, however, had been sharply cut by the force of the water. The water on the western bank yonder was a bit deep, but Gulab Singh's nose still stayed above the surface. Abdali's blue eyes took a sharp estimate of the flow, and they began shining with excitement. He removed the priceless necklace from around his neck and handed it over to Gulab Singh.

Abdali gathered the headmen, landlords and petty officials of the villages and set them to work. Huge trees were axed and their trunks rolled over to the bank within a couple of hours. Long bamboos were brought over and one of their ends was sharpened to a point. The soldiers used their swords to prepare these stakes; as they hacked and shaved the ends, they imagined they were hacking Maratha necks. Float-makers from four of the nearby villages were summoned. Najeeb, meanwhile, was seen hopping everywhere in excitement, goading the workers to hurry.

At the order of the emperor, a bunch of bare-bodied young men got into the water. They had with them a team of boatmen, float-makers and fishermen, all expert swimmers. Huge stakes were first hammered deep into the sand on the eastern bank. Ropes were then tied to the stakes and stretched forward from one stake to the next. With the help of the boatmen and the swimmers, stakes were lowered into the water and hammered in at intervals deeper and deeper into the flow. Soon there was a parallel row of stakes running across the water, almost like a road being built. Najeeb brought a heap of green flags and had them planted on top of the stakes. After the swimmers were done, Jahaan Khan signalled for the huge tree trunks that had been dragged over from the villages to be rolled in. One trunk followed another, and the green branches of trees were laid over them, creating a platform.

It was now well past afternoon, and Abdali was all ready to take his horse into the water. He rested his eyes on his Pathan horsemen. The roar of the water could be heard on the bank, and the fear of the river could be seen on the faces of the men. They stood looking through the corners of their lowered eyes towards their master, and Abdali could well read what was going through their minds. He got off his horse and walked up to the shrine on the bank, where he sat down. He replaced the turban on his head with a white handkerchief and immersed himself in prayer for the next half hour. He then called the mullahs and the maulvis of the army over and got them to etch the verses of the holy Koran on silver and copper plates. He placed sharp arrows on these plates and carried them to the riverside. He shot twelve arrows across the river one after another, returned to his place, and sat in meditation for another hour. He emerged from his meditation and addressed his men, 'There is no reason for us to tarry. Allah has given His promise: whoever dares receives His help.'

With that, he rode his horse energetically into the water. As the soldiers looked bewildered, the young Jahaan Khan shouted 'Allah-o-Akbar' and spurred his horse into the water. There was now no stopping the horsemen as they went into the water in bunches, with Abdali in the lead, sitting with his neck erect. His brocaded shirt was now completely soaked. As he reached the other bank, Abdali noticed the boggy ground in front. Instead of heading straight into it, he walked his horse downstream a little distance in the water and then brought it out.

Around fifty horses with riders had reached the western bank, among them Abdali, his commander-in-chief Jahaan Khan and his old Wazeer Shah Wali. When Abdali looked up, he was perturbed to see that some of the riders, in their excitement at the sight of the bank, had raced their horses straight into the silt mire and were now sinking. Five or six horses could be seen making last-ditch efforts to extricate themselves and failing. As many horsemen got sucked in too and died.

The horsemen who had crossed over safely frantically signalled the rest of them to halt. At the upper end of the bank were some waist-high bramble bushes. Young men and old began hacking them with their swords and throwing them into the slime. They also chopped limbs of some small growing trees on the bank and threw them on top of the bramble. Abdali noticed Shah Wali Khan standing on the bank wringing the water off his tunic and said to him, 'Shah Wali, what are you doing, standing there? Your wazeership and my emperorship depend on the soldiers crossing over to this side.' The old man too bent down and began uprooting the brambles. Layers upon layers of brambles and branches were thrown over the silt untill the heap was a few feet high. Abdali signalled the first horseman in the water to cross over. Tentatively, the rider urged his horse over the heap and made it to firm ground. The rest followed in a stream one after another.

Once the track had firmed, Najeeb lowered his horse in the water. Behind him entered the elephants, with cannons tied to their backs, and one by one emerged on the western bank. In the hustle-bustle of the crossing, those that turned left or right of the beaten track got washed away by the surge of the water, or sank into a slimy grave, man and animal, both. More than a hundred men drowned within an hour or two of the crossing. Abdali yelled at them to be careful, shouting, 'We have already lost many men in Kunjpura. We can't afford to lose even a single horseman from here on.'

Some seven or eight thousand horsemen made it to the western bank. Abdali immediately ordered them to undo the saddles and leave them out to dry. There were soon lines upon lines of saddles drying in the wind, while the bare-backed horses grazed on the soft grass.

⚛

About six miles down the river, a veteran of battles, Sakhroji Patil was minding the ford with a team of seven hundred horsemen. His post was on the exactly opposite bank of Baghpat, with the huge Yamuna flowing in the middle. It was after much thought that Shamsher had posted Sakhroji Patil there. Shamsher had warned him, 'Eat dust if you don't get food, but don't ever move away from your post, understand?' A few of his horsemen would ride into a nearby village for food, while the rest of them stood guarding the bank at all times. Sakhroji himself would never be found away from the wharf. He would get up at least three times during the night and check whether his men were awake on duty. The wide expanse of the Yamuna would remind him of the Panchganga that flowed by his village Wadingey. Sakhroji hadn't received his allowances for three months now, but he was not complaining. This campaign was an enterprise of moral worth, a mission for which all were fighting. Taming great cities like Delhi—a satisfaction worth starving for.

There was a wind blowing at twilight. Sakhroji had got a big fire going, round which sat a dozen or so of his men. The rest of the six hundred men were relaxing behind the bushes nearby. A fisherman had just come down from upstream with a basket full of fresh catch. The fish were now being roasted in the fire and eaten hot and crisp, head, tail, bones and all. With his entire fare sold off, the fisherman had sat down by the fire too, watching the soldiers feast. When Sakhroji noticed the man looking at him intently, he asked, 'Hey, am I a woman that you look at me with such interest?'

'What country have you set off to conquer?' asked the fisherman in the Hindustani tongue. 'Your king is bringing over horses and elephants to this side, thousands of soldiers are crossing the river. Where are you people heading, anyway?'

'Who could that be?' asked a few bewildered soldiers.

Oati's heart lurched. 'Up, up, boys, who else could it be?' he cried. 'It has to be our enemy. Up, quick! We have to block him!'

Seven hundred horses raced along the river at the speed of wind. Although the day was setting, Abdali's men could still be seen climbing out of the water like lines of ants, line after line after line. Sakhroji's men suddenly sprang out of the brambles and broke upon the surprised Afghans. They swung their swords and threw their spears and killed well over a hundred men. 'Har Har Mahadev!' they roared as they swung their weapons wildly. Najeeb and Abdali cried out in anger and shook the Pathans out of slumber. A thousand of them immediately surrounded the attackers and unleashed their weapons. A sword fell upon Sakhroji's nape and he fell; but even as he fell, he struck Ahmad Khan Khybari, a petty official of Abdali, on the neck and took him down.

'Kill every single one of them,' yelled Abdali. 'Don't let even one of them escape to carry the news to Bhau!' Seven hundred men were brought down. They lay dead in a pool of blood. Abdali's orphans then got into action and threw them towards the bank like so many dead mice, a veritable feast for the foxes and hyenas and kites and buzzards in the nearby woods. The blood spattered saffron flags lay scattered everywhere on the Yamuna bank.

Abdali camped that night at Fakhrubagh just outside Sonipat. The next evening, when Najeeb Khan and Shah Pasand Khan came to meet him, he asked, 'How many of our soldiers have crossed so far?'

'Aalam-panaah, three-fourths. We found some boats that these Margattha had collected on this side. They came handy in ferrying over food, fodder and tent material.'

'The entire army should cross over latest by tomorrow afternoon, understand?' instructed Abdali. 'How many of our soldiers drowned in the crossing?'

'Over a thousand.'

'Bad execution. What other news from the enemy?'

'There was a post of about five hundred men at Sonipat before we arrived. Our arrival scared them enough to flee north.'

'They fled north? That would mean to Bhausaheb, right?'

Najeeb and Shah Pasand bowed their heads. Abdali continued, 'Shah Pasand, set off tomorrow with adequate force, search out all ragged big and small posts of the Margatthas on the way up. Not one of them should go back to Bhau alive.'

Shah Pasand set off early next morning with a force of four thousand well-armed horsemen. Just five miles away they located the thousand-strong unit of Hari Deshpande, Bhagwantrao Kadam and Yesaji Bhoite in a state of complete unpreparedness. The unsaddled horses were grazing on the bank, while the men were loitering around without a worry. The Afghans wiped out every man in sight.

After three days at Sonipat, Abdali resumed his march. The unit bringing the rear ran into a Maratha patrol near the village of Ganor. A bitter battle ensued, leaving a thousand Afghans and fifteen hundred Marathas dead. Abdali continued his march over the dead bodies and entered Sambhalka. Three camps were stationed at Ganor, and Abdali moved on. He was accosted every now and then by units of five hundred to a thousand Maratha men that Shamsher and Damaji had planted along the path. The units fought bravely and well, but against the massive army of Abdali, they were no more than a few drops of water getting lost in the ocean.

On 30 October, Abdali left Sambhalka. A mile ahead was a village at a slightly higher elevation than the flat plains surrounding it. Abdali asked Najeeb, 'What village is this, Khan Saheb?'

'Panipat.'

※

It was the day of Dussehra. The entire army was in the mood to celebrate. Nobody could remembered the last time they had seen such a huge cache of loot. Seven hundred and fifty thousand in cash! Bhausaheb had ordered the immediate disbursement of a month's arrears to the men. Accountants and cashiers had set up fifty to sixty counters for distributing the overdue wages. With two hundred thousand sacks of wheat in hand, Bhausaheb had ordered the distribution of another month's worth of delayed wages in kind. The quantity of disbursement was so large that it had spilled over to the next day.

The happiest of them all were the six thousand horsemen who had lost their steeds during the Devgiri and Sindkhed battles or to disease. They had had to drag their feet across hundreds of miles, looking enviously at their colleagues who galloped past them while they trudged along like ordinary foot soldiers. Some of them had been lucky to land a camel in a raid, and some others had had to make do with a mule or a donkey. They were now astride sturdy Afghan horses, and could look back at their colleagues with pride.

When Bhausaheb gifted elephants with canopies to half a dozen chieftains, their faces turned bright enough to light up the night sky. Ibrahim Khan, on receiving an elephant as an honour for destroying the Kunjpura fortress, said, 'Bhausaheb, I will forever be grateful for your generosity. But, frankly, of what use is an elephant to me? I have to move with mortar-carrying Gardis all the time. I have to be nimble with my cannon carts. If I begin to fight my battles from atop an elephant, it would be the same as herding sheep from the back of a camel.'

'Khansaheb,' replied Bhausaheb with a smile, 'this gift is a mere symbol of love. We impose no restriction that this elephant be used only during battle. The animal is being gifted to you on the occasion of Dussehra.'

A good mile of the western bank of the Yamuna was chock-a-block with horsemen and troopers giving their horses a good scrub to wash away the months of dirt, slime and blood that had caked on their skins. A little downstream were the elephants frolicking in the water. Every time they slipped and fell, they would kick up a massive splash that sent sprays across to the bank. The mahouts that sat on their necks scrubbing the backs of their ears looked from a distance like flies on bullocks. Some sat scrubbing their howdahs. The herders had given their bullocks a scrub, and were crowding the waters now to give their animals a rinse. Every one of the soldiers was busy washing and polishing his weapons. The pilgrims had gathered upstream for their ablutions for the sacred festival. Still further upstream were the women taking their ritual baths. Some devotees were offering handfuls of water to the Sun God, while some others had brought together their palms in the water, chanting mantras to propitiate the river itself.

It was after ages that an army market had sprung up in front of the fort. The banias had set up shops under a canvas erected at two points by bamboos and laid out ware that would match anything sold in the city marts. Behind the rear curtain of one shop, the bania's wife was frying puran poli, the delicious sweet pancake that was the mark of the festival; and for all the lovely aroma that came floating into the shop, the man himself had no time to peek behind the curtain. With two months of arrears accounted for and the day being Dussehra, the crowds milling around the shops couldn't have been anything but dense. It was after an age, it appeared, that such a wonderful day had dawned upon the army, and soldiers, horsemen, troopers, and their women wouldn't let it pass without a fling in the market.

The army camp was easily ten times the size of the modest town of Kunjpura, making even the four hundred shop-tents of the bazaar altogether inadequate. Two additional bazaars had to be organized on either side with about fifty to sixty tents each, and they crowded up as rapidly as the middle one.

Setting up a shop-tent required a licence from either the Shindes or the Holkars or the Peshwa after the payment of a fee. The banias were agitated over this. They had been as much pauperized as the army in the previous few months. Anticipating a brisk business on Dussehra day, they had scoured the countryside and brought their wares, mostly on credit, on mules and donkeys. Their wares had still not been sold, and here were Gangoba Tatya and Dabholkar's clerks, going from shop to shop demanding money. 'Whose tent is it, Shinde's or Holkar's?' they went asking. There were skirmishes between the clerks of the two sides too, each claiming right of taxation. 'Never again will we set up shops in the Maratha army,' grumbled the harried traders as they divided their attention between their customers and the nagging clerks.

The entire army was drowned in tumultuous noise from everywhere. Horns and trumpets had begun blowing from early in the morning. Kettle-drums were beaten right through the day before the tents of the chieftains. In the hustle-bustle of an army on the move, they had not been able to keep the night-long vigil for the goddess Durga. They were determined now to expiate their sin of omission by worshipping some goddess on this holy day, never mind which one. The women of the royal household and the other pilgrim women hunted out the temple of Goddess Kalika in Kunjpura. They got into their nine-yard sarees, wore a nose-ring, filled the parting in the hair with vermillion, loaded their arms and ankles with bangles and chains, and went strutting down the lanes of Kunjpura in hundreds, inviting envious glances from the local women dressed in their simple shirts and pajamas. They lavished vermillion upon Goddess Kalika and offered her sarees and blouse pieces.

A big durbar was assembled in the evening for formal celebration. Vishwasrao was made to sit on the throne while Bhausaheb sat by his side. The chieftains made presentations to Vishwasrao. Bhausaheb thanked all present for their contribution to the victory they had achieved at Kunjpura. Chieftains, warriors, Brahmins, scholars and other notables were gifted clothes by Vishwasrao.

The day after Dussehra, Sardar Vinchurkar and Damaji Gayakwad paid a visit to Bhausaheb. Assessment of the wealth they had gained was still in progress. Holkar and Vinchurkar's men had been digging in the village and the fort, looking for hidden caches of treasure.

Gayakwad bowed and said, 'Bhausaheb, you granted amnesty to four thousand injured Rohilla Pathans and permitted them to cross the Yamuna. There is no doubt that their prayers for you will bear fruit soon. They couldn't believe at first that an enemy could be so generous. Now we request you to resolve the problem of the remaining two thousand Afghan slaves.'

'They are free to go wherever they like.'

'But what if they wish to join your services?'

'What does that mean?'

'Vinchurkar will tell you all.'

'Yes, Vitthal Tatya?'

'They are good slave boys; they were in the service of Najabat Khan. They are loath to be driven away from here. They have to make a living, they say, and it makes no difference to them whether it is with the Marathas or Afghans. I ask, Bhausaheb, what if I take them under my shelter?'

Bhausaheb sat silent for a while, mulling over the request, and then spoke, 'Look, Tatya, we already have thousands of extra mouths to feed, and we wouldn't want to add to that burden.'

'Bhausaheb, there's still time for the main war to begin. The Marathas and the Afghans are both marked by destiny to fight that. We have hundreds of thousands already with us; how will another two thousand make a difference? A mere fly sitting on an elephant. They will sweat and toil and earn their keep.'

'But all said and done, Tatya, they are basically slaves from Kandahar! What if they make mischief at the critical hour of war?'

'But who is talking of sending them to the front? They are strapping young lads, they can stay at the rear end, doing menial jobs, and collecting fodder for the animals.'

Bhausaheb didn't think it wise to stretch matters much and granted permission to Vinchurkar.

༺༻

It was now a week since the Marathas had arrived at Kunjpura. The pilgrims were getting restive, but Bhausaheb concentrated on the posts that reached him every day. There had been no news on Abdali in the past five days, but Bhausaheb was more concerned about what was brewing in the Punjab. If no information arrived from the scouts posted there, he would personally go and enquire in the afternoon.

The extension of the stay made not only the pilgrims restless but also Rakhmabai, Akkasaheb, her son Nana, the women of the royal pavilions and the wives of the chieftains. But Mahipatrao Chitnis and Nana Purandare too were itching to make a pilgrimage to Kurukshetra. Rumours began doing the rounds that Bhausaheb and Malharrao had had secret talks where they had decided to return to Delhi without covering Kurukshetra at all. Unable to restrain themselves any further, a group comprising Akkasaheb, Agnihotri, Jereshastri, Punalkar Joshibuva and Patankar Deekshit presented themselves before Bhausaheb. Rakhmabai began the conversation. 'Bhausaheb, I say this to you as a well-wisher: this degree of atheism is not good. After all, how far is Kurukshetra from here? A bare twenty miles! Coming right up to the doorstep of the lord, and returning without even peeping in, this is certainly going to hurt the Peshwa's reputation.'

'Shrimant, Kurukshetra is no way-side shrine. This is the land where the great gods Brahmadev and Indra themselves came and prayed. Ignoring it and turning round is collecting a massive load of sin against one's name,' said an agitated Punalkar Joshibuva.

All eyes were drilling holes into Bhausaheb, their anxiety increasing with every moment of silence. Finally, he sighed and said, 'All right, go, get busy. We leave tomorrow at dawn.'

The gathering was thrilled at hearing these words, and they trooped out excitedly to spread the word. The only person left behind was Vishwasrao, who stood looking at him with pain-stricken eyes.

'What's the matter, Rao Saheb? Why do you look so glum? Are you worried about something?'

'Kakasaheb, when I see liabilities descend upon the shoulders of an action-oriented man like you, my heart aches. Duties on one side, and religion on the other; finding a balance in the pull of these contrary forces is causing you great agony, I can see.'

'Rao Saheb,' responded Bhausaheb, placing an affectionate hand on the young man's shoulder, 'you are the future Peshwa. It won't do for you to worry so.

'Kakasaheb, I want to leave aside any consciousness of Peshwahood and look at your important duties as an ordinary man,' Vishwasrao said passionately. 'If there is important work to be done here, Kakasaheb, I suggest you forget this visit to Kurukshetra. I shall happily take over the curse of the three-hundred-and-thirty million gods on my conscience. But our first job is to get rid of Abdali.'

Bhausaheb looked at Vishwasrao with great satisfaction. Here was a boy perfectly suited to don the mantle of Peshwahood. He patted the young boy's back and said, 'Let me put the entire scenario before you. I have not been pushed into going to Kurukshetra by the pilgrims. Ala Singh Jaat is stationed at a place called Manku, very close to Kurukshetra. His envoys are going to meet me there. If the Sikh sardars and the landlords of the Punjab and Sirhind join forces with us, we will rout the Afghans and roast them alive. Besides, relations with this prosperous region will ensure plentiful food for our men and animals. Plentiful grains and plentiful grass—our entire army will return to good health. With the issue of hunger settled, all that we will have to worry about is the sword and the battlefield!'

⁌⁍

The army was up at dawn. The pilgrims were in a greater hurry today than the soldiery. People who were notorious for dragging their feet and bringing the rear—women, Brahmins, scholars—had suddenly turned nimble-footed like children. They were virtually floating in the air, as if their destination was not Kurukshetra but the abode of the gods!

By evening the army had touched Tarawadi, a spot twelve miles away. This was where they had decided to halt before doing the final lap to Kurukshetra. The troopers had erected four pavilions for the nobility. An exhausted Bhausaheb climbed down from his canopy with the help of a ladder and entered his pavilion. Just then, two horsemen came galloping up in a tearing hurry and pulled their animals to a screeching halt right in front. It was obvious from their appearance that they had been riding for long. Their shirts were coated with blood and dust. Without paying attention to the ushers, the two men barged into the pavilion. Bhausaheb turned round at the intruders, hand on the hilt of his sword, and shouted angrily, 'Who are you? How dare you get into my tent?'

'Forgive us, Shrimant,' the two panted and stuttered, 'we are from your army, Bhoite's battalion. We have come from Sonipat, escaping from the Afghans by the skin of our teeth. The Afghan has crossed the river and come over to this bank.'

Bhausaheb shouted in rage. 'Useless eunuchs! What were you doing when he was crossing over? Why didn't you die fighting there instead of coming running here?'

'Shrimant, every one in our battalion is dead. Not one left alive. These eyes have seen at least a thousand corpses stretched out on the field. We travelled this long distance to warn you. And we travelled in a pair only to ensure that if one of us died on the way, at least the other would survive to bring this news to you.'

Bhausaheb felt remorse for yelling at them. He thanked them and asked, 'How many Pathans have crossed over to this side?'

'Can't tell exactly, Shrimant, but we saw at least five to six thousand with our own eyes!'

The news spread like wildfire among the army. Vishwasrao, Jankoji, Shamsher, Pawar, Jadhavrao, Darekar, Yashwantrao Pawar, Gayakwad and a host of other chieftains went running to Bhau's pavilion. Parvatibai sat listening to the conversation from behind the screen. Bhausaheb ordered Balwantrao to send two units of the royal guard and two units of the Shinde-Holkar army back the way they came. 'They must keep running through the night and through the day. I should keep getting detailed information on the Pathans all the time. Only the Lord knows what happened to the units we had placed all along the way.'

Malharrao said, 'Bhausaheb, Abdali's arrival from Sonipat means that he has cut all our connections with Delhi. This can only spell disaster.'

'The trunk road will have to be opened up at all costs,' Shamsher said.

Noticing that this unanticipated development had rattled his associates, Bhausaheb spoke in a firm voice, 'Don't panic. We will find a way out of this calamity too. We had set out to trap him, but the tables have suddenly turned. So what? We too can play a few of our Deccani tricks on him. Bringing cannons and other heavy equipment across a flooded Yamuna is no easy task. It will take Abdali at least ten to twelve days to bring his entire army over to this side. We now have to move like the wind and catch his men in the act of crossing over. Let's drown them all in the river.'

Bhausaheb announced that the army would begin its return journey to Kunjpura at dawn. He then sat down to write a letter to Govindpant:

> ... news has just arrived that Abdali's forces have started climbing up the eastern bank about eight miles from Baghpat. We shall surely reach there in time and defeat them, but, Pant, you shouldn't sit idle there. Cut off his supplies, plunder villages, kill men, create terror. I have been writing this every day, but you have been doing nothing. What's the matter, Pant? We have been friends for so long! The Peshwa had thrown a grand pre-nuptial party when your daughter had got married, so close we have always been! It's during such desperate times that we need to reach out to each other. Come out and destroy our enemy!

The camel post left immediately. While Bhausaheb sat calculating his next moves, the usual leaders of the pilgrim party arrived mouthing abuses for Abdali. Akkasaheb was unsparing in her curses. 'That rotten Pathan will never come to any good, latching on to us like the devil. He will die a miserable death, take it from me!'

'Akkasaheb, with your blessings, we shall defeat him with ease,' Bhausaheb assured her.

'It's not our blessings that will help, Bhausaheb, but we will rope in the blessings of three-hundred-and-thirty million gods tomorrow at Kurukshetra. The fury of the gods and the Brahmins will burn him to ashes.'

'Akkasaheb, tomorrow we leave to chase Abdali away. We will visit Kurukshetra some other time.'

The faces of the assembled petitioners fell. Akkasaheb was particularly incensed as she said, 'Shrimant, Kurukshetra is barely another eight miles away! If necessary, we can leave right now and be back by tomorrow! It was from Kurukshetra that Lord Krishna went to heaven, and his five queens—Hemvati, Gandhari, Jambvati, Rukhmini and Satyabhama—all burnt themselves on his pyre to ashes. Take the blessings of the satis.'

'Bhausaheb, we will finish our prayers in no time!' Jereshastri pleaded. 'Soldiers who die there go straight to heaven!'

'So you want to send our soldiers straight there now?' Bhausaheb snarled in irritation.

Akkasaheb's face had turned red with rage. 'Bhausaheb,' she screeched, 'I have been carrying my husband's ashes in my pallu for two years now. You want me to scatter them on the street? If the Peshwa's brother refuses to stand up for his religion, who, then, will be the protector of our dharma?'

'I don't want to hear another word out of you, Akkasaheb,' roared Bhausaheb. 'At this point, duty is far more important than faith. There is just one religion I have to observe now, and that is the religion of war.'

Parvatibai, who had been listening to this exchange from behind the screen, came out and said, 'All right, now, we have said and heard enough. Let me take care of my husband first, we will see about your religion later. Standing up for the husband is the biggest dharma of all.'

The company left in a huff, with Jereshastri delivering the parting barb: 'When times turn sour, how will a person remember religion? You are bringing destruction on yourselves. If you care more for the throne than for faith, well then, all that you will get is a mouthful of dust.'

ॐ

By the next evening, the army had retraced its steps back to Kunjpura. There were a hundred thousand bags of wheat to carry. Those with sturdy horses tied a sack each to their backs. Despite loading all the carts, they still had a few thousand bags left. Half the night was spent requisitioning bullock and camel carts from the neighbouring villages. It took two days for the army to cross Karnal.

The army was resting next to the river in the afternoon when Bhausaheb met the first batch of news-carriers. The entire Afghan army had crossed the river and had set off from Sonipat. Bhau's face turned ashen at the news, but he didn't lose heart. He went near the canopy where Parvatibai was seated. In these last two or three days, he had been getting glimpses of a Parvatibai he had never known. It had been ten years since their marriage, but it appeared he had never seen the real woman in her. The woman who shrank herself into a ball with shyness, who never lifted her eyes when in conversation with him, she would now sit in the canopy with a naked sword in her hand, and sit straight as a ramrod, without a trace of fear on her face.

Bhausaheb went close to her and said, 'May I say something? I have never seen you in this incarnation before.'

'If I say something, will your lordship get upset?'

'No, never. What is it?'

'Your lordship used to look quite suitable for his role at the office table in Pune.'

'And now?'

'When I see this campaign, this passion, this bravery, I feel that those days in Pune were wasted. As you faced the conflict at the Red Fort, the manner in which you fought your way to victory in Kunjpura, the aura, the dignity, the grandeur of your personality has been increasing with every passing day.'

'Is this why your personality has also changed?'

'Yes, of course! If you have to live your life with a ball of fire, you have to get used to the heat, don't you?'

Bhausaheb laughed out heartily.

⚛

The army marched on till it reached Gharaonda. The Panipat fort had shimmered into sight from a couple of miles away. The news was that Abdali had reached Manor, and would be in Sambhalkha soon. His entire army, every unit of it, was marching in order. Bhausaheb got into consultation with Malharrao and Ibrahim. Malharrao said, 'Bhausaheb, turn to the left, and you have the flooded Yamuna. Go straight, and the Afghans block the way. The road to Delhi is properly sealed.'

'Huzoor,' Ibrahim spoke, 'the one single strong post on our way now is Panipat that lies in front of us. Let's capture it before the enemy gets there and keep the big village and the fort at our back.'

Bhausaheb stationed his four hundred elephants alongside the royal canal at Gharaonda. His own elephant then began moving rapidly towards Panipat.

CHAPTER FOUR

dance of death

Panipat's own population was fifteen thousand, next in line in terms of density to Delhi. But with the arrival of the massive forces of the Maratha army, with sixty to seventy thousand men descending on it, its narrow lanes and localities had begun to choke, creating the illusion of some great religious carnival in progress. The fort was tightly surrounded by residential neighbourhoods. There was some open ground adjacent to the Devi Lake, which Bhausaheb chose for the royal pavilions.

The news of the arrival of the great king of the Marathas having spread, the headman Arif Khan came over to pay his respects. A few Hindus of repute like Baleram Pandit had also arrived. Baleram Pandit stepped forward and began, 'Your Majesty, this town was established three thousand years ago by a king named Dandapani, and as the place of residence of King Pani, this town got the name of Panipat.'

'Looks like a truly old town, this!'

'Oh yes, Your Majesty, this town has often decided the fate of Hindustan, good or bad,' said Baleram with a laugh. 'The residents here say that when Panipat twitches its eye, Delhi's stomach turns to water. Plots have been hatched here for raising the prestige of the throne in Delhi or smashing it to pieces. Your Majesty, what we say here is not wrong: whoever wins Panipat wins Delhi.'

Bhausaheb laughed heartily and looked towards Yashwantrao and Shamsher, his eyes sending the message, 'So, friends, we have to guard with our lives this town we have won.'

'Your Majesty, Panipat is one of the five towns that Duryodhan had demanded from Yuddhishthir, along with Sonipat and Baghpat,' informed Pandit. 'The sight of Devi Lake seems to have given you a lot of pleasure. If you desire, we could go for a darshan, a holy sighting of Shri Mansa Devi at the opposite edge of the lake.'

'Pandit, we will do that another day. Let's settle accounts with the enemy first.'

The horses of the royal team rode through the town. Badiwad Mohalla, Sarai, Khirni, Onki Holi Mohalla, Panchkoran Mohalla, Maniyar Mohalla—one by one they trotted past the neighbourhoods and squares. Bhausaheb's eyes roved everywhere, silently measuring the potentialities of every nook and corner: which places could offer good cover, how the land rose and fell, how far away the peripheral wall was and how long, where his cannons could be placed and in what number. One aspect of the town that struck him was that a good eighty-five to ninety percent of the inhabitants were Muslims, and the number of the mosques spread across the town was surely upwards of forty. There were a few temples too, belonging to the Vaishnav, Satyanarayana and Bairagi sects. The fortification of the town was good. There was plenty of water too. Besides the big lake, there were around two hundred wells, and the imperial canal half a mile to the west flowed full. The army would not suffer any shortage of water.

The royal horses ambled over from Salarjung's mansion to Qalandar Square. The grocers had lined up their shops on both sides of the road. Past one more arch they came to the shrine of a holy man named Qalandar Baba, which, according to the locals, was four hundred years old. Two big structures covered with beautiful carvings stood on multiple pillars. Four of the pillars in front were made of touchstone, a stone against which gold was rubbed for testing its purity. When Bhausaheb heard this, he laughed, 'Well, Shamsher, we are the ones who will soon be rubbed against it.'

'What does that mean, Bhausaheb?'

'You've just taken a round of the town; what's your opinion on it? There are plenty of Muslims here, with the Hindus just a bare sprinkling. Who knows how long we will have to stay here, but till as long as we do, we will have to do so with great cordiality. A Hindu-Muslim skirmish won't do us any good. We will have to keep the confidence of the populace while we are here.'

The horses moved past Qalandar Square, took two or three sharp turns this way and that, and from Chandni Bagh, they began climbing the northern slope of the fort. Ibrahim Khan's horse quickly caught up with them. 'What's the news, Khan Saheb?' asked Bhausaheb after accepting his greetings.

'Your orders are being implemented, huzoor. We surveyed the moat round the village last evening, it's being given some minor repairs. Fateh Khan is supervising the work personally.'

Soon they were at the fort. Bhausaheb moved forward to survey the western side. The prosperous Panipat looked sturdily walled, and the land all around looked flat and green. The town was at an elevation. A path climbed up a mile from the south to reach it. The land to the north, however, looked broken, with a stream running on the other side. Bhausaheb then looked towards the east. The Yamuna took a crescent curve from the north about seven or eight miles away, and swung to the south. Glimpses of its expanse could be seen peeping through the gaps in the woods and the mango groves. It didn't look any less awe-inspiring even from this distance. Around two miles in front were mango groves and guava orchards. Despite the terrain being flat, there were plenty of trees and shrubs planted around plots of farms. Behind the trees in the east could be seen a number of villages and settlements. Bhausaheb turned to the headman and asked, 'What are these places?'

'That one at the foot of the dip is Rajakhedi, and the one on the rise is Ugrakhedi. The one between them is Suvakhedi. Beyond that, along the Yamuna are Chhajpur Khurd, Chhajpur Kala, Jwalapur, Jalalpur. Here towards the south are Risalu, and Siva, and below them is Bapuli. The entire region from this end to that is prosperous.'

Bhausaheb swept his eyes all across the sky and then began examining the fort. It looked quite like a fort in the Warhad province to the east of Maratha country. Its peripheral walls were made of bricks. 'Why do you make such brittle forts? One round of cannon fire will reduce your walls to powder.'

'What else can we do, Your Majesty? Ride for fifty miles in any direction and see if you can find a block of stone anywhere. There are no stones for miles across, so what do we do except build with bricks?'

Coming down from the fort to Panipat town, the nobles rode across the green meadows towards the east. The soil was white and loose. Bhausaheb said, 'Yashwantrao, we have grown up in regions with reddish-brownish soil. See the colour of this soil?'

'White as ash, Bhausaheb.'

'Looks like the soil has been mixed everywhere with flour,' said Shamsher.

'Not to me,' said Bhausaheb. 'To me it looks like holy ash. I feel like dipping my thumb in it and applying it on my forehead.'

There were any number of streams on the way, as also a few small lakes and puddles, requiring the horses to be carefully manoeuvred through them. There were a number of wells too, all of them walled round, and full to the brim. Bhausaheb commented to the headman, 'Farmers in your parts must all be very prosperous!'

'No such thing, saheb. You think the lands belong to the tillers? The feudal lords and sardars here are all servants of the Delhi crown and managed to get the lands on the Yamuna bank gifted to themselves. While they sit pulling at the hookah and lording over, bare-backed Hindu and Musalman families slave on the fields day and night.'

Straight down was a dense grove of mango trees. With so many trees scattered everywhere, the horses had to slow down considerably. As they moved ahead, they ran into a huge mango tree. It was more than sixty feet high, and had an umbrella wide enough to accommodate five or six threshing floors. A good hundred or so cattle sat under it contentedly chewing cud, while the cowherds sat under the same shade chatting. Bhausaheb brought his horse to a halt under its shade and looked up through the branches and leaves. He couldn't see an inch of the sky. The trees were covered with yellowish-reddish flowers. The flowers of this particular tree, however, were blackish, as if they had been burnt.

'Why did the flowers get burnt?'

'Your Majesty, you don't know the history of this tree. Four generations have played under its shade; people here call it the black mango. The flowers aren't burnt, they are simply black in colour. Its fruit is black too. Look at the leaves carefully, they look blackish too. It's not for nothing that they call it the black mango.'

Bhausaheb's horse Chandrasen went running past the woodlands of Ugrakhedi, Rajakhedi and Suvakhedi. The entire area was peppered with wells. Bhausaheb was particularly on the lookout for big, walled wells. Arif Khan and Baleram Pandit's horses were trailing a little behind, when Bhausaheb instructed Ibrahim, 'Make a careful note of all these wells, Khan Saheb, particularly the walled ones.' When Ibrahim looked quizzically back, Bhausaheb elaborated, 'It's not enough to have only Panipat; we should have all these villages behind us too.'

'But Bhausaheb,' enquired Ibrahim Khan, 'what if the enemy mounts an attack when they find our men out in the open?'

'Well, then, what are our cannons filled with, water? We'll set them on fire and roast the enemy out.'

'When we can safely place our men behind the walls, what would be the sense in pointlessly exposing our men to enemy fire?' wondered Shamsher.

'It's not pointless. There are two strong reasons to support this strategy. For one, we shouldn't get trapped for good behind those walls, we should have the land around under our control too. For another, if we fall short of water, these wells that are brimming over should be available for us if the occasion arrives.'

'Well, I don't think we are likely to fall short of water,' argued Ibrahim Khan. 'We have the imperial canal flowing full capacity barely half a mile up there.'

'Well, what about the huge number of men and animals we are carrying with us? About a hundred-and-fifty thousand people, sixty to seventy thousand animals if you count all the horses, mules, donkeys, elephants and bullocks; together they will need lots and lots of water. If something unexpected happens and if we find the water of the canal inadequate, out there we will have that poisonous snake, the enemy, whom we have angered greatly by poking a spear in its hole by plundering its provisions at Kunjpura. Why would it not want to strike back with all its force and venom at the spear that has so wounded it? Abdali is not going to walk away. He was desperate and courageous enough to enter his horse in a flooded Yamuna. He will not sit quiet, biting his nails. He has innumerable foreign tools and strategies to hurt us. We may have to stay stuck in Panipat for a long time, and that is why it is imperative for us to ensure our supply of food and water on priority.'

Bhausaheb continued, 'Which is why I tell you, Ibrahim, place your cannons at the big walled wells in the meadows. Plant your long-range five-metal cannons at as many places as you can. This side is a little exposed, so you should lay your cannons in a way that not a bird can fly within a couple of miles without being brought down.'

The nobles turned their horses towards the Yamuna, and reached Ramda Ghat in a couple of miles. At the upper end of the wharf was the Ramda village. One could see the entire expanse of the Yamuna from there. The floods caused by the rains during the hasta constellation had still not subsided. When Bhausaheb saw the overflowing river, he couldn't but admire Abdali's feat. Bhausaheb looked at the eastern bank and asked, 'Pandit, what's that region on the other side?'

'Your Majesty, the region a little beyond the other side is the land of the Rohillas—Rohilkhand and Saharanpur.'

Bhausaheb voiced the worries of all when he said, 'Yashwantrao, when the Yamuna subsides sooner or later, you can't rule out provisions reaching the Afghans from their Rohilla friends. Let's place live patrols here too from tomorrow.'

The survey now moved along the Yamuna bank. The horses travelled south five or six miles all along the bank, with Bhausaheb taking estimate of the expanse of the river, the lay of the bank, the position of the villages. Then they turned their heads west to return to Panipat, crossing the villages Sanauli, Chhajpur Khurd, Chhajpur Kala, Nimri and Ugrakhed on the way home. The natives didn't let the king of the Marathas go past unhonoured. The royal entourage was stopped at every village where water was poured over the hooves of the horses, aarti was performed and kettle-drums beaten. Bhausaheb gratefully acknowledged the affection and hospitality of the villagers. The sun had begun to set and the cold Yamuna air had begun to blow. It had begun to bite with vigour now, prompting Bhausaheb to comment, 'The cold in these regions is way harsher than ours.'

'Oh yes,' responded Shamsher, 'I've had considerable experience of this weather in my previous campaign with Dadasaheb. This time round, our army had crossed the Satpuda during the summer, so our men still haven't any idea how cold it gets here. The really chilly couple of months are still to arrive. It gets to be so bad that even if you were to bury yourself into the earth, you wouldn't stop shivering.'

'Bhausaheb, we must take steps against the cold,' said an alarmed Yashwantrao.

'How many things do we guard against, Yashwantrao?' laughed Bhausaheb. 'All of destiny seems to be descending upon us, unfavourably so. Well, so be it, what else can humans do except confront them?'

When they were close to Chandni Bagh, Bhausaheb got a clear view of Panipat up above from the farms on which they stood. The town looked tall and imposing, with its fortress sharply outlined. At its foot was an ancient moat—about ten feet deep and twenty-five feet wide—that sat encircling the town.

Years of neglect had resulted in the edges of the moat collapsing inwards at many places, and the rubble was now overgrown with bushes and weeds of all kinds. The utility of the moat as a line of defence was obvious, and it had been decided in the meeting the previous night that immediate work should begin for bringing it back into shape. Accordingly, work had already begun of scooping the earth out from the trench and laying it along the edge. Gardi and Maratha men could be seen working inside it with iron hoes and pickaxes. Ibrahim Khan's brother Fateh Khan, who was personally supervising the work, stood up respectfully at Bhau's arrival.

Bhausaheb was upset with what he saw, and turned towards his nobles. 'This is not the manner in which this work should be undertaken. This is no trivial work that can be handled by a few hundred people. The moat makes a circle of about three miles; how can we expect to finish in a day or two? With the enemy stationed four miles away, watching our every move, how can we be so laid back? Mahipatrao, issue a general order for all. As soon as their evening meals are over, everyone should get to work: cavalrymen, infantry, troopers, young, old, seniors, juniors, all. They should bring whatever they have with them—iron rods, hoes, pickaxes, baskets, buckets, and get to work under the light of torches. If some ten or fifteen thousand people get to work, we won't have a pebble left in the trench by daybreak. Get to work with such zest that the sun, when it peeps over the horizon rubbing its eyes, should blink and wonder how this miracle came about.'

Mahipatrao sped towards the army. Bhausaheb and Ibrahim Khan bucked their horses and left the others behind as they moved alongside the moat. 'Khan Saheb,' Bhausaheb asked, 'what's the update from the enemy's side? What's your estimation of their strength?'

'Bhausaheb, they have top quality cannons and plenty of gunpowder. Confronting them will require establishing strong fronts alongside the moat. We will have to prepare firm bases all along the trench and plant our cannons on them in two days' time.'

'You see any obstacles to doing so?'

'Bhausaheb, the earth on the edge of the moat is very dry and dusty. When the enemy begins firing his cannon, our horses and camels might get agitated. Their movement might disturb the earth on the moat's edge and make it crumble and fall into the trench. The trench can offer great cover, huzoor. To keep it strong, we will need to line it on both sides with stones, and stones are just not available in these parts.'

Bhausaheb was lost in thought. As they rode ahead, they noticed little clumps of brambles and bamboos scattered all around. Brightening up, he said, 'See those bamboo groves there, Khan Saheb? Chop them and hammer them in along the fringe of the moat. Scatter the stems and leaves all over them. That will give you a firm bed and prevent the earth from slipping. Make the edges so strong on both sides that even if horses were to dance all day, not a grain of sand will slip.'

As Ibrahim Khan got ready to take leave, Bhausaheb said, 'Get to it and finish the work before morning. Then you can build your bases along the moat and mount the cannons by sunset. You have Panse also to assist you. Prepare such a fortification that an ant should suffocate getting in.'

On way to his tent, he raised a call for an immediate conference. All his sardars presented themselves in quick time—Shinde, Holkar, Vinchurkar, Dabhade, Antaji Mankeshwar, Rethrekar, Nimbalkar, Pawar, Bande, Paigude, Darekar, Mehendale, and a few others. The issues under discussion were: with Panipat at their back, which sides should be covered and by whom, who should be doing the patrolling and when. Ibrahim Khan's gun-wielding battalion would be in the vanguard of the imperial highway that passed through the town on way to the Punjab and beyond. If the enemy broke through the obstacle and began moving towards Kandahar, Ibrahim Khan would be there to block him and blow him apart. Behind the Gardis would be stationed the Royal Guards, under the command of Vishwasrao. Shinde's forces would hold the area beyond the Royal Guards, covering the right side of the village and the fortifications to the east. The northern fortification behind would be under the Holkars and Pawar; to their left, leaning towards the west, the men of Damaji Gayakwad and Vinchurkar would keep a live patrol, while the forces of the other sardars would be planted in the gaps. The caravans of the pilgrims would be located right in the middle of the town.

The discussions ended late in the night, after which the chieftains set off towards their tents. 'Seen the battle formation?' remarked Gangoba Tatya snidely as he was putting on his footwear. 'When I say things, I am seen as a grouse, but isn't it quite evident how much dearer the Shindes are to the Peshwas than the Holkars? See where the Shindes sit, right in the lap of the Peshwas. And where are the Holkars? In the back of beyond. What I say, then, is not gripe, it is based upon facts and observation.'

Bhausaheb was keen that the sympathy of the people of Panipat should be with the Marathas. Accordingly, he issued orders that read, 'The army should behave with utmost decency with the locals, and no individual should be put to any inconvenience. If anybody is found behaving indecorously with them, his hands shall be chopped off.' Bhausaheb also invited the headman, the religious heads, the opinion makers and the senior citizenry of the town for a meeting at the royal pavilion. When the guests arrived, Vishwasrao and Bhausaheb went up to the door together and welcomed their guests inside. Arif Khan and Jagirdar Balwandar Singh were seated in the front, while right behind them were seated the mullahs, the maulvis and the other opinion makers of the town. Arif Khan assured Bhausaheb, 'Your Majesty, we do not see you as outsiders.'

'This is what I had wanted to declare in everyone's presence,' responded Bhausaheb. 'Please do not pay heed to the stories Najeeb has been propagating about us. We swear by everything that is holy to us that this war is not between Hindus and Muslims; it is a war between us Hindustanis and those foreign intruders. We are fighting for the defence of the Delhi empire. If our intention had been to swallow Delhi up, we could have easily done so during the four months that it was under our control. We could have appointed our nephew here as the emperor of Hindustan, but that is not what we are after—our mission is to make the foreign intruder bite the dust.'

Jagirdar Balwandar Singh assured Bhausaheb of the town's support. As the meeting was drawing to a close, Bhausaheb declared with all the humility he could muster, 'I once again give you my word, my men and I will happily die of starvation rather than cause the slightest discomfort to the populace here. Whatever calamity descends upon us, the mosques and temples of this town will remain unscathed even if we have to die for it.'

As the meeting got over, Bhau noticed Balwant Singh dragging his feet a bit. He went up to him and asked solicitously, 'Is there something on your mind?'

'Yes, your Majesty. I wish to remind you of our Dattaji Shinde.'

'Dattaji? What about him?'

'So many years have gone by since Abdali entered Delhi from the other side. That was when Dattaji had rushed towards Delhi along this route to protect Delhi. He had earlier taken the five-metal cannon called Attock from Ghaziuddin ...' Bhausaheb said, 'You are talking of that powerful, fourteen-arm long cannon, yes? As soon as he had taken possession of the cannon, he had written to me, saying that if we could have five such weapons, the empire could go conquer the world. Well, anyway, why did you suddenly think of that cannon?'

'It lies gathering dust right here at the edge of Panipat.'

'What are you saying?' Bhausaheb was surprised. 'My Dattaji's cannon lying in the dust here?'

'That's right. Three hundred bullocks had been yoked to the cannon in an effort to pull it, the ropes and chains pulling it had snapped, making it impossible to take the weapon to Delhi. Dattaji was in a hurry to confront the enemy, and he had to perforce leave the cannon behind here.'

'Please take me immediately to look at it, Jagirdar Saheb,' requested Bhausaheb.

They rode off with a handful of horsemen, flaming torches in their hands. They came to a halt at the southern end of the fortification where the long barrelled Attock lay under a thick coating of dust. Bhausaheb went up to the cannon and patted it as he would pat the back of his favourite horse. Letting his emotions run away with him, he said to Balwantrao, 'This cannon was not born to lie in the open, turning to rust. It was made to shatter to bits the enemy's chest, to turn impenetrable fortresses to rubble. Let's put four elephants to work if two are not enough, but tomorrow we will pull it and mount it at the front. We shall bring Dattaji's dreams to fruition. We shall make this cannon spit fire and blow the enemy to smithereens.'

Bhausaheb's Chandrasen began galloping along the fortification, searching for a suitable spot for mounting the Attock. Moving under the light of the torches, the patrol squad arrived at the eastern side and Bhausaheb looked down at the moat. He saw hundreds of torches flaring alongside the moat, and thousands of Maratha men working in their light. The sound of iron striking stone could be heard upto a long distance. When Bhausaheb looked closely, he noticed that not all of the men had iron hoes—a number of them were working with bamboos sharpened at one end, with which they were loosening the earth. The commitment of these men was amazing; as was the dedication of the men supervising them. Ibrahim Khan, Fateh Khan and Panse were there in person, egging the workers on. From a little on the other side came the voices of Shamsher and Vishwasrao, shouting, 'All right, men, get to it! Get it done!'

The trench in front was all aflame. Bhausaheb turned his gaze south and stared into the pitch darkness. He couldn't see the enemy in the black space ahead, but he could imagine them relaxing or hatching evil strategies. The thought of Abdali's forces there made Bhausaheb's blood come to a sudden boil. Grinding his teeth, Bhausaheb used the wind to send his message to Abdali, 'Go! Go tell my enemy that I have planted my feet firmly in the earth here. Only after I tear you apart and grind you in this dust shall I cross the Narmada and Tapti to go south. With the help of my hundred thousand Marathas, I have raised a fortification of fire around Panipat! Your horse would have kicked up the dust of a dozen countries before this, but you don't yet know the colour, the texture and the resilience of Maratha land. I shall be the one to make you taste that, I promise!'

※

The sun had been up for some time, but the fog was so thick that you couldn't see a person only a few feet away. Big and small bonfires were ablaze everywhere in the Afghan army camp. The soldiers had kept their weapons aside and were trying to thaw their fingers and toes that had turned stiff in the cold. To control the shivers, some of them had wrapped themselves tight in Afghani shawls long enough to drown their tall, conical Afghan caps in their folds. The cold had truly started getting under their skins.

A hundred thousand men and fifty to sixty thousand animals lay curled up in a stretch of one-and-a-half miles. Despite the dense fog, Abdali was out on his rounds. Following him closely were Jahaan Khan and Shah Pasand Khan, armed bodyguards in the lead and behind.

As he advanced, Abdali cast a distasteful glance towards Panipat, which wasn't really visible on account of the fog. Trenches were being dug in the flat terrain along the periphery of his camp. When Abdali stopped at a spot, the four soldiers doing the digging halted their work and looked up. Seeing the waist-high pit they had dug, Abdali instructed, 'Make the trenches wider and deeper. A soldier should be able to stand in there with a spear without the tip showing outside.'

Abdali rode ahead another half-mile. The fog had begun to lift now, and distant objects became clearer. It was on the third day of the Marathas settling themselves in front of Panipat that Abdali had planted himself across the imperial highway. He had set up camp about two miles away from the Maratha army near a village called Pasina Kala, which lay south of the villages Siva and Dahad. To ensure that the natives didn't cause nuisance, his soldiers had raided every single house in the three villages and confiscated not merely weapons, but all sharp instruments like axes, scythes and sickles. After Abdali's scouts had informed him about the powerful cannons that the Marathas had placed all around their encampment, he had moved up during twilight towards village Pasina. As his forces moved, they were instructed to chop big trees along the way. Their branches and trunks would be their cover in the open territory through which they were moving. The limbs of the trees were spread around the camp, the trunks pointing inwards while the canopies of branches and leaves faced outwards. Thus thrown one upon the other, these heaps formed a fortification, with wide passages left open at regular intervals for the men to pass through. Cannons were placed on both sides of the passages, charged and primed, ready to be set alight at a moment's notice. There were some cannons placed behind the leafy bulwarks too, with their mouths pointing towards Panipat. The barrels peeped out from between the branches and observed the movements of their Maratha targets. Smaller grenade launchers were planted between the bigger ones, with the gunners and grenadiers standing ready next to their loaded weapons. Enticed by the flat terrain, the Marathas were liable to launch an attack. Abdali had laid his gunners in place to mow them down if that happened.

It was now eleven o'clock and the fog had thinned so that one could see the town of Panipat with the fortification round it, and a few tents and pavilions too. He found a tree for cover, pulled his horse to a halt, and began examining the town with microscopic eyes.

Jahaan Khan said, 'See that, Aalam-panaah? Those Deccan rogues are sitting by their cannons on either side of the moat like so many monkeys on a tree. They bring some of their lighter cannons a furlong on this side of the moat early in the morning, sit it out all day, and carry their weapons back in the evening. Cheap tricks, these.'

'I know,' nodded Abdali.

'Are you aware of what happened last evening, your lordship? About twenty to thirty miles of the way from Panipat to Kunjpura is under Bhau's control. His provisions are supplied from the Punjab. Just yesterday morning, something like fifty carts of grains dispatched by that ruffian Ala Singh Jaat from the Patiala region reached the Margatthas.'

'I know all of that.'

ॐ

It was close to noon. The army inspection over, Abdali turned his horse round to return to his pavilion through the main gate of the camp. Just then, there was a series of explosions. As if an entire mountainside had been blown up with landmines. The earth shook violently and gave the horses such a scare that they came to a screeching halt, stood up on their hind legs and trod backwards, as if dreading to put another hoof forward. It was with the greatest of difficulty that a rattled Abdali brought his horse under control and stared wide-eyed towards Panipat. As he and his men stared, they saw streaks of light cut a parabola across the sky and come screaming towards their camp. The red-hot missiles shot from long-range cannons began landing on the outer side of the tree-barriers. It was raining sparks everywhere, sending men and animals scurrying for cover.

Red with rage, Abdali held the reins tight and surveyed his camp. Four of his own guns responded to the challenge, and shot out red balls of fire that, with a huge boom, went screeching across the sky towards Panipat. The missiles landed close to the moat, setting off an uproar among the units posted there.

Abdali spurred his horse and shot past the main gate towards his pavilion, with a hundred horses racing behind him. As he jumped off his steed, the grooms took the reins of his horse and carried it away. The guards bowed low in reverence and Wazeer Shah Wali Khan came out of the royal tent with hurried steps. A hundred horses stood in readiness with their saddles and harness in place, while two elephants stood by, swinging their trunks and flapping their ears. To the left and to the right stood two hundred and fifty armed slaves. As Abdali strode past them with strong, powerful steps, the ushers raised the cry of 'Alert, all! Eyes lowered!' Without so much as noticing the salutation, Abdali walked into his pavilion with his wazeer trailing behind him at a respectful distance.

'Shah Wali,' Abdali asked, 'how many of our men and animals fell victim to the bombardment from the other side?'

'Three horses died and five men, two of them on the spot.'

'I see.'

'Aalam-panaah,' ventured Shah Wali, 'that Ibrahim Gardi obviously possesses long-range cannons. Maybe we should shift our camp back a little.'

'Absolutely not!' the emperor barked. 'We have already retracted quite a bit from where we had pitched our tents on the first day for fear of being in the range of cannon-fire. It's now a fortnight since we shifted. The Marathas have got their spirits up only because they see no activity from our side. If we retract still further now, we will only make the enemy cockier.'

'But ... but, Aalam-panaah, our horses, our men ...'

'... are dying, right? Well, let them die. They must die. We are not here to play games.'

༶

Abdali was busy discussing the issue of provisions when Najeeb rushed unannounced into his tent. Abdali didn't like the impertinence and looked towards him with irritation. Pasting a forced smile upon his face, Najeeb said, 'Aalam-panaah, those Ayodhya donkeys have been stabled right next to the royal tent. Our Sunni Afghans do not like their living in such close proximity to you.'

'It's good for shirkers to be placed under the observation of a stern eye. Snobs like you call them donkeys, but when heavy loads have to be carried, it is these donkeys that prove useful.'

Najeeb had wanted to join in the discussion, but Abdali said brusquely, 'All right, Khan Saheb, you may leave. Come when I send for you in the evening.'

As Najeeb walked away with his head bowed, Shah Wali Khan allowed himself a silent laugh. In a little while, Hafeez Rahmat Khan was ushered in. The emperor welcomed him and continued with the discussion. Finally, as Shah Wali rose up to take leave, he said, 'Your Highness, there are wells here everywhere, but the thirst of our men is no small thing either. The wells that were full to the brim have now sunk to half.'

'Why are you worrying about the wells, Shah Wali? There is such a huge imperial canal barely two miles away. Its flow has not turned any leaner, has it?'

'What Aalam-panaah says is perfectly right. While our soldiers drink water from the wells, our bullocks, horses, elephants and all other animals use the canal. But your lordship forgets that this canal flows down from Kunjpura, and past the Maratha camp.'

When Abdali threw a questioning look, Shah Wali continued with a laugh, 'The Maratha camp is bursting with men and animals, Your Majesty. Some have come to fight, while some others have come for pilgrimage. There are hundreds of thousands of them, men and animals taken together, many more than ants in an anthill. They eat less and defecate more. They go and scrub themselves in the canal, some even wash their animals there, turning the water filthy. Our own animals that, till yesterday, were happily drinking the water, now turn their faces away.'

'All right, we shall personally go and see the state of the canal this afternoon.'

※

19 November 1760. It had begun to turn dark. The Marathas on the outer side of the moat could be seen gathering their cannons and carrying them inside. Torches were lit in Abdali's camp. The troopers quickly placed the cannons at the mouths of the passages leading into the camp. The camp guards got ready for the night vigil.

The army kitchens fired their hearths as the crickets began to raise a racket in the surrounding vegetation. It was over a fortnight since the camp had been pitched, and the dung heaped at one end had bred flies and mosquitoes in enormous numbers. Horses couldn't stand still for a minute without wild flies chewing at them from all sides. The bullocks too were spending more time swatting the pests with their tails than dipping into the fodder placed before them. The soldiers were at their wits' end, slapping their limbs and clapping their hands to get at the mosquitoes that buzzed around them. Emperor Abdali too was irritated beyond measure at this aerial assault, and his pavilion was filled with swirls of incense smoke every few hours to chase the insects away. The soldiers, meanwhile, were gathering round their bonfires to seek protection from the flies as much as from the cold.

The night wind began blowing, bringing bone-chilling cold along with it. It also brought with it a terrible stench that disturbed Abdali. 'Where is this foul smell coming from, Shah Wali?'

'Aalam-panaah, the wind is blowing from the direction of Panipat, so it has to be coming from the dung-heaps of the Marathas.'

Abdali began pulling at his hookah with greater urgency. He began to wonder whether he had made a wrong choice in selecting the site for his camp.

The Afghan horsemen, the orphans and slaves, the troopers and pages were sitting in separate groups finishing their dinner. Those who had finished their meals had turned sleepy, and sat nodding in front of their tents. Suddenly, the silence of the evening was shattered by the loud boom of cannon-fire coming from the west. Out of nowhere came loud screams of 'Catch them! Catch them!' 'Run, run!' 'Allah-o-Akbar!' A tremor ran through the entire camp. The nodders were jolted wide awake. The Afghans pulled their swords out and ran in the direction of the shouts. Cries of 'Har Har Mahadev!' could be heard at a distance. Abdali was startled, and immediately issued orders for the dispatch of Barkhurdar Khan's unit towards Panipat.

Barkhurdar Khan and Nawab Shuja-ud-dowlah rode in from the west with their men towards the emperor's pavilion, where the other chieftains had gathered too. Barkhurdar reported in a nervous voice, 'Your Highness, five to six hundred Maratha horsemen took advantage of the darkness and came right up to our fortification. They leapt over the barricades of tree branches and carried away with them a few of our smaller cannons. Shuja-ud-dowlah said, 'Aalam-panaah, I saw the raiders up close as they were running away. I even identified one of them.'

'Who was it?'

'Fateh Ali Khan.'

'Fateh Ali Khan? Who's he?'

'Ibrahim Khan Gardi's younger brother.'

'Barkhurdar,' snapped Emperor Abdali, 'how could you let him escape alive?'

'Aalam-panaah,' Barkhurdar responded timidly, 'we couldn't chase them too far. You had ordered us not to go beyond a certain distance.'

Commander-in-chief Jahaan Khan couldn't restrain himself. With his head down, but in a firm voice, he growled, 'Please forgive me if I sound impertinent, huzoor, but those two-penny Pendhari and Banjara tribals of the Marathas have been causing a lot of disruption. They sneak up to our army and run away with our horses, camels and mules. They have gone to the extent of stealing elephants too. Ibrahim Gardi has planted his cannons around Panipat and raised a mountain of steel. Our soldiers have begun to wonder whether the victorious forces of Islam are getting terrorized at the sight and surrendering to it.'

'Don't bring up the name of that apostate Ibrahim Khan,' barked Abdali. 'I haven't worn bangles to want to surrender to that blot on our religion. Just let him fall into my clutches; I shall then stuff him into my cannon along with gunpowder, and set it alight.'

Najeeb, who had maintained silence up till now, suddenly broke in, 'May I make a request, Aalam-panaah?'

'Speak. It is because of your request that an entire year has passed since I left my motherland, and am stuck here in this land.'

'Huzoor, those cattle thieves and tribal gangs of the Marathas have pinched twelve hundred of our horses, three or four hundred camels and four sturdy elephants within a fortnight. Aalam-panaah, but it is for your decree that we swallow our pride and stay quiet. Those sinners reached their limits today when they made away with twenty of our cannons. You should have seen how they were doing it, huzoor! Two horsemen were dragging a gun between them as if they were dragging a corpse! They have rubbed our reputation into the dust, your majes—'

'Where is your request, Najeeb?' Abdali cut him short impatiently.

'Why are we waiting, Aalam-panaah? Let's march up to Panipat with our cannons and blow them up! Why should the victorious army of Islam fear?'

'Take it easy, Najeeb. It will be foolhardy to drag our cannons up the slope and mount an assault now. We will launch our offensive when the time is right. A fully ripe fruit is easier to pluck and is always sweeter. There is no better virtue than discretion. Waiting a little longer is not going to cause us any grievous harm, but to those Margatthas it will. If the summer season is an enemy for us from the north, the northern winter is the arch-enemy of those bare-bodied Marathas from the south. The cold is going to turn severe in a week or two, and those infidels are going to freeze to death. That is when we shall roast them alive. Let's suffer a few losses now, and test out their stamina. Let's lure them into our net with these minor baits and then slaughter them when they are caught in it.'

The meeting over, Abdali turned towards his private quarters. He suddenly stopped and told Jahaan Khan, 'Jahaan, round up the men who were patrolling the parts from where the Marathas stole in. Strip them all, hang them by the trees at the same spots, give them fifty-one lashes each, then chop off their noses as a mark of their carelessness.'

Bhausaheb had finished with his bath and prayers, When he went to pick up his favourite Khorasani sword, he found Parvatibai standing with it in her hand. She pulled the sword out of its sheath and polished its glittering blade with the end of her saree. 'Why this sudden fondness for the sword?' Bhausaheb smiled and asked.

Parvatibai said feigning irritation, 'I am the daughter of the Kolhatkars of Penn, no less. While defending the coast, our ancestors stood in the ebb and flow of the sea and tested their mettle against foreign invaders, don't you know? A sword is no novelty for us; why shouldn't I be fond of this one, then.'

Bhausaheb burst out laughing at his wife's innocent vanity over her lineage. Her eyes teared up at that. He wiped her tears gently and asked, 'Have I offended you in some way?'

'How can you ever offend me? It's just that I heard you laugh with such unrestrained joy after so long, and that moved me. I beg of Lord Gajanan that He may keep your lordship happy for ever.'

'Has something else happened?'

'People have been talking ill of you, even the women of the noble households. When I hear their bitter, inauspicious words, I feel very hurt inside.'

'Who could they be?' Bhausaheb insisted on knowing. 'What do these people say? Let's hear.'

Parvatibai began hesitantly, 'All of us women of the camp were out on a round of Panipat. If you go down the eastern road, you come across a grand building called Kabuli Bagh. That was where our palanquins had gone yesterday. The foreigner king Babur had fought a battle here with a Hindustani king named Lodi. Babur won the battle and erected Kabuli Bagh to commemorate his victory. Our Akkasaheb was also saying that a king named Hemu had fought a big battle with Akbar, again in Panipat. It seems that Hemu was on the point of winning the war when a poison-tipped arrow struck him and he fell off his elephant. Believing their king to be dead, his men ran away, leaving Hemu behind to die.'

'What's special here? These are famous stories.'

'Akkasaheb said that the soil of Panipat is accursed. She said this soil doesn't like its own people. No native king has ever won here, he has always perished.'

Bhausaheb was startled for a moment, as if a streak of lightning had passed through him. He instantly got hold of himself and touched his wife's shoulder. 'Why blame the Panipat soil for this? This is the quality of our own soil too. The enemy doesn't wish you as ill as your own people do. But wipe those tears off your eyes. Get these thoughts of auspicious and inauspicious out of your head. You were talking of the courage of the Kolhatkars just moments ago, so why these unprovoked tears now?'

As he turned to leave, Parvatibai said, 'Today is Kartiki Shuddh Poornima, the full moon night of the month of Kartik. I propose to have some Brahmins pray at the temple of Goddess Shri Mansa Devi for the defeat of evil forces and for your success.'

Bhausaheb nodded and left straight for his office. He found Mahipatrao, Nana Phadnis and the other clerks grappling with the accounts. Along with senior chieftains like Vinchurkar and Holkar, younger ones like Shamsher and Nana Purandare were also present. As soon as Bhausaheb arrived, Purandare addressed him, 'Shrimant, you would have heard of yesterday's incident.'

'What incident?'

'There was an exchange of fire between us and the enemy. Our Sangameshwar Krishna Joshi was sitting at the front last evening when a cannon-ball landed there and killed Joshibuva on the spot. We have lost a good man.'

Bhausaheb was pained at the news. After a little while, he asked Holkar, 'Yes, Subhedar kaka, what's your opinion on the war?'

'Our fortune is in the ascendant, Bhausaheb,' the old man replied. 'The daily exchange of arrows, bullets and cannon fire continues. All signs look good. Our pendharis and banjaras have created mayhem among enemy ranks. The morale of our men is high. We hear that the supply of provisions to the Afghans has stopped. Flour is selling three seers to a rupee, gram is four, and clarified butter only half a seer. So expensive have commodities become there as compared to here: we get sixteen seers of wheat, twelve of gram and two seers and a half of clarified butter. If this continues, and if the enemy attacks us now, we should wipe them out in an hour or two.'

'That Abdulya calls himself a badshah,' laughed Vinchurkar, 'why, then does he sit at a spot three weeks at a stretch, till his butts go numb?'

This quip of Vinchurkar's produced all round laughter. Shamsher spoke in a grave voice, 'Truly, Bhausaheb, Abdali is trapped. Our army has blocked his way home. If he comes rushing at us, he will be roasted; but if he sits swatting flies at the same spot, how will he fill his belly? He seems to be locked in a pit, and doesn't know what to do.'

'Shamsher, we have to send our spies there to get reliable information on their next move. Who knows, these upbeat stories might be mere figments of imagination, the kind of stuff that our Sakharam Pant loves to weave?'

As the conversation continued, Mahipatrao came up with the account books. He told Bhausaheb, 'Shrimant, Fateh Khan, Ibrahim Gardi's brother, has made a number of trips since yesterday. There's a lot of unpleasant murmur among his men over the non-payment of this month's salary. Three visits they make in a day and sit grumbling.'

'Forget it, Mahipatrao, why bother Bhausaheb with unnecessary hassles? Our own horsemen and troopers have been going on with three months of arrears and yet they fight on uncomplainingly; and here are these Gardis, with just a fortnight's delay in salary, and they bang at the door like creditors. Let it hang for a little while more, how can it matter?'

'We can make payments, but our Kunjpura treasury is emptying out fast, and there's very little cash money left,' informed Nana Phadnis.

'All right. If there's enough left, pay the Gardis off,' declared Bhausaheb.

Subhedar Malharrao looked away, but Vinchurkar couldn't hold himself back. 'Bhausaheb, why so much more love for the neighbour's kids than for your own?' he protested. 'Why do your scales always have to tilt in favour of the Gardis?'

'You think they are fighting for the enemy?' riposted Bhausaheb. 'And since you talk of tilted scales, even in terms of sheer valour, their contribution has been greater. What did the assault on Devgiri show us? Who smashed the bulwarks of the Red Fort? Who brought down the Kunjpura walls? Why go so far? What about the events of two days back? Santaji Ghorpade fetching the crest from atop Aurangzeb's tent and Fateh Khan Gardi leaping into Abdali's camp and pulling cannons out from under his nose; is there any difference between the two acts? Don't these two feats require the same kind of raw courage?'

Vinchurkar could only look down and sulk. In a little while, he left with Malharbaba Holkar. Bhausaheb called over the files on food and fodder, took stock of the state of the treasury and his face clouded with worries. As he sat, he remembered Nanasaheb Peshwa. He was deeply upset at the nonarrival of resources from Pune, but that had in no way reduced his affection for his cousin. He picked up a quill and began pouring his heart out in a detailed letter. He described how the two armies stood face-to-face against each other; how there were frequent exchanges of fire and how there was no chance left of arriving at any kind of truce. He did not forget to seek the Peshwa's advice on how far he should go if there was ever a possibility of any agreement. He again made a fervent appeal to the Peshwa for help to be dispatched immediately. As he wound up the letter with enquiries about his health, his eyes turned moist.

ॐ

An urgent letter from Ibrahim Gardi reached Bhausaheb.

'*Huzoor, the army is in desperate need of gunpowder. If there is no dynamite and lead forthcoming in a hurry, the cannons are going to turn idle. With no gunpowder to feed into them, how are cannons any different from empty drain-pipes?*'

Bhausaheb's head was in a spin here, was he to go searching for gunpowder in this land? The person who immediately sprang in front of his mind's eye was Govind Pant. But instantly his face was clouded over in despair. 'Pant, oh Pant,' he muttered under his breath and reached out for his quill. Who else could he reach out to in this foreign land?

He addressed him with exaggerated honorifics, whose sarcasm, he hoped, wouldn't escape Govind Pant. He began:

To Rajashri Viraajit, Rajmanya, Rajashri, Govind Ballal Swami!

Respectful greetings from the helpless Sadashiv, son of Chimaji.

Know that I am doing well, and hope this letter finds you well too. The two armies are locked in confrontation with each other. As written to you earlier, the cannons have been laid out in formation, all ready for the battle to begin.

Pant, you have not been able to make any arrangement for provisions. You have merely been writing that you have made the arrangements, you are making arrangements, you are dispatching the wherewithal in a day or two, you are getting to work as per orders, and so on. No evidence of your effort however, is visible. Your words are pure hot air. No praise of your sense of responsibility is adequate. How much more can I write, Pant? I have exhausted myself.

Here, we have blocked the enemy's route home, trapped him. You need to stop his supply of provisions from behind. Rise and raid the territories of Najeeb and Shuja. Create mayhem there, set them on fire. What are you waiting for? This is not the time for you to sit with your eyes shut. A golden opportunity like this for earning your salt will never come calling again. Take Barve along with you.

We are in dire need of gunpowder here. Dispatch whatever gunpowder you have through Naro Shankar at Delhi. Of what use are you if you cannot come forward with help during these times of desperate warfare? You have grown by feeding off the Peshwa; is this how you want to return his favours? If you merely sit doing nothing, Pant, you will bring shame upon your name. Rise, Pant, get into Najeeb's land and raze it down. Pant, you can't wait any more....

Bhausaheb handed the letter over to the courier and leaned back upon his bolster. 'The soil of Panipat doesn't like its own people.' The words were pounding his head like a sledge-hammer. There was another voice that said that the ones who had lost before would have committed errors. Why, after all, were they stationed there, beating back problems at every step for the previous eight or nine months? Why did he fight it out with Dadasaheb and take the responsibility of this campaign on his shoulders? To turn his back on it half way? Never! Never under any circumstance! If it came to that, he would disperse in the dust, but the enemy and that Najeeb had to be squashed underfoot before that. 'Well, all right,' he said to himself, 'let me go and see what this Kabuli Bagh looks like.' With that, he walked out and mounted his horse. He rode off with his bodyguards behind him.

Since it was the day of the lunar eclipse, the pilgrims and the servant class were in a mighty hustle. All the temples in Panipat were abuzz with activity. The pilgrims had arranged for Brahmins to sit prayer for the fulfilment of their wishes: may the enemy be routed in quick time, and may the opportunity arrive their way for doing the rounds of the three important pilgrimages. Jereshastri, Agnihotri, Akkasaheb and the other spearheads of the pilgrims looked awfully busy. Long queues had lined up along the banks of the Devi Lake for a holy dip in its waters.

❦

22 November 1760. The Shinde forces were spread out on the right side of the Royal Guards, holding their flank tightly under control. Abdali's camp could be seen a couple of miles away from there. The Shindes were well known for their religious charities. It was the day of lunar eclipse, and Jankoji Shinde had gifted a baby elephant to the Bairagi temple in honour of the day, with the prayer that the sinister forces lurking over their heads should disintegrate. Jankoji had with him his two younger brothers Mahadji and Tukoji.

It was around five o'clock in the evening. Peace prevailed in the areas around the moat as well as the front. The occasion of the eclipse had perhaps made warfare undesirable, hence, not a single cannon had been fired, not a gun had crackled. There was no fusillade from the other side either. Abdali too had decided to adopt the strategy of lying low and merely observing. The sun was on its way down and a cold wind had begun to blow. The fear that usually reigned in the camp was not visible today across the two miles of flat plains in sight. The mules of the pendharis and the banjaras could be seen grazing everywhere happily. Far away, on the yonder side of the enemy camp, men and animals stood crowding the canal bank.

Jankoji Shinde leaned against the broad back of his horse and stood chatting with his men. Sardar Balwantrao Mehendale came riding from the side of the Royal Guards and pulled the reins on seeing Jankoji. 'So, Jankojibaba, what news?'

'Nothing in particular,' replied Jankoji. 'The blood races on furiously, but the battle refuses to get under way.'

'Huh?' snorted Balwantrao. 'The Shindes and Holkars shouldn't talk of racing blood from here on.'

'What do you mean?' growled a startled Jankoji.

'Well, yes, two or three of the Shinde-Holkar units have entered these plains before, but now they seem to vanish from the field at the name of the enemy. The earlier zest seems to have drained out of them.'

Jankoji was stung. 'Listen, you, Balwantrao!' he spat out, 'Don't you give yourself airs for being related to the Peshwas! Which Attock have you planted the flag on, anyway? How many victories to your credit?' Balwantrao raised his voice and said, 'The respect you get in the Peshwa house today is only because your Kakasaheb Dattaji did something worthwhile. And, yes, you are also a friend of Vishwasrao's. Other than preening yourself on these two assets, what else do you do except shoot the wind with big bombastic talk?'

Jankoji was beyond himself with rage. 'Hold your tongue, Mehendale!' he roared. 'You think there are differences between the Shindes and Holkars that you want to exploit? We haven't been passing time sleeping here in Hindustan. My grandfather Ranobaji died in an army camp, my father gave his life in Rajputana, and my Kakasaheb Dattaji was martyred at Buradi Ghat. When the time comes, our third generation of Shindes will also spill its blood in the service of the Marathas.'

'We'll see, we'll see soon enough.'

'Of course we'll see. We don't need to take lessons from you, Balwantrao!'

As the battle of words escalated, a few seniors intervened and separated the squabbling parties. Balwantrao turned round and headed towards the Royal Guards, and stood staring at the enemy camp in the distance.

Jankoji stood where he was, eyes flaming. His temper hadn't begun to subside when the person next to him pinched him softly on the forearm. Jankoji flared up, 'What's it?'

'Hush, Babasaheb,' he hissed. 'Just look down there!'

Jankoji looked down the fort wall towards the well in the southward plains below: it looked nice and big. His attention was suddenly caught by a well-built person standing next to the well. His head was covered with a blue, tapering cap of the Afghan type, he wore an expensive brown leather jacket and silk trousers loose on the thigh and tightly gathered round the ankles. Hanging on his chest was a double-string necklace, of pearls, perhaps.

'Who could it be?' asked one soldier of another. 'Wazeer or commander-in-chief?'

'Whoever he is, he is a big sardar,' responded the other.

'Hush!' Jankoji whispered, 'no noise at all! Just follow me quietly. Very likely, he has a thousand Afghans behind him, remember that!'

Jankoji turned his horse round and began descending with great caution. Immediately behind him trailed his men, advancing their horses as noiselessly as they could. By the time Jankoji had crossed the planks over the moat, he had behind him a force of seven to eight thousand men. Jankoji picked up speed. As soon as the Afghan stranger came in sight, he spurred his horse and leapt forward. When the men were half a furlong from the well, they raised a loud cry of 'Har Har Mahadev!' and launched upon the Afghans in the manner of a waterfall jumping off the edge of a cliff. Balwantrao standing at an elevation looked towards Jankoji's men and laughed.

When the Afghans suddenly encountered the Marathas breaking upon them with such loud clamour, they were rattled. But they swiftly organized themselves and jumped upon their horses and unsheathed their swords. Weapons swinging on strong wrists, they were ready to put up a good fight. The highly charged soldiers of Jankoji's forces had meanwhile encircled them. Weapon clashed against weapon and men rammed into men. The Afghans had begun by behaving like straws caught in the eye of a hurricane, but they summoned their courage and fought for their lives, as they slowly started pushing back in the direction of their camp. The horses' hooves kicked up the dry white dust and soon it became difficult to tell friend apart from enemy, ours apart from theirs. Loud cries of 'Arrey Deva!' and 'Ya Allah!' combined with shrill screams of agony as blade met flesh. Blood spurted everywhere, and the white earth was soon turning red in bigger and bigger patches.

Abdali's camp was in turmoil. People were screaming. 'The Margatthas have cornered the wazeer!' 'The wazeer's been caught alone!' 'The wazeer won't return alive!' Najeeb and Shuja's men got into action and sped off with loud shouts of 'Allah! Allah!' They were soon upon the Maratha men whom they pushed back about twenty feet. Jankoji was furious. He goaded his men with loud cries of 'What are you waiting for? Attack! Kill the bastards!' They began a counter-offensive and pushed the enemy back forty feet. Abdali dispatched a dozen cannon carts to the site of the battle. The bullocks let out loud belches and moved towards the conflict zone, but they couldn't sustain for long the Maratha assault.

They went berserk and ran helter-skelter upon the corpses that lay scattered on the ground. Najeeb and Shuja knew that they were beaten, but the darkness around them confused them, and the Shinde forces took full advantage by slicing wildly through the Afghans and pushing them steadily backwards. The Afghan men began retreating pell-mell, leaving the cannon carts unattended. The soldiers attending to the carts unyoked the bullocks by slicing off the holds and taking advantage of the dark, drove the animals away south, saving them from being plundered too along with the cannons.

Once they had driven away the enemy, the Marathas began gathering the lighter cannons they had left behind. But the Afghans were still not done with the skirmish. After they had retreated a safe distance, the gun-toting men turned round and started firing bullets among the Marathas. Jankoji's men, however, were not to be dissuaded from gathering their loot. There were four big cannons there, which it was difficult to drag away in a hurry; so they did the next best thing: they smashed them at the neck and spine, filled them up with stones and rendered them unusable.

The Marathas counted seventy of their own dead against seven hundred of the enemy. The soldiers lifted their injured colleagues on their horses and returned proudly to Panipat, Jankoji in the lead, accompanied by trumpeters blowing victory toots, and seven hundred Afghan horses bringing up the rear.

Jankoji marched with his men straight up to Bhausaheb, with their blood-smeared shirt-fronts on proud display.

Balwantrao arrived at the pavilion. Jankoji shot an angry look at him and said, 'Sardar Saheb, there was a battle being fought right in front of your eyes; how could you sit at ease instead of jumping into the fray?'

'Babasaheb,' laughed Balwantrao, 'I knew that you were good enough for the enemy, so I stayed out.'

'Or was it that you wanted us to be bested, Mehendale?' Jankoji asked in a raised voice. 'This was not what the gods wanted, though. Kakasaheb, let me say this straight: if this man had joined in to support us, we would have finished off the enemy, but he is such a coward—'

'Shut your mouth!' yelled Balwantrao, with one hand reaching for his sword. 'Janko, how dare you use that word for me? A tiny victory has gone to your head, so much so that you can't hold your tongue in check?'

'Please don't get so upset, Balwantrao,' Bhausaheb intervened. 'Jankoji is just a boy, you shouldn't take his words to heart. In any case, why did you stay out? Why didn't you join to help the Shindes?'

'Oh, that's wonderful, Bhausaheb!' Balwantrao cried. 'One grouse from this chit of a boy, and you have turned the service of a lifetime to dust. I am lost for words, Bhausaheb, truly!' He turned on his heels and strode out of the pavilion.

⚭

There were plenty of people assembled in Balwantrao Mehendale's pavilion: his sister Rakhmabai Akkasaheb, his sister's son Nana Phadnis, Nana's wife Yashodabai, and a number of others. Balwantrao's ten-year-old son Appa Balwant was playing around the room. Sardar Balwantrao looked heartbroken. Rakhmabai Akkasaheb thought it important to calm him down. 'Balwantrao,' she said, 'these are difficult times, and they are not for us to control. All that we can do is to face whatever comes our way. It's now a month and a quarter since the enemy has blocked us here, and the tension has now begun to show on your face. I had gone on my knees before your dear Bhausaheb, warning him that he should not fly in the face of religion. Calamity would descend, I had told him, obstacles would crop up everywhere. All of his conceit would come crashing to the ground, as it had for the King of Lanka! Well, he refused to pay heed to my words, and now destiny stands at the doorstep, whip in hand. How are you going to argue with it now?'

'When cannon balls begin to fall around us, a heavy knot develops in the stomach,' complained Lakshmibai Balwant. 'I then sit with Apparao on my lap, trying to pacify the terrified child. What does he understand who is fighting and for what?'

Nana Phadnis, who had been quiet all this while, adjusted his turban and said, 'Take what destiny serves. Our lordship Bhausaheb is otherwise a person of such great intellect and wisdom, but he seems to be slipping lately. Look at the way he is indulging those Gardis! Offering them caparisoned elephants, giving them cash advances while the rest of the army starves! If he doesn't care for advice from senior sardars like Vinchurkar and Holkar, what can small people like us say?'

'His behaviour has changed,' growled Balwantrao. 'I have always been regarded as his right hand, and now there seems to be no space on the left side either. Not much point in blaming Jankoji, after all he is just a kid, but Bhausaheb has known me all my life! So many expeditions I have done with him, and yet he does not understand me. Humiliates me in the presence of everyone because I didn't run to Shindes' help.'

'Everybody in the army has been shouting taunts!' added Lakshmibai.

'What do they say?'

'The most insignificant of the footmen and their brats say that if Mehendale had joined the Shindes that day, the Pathans would have been routed twelve days ago.'

'Nobody is willing to understand!' said Balwantrao in despair. 'I, who was close to the Peshwas, have suddenly been pushed away, and others have now become his confidantes. I didn't shy away from the battle out of any ulterior interest. I could see that Janko was winning effortlessly, and so I stayed out.'

Then he got up with a sudden decisiveness and headed towards Bhausaheb's pavilion with quick steps. He had not met him in the past four days.

Bhausaheb, meanwhile, was sitting with his nephew Vishwasrao. His face was glowing with joy. Vishwasrao was saying, 'Kakasaheb, here is an enemy that keeps count of every arrow, and it has suddenly decided to wind up camp and move back towards the river. Is that the reason for your happiness? Why do you think Abdali would have wanted to shift?'

'Rao Saheb, he was camped on a slope, while we occupy the stronger position on an elevation. His men and animals were becoming easy targets for our cannons placed on these heights. That's the reason why he has moved down to a safer distance.'

'Shall I tell you the truth, kaka? In all these months that we've been out on this campaign, I have never seen such happiness on your face as I see today. Surely, the reason for this joy can't be merely the enemy's moving six miles away.'

'Well, Rao Saheb, I am thrilled that the enemy's morale has been sinking with every passing day.'

'Come on, Kakasaheb, please don't feed me these tales. They are nowhere sufficient to explain the extent of your delight.'

Vishwasrao couldn't be shaken off, Bhausaheb knew. He laughed out loudly, looked around surreptitiously and leaned towards his nephew. 'This is a state secret, Rao Saheb,' he said in a low voice, 'and it should in no circumstances go outside of this room. The Peshwa himself has set off for the north with an army. He left on Dussehra.'

Vishwasrao felt a current of joy run through his entire body. It was with the greatest restraint that he did not pull his uncle into a hug. Bhausaheb went on, 'The news is confirmed. His lordship set off on Dussehra with a huge army towards Hindustan. He also dispatched letters last month to the Kolhatkars at Jhansi to buy plenty of bullocks.'

Vishwasrao's head was in the clouds. 'Could it really be, Kakasaheb,' he asked, 'that Shrimant is arriving to help us?'

'Why not, Rao Saheb? Why should you think that you and I don't matter to Shrimant? There are a thousand things that keep happening in life, so many ups and downs and twists and turns along the way, but can they in any way weaken the bonds of love? Rao Saheb, I have known your father well, and he has a heart loaded with love and affection.'

'But, then, Kakasaheb, why did he not respond to the desperate calls for help you sent to Pune in letter after letter?'

'That certainly is a mystery,' said Bhausaheb. 'Could the enemy have been intercepting them on the way? If that's the case, then it is a very serious matter. Letters reaching the wrong hands can spell disaster.'

Bhausaheb turned quiet for a while, lost in musings. Then he said, 'Rao Saheb, if Lord Gajanan does afford us this conjoining of forces, the next seven generations of Marathas would not be able to pay off this debt of gratitude. Just imagine! The Peshwa's forces pushing the enemy from below, and we blocking his way from the top of Panipat! Abdali will be ground to dust, I tell you, absolute dust! Why go so far, Rao Saheb, even if Govindpant and Barwe at the Antarved can choke his supplies coming from Najeeb's territories, we will drown out his army in the Yamuna with ease!' Just then, a page entered to announce the arrival of Balwantrao, who walked in with a long face. Bhausaheb hadn't met Balwantrao in four days, and he wondered whether he was still upset. 'So, Balwantrao,' he began pleasantly, 'what's new?'

Balwantrao responded glumly. 'I seem to have fallen out of favour with you, going by the manner in which I was put down in the presence of a mere boy like Jankoji! What's left of my dignity now?'

'Balwantrao, should you feel so upset because I raised my voice by a bare decibel? Who should I then talk with, Balwantrao? Who can I get upset with, then? Tell me this, Balwantrao, how many people can I handle alone all by myself? Look, you and I have always been close, there's a bond between us, so much so that seniors like Malharbaba Holkar and Vinchurkar take for granted that I act by your advice. They hold a grouse against me for that. Then there's the bad blood between you and the Shindes. The Shindes and the Holkars have for generations been at daggers drawn. Ibrahim and Holkar cannot see each other happy, cannot bear each other's success. And my lion of a brother, my Shamsher, the women of the royal household hold him in contempt as the son of a Muslim woman. The most ordinary foot-soldiers kick up a ruckus because I take Shamsher into confidence!

'Add to that the rifts among the Marathas. Each pulling in the opposite direction! The Brahmins are at loggerheads with each other. The Deshasth Brahmins crib that their position in the Peshwa's court has been undermined since the arrival of Mahadoba Purandare, and now the Konkanasth rule the roost. So many castes and sub-castes, each with their own temperaments and beliefs, every one of them starkly visible in the conduct of the army. A hundred faces looking in a hundred different directions. It is with the greatest difficulty that I have to make all these contrary strings pull together and have them stand up as one against our collosal enemy. There are times when my mind goes numb, I am at a loss to know how to handle things. Fate seems to be playing vicious games with me by raising a veritable mountain of problems at every step. Well, let Fate play whatever games it wants to, but one thing is certain, now that I have come so far, I am not going to back down.'

Balwantrao said, 'You and I have been together since we were children. I rode my horse with you to Mysore. Just three years back, we made the Nawab of Arcot eat humble pie. The very trees of Deccan shiver at the sight of our blades. And here's this brat of Jayappa Shinde, doesn't have enough hair on his upper lip yet and he wants to give me lessons on valour?'

'How many times do I tell you, Balwantrao, that the elders need to have bigger hearts?'

'I don't care for all that, Bhausaheb, but whether I live or die, this land will get to see the stuff the Mehendales are made of.'

༄

Bhausaheb rode off with his guards towards the fort by way of Qalandar Square. From the fortification on top, he surveyed the villages of Jalalpur, Bapauli and Goyla eight miles to the south-east. That was where Abdali had shifted his army eight days ago.

As his eyes swept over the landscape, his stomach churned. Could this be the verdant green land he had ridden through just a month and a half back? Could the turbulence of an impending battle have reduced it to this sorry state? Only a few weeks ago, both Jalalpur and Bapauli had been surrounded by thick woods. Even the little lanes and bylanes were lined then with dense trees on either side, home to abundant birds and fruits. In the ten days, those trees had been chopped down without restraint. Abdali had axed them to erect a fortification around his camp. Trenches had been dug too. With over a hundred thousand people to cater to, the need for wood was enormous anyway. What made matters a whole lot worse was the biting cold, which required fires to be burnt from sunset to sunrise; no surprise, then, that all the forests around those villages had vanished.

About three miles from Abdali's new camp was the village of Chhajpur, and between the two armies, the soldiers had chopped a massive tree and made a battle-pole out of it. The entire region had been flattened out. With the surrounding palaas trees also gone, it had become a huge playground. The excited Maratha soldiers would go galloping there and practise their battlecry of 'Har Har Mahadev!' Abdali, however, was being more discreet, and preferred, like the tortoise, to keep his legs tucked under his shell.

Bhausaheb's eyes travelled to the region below Panipat, and what he saw there startled him. In the village Suvakhedi that lay between Rajakhedi and Ugrakhedi, he could see bullock carts, big and small, covered and uncovered, making an exit from the village. Some camel-carts were on their way out too. Bhausaheb asked Nana Purandare, 'What do I see here, Nana? Where are these people going to?'

'Shrimant, how can the weak hope to survive when caught in the fight of two enraged bulls? With two huge, powerful armies in the battlefield, the lives of the poor locals are being torn to shreds. They are fleeing to save what they can, including their lives. Shrimant, there was a heavy exchange of cannon-fire last night, and Suvakhedi was caught in the middle of the crossfire. Four cannon-balls fell upon the village and burned houses, cattle and farms to the ground.'

Bhausaheb surveyed the desolate landscape with a heavy heart. The lake on the other side of Suvakhedi had shrunk to half, exposing the brownish silt all around it. The wheat fields surrounding it had been chewed and trampled out of shape by a steady assault of innumerable horses, mules and camels. The desperate farmers had pulled out whatever stalks they could salvage from the ruins. The mango grove had been swept out clean, except for the Black Mango tree, which was left untouched because of its legend of unleashing its fury on whoever showed it the blade. Its entire neighbourhood denuded, the tree looked all the more sinister in its loneliness. The guava orchards were being hacked and axed even as Bhausaheb watched. 'Nana,' he asked, 'those men in front there look like our Marathas!'

'That's right, Shrimant, those men among the guava trees are ours. They need fires in the evening to survive the chilly winds. They cuts down the forests nearby long ago; now they are left with no alternative but to go for whatever vegetation is in sight, dry or wet, big or small. It's now either the trees or their own lives.'

'Shrimant,' chipped in Mahipatrao, 'we have already lost a few hundred of the leaner animals to the cold. A dozen or so of the pilgrims have died too.'

Maratha posts could be seen spread all across Rajakhedi, Ugrakhedi, right up to Kabuli Bagh, with the saffron flags fluttering in the breeze across the meadows. Shamsher Bahadur could be seen engrossed in work as bases were erected alongside the bigger wells and cannons placed atop them. A few Gardi platoons had come up to help the Marathas with the work. Panse's men were there too. Bhausaheb looked up at the sky that was turning steadily desolate, and then turned his gaze from the northern side of Panipat to the east, where he could see a stream crawling along on its way to the mighty river. It now looked different; the leaping and gurgling of a month and a half ago, its wild swerves before it finally met the river had become a distant memory. Looking at its destitution, Bhausaheb remarked, 'This stream has shrunk too!'

'Why worry, Shrimant?' responded the ever practical Mahipatrao. 'The canal flowing to the west of the village is flowing to full capacity. The Maratha army is not going to run short of water, that's for sure.'

It was dusk. The occasion being the lunar eclipse of the month of Kartik, pilgrims and pawns had gathered whatever wood they could find and made their way back early to the camp. In this one month and a half, Bhausaheb's army had really spread its presence right across Panipat. East to west his camp stretched six miles, taking a good two miles of the southern part under its control. To the north, the thirty or forty miles of distance up to Kunjpura was under the strict surveillance of Bhausaheb's troops. As Bhausaheb's unit entered Panipat from the Chandni Bagh side, the Hindu and Muslim inhabitants chatting by the wayside quickly got up to pay their respects to him, who smiled back in acknowledgement.

⚭

7 December 1760. Under the pretext of arranging for provisions, Najeeb Khan and his brother Sultan Khan had set off with a force of a thousand horsemen and five thousand foot soldiers armed with loaded muskets. It was twilight, and Najeeb thought of exploiting the darkness to take a closer look at the Maratha camp. He went as close to the southern edge of Panipat as he could, using the bushes on the periphery as cover.

As a part of their drill, the Maratha troops had begun carrying their cannons back across the trench. Some were driving their bullocks over. A number of the troopers sat with the Gardis round bonfires that had just been lit. It being the night of the lunar eclipse, some of the valiant Marathas concerned with matters of sin and merit had gathered together in smaller groups.

Najeeb had always been allergic to the very mention of the word 'Maratha'. The very sight of them would make his blood boil, and he would take out his anger on whoever was within hitting distance. This time it was his brother at the receiving end. 'You, Sultan, you see them all the time, don't you, these Deccan monkeys strutting around? Dancing around the battle-pole every day, shouting slogans, challenging the Afghans with their cannon-fire, making a nuisance of themselves!'

'Brother, the badshah must surely have a good reason for holding off.'

'What reason?' growled Najeeb. 'A load of rubbish, I'm sure. I've begun to lose faith in that man.'

'What are you saying, Bhai-jaan?' Sultan was startled.

'How can I continue to trust this man? Here are these Maratha apes, dancing around him in broad daylight, and this emperor of Islam does nothing but sit and plan? Even if, as you believe, he does propose to fight the Marathas in due course, he is no blood relation of ours, is he?'

'How you do mean?'

'Isn't it obvious? How long, do you think, is that Afghani going to stay in Hindustan? He will leave one day, and we will be back to fighting our battles with these wretched monkeys! That's why I say, Sultan, let's make full use of this Kandahari while he is around. Let us ourselves set the spark of battle alight. If the tree is poisonous, it is never enough merely to cut it down. It is bound to sprout new leaves sooner or later. We need to pull these Marathas out root and stem from the territory of Delhi and destroy them altogether on the banks of the Ganga and Yamuna. You are my brother, Sultan, aren't you? You were the one who had gone to Kandahar to invite this Abdali to India, weren't you? Well, how long can we keep this enthusiasm alive? This dilly-dallying is breaking my dreams to smithereens. Why do you think I travelled all the way from Afghanistan to Hindustan on a lame mule? Why did I slowly rise from being a mere pawn to becoming a soldier, and then a commander? Why should it take so much sweat, so much blood and so many tears to convert my little dream into reality?'

Najeeb's steady haranguing was getting Sultan charged up. Adding more fuel to the fire, Najeeb went on, 'Look at those Maratha bandicoots there, how they sit by the fire warming themselves! Aren't you tempted to push them into the fire and roast them alive!'

'But Bhai-jaan, the emperor's instructions—'

'What emperor? What instructions? For whose benefit, do you think, is this entire game being played?' raged Najeeb. 'Sultan, that Ibrahim Gardi is an infidel, we all know; yet Allah has blessed him with a valiant brother like Fateh Khan, who had the gumption to sneak into the emperor's camp and make away with his cannons. And look at you! Why did *you* do this to me, Ya Allah? What kind of a brother have you dumped into my lot, a brother who stands staring like a girl instead of pouncing upon the infidels like a true jihadi should?'

Sultan was fanned into sufficient fury to pull his horse to a halt. As the soldiers marching behind him pulled their reins, Najeeb turned to them and screamed, 'My brothers in Jihad, don't just stand there staring at the infidels like impotent goats. These godless men have dug the trenches and thrown the earth on either side, waiting to be used. Launch yourselves upon them, unleash your holy jihad, massacre them wholesale, and bury these Margatthas in their own trenches.'

The Rohillas pulled out their swords and, seething with hatred, broke upon the unsuspecting enemy. The Marathas were caught unawares busy as they were carrying their smaller cannons back across the trench; a number of them paid for their unpreparedness with their heads. The soldiers on the inner side of the trench, however, jumped on their horses, swung their swords and spears and leapt forward. The cold had suddenly vanished from their bodies. As the horses broke out of the trench, the Rohilla frontline was pushed behind, but the men towards the rear of Najeeb's contingent were ready with loaded guns to mow down the advancing horsemen of Bhausaheb's Royal Guards. As the bullets pierced through their flesh, the horses began neighing in terrible agony and threw the riders off their backs. Many a rider was caught with his feet in the stirrup and dragged to his death in the trenches as his horse tumbled in. As Najeeb's men with their spent muskets withdrew, they were replaced by their colleagues from the row behind them with guns primed to rain a fresh round of balls upon the advancing Maratha horses. The Rohillas managed to gain control of a plank across the trench and began crossing over.

The night sky resonated with the agonized cries of dying men and animals. All of Panipat froze in fear, and doors and windows began banging shut. Maratha units were rattled. When Balwantrao heard the clamour, he jumped upon his horse and ran into the fire. Bhausaheb too galloped in like a streak of lightning. At a sign from Bhausaheb, a large bunch of men began swinging their sticks and whips upon the legs and backs of retreating horses. Thus blocked, the Royal Guards again turned round and went crashing into the Rohillas on the other side.

With Afghan guns in their hands, the Rohillas were clearly at an advantage. Then, all of a sudden, Ibrahim Khan's men ran in from behind and began firing their guns at the enemy. Gunfire answered gunfire and pandemonium reigned supreme. Ibrahim Khan yelled at his gunners and soon the cannons began booming too. But in a little while, both the forces had got so mixed up with each other that it became difficult to separate one's own men from those of the enemy, and Ibrahim Khan had to cry halt to the cannon fire.

Meanwhile, Balwantrao Mehendale had advanced with his men, swinging his sword to great effect and bringing down the Rohillas to the left and to the right. As he raced forward urging his soldiers to greater acts of daredevilry, a Rohilla bullet pierced his chest and he tumbled off his horse. A bunch of Rohilla horsemen immediately pounced upon the fallen man. One of them sliced off the buttons of his armour and another took a swing at his neck. When Khanderao Naik-Nimbalkar of Akhluj saw this, he immediately jumped off his horse and went rushing in with a loud cry. As he was driving the Rohillas off Mehendale, a few more Maratha men joined in and slaughtered the swarming men.

The Holkars and the Shindes were at some distance from the field of battle, but when they heard the uproar, they raced in with their men. The effort of the Rohillas to drag Mehendale's corpse away met with failure and they began falling to the onslaught of the newly arrived forces. More than half of the six thousand assailants fell to Maratha swords and the rest began fleeing the battlefield. But despite such a heavy loss of men, their leaders were delighted to have brought down a very important Maratha chieftain. To them, it was a victory deserving of celebration.

The battle stopped and the troopers carried Balwantrao's body and placed it before Bhausaheb. Bhausaheb touched his dead friend's face. He wanted to break into a loud lamentation, but steeled himself and ordered that Balwantrao's body be carried over to his tent.

The hour-long combat had inflicted great damage and cut down about a thousand of their best men. Dead bodies lay scattered everywhere coated in dust and blood, and it required considerable labour to identify their own dead from the mass of corpses and lay them out for cremation. 'Where are we going to get wood enough to cremate a thousand bodies, Pant?' a trooper asked Antaji Mankeshwar.

'Death and destruction is an everyday affair in times of war. We cannot have individual pyres. Make the pyres big enough to accommodate six or seven corpses in one lot.'

The Mehendale tent was in a state of complete chaos. Lakshmibai cried inconsolably. 'How could you leave me alone and depart, my lord?' She smashed her glass bangles and knocked her forehead against the floor at her dead husband's feet. There was no restraining the sister's grief either. 'My little brother Balwanta!' she bawled, 'you have left us all desolate, my valiant brother!' Little Apparao knew that a disaster had befallen him, although he could not fully comprehend the enormity of his loss, as he stood holding Nana's hand in a corner.

The news spread like wildfire that Lakshmibai would burn herself on her husband's pyre and become a sati. Bhausaheb said to Mahipatrao, 'I know that becoming a sati is an act of great merit, but wouldn't it put under pressure the wives of our other men?'

'How can you speak the language of a Musalman, Shrimant?' said a shocked Mahipatrao. 'For us Hindus, there is no greater act for a widow than to die on her husband's pyre. When Raghuji Bhosale and Shahu Maharaj passed away, their wives died with them. When Khanderao Holkar died, his three wives, five concubines and two dancers burned with him. When your own father Chimaji Appa died, your revered mother Annapurna Saheb climbed the pyre behind him, didn't she?'

Despite Mahipatrao's admonition, Bhausaheb went over to Balwantrao's tent to dissuade Lakshmibai. But she was firm in her decision. 'My lord has earned himself eternal glory by becoming a martyr, and I shall accompany him to the next world.'

'But your Apparao is still a baby. What about him?'

Hearing his name mentioned, Apparao ran forward and, clinging to his mother, cried, 'Mother, please don't abandon me.'

Bhausaheb held Apparao by the wrist and pulled him into his lap. He told Lakshmibai, 'All right. I shall not come in the way of your duty. Go without worry. I take responsibility of raising Apparao.'

A huge pyre was raised near Kabuli Bagh. Lakshmibai removed all the ornaments from her body and distributed them to the poor. A huge crowd had assembled to witness this act of supreme sacrifice. The other women of the nobility filled vermilion in the parting of Lakshmibai's hair, and smeared some on her forehead too. Lakshmibai turned over all her belongings to the Brahmins and climbed over the heap of logs. The pyre was lit to the sound of drums and gongs as the Brahmins chanted mantras to accompany the souls of the dead and the dying in their journey towards heaven. As Jankoji Shinde stood sobbing loudly, Vishwasrao put his arm round his shoulder and led him away. Women and children cooled the embers that had crackled off the fire and carried the pieces with them as mementos of a sacred event.

Bhausaheb stayed seated by the pyre for well over an hour. It was after much pleading that he was finally persuaded to leave. He got into his palanquin and was carried back to Panipat. On his way, he pushed the tassels aside to see innumerable pyres burning all along the way.

ঔ

The nobles sat with grave faces in the conference room. Since the evening of Balwantrao's martyrdom, the planets had begun to change their coordinates for the Marathas. Appaji Jadhavrao was saying, 'The enemy has begun to push its feet out from under its shell. Abdali's men are trying to block our supplies.'

'Yes, Shrimant,' Nana Purandare added, 'they stand everywhere on the road to Delhi, and not let so much as an ordinary post go past. They stop the camels and snatch away all letters.'

'What, then, are Naro Shankar and Baloji Palande doing, sitting there in Delhi?' Vishwasrao snapped.

'What can they possibly do? What's the strength of the forces under their command? Four or five thousand at the maximum. The land around Delhi belongs to Shuja-ud-dowlah, and the region upwards belongs to Najeeb, both committed to Abdali,' reasoned Shamsher Bahadur.

Bhausaheb, who had been sitting quiet all along, broke in, 'Right next to Panipat is the region of Kurukshetra. That's why, perhaps, I get the feeling that Mahabharat is manifesting itself on this land all over again. Both the armies have fanned themselves into red heat for a war. Abdali is not going to reach out to Kabul-Kandahar to keep his men and animals fed. All his provisions are going to come from the Antarved. At best, he will try to infiltrate into the Punjab. I have no doubt that the final outcome of this war will depend on which of us causes the other army to starve to death. Subhedar kaka, Janko, Shamsher, Antaji Pant, Nana, Manaji, we have to do whatever it takes to keep our supply routes open at all times.'

Nana Purandare had a scroll in hand. 'I received this from Ala Singh just yesterday. Ten days ago, he had dispatched five thousand bullocks with a pair of sacks on each back. He wants to know whether we have received the supplies.'

'Not a single bullock has reached us. What could that mean?' asked Vishwasrao.

'That somebody has been blocking the animals and pocketing the supplies, what else?' said a worried Bhausaheb, 'If there are no grains, no fodder, how will the army survive? The landscape around here looks as desolate as a desert now. If men and animals are wiped out, who will fight the war? Mahipatrao, write to Ala Singh immediately. He should not stop the supplies at any cost, whatever price we have to pay.'

'Leave alone the Punjab, Kakasaheb, but the grains in our vicinity are also becoming difficult to procure. Sumer Singh, the chief of the banjaras, is sitting outside, waiting for an audience with you. Let's call him in and hear from the horse's mouth how hell-bent the enemy is on starving us,' said Jankoji.

Sumer Singh bowed before the nobles and took his seat in a corner. For all purposes, Sumer Singh was no less than king to the banjaras. He always walked with his nose in the air, carried himself with the snobbery of an Arab horse. But in the past month, he had shrunk to nearly looking like a scrawny mule. 'What's come over you, Sumer Baba?' Bhausaheb enquired anxiously. 'You look unwell.'

Sumer Singh looked crushed. He spoke with a tremor in his voice, 'Huzoor, my hair has turned grey in the service of the Marathas. I've served my lord Holkar here, as also the Shindes right from the time of Ranoba to Dattaji. Never let the army fall short of food or fodder. I have never experienced times so devastating as now.'

'Yes, but tell us exactly what your problems are, Sumer Baba!'

'Just last evening those Afghans waylaid my men about fourteen miles down the riverbank. Camel-carts full of grains, horses, mules—the devils made off with about two thousand of our animals along with all the grain they were carrying.'

'Bhausaheb, the intelligence that our spies have brought is quite true,' Shamsher Bahadur began to say. 'The enemy has let loose a ruffian of a chieftain named Shah Pasand Khan. He raids the villages around. He doesn't sit counting gold coins like we do. Whatever the finds in sight, he takes away as his own.' Bhausaheb ordered Damaji Gayakwad, Shamsher Bahadur, Darekar, Paigude and the other chieftains to immediately constitute squads of strong and swift horsemen. 'Let's provide the banjaras with temporary replacements for horses, bullocks, mules and donkeys that they've lost. Every one of their units will now move under the protection of two thousand horses, each leading from the front. Not a single grain, not a single blade of grass should we lose from here on.'

After the meeting was over, some nomads from Kunjpura, Kurukshetra, Kaithal and Ambala came to meet Bhausaheb. He thanked them profusely for continuing to keep them well supplied through little known hinterland routes. He accorded them public honour by presenting them with shawls, necklaces and rings. He placed letters in their hands to be delivered to other herdsmen and landlords, requesting them to do whatever they could to add to the provisions. 'Please give them my personal message that we are fighting the foreign enemy to preserve the empire of Delhi. The dignity of Hindustan will survive only if we survive.'

Within minutes of the departure of the nomads, Yashwantrao Pawar arrived crestfallen. 'Yes, Yashwantrao,' said Bhausaheb, looking at his long face.

'Bhausaheb, the news is quite bad.'

'No difference left now between good and bad, Yashwantrao.'

'Saheb, mother Yamuna has suddenly turned quite benevolent to the enemy.'

'How do you mean?'

'I was surveying the villages along the riverbank in search of food and fodder when I noticed that the river has begun to abate rapidly, and boats and barges have begun to travel to and fro briskly. The supplies to the enemy has gone up substantially.'

Bhausaheb immediately sent orders to Shamsher that round-the-clock surveillance be posted all along the riverbank. It was true that the enemy was growing in strength, but he took heart from the fact that the western side of Panipat with its woods of thorny bushes, the imperial road in the north and the canal alongside it were still under Maratha control. He believed that if they strove, they could still move mountains, but the issue of food supplies had to be resolved first. He summoned Mahipatrao and announced, 'I propose to set off with five or seven thousand of the Royal Guards tonight in search of farms and fields. We will reach out to villages fifteen or twenty miles on each side of the Kunjpura road.'

Accompanied by his closest associates, Bhausaheb spent the entire night searching for sources where he could arrange for provisions for his beleaguered army.

※

A strange breeze was blowing near the Kunjpura post. The sections of the fortification walls that had collapsed had not been rebuilt, and a bitingly cold wind was whistling through the fort. Yesaji Daphale, the officer in charge of the post, and his eight hundred horsemen were going out of their minds trying to keep the warmth of their body from dissipating. The fires they had lit were proving utterly unequal to the task.

Around the same time, a young man of about twenty, sporting a fledgling moustache on his upper lip, stood in the mango grove nearby, sizzling in the fire of revenge. From the darkness where he stood, he looked with grief-stricken eyes at the bombed out walls of the fort. The cold air barely disturbed him; in fact, it only fanned the cinders in his heart to a new blaze of revenge. He had two-and-a-half thousand Rohilla Pathans with him. In a thick, passion-laden voice, he addressed his grandfather, 'Dadajaan, is this my father's Kunjpura? I see a big hole where the bastion used to be, where my father would stand and twirl his moustaches. He looked invincible, as did his fort, but those Margatthas have turned his pride to dust.'

'Do away with your lamentation, son. You are the cub of a lion, aren't you? You should sing the song of vengeance.'

'Yes, Dadajaan, it was because I had to fan my anger into red heat that for two full months I wandered from heath to heath, collecting intrepid warriors around me and fitting out an army. I won't rest before throttling to death those who have ruined my Kunjpura.'

'Move forward then! Launch your assault!'

'Dadajaan, how big would the Maratha garrison be inside?'

'Can't be very big. Sadashivrao Bhau would have assumed he's safe because Abdali is stuck on the other side, while the chieftains here have been slaughtered. Dileyr, we have been hiding under these bushes and observing them for two nights now. If there had been a large number of people inside the fort, wouldn't we have seen their commotion? No reason for us to delay.'

Dileyr Khan made a sign to his men, and they launched their offensive with a loud cry. They got in from the breaches that Ibrahim Khan's cannons had opened up and broke upon the unprepared defenders. The Marathas had turned stiff with the cold anyway, and seven or eight hundred of them were slaughtered before they had a chance to pick up arms. A large number of them ran in the opposite direction. Ranoji Jadhavrao of Kanpur yelled, 'How can you run, cowards? Bhau has ordered that we should leave our post only when dead!'

'What does it cost him to issue these orders? If we die in this wilderness, our bodies will not even get a decent pyre. If we die in our native land, there will at least be some women and children to cry over our corpses, however false their note.'

They ran through whichever dark lane afforded them an escape route. The Rohillas gave them chase and left a hundred Marathi corpses unclaimed.

Dileyr Khan slept peacefully after ages that night. The sun went well up the horizon, and he still lay snoring, while his grandfather sat pulling at the hookah. When the old man's gaze turned towards the imperial highway, he noticed a tiny cloud of dust at a distance. Could this be some enemy force riding in for a counter-attack? He quickly shook his grandson awake and pointed towards the steadily expanding cloud. Dileyr peered towards the advancing dust and wondered aloud, 'There are no Marathas left in the direction of the Punjab! Who could these men be, Dadajaan?'

'It could be Ala Singh Jaat and his Sikhs who supply provisions to the Marathas. That wretch must have set out to help Bhau. He wants to see the Maratha crowned the emperor of Hindustan, the shameless rascal.'

'Well, what do we do if he decides to come straight here?'

'Let's quickly move out of this post and hide behind the bushes along the highway.'

Grandfather and grandson hustled their two thousand five hundred men behind the bushes and watched the dust cloud turn bigger and bigger. Soon they could hear the rattle of hooves that steadily became louder. When Dileyr Khan began to discern the figures wrapped in the dust, he could hardly believe his eyes: countless green flags were fluttering atop the horses. In the lead was a rider carrying a flag with a crescent moon and star. Dileyr Khan uttered a loud cry of 'Allah-o-Akbar' and sprang out of hiding. His men followed suit. The horses were quickly pulled to a stop and a strong, big-built sardar astride a muscular Arab horse stepped forward and asked in surprise, 'Young man, who are you?'

'Dileyr Khan, the son of the Nawab of Kunjpura.'

'Najabat Khan—'

'I am his unfortunate son.'

'But this post had fallen into the hands of the infidels!'

'That's true, but we have just won it back,' informed Dileyr Khan and asked, 'Who are you?'

'I am Sher Atai Khan Baluch. My king has got caught in Hindustan, and I have set off with ten thousand men to extricate him.'

Atai Khan and his forces stretched themselves out in the Kunjpura Bagh. The two men discussed the reverberations caused in Kabul-Kandahar by the battle in Hindustan. After having rested sufficiently, Atai Khan got ready to resume his journey when Dileyr Khan barred his way and said, 'Khan Saheb, I have to avenge the killing of my father. Please take me along with you so that I may mow the Marathas down like grass.'

'Son,' responded Atai Khan, 'your passion is worth being sung in ballads. But you needn't head for the battlefield at all.'

'Why not?'

'Ten other chieftains joining him in battle is not the best way to serve the badshah. You can do greater service by staying back here.'

'What does that mean?'

'I have travelled for three days across the land of Punjab. I have seen so many caravans of bullocks and camels carrying grains. Thousands of bullocks belonging to Ala Singh of Patiala are moving along this route. My forces now possess four thousand bullocks they were carrying for the infidels. You stay here. If you wish, I can leave a couple of thousand fresh horses with you. Plunder this region, don't let a single grain sneak across this road. We can dispatch the infidels swiftly by guns or swords; but it will be much more fun to starve and kill them inch by inch. Let this be your service. This deed of yours will certainly please Allah and earn credit for your father in the Almighty's court.'

Atai Khan left behind a unit of two thousand men, and moved on towards Panipat. Dileyr Khan prepared a list of the villages from where the nomads passed, recruited more soldiers, and blocked the Punjab road. He didn't let a single sack of grain move south. The horses of the Rohilla Pathans roamed all night through the villages, set fire to huts and haystacks to terrorize the people. Swinging his naked sword that glinted in the fire, he issued dire warnings to the villagers, 'Remember this, right now you see only the haystacks burning. But if you supply provisions to those infidels, I promise I will roast you all alive in the same fire.'

※

Abdali looked extremely agitated. He had stepped out of his pavilion three times since morning. He would stare unblinkingly at the battle-post three miles away and Panipat, which was seven or eight miles away, as if struggling to come to a decision. He went back inside his pavilion and sat in conference with his Shah Wali Khan. After a while, he sent for Najeeb. Noticing the badshah in a temper, Najeeb made his bows particularly low. Before he could raise his head and straighten up, Abdali snapped, 'Najeeb, it's merely a game for you, while my men lose their lives.'

'But Aalam-panaah, I—'

'Shut up! Cut out your syrupy nonsense and listen. How many carts of grain have arrived from the Antarved in the last three days? How many villages have dispatched fodder? For months you've been saying, 'Aalam-panaah, just let the Yamuna subside and I shall clean out Antarved and Ayodhya and deposit it at your feet.' Now the river has ebbed; but where are your provisions? Such terrible shortage in the army that grain are selling for a rupee per seer?'

'Aalam-panaah, please hear me out. I've found out the reason for this shortage. That old sinner Govindpant has been raiding the Meerut province. He has destroyed our posts in and around Meerut.'

'Who is this Govindpant?'

'He is one of Bhau's courtiers. He's the same Govinda who had tried to block my meeting with Shuja-ud-dowlah. Sixty-five years old he is and—'

'Yet so energetic? And your officers there? What were they doing—sleeping?'

'Aalam-panaah, this is no time for squabbling,' intervened Shah Wali. 'Our supplies have to resume, otherwise a hundred-and-fifty thousand of our Rohillas will fall into Bhau's clutches. A year-long battle will come to naught.'

Abdali sat thinking for a long time and finally said, 'Najeeb, you must ensure that the supplies are resumed within the next twenty-four hours. We have the perfect man for this enterprise who reached our camp just this morning: Atai Khan, our wazeer's nephew. Take him with you and finish off with this Govindpant.'

Abdali also agreed to send Amil Musey Khan Baluch with the doughty Atai Khan. Musey Khan was familiar with every rill and hill, lane and bylane of the Antarved. Atai Khan also took along with him a chieftain named Karimdad Khan. The emperor addressed the two, 'Move like a raging storm. Do not stop anywhere on the way, eat your meals on horseback. Upon your speed depends the next meal of our army.'

Atai Khan was thrilled at being assigned such an important responsibility on the very day of his arrival. He assured the emperor with great pride, 'Qibla-e-aalam, I promise to return to the camp victorious.'

Nobody outside had any inkling of the plans that had been cooking in the royal pavilion since morning. Atai Khan and Karimdad Khan left the camp on the pretext of going for a hunt. On their tail were sturdy horses freshly arrived from Kandahar. Even the senior functionaries of Abdali's army were intrigued by the latest flurry in the camp. The ordinary soldiers looked in awe at the hunting team that was setting out. Some grand hunt, this!

※

17 December 1760. Govindpant had been camping near the highway alongside Jalalabad for three days. A fortnight ago, he had got news of

Balwantrao's martyrdom, and it had wrenched his old heart. Before Bhau had pitched camp in Panipat, Govindpant had been receiving a steady stream of letters from him: 'Pant, send money!' 'Pant, send gunpowder!' 'Pant, send bullocks!' 'Pant, block enemy supplies! 'Pant, burn villages!' Pant had begun to dread the arrival of these messages. He was more than twice Bhau's age, and although he admired Bhausaheb's resilience and determination, he didn't possess either the youth or the physical strength to keep up with his demands.

After Bhau reached Panipat, the letters slowed down and stopped coming after a while. But the ones that had arrived had been enough to shake the old man to the core. 'The Peshwa nurtured you since your childhood. Is this how you repay his debt?' 'Be true to your salt,' Bhausaheb had written, and that had galvanized Pant into action. He had rushed from Itaawa towards Delhi. He stepped on people's tails at Sikandra and forced them to cough up provisions. He collected sacks of grain and four hundred and twenty thousand in cash and handed them to Naro Shankar in Delhi, placing upon him the responsibility of making sure the provisions reached Panipat. He had then moved towards the north-east and barged into Najeeb's territory. 'Do what you have to,' Bhausaheb had written, 'but block the enemy's supplies. Loot highways, burn villages.' These words had cut a groove in his head. 'With Abdali having withdrawn from the Antarved, what prevents you from plundering a territory that has no protector?' Bhausaheb had asked. The only answer that Govindpant could give to that question was through action. Najeeb's influence on the Antarved had weakened, which Pant exploited and blew away their posts in the Meerut province. He had taken with him a nine-thousand-strong army, which he divided into smaller units and spread them around. They began waylaying horses and carts, camels and bullocks laden with provisions on the roads leading to Panipat. In his sunset hours, Govindpant had suddenly struck upon the verve and spirit of dawn, and got into the act with a vengeance. Hearing the passing of Balwantrao, he had suddenly registered the urgency and the import of Bhausaheb's admonition: 'Pant, you will not get again such opportunity to be of service.' In the last four days, he had hardly got off his horse, putting his creaking joints and muscles to a severe test.

It was a bone-tired Pant that hit the bed at night, and in the morning, his body would be reluctant to do his bidding. But what choice did he have except to yank it up and out? His entire force had been dispirited by the severity of the cold, and they wouldn't stir without their boss goading them from behind. Pant sat waiting through the day for the return of his squads that had set off in the morning in search of supplies. Bhausaheb had visited him in a dream last night looking desperate and forlorn, and Pant hadn't been able to shake off its effects. When his son Balaji entered his tent, he said, 'You know, Baloba,' he said, 'I saw Bhausaheb in my dream last night.'

'Really? What did he say to you?'

'What else could he say? He looked beaten, his clothes were covered in dust, there were lines of men and herds of animals around him, all looking weak and famished, as if they hadn't eaten for days.'

'Yes, but what did he say?'

'He came close to me and said, "Pant, you had once provided bread to my Kakasaheb Bajirao Peshwa that you had baked on cinders stolen from a pyre. Where has that zest and devotion gone? Today we lie starving in your province. Will you provide a seer or two of grains to my men, Pant? Even a sheaf or two of fodder will do for the animals. Look at the state we have been reduced to!"'

Pant wiped the edge of his eyes with a kerchief. 'I feel so hopeless, Baloba! A full thirty-five years I have spent in Hindustan, and for the last fifteen years at least, I have been writing to the Peshwa again and again: don't just conquer land, set up good administrative machineries everywhere. You keep moving forward, planting flags at every doorstep; and the next day, you can't even locate the staff on which the flag fluttered. If they had ensured good governance, why would this son of Chimaji Appa's have landed in this death-trap? They sowed only thorns and brambles of maladministration, and now sent this poor boy down the same road to go and conquer the world.'

Balaji had been avoiding getting into an argument with his father. But when Pant went overboard with his paeans of the Peshwa, he couldn't hold himself back. 'Dada, how can you forget the time when they confiscated your land and suspected your account books?'

'Baloba, with the Maratha Empire caught in a maelstrom, where is the point in cribbing over small matters? All right, they searched through the account books, so what? They handed over half our territory to a brother-in-law, so what? A master is a master. It's on account of his generosity that we became what we did. It was that Hingane who pointed a finger at us so as to distract attention from his own loot. But what came of it, finally? We didn't attract disrepute to our name as he did, did we? I had informed the Peshwa right then that we are humble lambs, our one single religion is to serve the Maratha empire to the end of our days.'

Pant then suddenly remembered the units that had gone foraging in the morning, and he asked, 'Baloba, the day is coming to an end, how is it that not a single unit has returned with provisions? We have barely arranged seven thousand sacks, a mere straw for an army that size. Bhau there would be waiting desperately. I know this land well, and I can imagine what state they would be reduced to without sustenance.'

'If you are so concerned, Dada, why didn't you send the supplies earlier?'

'Look at my age. My army is merely the army of our tiers. If I had two thousand strong men that warrior chieftains possess, I would have swallowed up Najeeb's province long ago. Yet I carry the weight of my age and health on my shoulder and continue to run for Bhau's sake: from Shukratal to Delhi, from Delhi to Itaawa, from Itaawa to Saagar. How much more can I run, Baloba?'

Govindpant was feeling exhausted, also a little feverish, but he stayed leaning against the bolster and prattled on. Balaji's attention had drifted.

Then he suddenly remembered something that made him start. 'Baloba, this Bhau has truly made me soft in the head. I still haven't had my bath and said my prayers! This hasn't happened to me before! How could I forget such an elementary thing?'

He forced his tired body up. He had never allowed anyone to heat his water for him, and now too he walked heavily out of the tent, placed a vessel on the makeshift brazier and got the fire going. He then walked back into the tent and brought out a plank and a change of dhoti. While he was doing this, three of his squads returned to report that they had collected eleven hundred sacks of grain. Pant was delighted. 'Just you wait, Bhausaheb,' he said to himself. 'Another two or three days, and I won't let you utter a squeak.'

The sun had begun its journey down and the early evening cold had arrived. The horses had come back from their forays and were busy dipping into the fodder; the horsemen were stretching their limbs. Pant's water had warmed up; he tested the temperature, found it too hot, and added cold water to the vessel to bring it to the desired heat. As he poured mugs of the warm water over himself, his joints and muscles began to relax. Suddenly, he saw a cloud of dust in the distance. It was heading in his direction. Their flags were saffron. It could be Naro Shankar. It had to be him! But why would he have left Delhi? Pant hurriedly finished his bath. By then, the saffron flags had reached the camp, and suddenly loud roars were heard. 'Allah! Allah!' 'Catch the bastards!' 'Slaughter them!' Pant's heart leapt to his mouth. The Pathans had mounted a raid from all sides.

Pant quickly wrapped a wet dhoti round himself. He slapped the horses on the rump and let them loose. He gathered all his strength to jump on his own horse and spurred it forward. By then the Afghans had slaughtered a couple of hundred Maratha men. The rest of them ran for their lives, with the Afghans chasing them like hunting dogs. Pant was shivering all over, and his rigid body rocked unsteadily on his steed that was galloping at great speed. He had done half a mile, and the Afghans were getting left behind when his horse stumbled against something and the old man fell off its back into the dust. 'Stop!' he yelled at his racing men. 'Don't leave me behind here! Baloba, stop!' When they heard his frantic cries, four or five of the horsemen in front turned round; Balaji turned round too. They lifted Pant and placed him back on the horse. Pant held the reins and sat leaning full forward, holding the horse's shoulder in his embrace. They would hardly have covered another furlong when he tumbled off again. 'Help me!' he screamed. Again Balaji and a few men stopped and put him back on the horse.

A hundred and more horses were racing away for life, with close to two thousand Arab-Kandahari horses in hot pursuit. The Maratha horsemen were being targeted one by one, and they fell under the hooves of the horses, wounds spurting blood. Now the horses were upon each other, and Pant fell again. He was instantly surrounded by Pathans. 'Baloba, Baloba!' screamed Pant. But the hundred or so fleeing horsemen had shot well past, Balaji among them. The old man's screams, whether they reached the fleeing men or not, couldn't have served any purpose. The prostrate Govindpant looked up at the setting sun and saw saffron flags floating in and out of his vision. That was when Afghan swords came swinging down and severed his head from his body. The head and body lay twitching for a while in the dust.

The Afghans razed the entire camp to the ground in an hour's time. The caravan of Atai Khan and Karimdad Khan began its journey back to the base camp, trumpets blaring and horses trotting in style. Amidst the general mood of excitement could be heard the raucous laughter of Atai Khan when his men lifted Govindpant's head on the tip of a spear.

❦

Bhausaheb's mind knew no rest. Govindpant's face swam before his eyes all the time. What could have happened to him? Why had messages from him stopped coming?

Bhausaheb had come to know that very evening that Atai Khan and Karimdad Khan's forces had set off from Abdali's camp towards Meerut. It hadn't taken him a moment to realize that the hunt was only a cover; it couldn't be anything but a raid on Pant's camp. The enemy had thrown a ring in the east and south, making it impossible for the Maratha men to stir out in that direction. The road to the west was a veritable jungle of thorns and brambles. After a moment's thought, Bhausaheb dispatched letters to Naro Shankar in Delhi, where a few good regiments of Meer Khan Thokey, Parvatrao Kadam, Lakshmanrao Gawande and Hiroji Shelke were stationed. All of them had a good four or five thousand men with them. It would be wonderful if anything over two thousand could be dispatched to help Govindpant. Pant himself had an army of about ten thousand men, and while they were not of the same quality as the Royal Guards, they could certainly be counted as warriors. Bhau had received intelligence of Pant having smashed the enemy supplies; hence it was obvious to him that the enemy would try to neutralize him.

Bhau had never felt this restless before. He couldn't guess why, but he could see anxiety hiding in the eyes of everyone he crossed: chieftains, their deputies, officials and clerks. Was that a sign of some imminent calamity? Nana, Purandare finally gathered courage and stepped forward. 'Bhausaheb, the scout has brought a worrying report.'

'What's that?'

'Abdali's camp has been celebrating the success of a major hunt.'

'What does that mean?'

'There's no way to get further details.'

In a little while, two camels were seen riding in from the direction of Abdali's camp, white flags fluttering. It could be an envoy. He was given immediate entry into the royal pavilion. He was carrying with him a box with carvings etched on it. He placed it before Bhausaheb and handed over the badshah's scroll. Heart beating wildly but face composed, Bhausaheb unrolled the scroll.

> We have dispatched your Govindpant to heaven. Your entire army is soon going to travel in the same direction. But since you are royalty, special arrangements need to be made for your reception up there; which is why we have sent one of your men in advance, so that you do not lack for any comfort there. Since your honour is not likely to believe that we are so deeply concerned about you, we are sending you the receipt of action undertaken, which you will find in the box. Please acknowledge receiving it.'

With hands heavy as lead, Bhausaheb lifted the lid of the box. It was topped up with fresh black currant leaves, below which was a brocaded kerchief. When he lifted the kerchief and saw what lay beneath, blood froze in his veins; numbness gripped him from the soles of his feet to the hair on his scalp. Dry, shrunken, carrying traces of recently wiped blood, lay the severed head of Govindpant. His eyelids were closed as the closed petals of a flower; his face had shrivelled and his cheeks had sunk deep. All who saw felt the earth pulled out from under their feet; some of the troopers broke down and cried. Gathering all his courage, Bhausaheb folded his hands before the head, lifted it out of the box and placed it on a cushion. All the assembled men folded their hands to mark their respect for the departed man. Bhausaheb then sat down to write his response to Abdali's letter.

> ... You have written that our entire army is going to travel in that direction. I humbly ask Your Highness: do you know of anybody who will not travel in that direction? We are all travelling down the same road, right from the humble groom who brushes the horse to the emperor of Kabul-Kandahar, who rides astride it flashing his proud sword. We are all fellow-travellers on that road. Who is afraid of the final destination?

I am neither king nor emperor. I am merely a cousin of the Peshwa, an ordinary soldier. How can it make any difference to a nobody like me whether the arrangements on the other side are good or bad? But your glory is of the highest order. You are the emperor of Kandahar, and arrangements for you have to be imperial in their grandeur. That is why Pant has had to leave in such a hurry.

Bhau handed over the missive to the envoy and sent him packing. A thick haze of grief had descended over the entire army. A pyre was erected for Govindpant's severed head and was lit amidst the chanting of mantras.

༺༻

The carts coming from the Punjab had begun to disappear. Bhausaheb lavished gold bangles and armbands upon the banjaras and pendharis. He raised the price for grains and fodder to four times, and finally persuaded them to stake their lives and step out surreptitiously to sneak in supplies. Abdali had begun encircling the Marathas as a farmer raises walls around his field to trap water.

While Bhausaheb sat in his office tearing his hair about what to do next, Vishwasrao and Jankoji walked in. The conversation began with Vishwasrao protesting, 'Kakasaheb, kakisaheb was complaining that you didn't return to your chamber last night. The servants tried to wake you up for meals, but you didn't respond. Kaka, I have never seen you in such a state of agitation before. The lines of worry, fear—'

'Not one bit, Vishwasrao, this Bhau has never feared anything. However, I do feel anxious for the hundreds of thousands of lives that depend on me, Rao Saheb. With the Yamuna having shrunk, the enemy supplies have resumed. After Pant gone, there is nobody left in the Antarved to create anarchy there or to block supplies. I have no idea where the rest of the fief holders have vanished. Sometimes I feel that we should blow the bugle of war and launch an assault. But then, I tell myself, if I want to give in to such knee-jerk impulses, why have I been patiently playing my moves all this time? A month has gone by, and the enemy has been waiting for us to step out so that we can walk into the net they have cast. They dare not launch an attack because we have erected a mountain of fire around us. In terms of war strategy, we are located in a position of advantage. Even if the food and fodder arrive late sometimes, we are well supplied with water. There is a canal that flows past us. We will survive on water. Abandoning this post will do us harm. I am quite confident that the Peshwa will arrive with his forces in the next few days. He left Pune on Dussehra. When his forces hit the enemy from behind and we attack from the front, the enemy is going to be crushed. They will be ground to a paste as spices are ground between a pair of grinding stones. Our Ala Singh Jaat is a brave man, too; and true to his word. His carts have not been coming in, but I'm sure some difficulties have cropped up on the way. Our supplies will perhaps resume as before very soon. Till such time, Rao Saheb, I feel we should look for some kind of a deal—'

'Kakasaheb,' said Vishwasrao, 'I'd rather lose my life than strike a deal with the enemy.'

'If it comes to that,' Jankoji joined in, 'let's get into battle bare-chested right now.'

'Sure,' laughed Bhausaheb, 'let's get into battle. That's exactly why we have crossed thousands of miles and arrived here. While we wait for the Peshwa's forces to arrive from the south and some supplies from the Punjab, let's fake an effort at truce. Rao Saheb, I wouldn't have used the word 'truce' even at the cost of having my tongue sliced from the root. But why even call it a 'fake' truce? A real 'truce' as an emergency measure looks like the only way out.'

'Why, Kakasaheb? Why?'

'If not for anybody else, for the sake of our men who sit looking at the sky and the animals who bellow on their leashes, a truce will have to be struck, however temporary. When the stomach begins to sing, nothing else is worth hearing.'

'But Shrimant, wouldn't we need a clearance from the Peshwa?'

'Yes, I had written and asked him whether we should agree to the enemy giving us one-fourth of the revenue from Chambal to Attock. His response was that we should not get into a truce out of fear. His argument was that Dadasaheb had run right up through Attock; he had established posts at Sirhind and Lahore in the Punjab. After all his conquests, I should not agree to a mere one-fourth. He alerted me not to do anything that would make me a laughing stock with Dadasaheb; instead, I should attack the enemy and destroy him.'

'Well, then, Kakasaheb, what should we do?'

'Rao Saheb, I shall give you the exact words of the Peshwa, 'The Peshwa has set off to come to your support. Do not worry.' So, Rao Saheb, he writes to tell us not to lose courage. Let's wait for that army to arrive. But the distance from Pune to Panipat is twelve hundred miles. Till such time as the Peshwa arrives, let us place a fishbone of 'truce' in the enemy's throat.'

⁂

When Bhausaheb began thinking in terms of truce, the person to spring to his mind was Kashiraj Pandit. Kashiraj Pandit was from the south, and Bhausaheb knew the weight this Brahmin's word carried in Shuja-ud-dowlah's court. Accordingly, he had written a couple of courtesy letters to Kashiraj from Panipat. Kashiraj had also responded by return post in a beautiful hand and well-chosen words. Even though Bhausaheb had never set eyes on him, he had formed a mental image of the man after reading those letters. Bhausaheb sat down and wrote two letters, one to Shuja-ud-dowlah and the other to Kashiraj Pandit, and dispatched them immediately to Abdali's camp.

Kashiraj read Bhausaheb's letter with great eagerness. As a mark of identity, Bhau had dipped his hand in saffron water and made an imprint on the page, which Kashiraj examined with great care. Bhau's words were reverberating in his head.

> *Do whatever you can, because the Marathi soil has never been in such peril before. It's now a matter of its reputation. You are joined to this soil by your umbilical cord, and this is your opportunity to repay your debts to it. Get Shuja-ud-dowlah to persuade Hafeez Khan and Shah Wali Khan to hammer out a truce that keeps our dignity intact.*

Kashiraj got up and headed for Shuja's pavilion. He found the Nawab still holding Bhau's letter. He was reading it over and over again.

> *I have written to you a number of times that we will resolve our differences to the satisfaction of both sides, but this foreign enemy has to be neutralized.*

I had also written that we are two arrows from the same quiver and that we should target the same enemy. I had tried to persuade you that the Afghans consider the Muslims of Hindustan worse than Hindus. But you rejected all my pleas, all my persuasions, and handed over your reins to rank outsiders. Unless the information reaching me is wrong, you know better than anyone else what kind of respect and honour you have been receiving and in what manner you are being felicitated since you joined them. Let me remind you once again of the affection that existed between our ancestors.

You may do a service to Hindustan even as you stay there. It is not possible that you are not aware of our strait circumstances. Persuade Hafeez Ahmad and Shah Wali Khan to talk to the emperor, and get them to bring about a truce that helps us retain our dignity. Pay your debt to Hindustan now.

. When Shuja looked up from the letter and found Kashiraj standing before him, he laughed and said, 'I was reading your master's letter.'

'I do belong to the same soil as Bhausaheb, but I have only one master, and that is you.'

'Pandit,' Shuja spoke gravely, 'I wouldn't want even an enemy to be caught in such a crisis. One can't deny that there has existed a bond of some kind between Bhau and me. The other things he has said are also true. We know how poorly these Afghans have treated us. Also, they will return home tomorrow if not today, and after that, it will be us and the Marathas again. They are in grave trouble, and I believe we should help them to the extent we can.'

'You are right, Nawab Bahadur; that's just what I was thinking.'

The two sat talking for many hours. The biggest obstacle to a truce, they knew, would be Najeeb. And they thought it would be best to try to soften him first. As decided, Kashiraj went to visit Najeeb in his tent that night.

❦

Under the dim light of the lamp, Najeeb's carrot-red face was looking redder still. Running his hand over his stumpy beard all the while, he heard out patiently all that Kashiraj had to say. He didn't miss registering the feeling with which the man was putting forth his arguments. After the Kashiraj Pandit had finished laying out his case, Najeeb began, 'I do not lay any blame at all on the Nawab Saheb, because the fault lies with his young age. How old would he be? Twenty-seven? Twenty-eight? His father was dearer to me than my own father was, and hence I do not blame him at all. He obviously hasn't seen the number of summers and winters in statecraft as I have, right? So, you now have to persuade him that a trapped enemy will twist and turn at your feet in whichever direction you want him to turn; but if you pity him and let him go free, is he not going to sting you at the very first opportunity he gets? A wise pandit like you should really be explaining these things to young Shuja, shouldn't you?'

Kashiraj Pandit knew that there was no point in reading the Holy Book before this donkey; he got up and left. Najeeb instantly called his brother Sultan Khan to his side and said, 'Listen, you have to keep a sharp eye on the movements of this man, his master Shuja, Hafeez and our wazeer. There are a few foxes in our army that have been thinking of truce. Sultan, you have to be on full alert.'

That very evening, Shuja paid a visit to Shah Wali Khan. The wazeer said, 'Nawab, what you say is quite right. What are we going to gain after all this bloodshed? Whatever we get will go to the share of that lying rascal, and all that we will be left with will be the loss of our men. My deep desire is to bring our prolonged stay in Hindustan to an end, wind up our tents and head back home.' Shuja, Hafeez Rahmat and Shah Wali decided that they would do all that they could to bring about a truce.

Chieftains like Barkhurdar Khan, Shah Pasand Khan, Shah Wali Khan and others had assembled in the emperor's pavilion. The emperor himself had still to arrive from his private quarters. Najeeb Khan sat next to Barkhurdar Khan throwing sharp glances in the direction of Wazeer Shah Wali Khan. Each time he looked at the old man, his bile would rise. Losing his patience after some time, he sent a barb loud enough for everyone to hear. 'The garland has been tied round my head and I am the bridegroom in this war. The entire responsibility of the war lies on my head. Whatever happens will happen because of me and for me. The rest of you are merely wedding guests and musicians. You begin to play when you are told to. Instead of playing your instruments, why are you talking of truce behind my back?'

The chieftains were startled at Najeeb's talk. Shah Wali looked towards Najeeb with distaste. Barkhurdar intervened and said to Najeeb, 'Why are you getting upset, Khan Saheb? Why should you take suchsmall matters to heart?'

'Small matters?' groused Najeeb. 'How can they be small when they have risen right up to my neck? That evening it was my five thousand men that the cannons of the infidels roasted alive near their trench. They were roasted on the spot like so many cutlets! It was my cousin who was dispatched to heaven, and now we have some stupid person among us who talks of truce? He is so timid, this person, so cowardly, so keen on shaking hands with the infidel that I wonder whether he is of Afghan seed at all!'

'Shut your mouth!' screamed Shah Wali Khan in rage. He pulled his Khorasani sword and swung it in Najeeb's direction. Certain that his last moment had come, Najeeb shut his eyes tight and froze in fear. But the alert Barkhurdar Khan pushed the shivering man away in the nick of time. A second's delay would have seen Najeeb's head topple off his shoulder. The other chieftains had enough time to recover and hold Shah Wali back. They surrounded him and tried to lead him out of the pavilion. But Shah Wali was far too angry to cool down. He tried to push the others away as he yelled, 'Worthless rascal! A mere pawn who has managed to move up the ranks, do you think that you can shoot your filthy mouth any which way you want? Wait till I slice you to pieces on the spot! Trying to mislead Aalam-panaah with your false talk of jihad? I can never fall for your delusional tricks. If ever any misfortune befalls the emperor, it is this Shah Wali that shall hold the reins of his horse and lead him out of the thorns, not you. You are no more than a monkey who is happy to dance with the drums in front of victory processions. What do you care for the badshah's good and bad? You try to undermine me because I can see through your schemes? You cultivate indiscipline and disrespect among us Afghans by using Commander-in-chief Jahaan Khan to suppress me? It's only on account of the badshah that I suffer you, else I wouldn't have hired a worthless person like you even to clean the dung from my stable!'

Red with rage, Shah Wali Khan strode out of the pavilion. A thoroughly rattled Najeeb went grovelling after him with folded hands, crying, 'Huzoor, forgive my impertinence, huzoor! It was because that snake Jankoji had attacked—'

'Silence!' Shah Wali whirled round and roared. 'Don't you try your monkey tricks on me! You will find enough idiots to admire your shenanigans. Go blacken your face there!'

☙❧

There emerged two clear factions on the issue of truce. Those who were in a hurry to return to Kandahar wanted the truce; while those whose minds were obsessed with religion wanted jihad. As the discussion among the chieftains warmed up, Najeeb's restlessness increased with every passing hour. He roamed agitatedly through the camp like an animal whose ears had just been clipped. Word of the ugly spat between his wazeer and Najeeb had reached the Badshah Abdali's ears. He called for a conference that very evening of all his chieftains and a select bunch of soldiers.

Najeeb was on tenterhooks. His dreams rested on which way the conference would go. After a little deliberation, he decided to visit Commander-in-chief Jahaan Khan in his tent. He reminded Jahaan Khan once again of the manner in which the Margatthas had slain his son in the Punjab eighteen months ago. Najeeb's next task was a chat with the ulemas. He went and sat with them, looking like an innocent cow. He consulted the chief maulvi Qazi Idris, took the blessings of the others, and finally turned in the direction of his own tent.

On the way, he received a piece of information that made him jump for joy. The noted cleric Shah Waliullah of Delhi had arrived and had gone straight to his pavilion. Nothing could have been more fortuitous than the arrival of this holy man; he had the power and influence to turn any argument in favour of jihad.

Shah Waliullah was the son of the sufi saint Shah Abdul Raheem, who had established an organization called Madarsa-e-Raheema. After his father had passed on, Shah Waliullah went on to establish a number of madarsas around Delhi. He had also done the pilgrimage of Mecca and Madina. He was convinced that the Marathas were hell-bent on wiping out Islam in Hindustan. In all his earlier campaigns to Delhi, Abdali would make it a point to pay his respects to Shah Waliullah. 'Islam is in danger!' was his abiding slogan, and he found Najeeb and Abdali among his most ardent supporters. Najeeb, thus, knew very well the kind of hold Shah Waliullah exercised on Abdali. No wonder there was a bounce in his steps as he raced towards his tent. Once there, he prostrated himself before the holy man and began to fuss over him.

As soon as dinner was over, the chieftains began to gather in Abdali's pavilion. The maulvis and the squad leaders assembled too. Qazi Idris and Shah Waliullah were seated next to the emperor. The conference began with the Wazeer Shah Wali underlining the huge overshoot in expenditure and the disruption of life caused by their protracted stay in Hindustan, and finished off by saying that a decent truce would put a stop to the miseries of their men.

After the wazeer had finished, Jahaan Khan rose from his seat and began putting forward counter-arguments. 'Aalam-panaah,' he said, 'even talking of truce does not sit well with a truly Islamic man, and actually bringing about truce is out and out anti-Islamic, since we have already declared jihad. Our Rohilla and Afghan brothers have already raised the cry of 'Allah-o-Akbar' and gathered under Your Highness's banner. These Margatthas are the sons of the devil. They were the ones who drove Prince Taimur out of the Punjab eighteen months ago? They smashed the throne of Delhi and devastated the beautiful city. They kept Najeeb Khan perpetually on the run and made life miserable for him. These monkeys from the Deccan have transgressed all limits and ground all of Hindustan under their heels. Under the pretext of offering governance in return for a quarter of the revenue, they wield the knife in the market place and indulge in outright plunder. As if this were not enough, they slaughtered Qutb Shah in Kunjpura, humiliated Najabat Khan and chopped him to pieces. How, then, can there be a truce? When our spirits and strength are on the ascendant, when our men and animals are ready for war, why talk pointlessly of truce? No, Aalam-panaah, no, that is no longer possible. Please don't talk of truce.'

Jahaan Khan's stirring speech got the audience's blood racing. Najeeb was thrilled. That was when Hafeez Rahmat Khan stood up to voice his thoughts. He listed out the benefits of a truce. Najeeb was livid. He sprang to his feet and screamed, 'Aalam-panaah, please first investigate why this old fogey wants to toss this stone of truce into the machine.

On one side of his property is the land of the Jaats, while on the other is the region of that sinner Govind Bundele. Clearly, it is to keep his own stomach full that this selfish man wants to obstruct the path of Islam.'

The Rohilla-Pathans created an uproar. As Hafeez Rahmat Khan sat down despondently, Najeeb sprang up again. Qibla-e-aalam, truce? The question uppermost in the minds of all the Afghan-Rohillas is, why truce? Truce with those Margatthas? Truce with this most dangerous set of people? Truce with those satans who washed their filthy horses on the sacred banks of the Attock river and polluted its water? People who assaulted the provinces of Chittod, Dwarka and Gujarat, and promptly tied them to their apron strings? Whose horses go rampaging into the hills of Damau and Kumaon? Who have taken into their control pilgrimages like Kashi, Badrikeshwar, Prayag, Gaya, and are plotting to raze the mosques in those regions to the ground? Aalam-panaah, Delhi, the seat of the empire, is a sacred place, and that satan Bhau had the temerity to smash the throne with a sledge-hammer!'

There were tears flowing from Najeeb's eyes as he sobbed aloud with a few hiccups thrown in. But his spiel had the desired effect. The Afghans were overwrought.

Najeeb wiped his tears, got his voice under control, and resumed, 'Aalam-panaah, if there has been any impertinence on my part, I seek forgiveness, but I shall tell you what the ultimate mission of these Margatthas is. Their dirty intention is to rock your very seat, to overthrow the throne at Kandahar itself, bring everything under a single umbrella, and ride their horses across the sky and the earth.'

'Well, we will see about that when they come visiting Kandahar,' laughed Abdali.

'Aalam-panaah, now that it is caught in a trap, this community will happily swear to all kinds of amity. This talk of truce appears to some like a colourful silken rope; but even if the rope is of silk, the knot on it is that of the gallows. One false step, and the knot will tighten around our neck and our tongue will leap out a span. Jahaan-panaah, all of the south has assembled here, and now is the time to tear apart and pound to a paste this arrogant, treacherous band of robbers. It is very rarely that an opportunity such as this presents itself to Islam. This is the time to grind these sons of Satan to dust.'

Abdali sat for a while with his eyes closed, then began in a measured tone, 'Listening to Ghazi Jahaan Khan and Najeeb would surely have provided succour to all of us here. I thank Allah for having given me the companionship of such valiant warriors of Islam as them. May every soldier's heart be filled with the zest, the passion they shares. But friends, an army does not survive on mere rhetoric. It's only for propping up Islam that we have been battling against unfavourable climates for the past two years. I have already snatched land from the possession of the Margatthas and handed it over to the Rohilla-Pathans. Yet, we have never received the provisions that we have wanted, and the quantity in which we have wanted it from the Rohillas. The Margatthas have been pushed to dire straits, they are famished, and yet they are ready to do battle. Crossing swords with such a resilient enemy needs strong wrists. Strong wrists come from a regular supply of food for the army. My insistence on this account makes the Rohillas groan and complain. This attitude of the Rohillas and the climate of this country have together stretched my patience to the limit, and I cannot take it anymore. My administration of Kandahar will gain nothing at all with the victories and defeats of these monkeys from the Deccan. By the grace of Parvardigaar, my throne remains intact. It's only for the sake of Islam that I have been battling these storms and suffering these inconveniences.'

'Nothing but jihad! Nothing but jihad! Aah! Wonderful!' Qazi Idris said, eyes filling up with tears. 'Oh Aalam-panaah, how sacred these words are! Nothing but jihad! Stay faithful to these words. Your Kabul-Kandahar is not beholden to the Rohillas for its sustenance. Oh badshah, the merits of Islam are great! Your brothers-in-religion, the Rohillas went to your door for help when the harassment of the Maratha infidels became too much for them to bear. If, such a great shahenshah of the Afghans, despite possessing such strength, does not reach out to help his brotherhood, he will have to answer in the court of Allah.'

Shah Waliullah Saheb picked up Idris's theme. His voice boomed like gongs being struck. 'O Aalam-panaah, doubt Qazi Idris's words at your own peril. When you ascended the throne, you took upon yourself the title of 'Durrani', which means the emperor of emperors. The very title of Durrani should be a refuge for Islam all across the world. Who else has the power left today to run to the defence of Islam except yourself and this poor Najeeb? When you summoned me four years back, I had alerted you to the danger that looms over Islam in Hindustan. The Jaats, Sikhs and the Marathas have let loose a reign of terror in this land, and if, under these circumstances, you shoo our brave jihadis away, at whose door then should they go with their begging bowl? O great crusader of Islam, pick up your sword in defence of Islam, and Allah will take care of your kingdom. Remember the great emperor Nadir Shah, who fretted night and day over his empire. He was your preceptor, wasn't he? At the tap of his horse's hooves, the frontiers of ten countries would shrink in fear, their thrones would rock, their capital cities would stand on their heads ... What was his end like? In one night, all of his grandeur turned to dust, didn't it? Remember, badshah, the world is perishable!'

The entire gathering was shaken at the declamations of Qazi Idris and Shah Waliullah. One chieftain after another stood up, thumped his chest and declared, 'What the qazi says is right. What Shah Waliullah Saheb says is the truth. O badshah, we will starve, but we will not abandon jihad. We shall die fighting on the battlefield for the sake of our brothers in Islam.'

Abdali's choices had disappeared. In a voice thick with emotion, he said, 'No talks of truce from today onwards. Let's sing the song of battle from here on.'

⁕

As they sat eating together, Naro Shankar asked Holkar chieftain Parashar Dadaji, 'Just the other day, I dispatched a hundred-and-ten thousand through Krishnarao Ballal. The money would just about have reached Bhausaheb. How come, then, he sent you over here in such a hurry?'

'What are you saying?' Parashar's hand froze mid-way to his mouth. 'Not a dime has reached there. They are in dire straits. I am not talking off the top of my head; the enemy's camp and our camp together have hundreds of thousands of people trapped in confrontation with each other. It's like a pair of lions growling and fainting and swaying for a leap against each other. Nobody in living memory has seen a war like this; it could well be another Mahabharat. The gods of those times may not have felt the pangs of hunger, but today, men are frantic from starvation. Men, animals, garbage, the stink of faeces and urine, human and animal corpses and skeletons scattered everywhere—it is a scene out of hell. It is after a long long time that I am sitting here in comfort, eating such delicious food, a complete meal, the kind of food that even the chieftains back in the camp can only dream of. That is why Bhau has sent me in such a hurry. Whatever can be procured will be worth its weight in gold.'

'All right. There is one-hundred-and-fifty thousand left out of what Govindpant had deposited with us, you may carry it with you. I would have sent the bags a couple of days back, but I wasn't sure whether the passage would be safe enough. Getting waylaid is the last thing we would want during times of such shortage. What is the route like now?'

'We had set off from Panipat late in the night a couple of days back. Noticed four small enemy squads and gangs of their orphans here and there till Ganor in the south. The way seems fairly clear, at least as of now. The enemy is about fifteen miles away along the riverside. Let me utilize this opportunity and quickly shift these funds to Panipat.'

'See, I have handed the funds over to you now, and I am free Bhausaheb's accounting is perfect, not a dime here or there. It's not for nothing that your Subhedar calls Bhau the guardian snake of the Peshwa treasury.

Both Naropant and Parashar laughed heartily. They then got up, washed their hands and sat back for some more chatting over paan and betel-nuts. The topic of Govindpant came up, how he finally met his end. Parashar then suddenly got up, prompting Naro Shankar to remark, 'What's the hurry? Rest for an hour or so!'

'I have to put the night to use and reach Panipat by morning. Bhau would be waiting. The slightest delay, and I would have to give explanations.'

'In that case, you'd better set off.'

Three hundred broad-backed horses stood snorting and shivering in front of Naro Shankar's manor. Even before the chieftains had finished with their meals, the clerks had given five hundred rupeesto each of the horsemen. The coins had been knotted up in a big kerchief, which the horsemen had tied round their waists, as a cowherd ties bread, and wound more cloth round it for added security. Not satisfied with that, they had also turned the end of their dhotis over it. That would ensure that not a single coin had any chance of slipping out.

Naropant bid Parashar Dadaji and his band of horsemen goodbye, and they rode out of Delhi with the battle cry of 'Har Har Mahadev'.

ॐ

Parashar Dadaji and his fellow riders, who had set off from Delhi in the afternoon, moved at a brisk pace and reached the vicinity of Sonipat by sunset. They dismounted at an inn outside the town for food and fodder. One hour of rest, and they were off again. Two hours later, the cold Yamuna air began to make its presence felt. Ears, fingers and toes began turning numb. The horses were pulled to a stop, and the men pulled out the warm blankets tucked in their saddlebags. They wrapped the blankets round their heads, undid the belts round their waists and tied them over the blankets. The blanket round the ears was similarly secured, thus blocking the wind. There was nothing, however, they could do to secure their arms and legs from being chewed to the bone by the chill. The horses ran on through the icy air, kicking up dust with their hooves as dogs do when trying to limber up against the cold. As they cut through the pitch dark, they had broken into sweat on account of the sheer exercise their muscles were getting.

They reached Ganor by midnight. 'Panipat not too far away now,' was the thought in their minds as they heaved a sigh of relief and pulled their horses to a stop. One more hour of rest, and they were off for their final lap. Dawn wasn't too far away; the heaths were blanketed in thick fog. One-and-a-half days of continuous riding had drained the animals; their knees, thighs and ankles had begun to turn stiff. Their speed had slackened and their gallop had begun to lose its rhythm. Luckily Panipat was now barely a few miles away. Even if they were to doze off on horseback, the riders knew that the animals would make it on their own to the camp. All night through, they had been straining every nerve in their body. Hopping in their saddles in time with their steeds had tied their guts into knots and made their spine ache at every vertebra. On top of it all was the bitter, biting, relentless wind stabbing at them from all sides, turning them numb in head, heart and body. The blankets did keep their torsos warm, but tthe mist in the air had turned everything damp: their blankets, their fingers, their stirrups, and the feet locked in them.

The horses were now cantering more than galloping. A number of the riders were nodding their heads in a semi-snooze, shrinking their bodies as much as they could as they cut through the thick fog. Dawn had just begun to break as this one-hundred-and-fifty thousand worth of treasure went floating through the white cloud. Soon they came upon fires twinkling at them through the haze. 'Ah, Lord Vitthala! You've seen us through! Home at last!' The horses headed straight for the fire and came to a halt when close enough. The riders jumped off their backs and scurried towards the fire on stiff legs. They spread their arms wide to gather all the warmth they could collect and instantly felt better. A bunch of these horsemen crowded around a fire and asked each other, 'Whose camp could this be?'

'This has to be Ibrahim Khan's, who else's?' responded a Muslim soldier.

Relieved, they opened themselves up yet more to the flames. That was when they heard the war cry of 'Allah! Allah!' that froze their blood. The entire camp had suddenly woken up with a jolt. The Maratha men leapt towards their horses with the cry of 'It's been a mistake! Run! Run!' 'We've walked into the enemy camp!'

But they were surrounded by Afghan-Rohilla soldiers in no time. It was as if a spark had fallen upon a stack of dynamite, setting up a chain of explosions as one stack lit the next one. Some felt the blade penetrate through their back as they leapt for their horses, others lost their heads to the well-aimed swings of Afghan swords. Horses were blocked mid-stride and their riders pulled down to be hacked to pieces.

An Afghan soldier located the money tied round his victim's waist. 'Don't let even one of them escape!' he yelled out to his colleagues. 'These rogues are loaded with money! Money going to that rascal Bhau, surely!'

Afghan swords swung with greater zest. Heads started tumbling and bodies were hacked. There were a few whose horses had some juice left in them; they made use of the haze and disappeared into the mist. But such lucky ones could be counted on the fingers.

The sun rose, and by and by the mist lifted. Within a radius of fifty or sixty feet were scattered almost three hundred horribly mutilated corpses. 'Bhau's treasure looted!' was the cry everywhere and victory bugles were blown. The village of Panipat, barely a loud shout away, heard with horror the noise of the rambunctious celebrations in Abdali's camp.

Abdali was noted for dispensing instant punishment at any sign of indiscipline, which would be commensurate with the gravity of the offence. He wouldn't hesitate a moment before sending steel rods up one nostril and out another, even beheading in public. But heartless as he was at chastising, he was equally celebrated for his munificence. When he was pleased, he would address his soldiers with pride and say, 'You are partners in my glory and grandeur. I am one of you. It's on the strength of your sword that I have managed to travel so far.' Today, he was particularly pleased.

It was only the previous evening that he had got his camp at the riverbank near Bapauli pulled out. In the darkness of the night, he had moved eight miles to the west and planted himself bang alongside the road to Delhi. He had then planted pickets around the imperial highway, and caught the Marathas in a trap. This was his third change of campsite. He had erected his tents by moving a little behind the first site, which he had abandoned on account of the stench that had settled in there. He had now parked himself just beyond the village Shiva, and his base spread across four miles right up to Saimla. His horses now roamed around from Risalu and Rasulpur up to the edge of Ugrakhedi.

At the front end of the camp, Abdali's chief of artillery Rehman Khan Barakzai was busy mounting the cannons on their platforms, while Abdali, standing next to him astride his horse, had his eyes fixed on Panipat, which could be seen a little distance away. 'Aalam-panaah,' Rehman Khan said, 'have a look at how this cannon has been mounted.' Abdali dismounted and began examining the 'Bangiyawali', the pride of his artillery division, a massive fourteen-and-a-half foot cannon with a mouth that measured nine-and-a-half inches. It had been cast out of molten copper and zinc at Baaroodkhana, an armaments factory that Abdali had set up in Kandahar. When Bangiyawali was being poured into its mould, Abdali had spent the entire night at the workshop in the company of his blacksmiths. This one single cannon had helped him turn to dust the bastions of many forts. Alongside Bangiyawali were mounted 'Lahori' and 'Taqdeer'. After finishing the inspection of his cannons, the emperor stood to one side, looked towards Panipat and said, 'Rehman, keep ready. Those Margatthas there are very proud of Ibrahim Khan's cannons. Ours should blow to smithereens their pride.'

'That they will, huzoor!' Having said this, Rehman Barakzai sidled up to the emperor and stood by him throwing surreptitious, sidelong glances at the master, as if he were priming himself up to say something. Gathering his courage, he swallowed hard and ventured, 'Please forgive my impertinence, Aalam-panaah, but your lordship just talked about the Maratha artillery. But more than their cannons, it is their chief of artillery Ibrahim Khan that has the greater firepower in him. A fearless soldier like him should have been in our army.'

'Shouldn't this thought occur to an intelligent man like him?' Abdali replied. 'How many times I have sent my agents to him! Reminded him of the Islamic seed of which he is the product! Admonished him to be true to his faith, invited him to become a chieftain of the Kandahar empire, but that unfortunate fool talks of loyalties.'

'Aalam-panaah, our fate is on the ascendance; which is why Bhau's treasure walked into our camp without even being invited this morning. Those hapless Margatthas had no idea that we had suddenly changed our campsite.'

'Quite true, Rehman; it's all Allah's benevolence, what else?'

'The Margatthas are going to flee in the next day or two. The news that has begun to arrive is that they are desperate for food.'

'Rehman, it irritates me to hear the artillery chief of our army to talk in such a childish manner,' Abdali said with asperity. 'Rehman, if fleeing had been their intention, the opportunities were always there; but that Maratha Bhau is made of very tough stuff. He is obstinate and he is proud. Such men would rather set fire to themselves than abandon their posts. I have seen many enemies and many wars, but this war has a character of its own. Only Allah knows how it is going to end. Let's not fool ourselves with delusions of certain victory. Let's stay alert.'

The sun had gone well up, and the mist that had lain hugging the ground had begun to melt. Bhausaheb, Ibrahim Khan, Shamsher Bahadur and Yashwantrao Pawar were riding around the camp, inspecting the security arrangements of the morning shift. Bhausaheb's horse, Chandrasen walked with a strut as it crossed the cannons mounted at the mouth of the trench. As Bhausaheb went past the bigger cannons—Mahakali, Sinhgadh, Mahalakshmi on one side and Varna on the other, all of Maratha land flashed before his mind's eye. Bhau began to miss his homeland and felt restless and distraught.

Bhausaheb's eyes turned south. What met his eyes caused him to stiffen and cry out, 'Khan Saheb, what's this I see?'

'Huzoor, I thought you would have heard of the enemy once again raising blockades on the Delhi highway.'

'Ibrahim, I know well enough when the enemy has advanced and how. Why look so far? See here in front, just a couple of miles away, the enemy's men and animals are roaming around with such abandon. How can you watch all this so passively?'

'So what would you have me do, huzoor?'

'What do you mean, 'What do I do?' Set those cannons on fire! If today the enemy doesn't care about being seen within a couple of miles, tomorrow he will turn brazen enough to walk into my pavilion!'

Ibrahim Khan's eyes turned moist. He asked Bhausaheb in a hoarse voice, 'Huzoor, how can we keep firing our cannons at every little incitement? Shouldn't we be conserving our gunpowder?'

The response stunned Bhau as if a cannon ball had fallen upon him. He rammed his horse into Ibrahim Khan's, held him by the shoulders and shook him as he said, 'What do you mean by conserving, Khan Saheb? Speak! How much ammunition have we still got? We couldn't have run out of it, could we?'

'No, huzoor, we haven't run out of it yet, but we now need to use it with discretion. When Abdali comes marching upon us, we have enough to last for a day. I have alerted you often enough about our supply of gunpowder steadily running out. Your lordship had even sent messages to Govindpant to that effect!'

Bhausaheb felt a constriction in his chest. In a heavy voice he responded, 'The supplier of gunpowder has returned to his Maker, and left behind sparks of vengeance. If we have to find a way out of this catastrophe, we now need every one of our bodies to pulsate like an ammunition dump.' He moved a little distance, stopped and turned round to observe the tense faces of his men. The distressing news had rattled them all. Bhausaheb's own heart had disintegrated like a lump of sod in water. There was turmoil inside him, but with superhuman effort, he kept the distress from showing on his face; what showed was the same resoluteness, the same determination to ride into the storm without flinching.

He entered his pavilion and took in hand some papers that Nana Purandare had placed before him. When he noticed Jankoji Shinde and Vishwasrao sitting there, his face suddenly turned stern. There was a rare harshness in his voice as he addressed them, 'What have you two been up to? What kind of letter did you send to the Peshwa yesterday?'

The two turned red in the face. Bhausaheb turned his attention towards the papers in his hand, which mostly dealt with the stock in hand of grains and fodder. Vishwasrao had turned nervous and fidgety; he couldn't think of another time when Bhausaheb had turned so angry at him. But what was there to get so upset about in what had he written? He could recollect every word of what he had written to his father:

> ... There couldn't be anybody as proud, resilient and firm as Bhausaheb kaka since Shivaji and Bajirao. Nobody would have seen such a person as him. The true worth of a diamond becomes evident only after it is rubbed against a grind-stone; so it is with kaka; ... every moment spent in Panipat can stand witness to the fact. Father, you will not be able to imagine, sitting thousands of miles away in Shaniwarwada, what kind of calamity has descended upon our army. Perhaps Kakasaheb, proud as he is, would not have written much to you about it, but both men and animals seem to be at the point of forgetting that there is something called food. They are dying of starvation. Their masters' state is no different. People have begun to stuff themselves with mere water to create a delusory sense of fullness. You can entertain hopes of meeting us in this world only if you dispatch a force of fifty thousand men and a billion rupees in cash. Father, you have—and may continue to have—any number of sons like me, but you will never have a brother like Bhau again, even after doing good deeds across seven lives.

Keeping aside the papers in his hand, Bhau rested his eyes on Vishwasrao and snapped, 'Rao Saheb, who has been advising you to write such ridiculous letters to the Peshwa? The battlefield is pumping fear into your heart, is it? Afraid for your life? If you are getting so terrified at the thought of battle, I can easily put five or ten thousand soldiers at your disposal, with whom you can set off for home.'

Vishwasrao's broke down. 'Kakasaheb, you seem to forget that it's under your tutelage that I have grown from a child to man. I am surely not such a coward as to abandon you, turn my back on the battlefield and flee. I am not a chicken-hearted flincher. I shall spill my blood and die fighting in this battlefield alongside you. I shall accept both life and death with equal joy as long as I can be by your side, Bhaukaka!'

'Why, then, did you write that letter at all?' roared Bhausaheb.

Jankoji, who had been hearing this exchange mutely, could hold his peace no longer. 'Why are you blaming Rao, Kakasaheb?' he broke in. 'When circumstances turn tough, who should a person turn to if not to his father? Besides, our writing this letter does not mark us out as cowards! We shall grind our bones to dust in this soil, Kakasaheb, but not get off the enemy's back. We shall hold death at bay with one hand as we strangle the enemy to death with the other. We shall die only after we have first dispatched him.'

Jankoji's words went straight and pierced Bhau in the heart. Not being able to trust his voice, he signalled the boys to come closer and placed his arms round their shoulders. Swallowing a couple of times, he finally said, 'Boys, where did you learn this wisdom? Even before the trace of downs on your upper lip has turned dark, how did you acquire the strength for such determination and sacrifice? Just the sight of you strapping young lads has increased my courage manifold, my pride in the Marathi soil that nourished you has doubled.... Forgive me for the harsh words I used, and don't let it hurt you. What upset me is something really quite different. Who am I, Rao, to stop a son from writing to his father? But we have definite information that it is only a rare letter that escapes from the net that the enemy has spread; all the rest of them get caught in the trap and become a source of information, letting him know in detail how we are doing here. Here you are, writing in the innocence of your heart to your father, but when the letters land in his hand, you can imagine what calamity can befall us. However hungry, harried and broken we may be, what the enemy should see is only our blazing eyes, our undimmed courage and our puffed out chests It is not as if all matters are decided only by the state of one's stomach. We can pull the cart of our mission across with only resilience and courage.'

Both Jankoji and Vishwasrao left for their regiments with Bhausaheb's words ringing in their hearts. Bhausaheb returned to his account books and got so lost in work that he did not realize that it was a few hours since noon had come and gone. A few assistants sat with him, coming up with whatever information he required. That was when an usher came running in and announced, 'Shrimant, Parvatibai saheb is on her way here.'

'What? She? Here?'

'That's right, Shrimant!'

The assistants got up with a start and discreetly stepped out of the tent. Parvatibai entered, balancing a plate in her hand, covered with the end of her saree. She signalled to her maid to leave the tent as Bhausaheb said, 'What a surprise, this! What's that you've brought me?'

'Your lunch,' she said, faking irritation.

'Lunch? And here?' he laughed. 'This is not the army mess; it is the war-room of the commander-in-chief.'

'Let the commander-in-chief ask his own heart: who has erased the dividing lines between the private chambers, the war-room, the army mess and everything else? You or I? Once his lordship sinks into this pit called the war, he completely forgets that there are other important things in this world!'

Bhausaheb laughed and sat down to eat. He paused and looked around to ensure they were alone, and then said, 'Hey, listen, you caught me by my hand and dragged me to wash my hands, didn't you? Well, then, how about using those beautiful hands to feed me a mouthful?'

Parvatibai turned red as a beetroot, tucked a corner of her pallu into her mouth and looked down shyly. Love and mischief played on Bhausaheb's face, as she slowly reached for the plate, rolled up a morsel and, without lifting her eyes, fed it to her husband. As one morsel followed another, and Parvatibai's shyness went away, she looked up and remarked, 'If anyone sees us indulging in this madness, what will they think about your lordship?'

Bhausaheb laughed with abandon and said, 'In the midst of cannon-fire and war bugles, I really do forget to have my meals. And the mistress of the house has come over today to feed her husband morsel by morsel ... Who knows whether this moment will ever return in our lives!'

Parvatibai had suddenly giggled shyly to herself.

'What is it?' Bhausaheb asked.

'Oh, nothing. Just remembered an event from long ago.'

'What event?'

'Do you remember the first Diwali festival for which your lordship had come to Penn? When we were in one of the top-floor rooms of the palace, and when you found no one was around, you had fed me a with your own hands?' She began to giggle as she finished. Bhausaheb also joined with a loud guffaw and said, 'Oh, yes. So how about a repeat performance?' So saying, he fed her a morsel, then another, and yet another, till Parvatibai could not hold her giggles. She blocked the next one with her hand across her mouth and said, 'I feel as if I am floating in the clouds.'

'Really?'

'Who knows if we'll ever have this moment together again?' Parvatibai bit her tongue as soon as the words left her mouth. It was as if an arrow had shot off accidentally and gone and pierced her heart. She burst into tears. Bhausaheb wiped her tears, and deftly changing the subject, he said, 'You remember how, when we were leaving Kunjpura for Panipat, you had sat in the canopy with a naked sword in your hand? I was so thrilled at the sight.'

'Yes, and if ever the time comes, I shall not merely carry the sword in my hand, I shall use it too!'

'Parvati, while you were at Shaniwarwada, you were so quiet. But now, another side of you has emerged from beneath your quietude in this war.'

'And I have experienced every bit of your glory at every step here on the soil of Panipat. What courage, what determination, what passion races through your veins!'

'What choice have I been left with, Parvati? With us Marathas, the custom is never to withdraw once the commitment is made. But I don't know why, Parvati, the riddle of this soil is beyond me. The traitors who sold the head of Santaji—the man who sliced off the emperor's crest—to the enemy in the hope of a base reward had sprung from the same soil too! The Red Fort was won with such sacrifice in blood, and there are people here and now, who were quite willing to hand it over to a pack of rogues for the reward of a mere hundred or hundred and fifty thousand rupees! Sometimes, as I sit here alone, thinking, I feel that this Panipat campaign is one of its kind: it is the coming together of the best and the worst aspects of the Maratha soil. Here are men who stand intrepid against the enemy even on empty stomach. The enemy has encircled us like the avenging gods, but has it stopped our internal bickering and nepotism? Our Maratha soil is full of contradictions. If the stones can be separated, this soil can be used to erect massive temples to the Gods of Victory, and yet, sometimes, these stones mixed up in the soil are so powerful that they can turn everything to dust.'

Parvatibai departed, and within a matter of minutes, Manaji Paigude, Darekar, Appaji Jadhavrao, Shamsher Bahadur and a few other leaders walked in. Sardar Darekar began, 'Shrimant, the enemy has penned us.'

'Shrimant,' added Paigude, 'till this day, we at least had the western jungle of brambles open to us for sneaking in and out; but Abdali has now gone and planted his Afghan pickets there too.'

'What are you saying?'

'Absolutely, Shrimant! I saw it with my own eyes.' Appaji Jadhavrao said, 'Shrimant, we are passing through terrible times. When our squads of banjaras, pendharis and lamhan set out to fetch fodder, they are immediately attacked by Shah Pasand Khan's troops and hacked on the spot.'

'But aren't they going under the protection of our own soldiers?' Bhausaheb queried.

'Bhausaheb, the enemy troops are unhampered and free, while our troops have to do the dual duty of minding the provisions along with fighting the enemy.'

Bhausaheb called over Nana Purandare and asked, 'Nana, how much fodder do we still have?'

'It is quite sufficient, Shrimant. It's all heaped up on the other side of Chandani Bagh. A good two hundred thousand bales stacked up. Quite sufficient.'

'You call that sufficient, Nana?' Bhausaheb raised his voice in frustration. 'But then, how can you be blamed? When were you ever required to look after cattle? Sixty or seventy thousand animals and two hundred thousand bales! Even if it is doled out with the greatest discretion, it won't last us beyond four days! What are we to do after that?'

Shamsher, who had sat silent all this while, spoke up, 'Bhausaheb, some thirty or forty thousand bales can be arranged to tide over our immediate needs.'

'How? Where from?'

'We received a message from Antaji Mankeshwar some while ago. The cattle grazers, along with the banjaras and our own men, have been reaching out to as far-out places as Asad, Karnal and Ganoha, and have managed to gather thirty or forty thousand bales of fodder in a little-known village in the east. Antaji has been able to requisition forty to fifty bullock and camel carts. They are now worried about safely delivering them to us, and have asked for a large, well-armed force as escorts.'

'Excellent news! Send instructions to Malharbaba and Jankoji. They have the manpower to ensure the delivery of this stock to the camp.'

Bhausaheb immediately met both Malharbaba and Jankoji. Malharbaba smoothed his grey side-burns, twirled his thick moustache and said, 'I'll set off immediately to escort all that provision here. Let's see who is feeling suicidal enough to stand in my way.'

The Holkar and Shinde contingents of five thousand horsemen each set off from their respective bases. As they were exiting Panipat on the north, they came upon Vitthalrao Vinchurkar's base, where they saw Vitthalrao sitting in consultation with someone. Malharbaba rode up to him, patted the rump of his horse and said, 'Out with a little tobacco, Vitthalpant.'

'Where are you off to, Malhari?'

'A small hunt. The tongue has been forgetting the taste, so I go looking for something worthwhile.'

As he rubbed tobacco in the hollow of his palm, he sent a cursory glance around Vinchurkar's pavilion. When he noticed upwards of a couple of thousand Afghans loitering around, he enquired with a laugh, 'Who are these new recruits?'

'Afghan boys from Kunjpura, who have sought shelter under me. They slog here for their daily bread. Where else could they go?'

'Be careful, Vitthalpant. When matters come to the crunch, you won't know whether these bastards are fighting for you or for the enemy!'

'Yes, I'll have to do something about that; blindfold them or some such thing. But where are you off to in such a hurry?'

'Off to fetch fodder.'

'Malharbaba, the enemy has spread out all over in this area.'

'Who cares, Vitthala?' Malharrao responded, giving his luxuriant moustache another twirl. While capturing the Wasai fort, it was I who set alight the fuse in that difficult tunnel. Bhau's father, Chimajiappa, was witness to it. Just watch me tame these bastards.'

⁂

Around dusk time, the horses were cutting their way to the north. Mahlarrao had only recently entered his sixty-seventh year, but a look at his still strong, well-built body would not have suggested anything more than fifty; blood still raced through his veins with vigour. When he rode his horse, he would bounce on the saddle with amazing vitality; it was the horse that was tested while handling its rider's weight and balance rather than the other way round. As it was turning dark, a couple of hundred enemy soldiers sprang upon them, but the Holkar force annihilated them as easily as pulling weeds out from the fence.

By dinnertime, Shinde-Holkar forces had reached Antaji Mankeshwar's contingent. Antaji had kept forty bullock and camel carts loaded with fodder, all tied up and ready to move. Everybody was of the opinion that they should set off on their return journey immediately. At a signal from Malharbaba, the wheels began to move with painful creaks and the caravan was on its way. Torch-bearers were distributed along the length of the caravan. The Holkars had brought the number of torches down to a bare minimum. Wherever the terrain was difficult, a few torch-bearers would stay behind to light the way for the passing carts till such time as the next torch-bearers reached them, and then race forward to their earlier positions. When the terrain turned flat, the torches would be extinguished so as to prevent any sudden and unexpected raid from the enemy. The Holkar-Shinde men rode on both sides of the caravan with swords unsheathed. The banjaras and the pendharis who had been reduced to trembling wrecks on account of the unceasing assaults of the enemy had suddenly regained their courage, and now walked with their heads up between their armed escorts. With torches and hurricane-lamps appearing and disappearing, the caravan moved on, cutting its way through the biting cold and the darkness, the creak of the wheels piercing through the night air and reaching across surprisingly long distances.

Panipat was now eight miles away. The path moved along the Yamuna, and as their home patch neared, the horses and men began to move more confidently and zestfully. The sods on the riverbank that came under the horses' hooves would roll into the water and sink with a plonk. Just then, two contingents of the enemy forces swooped down upon them like a kite descending upon a gaggle of chicks. Shah Pasand Khan was in the lead. 'Kill! Kill the Marathas!' he screamed as he leapt forward. The Shinde-Holkar men backed off a little bit at this sudden assault, and then the conflict began. Malharrao shouted to the men, 'Boys, you move on with the caravan! I'll handle these bastards!'

The creak of the cartwheels suddenly gained urgency as the animals were goaded into greater speed. Shah Pasand Khan bucked his men to block the progress of the carts as the Maratha men came back with a heavy counter-assault. The nomads were scurrying as fast as they could to stay out of the swords' way.

Old Malharbaba was as charged up as an elephant. 'Jai Malhar!' he roared, as he swung his sword and sent enemy heads flying off their shoulders. The old man's energy was infectious. Jankoji took inspiration and got into the midst of the enemy with murderous intent. The cart-track began to get liberally sprinkled with blood. The combined Shinde-Holkar forces swung their weapons with months of pent-up fury, bringing the enemy down like sitting ducks. When Shah Pasand noticed the scales tilting against him, he thought it prudent to get his forces to melt into the night. In a short while, the enemy had vanished.

As the Maratha men stood regaining their breath and mopping the blood off their shirt-fronts, the fleeing Shah Pasand Khan made his final dastardly move. As he ran, he tossed a few flaming torches towards the fodder-laden carts that brought the rear. One of them found its mark and set the dry stalks alight. Soon, the entire cart had risen up in flames. Its blaze spread and embraced two of the nearest carts. The entire expanse of the river flowing alongside dazzled in the light.

'Wait!' screamed Malharrao as he raced towards the flaming carts. When he reached the nearest one, he held it by the yoke by sheer animal force and yelled, 'Cut the ropes of the animals!' The men leapt in and hacked the ropes away. 'Now push these carts into the river!' The cart was rolled into water, where the fire fizzled out. In a little while, the other blazing carts were also pushed into the water. Only one pair of bullocks, however, could be saved.

It was around midnight when the caravan reached Panipat. Bhausaheb had been waiting in the office, with the instructions that Malharbaba should meet him immediately on returning. As the two chieftains headed towards the pavilion, Malharbaba told Jankoji, 'Janko, don't tell Bhausaheb about the burnt carts.'

'But concealing it from Shrimant means—'

'Doesn't he have enough to worry about? Why add another load?'

Malharrao entered the pavilion, and Bhausaheb said, 'Come, come, Kakasaheb! Has the fodder arrived?'

'Yes, Bhau, arrived safely.'

'Why don't you take a seat, Kakasaheb? Where should we stock it? I don't think we should heap it on top of the stock that lies in Chandani Bagh. If another place—'

'I've already made arrangements. I've told them to off-load today's consignment near Devi Lake.'

Bhausaheb sat silent for a little while before he resumed, 'Kakasaheb, I have some bad news for you.'

'What's it, son?'

'Your sardar Parashar Dadaji, who had gone to fetch funds from Delhi, just about managed to come back alive.'

'What are you saying, Bhau?'

'Yes, Kakasaheb. Not knowing where they were going in the dawn mist, our men rode into the enemy camp by mistake. They had no idea that the enemy had changed bases the previous evening. Some three or four hundred of our men were slaughtered and two hundred thousand worth of treasure was lost.'

'Our world seems to be going up in flames.'

'Yes, Kakasaheb. We just have to fight against it together!'

Their conversation went on till late into the night. It was with heavy steps that Bhausaheb finally made his way towards his private quarters. He had no idea when his eyes finally closed and he sank into sleep.

Suddenly, a loud uproar woke him up. The noise appeared to be coming from a distance. Heavy-lidded, he heaved himself out of his bed and rushed out. 'What's happened?' he asked the guard outside.

'Shrimant, it seems that our heaps of hay stored in the Chandani Bagh area have caught fire!'

Bhausaheb felt as if a heavy ball of lead had suddenly formed in his stomach. He jumped atop his horse and set off towards the east. The giant tongues of fire and the billows chasing them into the sky could be seen from a long way off. In fact, all of Panipat around it was flash-lit and glittering in the night. It had never witnessed a sight as awe-inspiring as this.

Bhausaheb stood and watched. Two hundred thousand bales of hay rushing into the sky like offerings to the gods! Mammoth dragons—red and yellow and white—leaping from the earth with a mighty roar and consuming the dark firmament with fearsome energy! There was complete pandemonium everywhere. The heat that emanated from this conflagration was such that it wouldn't allow anybody to step anywhere within a couple of furlongs of the periphery. All that the men could do was hold on to their puny buckets of water and watch with awe and fear the dance of destruction. Their hopes were going up in smoke.

⚜

Abdali had had a red tent erected for himself just a little distance from his pavilion. From there he could ascertain what was happening in the Maratha camp about five miles away. He would sit there pulling on his hookah hour upon hour, and regale himself with the sight of the enemy forces writhing in agony.

Things were moving at a rapid pace. A force of five thousand fearsome Afghan soldiers had stood alert all night, as always, to rush across land and water at a sign from their master. With the day having dawned, they were now being systematically relieved from their vigil by the fresh morning contingent.

Abdali had risen early today and returned from his morning ride across the camp on his favourite horse. He had taken an early bath and offered his morning prayers in front of his tent. That done, he entered the tent where the Rohilla chieftains Dundey Khan, Atai Khan, Hafeez Rahmat Khan, Ahmad Bangash, Saadullah Khan and a few Afghan generals had gathered for an audience with him. They greeted him by sending a prayer to Allah for the long life of their emperor. Hafeez Rahmat Khan sat next to him, while the rest stood around. The conference began with Dundey Khan, Saadullah Khan and the others pleading, 'Aalam-panaah, this is the time. The Marathas' spirit is broken. Their army is starving. This is the time when we should spring upon them and crush them altogether. What reason have we got for the delay, Aalam-panaah?'

The emperor had eased himself into a comfortable position and was pulling on the hookah with great pleasure. After letting them finish with their entreaties, he shifted his weight on his seat and said, 'Now get this clear, all of you. Matters of war are well beyond your intellectual capacity. When I sit pulling on my hookah, strategizing, fixing my moves, working out my game plan, I do not like it when people try to barge in. As a poet sits in a trance composing his poems, so do I sit fine-tuning my strategies. Don't you dare shove your noses into this! When the time is ripe, watch how we bring in the trophy. Your job is to stand and watch, is that clear?'

Abdali's brusque response sent the Rohillas into a gloomy silence. The discontent on their faces was not something he missed noticing. He laughed out loud and continued, 'The Marathas are like a thorn that has buried itself in the heel of Hindustan. This is what your Najeeb says, doesn't he? But gentlemen, there are ways and ways of plucking the thorn out. Very often the thorn is a tiny, insignificant thing, and people begin attacking it with knives and needles, causing more pain to the heel than to the thorn itself. The thorn sits unmoved, while the foot swells to the size of a pumpkin. Some others use thinner, finer needles, and often, instead of easing the thorn out, these needles push it deeper inside. The pain only increases. Then there are some smart fellows who recommend the use of one thorn to remove another. The result? Even before the first one comes out, the second one breaks inside, and again, you have a foot the size of an elephant. The wise person here is the grandmother. She lets the little one go to sleep, brings home a leaf the size of a palm from the forest, warms it in a pan and ties it on the affected spot. The embedded thorn slips out towards the leaf during the night, and without bothering anybody, it comes right out. In the morning, nobody knows how it happened—not the leaf, not the heel, not even the thorn. So, gentlemen, this is the wisdom with which the thorn lodged in the heel of Hindustan has to be extracted.'

The emperor's reply put all at ease. He then turned to Shah Wali Khan and asked, 'What kind of arrangement has been made around the Margattha camp?'

'Jahaan-panaah, everything is in perfect order. Jahaan Khan's contingent has been patrolling the bank of the Yamuna with six thousand men, smashing any efforts at reaching provisions to the enemy. Our lion Shah Pasand Khan has been moving around with his six thousand men, destroying the region to the west of the Marathas. He has even begun killing the animals that come to the canal for a drink.'

'Anything else?'

'Jahaan-panaah, our Barkhurdar Khan has also been prowling around the Maratha camp with his men, slaughtering any person that stirs in and out of the camp. Just the other day, he ambushed a ten-thousand-strong contingent of the Marathas who were sneaking back from Dhulkota with some fodder, defeated them roundly and brought hundreds of their animals over to our base.'

'Excellent.'

After this little conference, he called over his son Taimur, picked out a handful of horsemen from his slave cavalry, took a few trusted men from the slave regiment, and, thus, with a couple of hundred men around him, he rode for over fifty miles across the south of Panipat along an east-west axis. He came back to his red tent for lunch, and then stretched out to rest.

After finishing his dinner that night, he put on a warm jacket, picked up a naked sword, and with an escort of two hundred horsemen, he went riding out. His horse raced against the biting cold wind in the dim light of the star-lit sky. At a number of places, he encountered his men prowling around the Maratha camp. He rode deep inside from Ugrakhedi, from the lower end of Rajakhedi, along the black mango tree and from the direction of Gharaonda. His patrols now exercised complete control over the road to Kurukshetra and the Punjab, as also the imperial highway. Inspecting all these posts, Emperor Abdali moved southwards down the west of Panipat along the canal, observing every inch of the terrain with sharp eyes. All of Panipat had been completely encircled. The Maratha army had been trapped in a nut-cracker. A vagrant thought flitted through his mind of applying pressure and crushing the enemy right now, but he quickly drove it away. The nut was caught, of course, but it was a hard, resilient, unyielding nut, a nut that he feared could cause serious damage to the cracker. No, it was wiser to soften the nut a little more. It was a few hours past midnight now, and one could smell the dawn air closing in. This was the fourth day of the night vigil that he had begun, and it was now nearing its end. He began to gallop back towards his camp.

☙

Panipat had turned itself upside down in the darkness of the night; it did not sleep. The army's desperate state had shaken up the entire village. Dead or dying animals could be seen lying here and there. With the entire area denuded of trees now, there wasn't enough wood left even for a funeral pyre for the dying humans. Abandoning religious rituals, the soldiers had begun to dig pits in which to bury their dead. The clash of the two armies had left a lot of corpses scattered around; neither of the two armies had the courage to retrieve their dead from enemy strongholds. Besides, the strain imposed upon the living had transformed them into walking dead; bothering about the dead was a far cry.

Foxes would steal out of the jungles during the night and rip the flesh off the bones of the scattered corpses rotting in the open, after which the hyenas would arrive to crack the bones for whatever marrow they could extract. During the day, it was carnival time for kites and buzzards; they arrived in endless swarms to feast upon the dead and the dying. The flesh that lay unconsumed turned fetid, suffusing the air for miles around with an intolerable stink that made even the strongest of men retch and vomit. It was the misfortune of the Marathas that the wind too blew from the east to the west, heavily laden with the putrid stench of death. The diseased, pungent, malodorous air that drifted past the Maratha camp had gone and settled deep inside the hapless men and women, making even breathing a punishment. It was after two sleepless nights that somehow Bhausaheb tumbled into a nap, but he was jolted awake by horrible dreams. With her husband so distraught, Parvatibai too had no peace. As she lay with her head resting on his arm, a warm tear trickled down her cheek and rolled down his skin, scalding him, as it were, where it fell. He turned round, touched her cheek with the other hand and asked, 'Why do you cry, Parvati?'

'Your eyes have forgotten what sleep means.'

'I had a strange dream. I saw standing before me that bakul tree from Satara. It wasn't blooming as it always does. The buds had sunk their heads into the leaves in despair. Right under the tree stood Uma, looking very forlorn. Her eyes were streaming as she said, "Your lordship should take care of his health." What do I say, Parvati? I went a little farther beyond the tree, and my four children swam into sight—something that has never happened before! Two of yours and two of Uma's, all four of them mine! They came and put their arms round my legs, fixed their innocent little eyes on me and pleaded, "Father, why don't you have your meals, father, why have you stopped eating?"'

Bhausaheb's lips trembled, and he began to sob. Parvati gathered him into her arms. She ran her fingers through his hair, as if she were pacifying a child. Once the emotional outburst had subsided, Bhausaheb said, 'Parvati, as it happens, among our people, looking after the women and children of the household is considered the prime responsibility of the head of the family. In the army's rulebook, taking care of the women and children, the camp followers, the travelling pilgrims may be listed as unimportant work, but as the commander-in-chief here, I see it as my prime duty to ensure their comfort and security. Even now, in military terms, it is not at all late for me to gather my soldiers, launch a massive assault on the enemy and turn the tables on them, but for that I will have to abandon the non-combatants to fate, which neither my tradition allows nor my own conscience. If I hoist the flag of victory by exposing these women and children to the villainy of the Afghan rogues, will my homeland consider it as victory at all? Will they felicitate me or spit on my face? How do I say it, Parvati, but ... but ... these pilgrims, these camp followers, these women and children have ... have put manacles round my manly wrists. If I hadn't been carrying these chains, I would have leapt into the cauldron of war and burnt the enemy down, or gone up in flames myself.'

The cold this evening had scaled a new peak. The neighbouring regions had received heavy rainfall, it had been reported. Jereshastri lay next to the dying fire, a blanket wrapped tightly round his shivering body, an unsympathetic pillow under his head. As he lay staring gloomily at the starlit sky, he suddenly started. He had just seen a star fall. He got up and shook Punalkar awake. 'Up, up, Punalkar,' he cried hoarsely. 'Look what's happening!'

'Hmm? What? Whaat?' groaned Punalkar. 'Why are you waking me up?'

'Everything is going to blow apart, Joshibuva, why crib over the loss of sleep?'

'Why? What's the matter?'

'Look, look up there! I just saw a big, bright star shatter!'

'Did you, really?' Joshibuva was suddenly wide awake. 'Good lord! That's surely a sign! Pull out the horoscopes, quick!'

The two rummaged into their bags and extracted Bhausaheb's horoscope from it. They began examining it in the dim light of the cinders burning beside them. They had gone over the document many times over before, but in the light of this latest message from heaven, they did their calculations all over again. After Jereshastri and Punalkar had finished their arithmetic, Jereshastri placed a hand upon his heart and pronounced, 'I can say this on oath, I see nothing but death and destruction descending upon us. Punalkar, I have examined thousands of horoscopes in my life, but never has a more star-crossed, inauspicious document gone past my eyes.

'You shouldn't be using such words for Shrimant, Jereshastri!'

'Why shouldn't I, huh? Everybody is being sucked into this destruction, and I shouldn't speak? These are all sins from his previous birth, and now these are the returns.'

'Control yourself, Shastri—'

'What control? Whatever destiny has inscribed on the forehead is bound to happen, isn't it? Your good wishes and mine are not going to count for anything, are they? The sins of the previous birth have to be paid for in this one.'

'What rubbish! Just look at Bhau! Does he look like a person carrying the weight of sins from his previous life?'

'How can looks determine anything? Has anybody peeped into his previous life? Human bodies are infested with countless faults.'

'Well, let that be, Shastri, but tell me this: who did that star look like?'

'Who else but Bhausaheb? Bhausaheb, a 100 per cent!'

'Oh lord!'

All of a sudden, Jereshastri began to bawl like a child. Between sobs, he said, 'Joshibuva, sankranti, the zodiacal change in heavenly bodies! It is sankranti four days from now! Last year, in the village feast, what a royal treat had been served! And this year, it will be nothing but grief and starvation! The expiation of the sins of your previous life and mine! Today, lunch was altogether missing, and what we had for dinner hardly made for half a meal!'

'Jereshastri, if sankranti is really four days away, then our book of life is over!'

'How's that?'

'Shastribuva, sankranti has always been inauspicious for the Maratha community. It was on sankranti day last year that Dattaji of the Shindes was cut to pieces, wasn't he?'

'Well, yes, what you say is quite true!'

'Shastribuva, have you heard this news?'

'Which one?'

'Bhausaheb, it seems, wants to be able to make a lightning move upon the enemy, and for that he wants to leave all the pilgrims and camp-followers behind and move ahead with the army.'

'Just let him try ditching us! You think we will let him slip away? We will hold him by the legs. Tell him, we will, that he either takes us across or kills us, and then does what he wants with his battles!'

'Quite right! All this bluster! As if no Maratha warrior has fought battles before!'

As they lay chatting, they noticed a bunch of camp-followers approaching from behind. There were a few soldiers among them too. The unceasing draughts of bitterly cold wind were driving them witless, and they had set out in search of fuel. Fuel, however, was not to be had for love or money; the trees had been chopped off long ago. All that was now left to burn was their tents; but if that disappeared, where would they go for shelter? They were all in varying stages of starvation, some bad, others very bad. Some had chewed whatever leaves they could lay their hands on and downed them with water. The slicing wind on an empty stomach had reduced a number of them to near insanity. Since the area of Chandani Bagh and Black Mango lay in a state of devastation, they had formed into a bunch and set off to try their luck in the jungle of brambles in the west. It was just on the other side of the canal. Perhaps they would be able to bring some fuel back home.

As the group moved through the camp, others began to join them in ones and twos; till now it was a crowd of a good ten thousand marching towards the western edge of their settlement. As they neared the boundary, they were accosted by a chieftain of the patrolling contingent. 'Where are you fellows off to?' he growled.

'To fetch some fuel. This horrible cold won't let us live.'

'Do you have any idea that the enemy is lurking on the other side, baying for your blood?'

'Would it not be better to die with one stroke of the enemy sword, Sardar Saheb, than to freeze to death in this wind? Please do us this favour, saheb. Give us warmth, not obstruction. If you have to obstruct us, give us fuel then, give us warmth.'

The sardar mutely moved aside. The crowd advanced in big and small bunches, uncaring, unconscious of the thorns and grit that came under their feet, no food in their belly, no arms in their hands, in fact, not even adequate clothes on their bodies. Soon they got into the jungle. There were a few tufts of dry grass here and there upon which the men leapt like hungry cattle, uprooted it and began to lay it in a heap. They then struck a pair of flints and set the grass on fire. The quivering, shivering men began to crowd around it, heaving and pushing their way in.

⚛

Dawn had broken, but the darkness had yet to dissipate from the jungle. Shah Pasand Khan's men had taken position without revealing their presence, licking their lips as a wolf would at the sight of unattended sheep. Suddenly the air began to resonate with loud cries of 'Allah! Allah!' Shah Pasand's horsemen broke cover and descended on the emaciated, unarmed Marathas and swung their weapons in glee. Frantic cries of 'Arrey Vitthala!' set the jungle a tremble. The birds sat petrified on the trees, the leaves fluttered in terror, but there was no one around to call back, 'Hold on, I'm coming!' When they saw death lunging at them, the desperate men could think of doing nothing better than to embrace the nearest tree, making the slaughter so much easier for the executioner. The horizontal sword came swinging in and sent heads tumbling off shoulders with effortless ease. Only a few managed to escape the massacre; the rest of the ten thousand had found their warmth in heaven.

Shah Pasand Khan was overjoyed with the magnitude of the kill. He expressed the desire to have the emperor come over to witness the pools of blood that had gathered and the prodigious victory he had achieved. His men immediately got to work, dragging the corpses with their legs like the carcasses of animals and flinging them one on top of the other to raise heaps upon macabre heaps. Within no time at all, these mounds of headless men were shedding tears of blood.

※

The Maratha flags stood fluttering atop tents and pavilions against the biting dawn wind. Half-starved men rolled up in tight bundles lay inside their little tents. The animals lay rubbing their muzzles against the earth, all four of their legs folded under them, whisking their tails in the foolish hope of shooing away the cold. The guards on night duty were waiting with half-closed eyes for the sun to rise, which would bring their vigil to a close.

All of a sudden, the tents began to rock like lids on a boiling pot. The poles of the tents and pavilions, the flags atop them, the houses and shops of Panipat, even the remaining trees began to sway like drunken men. The men who had thus been shaken awake ran out of their tents, and the animals began to low in panic. Then, as suddenly as it had begun, the rocking ceased. Those who were awake immediately knew what had happened. 'It was an earthquake!' Once the word spread, everyone had abandoned sleep and gathered in a hundred groups to talk.

The grooms and herdsmen took their animals to the canal. It was a routine with them to drive their bullocks, camels and horses to the water to give them their morning drink. But what they saw there made their eyes pop out of their sockets. They couldn't believe their senses. Where had all the water of the imperial canal disappeared overnight? How could this ever happen? They turned their animals round in a daze and returned to the camp to spread the word of the sorcery they had just witnessed. 'The water in the canal has vanished!' people exclaimed to each other in disbelief. 'Nature has gone mad! The water has shrunk into the earth!' There was panic on every face. How could such an inconceivable phenomenon have come to pass?

The fortune-tellers were, of course, ready with their explanations, ten different ones coming from ten different mouths. 'This is a message from Goddess Durga, don't you see? An earthquake while our eyes were shut, and now no water to see when the eyes are wide open! What is there to wait for now except total annihilation?'

'When we talk of the future, we are not doing it for entertainment. There were two stars that blew up in the sky in the last two nights. You think it was for fun? You can see today what the heavens were pointing at. An entire canal getting swallowed up by the earth! When you display such arrogance, such pride, such scorn for the Gods, the Gods will surely let you know where true power lies! It's not for nothing that the Ganga has disappeared into the nether-world!'

Try as he might, Bhausaheb could not solve the riddle of how the canal had gone dry. It was solved when a Holkar soldier arrived and said, 'Shrimant, one of our scouts has brought information that Dileyr Khan has breached the canal near Kunjpura out of vengeance.'

Bhausaheb stood, looking puzzled, then asked, 'Who's this Dileyr Khan? And what does he have against us?'

'Shrimant, he is the son of Najabat Khan, the fort-keeper of Kunjpura. We tore the fort down and slew his father. This is an act of revenge.'

'While this man was cutting us off from the canal, what were our men doing?'

'Shrimant, Dileyr Khan destroyed our posts there quite some time back and brought the region under his control. He blocks provisions coming to us from the Punjab, loots the carts carrying fodder. He believes that the Marathas tortured his father to death and has sworn that he will not let grain or water reach his father's killers, and visit upon them as painful a death as his father suffered. He has only lived by his word by breaching the imperial canal.'

'Nana,' roared a livid Bhausaheb, 'can't we send an army right now and crush him?'

'No, Shrimant, I'm afraid we can't. The entire route from here to there is swarming with the enemy's soldiers. It will be suicidal to send our contingent all the way. The fact is, the sky has ripped open on all sides; how many tears can we go and patch?'

'But, Nana, where do we get the water for such a large army? Without water, whatever is left of our army will fall to pieces.'

'Shrimant, now is the time when we can reap the benefits of the plan you had put into place in our early days,' Nana Purandare said. 'As soon as we had arrived here, along with Panipat, we had taken under our control Ugrakhedi, Rajakhedi, and the region between Suvakhedi and Kabuli Bagh. There are at least a hundred wells within the boundaries of these places. As per your orders, Shamsher Bahadur has mounted long-range cannons by the side of those wells. There would be enough water in those wells to last us for the next four to five days.'

'What did you say? Just four to five days?'

'Well, Shrimant, we have all these animals—elephants, horses, camels, bullocks—and the thirst of hundreds of thousands of mouths; how can the supply last beyond five days?'

While the conversation was in progress, Mahipatrao Chitnis entered with a long face. 'Yes, Mahipatrao,' Bhausaheb addressed him, 'what have you got to say?'

'Bhausaheb, our treasury here has gone bone dry. We haven't a coin left in it; how are we going to pay the men? If they are not paid, how will they survive?'

Bhausaheb took some time organizing his thoughts. Then he began in a grave tone, 'These things had come to my notice last week when I was going through the accounts. There is no support coming to us from outside. The Shindes' wealth is all stationed in Gwalior, and all routes of accessing it have been blocked. Doom seems to be advancing on us. A decision will have to be taken in a day or two. Meanwhile, I can see only one way out.'

'What's that, Shrimant?'

'Send the basket round to the pavilion of every single chieftain, the pavilion of the royalty included. Gather all the gold that can be gathered from the women of the family and take it to the mint to get new coins minted. The army must be paid.'

Another two days rolled by. Men and animals now began to make a beeline for the wells at the end of the village. Looking at the size of the wells in the meadows of Suvakhedi and Rajakhedi, Shamsher had placed long-range cannons there. The cannons mounted along the side of the wells stood looking angrily towards Abdali's forces in the south. Each of these cannons was eighteen to twenty feet long, with a range of six miles. Ten gunmen were posted behind each cannon for loading it with gunpowder. Setting alight a cannon was not much different from dynamiting a tunnel. The sound was loud enough to blow away the eardrums, and its heat could make the eyes fall out of their sockets. Once they had loaded a cannon, the gunners would withdraw a mile before the fuse was lit. The main gunner would light the wick with a long hand, immerse himself in a pool of water and stay immersed till the gun exploded. Any delay or mistiming on his part would more or less guarantee deafness for a lifetime. It was around these cannons that the men and animals began crowding for their water.

The state of the army all of the previous fortnight had been bad. A very large number of them hadn't eaten anything at all for two days running. Whatever grain could be scraped was sold for a fortune, well beyond the reach of the ordinary soldier. The charan and the banjaras would risk their lives and manage to procure something from somewhere, but that would suffice for a mere five hundred men or so, and it would be immediately swept away by whoever had the resources. But food for a mere five hundred when there were hundreds of thousands of mouths to feed would have been a joke if it hadn't been so tragic. In stark contrast was the state of the Rohilla-Afghan camp. There was no Govindpant left to block access to their supplies, and plentiful arrived from the Antarved and Najeeb's provinces. Bonhomie reigned there in the same proportion as desperation in the Maratha camp.

It wasn't just food and water that had disappeared for the Marathas. Even the air in the camp had turned so thick with the smell of rotting flesh that breathing had become impossible. Nana Purandare went up to Bhausaheb and said, 'Shrimant, the very air that we breathe has turned traitorous.'

'What remedy do you suggest, Nana?'

'The remedy is to remove the dead bodies. Maybe we could suggest to Abdali that unarmed men from both sides get into the act and clear out their respective dead and dispose of them as per their individual customs.'

'I can send him a request if you say so, but I hardly expect him to agree.'

When Abdali read the letter that the envoy had brought, he laughed at what he thought was a good joke. Thrice before had he changed the spot of his base camp, and now he sat fresh and rested, as if just out of a bath. The malodorous air was blowing in the direction of the Marathas. What did he and his men have to do with it? He sent an immediate response that read, 'You are the one who is troubled by the stench, so your men should remove the bodies. You may remove ours too if you wish. We don't need them, so we won't object.'

※

It was dusk when Ibrahim Khan arrived at Bhausaheb's pavilion, upon which Bhau said, 'I apologize, Khan Saheb, it has never happened that your men have not been paid on time. But this month—'

'Please don't embarrass me so, Bhausaheb,' Ibrahim Khan said. 'This is no time for demanding salaries. We Gardis may be from another province, but we still belong to the Bheem-Kukadi creek. Consider us as natives of your Maval and let your good wishes stay with us.' A page came running in. 'Shrimant, some of our hungry men have gone towards Qalandar Square. They plan to raid the market place there.'

Bhausaheb was perturbed at the news. He ordered Yashwantrao Pawar, 'Leave instantly with your men for Qalandar Square. We have given word to the townsmen that we won't touch a hair on their head. Round up the rioters and chop them to bits.'

Yashwantrao got up, but before he had reached it, he heard Bhau's voice asking him to stop. 'I talked about chopping the rioters to bits,' he said in an embarrassed tone, 'but that is not what I truly mean. The poor soldiers have been starving for four days in a row; what else can they do except loot bazaars? We certainly have to stop them from going on a rampage, but let's not hurt them too much. Cane them. They should be taught a lesson, all right. We will live by the word we have given to the town. This place has so many mosques. Our war can easily acquire a religious colour if we are not careful. If that happens, our entire campaign will go to pieces.'

'We'll do what you desire, Shrimant.'

Yashwantrao set off and managed to drive away the mob of looters. However, he hadn't been fast enough. Four of the shops at Qalandar Square had already been broken into, pillaged and cleaned out. The natives had taken fright.

A few of the junior officials moved from tent to tent, pavilion to pavilion with a basket in hand. The sardars removed their gold wrist-bands, the chains round their necks, some even the studs from their ears, and deposited them in the basket. Their wives too undid the clasps of their necklaces, their bracelets and whatever other gold they had, and made an offering in response to Bhausaheb's call. All the gold thus gathered was sent immediately to the mint for converting into gold coins.

The lamps that were lit across the pavilion made the woebegone faces of the gathered nobles look spectral. They cried out in desperation.

'Shrimant! You have to find a way out of this, Shrimant! Our horsemen and troopers have cleaned out whatever leaves were left in the trees in the manner of goats. They have torn off the bark of trees and pounded it to make a meal. If this goes on, they will soon be fighting over the carcasses of dead cattle.'

Bhausaheb's eyes were blazing red. Pain and consternation had left deep furrows on his brow. He tightened his fists as he articulated each word with emphasis, 'These meadows, these winds, these trees, this earth, the entire universe has turned its back upon us. I can think of only one last hand that remains to played.'

'What's that, Shrimant?'

'One more effort at a truce, just one more!'

Bhausaheb decided to send Damajipant as an envoy. Damajipant was getting ready to leave for Abdali's camp when Bhausaheb's commanding words fell on his ears: 'For the sake of my starving men and distraught animals, we'll be willing to give away revenue rights of a few provinces. But even so—' Bhausaheb paused. Damaji turned round and looked anxiously at his face. Swallowing hard, Bhau resumed, '... but even so, arrive at a truce that does not compromise our dignity.'

Damaji left, carrying with him letters addressed to Kashiraj Pandit, Shuja-ud-dowlah and Wazir Shah Wali Khan. As soon as he reached Abdali's camp, he sought out Kashiraj. The man did all he could to hide his tears as he read the letter. Shuja too was deeply stirred by Bhau's words, and he went immediately to meet Shah Wali Khan. The two decided to present Bhausaheb's proposal in person to Badshah Abdali.

Abdali heard them out patiently. 'Find some way out of this mess, Aalam-panaah,' pleaded Shuja, as he finished.

Abdali heaved a deep sigh and replied, 'I am thinking of war alone right now. If all of you desire peace, I shall not say no to it; but this decision has to be taken by the Rohillas and their leader Najeeb.'

The wazeer refused to go to Najeeb, so Shuja dragged his feet towards Najeeb's pavilion. Najeeb narrowed his small eyes still further as he listened to Shuja's pleas, laughing all the while in his cheek. He then wrote a missive and sent his own special envoy to deliver it to the Maratha army.

It was past midnight, yet Bhausaheb was pacing his pavilion. The other nobles were also waiting anxiously when Najeeb's envoy presented himself before Bhau and proffered Najeeb's letter. Bhausaheb, instead of receiving the letter, ordered him to read it aloud to the assembly.

> ... It was a delight to hear that your arrogant, conceited heart still desires a truce. If you Margatthas really want truce, then pull down your tents, pack them on your backs and carry your wretched faces to the other side of the Yamuna. But in my experience, your community cannot be trusted. So I shall allow your army safe passage back home only if you leave Vishwasrao at my feet as my slave for one year. If your want a quarter of the revenue collected from certain provinces, we shall provide that too; but for that, you, that is Sadashivrao, will have to go to Kandahar as Badshah Abdali's servant and earn his goodwill....

'Silence!' thundered Bhausaheb, as his hand reached instinctively towards the hilt of his sword. It was with great effort that he managed to rein in his rage and roar, 'It's only because the rules of warfare have to be observed that I cannot chop this envoy into tiny pieces. Get out of here. Go tell your Najeeb that we shall send a befitting reply at the appropriate time and the appropriate place.'

Bhausaheb then took a few deep breaths before he could trust his voice, and said, 'This rat of a man, who has swelled from nibbling at Maratha land, he's become so crass and conceited that he has now gone and buried his poisonous teeth into the heart of Hindustan. The tongue that could send so humiliating a response to our offer of truce ... my hands itch to pull that tongue out of its root. If our chieftains from this land had held him by the scruff of his neck earlier, we wouldn't have had to come to Panipat. What terrible harm this monster has caused to the Maratha empire! What treachery, what insult! Najeeb, you impudent rake, the Marathas don't sit with bangles on their wrists. You have no idea of the hurt that even our women who wear bangles can inflict. We will show you on the battlefield what stuff we are made of.

'Mahipatrao, send this message to all the nobles, chieftains and other officials. We will hold a meeting as soon as the day dawns. Tell them to stay on high alert until then.'

༺༻

At the arrival of dawn, as Bhausaheb was walking with steady steps towards the office pavilion, he noticed hundreds of his men gathered around. Seeing him, they began to wail. 'Shrimant,' one of them began, 'please do not let us die of hunger and thirst. If we have to die, let us die fighting on the battlefield.'

'Shrimant, our limbs have swollen for want of food, we suffer dizzy spells of hunger. We cannot just fall here and become food for crows and vultures. Just give us the orders, and we will launch ourselves at the enemy.'

Bhausaheb said, 'Just a little while more, friends; the wait is coming to an end. I have called the officials over for discussion.'

The ushers let out a loud announcement of his arrival. He found Vishwasrao already ensconced in his seat of honour. Shinde, Holkar, Vinchurkar, Pawar, Shamsher Bahadur, Paigude, Dhaigude, Rethrekar, Darekar, Gayakwad, Bhapkar, Kadam, Phalke, Jadhavrao and all other chieftains were in attendance. Bhausaheb gave the signal, and the conference began.

Sardar Paigude was the first to rise and begin, 'Shrimant, the time has come. Instead of rotting here, let's fight the enemy. If not victory, let's embrace an honourable defeat.'

Shamsher Bahadur stood up next. 'We are now the arbiters of our own destiny. Chances of help coming from outside are now bleak. Let's forget about consequences, tighten our girdles and leap upon our enemy to cut our way out.'

Jankoji said, 'Bhaukaka, let's now show the enemy the power of our swords. Our weapons are thirsting for their blood.'

Having measured the mood of the gathering, Bhausaheb assumed his most commanding tone and said, 'I am well aware of the misery of our army. But our courage remains unshaken. Let death reveal all its hideous forms to us, but we shall not go begging to it for mercy. That is not the way of the true Maratha. We cannot be persuaded to sacrifice the Maratha army and break the spine of the empire by fleeing from the battlefield. Let's now step out, cautiously but with resoluteness and tenacity. Let's ram into the enemy and bulldoze our way past them, out to Delhi. Once there, we will gather our resources and rejuvenate the army. Thus reinforced, we shall return to decimate the enemy altogether.'

Bhausaheb's inspirational address brought energy flooding back among the gathered chieftains. They were unanimous in the opinion that Bhausaheb alone could retrieve them from the jaws of calamity. After letting his words sink in, Bhausaheb went on, 'I have been saying this again and again, if we hadn't had this dead weight of camp followers and women to lug around, we would have drowned that emperor of Kandahar in the Yamuna in two months' time.'

Subhedar Malharbaba came out with an involuntary 'Waah'. The proposal to move out of inauspicious Panipat, somehow make it to Delhi, and come back to fight the enemy with renewed vigour was approved unanimously by all present.

'The Yamuna bank is about ten miles from here. The best course would be to have the river covering us from behind, so that we can give battle to the enemy in front. All other routes are fraught with grave danger. The road to Kunjpura is infested with enemy soldiers; the route to Bikaner through the bramble jungle is impossible for such a large force to traverse. There would be no track for our cannon carts to move, our animals will not be able to cut through the bramble.'

Everyone was in complete agreement up to this point. Now came the issue of battle formation. Bhausaheb shot a questioning glance at Ibrahim Khan Gardi. He responded to Bhausaheb's glance and said, 'You Marathas are guerilla fighters, hit-and-run warfare is more your style. During times of face-to-face conflict, your regiment's horsemen might race ahead, and I will be left behind here with my eight thousand foot-soldiers.'

'How can you say this, Khan Saheb?' said a visibly annoyed Bhausaheb. 'We honoured you with rewards in Partud. Our lives are woven into the promises we have made to you. We shall bury ourselves on the battlefield alongside you. We shall get slaughtered, but distancing ourselves from you and sneaking out is not the Maratha principle.'

This pampering of Ibrahim Khan did not go down well with Vinchurkar, Holkar and Gayakwad, but Ibrahim was immediately enthused with Bhausaheb's appreciation of his worth. He cleared his throat and began to outline his battle plan. 'We shall have to fight as the Nizam fights in the south, as Bussey fought, as the French fight, and that is through artillery. That's the only way we will be able to extricate ourselves from Panipat. Unfortunately, our Maratha army does not possess enough guns and muskets of top quality. On the other hand, the Afghans are exceptional gunmen. Because of their proximity to the land of the whites, their weapons are lighter to carry and easier to fire. Our gunmen do not have the skill to handle the reins with one hand and fire with the other while riding. My Gardi contingent has guns of French make that can penetrate the enemy armour. They also have bayonets at the end of their gun-barrels, with which they can take an enemy down even as they fall. We should thus surround our people, our camp-followers, our women and children with our artillery men, plant our cannons, our guns, our grenade launchers and our bazookas in front, and move forward under their protection. With this battle-formation, we should be able to safely make it to Delhi.'

Subhedar Holkar found the plan overly clever. He exchanged looks with Vinchurkar, and decided to voice his protest, even if obliquely. Heaving a deep sigh, he said, 'Bhausaheb, if the enemy decides to block our passage, how are we going to manage, with all these camp-followers and women in company?'

'So what if they are women and non-fighting men?' countered Bhausaheb. 'Kakasaheb, that does not make them the pups of pusillanimous mongrels, does it? They are the product of the Maratha soil, aren't they? They will also take stout sticks in their hands and fight their way forward.'

Old guards like Antaji Mankeshwar, Damajipant Gayakwad, Vinchurkar and Holkar had no taste for these new-fangled, Moghul strategies of warfare. The younger lot of Nana Purandare, Vishwasrao, Jankoji Shinde and others, however, looked at Ibrahim with open excitement and admiration. The army was thus split into two clear factions: new and traditional, young and old. Vinchurkar, who had been seething inside at all the appreciation that Ibrahim Khan was garnering, could take it no longer. 'Bhausaheb,' he spat out, 'I have been observing you, for days and months, dancing to the tune of these Gardis. But what has been our style of warfare, Bhausaheb? Stake our lives in a sudden, fierce, unanticipated attack, or know when we are getting beaten and quickly withdraw into our hills and forests. We've lured the enemy into narrow gorges and beaten them lifeless; we've tied tinkling bells to the horns of our bullocks and led them astray; we've fried our enemies by pouring boiling hot oil on them from our bastions. This has been our style, this has been our speciality. Some have called it guerilla, some others have called it hit-and-run. Can you think of any Maratha general in the last seven generations digging a trench around his army and sitting trapped inside? Don't forget the Marathi tradition of combat that has been handed down to us from ancient times, Bhausaheb; if you get sucked into these foreign styles, it may destroy us all.'

After hearing Vinchurkar's oration, Holkar found his voice too. 'Don't wreck the army by indulging the fancies of adolescent boys and these Gardis, Bhausaheb,' he warned. 'I'm more than twice your age, my hair has turned from black to white wandering these lands. Bhausaheb, please take our advice seriously. I've spent my entire life fighting the guerilla warfare. How did Chhatrapati Shivaji raise his empire if not on the strength of these tactics? How else did great warriors like Santaji and Dhanaji bring glory to our land of Maharashtra? It was guerilla warfare all the way. How can you abandon this time-tested strategy for new-fangled ones?'

All eyes were now turned towards Bhausaheb, all ears cocked to hear how he would respond to Subhedar Malharba's points. Bhausaheb looked down and smiled to himself, organized his arguments and began, 'Subhedar kaka, it was such a pleasure hearing you wax eloquent on guerilla warfare. No one can deny that it was on the strength of guerilla combat that Shivaji Maharaj raised the standard of self-rule, even extended his dominion. But it surprises me, Kakasaheb, that the difference in the terrain between our Maratha land and Panipat should escape your sharp eyes. In Maratha land, the horses entered the Gajapur mountain pass near Vishalgadh, trotted hundreds of miles across and descended to drink water at the Kukadi, without the enemy getting any wind of it. Our land is a land of high cliffs, deep gorges, lofty mountains, invincible jungles and dense groves. There could hardly be any other land better suited for guerilla warfare. If Shivaji Maharaj, whom you have just named, had seen these Ganga and Yamuna plains, this terrain made of silt, hundreds of miles of flat land, a region where you can't find a stone to save your life, where not merely residential houses but forts too are constructed from bricks, where you won't catch sight of a single small hillock even if you were to go riding across hundreds of miles ... if the king had seen this land, he would have pulled us by the ears and asked how we could think of using guerilla tactics in such terrain. "Understand the tactics of the enemy, boys," he would have admonished us, "match move to move if you hope to save your army."'

'Kakasaheb, I swear by everything that is dear to me, I have never considered the value of my own life worth much. What I treasure is the lives of my army, whom I endeavour to save. It's only if we can save them that we will regain our strength and come back to destroy the enemy; else, the political presence of the Marathas in the north that took well over a decade to build will be blown to bits in minutes. The blood of thousands of brave men like Dattaji would have been shed in vain. If our overall mission has to succeed, then I can say with absolute conviction that this artillery warfare, however Moghul it may be, is the only option that gives our army any chance.'

Bhausaheb's arguments impressed the younger men, but the older ones remained suspicious. Subhedar Malharba Holkar refused to give up without giving it another shot. 'Bhausaheb,' he pleaded, 'think again.

Nobody in the entire Maratha empire has had the courage to even look you in the eye, and yet, there was that Gardi who had mounted an attack on you near Darpir.'

'Kakasaheb,' responded Bhausaheb with a tired laugh, 'Ibrahim Khan has shown us the power of his cannons plenty of times before this; how many times do you have to be reminded? Whose assault brought down Devgiri? Who demolished the Kunjpura bastion? Who brought the Red Fort to its knees? It was Ibrahim Khan and his cannons, was it not? In sharp contrast, what state were you reduced to in Rajputana when Abdali arrived with his cannons? You had to flee for your life into the mountains around there. So, please stop pointing fingers at a person's caste and faith. The fault is never of caste, it is of temperament.'

'You are absolutely right, Kakasaheb,' intervened Jankojiba Shinde. 'Talking of caste loyalties, haven't people from our own caste betrayed us to our enemies? Who was the one to give shelter to Najeeb?'

The jibe found its mark. Malharbaba turned livid. 'Janko! Hold your tongue, do you hear? Titch of a boy, you know who you are talking to? The family name you flaunt, its first sardar, Ranoba Shinde, your grandfather, what was he, after all? A mere page in the Satara court! Who brought him over to Pune? Who made him a sardar? It was I, Malharba, don't you forget!'

'And what were you doing at Holmuram before you became a sardar, sir? Herding sheep, weren't you?'

In no time at all, the argument caused an open, full-blown scuffle between the Shinde and the Holkar factions, with Vinchurkar and Mankeshwar siding with Subhedar Malharba Holkar. Matters came to a head when Malharbaba roared, 'Even if it means staking our lives, we shall fight according to the old guerilla practice. This artillery warfare is simply not acceptable to us.'

'We don't want any of your artillery! It's guerilla warfare for us!' screamed Vinchurkar and Mankeshwar.

This new twist in the scenario stunned everyone present. Even Bhausaheb was at a loss for words. That was when Ibrahim Gardi sprang up and bellowed, 'How dare you? You had given us your word as we were setting off from Partud! You think you can bolt away on your horses, leaving my footmen behind on the battlefield? I dare any son of his mother to just try! Till this day, my cannons have been trained at the enemy, snapped their spine, brought down their forts! I promise you, I shall not hesitate to turn their barrels on you and let them roast you alive! Don't … don't just run away like chickens! Come on, come together! Let's live together, fight together, die together!'

Ibrahim's words provoked the old guard still further. They glared at the Gardi, twirling their moustaches as they did so. Bhau shot a restraining look at Ibrahim, who immediately sat down grumpily. He then went over to Jankoji, Vinchurkar and Mankeshwar and had them sit at some distance from each other. He also pleaded with Malharbaba to take a seat. He then folded his hands before everyone and began, 'The enemy is sitting on our chests; how can we afford to squabble among ourselves? Abdali can only be vanquished if we stand united.'

The fire was doused. Before bringing the meeting to a close, Bhausaheb made one final pitch and said, 'Whether you like it or not, it is going to be artillery warfare this time. We all have to come together for a common purpose. The battle formations will be announced in the evening. Our army will set off tomorrow morning. If the enemy allows us free passage, then there shall be no face-off. But if he blocks our way, then God help him. We will slaughter without mercy.'

All the nobles dispersed except for Ibrahim Gardi, who stood alone in the now empty court.

'What is it, Khan Saheb?' asked Bhausaheb.

'Huzoor, how am I ever going to repay you for placing your trust in me?'

As Bhausaheb let out an embarrassed laugh, Ibrahim brought out a small bundle wrapped in a kerchief, pulled out some twenty-odd letters from it and handed them to him. The letters were from Abdali and Najeeb. Bhausaheb read some of them at random and laughed. 'What wonderful gifts they were, Khan Saheb!' he said. 'The title of Umrao, a province yielding two hundred and fifty thousand, a chieftainship in Kandahar, if you desire! The appeal to your faith is there, of course. They were grand offerings—'

'Shrimant, this Gardi will never budge from your side, in life or death.'

Emperor Abdali was returning from his evening survey of the camp. The Marathas, it appeared to him, had stopped stirring in or out of their camp. Despite having the upper hand on the enemy, he was in low spirits today. His hand went up to his ear, and as he felt around the lobe, he was reminded of Nadir Shah. The great man had clipped a part of his earlobe saying Abdali would remember him when he became an emperor himself. Nadir Shah's words rang in his ears, 'I haven't seen a boy as promising as Ahmad in the three lands of Iran, Turan and Hindustan.' These words, pronounced in open court, echoed in Abdali's ears, and they made him restless. It was now eighteen months since his Hindustan campaign had begun, yet there was no satisfactory progress to show for all that time. It was two months and a half since the Marathas had been confined to their camp; they were suffering, they had run out of food and fodder, but they were showing no sign of softening. They had gathered the courage to dig a trench round themselves, and now lay stretched out peacefully inside the enclosure. *I cannot find the courage in me to mount an assault and annihilate them. I've seen so many wars, but never run into such a resilient enemy. More than the boom of Ibrahim's cannons, it is that man Bhau's nerve. The audacity with which they brought down the Red Fort and ravaged Kunjpura! A community that vanquished Sirhind and Lahore, that scrubbed its horses in the water of Attock, can this community be expected to fall meekly on its knees? Their capacity to absorb pain is phenomenal. All right, then, I am in no hurry either.*

His thoughts pumped their wings and flew all the way to Kandahar. *Oh, how many months since I set eyes on my throne! Haven't heard the beats of the tambourine that come pulsating into the palace! The men and animals that have come with me, how many days have gone by since the wind of the motherland blew over them! How many more days will we have to stay here, nailed to Panipat?*

His horse suddenly missed a step, and a horrifying thought jolted him. What if he were to lose this battle? The thought was frightening enough to roll all of his life's work into a tight little bundle. The fate of the throne in Kandahar would be determined by the outcome in Panipat. The entire Afghan land was watching with great curiosity what their king had been doing these past two years in distant Hindustan. There were rumours being floated by his dissenters that he had lost the battle.

The intelligence that his scouts had been bringing from his court also included news of Zargari's Haji Jamaal Khan's flexing his muscles to take over the throne. He was strutting about in the provinces around Kandahar, claiming suzerainty over the Afghans. There was no shortage of rebellious cockatoos like Haji Jamaal Khan in and around Kandahar, was there?

The news of the gargantuan conflict had spread all over Hindustan too. Inayat Khan, son and heir of Hafeez Rahmat Khan, had just arrived from Bareili to join the army. What information had he brought? All of Hindustan was watching Panipat with bated breath. This battle was going to decide who would ascend to the throne of Hindustan, whether the Marathas were going to be rubbed out or whether they would gallop around every corner of Hindustan, planting their saffron flags. He was totally trapped in the pit of war. Earlier, the fate of Delhi hadn't mattered so much, but those days were long gone. If the throne of Delhi did not remain in Rohilla hands, the empire of Kandahar would also become difficult to hold. If he were to get defeated, how long would he be able to run? Kandahar wasn't an eight-day journey. Besides, who would let him flee in peace? Abdul Khalil Khan had gone and joined up with the enemies, and he was waiting for him to be chopped to pieces so that he could throw his ring round the Kandahar throne. This war had to be won. If his crown were to topple in the soil of Panipat, there would be nothing left for him to rule, not Hindustan, not Kandahar! He would then wander around the countryside like a mendicant, or would be dispatched into another dark dungeon. That would be worse than death!

He arrived at his tent and finished his dinner. Sleep eluded him. The gongs in his head refused to be silenced. The conference held in the desolate landscape outside Shaikh Sarkoo's shrine came to mind. This was immediately after Nadir Shah's assassination. What did he possess anyway, before he began his journey? There wasn't even a handful of flowers to celebrate his ascension to the throne, merely some blades of grass that were showered upon his head by a bunch of friends. And the throne to which he had ascended? A tiny mound of earth had done duty for that, and that was it! So, why worry? He had begun as a fakeer, and he would finish off as a fakeer! What was so earth-shattering about it?

Hey, but who were these people heading this way? Their faces looked familiar! They looked like landowners from Kabul, Ghazni, Hazara, Banu, Sindh and Dera Jaat.

... *What's there for you to laugh about with such scorn? People do suffer defeats, don't they? Summer, winter, rains ... seasons keep changing in men's lives, don't they?*

... *In men's lives, yes, but not in your life!*

... *What does that mean?*

... *We had told you right then, when you began this game of grass and sticks and took charge of Kandahar with the help of a few ruffians. We had told you then that getting the khutba read in one's name, getting coins minted in one's name, ascending the throne ... these are not things that would suit a roughneck like you.*

... *Why?*

... *Because you have no pedigree, you belong to the lowest class, you have no business occupying a throne. You are a mongrel, a mongrel, sprung from the poorest quality of seed, you have no lineage to speak of!*

It was as if somebody had overturned a drumful of hot embers upon his body. He jumped off his bed and began to pace the tent. His face contorted with rage, he clenched his fists as he shouted out, 'Good that those landowners woke me up from my dreams. I don't want to become a fakeer, I have to win this war! I have to show to the world the invincibility of my sword! I am not a mongrel! I belong to the highest pedigree! I'd rather give up my life than tolerate the slur of being low-born!'

He summoned Wazeer Shah Wali Khan and his general Jahaan Khan. When they arrived, he said, 'Shah Wali, Jahaan, you have to work without rest now—check our pickets, check the state of our squads, get the gunpowder carried to where the cannons are.'

'Aalam-panaah, everything is in perfect order,' Jahaan Khan said humbly.

'No, Jahaan, don't be fooled. Stay alert! The night belongs to the enemy. They are dancing all around you. Stay awake. The slightest drowsiness, the tiniest catnap, and you will never be able to sleep peacefully for the rest of your life.'

Stroking his white beard, Shah Wali Khan said, 'My lord, the scouts have brought information that the Maratha army has been hit by terrible famine; they are dropping like flies. I can see only two possibilities hereon: one is that they will come crawling to Aalam-panaah and seek your mercy—'

'Mercy? Let go of your naivety. This wretched community would prefer death to seeking mercy.'

'If they don't seek mercy, then they will come racing at us, all of them.'

'Well said,' responded the badshah with a clap of appreciation. 'Wazeer, your hunch has hit the mark. When a dam gets filled with more water than it can hold, its walls develop cracks. The Marathas' misery has crossed the limit. It is worse than even the bravest of men can bear, so they are bound to come rushing at us in a day or two.'

'Let them come, Aalam-panaah! We shall slaughter them all at the very first stroke!' said Jahaan Khan.

'Jahaan, you are a complacent fool. The lamp burns at its brightest before it dies down. The Marathas will fight with the greatest valour. If we fall short of withstanding their onslaught, misfortune will remove the mark of death from their brow and place it on ours. That is why I am alerting you—wake up!'

Jahaan Khan and Shah Wali Khan departed from the royal pavilion. Abdali summoned the warden of the harem. When the old man arrived, he shot off the instructions. 'Zulfiqar, sparks are going to fall on the arsenal storehouse in the next two or three days, and it won't take time for the whole thing to explode into flames. As soon as the battle gets going, you are to carry my begum and the other women of the tribe eight miles away.'

'Aalam-panaah, I didn't quite follow you.'

'You fool, it's time for the war, the like of which no one has seen before. Who shall win and who shall lose, how the shape of the war may change, no one knows. If we get defeated, if we are vanquished, then our women should not fall into the hands of the infidels. If something unforeseen happens to us, it shall be your responsibility to escort the women safely back to Kandahar.'

☙

Everything had begun to turn upside down after lunch in the Maratha camp. The gold ornaments that had been collected had been minted into

Bhaushahi, Holkarshahi and Jankoshahi coins and distributed among the men. The army was to leave at daybreak. Whatever grains were left in the Holkar-Shinde's and Bhausaheb's stocks were also evenly distributed, which amounted to very little per head. But the soldiers now had money, and they all made a dash for the grocery shops and bought off all the grain in little time. Hunger had settled so deep in so many bellies that they cleared out anything that could be eaten: dry dates, coconut kernel, gram and tur sprigs, and whatever else there was on offer. Within an hour, the shopkeepers had emptied all their sacks and tins. Around late evening, some of the men ran towards Qalandar Chowk, where the shops were still open. Those shops were emptied out too. And then they swarmed to the sweetmeats store. A melee broke out for the grams that were left, and a large number of the troopers ate those few fistfuls of gram, thanked the Lord for it, and washed it down with a few tumblers of water.

By around ten, the carpenters and masons got busy, and tents and pavilions started to come down. During the past few weeks of famine, a number of bullocks had died, and Ibrahim was hunting desperately for some animals to buy. He virtually fell at the feet of the traders and persuaded them to sell off their well-fed animals. The camp-followers were in a tizzy, running this way and that, seemingly without purpose. Lakshmanrao Panse and Ibrahim Gardi's men were engaged in taking down the big and small cannons from their mounts and placing them on the heavy carts.

On the other side, the court ordered by Bhausaheb had assembled in the main pavilion. Vishwasrao, as always, sat in the seat of honour, while the chieftains and officers sat in front of him with due observance of protocol and rank. Vinchurkar looked sluggish and Holkar couldn't keep his yawns under check. It being a public meeting, the entire place was overflowing with ordinary horsemen, soldiers, troopers, camp-followers and all the others who were not occupied with the task of folding up the camp.

After having finished the consultation with his generals, Bhausaheb got up and addressed the gathering. 'I begin by bowing in respect to the brave soldiers of my Maratha land, who have stayed by me through the extremely difficult months gone by. I want to acknowledge my deep gratitude to you for wading across streams and rivers, braving rains and storms, scaling mountains and crossing deserts with firm, determined steps to challenge the intruder and drive him out of Hindustan. While doing so, a series of calamities have buffeted us, and yet, not one of you has so much as thought of deserting our company. You cannot imagine how proud I am of the fact that despite the terrible battering you were receiving at the hands of fate, not one of you tried to rise up in rebellion.'

Bhausaheb broke down as he said this, stunning his audience into silence. Then someone shouted out and everybody else picked up the refrain, 'No, Bhau, no! We can never rebel against you and shall never desert you!'

'Bhau, we are not ingrates! We are not sinners!'

'We shall fight by your side, die by your side!'

Bhausaheb voice turned hoarse with emotion. 'I will never be able to repay this debt.

'Our Maker has not thrown us a challenge of such gigantic proportions before. A war like this may never be fought again. You have leapt into this conflict for the sake of your nation. However mighty our enemy, our mission is mightier, truer, holier. All the great warriors of Maratha land have assembled here in Panipat to defend Delhi: Paigude, Dhaigude, Morey, Pandhre, Kotkar, Shedgey, Shirkey, Pisaal, Misaal, Bargey, Bodhey, Kharaade, Lokhande, Hatkar, Waghmaare, Bhise, Rajput, Ranadive, Baagal, Kokate, Ayrekar, Kadamkar, Maney, Dabhade, Saatam, Wagh, Thorat, Palekar, Pol, Chauhan, Dhulap, Jadhav, Pawar, Bhosale, Gujar, Dafale, Ghatge, Kadam, Lingade, Yadav, Kharat, Shevale, Wabale, Aangrey, Aayrey, Bhapkar, Kakde, Jagdale, Rasaal, Gadhve, Katkar, Jagtap, Dhumaal, Gajare, Phalke, Nikam, Godse, Dudhe, Katey, Kadu, Ghugare, Padwal, Raney, Shirole, Shetole, Shelkey, Bolkey, Jirgey, Kaley, Gaajare, Raje, Gayakwad, Mohite, Patkar, Raaste, Patwardhan, Talekar, Dhamdhere, Palande, Kiturkar, Desai, Kolhatkar, Shingade, Shingte, Manjare, Gophaney, Algey, Kaapsey, Ghogale, Konse, Salvi, Murgey, Bandey, Bandgey, Mhaskey, Talkey, Navarey, Aabhley, Sonavane, Hovhal, Mohal, Haldey, Kuradey, Shinde, Bhoite, Walke, Chavle, Bhalekar, Chopde, Nalawade, Godey, Surve, Rasale, Mochale ... the list is endless! There is not a single village, not a single house, not one doorstep from the plateau of Maharashtra, not a single caste or sub-caste, that has not been represented today, here in Panipat. I see your eyes watering at the thought of God having bound us together here. The tears in your eyes, to me, are the waters of the sacred rivers Varna, Panchganga, Krishna, Koyna, Maan, Bheema, Mula, Mutha, Indrayani, Meena, Kukadi and Godavari. You have been exhausted by the unceasing onslaught of calamities; you have turned so lean that there's not much hold left on your waists for your dhotis; but by the grace of Lord Gajanan, your spirits remain undaunted.

'We will now set off towards Delhi. Once we get there, we shall re-energize ourselves and give battle to the enemy. But if he refuses to grant us passage on our way there, we shall teach him a lesson, and then continue south with our banners and our bugles. 'There's no reason for you gallant men to be considered as different from the great Maratha heroes who preceded us. King Shalivahan came back victorious, and we celebrate Gudi Padva in his honour. For hundreds of years now, houses are decorated with dolls and buntings, rangolis are drawn at our doorsteps. You have come this far giving battle to fate. If you can recharge yourselves one last time, my honourable Marathas, descendants of Chhattrapati Shivajiba and Dattaji, if you can tear through the enemy, then this victory will be celebrated for centuries to come as another Gudi Padwa, of that I have no doubt.'

'But,' here, Bhausaheb took a long pause, swept his eyes over the gathering, and then resumed, 'but we do not know what hides in the womb of time. We can only pray to our three hundred and thirty million gods and goddesses to give us help and protection and bring us victory. Human nature is such that it doesn't need much persuasion to sing ballads for the victorious, but failure attracts no sympathy or appreciation. There is nothing that succeeds like success, and nothing that sinks like failure. If our own people back home never get to know of the trials we have faced, if they are never told how our brave fighters embraced death like their beloved heroes, then our entire nation will simply throw stones at us and heap a thousand sins upon our heads. They will say the mad Bhau drowned himself and a hundred thousand men in his insanity. I shall be the one to carry the curse of having destroyed the youth of our country. So we must defend the dignity of our saffron flag.'

After Bhausaheb's soul-stirring speech, all the chieftains were presented with ceremonial clothing and paan. Ibrahim Gardi and Shamsher Bahadur had prepared elaborate maps that showed the positions of the different contingents. To the west of Panipat would be Holkar's forces, east of which would be Jankoji Shinde's men. In front of them, in the centre of the circle, would be the Peshwa's Royal Guards along with Bhausaheb's and Balwantrao's left-over men. Alongside them would move the battalions of Damaji Gayakwad, Vitthalrao Vinchurkar, Yashwantrao Pawar and Antaji Mankeshwar. The formation assigned Ibrahim Gardi's platoon to the far-east along the riverbank. The strategy was to place the camp followers, the pilgrims and the tribals in the centre and move forward giving battle as and when required. Bhausaheb reiterated again and again that whatever happened, whatever the provocation, no one was to leave their assigned place and break the circle.

The durbar got over and everyone began to leave for their tents to make arrangements for an early morning departure the next day. Shamsher Bahadur stayed back. He was so overcome by Bhausaheb's words that he cut through the crowd to reach him, kissed his hand and said, 'Bhausaheb, your image in my mind has grown to the size of a mountain.'

'Thank you, Shamsher, but what does it all ultimately add up to? When we were setting off on our campaign at Partud so confidently, did either you or I have any idea that such a string of calamities would befall us? But once we are in it, once the challenge has been accepted, there is no other recourse but to confront it with all our strength and determination.'

'Bhausaheb, your speech has suffused the blood in my veins with energy and courage. This son of Mastani will show the world that he is every bit the son of Bajirao too.'

'Shamsher, your status and mine are only marginally different. Where is my palace located in Shaniwarwada? In a small corner at the end of the setting sun. There were rows upon rows of people celebrating every one of the Peshwa's victories, but did the privilege ever come my way? I had to stand by the side and wait, hoping for some credit to fall to my lot. I had to argue long and hard to lead this campaign, and look how that has turned out. But, Shamsher, now that we have arrived on the battlefield, let's give it our all, and show to the world the worth of our blood.'

As he was leaving, his eyes fell on Vishwasrao's young, innocent face, marked with the anxiety of adventure. He placed an affectionate hand on his shoulder and said, 'Rao Saheb, I have so pointlessly dragged you into this war. The thought has been gnawing away at my insides.'

'Kakasaheb, you have not brought me here for sightseeing, have you? You have taught me never to shy away from one's duties. I will gladly lay my life at your feet.'

☙

The tents were being pulled out and folded into neat bundles, the bamboos piled up in stacks. The camp-followers were in a tizzy. Four of their women were in an advanced state of pregnancy, their bellies protruding like cooking vessels. The wind was freezing and the enemy was lying in wait. How would they manage to work their way through these obstacles with their precious cargo?

As the royal pavilions were brought down, their grass screens partitions were being ripped apart, and the dry stalks and grass were being fed to elephants and horses. Some foresighted horsemen had anticipated the fodder crisis and secreted little bundles of them in nooks and corners and holes in the earth. These now brought out those bundles and stuffed them surreptitiously into the mouths of their hungry animals. The less foresighted poked around here and there in the debris of the world dismantling around them, and placed before their animals whatever was even remotely edible. After that came water, a sacred duty for every single person who knew his animal; who knew when the next drink would be made available?

Bhausaheb stood in the dim light inside his pavilion, talking in whispers to a black mountain of a man named Visaji Krishna Jogdand. Bhau looked exceptionally tense. 'You have to bring her along with the utmost care as we make our way towards Delhi. You must be close to her at all times, do you hear? If anything untoward should happen to me, you know what to do. One single stroke, and her head should separate from the body.'

'Bhausaheb!' croaked a terrified Jogdand.

'Yes, Visaji, your five hundred horsemen should stay at our tail. Even in the other world, I should not get to hear that Bhau's wife fell into the hands of the enemy.'

Bhau finished with his bath and said his prayers just before dawn. A page entered and requested him to move to a smaller tent along with his wife so that his pavilion could be dismantled before it became light.

As soon as the two entered the tent, Parvatibai said, 'You must eat something, my lord!'

'But, love, my men and horses—'

'No more of that! I've been hearing those words for the past four days! A little bit of fruit, at least! I will not let you leave the tent otherwise.'

Left with no alternative, he sat down to eat. Parvatibai rushed towards the plate of fruits she had kept ready and handed it to Bhau. As she straightened up, the dagger that she had kept concealed at her waist slipped and fell clattering to the ground.

Bhau was startled. 'What's this?'

'A dagger,' she responded calmly. 'If Jogdand can't reach us in time, we must be prepared to defend ourselves, mustn't we?'

'Jogdand?' A pause, and he went on with extreme trepidation, 'Parvati, you overheard our conversation, did you? How can you be so calm after hearing all that?'

'What choice do we have? Once we have accepted the Kshatriya way of life, there's no point in rejecting its consequences, is there?'

Bhausaheb's heart suddenly felt heavy. He just looked down at the plate and began to eat the fruits without looking up. Parvatibai placed a hand on his shoulder. 'I am your fellow-traveller on the journey of life. Wherever you go, I go too. Don't ever play foul by slipping out without me. In this field of battle, I cannot ask any other favour of you except this: I will live or die with you. Don't you disappear without taking me along!'

Dawn had broken. Criers had begun going round the camp, shouting, 'Come on! Wind up! Get moving!' Bhausaheb's elephant Gajendra, suitably ornamented, stood before the tent shaking its trunk, waiting for its master to come out. The horse Chandrasen too stood dancing on impatient legs. Bhausaheb put on his helmet and tightened his sash round his waist, after which Parvatibai lifted his favourite Khorasani sword, buffed its blade with the end of her saree, placed the belt over the sash round her husband's waist and buckled it in place. She then brought out the prayer tray with a lamp burning on it, applied vermillion on Bhau's forehead and swirled the tray round before him, as was custom. Bhau was about to get up when a draught from outside blew the lamp out. Parvatibai's heart sank. Bhau, however, did not notice the flame going out. As she saw his broad back retreating from her in the direction of Gajendra, her dam burst. She could contain her tears no more.

⁂

The campsite looked like it had been hit by a hurricane. 'Wind up! Wind up!' screamed the criers as they roamed around, nudging and prodding the laggards. Kettle-drums and war bugles had been strictly ruled out so as not to alert the sleeping enemy. Vishwasrao's elephant Shamsundar was swaying rhythmically as it carried its royal burden. In the canopies that followed were seated the women of the nobility: Akkasaheb, Parvatibai, Nana Phadnis's wife Yashoda, Paigude's family, and others. The grooms, the mahouts, the riders began to poke the animals to move faster as they crossed the trenches and entered the plains of Panipat. As Gajendra walked forward with Bhausaheb sitting atop, the chieftains hurried to offer their respects to their commander-in-chief. Gajendra acknowledged each of these salutes by raising its trunk. Alongside the elephant trotted Chandrasen, as if it were setting out to conquer the world.

The journey would be difficult and fraught with danger. Accordingly, everything that was inessential and bothersome to carry was left behind, making the grounds look like a refuge dump of broken carts, palanquins, tattered tent-covers, tarpaulin screens, drapes and lumber.

The platoons began to move in the still air with their banners and shields in front of them. Shamsher Bahadur rode up from one side, halted his horse across Gajendra's track and got it to rise on its hind legs in a salute to his master. Gajendra lifted its trunk and trumpeted loudly in acknowledgement.

The squadrons assembled in the open field outside the trench and began to take up their battle positions in the pre-decided concentric formation.

His armour concealed under his loose-fitting shirt, Ibrahim Khan could be seen running everywhere. He was required to keep under control the outermost left wing of the formation, right alongside the riverbank, and he was doing it in the manner of a cart-man keeping the main stem of the cart pressed tight on the yoke. As soon as he was sure that his carts were nicely aligned, he rode up to Bhausaheb and offered his salute. Acknowledging his greeting, Bhausaheb said, 'Khan Saheb, let's exercise all the caution and care that we must. Our army is still not accustomed to fighting in this circular formation. We need to strike a good balance between the fast-moving animals and the slower moving foot soldiers.'

'Huzoor, this formation has been designed with exactly the same intention. If our battalions stay in their assigned positions, we should be able to make rapid progress. If the enemy blocks our way, we will blow him away and touch Delhi in the quickest possible time. I shall see to it.'

It was getting to be light now. The eastern horizon had turned noticeably brighter, and the army had begun to move. Ibrahim Khan's eight thousand men were marching in order on the left with their muskets on their shoulders. Alongside them moved hundred and fifty cannons. It had been decided to leave the biggest of them behind, at the trenches, beside the wells, because it would be impossible to cart such heavy artillery at a time when speed would be of the essence. Dattaji's cannon, Attock, was also left behind, looking sad and uncared for at the edge of Panipat. Even the ones that were being carted were testing the strength of the tired, emaciated animals, and it was only the prodding and tail-twisting by the cart-men that compelled them to keep moving. Wherever the army fell short, the traders' bullocks had been yoked for an exercise they had never performed, and who lodged their protest with frequent burps and vigorous shakes of horns. Right behind Ibrahim Khan danced the shields of Gayakwad. Along with the Gardis rode two and a half thousand of Damaji Gayakwad's horsemen and another fifteen hundred of Vinchurkar's. The two thousand Afghan orphans who had taken shelter under Vinchurkar at Kunjpura were moving in the vicinity too. In case the two armies got mixed up with each other during an attack, Vinchurkar had made his Afghans wear saffron bands round their brows to make identification easier.

Ahead of the Gardi battalion, somewhat to the right, walked the elephant that carried the royal banners. Here was located the Peshwa's Royal Guards, the very heart, the nerve centre of the Maratha army. Its fourteen thousand horses walked as if intoxicated by the spirit of war.

The Royal Guards was under the direct command of Sadashivrao Bhau and Vishwasrao, and it had as its officers warriors of such eminence as Satvoji Pilaji Jadhav, Sonaji Bhapkar, Shamsher Bahadur, Manaji Paigude, Antaji Mankeshwar, Subhanrao Mane, Santaji Wagh, Dadaji Darekar, Shahaji Zhambre, Khanderao Naik-Nimbalkar, Baji Hari Supekar, Dhamdhere, Yashwantrao Pawar, Kakade, Kadu, Kamthe, Muthe, Harphale, Kadam, Shitole, Dhaibar and Chauhan. All of them rode with a strut that suggested that the encounter with the enemy was due in the next ten minutes, and they would prefer to eat him raw. They carried naked swords, rapiers and spears in their hands, all ready for action. Some even carried bows and a quiver full of arrows.

The fighting men among them were around forty-five thousand; but the hat was bigger than the head; the non-combatant camp followers that moved with them were in the region of a hundred to a hundred and twenty-five thousand, consisting of a mind-boggling assortment of people such as tribal chiefs, personal attendants, water carriers, religious teachers and their disciples, fiddlers, dancers, cobblers, blacksmiths, palmists, astrologers, traders, pilgrims, cart drivers, clowns, cooks, herders, jugglers, entertainers, highwaymen, nomads, grocers and petty shopkeepers. There were also big flocks of injured soldiers and animals, palanquins of pregnant women as well as the women of the royal and noble households. The non-combatant force was shivering in the cold of the morning; there were plenty among them, of course, who were shivering for other reasons.

To the extreme right towards the Panipat side were the regiments of the Shindes and the Holkars. Jankoji seated in his canopy was virtually dancing with excitement, eager to confront the enemy and wipe him out sooner rather than later. His two young cousins Mahadji and Tukoji were racing alongside him in equal excitement. In front of the Shinde forces marched Holkar's men. Seated in his canopy, Malharjiba looked grave and preoccupied. Gangoba Tatya, sitting in his seat behind the canopy looked at the army and blinked. Towards the rear end, the non-combatants were placed in the middle, with seven thousand of the Royal Guards bringing up the tail along with a few contingents of some of the chieftains.

This vast mass of humanity measured two miles across and trailed at least two miles behind the van. With the vow of protecting Delhi and safeguarding the dignity of the Marathi soil, this colossal army was moving apace towards the abyss of war.

༻❀༺

The cold early morning wind was not letting Najeeb sleep in peace. He lay tossing and turning, searching for some position that would give him the warmth he sought. Abdali's army, a procession of idiots! *Please friend, come and bail me out of this, friend! You call them over, and they now sit dismantling your house! And what a faithless pack! Happily eating off my larder two times a day and doing what the rest of the time? Nothing but sleeping and farting! They have eaten all of the Antarved to beggary and turned it to crap, and now loaf around the place burping like stray bulls! When I get after that Afghan and beg him to get into battle, the smartest thing he can say is, 'We will pull the thorn out at the appropriate time!' Yes, then, keep taking us for a ride with this rubbishy eyewash, and when the time comes, call me out and pluck* me *out as the thorn!*

As he lay wallowing in self-pity, the sound of a scuffle caught his attention. What could that sound be? Just ordinary bullock carts or cannon-carts? Could it be that those Margatthas had walked over to his house? He leapt out of bed, went to the door of his pavilion and stared in the dark. The sky had just begun to light up. Then he saw four horsemen come racing towards him. They quickly jumped off their horses and began to shout, 'Khan Saheb! Khan Saheb!'

'Stop blabbering and start talking!'

'Khan Saheb, the Marathas have marched out in full battle readiness; they are coming with their artillery in the lead!' Still in his nightclothes, Najeeb leapt upon the nearest horse and galloped towards Abdali's tent, shouting all the way, 'Wake up, Kibla-e-aalam! Wake up! The deluge has arrived! The world is drowning!'

The king was awake anyway. As soon as he stepped out with his hookah in hand, Najeeb cried out in agony, 'Aalam-panaah, we are done for! Sunk! The water has started rushing in through the nose and mouth. My lord, we have begun to choke.'

'What is the matter, Najeeb?'

'Matter, my lord? The matter is simple: we are dead! Those monkeys from the Deccan are marching upon us with their army!'

Shah Pasand Khan was in charge of surveillance duty that night. His men too came running with the news. The sound of the creaking cartwheels and the jangle of the chains could be heard now. The emperor cocked his ears and looked towards the north. He pulled two long drags on his hookah as he let the news sink in. Then he handed over the hookah to his page, jumped on his steed and slapped its rump. He went galloping to his court pavilion four miles away and stopped there. From there, he could distinctly hear the sounds of a massive body of men, animals and vehicles on the move. At his instructions, bugles were blown and kettle-drums beaten, which awakened his entire camp with a jolt.

Abdali had anticipated that the starving, desperate Marathas would break out from their confinement and come barging into their camp, so a plan to handle the contingency had been lying ready in his head. He now only had to put it into effect and point the way to his befuddled men. Accordingly, he collected all his chieftains and officials and began to shoot off instructions. 'Najeeb, you must set off immediately with your fifteen thousand foot soldiers, go to the rear left corner of our army and park yourselves right along the Delhi road. The infidels may try to ram into us, crack a way open and pass through it. Your job is to block their way and beat them back. You have been letting off such quantities of gas for so long, the time has now come to let sparks fly off your weapons. Get your soldiers to do some good work.'

Then his eyes rested on Shuja-ud-dowlah. As he looked, he thought, This man still has a soft corner for the Marathas. The bastard can change sides at the critical moment. He needs to be yoked to a solid, dependable mate, so that he cannot drag the cart too much his way. Best to pair him with Najeeb. Who better than Najeeb to keep him on track or to kill him if he decides to defect? He laughed aloud and said, 'Nawab Saheb, why don't you ask your three-thousand-strong cavalry to move alongside Najeeb's? Your Gosavi regiment should bring glory to the name of Ayodhya. Keep your sixty cannons to the front too.'

The spine of the army would be the emperor's own men, operating from the centre. In his mind, he had long ago handed the reins of his main cavalry to his Wazeer Shah Wali Khan, a cavalry that had Kabuli and Kandahari horses capable of pulling victory out of any conflagration. Countless were the conflicts where Shah Wali had stood shoulder to shoulder with his king. In the matter of truly knowing what was best for the king, for sheer readiness to lay his life for his welfare, there was no person in the entire army who could come anywhere close to the trusty, crusty old wazeer. Throwing a look of extreme confidence towards the old man, Badshah Abdali said, 'I am placing in your trust the control of my nineteen-thousand-strong cavalry that has turned to dust the arrogance of countless capitals. My sturdy Irani-Turani horses have never known defeat. They have this terrible habit of rubbing away the boundary lines of parganas and of countries with their iron-hooves. These are the horses I hand over to your charge. Besides, I place at your disposal the services of your valiant nephew, Atai Khan, who so efficiently put paid to the machinations of Govindpant Bundele.'

Next, he turned towards where Faizullah Khan, Dundey Khan, Saadullah, Ahmad Khan Bangash and many of the other Rohilla chieftains were sitting, and addressed them with a hint of sharpness, 'You are my brothers who have made Hindustan your own. It is for your sake alone that we have stayed behind, away from Kabul-Kandahar, under these testing conditions. The other day, when I merely expressed my wish to return to my homeland, you came down on me like a ton of bricks. The time has arrived for you to really put on show your proclaimed love for jihad and Islam and toss those infidels into the Yamuna. I will place all of you chieftains to the extreme right, alongside the river, with a strength of fifteen thousand Rohillas. It is possible that if they find the road to Delhi difficult to travel, the Maratha army may want to cross over to the other side of the river; or if they enter the Antarved, who knows the lanes, the by-lanes, the riverine tracks and the various alleys and paths better than you, my valiant friends? You should really be able to raise pyramids out of the severed heads of these infidels!'

Abdali thus assigned positions to almost everybody. He instructed Shah Pasand Khan to stay to the left of Najeeb with his five thousand horses. He told Commander-in-chief Jahaan Khan to help the main force that would move under the wazeer. Barkhurdar Khan was looking a little miffed because he had not yet been assigned an important position in the battle formation. After having looted so much of the enemy's supplies and diverting them to Abdali's forces, he didn't seem to count for much in the emperor's eyes. The emperor noticed the disappointed look and said to him with a laugh, 'Barkhurdar Khan and Amir Beg, it doesn't suit crusaders like you to look so disheartened. I am placing upon you the responsibility that matches your stature. We have to make full use of your three-thousand-strong artillery and your lightning-fast horses from Persia. I have to test the faith of that incorrigible renegade Ibrahim Gardi. He spills the blood of his own brethren to please his infidel masters. That filthy bastard has already dispatched thousands of our Rohillas and Afghans into Allah's shelter. Barkhurdar and Amir Beg, he may yet cause the biggest destruction to our men of faith. You have to swoop upon him like a hawk and tear out his entrails! You have to turn his name to dust.'

The entire Abdali army took its battle position. Starting from the Delhi road on the left where Shah Pasand stood with his forces, right across up to the riverbank on the right where Barkhurdar stood alongside the Rohilla men, Abdali's army stood stretched out across fifteen odd miles in a crescent formation. Abdali's sharp eyes surveyed the land to the north in the direction of Rajakhedi and Ugrakhedi. He sat on his horse, pulling vigorously at a hookah, without taking his eyes off the northern plains.

※

On the eighth day of the Hindu month of Paush Shuddh, 14 January 1761, the Panipat sky that had been lulled into silence by months of inactivity suddenly came alive. The sun decided to make an appearance at 7 a.m. The mist too let up, as if it had decided to offer an unobstructed arena to the mighty armies that were to clash today. Abdali could see the Maratha army from eight miles away. One hundred and fifty thousand men seemed to be rolling like a giant ocean wave towards him. The cannon carts could be seen moving forward, creaking and heaving, straining, as if, to turn the direction of the wheel of fate. If one were to look merely at the flags and pennants atop the massive wave, one could easily mistake it for the Dnyanoba or Vithoba processions on the point of hitting Pandharpur. The tips of the spears and the raised swords caught the sunshine and dispersed all across the plains to lend the wave a long silver crest from one end to the other.

It was 9 a.m. by the time the Gardi battalion, after covering a distance of fifteen miles, reached Chhajpur. A bare two and a half miles separated the Gardis on the left flank of the Marathas from the Rohillas on the right flank opposite. The royal regiments of Shah Wali Khan and Bhausaheb were facing each other across a distance of about three miles. The right tip of the Maratha forces was under the command of the Shinde-Holkar combine, confronting Najeeb Khan and Shah Pasand Khan on the left wing of Abdali's army, still about four miles away.

Grinding down the foot-high embankments that separated one field from another, the Gardi regiment appeared to be bouncing as it moved. Abdali's forces stood across their way in the crescent formation, eyes flashing at the enemy. About three miles in the rear of the army sat Abdali himself in a tent on an elevated spot. He had spread hundreds of scouts across every part of the army; their sole job was to deliver the latest developments to him from every front. He had a panoramic view of the plains. The Maratha soldiers in their circular formation measured up to about forty-five thousand, which made them a good fifteen thousand less than his own; but Abdali was not the kind to underrate the importance of the raw courage of the Marathas, as also the do-or-die desperation born out of prolonged suffering.

As they were halfway between Chhajpur and Nimbdi, Ibrahim looked at the enemy forces that stood blocking them two miles away like an iron wall. He resolved to blow up the iron wall. He asked for the barrels of the cannons to be turned in the required direction. The cannons were brought down from the carts. The masons immediately got busy, scraping up the earth around them into a heap to form tall mounds for mounting the cannons. To ensure that the cannons didn't jump out of their bases with the recoil, stakes were dug deep into the ground and the cannons were firmly secured to them with heavy ropes. A hundred cannons soon stood lined up shoulder to shoulder. Lakshmanrao Panse also had cannons lined up near the Royal Guards. The cannoneers got into a frenzy and began to tamp gunpowder, lead and paper into the mouth of the guns. The gunpowder was then tapped down with a light iron peg. The guns now stood loaded. A little behind the cannons, next to Bhausaheb, stood two thousand camels carrying on their backs the smaller cannons, bazookas and grenade launchers, all stacked and ready for use. Knowing that the spark would soon be lit, the grenadiers steadied their animals.

Abdali's chief cannoneer Rahman Barakzai had also got his cannons into readiness. His smaller cannons stood rocking softly on the backs of seven or eight hundred camels. Bhausaheb's fourteen thousand horses, the backbone of the Maratha army, stood snorting and hopping from one leg to the other, staring ahead with inflamed eyes. Shah Wali's nineteen thousand horses also stood tense and ready. Shah Pasand's men from the south and the Shinde-Holkar men from the north were slowly and cautiously closing in on each other.

Around 9.30, whatever birds there were on the plains had turned completely silent. The sack-like pockets of mist that had lingered till a while ago had thought it best to vanish before the combat began. As the sun rose up, the soldiers on both sides felt their temples throb with tension. Soon, the air began to resonate with loud battle cries of 'Har Har Mahadev!' and 'Deen! Deen!' Ibrahim Khan took the light to the wick of the cannon Mahakali. The explosions that followed the setting alight of a few other cannons made the earth tremble in fear and consternation. Huge balls of fire went arcing across the sky, sparking and shrieking horribly as they flew. A few of the shots fell among the Rohillas gathered two miles away, while a number of balls had overshot their target by a distance. The Mahakali had begun to belch and roar with such passion that, along with making life hell for its feeders, it had stretched its ropes and jumped a few feet in front. Within minutes of Mahakali getting into the action, the cannon Taqdeer on the Rohilla side had begun to spit fire too. While the cannons boomed like thunder, arrows began to descend on both sides like a rainstorm. The horses danced in a trance to the beats of kettle-drums, bugles and trumpets. The Gardi drums too beat a wild tattoo, whipping their gunners into a frenzy of action. Empty powder kegs were being swiftly kicked behind. Up in the sky, one could see nothing except huge mountains of smoke and dust. Smoke bombs were being hurled from both sides. Najeeb had a plentiful supply of these smoke bombs, with which he was trying to unnerve the Marathas.

It was getting to be 11.30 now. The terrorized sun hung in the sky, wiping its sweaty, sooty face, as it watched the scene down below. It hadn't seen such mayhem since the Mahabharat was fought thousands of years ago, and it was trying to find a safe spot for itself behind the billowing clouds of smoke and dust. It was dusk at noon, and the goddess of war was swirling around the plains hysterically, her flame-red tongue hanging down to her powerful bosom as she gathered men and animals in her fearsome embrace. Scorched horses and camels lay dying, scratching out absurd patterns in the dust with their hooves.

The Gardi cannoneers were on a rampage, firing a steady stream of fireballs into the enemy cluster. And yet, Ibrahim Khan noticed that even after ninety minutes of relentless bombarding, the damage wasn't as grave as it should have been. A number of his shots were flying over the heads of the Rohilla men and falling on the other side, he guessed. That could be the only explanation for the Rohillas continuing to crawl ahead. He ordered the cannon fire to cease instantly. 'Pull the smaller guns to the two edges of the formation,' he yelled. 'Open up the way for the musketeers to move forward!'

Seven battalions of the Gardi musketeers leapt forward, each consisting of a thousand men. Seven thousand muskets set up a noisy crackle. Barkhurdar Khan and Amir Beg on the other side had been waiting since morning to get their teeth into the Maratha jugular. They had been planning to move to the extreme right and throw a ring round the Gardi men. The move hadn't escaped Ibrahim's shrewd eyes, and he had planted two thousand of his gunmen to tackle the advancing enemy.

Right in front of Ibrahim stood eighteen thousand Rohilla men, among them such seasoned fighters like Dundey Khan, Saadullah Khan, Inayat Khan and Faizullah. To keep them at bay, he had merely eight thousand of his Gardis, who kept firing at the far mightier force with relentless courage. Pushing the butt against their shoulder, the men would fire in standing position, handing the empty musket down to their mates sitting at their knees, who instantly handed them freshly reloaded weapons. As Ibrahim stood guiding his men, a slave came running and shouted, 'Khan Saheb, your brother-in-law has been killed!'

'We'll see about that later,' he shouted back, without taking his eyes away. The Gardis had begun to find their rhythm; their bullets were bringing the Rohillas down like leaves off an autumnal tree. The slave boys working right behind the Gardi musketeers were keeping them supplied with fresh boxes of gunpowder and clearing the empty boxes away. The Rohillas were getting mowed down like crops being harvested. Blood spurted everywhere; the field was littered with corpses. Gaps appeared and steadily began to widen in the wall that the Rohillas had erected. The Gardis were now ready to barge in through the gaps. Trumpets of victory began sounding in Ibrahim's ears. Out of the eighteen thousand Rohillas that had stridden out, barely seven thousand were left. Within two and a half hours of the storm that he had let loose, Ibrahim had virtually demolished the wall of humanity that the Rohillas had erected. Behind Ibrahim's men stood the forces of Vitthalrao Vinchurkar and Damaji Gayakwad. Meanwhile, the contingents of Barkhurdar and Amir Beg had been making desperate attempts to sneak past the enemy from the left flank and launch an attack from behind.

Old Vitthal Vinchurkar had been watching from behind the havoc that the Gardis had been wreaking upon the Rohillas, creating a new high-water mark in bravery. Vitthalrao was not going to be found wanting. 'If these Gardis paardhis can do it, I can certainly do it better,' he muttered under his breath as the blood rushed into his head. 'After spending an entire lifetime in wars and on hunts, if I don't step up now, I will bring shame upon my white hair! People will laugh at me!' He tucked a little tobacco powder in his cheek, pulled out his broad-bladed sword and yelled 'Har Har Mahadev!' as he spurred his horse into a gallop, breaking the impenetrable circle that Ibrahim Khan had formed. His fifteen hundred men rode full pace at his heel, reverberating their leader's cry of 'Har Har Mahadev!'

Damaji Gayakwad, who had been watching this, signalled to his twenty-five hundred horsemen, and they set off, hot on the trail of the contingent ahead. As the saffron flags went fluttering forward, Vinchurkar's asylum-seeking Afghan boys got confused and dispersed into the rest of the Maratha army.

Hearing the sudden commotion, Ibrahim turned round to see what was happening. What he saw formed a lump of fear in his gut. He yelled, 'What are you doing? Don't dash out front! Don't break the circle, you idiots! It will be disastrous! Stop!'

Hearing Ibrahim's desperate calls, his brother Fateh Khan, who had been handling the cannons, looked up and immediately tried to stand in the way of the riders closing in upon him, yelling frantically, 'Stop! Please, I fall at your feet, stop! Don't break the circle! We'll be devastated!'

But drunk on their egos and hell-bent on proving a point, Gayakwad and Vinchurkar did not pay heed. Who's screaming? What's he screaming about? Who cares? Our job is to come crashing down upon the enemy, teach the bastards a lesson! The distance between the Gardis and the Rohillas had shrunk substantially, which Vinchurkar and Gayakwad filled in. Their horsemen now suddenly created a screen through which firing became impossible. The Gardis could do nothing but hold their fire. How could they fire at their own men? They simply stood there letting off the steam that the war-fever had induced, while their guns let off whatever smoke was left in the barrels. What else was left to do except chew their nails and bang their heads against their guns?

The fleeing Rohillas turned round to see why the gunfire had suddenly stopped. What they saw brought the light twinkling back in the eyes of their young commander Inayat Khan. 'Stop!' he yelled to his men. 'The Marathas chasing us do not have guns. Go get them, boys!' The Rohillas didn't need a second invitation. They turned round and fired their guns. The missiles went whistling out of the barrels and found the broad chests of the rushing Marathas and their horses. Their flashing swords were desperate to get a taste of the enemy's blood, but how could they move forward with bullets flying all around? In the chest, in the back, in the head—the bullets found their mark and brought the riders down like they had been put there for target practice.

When Barkhurdar Khan and Amir Beg saw the Gardis standing there, confused and dumbfounded, they saw the opening created by the disappearance of Vinchurkar and Gayakwad's men and penetrated the circle from the left. The Gardis were jolted by this sudden onslaught, but Ibrahim and Fateh Khan made desperate efforts to reorganize themselves. The two Rohilla generals had, however, blocked their way from the north and cut them off from their supply of gunpowder. All this time, Inayat Khan had been making mincemeat of Vinchurkar and Gayakwad's men. Once they had been slaughtered, Inayat Khan, Ahmad Bangash Pathan and Dundey Khan rushed with their remaining Rohilla warriors and attacked from behind the Gardis, who were now turned north, battling Barkhurdar Khan and Amir Beg.

Vinchurkar and Gayakwad fled in panic towards where the Royal Guards were locked in mortal conflict with Shah Wali's battalion. They instantly got sucked into the conflict alongside Bhausaheb, none of them with any thought about how the Gardis' forces three miles to the left would be faring. With Shah Wali Khan's assault giving the Marathas no time to think of anything else, Ibrahim Khan Gardi was left utterly helpless. The man who was on the verge of victory a little while ago was now caught between the enemy pressing upon him from both directions, staring at certain defeat. Even so, he decided to buck up and fight until his last breath.

Barkhurdar Khan, Amir Beg, Saadullah, Faizullah, Bangash Pathan, Dundey Khan and the other Rohillas had now got the Gardis in a pincer grasp, and they were steadily pressing it tighter. There was no distance left now for any use of firearms. Men were now in head-on collision with men, and the Gardis fought on. Their beloved cannons, which had been their companions for life, were standing useless. As Ibrahim fought, he saw his brother Fateh Khan being bored with one spear in the stomach and another few in the back. As Fateh Khan fell, the spears prevented his body from making it all the way to the ground.

There were barely seven or eight hundred Gardis left now. Gunfight distance had vanished long ago, and they were now making as much use of the bayonets as they could, disembowelling whichever Rohilla danced into their range before falling to their death. Heads were being lopped. More and more Gardi corpses had begun to litter the ground. The Rohilla groups that had earlier withdrawn due to the ferocity of the Gardi assault had all begun to ride back in and settle scores with their nemesis. Barely three hundred Gardis were left standing and battling, among them their leader, Ibrahim Khan Gardi. Bleeding from multiple wounds, clothes soaked in blood, Ibrahim Khan continued to swing his blade with all the fervour he could muster.

⚛

Bhausaheb had planned to move along the Yamuna bank and somehow push his way through to Delhi, but looking at how the main enemy forces—Irani and Turani included—had blocked his passage and were bent upon a fight to the finish, he had changed his plan. He turned sharply towards the south and now stood in direct confrontation with

Shah Wali's regiment. Emperor Abdali had assigned a battalion of battle-hardened Irani and Turani cavalrymen to Shah Wali Khan. Except for four or five days at the most, Abdali's forces had never had to face any serious shortage of food and fodder; as a result, the nineteen thousand horses that stood snorting and glaring at the Maratha forces were strong, healthy and battle-ready.

Bhausaheb had thirteen thousand horses of the Royal Guards under his direct command. To his immediate right stood Satvoji Jadhav with his fifteen-hundred-strong cavalry, as also fifteen hundred horses each of Yashwantrao Pawar and Shamsher Bahadur. These animals had run into the battlefield with barely a handful of hay that their grooms had procured for them in the dead of the night, washed down with plenty of water. The poor animals had not had a healthy feed for a long time before that, but since the dawn of that day, they had been taken over by the same spirit of raw courage as their masters had. A good fifteen miles of run after so many days of being tied to the stake was making them feel light and frisky. Whisking their tails now and then, they stood glaring at the distant enemy and snorted back.

Rival shields stood reflecting sunlight over each other. The battle cries of 'Har Har Mahadev!' were equally vociferously echoed by cries of 'Allah-o-Akbar!' Both sides glared at each other, looking for an opportunity to make the first move.

Four miles down, the conflict between the Gardis and the Rohillas had flared up, and soon the spark was lit here too, literally, when Lakshmanrao Panse set fire to the wick of his best cannon. Huge balls of fire began to rain on both sides. Every ball that landed instantly tossed up twenty-five to thirty healthy men as pieces of flesh and bone. The Kandahari soldiers were being fried crisp by the unrelenting fusillade. There was dense smoke everywhere. The ferocious assault by the Marathas put Shah Wali on the alert. It didn't take much time for the seasoned wazeer to understand that the absence of the Gardis suggested this was not their main artillery force. His cannons started to respond with equal ferocity. Thus, the two mortal enemies advanced threateningly towards each other. The Afghans made seven hundred she-camels go down on their front knees and began to fire their smaller cannons into the mass of the enemy in front. Rehman Barakzai went around with a cane in his hand and rained it upon the backs of his cannoneers and grenadiers, admonishing them to aim with care. Singeing and roasting in this rain of fire, the Marathas kept hitting back as they crept forward.

Angry red balls of fire kept crossing each other in the air, kicking up mountains of dust and human and animal flesh when they found their mark. A few of these shots went over the heads of the soldiers and fell among the non-combatants ranged right behind, letting loose terrified screams and roars. A large number of them scampered backwards to what they hoped and prayed was a safe enough distance, squatted on the ground and wailed. They held each other tight and looked up at the sky to watch the dreaded fireworks. Jereshastri and Agnihotri were trying their best to burrow themselves into the ground. 'Find a way out of this catastrophe,' they screeched at each other, putting their heads on each other's shoulder and crying inconsolably. The women and children bawled and stared at each other with petrified eyes.

The strong, big-boned, well-fed Afghan horses were bursting with energy. There was no shortage of gunpowder either, and it could be used without any concern for conservation. The Afghan gunners let loose volley after volley, never caring if some of their blasts missed their mark. Pansare's arsenal, by contrast, was woefully short of ammunition; in more or less the same state as the emaciated Maratha horses. The powder had to be used with extreme prudence. The enemy fire had blocked forward movement. Panse's artillery began to peter out, and the enemy had begun to creep closer and closer with the avowed intention of feasting on their blood. Bhausaheb, standing in his canopy, had been bucking his soldiers with loud cries of 'Har Har Mahadev!' and urging them to hold on to their courage.

With the distance between the Royal Guards and the enemy steadily shrinking, the gunpowder running out, men and animals falling as they stood, the horsemen began to veer round to the opinion that it was better to rush into the conflagration and make something out of it than just get swatted to death like flies. The intrepid soldiers firmed their will, tightened their fists on their swords and spears, tested the reins of their horses and leapt forward with loud cries of 'Har Har Mahadev!' Uncaring of what the flames were doing to them, they swept on like a river in flood and broke upon the astonished Durrani army. They were falling by the hundreds, both men and animals, but a large enough number of them were now within attacking distance of the camels with their bazookas. Raw, desperate courage and the element of surprise helped them slaughter a number of the enemy gunners, till at last they had silenced all of them, although at a terrible cost of life.

It was now face-to-face combat. The bullocks from both groups had found their independence and were searching for ways to escape the inferno. It was now the relatively fresh, well-fed, battle-hardened Durrani horses that kept pushing hard, ranged against the debilitated but resilient animals from the Bhima basin who refused to step back. Whenever the Maratha horsemen were pushed, they would move five or ten steps back, turn round like dancing pigeons, let out a battle cry and launch themselves all over again at the enemy. The men on both sides were charged with the spirit of battle, and they threw themselves upon each other with eyes glaring, swords flashing and arms swinging. The Afghans who had come from much colder lands had put on their leather jackets, which the enemy's weapons could not easily penetrate. The Marathas, in their home-spun cotton, were at a disadvantage. The dark Maratha skins turned red with blood as the blows found their mark. The combat went on for well over an hour, blades cutting through flesh. Suddenly one of the Maratha men broke the news, 'Hey, the monster who murdered Govindpant, the guy who prevented our provisions from reaching us, that rogue Atai Khan is in the contingent in front!'

'Kill! Kill! Kill Atai Khan!' 'Ataya re Ataya!' 'Kill him! Kill him!' The Bhima basin horses were spurred into greater speed, and they rammed into Shah Wali's men. Yashwantrao Pawar suddenly espied Atai Khan shooting arrows from his canopy atop his elephant. He instantly bucked his horse, reached up to the elephant and leapt at the howdah. Atai Khan dropped his bow and pulled out his sword. Yashwantrao's four-arms-long sword didn't give Atai Khan any time to organize his defence. It pushed him into a corner and fell on his arm with such force that Atai Khan lost both sword and the arm holding it. Quick as a flash, Yashwantrao saw the opening and thrust the tip of his sword deep into and across Atai's guts. The wound squirted blood on Yashwantrao's face as he pulled the sword out, lifted the dying man and tossed him to the ground below.

Atai's swift and brutal slaughter did two things: it filled Yashwantrao's men with new energy, and it took the wind out of Atai's army's sails. His three thousand soldiers were getting shredded and bloodied by the minute. Their canopies and howdahs were being pulled to the ground. With the leader dead, they had shrunk in spirit and begun to flee. This gave Marathas a new high, and they began swinging their weapons with a vengeance. Shah Wali Khan, who had noticed the resurgence of Maratha energy, looked anxious, and when he saw his men turning tail and fleeing, he was alarmed. His vision turned dim. 'Things don't look good at all,' he said hoarsely to himself and got down from his canopy.

There were barely a thousand horsemen and fifty or so camels left around him. He first tried to block the way of the horsemen with the cry, 'Stop! Don't flee!' but with defeat staring them in the face, no one felt it worthwhile to listen to an old man's entreaties. Mortified, he went and sat next to a heap of corpses and screamed at his fleeing men, 'Treacherous fools! Where will you run to? And how far can you run? You think the land of your fathers is close enough to reach in a few days?'

That was when Kashiraj Pandit came to where he sat. Shah Wali beat his breast at seeing him and cried, 'Go, run, son! Tell your master and my foster son to rush to my rescue. Without his help, I shall certainly be killed.'

Kashiraj sped away and delivered Shah Wali's message to Shuja. The Nawab raised his hands in despair and said, 'The Shindes and Holkars are standing right there with a noose to swing me by; won't they be waiting to swallow up my army? This is war, Pandit, and in the middle of war, there's no father or son, no natural nor foster.'

The wazeer, meanwhile, was in a terrible state. 'I will be wiped out! Dead, for sure!'

With the enemy's main Irani army brought to tatters, Bhausaheb could see huge gaps emerge right in front of him, the escape route becoming wider and wider. 'This is the opportunity you have been fighting for!' he told himself. 'Barge through this opening, and you will be in Delhi before you know it!' As soon as this thought struck him, he turned his head round to see hordes of camp followers a couple of miles away, terrified as a bunch of sheep surrounded by a pack of wolves. There were helpless women there with their brood, pilgrims and non-combative artisans, who would be gobbled up with great relish by the enemy smarting for revenge! How tall could a tall person be? Six feet? Seven feet? How tall should a mission be? Was any measure invented that could measure its height?

Bhausaheb's was clear on this: as the commander-in-chief and the patriarch of this vast multitude, he had to take them all across to safety. It was an hour past noon by now. A thick blanket of smoke and dust hung in the air. All across were fighting men of both sides, milling around to secure whatever advantage could be gained. The Maratha steeds, however, had turned decidedly listless. They had been slowing down for some time, but the heat of the sun, ordinarily welcome in such cold conditions, seemed to be sapping their inadequate juices. They had begun to respond less and less to the persuasions of their riders. The men pummeled them with their fists, twisted their tails, dug their spurs into the belly, but the dead-beat animals had little energy left in them to move. The fortnight-long starvation could in no way have been compensated by the handful of fodder they had received the previous night. Above all, that was the maniacal running they had been doing since morning; no wonder, then, whatever water there was in their bellies had evaporated as sweat. A number of them turned dizzy and began to collapse where they stood.

The men on their backs were in no better state. 'Water!' they croaked, 'water!' There were not enough water-carrier boys around to distribute the life-saving fluid, not enough bags either. Men were frothing at the mouth, looking deathly pale and drawn. With the opening in front of them invitingly wide now, there was no excitement to rush through it to the other side. A little more of the sun, and the men were collapsing too. It was as if an unknown power was mesmerizing them to fall in a swoon, a poultry farm struck with sleeping sickness. Bhausaheb was alarmed at this sudden turn in his forces and asked, 'Nana, what disease is this? What black magic?'

'No sickness or magic, Shrimant; if you will notice, the sun takes its arc with a southern tilt this time of the year, and our army is moving south too. Our men have been starving for so long, as it is, and now this slanting sun!'

'The sun god too had to go and join the conspiracy to finish us!'

Undone by their belly, men and animals looked around frantically for a few swigs of water. There was no strength left in them to make a dash through the opening in the enemy's army that beckoned them.

A few miles to the south, Abdali stood on his elevated spot, a European telescope in hand, seeing the dismal scene unfold before him. His scouts would come running in rapid frequency bringing information from every corner of the field. Whose contingent was getting wiped out, which chieftain had been slain, in which part his men were dominating, in which part the enemy's, what the state of the ammunition was—all information was reaching up to him within minutes of the occurrence. The instruction to these couriers was quite clear: 'Even if the entire army is getting wiped out, you should not tarry. Keep running without a break!'

He could see the Rohilla forces fall. When the Kandahar cavalry under Shah Wali Khan began to get decimated too, Abdali's heart sank. The news from the scouts was getting worse by the minute. There were barely a couple of hundred men left around his wazeer. The rest had either fled or been killed.

Seeing his impregnably laid out crescent formation of the morning collapse under a few hours of hammering, Abdali was unnerved. The murderous assault of the Maratha storm was rocking his ship violently. It was ripping off his massive sails and stretching the ropes; they had begun to snap. The vessel carried as cargo all his army, his reputation, his very future as the emperor of Kandahar and Kabul. Suddenly, he thought of his harem and sent for the chief warden Khoja Mohammad Khan and his assistant Zulfiqar. 'Where are the women?' he yelled as soon as he saw them.

'As per the royal orders, they have been safely sheltered four miles behind us, Aalam-panaah. Please do not worry about them.'

'Take them further behind by another four miles. Keep the sturdiest horses ready for them in case the need arises. Under no circumstances should the ladies fall into the hands of these Margatthas! Keep a sharp eye on the battlefield, and if things get worse, depart for Kandahar at full tilt without waiting for instructions.'

After settling the issue of the harem, Abdali turned his attention back to the war zone. A good six or seven thousand of the Afghan fleers had assembled a little distance from the royal tent, still shivering and cowering with the fear of the slaughter they had escaped from. When he saw those deserters, Abdali felt like vomiting. He had a mechanism for setting this kind of cowardice aright. He carried with him a special squad of five thousand men known as much for their phenomenal strength as for their brutality. These men had been handpicked for the utter insensitivity they possessed for the human condition. These executioners did not turn a hair while breaking a person's limbs or beating him to within an inch of his life. They just had to be told how far to go, and they never failed to travel that distance. He sent for fifteen hundred of these executioners to look around for deserters and settle accounts with them. Another two thousand he sent to the battlefield so as to ensure the full participation of the soldiers in the battle at hand. The remaining fifteen hundred he set upon the seven thousand fleers that stood by his tent.

The batch of executioners who had been sent to stem the leak had taken positions that afforded them high visibility. When the Afghan deserters saw them from a distance, they knew they had nowhere left to go except the battlefield. Death there would surely be painless relative to the end that these demons could bring to their wretched lives. The contingent of executioners on the battlefield ensured that they got back into the fray. Abdali had kept three thousand men in reserve whom he now dispatched, rested and fresh, to help the tiring men on the front.

Najeeb Khan's fifteen thousand pawns stood four miles in front of where Abdali stood. The Shinde-Holkar team was still about eight miles away. The face-to-face combat had already begun at the river end and the middle, but on this Delhi road end, the battle had still to begin. Najeeb, however, had whipped himself into a state of high excitement. He had all along been carrying himself as the bridegroom of the party; he had kept the flame of hatred against the Marathas burning bright. Now that the moment had arrived, he was eager to be up there in the forefront and get busy smashing the faces of his mortal enemy. His restlessness to get into the action was such that even at this distance, still eight miles away from the enemy, he had begun to shoot smoke bombs three or four hundred at a time. They went crackling and smoking all the distance, creating an immense amount of rattle, besides releasing thick, acrid smoke. The idea was to put the fear of God in the Maratha forces, reduce them to tears even before they met face to face.

By 1.30 p.m., Shah Wali Khan's forces had been reduced to dire straits. The goddess of victory had pulled out her garland and was all ready to put it round the Maratha neck. If only they could have stretched the tiniest bit, victory would have been theirs. But coming at the heels of deprivation, this last, superhuman effort had so drained them that their knees refused to hold them up any further. Fortunately, Abdali reinforced his debilitated forces with fresh men and was ready to fight again.

As Bhausaheb continued to urge his men to another round of combat with battle cries of 'Come on! Kill! Slaughter!' a horseman rode up to his canopy and yelled, 'Shrimant! Our Ibrahim Gardi—'

'What about Khan Saheb?' Bhausaheb nearly stopped breathing.

'The enemy has taken him prisoner and taken him away in chains. Despite being riddled with grievous wounds, he was seen struggling like a wounded tiger as he was dragged away. Thirty or forty of the enemy men have been assigned to take him behind the battle line.

'What about his battalion?' he asked, his heart sinking rapidly.

'They have been slaughtered to the last man. Every one of them died fighting.' Bhausaheb shut his eyes tight, as if trying to regain control over his thoughts. When he opened them again, he saw that the rifts his army had created in the enemy's battle formation had repaired themselves. The wall once again stood solid and forbidding, and the Afghans were once again snarling and straining to reach up to them. This was no time for him to stand grieving. This was his moment of reckoning. With a loud cry of 'Har Har Mahadev!' he jumped off the canopy on to the back of Chandrasen, drew out his sword and, swirling it in the air, rushed forward to destroy the enemy. Vishwasrao raced in tow. The Afghans and the Marathas were now so locked in each other's fatal embrace that death for at least one of them could be the only outcome.

The clash that ensued was the bloodiest yet. Horse rammed into horse and men leapt on each other with fearsome weapons flashing. Heads began to roll off shoulders, intestines were sliced out to fall trailing upon the ground. Eyes, ears, noses, chests, limbs were slashed, pierced, hacked and thrown across the battleground, some still pulsating with the last spark of life left in them. Skulls were cracked open, and the brains oozed out in a macabre parody of smashed melons. The air rang with frightening screeches of 'Hey Bhagwan!' and 'Arrey Deva!' and 'Ya Allah!'

and 'Ya Parvardigaar!' as what were once human beings departed to meet their Maker in a messy salad of flesh and blood and gore.

The fervour with which the Marathas had renewed their attack pushed the Afghans on the backfoot once again. Shamsher Bahadur was swinging his sword with deadly effect, slicing and cutting through enemy flesh, compelling them to make way for him. 'Look! That's Bajirao's son!' they told each other in awe as they tried to get out of his range. Yashwantrao Pawar was in a zone of his own. The forty bleeding wounds on his body had not slowed him down. He was a slaughtering machine that had been wound tight and then let loose to wreak havoc.

While Bhausaheb had thrust himself deep into the roaring melee of enemy soldiers, slashing and chopping as he went, Vishwasrao had also decided to make this his day of arrival into manhood. He took his horse ramming into the enemy fold and swung his sword to make heads fall like overripe fruit on a windy day.

After an hour of vicious counter-attack by the Marathas, led by the delirious, intoxicating excitation of their chiefs, the tables had once again begun to turn. The chariot of victory was veering in the direction of the Maratha army when a bazooka shot came whistling in and hit Vishwasrao straight on his brow, killing him instantly. He slumped forward on his horse's mane, instinctively tightening his grip on the animal's ear. Blood gushed out of the hole from where his life had fled.

When Bhausaheb heard the news, he let out a piteous roar of 'Rao Saheb! Rao Saheb!' and leapt forward. He brought the corpse down from the horse and sat down with Vishwasrao's body cradled in his arms. He looked at the delicate face of the adolescent boy and ran his blood-smeared fingers through his soft, golden-brown hair. Vishwasrao's eyes were half-closed and the jaw hung half-open. This blow drove Bhausaheb to distraction. He handed the corpse carefully over to the others and sat in a daze, hallucinating the sudden appearance of Nanasaheb. The father threw a grief-stricken, accusatory look at Bhausaheb and wailed, 'Is this why I had left my seventeen-year-old boy in your charge, Bhau?'

Bhau could not raise his head to meet Nanasaheb's eyes, however hard he tried. 'Shrimant,' he stuttered incoherently, 'Rao's passing has broken the pearl necklace that hung around the Maratha empire.'

The soldiers placed Vishwasrao's body in the canopy atop Gajendra and covered it with a velvet sheet. Bapu Hingane sat beside it. Bhausaheb felt volcanic anger build up inside him. He knew that there was only one way in which he could release it. He once again leapt upon Chandrasen, tightened his grip on his Khorasani sword, and roared into the sky, 'How far can you run, bastards? Abdalya, Najeeba, I shall not turn my back to the battlefield without first dispatching you to hell!'

⁕

It was now past 2.30. The plains of Panipat seemed like they were going up in flames. Najeeb, marching along the right wing of the Afghan force, was making a steady advance. His pawns led the march with heavy matchlocks and bazookas on their shoulders. They had with them a team of masons and diggers who would quickly dig small trenches, into which the gunners stepped. They would take cover behind the protection of the dug-up earth, rest the barrels on the rim and let go a few volleys. When news reached them of Vishwasrao's death, Najeeb went delirious with joy. He forgot all dignity and hopped around, dancing like a drunken ape. His regiment gathered speed as it neared the Shinde-Holkar formation.

The news of Vishwasrao's passing had hit the Maratha army like a blast of chilly wind. The non-combatants were shell-shocked too. While Bhausaheb had placed Vishwasrao's corpse on the canopy atop Gajendra and thrown himself ferociously into the battle, the elephant began to get left behind, trudging along with its lifeless burden covered under a velvet sheet. Bapu Hingane sat next to it with a heart, too wounded to even cry. A few canopied elephants caught up with Gajendra from behind, one of them carrying Parvatibai, Rakhmabai Akkasaheb, the Paigude family and a couple of others. As they caught up with Ganjendra, Parvatibai pulled the curtain of her canopy back to see the velvet-wrapped body. Her heart throbbed wildly with fear as she asked, 'Whose corpse is that, Pandit?'

The dam burst for Bapu Hingane. 'Vishwasrao Rao Saheb is no more with us!' he lamented aloud. 'This is his body that I carry.'

The sky swam before Parvatibai's eyes. She let out a loud wail of grief. An equally broken Akkasaheb gathered Parvatibai in her arms and consoled her through her own tears, 'Don't cry, my girl, there's nothing we can do. God lured us into this land with such grand invitation, only to crush us under His heel. His rage hasn't cooled off yet. Who knows who else He proposes to gather unto Himself!'

The news of Vishwasrao's death fired up Abdali and his men. He dispatched his remaining force of six thousand musketeers under the command of his favourite slave, Kizal Baksh. The regiment was split into three units of two thousand each: one was deployed on the eastern side of the Maratha Royal Guards, the other on the western side; the third launched a frontal attack on the centre. He also released the last two thousand of his bazooka-laden camels that began raining hell-fire upon the helpless Maratha horses, bringing them down like flies. The heaps of their dead assumed frightening dimensions.

The non-combatants had been rendered distraught by the news of Vishwasrao's death. The two thousand slaves of Vinchurkar's took off and tossed away the saffron bands from their foreheads and roamed through the Maratha army and among the camp followers yelling, 'Vishwasrao is dead! The Marathas have lost. The Marathas have been beaten!' Along with creating this ruckus, they also snatched away whatever they could find, beating whoever showed the least resistance. The saffron band no longer on their brows, they were mistaken for Afghan soldiers who had penetrated deep into the enemy camp. The chaos and confusion deceived even some seasoned soldiers into believing that all was over. They quickly turned their horses in the direction of Rajakhedi and bolted.

⚛

The Shinde-Holkar regiment was to the right of Bhausaheb, a large number of them on horseback. This regiment had seen nothing but defeat in the past eighteen months, and Bhausaheb had anticipated that their morale would be low, which could even lead to desertion. That was why he had placed himself in the middle, so that their contagion didn't spread among the rest of his forces. The situation with his own Royal Guards, however, had turned desperate. While the Gardis to his right had been wiped out, the forces on the left along the Imperial highway still hadn't clashed. It was just long-distance missiles travelling mainly from south to north, most of them Najeeb's smoke-bombs. The distance between the two combatants had been the biggest to begin with; added to that was the slow progress on both sides. Najeeb had been moving carefully, fearing that the Shinde-Holkar horsemen would take a heavy toll of his pawns if he dashed forward in too much of a rush. The news of Vishwasrao's death changed all that, and now his musketeers had begun to move with dispatch, firing at the enemy as they moved along. Jankoji, closing in from the opposite side, would have wanted his force to show a good deal more urgency, but he was handicapped by the Holkar men, who did not seem to be in any hurry at all. Right since morning, Malharba had not shown any great enthusiasm for the conflict ahead. With him not awfully charged up, his men had taken their cue from their leader and slackened their pace. It was almost 3 p.m. The news of Vishwasrao's passing away had reached the Shinde-Holkar regiment, and it had spread a pall of gloom everywhere. Najeeb was now barely a couple of miles away, marking his march all the way with volleys of gunfire. Meanwhile, Shah Pasand Khan, who had been holding the fort on one end of the Delhi road, had begun to slip into the right nook of the Shinde-Holkar forces, which would mean that they would be hemmed in from all four sides—a thought that gave shivers to the soldiers and their masters. Gangoba Tatya, standing next to Malharba, was sweating profusely and mopping his face every now and then with his long kerchief and looking in all directions, fear writ large on his face. Malharba asked him in a tense voice, 'Gangoba, is the war turning in their favour?'

Gangoba snorted sarcastically and said, 'Subhedar, it doesn't really matter whether the war turns or not, but is it all right for heads to turn during such desperate times?'

'Meaning?'

'What else can it mean, Subhedar? What's the point in trying to argue with people whose heads are muddled up with fancy ideas? I believe that if the head stays in place, some hat or the other will arrive!'

Gangoba's suggestion made a lot of sense to Malharba. Around three o'clock, they turned their horses round. Once the men saw the two moving in the opposite direction, the men of the two forces did the same. Jankoji was dismayed by what he could see happening all around him. Mad with rage, he tried to block the passage of the fleeing men and screamed, 'How can you leave our leader halfway and run, you treacherous bastards? Loyalty to your salt, wretches, loyalty to your salt!'

He didn't find anyone responding to his call. The Punjab, Shukratal, Buradi Ghats and then the escape into the deserts of Rajputana, for the past two years it had only been a story of defeat and flight for the Shinde-Holkar men. Fear had not loosened its grip of their hearts. The chase that they had barely kept ahead of on the evening of Dattaji's slaughter was still their favourite nightmare. They dreaded the thought of having to go through it all over again, and they prudently turned round and fled.

Mahadji also joined the team of fleeing horsemen, leaving his cousin fretting and fuming in helpless rage. He then turned his gaze towards where the Royal Guards, now four or five thousand of them, were tenaciously giving a tough fight to a far superior enemy. A few saffron pennants, surrounded on all sides by the Afghan forces, could still be seen bobbing atop their elephants. Bhausaheb in the inner ring was fighting the battle of his life. The slaughter of Vishwasrao had already killed something deep inside Jankoji. He still had his cousin Tukoji with him along with a few dozen of his closest friends. He cast a look at the skirmish that was happening round the royal flag, fanned the fire to seek revenge for Dattaji's death, tightened his sword round his waist and shot off in that direction, with his loyal friends on his tail.

The last leg of the war was in progress. Bhausaheb was in the middle of it, letting out loud battle cries of 'Come on, boys, fight! Strike! Kill!' as he himself swung his sword in a fever of excitement. A vast number had achieved martyrdom and a number of them had turned tail and fled, but Bhausaheb and the loyal men around him knew that this was their last stand. They were uncaring of the smoke and dust that had enveloped them, or the strength of the enemy that confronted them; they would fight for as long as there was breath in their bodies. *Rao Saheb is now with the gods; how will I face the Peshwa? It is possible the forces in front will deny us victory, but neither they nor the gods above can deny me my sacred right to martyrdom.* His mind had drifted well beyond the realms of life and death. He remembered what he had told Nana Purandare again and again, 'I have no fear of death at all. I have met him many times in this short span of life, as one meets a friend from the other side of the river. What's there to fear about him?'

Bhausaheb was in a trance as he swung his sword at the necks and shoulders of whichever enemy fell within his range. He shouted words of encouragement to his colleagues fighting alongside him. 'Come on, Darekar, Pawar, Kadu, Kakde! Good show, Daphale, Bhosale, Bhoite! Don't stop! Just keep going! Kill! Slaughter!' The wave of enemy forces rolling over these braves was, however, just too powerful to be held back. It kept pushing the Maratha fighters farther and farther back.

⁂

Parvatibai, sitting in her canopy, could see nothing through the blanket of dust and smoke that had settled so heavily on the battlefield. Visaji Jogdand, who had been given the responsibility of her security, was nowhere to be seen either. Through the devastation that spread everywhere, she could not see where her husband would be. Her heart was in turmoil. The confines of the canopy had begun to suffocate her; she was finding it hard to breathe. Her anxiety reached such a pitch that she leapt out of the canopy onto the ground. She noticed the horse of a slain soldier nearby. Picking up the sword that lay next to him, she jumped up on the horse and set off towards where the conflict was thickest. Every pore of her body was aflame. 'I shall be your partner in martyrdom, my lord! I shall not be denied that right!' she said to herself as she spurred the horse.

Bhausaheb and his Royal Guards were steadily getting isolated. Amir Beg and Barkhurdar Khan began moving in from the river end. From the imperial road end came in Shah Pasand Khan, while Najeeb's force of over ten thousand foot soldiers came from the left. In front was Shah Wali Khan, now bolstered by fresh reinforcements, while from his right side closed in the Rohillas Dundey Khan, Saadullah Khan, Faizullah Khan and Inayat Khan.

Damaji got hit on the leg by a bazooka shot, and he quickly turned his horse round and moved out of the battlefield in the direction of Malharba. Vitthalrao Vinchurkar, who had suffered grievously at the hands of the Rohillas, also found the opportunity to sneak out and head Malharba's way. Shah Pasand had already moved out of the imperial road and was heading towards the main force in the middle; the contingents of Najeeb and Shuja had also left their corner, rendering the road to Delhi open for the first time in many weeks. That was the road that the deserters hit—Malharba, Sabaji, Vinchurkar, the wounded Antaji Mankeshwar and many other sardars and their contingents—and began to make rapid progress towards the south down a now-unhindered road.

Jankoji and his fifty-odd braves were giving hard, unrelenting fight to the enemy. Shamsher Bahadur was swirling his sword, bringing down one soldier after another in a maniacal rush. His hands were coated with blood right up to his elbows. He had noticed the rats who had been quietly edging away, and he vented his rage upon the hapless Afghans who fell in his way. Only a miracle could have made his mad dispensation of death carry on for very long, and miracles had long stopped happening for the Marathas. A desperate swing of an Afghan landed on his thigh and another landed on the head. Shamsher collapsed under those two blows and fell to the ground in a swoon. Yashwant Pawar's frenzy was bringing the enemy down like flies, too, when a Kandahari spear came flying in from nowhere, penetrated from his back and pushed its tip out from the chest. He died as he fell from his horse.

Bhausaheb's horse, Chandrasen, was as intoxicated with the spirit of war as its master, and it leapt hither and thither over heaps of corpses at its master's orders. Four enemy soldiers approached from behind, two of whom swung their swords and found their mark. They tore through the muscles of the horse's rear legs and cut open the main arteries. As the doubly lamed Chandrasen collapsed, Bhausaheb jumped off its back, looking for another horse. He had no time to lament the fate of his favourite horse. His men were falling like leaves hit by the autumn wind.

Those who stood fighting were being relentlessly pushed back. Some of Shamsher's men had reached the wells where the cannons still stood on their mounds. The direction in which the guns faced was mainly teeming with enemy soldiers. They somehow managed to find enough gunpowder to stuff two of the cannons and set the wicks alight. In the fever of excitement, they had lost the sense to distance themselves from the cannons before they exploded. The cannons found their mark and blew away huge swathes of the advancing enemy, but alongside, they also shattered the eardrums of those even twenty feet away, while the heat that emanated from the flaming guns roasted the ones who had lit the wicks. Bhausaheb's most trusted men were either falling, fighting or were slowly sneaking away from the battlefield. Among the remaining who were staking their all to keep the royal flag flying was the bloodied Jankoji. As he strode forward to steady the flag that was teetering on the back of its elephant, he found himself surrounded by thirty or forty enemy horsemen. Leaping upon him from all sides, they managed to pin him down and capture him alive. His one regret as he was being dragged away into captivity was that he was leaving Bhau behind to fight his desperate battle instead of dying fighting by his side.

Seeing the entire army falling apart, Jankoji's cousin Tukoji Shinde rode up to his leader and said, 'Bhau, you have fulfilled the dharma of a kshatriya. There has been no warrior in Maratha history who has battled as you have. Would it not be prudent for you to withdraw and come back to fight another day?'

'In which direction do I withdraw, Tukoba?' responded Bhausaheb. 'With Rao Saheb martyred, how do I show my face anywhere in Pune? Why should I bother about this worthless body of mine? The only thing left for me to do now is to keep fighting, die fighting.'

Bhausaheb now stood in the midst of a dense crowd of Abdali's men. He fought on, swinging, slashing, cutting, slipping, recovering, swinging again. He was so caked in dust, sweat and blood from head to toe that the only way by which the handful of his men identified him was the frenzy with which he swirled and lunged and thrust. Suddenly, the shot of a bazooka fired from somewhere came and hit him on the thigh. Bhausaheb roared, 'Hey Bhawani! Shrimant! Shrimant!' as he slid off his horse and fell to the ground, writhing in agony.

The near invincible Bhau was down, but not yet out. The fire that burnt in him was flaming still. Using the spear in his hand as support, he stood up to stare with blood-red eyes at the four enemy men closing in upon him. They were eyeing with greed the diamond- and emerald-studded pendant that hung by a chain round his neck. Bhau gathered whatever little strength was left in him, balanced himself on one foot, and raising the spear, he swung it among the advancing men and managed to bring down all four. Then he collapsed like a sack of coal. His corpse now lay among the heap of the corpses of his other brave warriors.

That very day, at that very moment, the festival of sankrant was being celebrated in Maharashtra. While puran polis, the famed sweet pancakes of the land, were being fried in every household, the brave son of Chimaji Appa named Sadashiv Bhau had finished his battle with destiny, and had fallen into eternal sleep in the distant land of Panipat.

❦

It was the sunset hour of the day of Paush Ashtami Shuddh. It was barely 5 p.m., but the sun had gone under the skyline. Not a single Maratha could be seen standing anywhere across the Panipat plains. Thirty-five thousand of them had been slaughtered. The place had been given a sprinkling of decapitated heads. The corpses at some places were lying in heaps. The darkening evening gave the entire place a macabre, surrealistic, eerie feel.

Abdali began to feel tiredness descend upon him. He wanted to return to his base camp. He scanned the devastated plains with wide-open eyes as his horse made its way past scattered bodies and puddles of blood. He had for company the loyal Wazeer Shah Wali Khan and a couple of other chieftains. A shadow of worry flitted across his face, and he stopped. He turned round and asked, 'Shah Wali, are any Marathas hiding around likely to return in the darkness of the evening?'

'No chance of that, Aalam-panaah, all of the Deccan has been destroyed. Who is left to return?'

The tired horse and horseman finally turned round towards the camp for rest. The crowd outside the royal pavilion was milling with jubilant chieftains and officers. The relief at having come out alive was evident on every face. Hafeez Rahmat Khan's son Inayat Khan had particularly distinguished himself on the battlefield that day. Abdali honoured him by gifting him with ceremonial robes and said, 'My heart swells with pride at honouring this valiant man. I congratulate you, Hafeez, for being blessed with a son like him.'

The gesture of appreciation touched the hearts of all present. Inayat Khan was not so overwhelmed with the honour as to forget himself. He responded to the emperor's praise with words of gratitude. 'Aalam-panaah,' he said, 'who are we to flaunt our bravery in your presence? What are we in comparison to your valiant self? Despicable insects! If you hadn't subdued the battlefield today with your gallantry and wisdom, these sinning infidels would have been running all over the place in glee. A war like this one is fought only once in a few centuries, and it is your valour alone that has brought victory to us. Please accept our congratulations for a victory that has dazzled the entire world.'

The assembly was impressed by the young man's judicious response and turned to see how it had gone down with the emperor. Instead of preening himself over the praise, Abdali looked strangely distracted. It appeared that he was at a loss for words. Finally, after a swallow, he began, 'Victory? ... Yes, victory it is. But the fact remains that till late in the afternoon, I was not sure whether there would be a way out of this flaming, exploding, disintegrating patch of land. It was Allah alone who made the way out for us; a lump of earth on the heads of the sinners and a crown on our brow. It could have gone in any direction, and it was Allah's mercy that gave us this phenomenal victory. What are you and I except lumps of clay? The One who makes things happen is the Almighty Protector of us all.'

He let his words sink into the minds of his stunned audience. Then he turned towards his wazeer and said, 'I carry all of Hindustan in the hollow of my palm, but even at this moment of victory, we cannot forget the extreme valour that the Marathas displayed. Despite having gone hungry for so many days, despite being hit by famine, they threw all they had into the fight. History may have no parallel to their heroism. The image of the battle refuses to leave my mind. Those gallant men, leaping upon us like tigers and lions! The boom of the cannons as they threw crackling flashes of lightning across the sky! Shah Wali, if I truly have to bare my heart, if our legendary heroes Rustam and Isfindar had been present on the battlefield today, they would surely have bitten their nails at the sight of the gallantry that these infidel Marathas put on show.'

Abdali suddenly felt tired to the bone. He dispatched a slave to arrange for some hot water for his bath, instructed another to fetch a prayer mat, and told his sardars, 'Leave me alone now. I have to meet my Allah in private.'

The audience dispersed and the emperor began to ready himself for prayer. Before he had settled, he was informed of the arrival of Qutb Shah's son and Abu Samad Khan's son along with a bunch of other youngsters. They wanted to meet him urgently, and though the emperor was not in the mood for it, he thought it fit to indulge them. The two boys looked quite incensed. Qutb Shah's son began the conversation by saying, 'Your lordship, we need permission from you to massacre whatever infidels are still alive.'

Emperor Abdali let out a soft laugh and said, 'How are you going to kill those that are already dead?'

'Jahaan-panaah,' growled the boy, 'did this thought cross their filthy minds when they chopped off my father's neck?'

'The prince is stating a fact, Aalam-panaah!' joined in Samad Khan's son. 'What happened to his father was no different from what happened to mine. Besides, as we were setting off from Kandahar in your army, our mothers and sisters had told us over and over again to kill as many infidels as we could lay hands on and earn merit. We lay our request at your feet that we be allowed to go on indiscriminate slaughter. Your lordship should not stand in the way of our desire to earn merit.' The emperor granted them permission to kill as many as they wanted to in one night within the radius of twenty miles. Satisfied, the excited youngsters set off in search of their victims.

ॐ

The battlefield was covered by the diffused light of the stars in the sky. In that light, the Afghan slaves were roaming the battlefield, looking for whatever treasure they could glean from the dead lying scattered all over. They would snatch a gold chain off one neck and slide a ring off another finger. If the ornament refused to come out with ease, knives and axes were freely used to disengage it from the wearer. A large number of Marathas had somehow found shelter in some corner of the plains while the war was in full flow. Now that it was over, they had sneaked out of their hiding places and were moving towards the village of Panipat. They had no idea whether their leader Bhausaheb was alive or dead. They had faith in the commitment he had often given them by saying, 'I am always thinking about you all.' They were hoping, as they moved, that Bhau would be waiting for them on the outskirts of the village.

The place where Shamsher Bahadur had fallen was now enveloped in darkness. He hadn't altogether regained consciousness, but he could feel the multiple wounds on his body throbbing mercilessly. He would let out occasional groans of 'Bhau, Bhau!' and imagine that Bhau was softly running his healing hands over his injuries. Suddenly, he reached out and held that hand in his own. 'Bhau,' he asked anxiously, 'is the enemy dead? That Najeeb, has he been torn apart from limb to limb? If not, you should do it instantly. As long as he continues to walk on his two feet, the rest of the world will be compelled to walk on its head. He is the devil incarnate. Why worry about my state, Bhau? Please think of your own health! But what's this, why is your hand so cold to the touch?'

The cold night wind was digging deeper and deeper into his wounds. Suddenly, a particularly sharp pain jolted him into consciousness. He opened his eyes to realize that there was a dead body lying over him. The hand that he had been holding was that body's. He flung the hand away and pushed the body off his own. As he sat up, he realized that there was another body lying over his legs. Pushing the other one away too, he gathered all his strength and determination to stand up. Every bone, every joint, every muscle inside him was shrieking with agony, so much so that for a minute, he almost blacked out again. He stood still, took deep breaths and applied his will power to retrieve his balance. He then looked around, and even in the dim starlight he could see the wreckage that lay all around him. As he slowly began to walk, if he was not stepping on a body or a dismembered limb, he was putting his foot into earth made thick and slimy by all the blood it had soaked.

As he made his way forward across a few fields in the dark, Afghan voices reached him from a neighbouring field. He crept forward cautiously till he was close enough to see what they were doing. They were Afghan scavengers, who were sifting through the dead bodies and retrieving whatever valuables they could find on them. So, the war was over and the Afghans had won! What had happened to Bhau? Could he have somehow found an opening and made a dash for Delhi as planned? Shamsher exploited the darkness and whatever shelter the embankments around the fields offered and moved away, managing to put some three or four miles between himself and the scavenging Afghan bunch. As he was walking through a field, he heard a groan. He went closer and found one of the Maratha travellers writhing in pain. The bitterly cold wind was making his agony worse. Shamsher looked around, saw plenty of dead bodies scattered everywhere, retrieved whatever clothing he could from those who would never need it again and placed it upon the shivering man. The man, however, was beyond benefitting from this small act of kindness. As Shamsher held him in his arm, the old man's head drooped and he died. Shamsher laid him back on the ground and walked on.

Where could Bhau be? Wherever he was, hopefully in Delhi, he would be searching for him. Just the other day he had said to him, 'Shamsher, you and I are travellers of the same unfortunate road. Whatever happens to us, we will never abandon the road that leads us to our goal.' Bhau was not born to die like a bubble-burst. He was waiting for Shamsher somewhere.

After walking about ten miles, Shamsher arrived at the riverbank where he saw a horse. He hurried up to it and noticed it was from his own parts. It would have belonged to one of his own soldiers. Its saddle, Shamsher noticed, was still sticky with blood. With the river in front, he now had a sense of direction. He carefully lifted himself onto the saddle, turned the animal southwards and patted its rump. As the horse moved on, Shamsher involuntarily slumped forward and held it by its mane. He lay there groaning and wincing as the horse kept moving forward.

⚜

In another part of the field, Parvatibai was carving her passage through the night southwards. As she moved, she was sending frantic appeals to her gods. 'Hey Parmeshwara! Where is my husband? What kind of a sankranti have you sent to my share?' Tired, hungry, distraught, she was only hazily aware of whatever she could see around her. The pressure of the Afghans chasing from behind had slackened, and so had her grip on the sword. Wouldn't she be better off dead than roaming directionless in this foreign land? Where was that Visaji Jogdand, who had been appointed as her guard and executioner? If only he had lived by the word he had given his master, she would have been spared this agony. Where was he? Where was her lord and master?

Parvatibai had noticed a number of fellow Marathas heading in the same direction as she was moving. These were the petty chieftains and their men, who had taken the route to Delhi during the final moments of the conflict at Panipat. Parvatibai went closer in the hope of getting some information from them about her quest. One of them informed her that Bhau had gone in the direction of Delhi. But then, she remembered distinctly how she had dinned it into her husband's ears, 'You are not to go anywhere leaving me behind! I don't care whether you go towards life or death. You have to take me along! I shall imprint my footprints on yours all the distance, no matter where they fall!'

She ran into an old slave called Jaanu Bhintaada. In fact, it was Jaanu who recognized her. Jaanu was a tall, big-boned, well-built man with the heart of a lion. The two of them rode alongside in the dark night. Parvatibai hadn't had a grain of food since morning. Also, the exhaustion of the travel and the anxiety about her husband had started making her feel dizzy. 'How far away is Delhi, mamaji?' she asked.

'Baisaheb, Delhi is very far away. At least another one and a half days away.'

'Mamaji, is his lordship going to be there?'

'God alone knows!'

'What does that mean?' A lump of lead had just formed in her stomach.

'I mean,' Jaanu said with greater discretion, 'I mean, if he is not in Delhi, he could then be in Buland Shehr or one of the neighbouring towns.'

'But, mamaji, how could his lordship have left me behind and gone?'

'Baisaheb, all of us would carry our women along, what's so special about that? But Bhausaheb had to carry destiny riding piggyback on him. In any case, he would surely make a stop at some village on the way. He cannot go south without taking you along with him.'

'Absolutely true,' she said with a laugh. 'These desperate circumstances would have required him to rush forward in a hurry. Otherwise, you can ask me what he is like. He could be the strict, no-nonsense leader for you, who has zero tolerance for laggards. But where I am concerned, he would loathe himself if I missed a meal. How he sits with a long face like a small child, ask me! He is standing under a tree, very likely, eyes moist, waiting for me to arrive!'

As they rode along, Parvatibai's horse stumbled, and being in a starved and tired state, it collapsed. Its sphincter lost control, it evacuated copiously and threw its head down, dead. Parvatibai had fallen to the side and fainted. Jaanu rushed to her. He placed her head in his lap and affectionately pushed her hair back into place. 'She looks so much like my elder daughter!' he said to himself. Water had to be found, and with that intention, he got on his horse. He would have travelled a couple of miles when he heard the loud cries of a chase. He saw that the Marathas who were trailing him were now close to being overtaken by a posse of the enemy horsemen. Jaanu froze in his track. 'No,' he told himself, 'I can't let this happen. Filthy bastards, you may take my head, but I shall not let Bhau's woman fall into your hands.'

Old Jaanu quickly turned round and went to where Parvatibai lay. He loaded her on his back like a sack and secured her with a band round his midriff. With the greatest care, he mounted his horse and galloped. Carrying a double load, the horse raced forward with as much speed as its weakened state allowed. The noise of the enemy had by no means disappeared.

❦

The starlit night seemed to have sold itself to the enemy. In the panic of saving their lives, the Marathas had left a huge quantity of wealth and material behind. Thousands of camels, a hundred and fifty elephants, cannons, bazookas and other big and small guns, and most of all, a vast number of Maratha and Brahmin women had fallen into the hands of the marauding Afghans and Rohillas. Except for the pavilions of the emperor and his wazeer, every other pavilion and tent had a bunch of these unfortunate women, rounded up and herded in, like cattle in a pen—broken, terrorized out of their wits. They were under the charge of their minders, who cracked whips at anyone who so much as whimpered.

The sons of Qutb Shah and Samad Khan entered Panipat a little after nine. It looked more deserted than a graveyard because an exodus had begun four days ago. But it still housed around eight thousand women and children with a smattering of skin-and-bone soldiers, who had hoped that Bhausaheb would come and take them out of there. The two princes got in with their demoniac squad, and the first thing they did was to bolt the city gate from the inside. Then they set off on their carnage, running a tooth-comb through every lane and bylane, knocking down doors and windows, poking their swords through garbage, peeping into pits, drums and barrels, and flushing out petrified bunches of ragged humanity from wherever they had found refuge. They chased them down the streets, brought them down in their thousands through wild swings of their weapons and broke them under their horses' hooves. The women and the young ones were gathered up, screaming and kicking, bound by ropes and carried off as booty, to be sold as slaves at the appropriate time. The women who could make it to the wells and to the Devi Lake were lucky to find refuge in death, but a vast majority of them didn't have luck running their way, and they finished off being driven before their captors like sheep being driven to the market.

As they were departing after two hours, Qutb Shah's son asked Samad Khan's son, 'How many did you kill?'

'I could just manage a hundred and fifty. And you?'

'Only marginally better. I chopped two hundred.'

⁂

While most of the sardars in the Afghan-Rohilla army had gone to sleep after a night of revelry, Shuja's camp was still awake. Around six thousand desperate Marathas had taken shelter under him. He had planted the men of Umraogiri and Anupgiri Gosawi around his base for security and provided the refugees succour. He had ordered for the entire stock of flour in his kitchens to be used up so that the starving Marathas could be given a chapatis. After they had washed it down with water, the hapless refugees sat huddled close together outside, trying to find some warmth in the crowd around them. Next to them sat the elephant Gajendra, sensing, perhaps, the tragedy that had descended upon the house of his master. Vishwasrao's body had been taken out of the canopy and placed in a palanquin that sat in the middle of this devastated crowd. Shuja had paid Barkhurdar Khan three hundred thousand in cash to buy off the martyr's body. But just a little while ago, a message had been delivered to him from Abdali, demanding that the corpse be presented before him the next morning.

As the Maratha men sat worrying about the fate of their prince's body, an old man pleaded with Bapu Hingane, 'Do what you can, Pandit Bapurao, but we must cremate Rao Saheb tomorrow. We can hardly call ourselves human beings now, just a bag of skin and bones, without any strength left to make it back to our homes. But we want the solace of having done right by our prince. Please, Parmeshwara, grant us this one reward. Do not let the body of the scion of the great Maratha empire be thrown to vultures!'

Shuja had been badly shaken up by the information that had reached him of the demoniacal massacre of the helpless and the innocent. He was assuaging his conscience by doing whatever lay within his means. He had no idea what had happened to Bhau. Sleep had deserted him as he was tortured by the memory of the efforts that Bhau had made to get him to his side. His head had turned numb. Next to him sat Kashiraj Pandit, who himself was too shattered to help Shuja.

Some time after midnight, Phuli Khan sneaked into the Nawab's pavilion. Whispering to them that he had information worth a hundred thousand, he took them across to his tent. Phuli Khan was a trusted fiefholder, and Shuja had no hesitation in taking him for his word. There was a single torch burning inside his tent, in the light of which Shuja and Kashiraj noticed an extremely dark man stretched out on a plank. Three doctors were applying pastes and potions to his wounds. The man was in the throes of agony, struggling for breath. One look at the prostrate man and Shuja was overcome with emotion. He cried out in a hoarse voice, 'Ibrahim Khan! Ibrahim Khan!'

As he placed his hand on Ibrahim Khan's burning forehead, Shuja was transported back to a time when Ibrahim Khan stood beside him at the fort walls that surrounded the city of Ayodhya. Ibrahim had raised a mountain range of steel cannons all around, making it impossible for anyone in Hindustan to so much as look angrily towards Ayodhya. Shuja touched Phuli Khan's shoulder and said, 'Let's thank the lord that this gem has reached us. Nobody should get to know he's here. This priceless jewel will look best on the Ayodhya's crown. Get the best doctors, fetch the best medicines. He has to be saved at all costs. Get him fit enough to travel in a palanquin in the next two or three days. We should quietly smuggle him away to Ayodhya before anyone here gets wind of his presence. Do whatever you have to, Phuli Khan, but he has to be secured for me.'

As Shuja-ud-dowlah set off with Vishwasrao's body placed in a canopy atop Gajendra for presentation before the royal pavilion, the six thousand Marathas who had taken shelter under him created a hullabaloo. Some even fell at his feet and began to cry uncontrollably. 'Nawab Saheb,' they cried, 'please do not leave us and go anywhere. These sons of the devil will wipe us out in no time.'

'Stop worrying on this count,' the Nawab reassured them. 'The Gosawi brothers, Umraogiri and Anupgiri, are my chieftains and my right and left hand. Their men have placed you inside their security ring. They will stake their lives to ensure that nobody touches a hair on your head.'

'But Khan Saheb, you will get back the body of our Rao Saheb, won't you?' came a voice from the crowd.

'Yes, I will,' Shuja responded without much conviction.

Shuja's horse led the cavalcade, with Gajendra tailing him with Rao Saheb, in its canopy. A sizeable crowd of Rohillas followed, curious to get a glimpse Vishwasrao.

Shuja had been jolted by the malice the Afghans had been displaying. There were times in the night when he had been shaken out of sleep by the heartrending cries of the Maratha women. The had heard of some of the women committing suicide by banging their heads against the posts. The Afghans had tied them up so as to keep them from doing that.

As he rode past an Afghan tent, he was shocked to see a young woman standing against the points of swords ranged around her. An Afghan standing next to her was bellowing her price, 'Four rupees, just four rupees for this piece!' to a group of people assembled around her. Four rupees for a pretty woman and six rupees for a sturdy horse, that was the going price in the Afghan market. The best of the women and horses the Afghans had kept aside to carry with them to their native land. 'You should have crossed the Yamuna and come to Ayodhya a little earlier, Bhausaheb!' wailed Shuja under his breath. 'The auction of Hindustan's dignity could then have been prevented.' Despite knowing all, he had been helpless in preventing these things from happening. On the contrary, he had been made the butt of Afghan curses for sympathizing with the infidels.

A white sheet was spread in front of the royal pavilion alongside the cannons on which Vishwasrao's corpse was lowered. Strong-smelling herbs were strewn around to overpower any stench the body would be emitting. Abdali himself emerged from his tent along with Shah Wali Khan and Barkhurdar Khan to have a look at the slain prince. They all broke out into involuntary 'Waah!' and 'Subhan Allah!' seeing Vishwasrao's handsome face. The fair complexion, the pink lips now turned pale, the trace of a moustache on his upper lip, graceful build and hands reaching up to his knees, Vishwasrao had the looks to make people forget their worries and keep looking. Wazeer Shah Wali commented, 'I've been to so many countries and seen so many people, but never have I come across a boy more handsome than this one!'

'Somebody was saying the other day that the most beautiful Maratha woman was Mastani, and the most handsome man was this Vishwasrao,' said Abdali. 'I see that he was absolutely right here.'

'Aalam-panaah' suggested Barkhurdar Khan, 'we should carry this prince of the Deccan with us to Kandahar as a symbol of your victory. We can mummify the body and put it on display in Kabul.'

'That's right, my lord!' piped another. 'We could even stuff straw in his beautiful skin and keep it as an exhibition piece! It will draw crowds for sure!'

'I cannot accept these ghoulish suggestions!' screamed Shuja loudly, but there were not many who cared for his opinion. The hubbub increased to such an extent that Abdali decided to postpone making a decision on the issue for a later date. He agreed to let the corpse stay in Shuja's custody.

☙

Out of habit, Badshah Abdali set out to take a round of the battlefield. Wherever he turned—the Kurukshetra road in the north, the road to Muzaffarnagar along the riverbank, towards the bramble forest in the west, the road to Bikaner or the southern side towards Delhi—he saw heaps upon heaps of dead bodies lying everywhere. By the time he crossed Rajakhedi and Ugrakhedi, even he was disgusted with the scale at which the slaughter had happened. The foul smell that sat thick on the air was making breathing impossible.

Nobody, however, had any idea where Bhausaheb could have disappeared. Shuja-ud-dowlah was as anxious as the Marathas to know about the fate that could have befallen the man. Finally, seeing that even Abdali was curious to resolve the mystery, Shuja constituted a team of the two Maratha envoys, Shakhdhar Pandit and Ganesh Pandit, along with Kashiraj Pandit, identified those among the prisoners who could recognize Bhausaheb, assigned to them a hundred and fifty water-carrier men, and worked out a plan for a systematic search. They decided to begin from one end and divided the patch of land into smaller units. A few persons were detailed to collect the heads covered in dust and blood. Another set would try to peel off the muck collected on the faces, after which the water-carriers would give the faces a wash. Some others would look for identification marks on the body. They would keep tossing away the scrutinized heads and bodies and move on to the next lot.

After two or three hundred cadavers and heads were examined and thrown away, they came across a body that had been pierced by a spear, which had prevented the body from properly falling to the ground. It was immediately identified as the corpse of Yashwantrao Pawar. Further ahead, they came upon another body that was punctured with countless wounds. After the face was scrubbed a couple of times, Bapu Hingane recognized it and shouted, 'This is Santaji Wagh!'

'Who was Santaji Wagh?' asked Shuja.

'He was a chieftain of the Holkars.'

'Look at the number of wounds! See if you can count them!'

Bapu Hingane began the count and had counted more than forty wounds when he finally broke down. 'Just tell me, Nawab Sahcb, what did this man get out of such incredible bravery and tenacity?'

Shuja was reduced to tears too. 'You Margatthas, what are you, human beings or demons? How many wounds can a person take? That too under starvation? And what kind of a leader was Bhau, to instigate his men to such madness?'

An entire day of search went by, but Bhau's body was nowhere to be found. As it was turning dark, Tukoji's body came into sight.

☙❧

Meanwhile, Vishwasrao's body had begun to bloat. There was every indication that it would begin to reek in a few hours. Shuja took Shah Wali along and went straight to the emperor. He pleaded with him, 'Your Highness, you have won this great war in the land of Hindustan. But it is important to let your vanquished enemies observe their revered rituals.

One of the values dear to this land is that an enemy, however bitter and however old, remains an enemy only till he lives. However you may hate Vishwasrao, you cannot hate his dead body. The body is beginning to fester. Please let them consign Vishwasrao's body to the elements according to their ancient customs.'

Abdali was finally made to agree. A pyre was built and the corpses of Vishwasrao, Yashwantrao, Santaji and Tukoji were given the torch.

Kashiraj Pandit had contributed all he could to the negotiations. When he returned to his tent in the evening, he found Barkhurdar Khan's accountant Motilal waiting for him. He looked a bit flustered. Shooting surreptitious glances to either side, he signalled to Kashiraj to follow him. They crossed a few camps soft-footedly in the dark and stood in front of one of the many tents that had been pitched close to Barkhurdar's pavilion. The two quietly slipped into this tent, from the other side of which, they could see the corridor at the back end of the pavilion. They then sneaked up to the pavilion where Motilal softly pushed aside a heavy partition screen and asked Kashiraj to take a peep inside.

Heart pounding violently, Kashiraj saw that the space was lit up by a few dim lamps, and in the middle of the floor sat a solitary Maratha gallant, his royalty indicated by the expensive, brocaded shirt and jacket that he wore. The clothes, however, were torn and shredded by numerous cuts made by swords and spears, and smeared with congealed blood and dirt. There were fetters on his wrists and ankles. The man sat forlorn, dejected and broken, with his knees gathered in the fold of his arms and his head resting on them. In spite of the grime that covered his face, neck and the rest of the body, Kashiraj recognized him as Jayappa's son and Dattaji's nephew Jankoji Shinde.

Kashiraj was far too overcome by this sight to hold himself back, and stepped in. Jankoji instantly recognized Kashiraj and hid his face in shame between his knees. Placing a soft hand on the distraught man's head Kashiraj said, 'Why hide your face, Rao Saheb? What if you have been defeated? The kind of battle you put up has made us feel small. You have displayed the valour of the seed from which you have sprung. You have no reason to feel any shame!'

Jankoji, however, couldn't get over the circumstances in which he was being seen. 'What's the point of living in this state, Pandit?' he cried.

'Instead of dying by inches in these humiliating conditions, I should have been blown up by a cannonball. I don't know why death has always managed to side-step me after coming so close! I fainted at Buradi Ghat at the critical moment and Dattaji gained martyrdom without meeting his heart's desire to kill Najeeb. In this war too, my limbs turned stiff at the moment of reckoning. Look at the record of the Shindes, otherwise. They have a tradition of seeking out death as a friend rather than ducking it. Why am I alone left behind as a grieving widow? My mate Vishwasrao is gone, no one knows where Bhausaheb is. What do I do with my barren life now?'

Kashiraj sat by the inconsolable young man, placing his hand affectionately on his back. 'Rao Saheb,' he said. 'I am from your homeland. Unburden your mind if you want to.'

'These Afghans, are they human beings or the devil's rabid pups? Do you know why this wicked Barkhurdar has kept me hidden from Abdali? He is demanding a huge ransom from me.'

'How much is he asking?'

'Seven hundred thousand!'

Kashiraj was stunned. Jankoji went on, 'These chains, these rods strapped to every part of my body, they are impossible to endure. Let me loose, I say, make me duel with the best Afghan they can find, but don't kill me by squeezing me like this! Where does this Satan expect me to get the money from? Please inform your master of the state in which you find me. Tell him to remember the favours he would have received from my ancestors and help me out of this hell.'

'I shall do that, Rao Saheb, you can be sure. The recent political equations have placed us on opposite sides, but my master Shuja-ud-dowlah has not forgotten the cordial relations he enjoyed with the Marathas. He will certainly find you a way out of this.'

After thus reassuring the prince, Kashiraj took leave with a heavy heart. His immediate task was to contact Shuja. Shuja would not have forgotten how Jankoji's grandfather had extricated his father from the trap of the Rohillas. He would throw at Barkhurdar Khan the seven hundred thousand like pebbles to save Jankoji's life, of this Kashiraj was certain. It was already past midnight, and Shuja could have gone to sleep. But this was too urgent a message to be delayed. What should he do? That was when a servant informed him that Shuja was sitting in Najeeb's pavilion. Kashiraj immediately headed in that direction. The pavilion was alive with raucous celebrations going on inside; a young girl was dancing to the beat of ankle-bells and drums, while the august gathering—including Najeeb and Shuja—sat soaking in the girl's beauty and dancing. Despite the awkwardness, Kashiraj reached up to Shuja and whispered the message in his ear. Shuja's face suddenly flashed, which Najeeb did not fail to register. When the performance got over late in the night, Najeeb nudged Shuja and asked him, 'What news had your man brought?'

'Oh, it was just one of the routine activities at our camp.'

After Shuja had left, Najeeb called one of his scouts and said, 'Keep a sharp eye on all pavilions and tents, begin a quiet search and let me know by tomorrow. Pay particular attention to this rotten egg Shuja and his lackey, that Pandit fellow.'

⚜

The very next day, Najeeb's spy returned with news. Barkhurdar Khan had hidden Jankoji Shinde in the back of his own pavilion. He was well aware of the bad blood between Shah Wali Khan and Barkhurdar Khan, and he knew how to exploit it. He instantly went to Shah Wali, who was left with no choice but to ask him to take a seat.

Bringing his most supplicant tone into play, Najeeb said, 'Huzoor, I am aware that there are a number of things about me that you don't like, but I am always committed to speaking the truth, however bitter. Look at this case: I remember that no-good chit of a boy Jankoji, nephew of that rascal Dattaji Shinde had the temerity to corner you near the well a month ago. Now tell me if it is right that one among us should offer shelter to a sinner like him.'

'What are you saying? Is that scoundrel still alive?'

'Not only alive, huzoor, but he is relaxing right now inside our camp!'

As expected, Shah Wali was furious. 'Who's doing is this?'

'It is your "guest" Barkhurdar Khan. Although he claims himself to be the Nemesis of the Marathas, he has the cheek to give refuge to this Janko.'

'All right. We shall be meeting in a little while for the dinner that the emperor has organized. I will ask the emperor to seek an answer for this audacity.'

※

They were all there for Emperor Abdali's dinner: chieftains, generals, princes and officials. The fare, as was to be expected, was sumptuous, to suit every taste. There was meat of all kinds, cooked in a variety of styles, Afghan, Persian and Indian. There were sherbets and fruits and sweetmeats. As the Afghan and Rohilla nobles tucked it in with relish and abandon, their conversation was mainly centred on the great exploits in the battle. Most of all, it was praise for the courage, the acumen and wisdom of their emperor that had made this phenomenal victory possible. It was during this feasting that Shah Wali sought the attention of the emperor and said, 'Aalam-panaah, I thank you for the grand feast you have hosted for our worthy generals and their subordinates, but as I partake of the delicious fare, somehow the taste vanishes at the thought that there are big infidel sardars being sheltered in our very own camp as we sit and eat here, waiting for the opportunity to make a meal of us all.'

'What are you saying, Shah Wali?' responded the astounded emperor.

'Only the truth, Aalam-panaah. That wretched Jankoji Shinde, that sinner is right now enjoying a royal repast in our camp.'

'Shah Wali, don't beat about the bush. Come out straight with the name of the person who has given him shelter.'

'That, Aalam-panaah, Barkhurdar should be able to tell us best.'

Barkhurdar Khan froze. Then he stuttered, 'No, Jahaan-panaah, this is not true.'

'All right, then, we will come and inspect your pavilion. That will settle what is true and what is not.'

Barkhurdar got into a panic. He had seen the punishments the emperor meted out to offenders, and the very thought made him sweat profusely. He was racking his brains to find a way out of the jam when he noticed his accountant Motilal standing behind the emperor. The man had his eyes nailed on his master, expecting for some signal to arrive. Barkhurdar winked and Motilal sneaked out to do the only thing that could be done.

Motilal immediately called over the most trusted of Barkhurdar's men and explained the circumstance to them. Five or six of the strongest of them got together and entered the corridor where Jankoji was trapped. A couple of them leapt at him and tried to reach for his throat. The prince still had enough spirit left in him to throw them off him, in spite of the restraining chains. Recovering his breath, he barked, 'Why get after my throat, you lousy cowards? Don't drown me like an unwanted pup. Kill me like a man, if you have to. Slice my head off my shoulder with a sword. I am a soldier, and I want to die like one.'

'That doesn't suit us, huzoor. We cannot have your blood spilt all over the place.'

This time when they attacked him, they did so with caution. Two of the men pinioned him by the chains on his arms, two others sat on his legs and another two descended on his throat. Jankoji tried to kick and twist and turn, but as the pressure of the thumb went deeper, his breath choked. As his mouth started to froth, he gave a violent shiver and then went still. The killers maintained the pressure till they were sure that life had fled out of him. The eyes had bulged out and the tongue had popped out.

The cowardly work done, they now got busy disposing of the body. A pit had been dug close by to throw away the skin, the entrails and other inedible parts of the animals that had been getting slaughtered over the past couple of days. It had already become two-thirds full. A couple of men had scooped out the muck so as to widen and deepen the pit and create space for a human body. When they found that Jankoji's body would still not fit in, they chopped it off from the legs and threw the dismembered corpse inside. Then they lowered on the dead man all the muck they had scooped out earlier, so that nobody could be the wiser on what lay beneath.

Within minutes of the deed being done, the executioner squad of the emperor arrived at Barkhurdar's pavilion for the. The search was intense. They would have moved up and down the burial spot any number of times, but the crime had been hidden well. Barkhurdar heaved a sigh of relief.

Under instructions from Shuja, teams of water-carriers, the bhishtis, continued uncovering corpses for the third day. Water was splashed on the face for identification and then the body would be tossed away. A terrible stench had settled on the field. The bhishtis were sick to death of the intolerably foul smell but could do nothing except retch and vomit and continue to work. Shuja and Bapu Hingane still had hopes of finding Bhausaheb; which meant that there was no relief for the bhishtis till all the corpses had been examined.

Tossing and turning the bodies around, the squads had moved eastward towards Black Mango. As protection from the stench, they had wrapped their turban across their noses. Hingane had tied a kerchief round his nose too. Warm puffs of air escaped the piles when the dead bodies were turned this way and that. Maggots scurried out of the carcasses and crawled right up to the elbows of the workers, who were going crazy flicking them away with the other hand.

Hingane suddenly came upon the muzzle of the horse Chandrasen, lopped and singed by cannon fire. The hopes of the foragers shot up instantly. If Bhau had fallen, his body should be somewhere close around here. The bhishtis kept moving forward, tossing about bodies like burnt bricks being tossed out of kilns. The black mango tree had taken quite a few cannon hits too, burning the naturally dark coloured leaves into darker shades of black and blue. It seemed as if the multitudes of human bodies laid out to dry had shamed the tree into shedding its leaves too.

Just then, as a bhishti was in the act of tossing away a strongly built, headless body, three priceless pearls rolled off the corpse. That alerted all those in the vicinity. They threw buckets upon buckets of water on the carcass till a completely blood-bespattered, gold-embroidered jacket began to emerge out of the grime, with just a trace of yellow showing. One thigh showed marks of deep cuts; punctures made by bullets became clearly visible too. Hingane turned the corpse on its stomach and examined the back. A thick, reddish-brown mole on the back the size of a berry, the tattoo of a fish on the foot, and what clinched the issue—the old dagger-wounds on the back. Hingane could hold himself no longer, and bursting into loud lamentation, he said, 'This is the exact spot where Muzaffar Khan had wounded Bhau, and this is the scar. Alas, alas, that the prince of Deccan should die in this wilderness!'

As soon as news reached him, Shuja went running to the spot. The sight of Bhausaheb's headless body overwhelmed all who saw it. Kashiraj and Shuja did all that they could to arrange for the funeral pyre. With no lumber anywhere, they collected the broken wheels of cannon-carts, smashed-up howdahs and whatever wood they could scrounge out of the scattered tents and erected a pyre. There was no shroud either, so Kashiraj opened up his trunk and pulled out a brand-new shawl to spread over the corpse. Water needs to be poured into the mouth before a dead person is consigned to the flames, but how does one do that if the head is missing? Where's the mouth? Bapu Pandit rolled up some palaas leaves and inserted the roll into the severed neck. Shivering with terror as much as with cold, the Marathas poured some water in. As Bapu Hingane set the pyre alight, all the Marathas under Shuja's protection stood to offer their respect to the departed hero. Some threw their earrings into the flame, some others offered their bracelets, but for a large number of them, all they had to offer as homage was their tears. Kashiraj distributed dakshina to the Brahmins.

The assembled men decided to finish off the tenth-day ritual that very evening, as there was no surety of them being alive the next day. Shuja said, 'Let me take the responsibility of hosting the dinner.'

'Food cooked in your kitchens can't be accepted,' objected Joshibuva of Pune. 'At best, you may provide the grains. We'll do the cooking ourselves.'

That's how the tenth-day ritual got to be performed that evening.

༺༻

Bhau's head was found the next day. The Afghan at whom Bhau had last aimed his spear as he collapsed had buried it near his tent. This Afghan confessed to Shuja that he had chopped the head off Bhau's corpse in the hope of pocketing the diamonds and emeralds round the neck, and buried it so that nobody would get to know. Another pyre was arranged and the head was given a separate cremation.

That evening, Badshah Abdali called Shuja over for an audience. As Shuja stood before him, he cast a sharp look and exclaimed, 'Nawab Saheb, when you first came and met us, we instantly conferred the title of

Farzand Khan upon you. In the presence of the entire court, we showered praise upon you by comparing you with our dear Taimur. We ask you as our son, so tell us the truth: where have you hidden Ibrahim Gardi?'

Shuja's legs turned to jelly. It wasn't as if he was afraid of Abdali any more, but the thought of the priceless diamond he now possessed slipping out of his hand made him shudder.

'Yes, Nawab Saheb, where is Gardi?' barked Abdali.

'Who is this Gardi, huzoor? Why should anyone come to me?' Shuja tried to fend him off.

But when Abdali called for a copy of the Koran, and asked him to swear on the holy book, Shuja was left with no choice. He confessed that Ibrahim was in his camp. At that, Najeeb's Rohilla men, the Afghans and Barkhurdar's soldiers gathered in front of Abdali's tent and began to shout:

'Turn that infidel Ibrahim over to us!'

'His cannons have sent thousands of our men to the house of God!'

'We want to drink that devil's blood!'

When he heard this clamour, Shuja was beside himself with rage. He went red in the face. Clenching his teeth, he spat out in passion, 'I'd rather give my life than turn Ibrahim over!'

'We shall make war over whoever gives shelter to that infidel,' roared Shah Pasand Khan.

'Then so be it,' snapped back Shuja and pulled his sword out of its sheath. 'If anyone so much as touches a hair of Ibrahim's head, I shall chop both his arms off the elbow.'

Shah Wali Khan intervened with a Koran in his hand. Swearing by the holy book, he assured Shuja, 'Nawab Saheb, you hand Ibrahim over to us. I give you guarantee that not a hair on his head will be harmed.'

'What prevents you from betraying me?' shot back Shuja.

'So you think swearing on the Koran is child's play?' the wazeer asked, raising his voice a few decibels.

Shuja was now helpless. In a beseeching tone, he addressed Badshah Abdali: 'Jahaan-panaah, forgetting all the bitterness of the past and ignoring the heartrending pleas of Bhau, I came over and joined you. He never went back on the word he had given. Please bestow this favour on the people of Hindustan. Ibrahim Gardi is the Kohinoor of Hindustan. Do not visit any treachery upon him.'

He then handed Ibrahim over into Shah Wali's custody. Abdali's curiosity kept mounting steadily that evening. Who was this Ibrahim that had sent thousands of Afghans roasting to their deaths? What did he look like? Could he be taken into employment and carried back to Kandahar? Or should he be diced right here and thrown to the dogs? Around midnight, he expressed his desire to see the man. Without letting Shuja get wind of it, under tight security, Ibrahim was presented before Abdali.

In the flickering flame of the torch, Abdali subjected Ibrahim to repeated inspection. The red of Ibrahim's eyes looked redder against his dark face. He was staring unblinkingly at Abdali with sharp, piercing eyes. His entire body was covered with wounds. Some appeared to be bleeding even now through the rags tied round them. A broken bone had rendered one foot lame. So many of the pockmarks on his face had been obliterated by scabs of later wounds. His son-in-law, son and beloved brother Fateh Khan had all fallen in Panipat.

There was nothing left for him to live for. The energizing image of Bhau that had sat in a corner of his heart had faded too. The hand that had patted him on the back for bringing down the ramparts of so many forts had disappeared. The patron who would inspire him to fight on through rain and sunshine, through winds and storms, was no more. Ibrahim was now reduced to the state of a massive tree trunk that had been eaten hollow from the inside. Emperor Abdali cast a searing glance at Ibrahim and asked, 'So you are Ibrahim Gardi?'

'Hmm,' growled Ibrahim.

Abdali looked piteously at Ibrahim, and said, 'You unfortunate man, if you had shown sense while there was time, you could have asked for the post of commander-in-chief of Kandahar, and I would have happily showered it upon a valiant person like you. But look, what state you have been reduced to, you hapless brave-heart.'

Ibrahim returned Abdali's pity with an unrepentant glare and said, 'Oh, you king of Kandahar, what control over heaven and earth could you have given me? Even if you had offered me the suzerainty of Kandahar, I would have tossed it away like food gone bad.'

Abdali was in a dilemma. For a moment, it seemed as if he was debating whether he should speak or stay mum. If Ibrahim could be brought over, the ordnance of Kandahar would gain great prestige and power. The Kohinoor of Hindustan would truly glitter in the setting of Afghanistan. He finally could not hold himself back and said, 'Listen, Ilah may well be willing to set aside a thousand of your sins and visit His blessings upon you. If you agree to give your services to the crown of Kandahar ...'

Ibrahim felt a gush of pity for Abdali. He broke into derisive laughter that made the chains on his arms rattle. Loading his voice with all the scorn he could gather, he looked straight into Abdali's eyes and said, 'Loyalty and trust, to me, are not so cheap as to be changed like the clothes on one's back. We happily stake our lives to stay true to our word. My master's feet stayed rooted to the soil of Panipat only so that he could stay true to the fidelity he had sworn for me. He became one with the soil. The flowers of fealty that lie scattered at my master's feet ... you expect me to shower them at any passing riffraff? I'd rather die a thousand times than even once desecrate my pledge.'

For a passing moment, Abdali stood stunned and dazzled by Ibrahim's response. Then he said, 'All right, you hold service with us in such contempt. Even after this insolence, if, out of magnanimity of heart, we were to let you go free, what would you do?'

Like a lion, Ibrahim roared, 'If you ever display this largeness of heart and let me go free, there is nothing else I will do but this: God willing, I will gather another army and mount an attack on Kandahar. I will avenge the murder of my master.'

'Silence!' screamed Abdali in an uncontrollable rage. 'Take this foolish man away. Put him in fetters and throw him in a dungeon, like a rabid dog!'

Ibrahim's battered body was thrown like useless lumber into a tent close to Barkhurdar Khan's privy. Abdali could easily have hacked Ibrahim to pieces in open court or have him trampled to a pulp under an elephant's feet. In fact, Barkhurdar had even suggested that to him. Abdali took him aside and admonished him, 'That Shuja is young and immature. Why invite his ire? We still need him for the food and fodder he can provide. Why should we pointlessly provoke the Shias and the other Muslims of Hindustan?'

'But, Aalam-panaah, this sinner ...'

'I accept all that. But our army is due to move towards Delhi in the next four or five days. Finish him off in slow degrees during this period.

Once we have decided to eliminate him, why be impetuous like the Margatthas? Keep the head cool.'

Ibrahim's body lay like a bundle of twigs on a tattered spread. Thrice he had been grievously injured during the battle. It was through a combination of luck and effort that, jacket soaked in blood, he had hoodwinked the Afghans and landed into Shuja's hands. Shuja had immediately put him under the round-the-clock care of doctors. The wounds had started to heal, and he had begun to sleep well. The plan was to smuggle him away to Ayodhya in the next four or five days. But suddenly, the enemy had got wind of his presence and all plans had fallen apart.

But now, Ibrahim was in a piteous state. Small doses of poison were being administered to him with food and water. In the name of medicine, poisonous leaves were being applied to his wounds. His head would buzz with all the poison seeping in. His limbs had turned limp. The wounds that were on way to healing had again turned runny. Pus had begun to form all over his back, his stomach, his calves. His skin was peeling off like banana-skin, exposing the flesh. His colossal frame now reminded one of patches of turbid water showing on a stretch of deep-brown slush.

There was nothing left for him to live for. The battlefield had swallowed up eight thousand of his fearless companions; his lion-hearted younger brother Fateh Khan had become one with eternity; his lineage had been brought to a halt; his son-in-law had perished; Bhausaheb had gone missing. So why live then?

The poisonous leaves shot strange pains through his body, giving the sensation of being roasted at the mouth of a belching, smouldering cannon. He would try to stand up, but his limbs had turned into jelly. His spirit, however, remained strong as ever. Once in a while, he would surface from his torpor and wonder what would have happened to Bhausaheb. He finally received its answer one afternoon. The Afghan slaves who came to feed him his bitter meals were discussing among themselves how the body and the head of Bhau had been discovered, and how they had been separately cremated. Ibrahim sank back into his torpor. His breathing became fainter.

The army drums had begun to roll. Abdali was ready to set off for Delhi. Afghan and Rohilla regiments left the camp.

A terrible stench had begun to rise from every part of Ibrahim's body. Flies had gathered in swarms on the suppurations. The slaves posted to keep watch on him were nauseated too. Some little chore brought a slave closer to his head. As he approached, nose held tight, something aroused his suspicion. He immediately called over his colleagues, who together confirmed that Ibrahim's soul had fled. On receiving the message Barkhurdar arrived instantly. There was the tiniest palpitation still, the body still indicated the presence of life. But the flies buzzing around him and the insects crawling over the limbs were enough evidence for Barkhurdar. He signalled for the body to be thrown out and rushed away to deliver the good news to Emperor Abdali. The regiments of Abdali had set off towards Delhi with trumpets and fanfare.

Ibrahim's mutilated, half-naked body lay on the Panipat soil like a massive, grounded five-metal cannon. The vultures there, grown fat on a daily diet of blood and flesh, had become disdainful of stale flesh. Now, as their eyes lit upon this living corpse, they flapped their mighty wings in glee and closed in on the fallen hero with loud, raucous screeches and cawings. For the next hour, the air was taken over by their noisy feasting.

CHAPTER FIVE
white cloud

How does one patch up a torn piece of the sky? How many patches can a ragged sky take? The eighth-night moon had turned traitorous too. The moonlight stayed till well beyond midnight, cutting down escape opportunities for the fleeing Marathas. It was only after the starlight had faded that the enemy slackened its chase. Both of Jaanu's horses had died of sheer fatigue and starvation, leaving him with no choice except to carry Parvatibai on his back, as if she were his little daughter. Jaanu Bhintaada, now past sixty, was an old retainer of the Peshwas, a native of village Bhidvi in the province of Purandar. He had spent his entire life in the service of the Peshwas, forever in the saddle, either on a campaign or a hunt with his masters. As a result, he had turned strong as an ox and tough and resilient like rawhide—so tough that for a bet he had climbed a wall in Bhidvi with his back against it. That had earned him the nickname Bhintaada, from the Marathi word 'bhinti' for a wall. But tonight's task had begun to test even his resilience. He had the satisfaction, however, of carrying no less a person than Bhau's wife to safety, and for this piece of good fortune, he would readily lay down his life.

Near Sonipat, they ran into two Maratha horsemen, Viroji Baravkar and Piraji Raut. The two mounted Parvatibai on a horse and began walking alongside. Sorrow had transformed her into a whimpering child. 'Mamaji,' she asked Viroji, 'could you have seen Bhausaheb anywhere?'

'What do I say, Baisaheb? Times have turned so dark that it is impossible to trace anybody's whereabouts.'

Nana Phadnis was clad in a loin-cloth like the rest of them. The Afghans had blocked their passage a number of times, but finding nothing worth looting on them, they had only beat them and let them move on. Each time that they were manhandled, a dozen or so of the starved Marathas would die. Hunger had driven them to distraction anyway.

As the ragged bunch walked on in the darkness, another lot of fifty to sixty Afghans came up from behind and broke upon them with swords and stout canes. Ramjipant and Bapujipant fell to the ground writhing under the blows that fell upon them. Nana, however, managed to escape into the tall grass that grew by the wayside and escaped detection. He sat shivering there, shrunk into a ball, and emerged only when he was sure the attackers had moved on.

He had managed to escape the beating, but there was no relief from the gnawing in the belly. As he walked desperately looking for some sustenance, he spotted a tree of Indian berries. He plucked as many leaves as he could and began chewing on them. A little further ahead, he noticed a pool of water and scooped a few handfuls to wash down the leaves. Where was his mother Akkasaheb? Where were his dear wife Yashoda and their son? Tears rolled down his cheeks as he walked on, wondering where and when this macabre journey would end.

When the horrible night came to an end, news had reached the towns and villages of the Antarved region that lay between the Ganga and Yamuna—Bahadurgadh, Hissaar, Sonipat—of the defeat suffered by the Maratha forces, and it was spreading like wildfire in the direction of Delhi. The formidable empire that had only a few months ago hoisted its flag at Attock and had held sway all over Hindustan now lay with its spine broken, and its remaining rump was making a mad dash southwards to escape from the clutches of the victors snapping at their heels. This became an open invitation for all the rogues and scoundrels of the region to swoop down on them and help themselves to whatever came to hand. The animals and ornaments had been snatched away long ago; now, even the clothes on their backs, their dhotis and their turbans were considered worthwhile loot. Every couple of miles the fleers were accosted by cane-wielding gangs that divested them of one more item, or beat them up just for the pleasure of seeing them roll in pain. The survivors of these bitter encounters now abandoned the main routes and began moving through fields, heaths and woods.

The Maratha sardars Antaji Mankeshwar and Baji Hari were traversing the heaths of Farooqabad on their way to Delhi. They still had on them heavily brocaded shirts liberally smeared with blood. Some thirty or forty horsemen had joined them in the hope that the presence of the grandees would offer them some kind of protection. Antaji, now in his sixties, had spent almost four decades in the upper reaches of Delhi politics, the previous ten years at the head of a five-thousand-strong force appointed for the defence of the emperor in Delhi. Once past Farooqabad, they had calculated, they would be able to reach Delhi by afternoon. If he could escape the mayhem en route and reach Delhi safely, Antaji was sure he would be able to work something out.

The horses crossed a biggish stream and entered the plains on the other side. They could hear the calls for prayer from the mosques of Farooqabad and the ringing of the temple bells. What they saw at the boundary of the town, however, made their blood freeze. Ranged all along the outskirts was a crowd of some two hundred townsmen, the landlord at the centre, armed with sticks and pickaxes and stone-throwing slings, waiting for them to close in. Some thirty or forty of the shelter-seekers hurriedly turned their tired horses round and got back into the stream to cross back to relative safety.

༄༅

The news of the decimation of the Marathas reached Delhi early Thursday morning. The eight-hundred-strong unit of Baloji Palande and Meer Khan Thokey stationed inside the Red Fort began to gather its belongings in a hurry to make a quick exit. Down below the Asad bastion, the three thousand men of Parvatrao Kadam, Govindpant's son Baloji Govind, Hiroji Shelke Lakhoji Bodhe, Lakshmanrao Gawande and Narayan Bapuji Rethrekar had set up their tents on the sands of the Yamuna. Once the news of the Maratha bloodbath reached them, they instinctively ran for protection inside the Red Fort. It was pell-mell everywhere: the soldiers inside rushing out, the men outside rushing in. The story began doing the rounds that the entire one-hundred-and-fifty-thousand-strong army had been wiped out to the last man, every chieftain dead. And that both Bhausaheb and Vishwasrao had been put into chains and dispatched to Kandahar. With no firm evidence to go by, nobody knew how much to believe and how much to reject as fabrication. Subhedar Naro Shankar didn't know what to say to the agitated soldiers who came running to him with frantic questions.

It was dusk when Gangoba Tatya Chandrachud managed to make it to the Red Fort exhausted to his last breath, and that was when the picture of the total annihilation of the Maratha army became clear. As the famished Gangoba sat gobbling the food Naro Shankar had placed before him, the gory details of the rout came tumbling out. The terrified and bewildered Naro Shankar asked, 'What do we do now, Tatya?'

'Put your faith in God and belt down southwards.'

'But I am the subhedar of Delhi! I have given my word to Bhausaheb not to abandon it even at the cost of my life!'

'But, Naroba, with Bhausaheb dead, who are you now answerable to?'

'But, Tatya, it doesn't sit well on my conscience!'

'Very well, then, do what your conscience tells you to do. As far as I am concerned, as long as there is life, there is hope. If a companion of the Peshwas across three generations like Subhedar Holkar thought it wise to withdraw, where do people like you count? Wisdom lies in saving one's precious life and planning for another day.'

Not knowing when his next meal would arrive, Gangoba Tatya gorged himself to bursting point and left with a couple dozen of his companions in the direction of Mathura.

The situation in Delhi deteriorated rapidly. Small-time louts began fancying their chances and waylaid the Marathas with whatever came to their hand. Naropant took cognizance of the changed circumstances and got busy gathering whatever he could for a quick exit. There was three thousand worth of treasure in the fort, which he had to carry safely out. By around midnight, the law-and-order situation around the town had taken an ugly turn. He would keep the treasure aside for another day. As for now, the best he should do for the good of all concerned was to sneak away and hit the road to Mathura. 'Dig your feet into Delhi and fight till the last breath,' Bhausaheb had hammered into them again and again. But it was clear to all—chieftains, lords, officials and servants—that the circumstances on the ground demanded an altogether different strategy: run while the running was good.

By Friday morning, not a single Maratha could be spotted anywhere inside Delhi. Another four or five days later, the tattered remnants of the once invincible Maratha army began to assemble at Mathura. Malharrao Holkar became the nodal figure around whom people gathered. Jaanu Bhintaada, Baravkar and Piraji Jadhav had somehow managed to bring Parvatibai safe, if not altogether sound, to Mathura. Her arrival there immediately attracted all the notables to her. When she spotted Malharba, she broke out into unrestrained sobs and wailed, 'Mamaji, what's happened to his lordship? Where is my husband, mamaji? When can you arrange to take me to him?'

'What do I tell you, Parvatibai? Towards the later moments, such a huge crowd of soldiers had gathered around the royal flag that Bhausaheb had completely disappeared into it. When even the eyes of the gods could not have penetrated through the dense crowd, what could human eyes do?'

Malharba had decided not to tarry unduly in Mathura. He decided to move towards Bhind and past Bhind to Gwalior. He sold whatever he had on him and raised some money from local traders to buy fresh horses. As Malharba and Gangoba Tatya got ready to set off for the ravines of Chambal, and move along the riverbank towards Bhind, a bemused Baravkar asked, 'Subhedar, I would have thought it simpler to go straight through Jaat territory towards the south; why, then, go through this circuitous route via the badlands of the Chambal?'

'Viroba, time is not on our side today, compelling us to be always on the alert. Who knows whether the changed circumstances would have altered Surajmal's allegiance? What if he decides to take us captive and hand us over to the enemy? It's best not to tempt fate in these difficult times.'

☙❧

Tall and big-built, heavy-whiskered, this young horseman was moving towards Bharatpur, the capital city of the Jaats. In his late twenties, the man looked so deadbeat, stretched out on his horse's shoulder, that passersby couldn't be sure whether he was alive or dead. The heavily brocaded shirt on his back was soiled and blood-soaked. The blue and black marks all over his body looked a good week or two old. The man was barely conscious of being carried along. He had vague memories of dismounting now and then to quench the fire in his belly by eating grass and wild leaves. Every time he had gained some degree of consciousness, he had been struck by the pain that racked every inch of his body, as if his bones had cracked and muscles had been torn to shreds. Though his wounds had stopped suppurating, a putrid smell seemed to have settled deep inside his skin.

As he moved along in a semi-conscious state, the loud call of the town-crier rang in his ears, 'Hear, hear, hear! Citizens are forbidden from causing any harm to the Marathas coming from Panipat! Feed the hungry, offer them shelter, provide them with clothing. This is by order of the king! Hear, hear, hear!'

The words 'Maratha' and 'Panipat' had penetrated past the young man's semi-conscious state. He straightened his back by pushing himself against the horse and looked around with heavy-lidded eyes. Whose town is this? Who is the king? When he saw a passerby, he asked, 'Whose land is this, friend?'

'The Jaat king's.'

'What town is this?'

'Bharatpur.'

The Maratha chieftain was visibly overwhelmed, to the point of turning teary-eyed. The sun had begun to rise as his horse trodded on towards Bharatpur. The aches and pains were well beyond his threshold. He had lost a lot of blood too. He once again laid his head on the horse's mane and passed out.

As the horse entered the main town, heads began to turn. Going by his brocaded attire, this was no ordinary soldier; he was more likely to be the young prince of a powerful kingdom. Soon, there was a bunch of curious kids trailing him. This procession happened to cross a cluster of hungry, woebegone Maratha men, who had sat down to consume the fare that a generous citizen had laid out before them. One of them noticed the horse and its burden, and he sat up electrified. He instantly left his leaf-plate and hurried towards the horse. One look at the man and his eyes popped out. 'Look what we've got here!' he yelled out excitedly to his compatriots. 'It's Shamsher! Bajirao's son Shamsher Bahadur!'

The others sprang up from their meals and rushed to stand in a circle round the horse. One of them ran back to fetch some water and tried to pour it down the young man's parched lips. Many of them broke into loud laments at seeing their prince in this state. They turned the horse's head in the direction of Surajmal's palace and nudged it forward, chattering along as they followed. Their meal lay forgotten. By the time they had reached the palace, news had already reached the king of the arrival of the royal refugee, and he was waiting at the gate with servants in attendance. The sight of the beaten hero made Surajmal's heart turn to water. He placed an affectionate hand over the limp, listless body, turned towards his doctor and said, 'Looks like he is running a high temperature. He is a royal guest. Spare no efforts at treating him.'

'It shall be done, Your Highness.'

'Do you know who this man is? He is the son of the man who made all of Hindustan tremble under his horse's hooves! He is Shamsher, the son of Bajirao Peshwa!'

Shamsher was taken off the horse's back and placed in a palanquin. He was carried to a palace that was readied for him, with the Marathas following him all the way unbidden. The ones in front leapt forward to remove his shoes and broke into sobs when he yelled at the pain when they were peeled off his blood-caked feet. With liberal use of a pair of scissors, the medicine man removed the clothes off his trunk with the greatest difficulty and carefully began to mop the congealed blood off his chest and back with cloth dipped in warm water. His entire body was one big, raw mass of flesh, some of the cuts having gone right up to the bone. Surajmal stood by the side as the doctor did the cleaning and winced each time the man shuddered with pain. 'Is he going to recover?' he asked hoarsely.

'Difficult to say,' responded the doctor. 'He's lost a lot of blood. Look at the mess his back is in. And then the long distance he has covered without food. We don't even know of the cracks and concussions inside.'

'He must be saved!' Surajmal snapped unreasonably at the doctor. 'It was stupid differences that kept me from jumping into the war alongside his family. But for the sake of my own self-respect, I must earn the merit of saving this young man! Do what you have to, but save him for me!'

'Your word is my command, Your Highness.'

The doctor applied all kinds of poultices prepared from wild herbs, and painstakingly lowered some bitter potions into the man's mouth. The palace was getting crowded with Maratha men, but Surajmal didn't have the heart to shoo them away. As he stood there watching, his favourite queen Hansiya came and stood beside him. Realizing after some while that they were more a hindrance than help, they walked away. 'What a resilient breed these Marathas are!' she remarked on the way out. 'Just last year, we had that other gallant Dattaji's widow staying with us. Despite her irreparable loss, what courage and tenacity she displayed! I can't think of many such strong-fibred communities in Hindustan. Indestructible!'

King Surajmal and his queen Hansiya had made good arrangements for the Marathas who had fled from Panipat. Soldiers as well as pilgrims were housed in the rest-houses in the precincts of temples and manors. Every person was given a quilt and a set of clothes, along with five rupees for expenses. Those who wanted to move on homewards were given a travel allowance. Queen Hansiya had made announcements in the nearby provinces offering refuge to all in her land.

Bharatpur having turned awfully cold, Shamsher was put under four quilts, one on top of the other. The Maratha seniors had sent the men away and seated themselves on the floor in a kind of vigil at the head and foot of his bed. Around midnight, Shamsher opened his eyes, looked around in the dim light of the lamp and groaned, 'Bhau! Bhau!' Nobody had the courage to look into his eyes. He felt a soft hand caressing his head, and he was sure it was Bhau's. He reached up to the hand and turned his eyes upward to see that it was Surajmal. Shamsher's eyes were swimming in tears as he asked like a lost child, 'Your Highness, where is our Bhau?'

Neither Surajmal nor those gathered around him knew what to say and where to look. Shamsher's heart turned heavy as lead. He pulled Surajmal's hand to his chest and wept inconsolably.

Surajmal softly touched Shamsher's brow. 'Sardar Saheb, please try to put behind what is past. The grief is huge, I confess, but you are in no state to suffer more than you already have.'

Shamsher made visible efforts to suppress the scream that had wanted to escape from his chest. He bit his lip, shut his eyes tight, took a deep breath and held it for a while. Realizing that it didn't help, he broke out in a loud bawl and said, 'How can I stop myself from grieving, Raja Saheb? My life has lost its meaning. He taught an unfortunate boy like me the purpose of existence. He taught me that the battlefield was the final fulfilment, the ultimate justification and the last resting place for a man of courage and valour. Hundreds of thousands of men and animals he had gathered around him to turn all of Hindustan upside down; he inspired countless people like me to forget thirst, hunger and pain, and plunge into the sacred mission of driving the foreigner out of our land. Where will I find another man like him, Raja Saheb? With Bhau gone, I see no purpose in living. I'd rather die!'

He again fell into a swoon. Groans of 'Bhau! Bhau!' kept escaping his lips from time to time. As the night advanced, his fever worsened, and no amount of cold swabs could bring it under control. Shamsher Bahadur stopped groaning just after dawn. The palace reverberated with loud cries of his grief-stricken countrymen; the king and queen couldn't hold their tears back either. After a while, Surajmal instructed his administrator, 'Let a monument that matches the dignity of this great warrior be built in Bharatpur. Let his soul not feel the pinch of having died so far away from his motherland.

☙

Nanasaheb Peshwa was on his way to Malwa with an army of twenty thousand men. He had crossed the Satpudas at Hivarbari, and after leaving behind Godhadi, Kaigaon and Kasba Nemawar, he was closing in on Bhelsha. Having handed over a substantial army to Raghunath Dada for the Nizam's administration, he was left with a rather small force. He, however, still had for company friends and well-wishers like Sadashiv Ramchandra, Yamaji Shivdev, Gopalrao Patwardhan and Babuji Naik Baramatikar along with their men.

Nanasaheb was barely forty years old, but he felt tired in mind and body, and had begun labouring under the notion that he was now an old man. The burden of running the Peshwa's office had fallen upon his shoulders when he was merely nineteen. The first ten or fifteen years of office had been tough, stressful and difficult. Major campaigns starting from Malwa, across Prayag right up to Bengal were undertaken, the strain of which had burnt out much of his enthusiasm. With Dadasaheb and Bhausaheb coming of age, he had heaved a sigh of relief and handed over much of his responsibility to them.

He had spent the last ten years in great luxury, relaxation and indulgence of the flesh, but that hadn't led to any sense of contentment. On the other hand, he and Gopikabai had been in a state of confrontation for a fairly long while now; the sparks that flew between them refused to die out. Meanwhile, he had contracted tuberculosis, and that meant consuming pills and potions all the time. Panipat had now become an ever-present ghost that harried his mind. A hundred thousand men, most of them young, the bloom of Maratha land, had stood up to confront the enemy at Panipat. How could an entire generation have been mowed down so ruthlessly?

When the circumstances in Panipat had turned knotty, when vultures had been circling around the hungry and thirsty Maratha army, when nature was giving them no respite either, when strong winds had begun to blow into their faces, when the noose thrown by Najeeb-Abdali was tightening by the minute, wedding bells were ringing in Paithan on the banks of the Godawari to celebrate the Peshwa's second marriage. The day was 17 December 1760. Well before this, the enemy had blocked the movement of letters, with the result that neither side knew what was happening at the other end. Disgusted with the endless bickering with Gopikabai, Nanasaheb had put the garland round nine-year-old Radhabai, the daughter of a Deshasth Brahmin money-lender of Paithan named Naroba Naik.

So thrilled had the Peshwa been with this new step that he had pushed his close friends Aba Purandare and Veereshwar Deekshit to get into second marriages too. Wild celebrations had followed. Getting the Peshwa himself for son-in-law was no small thing for Naik, and he hadn't grudged expenses to make the event a memorable one for the entire town. The chieftains and senior officials gathered for the occasion were bestowed with feasts and clothes and entertainment of every kind. The whole town was lit up and resonated with firecrackers. The marriage procession was led by the groom atop a dazzlingly caparisoned elephant, with the citizenry throwing flower petals at the retinue all the way. After four days of merry-making, the Peshwa's party was seen off on the fifth day with appropriate fanfare.

But all this gold-plating didn't bring comfort to the Peshwa's disturbed mind. The auspicious turmeric paste was an embarrassment. The laughter, the feasting, the wedding songs, the firecrackers and the musical instruments failed to suppress the war-bugles that were blowing inside his head. Clashing swords, booming cannons, men and animals screaming in pain, smoke and dust all around, these were the sights and sounds that had taken charge of his thoughts. He was like a man who had suddenly been jolted out of a nightmare in the middle of the night ...

Days rolled by as the Peshwa's battalion sped northwards. As he sat in his canopy, the Peshwa's eyes would bore as far into the land ahead as possible, but there was no sight of any courier closing in. More than a month had drifted by without any news arriving from the battlefront. What could be happening at Panipat? Why wasn't he being kept informed? Nanasaheb turned his desperate eyes towards his friend and cousin Veereshwar Deekshit and said, 'It was so long ago that we had heard of the two armies standing face to face. Why has news stopped coming since then?'

'A deal may have been struck!'

'That's what I say, Veereshwar, if there is no news of war, why don't we then get news of a truce?'

'Something untoward may—'

'No, no, Veereshwar, none of that inauspicious talk! Every single household of the Deccan has its bread-earner standing there in Panipat. The entire younger generation has assembled there. My own flesh and blood, people who occupy the deepest corner in my heart—they are all gathered there. They must come back victorious. If someone so much as touches a hair on their head, I shall set fire to the entire world!'

Veereshwar stayed quiet. The Peshwa, however, knew no peace. His brow had broken into beads of sweat as he continued, 'Veereshwar, am I not already very late for the campaign? I had left the wada on Dussehra, and now sankrant has gone past, but we are still travelling. It's been so long since I sent the instruction to Kolhatkar at Jhansi to arrange for bullocks; it's been so long since I sent a letter to Bhau, telling him of our entering the north with an army of twenty thousand men. It's so many months since I last saw Bhausaheb, Vishwasrao and our Shamsher. They would be sitting with their eyes glued to the south ... Veereshwar, why should we think only of war and truce? Perhaps they have won. They are great warriors, all of them.'

'That probability cannot be denied.'

But it was too fanciful a thought to stay for long in Nanasaheb's troubled mind. 'But in that case, they would have informed us.' Nanasaheb Peshwa issued a diktat to his men: every single traveller, trader, pilgrim coming from the north should be stopped and questioned, checked for any information that could be extracted from him. But that exercise didn't bring any satisfactory answers either. The deafening, deadening silence emanating from the north had now got the entire army worried. Gopikabai had stopped talking to the Peshwa, but her anxiety for news from the north was no less. Everybody was on tenterhooks.

The army kept pressing on in the direction of the Narmada, crossing Burhanpur and Handia on the way. As they crossed the hump of a ridge, suddenly they were greeted by the sight of dense woods, and on the other side of the woods, the long, shimmering line of water stretching from the east to the west. The chant went rolling up and down the entire army, 'The Narmada! The Narmada!' The constant craning into the distance northwards had turned the Peshwa's neck stiff. On hitting the waterfront, he finally made a sign for the army to stop for rest after crossing to the other bank. The men surveyed the vast expanse of the river and went splashing into it with their horses, bullocks and camels. The other side looked like an unbroken stretch of sand. The horsemen waded through the cold, refreshing water and stretched themselves out on the other side to rest their tired limbs. The tent-makers quickly located a few shady trees under which they erected tents for the royalty and the nobles. Nanasaheb went into his tent and sat staring unblinkingly at the massive river. He had no appetite for the food that was placed before him. A month had gone by, and yet no news from the north; what could it mean? 'Shrimant!' a voice broke his reverie. 'Shrimant!' It was his friend Aba Purandare standing panting at the door of his tent, as if he had rushed in with something important. 'Yes, Purandare, what news have you brought?'

'Shrimant, there's a money-lender travelling south from Sonipat-Panipat. We've just blocked his four horses and a couple of camels on this side of the river.'

'A money-lender from Sonipat-Panipat?' Nanasaheb's heart gave a lurch.

'Yes, Shrimant.'

'What information does he have?'

'We've been grilling him, but he's not being forthcoming. Looks bewildered. But I suspect he knows quite a bit.'

'Bring him here immediately.'

An old Muslim man in his mid-sixties was brought before the Peshwa. He looked tense and uncertain. The deep furrows on his brow and a spider-web of lines across his face suggested he was a man of much knowledge and wisdom. Nanasaheb walked up to him, placed a reassuring hand on his shoulder and asked, 'Where are you coming from, Sonipat or Panipat?'

'From Sonipat, huzoor.'

'Where are you headed?'

'To Aurangabad, huzoor.'

'When had you set off from Sonipat?'

'About two weeks ago, huzoor.'

'Any news from those parts?'

The man looked frightened like a trapped animal, not knowing what to say. Nanasaheb feared the worst. However, in a choked voice, he went on, 'Look, our Maratha army, all our wealth and prestige have been locked in that region, fighting a war. You belong to that region, so please tell us all that you know. Even if the news is bad, please tell it to us. We promise that you shall not be harmed.'

A big crowd had assembled round the tent by now, tense and silent, waiting for the man to start talking.

The money-lender began, 'Huzoor, I am an ordinary trader, what do I understand of your politics or wars? But I'll tell you whatever I heard.'

'Yes, please! Quick!'

'All that I could understand was that there was a battle in Panipat between the Afghan king, Abdali and the people from the Deccan. The Deccan people, I heard, were vanquished.'

Everyone's face fell. Nanasaheb felt a tight knot develop in his chest. Aba Purandare asked the trader, 'Why do you say that the Deccan people were beaten? A lot of blood-smeared men were running towards the south. If it had been the Afghans, wouldn't they run northwards?'

Nanasaheb composed himself and asked, 'Any other news? Any names of the chieftains who died?'

The old trader said in a level voice, 'Please don't ask me any more. I have told you whatever I knew. I haven't heard of the people who were slain. All that I heard from the people of my town was: two pearls gone, a couple of dozen guineas and countless small coins.'

Nanasaheb felt as if somebody had pushed him off a ragged cliff into a bottomless abyss. He began shivering uncontrollably. He had no consciousness of when the trader departed. His throat had gone completely dry. His knees gave way, and he would have collapsed where he stood if Yamaji Shivdev had not lunged forward to hold him. As Nanasaheb clung to his shoulders and cried, Yamaji tried to calm him. 'Please, Shrimant, don't give in to grieving at this unconfirmed news. Let's wait for some more authentic information.'

But Nanasaheb was inconsolable. 'Who else can the two pearls be except the two people dearest to my heart?' he cried.

Nanasaheb was so shattered that he simply fainted. The servants carried him to his bed and sprinkled a little water on his face. When he came to, his friends gathered around him. 'Shrimant, please get a grip on yourself. We still don't have any definite information.'

Nanasaheb calmed down a little. A flash of determination lit his face, and he somehow managed to get up by leaning against Yamaji Shivdev's shoulder. 'Come along, up, all of you, we have to get moving! Let's see what calamity has fallen upon the boys.'

❦

The Peshwa's caravan resumed its journey northwards. On the third day, they came upon the fleers from Panipat, who had been running relentlessly south—hungry, wounded, broken. The Maratha army had been completely decimated in the war, they confirmed, but these were people who had abandoned the battlefield around afternoon, hence they couldn't say who among the chieftains had died and who survived. In the hurry to escape with their lives, they hadn't bothered to collect details. Some talked of Bhausaheb and Jankoji being alive, but most of the others stood with their hands clapped on their ears.

Nanasaheb showed presence of mind and sent some of his best scouts in different directions to bring back whatever news they could collect. Deep inside, however, the Peshwa had started disintegrating fast. The moment he fell asleep, he would wake up with a start, crying, 'Bhau! Bhau!' The absence of information on both Vishwasrao and Bhausaheb had shaken Gopikabai too to distraction. She had gone into a shell, crying incessantly and refusing to communicate with anyone.

It was on the first day of their halt at Bhelsha that a piece of good news reached them. When Nanasaheb was informed that Vitthalrao Vinchurkar, Nana Purandare and Parvatibai had found a safe haven in Mathura, his spirits lifted and he said, 'Surely my Bhau and Vishwasrao would also have found some shelter!' He instantly issued the order that the army would stay put in Bhelsha till such time as they had some information on Bhau. He wrote a letter to Nana Purandare instructing him to send scouts to Ajmer and Gwalior and the valleys of the Chambal and the Yamuna. As he was finishing, he added with a quivering hand, 'If Bhau is not in this world, there is no point in living on. The world and all its wealth are meaningless without Bhau. I shall spring back to life only after I see a letter in his hand.'

One night, as he lay in his tent grieving over Bhau, Veereshwar Deekshit and Babuji Naik rushed in with a couple of letters. They were from Shuja's confidantes, Kashiraj Pandit and Anupgiri Gosawi. The Peshwa took Kashiraj's scroll with trembling hands, undid the knot and began to read each word with hungry eyes:

The humble servant Kashiraj Shivdev offers his deepest obeisance to His Excellency the Peshwa.

The great conflict that took place between the Maratha forces and the forces of Abdali has just come to an end. My master Shuja-ud-dowlah was deeply desirous of joining the Marathas' side, but God works in His own mysterious ways. Your lordship would by now have heard of the disastrous results of that war. My master was persuaded to launch a massive search through the bodies that lay scattered in the battlefield, at the end of which the bodies of Shrimant Bhausaheb and Rao Saheb were recovered. Their last rites were performed as per the customs by the Brahmins, and their remains were consigned to the flames of sandalwood. My master Shuja-ud-dowlah is deeply aggrieved at the manner in which things transpired. There is no doubt that this will be a heavy blow for your lordship to bear, but we are all helpless against God's will. Nothing more left to write. Please continue to keep us in your grace.

Every word of Kashiraj's letter fell like a sledge-hammer on the Peshwa's heart. His grief overcame him. 'Bhau!' he wailed, 'Bhau!' He had lost all awareness of the company that stood round him, and he went about the tent with his arms beating his chest. He put his arms round the post that held the tent up, banged his head against it, and suddenly imagining the post to be Bhau, perhaps, he kissed it again and again, wailing all the time, 'Bhau! My Bhau!' Sadashiv Ramchandra, Vitthal Vishram, Veereshwarpant, Yamaji Shivdev, Babu Naik and others stood around him in a circle and tried to lead him towards his bed. But Nanasaheb, at this point, seemed to be in a delirium. 'I am responsible for the boy's death,' he wailed piteously. 'I am the impotent one here, addiction-ridden, sinner. Bhau, Dada, Shamsher, these have been the brave ones, God's own warriors! Look at my worthlessness! I have beaten Dada, said unspeakable things to Bhau, behaved obnoxiously with them all! Will they ever forgive me, oh Lord, will they ever forgive me?'

'Please, Shrimant, please calm down! Don't be so harsh on yourself! When have you ever fallen behind in your duties?'

Nanasaheb's grief, however, refused to be contained. 'Bhau,' he wailed, 'with you gone, all my wealth and power have been reduced to mere dust. My son too was just an adolescent, and the two of you have shot past the stars and disappeared.'

⁌⁌

Abdali had ensconced himself along with his begums in the Delhi palace. His army had set up its base camp in the Ahmadgunj area. It was around two decades ago that the nizam of Hyderabad had prophesied before Nadir Shah at the Deewaan-e-Khaas, the Hall of Private Audience, that the boy Ahmad would rise to be emperor. It was in the same Deewaan-e-Khaas that Abdali had called for a special durbar after wiping out the Maratha army.

The Kohinoor was acknowledged the world over as the biggest and the most beautiful diamond ever mined. Nadir Shah had carried it with him to Persia, where Abdali had managed to get hold of it on the night of the Shah's assassination. It was on the rarest of rare occasions that Abdali would wear it on his person, but after the victory at Panipat, he would strut around flaunting it every day.

When Zeenat Mahal, the mother of Delhi's emperor Shah Alam, had heard of the arrival of Abdali from Panipat, she had rushed with her grandson Jawaan Bakht from the village of Narela, seven miles distant, to offer him her fealty. The imperial family had obviously no memory left of how Bhausaheb had declared the Bengal-based Shah Alam the emperor of Hindustan and sacrificed the hundred-thousand-strong Maratha army while fighting for the emperor's rights to the throne. On the contrary, Zeenat Mahal, grandson in tow, was raring to fall at the feet of her one-time tormentor.

Destiny had certainly been kind to Abdali. It had rescued him virtually from the jaws of death and placed the crown of victory on his head, all within an hour of the battle being turned upside down. He was convinced that there would never be a repeat of the war he had won by the skin of his teeth. A rare thrill had raced through his veins at the thought of holding Iran, Turan, Kabul and Kandahar under one heel and planting the other heel on the jugular of Hindustan. But it hadn't taken him long to realize that this couldn't go on for long. As the smoke had dissipated, the practical man-of-the-world had taken over.

A considerably toned-down Abdali had called his wazeer over to his tent before setting off for Delhi. 'What is your opinion on the arrangement I have made for Hindustan, Shah Wali? The imperial throne for Shah Alam, wazeership for Ghaziuddin, and the post of Meer Bakshi for Najeeb; how do you find this new dispensation?' he asked the old man.

'Jahaan-panaah, it speaks of your large and forgiving heart that you have handed wazeership to Ghaziuddin in spite of his thousands of faults. Shah Alam was, of course, the most popular choice for emperor. As for making that scoundrel Najeeb the Meer Bakshi, putting the maintenance of the imperial army into that rascal's hands, could Your Highness have made a mistake?'

'Most certainly not,' laughed Abdali. 'Tomorrow, if the Jaats launch an attack, or if the Marathas rise up once again from the dust, or if the Sikhs suddenly get fired up, you can be sure that neither that itinerant Shah Alam nor the chicken-livered Ghaziuddin will come to the party. The only person we are left with, then, is the rascal that you so rightly detest. He will come, and he is the only person in sight who can stand up to the Marathas.'

'Jahaan-panaah,' said the wazeer in a low voice, 'you had given word to Nawab Shuja-ud-dowlah that he would be the wazeer. Why did you not consider him?'

'That was simply not possible,' Abdali retorted conspiratorially. 'I would never have given him any power or prestige. He is young, he is ambitious and he is hugely more talented than the rest of the crowd, and these are grievous faults to possess.'

Having silenced his wazeer by his devious calculations, he turned to the main subject and asked, 'What's the state of our army?'

'Not very good. Aalam-panaah, it's been two years since our men last felt the wind of their land blow through their hair. They are eager to be back with their wives and children. Many of our soldiers are upset at their salaries falling into arrears by two years. A revolt is not inconceivable. Never mind what happens to Hindustan, we need to take care of our men. We have to arrange for their salaries.'

'And how do we do that?'

'Aalam-panaah, that's exactly why we have called over Najeeb and Zeenat Mahal. They are waiting in the tent behind.'

'You think it's possible to get a pie out of that skinflint? In any case, call them over.'

Najeeb arrived in his customary fashion, bowing and grovelling all the way. He was carrying an elaborately carved box, wrapped in heavily brocaded cloth, under his arm.

'What do you bring with you, my friend?' Abdali asked with a laugh.

'Your Highness, I had sent a man to the inner reaches of a Himalayan kingdom to procure these for me. These are some of the best perfumes one can get anywhere in the world. Your Highness is going to be delighted at the fragrance of these exquisite attars, of that I am sure.'

'Don't you try to dupe me by your sugary talk and your heady perfumes, Najeeb,' snapped Abdali. 'Tell me, instead, what you propose to do about my men who are fainting of hunger? They haven't received their salaries and allowances for the past two years. Why has your tongue that talked of raising millions in a minute gone limp?'

'Aalam-panaah, please do not be upset with your slave. While your men go hungry, how can I down even a mouthful? I have been spending sleepless nights trying to figure out how I can be of help to Your Highness. I would happily have emptied out bags upon bags of gold coins and thousands of sacks of grains at your blessed feet, but as you will appreciate, for these two years I too have been caught in the maelstrom of war. I have not been able to pay attention to my province, nor have I been able to collect revenue. I am starved for cash right now!'

'What all this means, Najeeb,' said the emperor with severity, 'is that you have begun to show your true colours.'

'Not at all, Aalam-panaah,' grovelled Najeeb. 'I shall present at Your Highness's feet all the money I had promised to the last paisa. But I suggest, huzoor, that you don't let Surajmal Jaat and Shuja-ud-dowlah go untapped. Why snatch at a petty thief's loin-cloth? The Jaat's land can yield gold!'

'But how can you collar the Jaat at this late hour?' asked Wazeer Shah Wali.

'I have taken his two envoys Nagarmal and Majlasrai into my custody. Your lordship should haul them over the coals. Pinch their noses and they will open their mouths.'

The badshah issued orders for the two to be presented before him. Zeenat Mahal, the queen mother of the emperor of Delhi too crawled into the presence of the emperor of Kandahar. As soon as the Jaat's men arrived, Abdali shot off a direct question: 'How many millions do you people propose to offer to us?'

'Huzoor, we shall send our scouts to apprise King Surajmal of Your Highness's desire.'

'I don't care what your scouts do, I want the answer from you.'

'Your highness, this kind of decision is taken by the king; we are merely servants. Surely, we cannot be expected to have an answer to your question. We assure you, however, that your desire shall be conveyed immediately to Bharatpur for the king to take action.'

'Can't take decisions? Which fool then appointed you as envoys?' snarled Najeeb.

'Throw them into prison, huzoor,' Zeenat screeched, 'otherwise, there won't be a single coin coming your way!' Emperor Abdali ordered for the two to be placed under arrest. They were put under chains and dragged away from his presence. His face was turning darker by the minute. After the sensational but costly victory he had achieved, what had he got to show for it? Noticing his mood flipping dangerously, Najeeb came back with his fawning notes, 'Your lordship, for two years I have been circling around you, washing your feet. The desire to continue to serve you is still as strong as ever. I shall most certainly bring money for you any which way I can, but meanwhile, you shouldn't let that Jaat escape scot-free.'

'Wonderful, Najeeb, wonderful!' grimaced Abdali. 'For sheer wiliness, nobody can come anywhere close to you. I break the Jaat's back so that you may enjoy unhindered power in Delhi, right? Your reputation as a smart operator is not at all undeserved.'

Najeeb thought it best to put his head down in embarrassment. It was now time for Shah Wali, Jahaan Khan and Zeenat Mahal to get into the conversation. 'Aalam-panaah,' the queen mother submitted, 'the Jaat is not going to part with a single dime without military pressure being built over him. I request that a regiment be sent immediately to teach him a lesson.'

The discussion went on for a long while, after which Abdali announced his decision: 'The Afghan army will march upon the Jaat in the next three or four days. Begum Saheba, both you and Najeeb should accompany the army. After all, when they get into the pillaging, who can guide them better than you two on where the gold lies secreted, where the treasure houses are?'

With that arranged, he dismissed the two from his presence and stayed on with Shah Wali and Jahaan Khan. The two were observing their emperor's face closely, watching a wide range of thoughts flip past his countenance. He finally collected his thoughts and said, 'Shah Wali, this Najeeb is one of the most cunning human beings I have come across.'

'He is wicked to his fingertips.'

'I thought him fake from the day I first set my eyes on him, but I had never imagined him to be as vile as this. What I am worried about, Shah Wali, is the safety of Islam in Hindustan.'

'Aalam-panaah, we didn't quite understand.'

'However loudly this Najeeb has proclaimed his concern for Islam, all his jihad is exclusively for his own welfare. His call for the defence of Islam is really a call to have himself defended. I have to stand before my Allah and answer some day, and I must do something to ensure my religion isn't wiped out of here. The only way the Rohillas can thrive, and through them Islam, is by having a cordial relationship with the natives of this land.'

'What does that mean, huzoor?'

'It means that it will do the Rohillas good to stay on friendly terms with the Marathas. From the experience I have had of these men, I can say that they are not easy to incite, but once aflame, they are not easy to douse. Could you have forgotten so early, Shah Wali, the men you saw on the battlefield so eager to embrace death?'

Abdali finally muttered to himself, 'This matter I alone will have to set right,' and sent instructions for Yaqoob Ali Khan to be sent to him immediately. When Yaqoob arrived running and panting, Abdali said to him, 'Yaqoob, this battle with the Marathas has drained us; we now place the responsibility of making peace with them on you. Write a letter to that Nanasaheb. Win him over. A lot of great work can be done without brandishing the sword.'

Shah Wali Khan and Jahaan Khan were both stunned by this new side of their king. As Abdali pronounced each word with care and precision, Yaqoob took the dictation in a neat hand:

> ... *Shrimant Nanasaheb Peshwa, Wazeer, there is no reason for enmity between us. Your beloved son Vishwasrao and your dear brother Bhausaheb died in the battlefield, for which we also feel the deepest regret, but, really, we had been left with no choice over what happened. It was Bhausaheb who first mounted an assault on us, and we were forced to use our arms in self-defence. That your gallant men should have died in the action is most unfortunate. If you decide to run the affairs of Delhi as before, we shall have no objection. But the land of the Punjab beyond the Sutlej should please be allowed to stay under our control. Out of the greatness of your heart, please try to wash away the bitter memories of the unfortunate battle from your mind. I wish that affection and goodwill continue to stay between us....*

Abdali had also invited Shuja-ud-dowlah over, and was now mulling over how to broach the subject that was bothering him most. Riots had broken out in Delhi a couple of days back between the Shias and the Sunnis, which, he knew, had been sparked off by Abdali's men. Shuja had not been able to stand for long the looting and arson the soldiers and the citizens had indulged in, and had left the scene with great bitterness. Matters had not stopped at that. Shuja's army had been pilloried too. The nawab was livid that while Abdali had brought the riots under control, he had not exerted as much pressure upon the Sunnis as he could have.

When Shuja arrived, Abdali got straight to the point and said, 'Nawab Saheb, I will have to trouble you a little bit more. You are very well aware of the desperation to which our men have been reduced. They have not been given their salaries for two years now. Najeeb has no money, and the Marathas whom we defeated were already famished and penniless. Their land is thousands of miles away, impossible for mounting a raid. Will it be wrong, then, to expect some help from a friend like you?'

'Aalam-panaah, the situation is rather difficult—'

'That it is for us, not for you! Your province on the bank of the Ganga has soil soft as butter. Rivers of nectar flow through your land twice a year, and you have a revenue collection of twenty million a year. What difficulty can you have?'

Shuja let him speak on for a while and broke in with a soft voice when he found his opportunity, 'Please forgive the impertinence, Aalam-panaah, but let me refresh your memory. Do you remember how hard you tried to turn us away from the Marathas and join your forces? You had made loud declarations then that you didn't want a pie out of us! You had conferred upon me the title of Farzand Khan amidst loud clashing of drums and cymbals. In spite of all your proclamations, during the campaign, you compelled us to supply you with provisions. Now that the war is over, the same theme continues? After all, what has been our fault? That we joined your forces? Or are we the defeated country? Why, then, these compulsions? Are these the rewards for having marched with you?'

As Shuja's voice rose in excitement, Abdali too lost his composure and said in a rough voice, 'What, exactly, do you want to say, Nawab Saheb?'

'Aalam-panaah is well aware of that. That Ghaziuddin had been rolling in the dust before the Marathas for procuring the wazeership of Hindustan, but Bhausaheb had refused outright to throw even a stale piece of bread before that dirty dog. However, what have we benefitted by abandoning so many years of cordial relationships with the Marathas and joining you? This talk of giving you tribute? We did not help the Marathas by so much as a dime, yet, in spite of our being in your camp, Bhausaheb had openly declared the wazeership of Hindustan for me. It's threats and pressures for me even now, but that treacherous, cowardly thief, that man who was nowhere within miles of Panipat, he walks away with the prize of the wazeership of Hindustan?'

The badshah stayed silent for a while. He then laughed and said, 'Why are you so enamoured of this empty wazeeri? The emperor of Kandahar has the power to load you with more precious gifts.'

'That's not possible, because I know my limitations.'

'Limitations? What limitations?'

'Just this, that Shuja is a Shia, not a Sunni.'

Shuja's response left Abdali speechless. It took him some time to organize his words and resume, 'Nawab Bahadur is labouring under some misconception. You appear to be deeply disappointed in us.'

'Because we did not receive even the basic civil behaviour that one expects as a human being.'

'Meaning?'

'What do the Shia-Sunni riots that flared up in Delhi indicate? What did you do to curb your Sunni brothers from humiliating us?'

Abdali had run out of arguments. He sat silent for a long time with a worried look on his face. Then, as if he had arrived at some decision, he said, 'All right, Nawab Saheb, we would have committed some errors in the rough and tumble of the times. You may not have even received the justice you deserved for having suffered on our behalf. But don't let this make you angry. Keep your heart clean. We are running short of grains in our army; our soldiers have not received their wages. One of our battalions has left for raiding the land of the Jaats, but we don't expect them to come back with much from there. Even if it is in the shape of a loan, you will have to help us with a few hundred thousand.'

'Have to, is it?' Shuja asked tauntingly.

'Yes, you will have to.'

'Very well, Your Majesty,' Shuja sighed as he got up to leave. 'This slave shall certainly comply with the orders of the emperor. But you know well enough how far Ayodhya is from here. I request that I be granted a compliance period of at least four days.'

Shuja took leave of the emperor and headed for his camp. He had already got clear indications of the direction in which the political winds were blowing and had begun making secret preparations for leaving Delhi with his army that very night. When a person gets very hungry, he may not much care for how he gets his food and what he eats. If Abdali did not get provisions from elsewhere, he would certainly come and squat on his chest, and this was an open secret. That was why he had brought his cannon carts to the bank of the Yamuna under the pretext of getting them washed and repaired. Easy availability of water for the animals was a believable enough excuse.

Abandoning all thoughts of consequences, as soon as it was dark, Shuja sneaked off with his army in the direction of Ayodhya. He had for company his loyal generals Umraogiri and Anupgiri, and his trusted adviser Kashiraj Pandit. All that he wanted to do was to escape from the clutches of Abdali and run his kingdom well. As they rode on, the Nawab slapped the rump of his white horse and said to Anupgiri, 'Bhausaheb was an honest man. I still remember the appeals he made through his letters. 'We are two arrows from the same quiver.' But we became puppets in the hands of cruel fate and landed in the camp of the outsider. My desire, otherwise, was to fight shoulder to shoulder with Bhau. What have we gained from joining Abdali except badly burning our fingers? If Bhau and we had been able to come together at the right time, the map—and the destiny—of Hindustan would have been quite different. Arrows of the same quiver are meant to pierce through the common enemy's chest, but what actually transpired was something altogether different.'

A fair distance had been covered away from Delhi. By the time day broke, the horses' movements slowed down. Shuja resumed his conversation with his chieftains. 'I have heard from our historians and scholars about the earlier two battles fought in Panipat. The first was between Ibrahim Lodi and Babur. The second happened twenty-five years later between Akbar and Hemu. Now we had this one after two hundred years. After the war between the Kauravas and the Pandavas, there never has been a war of this scale, a war this bloody, in modern times, and it's not likely to be repeated.'

'Yes, we too have heard of the earlier two battles,' said Anupgiri, 'but Nawab Saheb, we cannot underrate the great warriors Babur, Lodi, Akbar and Hemu, can we?'

'There's no question about it. But time, in this battle, had caught both Bhau and Abdali in a long spell of two months and a half. In the first two, the conflicting forces merely ran in and clashed and the outcome was settled in a day or two; but the human body was never subjected to such terrible handling over such a protracted period. The soil of Panipat had never before witnessed famine of this dimension, such shortages, such profane abuse of man and beast.'

'Nawab Saheb, destiny strikes in the most incomprehensible manner. No native prince has ever been victorious on the soil of Panipat.'

'This is what pains me to no end,' said Shuja with a sigh. 'I tried with might and main to bring about a truce between Bhausaheb and Abdali, but failed miserably. Truth be told, when death was dancing its macabre dance that afternoon, when the heat of the battlefield had begun to spread in all directions, when smoke and dust had turned thick and jammed the heads and lungs of the warriors, so many times the thought had crossed my mind of breaking rank with Abdali and crossing over. I felt like joining forces with Bhausaheb, with the men of our soil and turn on the Afghan forces. But I couldn't manage it. In fact, there was one moment when I actually pressed my feet in the stirrup and pulled the reins, but I found my way blocked.'

'Why did that happen?'

'Because that Najeeb guessed that I was likely to turn on them. He and Abdali had arranged for our men to be positioned by his side. If I had made the slightest move, our men would have got into conflict with his smoke-bombs. That wretch would have died pulling me by my leg, but would never have allowed me to cross over.'

The hoof-beats had turned considerably weaker. 'Are they likely to give us chase?' asked a worried Anupgiri.

'Where do they have the manpower for it?' laughed Shuja. 'Abdali's main unit has gone to raid Surajmal Jaat's land; the army is hugely upset at the lack of provisions and arrears in payment; almost all of them are pining for home. There is serious unrest in the army, a revolt is a distinct possibility. What, finally, has Abdali gained from such a massive victory? Where do they have the strength in their legs to run after us?'

⊕

The Peshwa camp had been erected at Pachhor, a little beyond Siroj in the central region. The question that was taxing all of them was whether or not to proceed towards Delhi via the Chambal ravines, Agra and Mathura. Nanasaheb's own opinion was to gather the scattered forces and launch an immediate attack on the enemy, but news had just arrived that Malharrao Holkar, Vinchurkar and Naro Shankar had already set off in their direction, and should be with them in the next two or three days. So they had decided to stay on in Pachhor.

Nanasaheb was still in the infirmary. He had plenty of people for company: his immediate family of Gopikabai, his two sons Madhavrao and Narayanrao, his new wife Radhabai, Dada's wife Sagunabai, his close associates Veereshwar Deekshit, Yamaji Shivdev, Vitthal Vishram and a few others. Yet, Nanasaheb's fevered mind knew no calm. He opened his mouth only to groan, and the only words he said were 'Bhau! Bhau!' The tuberculosis was taking its toll on him anyway. And now the double tragedy of the loss of son and brother had shattered him. Living every moment under the dense shadow of grief had made even breathing difficult. His once strong chest and muscular body appeared to have withered, leaving behind a sickly pale, limp bag of skin and bones.

Gopikabai sat at the foot of his bed, looking equally emaciated and distraught. The loss of her young son and the breakdown of her husband's physical and mental health had hit her very hard too. She would just sit looking at the Peshwa, massaging the soles of his feet. Every once in a while, the Peshwa would be racked by a paroxysm of cough. He would roll himself into a bundle and cough and cough till his face contorted and his eyes flowed. He would then fall back listlessly, chanting the same chant: 'Bhau! Bhau!'

'Shrimant, please give yourself some rest. It is not unlikely that both Bhau and Jankoji are still alive. There is a pair by these names roaming in the north, I have heard,' said Vitthal Vishram.

Nanasaheb's mind suddenly went off on a tangent. He looked at Vitthal Vishram and said, 'While leaving the south, the nawab had given me his word that he would follow if we took the first step. Our empire then was at its peak. But now we have had Panipat; why would he want to come along with us now, Vitthalpant?'

'That's true, Shrimant. All fair-weather friends.'

The Peshwa was exhausted. He signalled for the gathering to leave, with the message that Malharba should be sent over as soon as he arrived. With that, he slipped back into his bed and Gopikabai covered him with a quilt.

Nanasaheb's senior friends sat chatting in a tent close by. 'What fraternal love!' commented Yamaji Shivdev. 'The son born of him also died in Panipat, but Shrimant doesn't mention him as much as he does Bhausaheb.'

'It's history repeating itself. Once Bajirao was gone, how long did Appa last? This was another pairing of Nana-Bhau.'

'Looks like Shrimant is beginning to lose his senses. Often he doesn't recognize his close ones. Talks sometimes of setting off immediately for an assault on the enemy, writes to Rana Madho Singh asking him to form a confederation, and so on.'

As they sat chatting, news came of the arrival of Malharrao and Vitthalrao. They rushed out and brought the two back into the tent. As the Peshwa had just fallen asleep, they brought out some fruits and began to converse. Both the chieftains were touching seventy, but they looked as alert as before. The exhaustion of their latest misadventure was evident on their faces. After a little bit of chit-chat, Veereshwar Deekshit asked a question that had been bugging him, 'The rumour doing the rounds here is that mid-way during the battle, senior chieftains like you abandoned Bhausaheb and Vishwasrao, and cleared out of the battlefield. Sounds hard to believe.'

Malharba's jaws clenched. A shadow of guilt, however, passed across Vinchurkar's face. In a tone of regret, he said, 'Veereshwar, I feel terrible shame at hearing such stories. We held the fort in Panipat through such trying circumstances, but moved out at the critical time and brought disgrace on our white hair. It hurts. Actually, the fault was not ours. When we saw many groups moving out, we thought the royals were among them, so we left too. But what further acts of valour are we going to perform now in the little time we have left on this earth? If God had arranged for us to be martyred on the battlefield instead of having to leave it halfway, I would have offered a million thanks to the Almighty.'

Malharrao's face had turned red with suppressed rage. 'Instead of talking of 'leaving' the battlefield, why don't you come clean and say we deserted? It will lighten your heart. What can we say, anyway? You happen to be a relative of the Peshwa. If it had been anyone else, I would have pulled his tongue out from the root.'

Veereshwar simply turned his eyes down. Malharrao Holkar took a few deep breaths to get a grip on himself and continued, 'Well, all right, there have to be a large number of people who have questions regarding our behaviour on the battlefield, and this is what I have to say in response. My entire philosophy of life is of a different mould. I don't believe in upturning a boiling vessel upon myself. I prefer to let the vessel cool before I work out what to do with it. My strategy has always been based upon practicality, and I prefer caution to foolhardiness. My hair has turned white playing the game of politics; these eyes of mine have seen close to seventy cycles of seasons, but I'm not the kind to stretch things to a snapping-point. Nor am I the kind to live in a world of dreams. I would never yearn, like Dattaji did, to go riding against fire, sword swinging, bent upon embracing death and becoming a martyr. While there is life, there will always be opportunities, this is my driving principle. If circumstances require me to withdraw, I shall most certainly withdraw, so that I can be there to leap forward with alacrity when the right opening arrives. I don't find anything wrong with this principle. The motto is: stay alive and keep the kingdom alive. Beyond this, I don't care what blame people want to heap on me.'

The Peshwa had woken up after an hour's nap. As soon as he got to know of the arrival of Holkar and Vinchurkar, he sent for them. His wounds were raw and bleeding. Even before the two arrived, he had broken into sobs. When he saw them through a haze of tears, he wailed, 'You've arrived, Malharba, Vitthalpant! But why alone? Where have you left my Bhau? And in which wilderness have you left my son behind?'

The two neared Nanasaheb's bed. Was this their Nanasaheb Peshwa? His grief had reduced him to skin and bones. They embraced him by turns. Holkar took the Peshwa's thin hands in his as the sick man moaned,

'Malharba, Vitthalpant! Where is my Bhau? How is he? If you don't fetch him back, I shall certainly go insane … And where is Parvatibai?'

'She's is in Gwalior, Shrimant. She's safe.'

'Safe? How can she be safe? Poor girl, who will she lean upon for the rest of her life?'

'Please, Shrimant,' murmured Holkar as he patted Nanasaheb's hand, 'you have to find the strength to come to terms with what's happened.'

'Malhar kaka, had Bhau received the million rupees I had dispatched to him?'

'Shrimant, if we had received this sum, we would have dispatched the entire Afghan army to Yama's abode. Our men died waiting for provisions. What little we received from the Punjab vanished in no time. It was on sheer will-power that they survived for as long as they did. But let's move on, Shrimant, you must take care of your health.'

'At least, how Bhau and Vishwasrao fared. I have to hear that out, however painful it is.'

'How do I describe the courage and passion with which Vishwasrao fought? He fell upon the enemy like a tornado, tearing through the hordes that surrounded him, destroying them as if he had been taken over by some divine spirit. That was when a shot came from nowhere and pierced him in the brow. All came to a sudden end.'

The loud lamentation of a heartbroken Gopikabai filled the tent It was only when she saw the state of her devastated husband and the terror on her son Narayanrao's face that she managed somehow to rein in her grief, and covered her face with the end of her saree.

'What about Bhau, Malhar kaka?' The Peshwa wouldn't stop.

'It was unfortunate that Bhau did not listen to our advice. We begged him not to get into the battle in the Moghul manner, but he was far too enamoured of those Gardis to pay heed to us. If only he had listened, we could have won. Vishwasrao's sudden fall rattled the army. Not knowing how to face you, with Vishwasrao gone, Bhau jumped off his elephant on to his horse and galloped off to where the enemy was most densely gathered. Once he disappeared inside that mass, we lost sight of him.'

'But how could you have left the battlefield without Bhau, Subhedar kaka?' persisted the Peshwa.

'He sent us a message, Shrimant, that we should clear Parvatibai out of the battlefield, which left us with no choice but to obey. It was with the greatest difficulty that we finally made it to Gwalior.'

'What finally happened to Bhau, can't you tell me?' the Peshwa went on doggedly.

'I beg your forgiveness, Shrimant, we don't have any concrete information. We keep hearing all kinds of contradictory stories.'

'I shall never know peace till I hear the final word on Bhau.' With that, he stretched his arm out for Veereshwar to help him up. He seemed to have made up his mind on something. He swayed as he stood and clenched his fist. His eyes had stopped streaming and turned blood red. 'Subhedar kaka,' he said with as much iron as he could muster, 'you are there, as are my other compatriots like Vinchurkar, Baramatikar, Yamaji, Vitthal Vishram and Veereshwar. Let's steel ourselves once again, temper our weapons and get into a gallop. Let's block the enemy on its way to Kandahar, cut him to pieces and drown their entire army in the Yamuna. We have to avenge Bhau's blood, we have to, do you hear?'

Malharrao stood speechless. Gopika stared, wide-eyed with fear. The other sardars too watched nervously. When there was no response forthcoming from the Malharrao Holkar, the Peshwa screamed, 'Why don't you say something?'

'What's there to say, Shrimant?' Malharrao said in a low voice. 'As for the enemy, they have taken a battering too. Revolt has begun to break out in their ranks, we hear. He is not going to tarry in Hindustan for too long. Where is the point in steeling ourselves now? The few survivors we have in our Maratha army are already starved and broken. They have fallen into a stupor. Their homes have gone into a spin. The vanquished have no friends. We won't find anyone who will step out to help us in this venture. Even here, within our own lands, we are having problems gathering revenue. We shall certainly wreak vengeance upon the enemy, but right now, we need to pick up our pieces.'

The Peshwa was so far gone that he couldn't believe his ears at what he considered was Malharrao's insubordinate talk. When he began shivering with anger and helplessness, Gopikabai rushed forward and held him. 'Your lordship should take care of your health!' she pleaded through her tears. Please think of our sons, this little Narayanrao here, look at your terrified Madhavrao there. If you stay well, we all stay well. Let's turn back south. You alone cannot stem the crack in this massive dam!'

※

The tents of both Malharrao Holkar and Vitthalrao Vinchurkar had been pitched quite close to the Peshwa's pavilion. For the last four days, they had spent hours on end with the Peshwa, talking of times past. Vitthalrao Vinchurkar had just left for his tent after spending some time with the Peshwa, and stretched out on his bed. Despite having crossed sixty-five he stood with good carriage, back always upright, head held high with pride. When he went around the empire, he would stroke his white beard and twirl his dense moustache with pride. But as he was walking back today from the Peshwa's pavilion, the pride of old, the strut in his walk had been missing. While young boys had been falling in the foreign field of Panipat, he had deserted it mid-action. He had brought shame upon his white hair. He felt as if the entire country was now looking at him with scorn, as if asking him why he had fled like a woman. The self-loathing was stifling him. What have you made me do, God? Blackened my face in my last innings ...

While he was sitting with the Peshwa that afternoon, a bunch of the Panipat survivors had arrived for an audience, eyes filled with tears. As they were relating the deeds of the martyred youngsters, Vitthalrao had had to struggle to meet their eyes. Nanasaheb had turned to him and asked, 'Vitthalrao, the Afghan slaves that you had taken under your charge at Kunjpura—they wreaked mayhem later, I hear. Started spreading the word of defeat much before the war got over and did a lot of looting too!'

Shame and remorse made him bend his head. 'That was a terrible mistake on my part, Shrimant,' he had confessed. 'I had given them shelter out of pity, not taking into account that they could betray us.'

'That seems to be an inherent fault of us Marathi people, not reading a person's character till he places a knife across our throats. By the time truth dawns, the earth has been pulled from under our feet.'

Vitthalrao kept tossing and turning that night. Just as he had dozed off, he heard Ibrahim Gardi's frantic cries. The man had brought Abdali to his knees in the very first round of conflict. That was when he and Gayakwad had broken the circle and dashed ahead. He heard Fateh

Khan crying out in panic, 'Stop! Stop! I fall at your feet, please don't break the circle!' The desperate cries of the young Gardi jolted him back into wakefulness. What a fatal error he had committed by giving in to his false pride that day. It had wiped out the entire Gardi battalion and changed the course of the battle. He got out of bed, wrapped a thick blanket round himself and walked out into the cold wind towards the Holkar tent to find his friend awake too. 'The night rises up like a cobra to snap at me, Malharba. I have forgotten what a sound sleep feels like. The most frightful events haunt my dreams. The shame of Panipat seems to have stained my character. What do I do to wash it off, Malharba?'

'You can't turn the clock round, Vitthalrao,' Malharba tried to pacify him. 'The only thing you can do about the unfortunate events of the past is to leave them behind and look ahead.'

Vitthalrao sat nodding for a while and then burst out in anger, 'You tell me, Malharba, where have I fallen short in my service to the Maratha empire? Who was the one who broke the Siddhis' back at Janjira? Who joined with Appa to finish off Daya Bahadur at Malwa? Who ran neck to neck with Bajirao when he assaulted Delhi? When Wasai was besieged, who was there alongside Appa other than you and me? But then, where did all our valour and gallantry disappear in Panipat? If only all of us had stiffened our resolve and come down upon the enemy with all our fury, we would have made that Abdali shit bricks as I had made that pig shit in the heath at Jawali long, long ago. This one miscalculation has wiped out our loyalty of decades.'

'You are right, Vitthala, we did seem to have erred. But what can we do now? When all that water was flowing past, that was the time to divert it into our farms and reap a rich harvest. Now there is no water, no paani, and no Panipat. What is left now in our old age except to sit watching all the muck that the water has left behind?'

☙

Abdali sat in the palace leaning against the bolster, fuming with rage. Before him stood Shah Wali Khan, looking flustered and shame-faced. The emperor slapped his thigh in anger as he said, 'How do you forget that you are the wazeer of Kandahar? With what confidence I had handed over the charge of the raid on Jaat territory to you! Not only had I given you my best horses, but also sent along Najeeb and Zeenat Mahal, who knew the lay of the land! And here you stand before me, returning defeated after having barely travelled twenty-five miles! Don't all of you feel ashamed?'

'You are mistaken, Qibla-e-aalam,' the wazeer responded in a calm voice. 'Your forces do not know the word "defeat". I myself am not the person to accept defeat till as long as there is breath in my body. But when the army was consumed by the flame of revolt—'

'Revolt?' screamed Abdali.

'Yes. What could I do to quell the internal revolt?'

'Shut up!' roared the emperor. 'How dare you give me such a lame excuse! As my wazeer, don't you know the punishment that is meted out to rebels in the Durrani army? Why didn't you first blow up the rebels with cannons or trample them under elephants before you came to me with this news, Shah Wali?'

'Aalam-panaah, we have handed down this punishment numerous times before, but this was not the occasion for it; in fact, it was impossible.'

The emperor threw a worried glance at Shah Wali. The old man returned a beseeching look and said, 'How many could I have handed this punishment down to? If I had been indiscriminate, would a single groom have been left in your stable for brushing your horses or a palanquin bearer for the ladies? Would we have been left with four soldiers to travel back home with us?'

'How do you mean?'

'The entire army is preparing for a revolt. A slave had brought the news yesterday that our two chieftains Dilawar Khan and Jaal Beg are already on their way back to Kandahar, taking with them ten thousand horsemen each.'

'The discontent among the men is really strong, then!'

'That's right, Your Highness.'

'Shah Wali, these stories sound unbelievable to me. My men are partners in my destiny; and though I can be harsh in my punishment, I have loved them like my own blood. Why should, then, my army be so upset?'

'The battle of the belly is always the tougher one to fight, Aalam-panaah. A hungry man may well test his teeth on a cannon. The wretched and hungry have shaken many a throne across the world, torn the banner to shreds.'

As the emperor listened with a darkening face, the old wazeer went on, 'There is nothing surprising about the ferment among the men, Aalam-panaah. Their biggest enemy, the summer of these parts, is coming back again. Not only have they not received their allowances, but they have also forgotten the feel of the cool wind of Kandahar. They think of their loved ones back home and turn morose. I have seen some of the men cry.'

Noticing that the emperor was hanging on to his words, the wazeer cleared his throat and brought up another matter of concern. 'Qibla-e-aalam,' he continued, 'those who had wanted to leave have left. The ones that are left now are not outside the scope of your influence. What I am more worried about is the news I am getting from our country. Your nephew Abdul Khaliq Khan Girishk has already started strutting around, projecting himself as the emperor of Kandahar. There is news that he is slowly progressing towards our capital city and a few small-time rebels have joined his forces. Under such circumstances, the two chieftains suddenly detaching themselves and heading homewards can't be a good omen. Anything can spring out of this. But I have a worse piece of news.'

'Tell me, Shah Wali. I don't want a single word held back!'

'Aalam-panaah, our enemies, the feudal lords of back home, have spread the rumour everywhere that Aalam-panaah has suffered a crushing defeat in Panipat, a more coloured version being that you have been taken prisoner, another saying that you have been slain.'

Abdali was stung. 'Wazeer, here I stand before you hale and hearty after having razed all of Hindustan to the ground in Panipat. Who is left now to dare raise arms against me?'

'Aalam-panaah, if the husband has been away for a couple of years, the wife's virtue cannot be trusted. She either strays herself or others lure her into infidelity. Here it is a matter of the entire country's character. If the king is out for so many years, whom do the subjects look to? That treacherous Shuja-ud-dowla deserted us, our trusted chieftains have ditched us. Aalam-panaah, I too am being assailed by all kinds of fears.'

'What fears? What fears after our army has crushed Hindustan so completely?'

'Aalam-panaah, was Alexander any small a conqueror than you? But this soil of Hindustan is bad.'

'What do you want to say?'

'Huzoor, where did the all-conquering Alexander die? On his way home, didn't he? I seek your forgiveness for speaking straight, Aalam-panaah, but what has your army really gained by hoisting the flag of victory in Panipat? Those Margatthas were paupers anyway, what could you have got out of them? That cunning, lying fox Najeeb, who talked of presenting millions to you, has stopped coming before you. Surajmal Jaat is not likely to even look in our directions. Shuja has left. Our army is going hungry. The Sikhs have begun to raise their heads in the Punjab. You have achieved such an unparalleled victory here, and yet the air in your home country is rife with stories of your defeat.'

Shah Wali stopped to give his words time to sink in. After a while of silence, Abdali heaved a deep sigh and said, 'Shah Wali, it really is Allah's mercy that victory fell our way; otherwise it was always neck to neck between the Afghans and the Margatthas. We were both determined either to kill or to die. Victory in such a conflict is so much a matter of luck. I know well that if we had been defeated here, the crown of Kandahar too would have toppled into the soil of Panipat. Agreed that nothing came out of this battle for us as such, but we saved our Kandahar empire from disintegrating and our reputation from getting rubbed into dust. That is no mean achievement.'

He called Shah Pasand Khan over immediately and instructed him, 'Leave for Kandahar right now. Move like the wind, hunt down that Abdul Khaliq, and strangulate him the moment you find him. Stuff his corpse with hay and take it around in procession in Herat, Farah and Kandahar. Quash the revolt before its sparks spread. I shall be following at your heels. Make lavish arrangements for my welcome. Raise victory gates at every village that we cross, strew the streets with petals, have victory drums played everywhere till such time as we arrive. Leave right now with the strongest regiment you can gather. Go!'

22 March 1761. Abdali had set up a temporary camp in Shalimar Bagh after setting off on the way home a few days ago. Small units of the army had already begun to move on the imperial highway. The emperor's horse was to hit the highway in the afternoon, and arrangements were being made for the event along the route. The big-wigs of Hindustan had gathered to bid the emperor adieu: Zeenat Mahal, Yaqoob Ali Khan, Najeeb Khan, Wazeer Ghaziuddin and others. This would be Emperor Abdali's last address to them.

Although Ghaziuddin had been made the wazeer of Delhi, he would be that only in name. The real power would lie in the hands of Najeeb. As the Meer Bakshi, Najeeb would be in control of the army, he would be the chief security officer of Delhi as also the chief administrator of the empire. The wily man had tried to please Abdali with the gift of a million and a quarter, but it hadn't really worked magic.

As he now stood to say his farewell, Abdali looked at Zeenat Mahal and Najeeb and said, 'All the land of Hindustan north of the Sutlej shall be mine. Whoever sits on the throne of Delhi, I don't care who, should send to me an annual revenue of four million rupees. It will not be possible for me to send an army over to collect it, so the responsibility shall lie with the Delhi emperor to have the tribute reach me in Kandahar without delay. Any neglect in this matter, and I will make the person in charge repent.'

This said, Abdali looked with distaste at Najeeb and said, 'Najeeb Khan, the money you brought over the other day will not be enough for even distributing grams to my army. Tell me what you have done about the millions of rupees you had promised.'

'Aalam-panaah,' Najeeb beseeched, 'your lordship has borne a lot of hardships these two years, but I request his patience for another month or two. We will cross the Vindhyas and the Satpudas and travel south. We will plunder the palaces and temples of gold- and silver-laden towns like Paithan, Pune and Pandharpur and—'

'Najeeb,' Abdali cut short his fanciful talk. 'You are of the Afghan race, and you belong to the Yusufzai clan. You came over to Hindustan to make your fortune. But you turned out to be a traitor of the worst kind.'

'Aalam-panaah,' Najeeb went on his knees and placed his brow on the ground, 'please don't read me so wrong. Irregular it has been, I confess, but I have done all that I could to provide for such a huge army as yours.'

'Have you done us any favour by doing that?' roared Abdali. 'You have the gumption to stand here and show us the carrot farms of the Deccan? You expect that we will be lured into doing this run for you? Our forces are here only in flesh; in thought, they have already reached their native land. You are very well aware of the impossibility of turning their heads in that direction, and yet you make this fraudulent offer!'

The emperor was so livid that none dared look up. After a minute of tense silence, Abdali resumed, 'Najeeb, there is not much point in blaming you either. I was not wrong in my calculations about my army and its involvement in this mammoth campaign. There was just one thing that went a little wrong.'

'Have I erred somewhere, Your Highness?' asked Najeeb.

'The fault is not yours, Najeeb,' the emperor pronounced in a voice dripping with scorn, 'the fault has been mine. I could not correctly judge you for what you are.'

Najeeb hung his head. Abdali went on, 'You went on deluding me and my men with your talk of jihad. The Margatthas have always referred to you as a snake, and they have been right. You are no ordinary snake at that, you are a cobra and python rolled into one. Who you would mark out as your enemy, who you would roll into your coils, who you would get your fangs into—I guess the best of snakes can take lessons from you in the art. Then again, you are not just a snake, you are also a snake charmer. When you begin to blow on your pipe, the best of them cannot save themselves from getting hypnotized. My own men have pushed me away and run after you and fallen into your net of jihad.'

'Aalam-panaah, there's some mis—'

'Cut out your rubbish!' Abdali snapped. 'The one sincere advice I want to give to all of you is that if you wish to stay in Hindustan, you must build cordial relations with the natives. I am no groom from your stable to come running every time you call. Come to an agreement with the Jaats. Najeeb, I have already sent a letter of reconciliation to the Marathas. Make bonds with them. It is a very tough breed of people. Remember how they had subdued even Shah Wali's soldiers, even if for a short while. If you don't behave decently with them, Najeeb, they won't let even your grave rest in peace.'

Abdali was getting late for his ride home. He got up and moved towards his soldiers, who were waiting for him excitedly to get a move on. As he reached up to his horse, before easing his foot into the stirrup, he turned round, placed his hand on Najeeb's shoulder and said, 'Najeeb, I have this one final advice for you.'

Najeeb looked up at the emperor tensely.

'You hoodwinked thousands of soldiers into sacrificing their lives for jihad; you even managed to dupe a true Muslim like Shah Waliullah Saheb into falling for your wiles; you fooled the entire country into standing on its head in the name of Islam. If you can even now find the time to truly serve this holy religion with honesty and sincerity, you may well be able to save your soul from going to hell. That is all.'

☙

Nanasaheb Peshwa was camping at Burhanpur. Nana Phadnis and Parvatibai had arrived there the previous evening. Nana Phadnis had found the opportunity to present himself before the Peshwa but Parvatibai was still to meet him. The Peshwa had turned shockingly weak and thin. The strong, muscular frame of merely five years ago had melted into sunken cheeks, shrunken chest and knobbly, bony limbs. New information arrived every day on the events that had unfolded in Panipat. Four months had gone by, but the wound showed no signs of healing. The non-stop haemorrhaging had thoroughly emaciated the Peshwa in both spirit and body. He had become unpredictable. No one was sure when and with whom he would get upset or angry, and for what fault. The chieftains and officials had begun to avoid being within his range.

While he lay in one of the inner apartments of the royal pavilion, his friends and associates would sit in the adjacent office pavilion and brood over a single subject: Nanasaheb's health, and its potential to reduce the entire Maratha empire to dust.

Looking deeply anxious, Veereshwar Deekshit said, 'Only Lord Omkareshwar knows what the Peshwa may do next. He hardly eats anything, gets wild over all and sundry, has no consciousness of anything that he does.'

Yamaji Shivdev looked a little uncertain as he said, 'He gets into bouts of insanity, actually. If you remember, on the festival of Gudi Padwa, he had hugged Holkar in Indore, entrusted to him the safety and well-being of the empire, but as he moved south from there, he had no compunction in confiscating the Holkar palace that lay on the way. How do you explain this behaviour?'

'What about the contribution of the Shindes to the glory of the empire?' said Vitthal Vishram. 'Some of their best princes like Ranoba, Jayappa, Dattaji and Jankoji laid down their lives on the battlefield in the service of the empire. But look at what our Peshwa gave them in return! Went to Ujjain and snapped up their entire property! Our Yashwantrao Pawar actually fell fighting in the battlefield of Panipat, and the Peshwa goes and confiscates his palace? How can a person stand up to this kind of erratic, unfair behaviour?'

'He keeps a cane in his hand these days, and one can never tell who will become the beneficiary. It has become so exasperating!' said Veereshwar.

As the conversation progressed, suddenly, they heard some noise from the Peshwa's pavilion. Everyone rushed in that direction to be greeted by a strange sight. The Peshwa stood leaning against a post, trembling with anger. Two of his servants were holding down his hand that held his cane, but the Peshwa was still managing to give it some swing. Gopikabai stood behind a screen, shivering in fear. Next to her stood two of her maids, also shivering and looking terror-stricken. Nanasaheb, it appeared, had used his cane on Gopikabai. The shocked spectators could see that he was trying his hardest to free his hand and hit her again.

'Wretched woman,' he yelled, 'it was because of you that Panipat happened! I lost my boys because of you! You were forever running down my Bhau! You bullied and hounded the poor orphan boy out of greed for power! You pestered me into sending Vishwasrao into the campaign! You alone pushed them to their deaths. How many more do you want to swallow up?'

Could this be the Nanasaheb they had known and loved? A person who had been known for his compassion and wisdom? None of those assembled had the courage to intervene in the domestic tiff. With Nanasaheb bent upon chastising his wife, all they could do was to stare at each other helplessly. Suddenly there was a loud murmur at the entrance of the pavilion, and the crowd parted to allow passage to Parvatibai. Her eyes were a little sunken with grief, but the strength of character was still evident.

Parvatibai cast a sharp glance at Nanasaheb. As he returned her looks, the cane slipped out of his grasp and fell to the ground. He noticed the vermillion mark on her forehead, the gold mangalsutra round her neck, and other items of jewellery common to a married lady of the royal household. Tears welled up in Nanasaheb's eyes, and he began to look dizzy. Gopikabai noticed his state and helped him to his bed. Parvatibai swept a sharp glance at the gathering, which was a signal for them all to melt away. She then went to Nanasaheb's bedside and placed her palm on his forehead. Nanasaheb replied in an anguished voice, 'This is all the curse of the gods. I am sure I am expiating for the sins of my previous life.

The conversation between the two went on for a long time. Finally, the Peshwa said, 'Gopikey, Parvatibai, this town seems to rise up and tear my heart asunder. I can't stay here anymore. I want to be taken to Pune. Whatever good or bad has to happen to me, let it happen in my Shaniwarwada, on the bank of the Mula-Mutha, in the sanctum-sanctorum of one of its temples. I must end my exile here and return home immediately.'

Everybody knew of the deep affection that the Peshwa had for Pune. The huge gardens, the wide roads, the Parvati temple complex, these were all Nanasaheb's ways of expressing love for the city. Pune had gained a reputation across Hindustan as a city of knowledge, culture and religious affairs. He looked at Parvatibai with desperation and said, 'Let's leave tonight itself, or latest by tomorrow morning.'

Parvatibai's eyes turned moist. In a sorrowful but firm voice, she said, 'How can I come over to Pune before my lord and master arrives?'

His eyes filled up with distress at Parvatibai's words. She continued, 'How can I leave till I find out where he is? He is sure to pass this way one day. News keeps coming from Hindustan about his being in one place one day and another place the next. In whichever part of the world he may be, there can be no better news than that he is happy.'

She remembered clearly the time when they were setting off from Kurukshetra towards Panipat. When Bhausaheb had expressed his admiration at finding a sword in her hand, she had said, 'If one is married to fire, then one should get used to the heat.' The memory of that moment on the eve of the battle had made a permanent home in her mind. She had put him on oath that he would not leave her behind, and the man was known never to go back on his commitment.

The Peshwa watched the changing expressions on Parvatibai's face as she stood lost in her thoughts. 'How long can you continue to live with false hopes, Parvatibai?'

'How can you call my hopes false, Shrimant? Please read this letter he had written to me and then you will understand. If I return to Pune without him, he will be very upset.'

Nanasaheb took the letter. The handwriting was exactly like Bhau's. It was sent by the envoy of Jaipur to a Peshwa clerk named Lakshman Appaji Ekbote, who had gone to Sirhind. The letter had brought the bloom back on Parvatibai's face.

He looked at her with great sympathy. How was he to explain to her that it was a ruse played by some of his officials after the mass slaughter at Panipat? The idea was to keep adversaries like Salabat Jung, Nizam Ali, Maisurkar—in fact, even people like Udaji Chauhan—under check. It would be dangerous for them to get the idea that the spine of the Maratha empire was broken, hence the myth was being perpetuated that great warriors like Bhausaheb and Jankojiba were alive and well. The unintended consequence was that a number of imposters had begun to exploit the situation, and information on sightings would keep arriving. Concerned about the Peshwa's health, the conspirators and the forgers had even hoped to include him in this deception, but Kashiraj's letter had put paid to that expectation. The Peshwa could now only look at Parvatibai's innocent conviction and feel a little more shattered.

ॐ

It was four days into the Orion constellation that Nanasaheb's procession touched Yerwada and pitched camp close to the Dharmshala. On Thursday evening, he had reached the outskirts of Pune and had planned to set off for Shaniwarwada on Friday morning, but Punalkar Joshibuva had declared Friday inauspicious for returning home after eight months of staying out, and that had been that.

The tradition had been for the Peshwa to enter the capital city of Pune with great fanfare, but the circumstances this time were different. Nanasaheb Peshwa had set off from Kaigaon after offering ritual prayers for his father the late Bajirao. As he traversed the Maratha land, the destruction that Panipat had wrought hit him with stunning force. Every single village on the way had sent a couple of hundred of its youth into the war. The vast majority of them had been annihilated. A number of those who had managed to return home had lost all interest in life and sat at home in a stupor. There were the crippled ones who had become a dead-weight upon their impoverished families. A huge number of them had simply disappeared. Whether they had fallen on the battlefield or had turned mendicants no one knew. A vast number of young women were in the same state as Parvatibai, still observing the dress code of women with living husbands, wearing vermillion on their foreheads and in the parting of their hair, waiting for their husbands to return some day. Whenever any army unit crossed, everyone would rush up to it and make frantic enquiries. 'Have you heard from my husband?' 'Any news of our son?' 'Could you have run into my brother?'

As Nanasaheb had passed through these villages, observing the widespread devastation through tear-filled eyes, he died a thousand deaths. Two days had passed since he had arrived in Yerwada. He could see from there Pune, half covered in dense green vegetation, with the spires of temples and the taller buildings spiking into the sky. He would sit for hours watching the Parvati hill far in the distance. His eyes would drift to the saffron flag flying atop Shaniwarwada and he would break into a sweat. Returning to Shaniwarwada had always been exciting, but that was before the blight had struck. Without Bhau or Vishwasrao or Shamsher Bahadur waiting for him, what would he do there? How would he be able to walk its corridors without their images leaping at him at every turn?

Gopikabai had now become a regular fixture, sitting by her husband's bedside day and night. Her heart and mind knew no peace. The prince she had brought up to become the next Peshwa, on whose account she had caused pain to so many innocent people, in which part of Hindustan had she lost her dear Vishwasrao? How would Shaniwarwada look now without his happy presence? She could not shake away the image of

Bhausaheb as he stood before her, desiring her blessing before setting off on the campaign. The picture of that orphan boy Shamsher standing before her refused to leave her mind too. In her blind obsession for her son's welfare, she had been grossly unfair in her treatment of two wonderful people. Destiny had removed all three of them from her life now, and her conscience allowed her no place to hide from self-loathing.

Raghunath Dada was as lost as everybody else on how to bring normalcy back into Maratha life. He took Sakharam Bapu, Krishnarao Parasnis, Trimbak Kanhere and a few others with him to visit the Peshwa at Yerwada. Nanasaheb's state left him speechless. 'What have you done to yourself, Shrimant?' he cried in agony as he took the Peshwa's hand in his.

'Arrey Dada,' groaned Nanasaheb, 'if we had all got together and fought as a single unit, crushing the enemy was no big thing. It was our dissensions that brought the empire to ruin at Panipat.'

After tremendous effort, Raghunath had managed to get the Peshwa to get a grip on his grief, and persuaded him to have a doctor see him. Prayers had been organized at a number of temples seeking divine intervention. Baburao Phadnis had left to plead with the Ganpati at Ballaleshwar, while priests chanted slokas and performed havans at the temples in Wadgaon, Pabal, Thevoor and other places.

An auspicious moment was identified and the Peshwa was placed in a canopy atop an elephant on Tuesday evening. The procession crossed the river and entered the city. There was a light but steady drizzle, converting the streets into a slurry of mud. While there were no music, drums or dancing, the crowd on both sides was as dense as always, watching the Peshwa move towards Shaniwarwada. There was no cheering either. The usual spirit of joy and pride was missing. Nanasaheb Peshwa looked nervously at the people lined on either side and asked Sakharam Bapu, 'Bapu, why are these people glaring at me so?'

'It's not that at all, Shrimant, it's just that they are grief-stricken.'

'No, Bapu, no. The people are interrogating me with their eyes. They are asking why I am coming back alone. Where is Bhau? Where is Shamsher? Where is Vishwasrao? Where are the young boys of every household?'

It was around dinnertime that they reached Shaniwarwada. The Peshwa was brought down and placed in a palanquin, which was carried in through the Delhi Gate. He instructed them to carry it past the office and asked it to stop there. Raghunath Dada helped him out of the palanquin and took him to where Bhau used to sit. This was where Bhau would place his finger on a page of the ledger and make the biggest chieftains and their accountants break into a sweat. The place wore a deserted look now. The Peshwa was so overcome by the memory of those times that he simply went down on his haunches with a loud cry of 'Bhau! Bhau re!'

༄

Work on the Lakdi Pul, the wooden bridge that was being built on the Mutha river, was still in progress when Nanasaheb returned to Pune. He would sit for hours watching the construction work with empty eyes. Raghunath Dada, Sakharam Bapu, Kanhere and a few intimates would always be around as he sat.

As they sat once, Sakharam Bapu pointed at the bridge and said, 'Shrimant, this bridge is going to be very useful for the town. More settlements will come up on the other side. That Patil Wadi over there, those other four or five wadas around there; look at the lives that this one single bridge will connect with each other!'

'Arrey Bapu,' said the Peshwa, 'is this bridge of yours going to connect me back to my Bhau?' Then he added, 'This wada seems to be squeezing the breath out of me! Move me out of here!'

Arrangements were made, and the very next day, the palanquins set off for Parvati. The Peshwa had been wanting to go there for a long time. After they had come out of the thick woods, the Parvati hill came into sight. There used to be just one ancient temple of a goddess atop the hill to begin with, which an old devotee would visit regularly for performing his prayers. Gopikabai had come down once with a terrible sciatic pain, which no amount of treatment would relieve. Nanasaheb had gone begging at the feet of the goddess and the relief was immediate. From that day onwards, daily offerings began being made to the goddess. Nanasaheb had always believed Shahu Raja to be the incarnation of Lord Shiv and had laid his devotion at the king's feet. When the king passed away, he had a huge silver statue made of Lord Samba, an incarnation of Lord Shiv, which he got installed atop the hill. After six years of continuous activity, a grand temple was constructed to house the statue. A gold statue of

Goddess Parvati was placed upon one thigh and another of Lord Ganesh was placed upon the other thigh of Samba. The statues would be given their holy baths at state expense and holy offerings distributed every day. Two other temples followed: one of Lord Vishnu and another separate one for Lord Ganapati right behind the main temple. A huge manor was built there too, and a proper religious foundation was established. A proper court had begun to assemble at the temple after Nanasaheb's arrival. There were priests and pundits, watchmen, singers, scholars, disciples, watermen and a host of others. Nanasaheb was convinced that with so many gods, goddesses and holy men nearby, his health would improve. His palanquin would make innumerable trips to the durbar hall, where prayers and discourses would be in progress. He would sit there, lost in contemplation of the divinities that he had been instrumental in bringing together on that altitude. In the evening, the palanquin would be lowered next to the railing outside the temple; he would sit in the cold wind, watching his Pune unblinkingly for a long, long time.

But three days into the visit, and his restlessness returned. His health also took a turn for the worse. Whatever energy he had gathered in the past few days drained away. He found it impossible to sit in the palanquin in spite of all the bolsters placed around him for support. The bouts of racking cough became longer and more frequent. Parvati was no longer a good place to stay in. He was moved back into Shaniwarwada immediately.

❦

Nanasaheb Peshwa lay in bed one afternoon, eyes half closed. Gopikabai sat next to him, her head sunk, her eyes closed, looking defeated from incessant stress and sleepless nights. She had slipped into a drowse before her husband did.

Nanasaheb was suddenly back in full form. He mounted the stairs of Shaniwarwada right up to the seventh floor. From that height, he could see thousands and thousands of horsemen come galloping in. Their saffron pennants were fluttering wildly in the wind, and their cries of 'Har Har Mahadev!' was resonating all around. As he watched, he saw the army get into the Mutha river. In a little while, it had climbed out of the near bank and was heading straight for the wada.

Right in front was riding a gallant horseman on a spirited horse. As they neared, some of the soldiers shot forward, brought down the saffron banner that was riding atop an elephant, and handed it over to their leader. Loud cries of 'Har Har Mahadev!' rolled forward with the wind. The musical instruments and the war-drums lifted the cries high up in the air and scattered them in all directions. When they had reached Shaniwarwada, the horseman jumped off, raised the banner aloft, stuck his chest out and stepped into the wada with strong strides. His clothes and the banner in his hand were spattered with blood. There was blood on his glowing face and muscular arms too. Who was this man leaping rather than walking towards him with such energy?

Was it? ... Could it be? ... It most certainly was!

It was his beloved Bhau, walking towards him, a blinding smile playing upon his lips. The Peshwa suddenly felt as strong as an elephant. He flew down the stairs. Once out of his palace, he raced towards the courtyard near the office and came face to face with the man. With a loud cry, the two stretched out their arms and locked each other in a tight embrace, rocking slowly as tears of joy and pride streamed down their cheeks.

'Most revered brother, look at this banner,' Bhau cried. 'I soaked it in Abdali's blood before bringing it to you. We have won the battle! Panipat is ours!'

'Bravo, dear Bhau! You have vanquished the three worlds. You have truly brought glory to Appa's name and to the Maratha empire!'

In their excitement, banner in hand, the two ran back to the palace and all the way up the seven flights of stairs. There, on the main flag-post, they hoisted the flag and saw it flapping wildly in the strong wind.

Suddenly, the Peshwa began to cough. He saw thick black smoke rising up the stairwell. The acrid smoke was choking him. 'Run, Bhau, run!' he screamed through his coughs. 'The palace has caught fire!' Bhau had suddenly vanished! Could he be caught in the fire? The wind was fanning the flames, and the blaze was turning wilder by the minute. 'Where are you, Bhau?' he screamed at the top of his voice. The palace had begun to crackle, and the smoke swirling up the stairwell had covered everything that lay below.

Nanasaheb yelled to himself. 'I must go down and see him to safety!'

'Hold on, Bhau,' he bellowed into the fire, 'I'm coming!' With that, he leapt into the inferno ...

Gopikabai watched with horror as the Peshwa suddenly sprang out of the bed and fell with a thump on the floor. She let out a loud shriek and gathered the fallen man into her arms. The other chieftains and officials came running in hearing her scream and lifted the flailing Peshwa back into bed. His clothes were soaked in perspiration, and he screamed incessantly, 'Fire! Fire!'

Then suddenly, he went limp and passed out.

The doctor arrived and mopped his wet face with a piece of cloth. He gave his palms and soles a vigorous massage. When consciousness began to return, he persuaded him to drink a few mouthfuls of the potion he had prepared. Little by little, Nanasaheb came to. He signalled young Madhavrao to come closer and ran a hand over his face with great affection. 'All is not well with me, son,' he said, struggling for breath. 'I don't think I have more than a few days left. You will now have to take charge of the empire.'

At these words, the entire assembly broke out into loud sobs and protests. Gopikabai began to wail. Raghunath Dada couldn't hold his tears back either.

'Please don't say such things, Shrimant,' Neelkanth Purandare pleaded through his sobs. 'The entire kingdom calls you and Bhau a reincarnation of Lord Rama and his brother Bharat. With Bhau nowhere to be found, how can you too walk out of your duty to your people?'

'Neelkanthpant, this is a slightly different Ramayan. Here, it was my Bharat that left with my footwear for the exile. Through the summer heat and through rains and through the winter wind, this Bharat, my Bhau walked on, holding my footwear close to his heart, and never returned from his exile.'

The Peshwa could be calmed down. 'This wada wants to rise and swallow me up,' he cried through the day. 'I get nightmares every time my eyes shut even during the daytime. My marrow has begun to freeze in my bones. I want to be moved out. I want to be moved out, do you hear?'

The Peshwa was again shifted back to Parvati that night.

Monday, the day of Lord Shiv. Nanasaheb Peshwa was feeling better today. He called for his palanquin and set out for a round of the temples. He then made his usual halt at the railing outside the main temple and looked long and deep at the Pune he loved so much.

The evening found him sprightlier than he had been in a long time. He talked endlessly, with Raghunathrao, Gopikabai, Madhavrao, Narayanrao, and all the servants and maids gathered round him.

He looked at Raghunath and said, 'Dada, Kurukshetra is very close to Panipat. That was where the great conflict between the Kauravas and the Pandavas happened. That entire region lives under the hypnotic influence of the Mahabharat. Our own battle was quite like the Mahabharat. It was my misfortune and the misfortune of the Maratha soil that we did not receive information on time, and therefore, I could not dispatch the provisions. Bhau, Vishwasrao, Shamsher, Jankoji, Dattaba, every one of them fought with the same passion as Bhima and Arjuna, whose exploits gave the gods their godhood. Our boys fought with the same valour, but what did they gain for their sacrifice?'

'Shrimant,' suggested Raghunath, 'you should try to rest now. You are not in the best of health; a little rest will do you good.'

'Dada,' the Peshwa went on, as if he had not heard a word of the admonition, 'the Panipat episode reveals the best as well as the worst aspects of our people. But let me tell you this, Dada: till as long as we continue with our nepotism, our indifference, our treachery, till as long as we don't give a burial to our helplessness and complacency, Panipat will keep on happening to us over and over again. It will happen a thousand times.'

Suddenly, Nanasaheb's breathing became laboured, and he began to sweat profusely. As the night advanced, his health worsened. Madhavrao, Raghunath Dada and Narayanrao panicked. The women wailed. In spite of being short on breath, Nanasaheb continued to call out: 'Bhau! Bhau!' Raghunathrao placed the Peshwa's head in his lap. As the Peshwa looked up, he saw Bhau's face in Raghunath Dada's eyes. Bhau was smiling. Midnight came and went.

On Jyeshth Vadya, 23 June 1761, Nanasaheb Peshwa made a giant effort to lift himself up, put his arms round Raghunath and croaked 'Bhau! Bhau!'

His last call went rolling out into the night. Then, his head went limp and fell back into Raghunath Dada's lap.

The Peshwa had found his release.

Till about thirty-five years ago, a small stone memorial stood quite lost in a sugarcane field near the modern township of Panipat. It was seen as a reminder of defeat and shame, and was consequently ignored. Vishwas Patil's Marathi novel *Panipat* was published in 1988 and was soon translated into Hindi and other regional languages. The hundreds of thousands of copies that got read completely changed the perspective of the readers towards this historical episode and the structure that stood in its memory. It was no longer regarded as a mark of shame, but as a symbol of the undying spirit and the super-human ability of the Maratha warriors to fight on and on in the face of imminent annihilation. People now assemble on 14 January every year to pay their tributes to this symbol of heroism.

notes

1. Jayappa Shinde and Malharrao Holkar signed a treaty called the Ahmadiya Agreement with the emperor of Delhi between 1751 and 1752. Accordingly, Antaji Mankeshwar established himself in Delhi to take over the responsibility spelt out in the agreement. Information on the roots of Panipat may be gathered from here.
2. Raghunath Dada had mounted two northern campaigns before the battle in Panipat occurred. He had reached up to Attock in the second campaign. Najeeb-ud-dowlah and he had been caught in a skirmish before this event. The cow-slaughter episode that occurred in 1757 and the confrontation that followed between Raghunathrao and Malharrao has been discussed at length in Najeeb's biography. A number of things written by Najeeb's biographers Biharilal and Nooruddin match well with the *bakhars* and the *kaifiyat*, the annals and narratives on Bhausaheb. For example, there is remarkable consonance between Bhausaheb's *bakhars* and Najeeb's biography on the description of Najeeb moving away from the conference pavilion at Shaamli without entering the tent, because he thought that 'the eyes of these Marathas indicate danger'.
3. Najeeb played a central role in the Panipat conflict. If not for Najeeb, the battle, perhaps, would not have happened. Obviously, therefore, both Nana and Bhau were well aware of the potential of Najeeb to play mischief and cause destruction. That is why such references occur in their writing: 'Najeeb is Abdali', Najeeb is a 'delusionary demon' and a 'snake'. The Peshwa had instructed that he should be killed first; but Raghunathrao, and during the early days, even the Maratha representatives in the north such as Govindpant, Hingane and Malharrao disregarded these instructions. It is commonly accepted that Malharrao even regarded him as an adopted son. I realized very early during my research that Najeeb's character should be

studied thoroughly. Sources, however, were not readily available. Finally, I managed to land Jadunath Sarkar's translation of Najeeb's biography written in Persian by Nooruddin and Biharilal in the 1932 to 1934 files of *Islamic Culture*. After great effort, I also managed to procure an English translation of Ibdur Rashid. The delusionary, disruptive and mischievous character of Najeeb is also starkly evident in the original Maratha papers of the decade extending from 1756 to 1765.

4. S. N. Joshi considers the Buradi and the Panipat conflicts as two parts of the same war, and this is quite true too. Both these conflicts were against the same enemy. I had to spend many days in the Delhi area in search of Buradi or Badau Ghat, which I finally located near the Badali station. Dattaji had gone to the north with the following missions in hand: taking Najeeb to task, capturing new territories, setting up an administration in the Punjab and moving on to Bengal to bring an end to the Peshwa's debts. To begin with, Dattaji roundly rejected Malharrao's advice that it would demean the Peshwa's stature; but later, in his effort to bring down the debts and to raise money, he decided to make use of Najeeb, and this was where he erred. Muzaffarnagar is an important district place in Uttar Pradesh, and Shukratal is located about twelve kilometres from there. A visit to the place confirms the accuracy of its description in the *bakhars*. The river looks like 'the beam of a palanquin' from there. However, no signs of any fort are visible now. A big temple of Mahadev concealed among the trees at Shukratal gives evidence of its antiquity. It is difficult to say whether the writer of the *bakhars* travelled everywhere during the Panipat campaign, but he would certainly have accompanied the army in the region that stretches from Delhi to Kurukshetra. Recent research has begun to dilute the suggestion that Dattaji Shinde would have dashed into the conflict in a state of high passion. The three units he had planted at Rajghat, Majnu-ka-tilla and Buradi suggest that he entered the battlefield with sufficient discretion. But when he got to know of the slaughter of a very large section of his army, he tossed away his chieftain's jacket and threw himself into the battle like an ordinary soldier.

5. We do not have much information on the conqueror Ahmad Shah Abdali. It was in 1959 that Prof. Ganda Singh's biography of Abdali became available in English, and it became possible to understand Abdali as a general. Ganda Singh has put together this beautiful work by drawing on Persian, English, Urdu, Hindi, Marathi and Punjabi sources. This book was of great help to me in creating the character of Abdali.

6. In the tradition of *bakhar* writing, the writer has presented the events at Partud in a rather dramatic manner. Dadasaheb insisted on going on the campaign with the entire royal paraphernalia, as an alternative to which it was decided that Nanasaheb himself should set off on the campaign along with Bhausaheb. The letter of Nanasaheb, dated Phalgun Vadya 9 of the Hindu calendar year 1681, that was unearthed recently from the office of the *Chitnis* (Scribe) at Sangli, brings considerable clarity to the issue. Nana writes to Bhau, 'The best thing for you to do is to find an auspicious day in the next two or three days and set off separately from me. You had better not take me because of my bad physical state. It is not proper right now to send the boy with you.' The letter suggests that the original plan was for both Nanasaheb and Bhausaheb to set off together for the north. The 'boy' would refer to Vishwasrao (S. N. Joshi). It also suggests that the Peshwa had not wanted to send Vishwasrao to the north. Thus, the assertion of the *bakhar* begins to sound plausible that it was Gopikabai, who pushed Vishwasrao into going so as to keep Bhausaheb in restraint.
7. The impression that the Marathi people carry about the events that transpired at Panipat is based primarily upon the reportage of those who had run away from the battlefield. The senior chieftains who had deserted the battlefield would have wanted to throw a screen upon their own cowardice. The best way to save their skins would be to paint Bhausaheb as proud, arrogant and insensitive. Bhausaheb, who had fallen in the battlefield anyway, was not going to appear to present his side of the picture. The rather colourful presentations of events made in the *bakhar* also stamped Bhausaheb as conceited and overly arrogant. I too had decided to go along with this picture and lay the blame on Bhausaheb's head. However, when I studied the letters and documents of that eventful decade, especially the events related to the Panipat campaign, quite a different picture began to emerge. Success and failure do not lie in anybody's control, but the dedication with which Bhausaheb set about preparing for the success of the campaign and the hard work he ploughed into the effort are utterly unique. A serious study of Bhau's personality is sadly missing. There is need for sufficient light to be thrown on his childhood days, his education, the suffocation he felt during his early days at Shaniwarwada, his experiences on the battlefield before Panipat, his readiness to go to Karveer, and such other areas. In this regard, I find an article titled 'Sadashivrao Peshwe—Jeevan Vruttaachey Dhaagey-dorey' (Sadashivrao Peshwe—The Story of his Life) extremely illuminating. This article appeared in the January 1933

issue of the magazine *Hita-chintak*, brought out by Riyasatkar Sardesai. The picture of Bhau drawn in this article on the basis of original documents of Bhau's times is not to be found anywhere else in Riyasatkar Sardesai's writings. Nobody seems to have much affinity for Bhau; once a person has been branded as mad and conceited, why look in his direction again? It was this lack of affinity that made great scholars issue pronouncements like: Bhausaheb had no experience of the battlefield, or that he was best suited for the Peshwa's office.

8. The library of the Bharat Itihaas Sanshodhak Mandal, a renowned institution dedicated to historical research at Pune, was of great help to me. That was where I met Pramod Oke, a young research scholar of history. It was during discussions with him that a number of aspects of Shamsher Bahadur's personality came to my attention. The books by Dr. Gorelal Tiwari and Dr. Bhagwandas Gupta relevant to the subject and the perusal of some contemporary documents provided additional information. It has been getting clearer in recent times that Gopikabai's concern for the legacy of her sons caused her to treat both Sadashivrao Bhau and Shamsher Bahadur quite shabbily.

9. It was fifty years ago that Dr. Ashirvadilal Srivastava had written the important two-volume biography of Shuja-ud-dowlah. His article that appeared in the *Sardesai Gaurav Granth* (commemorative volume) is also remarkable. The article carries detailed information on the dramatic tug of-war that took place in Ayodhya between Najeeb and the Maratha agents to pull Shuja over to their side. S. N. Joshi, while commenting on the Sangli letters, has also thrown plenty of light on the relations between Shuja and the Marathas.

10. 'The proud and arrogant Bhau refused to listen to the advice of the Jaat king; he smashed the Delhi throne.' These are the main accusations levelled against Bhausaheb. These accusations, however, collapse on the reading of Bhausaheb's own letter, which was among the papers found in the Chitnis's office at Sangli. The letter, dated *Bhadrapad Vadya 3* of the year 1682, (27 September, 1760), stretching up to six or seven folds plus two attachments, throws sharp light on the Panipat campaign. The letter makes clear that Wazeer Ghaziuddin and SurajmalJaat had wanted Delhi and the surrounding territory for themselves. Not wanting a competent person like Bhau to lay claim there, they had been insisting that he should halt on the other side of the Chambal. Even after Bhau had won the fort, the Jaat king had wanted possession of the keys of the treasury, and had

bought over Gangoba and Dabholkar for the purpose. In Bhausaheb's own words, 'The Jaats made a deal with these officials to get the wazeer's men inside the fort ... These officials collected a hundred or a hundred and fifty thousand and committed themselves to make him the wazeer.' This letter suggests that not only did Bhau not disappoint the Jaat, but he accepted his other conditions and made an effort to bring him round. Surajmal Jaat later did give his services to the Marathas who were escaping from Panipat, but in the above instance, there were thoughts in his mind.

11. Prof. T. S. Shejwalkar wrote a special article a few years ago to tell everyone that Bhausaheb had not smashed the Delhi throne. A terrible famine was raging in Delhi then, and Bhausaheb carried the responsibility of saving the lives of men and horses. He did tear off the silver ceiling so as to meet his dire needs, it is true. It would be a creditable act for any commander-in-chief. Bhausaheb has himself clarified in the above mentioned letter, 'The ceiling was worth eight or nine hundred thousand, some of which the wazeer had ripped out anyway. The rest we tore out with the consent of the chieftains. We gave some to the chieftains for meeting their expenses, the rest was used for food.' In the same letter, he informs, 'Malharba holds the strings of Najeeb.' Finally, he also exclaims with regret, 'We are comrades-in-arms.'

12. The devious machinations of the officials mentioned in the above letter are a family trait sticking permanently to the Marathi soil. The kind of patriotism displayed by Gangoba and Dabholkar is of the same calibre as Suryaji Piaal's. Bhausaheb had handled the office at Pune with great efficiency. He had examined the account books of power-drunk chieftains and officials of the north like Naro Shankar, Hingane brothers, Mankeshwar, Bundele and others and put the fear of god in them. As a result, none of the representatives of the Maratha empire in the north appear to have offered much help to Bhausaheb, except for the sacrifice of Govindpant.

13. At Wai, the late V. K. Rajwade found a lot of letters that were written by Bhausaheb to Govindpant Bundele, accusing him of being a shirker. Prof. Shejwalkar, on the other hand, took Pant's side, which led to the well-known battle royale between the two historians. This confrontation would occasionally be allowed to slip to the level of caste conflict. During the time that I was researching for the book, Prof. Shejwalkar's nephew Shashikant Shejwalkar gave me an unpublished article written by his uncle titled 'Govind Ballal Kher, alias Bundele'. The article is quite expansive, in spite of being a little incomplete. Govindpant did not possess a proper

professional army, it was just a second grade force for meeting his needs as a revenue collector. He would write endless letters to the Peshwa, exhorting him to not just focus on winning new territories, but to place a permanent army in the north and improve the administration. The assaults he mounted near Najeebabad, as also his efforts in the Meerut province of trying to gather provisions show him to be a sincere servant of the Maratha empire, particularly in comparison to all the others. His old age and his heavy body prevented him from mounting the kind of lively raids that Bhau expected from him, but he remains the only northern chieftain to have sent a few hundred thousand to help Bhau.

14. The occasional Shia-Sunni skirmishes in Abdali's army, the stifling of Shuja-ud-dowlah by Abdali and the Muharram riots find mention in a few Persian *bakhars*. They have also been endorsed by Shuja's biographer Srivastava. The eminent Urdu litterateur Mushtaq Qazi was of great help to me in understanding the language and Islamic customs. In the course of his review of the Sangli letters, S. N. Joshi has done a very sensitive analysis of the two or three efforts at truce that were made by Bhausaheb and Abdali. Shah Waliullah, Najeeb and their friends had mounted a campaign of jihad for the rejuvenation of Islam in Delhi and its precincts. Hariram Gupta, in his book *The Marathas and Panipat*, provides important information on this campaign.

15. Entering his horses into a raging Yamuna near Bagpat is a fine example of Abdali's courage and military leadership. We meet this episode in Najeeb-ud-dowlah's biography, as also in a few Maratha letters. We also encounter it, along with the name of Gulabsingh Gujar, in the ballad procured by Shejwalkar. I walked north for a few miles along the right bank of the Yamuna near Bagpat. Time could certainly have left its impact on the expanse of the river, but after all that, its width there does give us an idea of the man's courage.

16. One of the reasons for establishing an army post in Panipat could have been Bhausaheb's conviction that provisions would continue to arrive without interruption from Alasingh Jaat at Patiala. That there was a correspondence between Alasingh and Bhau is quite clear (*Peshwe Office* 27, Article 262). The supply for the first month would have come without break. The reason for Bhausaheb to move towards Kurukshetra after Kunjpura, besides pressure from the pilgrims, could have been a meeting with Alasingh. Alasingh was located at the Manku fort nearby during that period. Alasingh's biographer Prof. Gupta writes that as soon as Abdali had

learnt that Alasingh was supplying provisions to Bhau, he had set some of his soldiers after him; that could also be the reason why the supplies from the Punjab stopped. The authentic letters of one Lakshman Appaji Elbote, a Maratha horseman, indicate that after the rout at Panipat, a number of horsemen had fled to Alasingh for shelter. Alasingh, the founder of Patiala, continued to help the Marathas even after the defeat, which suggests that Bhausaheb would have left a favourable impression on the man. Once the Marathas were caught in the Panipat trap, Bhausaheb made back-breaking efforts for procuring food and fodder through the agency of the herders. 'The *Bakhari* of Bhausaheb', by their very nature, are a dramatized and colourful but selective rendition of 'The *Kaifiyat* of Bhausaheb'; hence they do not carry sufficient details of this effort. But these *bakhars* have gained more popularity on account of their dramatic episodes and ornate language. That may be the reason why the exertions of Bhausaheb mentioned in the *kaifiyat* have not caught sufficient attention of the scholars.

17. The sources for knowing what actually transpired on the field of battle at Panipat are very few. The main sources are: the twenty-five to thirty letters that the soldiers wrote home from the battlefield, Nana Fadnis's autobiography, and the Persian chronicles of Kashiraj Pandit who was present on the scene. An important contribution was made to this in 1961 by Setu Madhavrao Pagadi and N. R. Phatak, who gathered about twenty-five primary Persian sources, including a few letters and mostly *bakhars*. Some of these Persian sources have been translated by a few Englishmen, which I read with great care. I also read the *bakhars* of Kashiraj as translated by James Brown, H. G. Rawlinson, Lokhitwadi and Jadunath Sarkar. The Marathas were in dominance during their first month in Panipat, but the situation changed later. Bhau is accused of having used very heavy cannons, but a number of Persian sources tell us of the kind of terror these artillery pieces had struck in the minds of the enemy. It was these guns that had put an abiding fear of Panipat in the heart of Abdali. Nanasaheb Peshwa and Bhau had caught a glimpse of the power of the French cannons on the bank of the Kukdi river, and the two brothers had decided right then to procure these weapons for their army. Parvatibai is shown as rather masculine and aggressive in the Persian sources, while among us, she is presented as the personification of innocence and simplicity.

18. Prof. Shejwalkar's research brings home to us the important role that nature played in the battle of Panipat. The south-tilted movement of the sun causing dizziness to the soldiers and the reek of rotten flesh blowing

in the direction of the Maratha camp are important observations. It is difficult to say whether Fate itself had stood up to test the resilience of the Marathas. Nana Phadnis writes in his autobiography, 'An earthquake occurred as I sat near Shrimant.' Another letter reads, 'A big star exploded and twice the earth shook as a consequence.' (*Maharashtra Itihaasachi Saadhane*, Volume 6, article 409.)

19. Guerilla warfare versus circular battle formation: Bhausaheb is accused of having 'abandoned the native style of warfare in favour of the Muslim style'. But it needs just one look at the uniformly flat plains of Panipat to realize that this was no land for guerilla warfare. A conflict had arisen in the army just before the battle began with regard to these two modes of warfare. The argument that had erupted between Ibrahim Khan Gardi and the Maratha sardars can be seen from the letters of the Holkars gathered by Pagadi and Phatak.

20. The army was in a state of near-starvation four days before the battle erupted. 'Grass has altogether disappeared. The grass roots are brought from places, ground and fed to the horses. For the men, however, it is fasting times,' reads Moroba Dada's letter. One comes across a number of Persian letters and Maratha sources with the same theme. 'Bhausaheb has abandoned food, drinks only milk' is a new information that has emerged. Taking all sources into consideration, it appears that Bhausaheb had entered the battlefield with firm determination.

21. 'Shrimant Vishwasrao passed away after being hit by a bullet. Bhau, however, went on fighting. 'I was with him till such time as barely seventy-five horsemen were left,' writes Nana Phadnis in his letter. This confirms that Bhausaheb continued to fight when all his near and dear ones had cleared out. The *bakhar* writer of Bhau dusted his hands after stating, 'If even the gods do not know whether Bhausaheb rose up to heaven or descended into Hades, how can human beings know?' For my delineation of Bhausaheb's martyrdom, I have drawn on Kashiraj Pandit. Kashiraj was himself present on the battlefield. Even after the battle got over, he did a lot for the Marathas. He gives such minute details like how many Surya-namaskar exercises Bhau would do. I have relied on Kashiraj for the martyrdom of Ibrahim Gardi and Jankoji Shinde too. Prof. Shejwalkar says, 'There is not much material for authenticating what Kashiraj has narrated, but going by the kind of person he was, there is no reason for distrusting him.' At least about Bhau, it can be stated without a doubt that he was not the kind of person to stay closeted in the womb of Time; if he had

survived, he would certainly have materialized in Pune. His imposters are a good example of the intellectual level and the innocent credulity of those times. Both Jadunath Sarkar and Hariram Gupta appear to have taken for granted that Bhau fell on the battlefield.

22. Abdali seems to have taken such fright of Panipat that although he made later raids on Hindustan, he never went anywhere close to Panipat. Although Najeeb ruled over Delhi for the next ten years, he never declared himself emperor. After his death, when Mahadji Shinde visited the Antarved, he made it a point to raze Najeeb's tomb to dust. Till the day of his death, Vinchurkar carried the regret of deserting the battlefield and not dying the death of a martyr.

Obviously, my work is a novel and not a historical document. My intention was to write without going against historical facts. That was the reason why I had immersed myself in this work for four or five years. In order to get the language right, I studied the *bakhars*, but I also made a careful study of the original letters of the soldiers and chieftains of those times. A good part of the subject matter of letters may not be considered very reliable for the historian, but it is often very useful for a novelist. I took special pains to familiarize myself with the Marathi dialect in which correspondence took place during those times.

23. My friend Bal Ghevare and I visited Panipat, which is a town in the revenue sub-division of the district of Karnal. A deputy collector had arrived from far-away Maharashtra for some research work; maybe that was why Mr. Singh, the deputy collector of Panipat, extended to us all kinds of hospitality and cooperation. The tehsildar, Narsingh Dhool, the naib-tehsildar, Baleram, and others went to the extent of providing a car for us to visit the fifteen or twenty villages that fell within the battle-range of Panipat. It was an extraordinary piece of luck that I could visit about twenty-five spots related to the battle. Mr. Ganpatrao Tapase, the then governor of Haryana, has done a great favour to Maharashtra by getting the then chief minister of Haryana Mr. Bhajanlal to sanction 4.2 million rupees for a Panipat memorial. The work on the memorial was in full swing then, and it would very likely have reached completion in the following two years. Even now, one finds the wheels of small cannons and the hilts of swords in the excavations made for laying the foundation of the memorial. People talk of the big Maratha cannons that were laid out along the wells there. The bases prepared for mounting the cannons were in existence till as late as twenty-five years ago, people say.

24. There is a village too by name Bhaupur in Panipat sub-division. There is also a dilapidated fortress called Bhau ka Qila (Bhau's Fort) on the Yamuna bank. Ballads of Bhausaheb are sung even today in the villages around the place; no such songs are sung for Najeeb or Abdali. Bhau is referred to as 'Dakkhan ka Raja' (the king of the Deccan) in these ballads. In the manner of troupes in Maharashtra called Daangat that sing traditional ballads and epics, the Jogis are the balladeers of Haryana. Shejwalkar managed to procure an entire ballad from one such Jogi. Qanungo also managed to gather a few epics and poems of valour. S. N. Joshi too had made efforts in this direction in 1930. I also searched around the villages there, but with the Jogi breed of singers in the process of disappearing, there was not much that fell in my hands. Camping in the region for a few months and launching an intensive search may uncover a few such poems. 'Dakkhan ki Rani', (queen of the Deccan)—by which they mean Parvatibai—is an extremely valorous and resplendent woman in the ballads of the Jogis. In one of the ballads, as Bhau is setting off to conquer Hindustan, his mother stops him at the threshold of Shaniwarwada and asks him in a worried voice:

Tu kya shah se ladega mann mey garvaaya
Bade Rao Datta Patel ka shir tod bhagaaya
Shukratal mein bhuratiya dhoondha na paaya
Beta, Dakhin baitho karo raaj, meri bahut hi maaya

The loving mother tells Bhau, 'Son, give up your arrogance that you will be able to defeat Abdali. Look at what he did to the valiant Datta at Shukratal by chopping off his head!'

Bhau maata sey kahey ek arj sunaavey
Kahey kahaani baavari kyon hamey daraavey?
Mera nav-laakh nejya dakhani kon saamney aavey?
Sooyenkey sunkey maskaley jar saavar gaavey
Atak nadee meri paaiga ghodon keh jal pyaavey
Toph kadak-keh khuney desh ganiyar garjaavey
Dakhan to soyi aavengey jinhoney harlaavey

Bhau responds: 'Oh mother, why do you try to scare me by blocking my way? Trying to frighten me? I shall make my horse drink the water of the river Attock. I shall blow the enemies of the land to shreds with the boom of my powerful cannons. I shall not only return to the south, but I shall destroy the enemy as I return.'

www.ingramcontent.com/pod-product-compliance
Lightning Source LLC
LaVergne TN
LVHW020417070526
838199LV00055B/3641